AGING A–Z

This provocative, intellectually charged treatise serves as a concise introduction to emancipatory gerontology, examining multiple dimensions of persistent and hotly debated topics around aging, the life course, the roles of power, politics and partisanship, culture, economics, and communications. Critical perspectives are presented as definitions for reader understanding, with links to concepts of identity, knowledge construction, social networks, social movements, and inequalities. With today's intensifying concentration of wealth and corporatization, precarity is the fate for growing numbers of the world's population. Intersectionality as an analytic concept offers a new appreciation of how social advantage and disadvantage accumulate, and how constructions of race, ethnicity, class, ability, and gender influence aging.

The book's entries offer a bibliographic compendium, crediting the salience of early pioneering theorists and locating these within the cutting-edge of research (social, behavioral, policy, and gene–environment sciences) that currently advances our understandings of human development, trauma, and resilience. Accompanying these foundations are theories of resistance for advancing human rights and the dignity of marginalized populations.

Carroll L. Estes is Professor Emerita of Sociology at the University of California, San Francisco (UCSF) where she founded the Institute for Health and Aging and chaired the Department of Social and Behavioral Sciences in the School of Nursing. Dr. Estes is a member of the National Academy of Medicine and past President of three national organizations in aging: the Gerontological Society of America (GSA), the American Society on Aging, and the Academy for Gerontology in Higher Education (AGHE). Credited as a founding scholar of the "political economy of aging" and "critical gerontology," Estes has Distinguished Scholar Awards from the American Sociological Association, Pacific Sociological Association, American Public Health Association, American Society on Aging, GSA, and AGHE. Receiving UCSF's highest honor, the UCSF Medal, Estes' awards for public service and action include Sociologists for Women in Society, Justice in Aging, National Organization of Women, Gray Panthers, and honorary Fellowship in the American Academy of Nursing.

Nicholas B. DiCarlo, LCSW, writes about aging and social policy at the Institute for Health and Aging, UCSF. They* have degrees in Media Studies and Film (BAs) from Vassar College and received their Masters of Social Work at Hunter College, specializing in global social work. Writing with Carroll Estes, their critical gerontological work has grown to reflect the ways in which the psychic and social are invariably bound. DiCarlo has a private psychotherapy practice in Oakland where they bring this lens on aging, inequality, and generational trauma.

* They/them pronouns are part of embracing a non-binary gender identity. As the language and practice surrounding gender and identity change, we can take opportunities and risks to share this change across generations.

Monumental in scope, painstaking in detail, penetrating in depth and really accessible in style, this is the book to refer to for anyone interested in what aging means for society, and how much more it could mean if radically new policies were introduced by governments. Written with an enthralling vibrancy and heartfelt dedication to critical analysis, Estes and DiCarlo have performed a near miraculous feat in crafting the essential source for both newcomers to the aging field and more experienced hands. Congratulations to them both. I could not recommend this book more strongly.

Alan Walker, *Professor of Social Policy & Social Gerontology,*
University of Sheffield, UK

The authors provide an unusual and welcomed project to infuse critical sociology and political economy to the study of gerontology. The encyclopedic entries are well written (and fun) to read. Highly creative, refreshing, and compelling.

Teresa Ghilarducci, *New School for Social Research, and coauthor of*
Rescuing Retirement: A Plan to Guarantee Retirement
Security for All Americans

Whatever depth of knowledge and expertise one already possesses, and whatever perspective one brings to the study and understanding of aging, it can be guaranteed that every reader will find much that is new and provocative in *Aging A–Z*. For scholars, policymakers and others interested in the future possibilities of age and aging, this book's breadth and the extensive range of concepts is both challenging and inspiring.

Dale Dannefer, *Selah Chamberlain Professor of Sociology,*
Case Western Reserve University

Aging and Society
Edited by Carroll L. Estes and Assistant Editor Nicholas B. DiCarlo

Aging A–Z
Concepts toward Emancipatory Gerontology (2019)
Carroll L. Estes with Nicholas B. DiCarlo

Forthcoming:

The Privatization of Care
The Case of Nursing Homes (2019)
Pat Armstrong, Hugh Armstrong et al.

Age and the Research of Sociological Imagination
Power, Ideology, and Life Course (2020)
Dale Dannefer

AGING A–Z
Concepts toward
Emancipatory Gerontology

Carroll L. Estes
with Nicholas B. DiCarlo

Routledge
Taylor & Francis Group

NEW YORK AND LONDON

First published 2019
by Routledge
52 Vanderbilt Avenue, New York, NY 10017

and by Routledge
2 Park Square, Milton Park, Abingdon, Oxon, OX14 4RN

Routledge is an imprint of the Taylor & Francis Group, an informa business

© 2019 Taylor & Francis

The right of Carroll L. Estes and Nicholas B. DiCarlo to be identified as authors of this work has been asserted by them in accordance with sections 77 and 78 of the Copyright, Designs and Patents Act 1988.

Library of Congress Cataloging-in-Publication Data
A catalog record for this book has been requested

ISBN: 978-1-62958-449-2 (hbk)
ISBN: 978-1-62958-450-8 (pbk)
ISBN: 978-0-429-05518-8 (ebk)

Typeset in Baskerville
by Apex CoVantage, LLC

Visit the eResources: www.routledge.com/9781629584508

Dedicated to
Duskie Lynn Estes
and to the next generations
Brydie and Mackenzie

the best reason for
Emancipatory Gerontology

The "generation gap" is an important tool for any repressive society. If the younger members of the community view the older members as contemptible or suspect of excess, they will never be able to join hands and examine the living memories of the community, nor ask the all important question, "Why?" This gives rise to a historical amnesia that keeps us working to invent the wheel every time we have to go to the store for bread.

(Lorde, 1984, p. 117)

Lorde, A. (1984). Age, race, class, and sex: Women redefining difference. In *Sister outsider: Essays and speeches* (pp. 114–123). Freedom, CA: Crossing Press.

Contents

Preface

From the earliest days of my academic work I have been directed to the practical aspects of my discipline, infused with multidisciplinary and interdisciplinary scholars and practitioners. Although deeply schooled in and drawn to the history of social thought, my teachers, collaborators, and mentors crossed lines and boundaries with ease. Always working with people in settings, projects, and institutions that were breaking out of disciplinary boxes, my work pulled me toward the application of my learning to present-day affairs, which in my case seemed to be rife and roiling with controversy and social action. The politics and policy in the classroom I was learning was in many ways inseparable from the daily news. Remember, in my undergraduate years, I was in the so-called Silent Generation of the late 1950s. The ivory tower was never the reality I understood or made much sense to me. My formative graduate education and academic exposure was in the 1960s and 1970s, where all hell was breaking loose on Vietnam, Women, Civil Rights, the War on Poverty, and Question Authority (seriously) on the streets, in the canons of law, and against institutional probity and propriety (Estes, 2008, 2018). In academia I saw what amounted to the university faculty and students orchestrating their own "throw down" against the "taken-for-granted" ways of thinking, speaking, and acting about the central sociological questions of the time: How do social order and social change come about and how are we and they transformed? Paradigmatic wars among scholars in and out of the university were brutal and in many ways unforgiving. The organization of the mind and meaning jarred human consciousness. The contradictory reach was for the security of scientific objectivity and the certainty of fact and truth, as if these stood independent of our beliefs and life worlds. Critics of the status quo demanded that the "taken for granted" be "interrogated." Sociologists of knowledge (presently called "knowledges") broke the news that our perspectives, questions, assumptions, research, and findings were partial – and that this was consequential (Estes, 2001). Fast forward to today: there is an uncomfortable familiarity with descriptions of social uprooting, disruptions, conflict, hope, and despair of the 1960s.

Aging A–Z strives to situate the unfolding surprise and jolting journey presently underway, with old age and aging destinations uncertain and worrisome. Many of our concepts, policy questions, and analyses "go big" in confronting the broad scope of concerns. Our commitment is to critical perspectives, with theoretical and empirical grounding linked to human rights, social justice, democracy, equality, fairness, and "the social" which affirms the rights of all peoples and the preservation and protection of our commons.

With respect to older persons, each of the entries is loaded and cognizant of the stakes bound up with the mal-distribution of advantage, disadvantage, security, and life chances in every sense of these words. Issues of race, class, and gender in the early days of the "social problems" literature have been "complicated" in the world, and our realities in it. Presently our diversity discourse extends to race, ethnicity, gender, sexualities, age, generation, ability, native and indigenous peoples, immigrants, and more. As a critical scholar, I am shocked and deeply motivated by the relevance, strength, work, and *possibility* of social theory as part of our consciousness and efforts to change the world. The special gift of *A–Z* has for me been the necessity to reread classics and open up to some amazingly provocative rethinking, truth telling, and alternative, even extreme perspectives, via Podcast, and everything internet, digital, and social media, including fake news. In the latter respect, I owe much to my young collaborator Nicholas B. DiCarlo, with whom our age difference spans more than 40 years.

– Carroll L. Estes

References

Estes, C. L. (2008). A first-generation critic comes of age. *Journal of Aging Studies, 22*(2), 120–131.

Estes, C. L. (2018). A first-generation critic comes of age revisited: Reflections of a critical gerontologist. In C. Wellin (Ed.), *Critical gerontology comes of age* (pp. 19–34). New York: Routledge.

Estes, C. L. & Associates. (2001). *Social policy & aging: A critical perspective.* Thousand Oaks, CA: Sage.

Collaborator's Comment

I grew up in West Virginia, where I cherished an Appalachian familiarity and closeness with many, yet also faced many threats to queer and non-conforming parts of my identity. Life events and incredible opportunities have led me to search for meaning in theory. These academic influences have emboldened me to resist the violence of our social order, heal wounded parts of myself, and extend myself as an ally to marginalized populations.

My undergraduate work at Vassar College grounded me in the social construction of abjection. Media theory introduced me to conceptual models concerning representation, authenticity, and capitalist spectacle (Barthes, 1957/1972). Film theory named the "male gaze" (Mulvey, 1989) and Judith Butler's (1990) concept of *performativity* radicalized my understanding of the fluidity and context of identity. These led me to interrogate messages about fat bodies through theoretical lenses looking at power, particularly through control of the "unruly" by fetishism strategy (Kaplan, 2006) and the carnivalesque (Bakhtin, 1965/2009).

Social Work school (Hunter College) insisted on anti-oppressive lenses which invigorated these perspectives on power. Reading Freire (1970) in a parking lot at my temp job, I could feel an intellectual shift – I could see in new ways my privilege and complicity in oppressive systems, especially within education. Psychoanalytic theory provided a strong foundation to examine my disavowed racism, sexual trauma, and unconscious anxieties regarding aging. My clinical work and training made these knowledges operational. Working with children at an afterschool program in the South Bronx and critically ill patients of all ages in a

Washington Heights hospital illuminated how opportunity, precarity, and community inform embodiment and the life course perspectives I have studied.

My work feels as if it is just beginning, as I continue to gather an awareness of what has been given to me through the wisdom and generosity of my elders. In my private psychotherapy practice, my clients perpetually humble me as they share precious parts of themselves and bravely explore new selves. And I am dazzled by whatever alignment of stars positioned me with the affinity network of critical gerontologists. I am so grateful for Carroll Estes' invitation to participate in this, which I now understand to be one of the broadest and most expansive resistance movements in thought, recognizing that we are all aging peoples in this together.

Nicholas B. DiCarlo

References

Bakhtin, M.M. (2009). *Rabelais and his world* (H. Iswolsky, Trans.). Bloomington, IN: University of Indiana. (Originally published 1965.)

Bakhtin, M. M. (1984). *Rabelais and his world* (Vol. 341). Indiana University Press. (Originally published 1968.)

Barthes, R. (1972). Mythologies. 1957. Trans. Annette Lavers. New York: Hill and Wang, pp. 302–306.

Butler, J. (1990). Performative acts and gender constitution: An essay in phenomenology and feminist theory. In S-E. Case (Ed.), *Performing feminisms: Feminist critical theory and theatre* (pp. 270–282). Baltimore, MD: Johns Hopkins University Press.

Freire, P. (1970). *Pedagogy of the oppressed.* New York: Herder and Herder.

Kaplan, L. J. (2006). Cultures of fetishism. In *Cultures of fetishism* (pp. 175–190). New York: Palgrave Macmillan.

McIntosh, P. (1988). White privilege: Unpacking the invisible knapsack. Retrieved from www.racialequitytools. org/resourcefiles/mcintosh.pdf.

Mulvey, L. (1989). Visual pleasure and narrative cinema. In *Visual and other pleasures* (pp. 14–26). Basingstoke: Palgrave Macmillan.

I

Opening

Aging A–Z offers an overview of central dilemmas and social problems in critical gerontology and social policy. The critical speaks to the imperative for a gerontological imagination that probes the existing social order and challenges normal science and what we take as the truths about old age and aging. The timeliness and significance of such questions demand sensitivity to what is possible and how social change may be produced.

Crises in the world delineate social struggles and create urgency for *"epic theory."* In calling for epic theory, Sheldon Wolin insists that theory be a public enterprise as much as an academic one. Theory is not dead, frozen, cloistered in the ivory tower. Theory can and must contribute to American politics, economics, and social existence, helping to catalyze and realize publics. *Epic theory* moves beyond isolated incidents as single events, and instead grasps and advances theory through "attempts to change the world itself'" (Wolin, 1969, p. 1080). In our time, the need for epic theory resonates with the idea of emancipatory gerontology. It follows up and deepens previous work on the political economy of aging (Estes, 1979, 2011, 2018).

Political economic and cultural theories may call into being and lend analytical categories that will draw intellectuals, politicians, and social movement activists into the base, disturbing the roots of the really existing social order. We see the ways in which multinational capitals, nation-states, and elite power networks are implicated in global crises now extending through the life course of generations. How do theories of aging connect to these times and social forces? The perspectives of a critical political economy of aging provide a foundation for this treatise *Aging A–Z*. We hope it contributes to opening up fields of work, theory, science, and practice that advance what we call an emancipatory gerontology. In this respect theory may offer guidance in questions of justice and obligation in crisis and war; it may shed light in dark times.

Wolin warns that dominant elite interests may be precursor to authoritarian regimes, politicizing and policing many life spheres. He observes that democracy is not a fixed state form, but a political experience in which people are active political actors. He charges political theorists with hunting down "fugitive moments of democracy," reminding us that democracy may become a momentary political experience. Howard Zinn, late author of *The people's history of the United States*, offers guidance on "how-to use the past to change the world." We may engage and widen our view as we examine:

the silent voices of the past so that we can look behind the silence of the present. It can illustrate the foolishness of depending on others to solve the problems of the world – whether the State, the church, or other self-proclaimed benefactors. History and theory can reveal how ideas are stuffed into us by the powers of our time, and so lead us to stretch our minds beyond what is given. It can inspire us by recalling those few moments in the past when men [and – yes – women] did behave like human beings, to prove it is *possible*. [...] [I]t can sharpen our critical faculties so that even while we act, we think about the dangers created by our own desperation.

(Zinn, 1970 [2012], p. 103; see also Birkenkamp & Rhudy, 2009)

See also: Radical History, The Closing

References

Birkenkamp, D. & Rhudy, W. (selected and introduced). (2009). *Uncommon sense: From the writings of Howard Zinn*. London and New York: Routledge (Taylor & Francis Group).

Estes, C. L. (1979). *The aging enterprise: A critical examination of social policies and services for the aged*. San Francisco, CA: Jossey-Bass.

Estes, C. L. (2011). Crises and old age policy. In R. A. Settersten Jr. & J. L. Angel (Eds.), *Handbook of sociology of aging* (pp. 297–320). New York: Springer.

Estes, C. L. (2018). A first-generation critic comes of age revisited: Reflections of a critical gerontologist. In C. Wellin (Ed.), *Critical gerontology comes of age* (pp. 19–34). New York: Routledge.

Wolin, S. (1969). Political theory as a vocation. *The American Political Science Review*, *63*(4), 1062–1082. (David Marcus, Wolin review, *Dissent Magazine*, November 2, 2005.)

Zinn, H. (2012). *The indispensable Zinn: The essential writings of the "people's historian"* (ed. T. P. McCarthy). New York: The New Press. (Original chapter "What is radical history?" published in H. Zinn, *The politics of history*, 1970.)

II

Why *Aging A–Z* Now?

There is an urgency within and across the field of disciplines that comprise aging knowledge, practice, and advocacy. While studies in aging and methodological advances and interventions are flowering, a vital range of critical connections remains opaque. A penetrating uncertainty and anxiety underlie the deepening personal and collective risks as austerity ideology and politics swamp social policy on multiple fronts. As blame, shame, and inequality skyrocket, the lives of our kin and many of those around us seem almost malignantly misshapen, denied dignity, and absent any sense of fairness.

Gerontology and geriatrics sit within the broad social, behavioral, and policy science fields as well as biology and medicine. The practices that build upon them are being reshaped, deconstructed, and reconstructed. Bridging across disciplinary fields and intricate specialties and sub-specialties are rapidly producing entirely new niches and opportunities. The significance and acceleration of these dynamics of knowledge production and practice innovations highlight the value of enumerating classic principles as well as unfolding gerontological studies and innovations. *A–Z* contains theory because it aims to make sense of the world in which we live and to enable us to live in it and leave it in a better place. The connections are not random or haphazard

between the knowledges (plural here is intentional) gained from scientific pursuits and practice inventions.

As A–Z concepts show, scientific work is articulated through and seen in the distribution and mal-distributions of resources through society, the State, and the economic institutions of capital and global nations. The rewards are not random.

On an institutional level, critical gerontology and the political economy of aging gained ground in the late 1970s and 1980s, and this approach is acknowledged as one of the theories in gerontology. Yet the volume and vibrancy of this work has struggled since. Today, there are few scholars, theorists, researchers, and practitioners dedicated to pushing the substance and boundaries of this approach. A cursory review of annual meeting programs of the major gerontological societies and associations in the USA and Western Europe (e.g., the GSA, IAGG, ASA, and the British Society of Gerontology) reveals sparse attention to critical research and theory. We lack ethnological inquiry in systematic depth within critical perspective frameworks. We lack stable institutional support for training programs and higher educational commitments to train, foster, promote, and provide career rewards for such work. Although critical scholarship is in some sense rebounding, it remains at the contested margins – in gerontology as in many other fields. In contrast, schools and programs of entrepreneurship and free enterprise, especially technology "startups," are recruiting and turning out large cadres of graduates at premier institutions of learning.

Resistance on multiple fronts is percolating more boldly, largely outside established educational institutions. Resistance practice operates in and through think tanks, Google groups, advocacy organizations, coalitions, marches, and protests (Estes, 2017). While gerontology and geriatrics professional association meetings offer direct policy information and calls to action, gerontologists, geriatricians, and all health and human service workers are affected by threats to the existence and continuing support of basic federal and state-level programs, policies, and regulations in both research and education.

Welfare state policies in the United Kingdom, Canada, and the European Union as well as the USA varyingly confront the constraints of globalization and capital markets, austerity policies, deep inequalities, and a growing diaspora of stateless peoples migrating in search of safety and security.

In the USA, neoliberalism, big money, big capital, and their ever-larger multinational conglomerates have promoted deep corporate and billionaire tax cuts. The pattern appears to be one of diminished corporate responsibility for the US nation-state and its working people as our industries, products, jobs, and profits flee, circling the globe in constant search of more and more financial capital accumulation. There is a disturbing lack of policy attention and concern about the declining income, wealth, health, and quality of life of most Americans compared to the top 2 percent, despite incessant rhetoric of worry about it.

These forces and the Supreme Court's "Citizens United" decision (equating corporate money with free speech) have endangered the Big Four: Social Security, Medicare,

and Medicaid, and the Affordable Care Act (ACA) as well as countless other vital programs. Under conservative government leaders, attacks on immigrants, citizen rights and nation-state membership, and impediments to the franchise of voting rights are justified by repeated rants of being fiscally "unsustainable." This ideological framing promotes the perception that austerity, debt reduction, privatization, and other forms of "structural adjustment" and massive job losses are requisite to economic survival.

Aging A–Z is designed to assist in unconfounding and locating the central forces driving the growing chasm of inequalities as well as possible individual and collective actions that may alter the present course for better or for worse.

Framework

A–Z seeks to inform the reader in navigating a vast and contentious literature on contemporary social policy and aging. Crafted in the format of a Glossary of key terms, *A–Z* draws us into central debates and issues within and across disciplines, as most relevant to the life course and old age and aging in society and around the globe. According the stark social inequalities their formidable significance, the book offers brief and readable perspectives on old age policy and critical theory.

A–Z is organized as a reference volume that belongs on the desk of anyone interested in older persons or who is involved in making, engaging, implementing (or lamenting) social policy and the politics of aging, as well as those of us working in programs and institutions, or with persons who are affected by them. Our audience is newcomers, students, professionals, and established scholars in the disciplinary fields of social policy, sociology, anthropology, political science, economics, social work, law, media studies, health policy, public health, medical humanities, race and ethnic studies, and women's and intersectionality studies. Each of these fields is integral to advancing and expanding the political economy of aging and critical gerontology.

Succinct descriptions of 100 to 500 words illustrate the interplay and development of the concepts, material and symbolic. The text shows that knowledges are not static, but recursively inform and expand our ways of seeing, understanding, and living.

How to Read A–Z

There is no single way to read *A–Z*. It may be read alphabetically, but we encourage readers (especially those coming with a specific question or interest in a topic) to explore the interrelatedness of the policy, theory, and practice through cross-references (in *See also*). Readers are advised of the pivotal import of following the additional related concepts cited at the end of each concept under *"See also"*. Readers may further examine concepts through the references provided. The *Further Reading* sections are a mix of government websites and data sources, non-profit institutions and advocacy newsletters, scholastic peer reviewed articles and books. There are also occasional *fugitive documents*, references that are not part of established citation practices.

The book invites readers to participate in the living body that is theory, policy, practice, and action. The dictionary's function is to document and promote words, definitions, and conceptualizations that (1) highlight gerontological and critical discursive contributions as well as confrontations and conflicts. The references introduce a breadth of gerontological thought and study, and explicitly reach into and beyond the normal science of aging. Throughout, key thinker-doers provide stepping stones of scholarship and praxis that (2) illuminate forms of expression people employ to describe their experiences and meanings. This is especially important to locating and hearing the voices of older persons and their advocates; (3) identify institutional program and research practices that

bear on the relationships between aging peoples, society, and policy; and (4) encourage ourselves as students, teachers, researchers, practitioners, elders, and policy-makers to reflect on our own subjectivities and experiences as a way to incorporate critical and culturally inclusive vantage points in the gerontological lexicon.

An extensive Appendix on *Teaching and learning from* Aging A–Z suggests ways to organize courses on selected topics utilizing specific concepts, current events, and public issues. Also included is a template and sample syllabus for teaching a course on Theories of Aging. Pitched to modalities of co-learning, self-reflection, memoing, and learning objectives for each topic, the approach adopts the principles of critical pedagogy and applied adult learning. A Practice Toolkit incorporates relevant A–Z concepts in reference to "Age and Disability," "Trauma, Inequality, and Vulnerable Populations," and "Critical Care, Medical Environments, and Social Welfare." There is a selective brief Legislative Appendix of proposed Congressional Bills and Resolutions designed to stabilize social insurance programs and expand health and retirement security for elders, the disabled, and the marginalized. Party leadership in the 114th and 115th Congress has not permitted the release of these for Congressional committee or floor votes. The Legislative Appendix tags the active and furtive federal initiatives in support of rights and entitlements to basic health and retirement security, and the end of extreme poverty.

Aging A–Z offers perspectives for thinking critically. *Critical* may be used in reference to any concept, idea, action – signaling that it is only partial and that its "essence" is in its potential, what it might become. Reality is never completed. This is part of a critique of society and the exposition of what its potential might become via a higher form (R. Collins, 2004, p. 104). We concur with Luc Boltanski (2014) that "theory must always remain *open, incomplete, and underdetermined*" (italics in original).

In the context of contemporary events, *A–Z* articulates terms with examples of policy issues, debates, and synthesizes cross-disciplinary perspectives of evolving social movements and knowledges. The format depicts the multifaceted elements: event rituals, ideas and constructions, structural elements and social formations, as well as how these relate to the aging of individuals, communities, and society. *A–Z* overviews the phenomena and consequences of globalization, financialization, and the dominion of capitalism.

The text uncovers major institutions and networks of power as well as the spheres and peoples subject to domination, and the actors running the gauntlet of resistance to subjugation and oppression. Central to our exploration of power, the Glossary incorporates terms relevant to how markets and nations implement borders that restrict citizenship and capitalize on the precarity of statelessness.

With conflict and critical theories guiding the *A–Z* framework, core elements include the dynamic, dialectical, and dialogical relations of power, ideology, structure, and agency as implicated in struggles for and against social policy (Estes, 1979, 1991, 2001, 2016, 2017, 2018) and the socially constructed problems and practices upon which policy rests. With an intentional focus on marginalized voices, contrasted with mainstream politics and economics, *A–Z* underscores the lens of intersectionality in policy analysis, practice, theory, and social change. Our critical perspective attends to the interactions and false dichotomies of structure and agency. Age, race, ethnicity, class, nation, genders, sexualities, (dis)abilites, and generations are best understood, as Patricia Hill Collins writes (2015), "in relational terms" rather than as isolated "categories of analysis."

The Glossary index is selective in the vantage points of specific concepts, chosen in relation to critical thought; yet the descriptions attempt to preserve fidelity to the relevant key authors' ideas. Paradigm conflicts and contradictions exist and are taken as significant rather than suppressed. The text signals the tensions and dilemmas pertinent to the viewpoints in *A–Z*. Each entry could be a chapter or dissertation. Examining related and/or contradictory terms and concepts together offers an opportunity for encounter; two or more terms could be in dialogue with each other for hours. The reader may be struck by our specific "take" on topics, such as "healthy aging" or "inequality," despite other available large and diverse literatures elsewhere. Our concept choices and descriptions link to the larger critical space of *A–Z*. Overall our perspective brings with it warnings about the short-sighted trends in the psychologizing (individualizing) and geneticization of everything aging. Our admonition is that, taken whole cloth, narrowed thinking tends to obscure and obviate the social rootedness of issues and the embedding of solutions within dominant structural and power arrangements (which themselves are contested).

Writing on the concepts, issues, and ideas in *A–Z*'s idiosyncratic dictionary format is designed specifically as a major curricular resource for undergraduate, graduate, and professional-level courses – either for formal or informal classroom learning and teaching, or self-study. *A–Z* covers limited history and content, opening up possible reimagining of new scenarios for key ideas and issues. As we discover similarities and competing concepts, we expect that communications within and across the fields will grow and broaden our understandings and potential to act in ways that promote social and democratic innovations.

This writing is part of our urgent call to fill our roles and responsibility as public intellectuals in the best tradition of engaged social science (C. Wright Mills, Alvin Gouldner, Randall Collins), organic intellectuals (Antonio Gramsci), communicative ethicists (Jürgen Habermas), black feminists (bell hooks, Patricia Hill Collins), race theorists (Michael Omi, Howard Winant, Joe Feagin) and others. Our shared commitment is to foster a critical imagination, scholarship, practice, and engaged empowerment to advance the reality of a just society.

We seek to advance the promise of *emancipatory gerontology*. **The Closing** offers brief notes on *emancipatory gerontology* and the future challenges ahead.

References

Boltanski, L., Honneth, A., & Celikates, R. (2014). Sociology of critique or critical theory? Luc Boltanski and Axel Honneth in conversation with Robin Celikates. In S. Susen & B. S. Turner (Eds.), *The spirit of Luc Boltanski: Essays on "pragmatic sociology of critique"* (pp. 561–589). London: Anthem Press.

Collins, P. H. (2015). Intersectionality's definitional dilemmas. *Annual Review of Sociology, 41*(1), 1–20.

Collins, R. (2004). *Interaction ritual chains.* Princeton, NJ: Princeton University Press.

Estes, C. L. (1979). *The aging enterprise: A critical examination of social policies and services for the aged.* San Francisco, CA: Jossey-Bass.

Estes, C. L. (1991). The Reagan legacy: Privatization, the welfare state, and aging in the 1990s. In J. Myles and J. S. Quadagno (Eds.), *States, labor markets, and the future of old age policy* (pp. 59–93). Philadelphia, PA: Temple University Press.

Estes, C. L. (2016). Older US women's economic security, health and empowerment. In S. Dworkin, M. Gandhi, & P. Passano (Eds.), *Women's empowerment and global health* (pp. 232–250). Oakland, CA: University of California Press.

Estes. C. L. (2017). Women's rights, women's status, women's resistance in the age of Trump. *Generations, 41*(4), 36–44.

Estes, C. L. (2018). A first-generation critic comes of age revisited: Reflections of a critical gerontologist. In C. Wellin (Ed.), *Critical gerontology comes of age* (pp. 19–34). New York: Routledge.

Estes, C. L. & Associates. (2001). *Social policy & aging: A critical perspective.* Thousand Oaks, CA: Sage.

III

Critical Concepts

A

Abjection

Organizes around the rejection of weak or unworthy people or bodies deemed out of control or disgusting. Mechanisms of abjection include being deprived of social inclusion, citizenship, and rights. Race, ethnicity, gender, body size, and ability are some of the identities that dominate mainstream culture attacks. Abjection is not static. It changes through time and responds to political motivation and mobilization.

Abject bodies may include: black bodies at police traffic stops, older bodies in crosswalks, fat bodies in ice-cream parlors, unaccompanied women, trans-bodies, people without money or new clothes, people sleeping in their car or the street, refugees and immigrants without documentation. These are the unwanted bodies that sow fear in those with the comfort and safety of privilege.

Kristeva (1982) employs a psychoanalytic lens to suggest that through abjection dominant culture attempts to cast aside the materiality of death, so that susceptible or vulnerable peoples are further marginalized. She writes, "by way of abjection, primitive societies have marked out a precise area of their culture in order to remove it from the threatening world" (Kristeva, 1982, p. 10). Social insurance directly implicates this "materiality of death" – the physical evidence of embodied vulnerability and mortality. This fear and disgust fuels the anti-aging industry.

Abjection also plays a role in determining the content of academic study of marginalized identities and groups. The rejection of certain identities as unworthy of study or analysis further isolates communities.

See also: Anti-aging, Disability, Fascism, Intersectionality/Intersectional Knowledge, Oppression, Privilege, Psychoanalytic Social Theory, Welfare State

Further Reading

Becker, H. S. (1973). *Outsiders: Studies in the sociology of deviance*. New York: Free Press.
Gilleard, C. & Higgs, P. (2011). Ageing abjection and embodiment in the fourth age. *Journal of Aging Studies, 25*(2): 135–142.
Kristeva, J. (1982). *Powers of horror: An essay on abjection*. New York: Columbia University Press.

Ableism/TABS

Manifests in discriminatory behaviors or beliefs that favor able-bodied individuals to the detriment of individuals with disabilities. A reframing of abledness is identifying Temporarily Able Bodies (TABS), since all bodies are susceptible to injury or illness (Shildrick & Price, 1996). A critical gerontological approach to abledness entails looking at the intersectionality of oppressed identities and critical political economy analyses of the physical body as a resource exploited for profit. These analyses extend to identifying fascist trends of destroying bodies that cost but cannot produce profit. This is historically seen through forced euthanasia of disabled individuals in Nazi Germany, and the withdrawal of support for disabled pensioners in Fascist Italy (Quine, 2002). In the USA, Mia Mingus (2018) and Alice Wong (2018) are bringing forward disability and transformative justice.

Example

Society (via the welfare state) neglects an older woman with osteoporosis which results in vertebral collapse. She physically embodies oppression potentially informed by (1) inadequate access to nutrients and medical care which could prevent or delay such collapse; (2) beauty standards which have encouraged frailty through dieting; (3) exclusion from a labor force that leaves her financially precarious; (4) not qualifying for Social Security Disability because she didn't earn work credits for the years she was a homemaker and mother and has not been in employment over the past five years, and (5) Social Security payments have not kept up with the cost of living, especially in her quickly gentrifying neighborhood.

See also: Abjection, Embodiment, Cumulative Advantage/Disadvantage, Fascism, Inequality, Precarity, Welfare State

Further Reading

Benjamin, R. (2016). Interrogating equity: A disability justice approach to genetic engineering. *Issues in Science and Technology*, *32*(3), 51–54.

Campbell, F. K. (2009). *Contours of ableism*. Basingstoke: Palgrave Macmillan.

Charlton, J. I. (1998). *Nothing about us without us*. Berkeley, CA: University of California Press.

Mingus, M. (2018). Retrieved from http://leavingevidence.wordpress.com.

Quine, M. S. (2002). *Italy's social revolution: Charity and welfare from liberalism to fascism*. New York: Palgrave.

Shildrick, M. & Price, J. (1996). Breaking the boundaries of the broken body. *Body & Society*, *2*(4): 93–113.

The Arc. Retrieved from www.thearc.org/.

Wong, Alice. (2018). Disability Visibility Project. Retrieved from https://disabilityvisibilityproject.com/about/.

Actuary

An occupation geared toward the assessment of risk. Life actuaries assess risk for insurers (social and for profit), governments and the State, Wall Street and businesses, politicians and the public. Actuarial statisticians analyze mortality risk, morbidity risk, and investment risk for life insurance, annuities, pensions, short- and long-term disability insurance, health insurance, health savings accounts, and long-term care insurance, the Affordable Care Act (ACA) and its Repeal and Replace proposals (Bureau of Labor Statistics, 2018). Complicating and augmenting the significance of actuaries and their sciences as a top-ranked profession are big data and technological advances in statistics and digital capabilities that have opened up the availability of longitudinal and cross-sectional datasets, including real-time opinion, health, and retirement surveys. Economists, demographers, statisticians, epidemiologists, sociologists, and financial, health and aging policy analysts, and other disciplines form the backbone of the sciences here. The accuracy of projected risks is also dependent upon and, influenced by politics, budget constraints, changing demographics, and other factors such as epigenetics, precision medicine, profits in the medical industrial complex, inflation, and cost-of-living considerations.

Actuarial work is fundamental to this day, with blazing debates on the federal budget, raising the age of eligibility for Social Security (again), and for Medicare, whether either (or both) are going "bankrupt", or can attain long-term actuarial balance (Diamond, 2004; Aaron, 2014). Controversies concern the use and even *the legitimacy* of various concepts and techniques of measurement, such as infinite horizon budgeting, demographics to consider, generational accounting, and generational equity. The scientific debates over method, stats, and interpretations themselves are as formidable as are their respective consequences. Public and private pension reform and retirement security are steeped in public debate (Ghilarducci, 2010/2011).

Historically, Social Security and Medicare actuaries have been influential, sometimes drawn into debates and ideological battles as, if, and when such conflicts intensify and polarize. Robert Meyers worked with President Roosevelt and his administration, tasked with measuring risk to ensure that government could build a self-supporting old age program that would deliver what it promised. As Chief Actuary from 1947 to 1970, consultant, and briefly SSA Deputy for Reagan, Meyers twice resigned over the politicization of Social Security and what he called meddling by the Office of Management and Budget (OMB). As director of the successful 1983 Greenspan Commission on Social Security Reform, Meyers was aghast at privatization talk: "To me, the translation of the word 'privatization' is 'destroyed'. . . . If it won't do it immediately, it will do it inevitably" (DeWitt. SSA Archives, 1996).

Actuarial statistics in Medicare, Medicaid, the ACA, and long-term care (including the now-repealed CLASS) are as important and politically considered (see Richard Foster, Chief Actuary of the Center for Medicare and Medicaid's/CMS alternate scenarios of the ACA's "potential cost understatement"). Congressional Budget Office (CBO) cost estimates on legislation mark pivotal conflicts in policy.

See also: Crisis, Demography/Demographics, Economics, Insolvency, Morality, Political Economy, Risk

Further Reading

Aaron, H. J. (2014). The economics & politics of long term budget projections. *Brookings Hutchins Center Working Paper #8*. Washington, DC: Brookings Institution.

Bureau of Labor Statistics. (2018). Employee Benefit Survey/EBS publications and latest bulletin on Benefit plan details. Retrieved from www.bls.gov.

DeWitt, L. & Myers, R. J., "Social Security Administration Oral History Interview with Robert J. Myers," SSA History Archives. Baltimore, MD: Social Security Administration. https://www.ssa.gov/history/ret2.html

Diamond, P. (2004). Social Security. *American Economic Review, 94*(1): 1–24.

Estes & Phillipson, (2002). (See Carroll L. Estes' Selected Works, Appendix 4, page 395.)

Ghilarducci, T. (2010/2011). The solution to the pension crisis is more pensions. *Perspectives on Work, 14*(1–2), summer 2010/winter 2011: 34. Published by the Labor and Employment Relations Association (LERA). Retrieved from www.economicpolicyresearch.org/images/docs/Teresa_Ghilarducci/The_Solution_to_the_Pension_Crisis.pdf.

Society of Actuaries. (n.d.). Financial perspectives on aging and retirement across the generations. Retrieved from www.soa.org/research-reports/2018/financial-perspectives-aging-retirement/.

Administration for Community Living (ACL)

A federal agency within the Department of Health and Human Services (HHS) that oversees a variety of programs and agencies related to aging and disabilities.

The ACL oversees the Administration on Aging (AoA), the Administration on Disabilities (AoD), the National Institute on Disability, Independent Living, and Rehabilitation Research (NIDILRR), the Center for Integrated Programs (CIP), the Center for Management and Budget (CMB), and the Center for Policy and Evaluation (CPE).

See also: Abelism/TABS, ADA, Disability, Medicare, Older Americans Act

Further Reading

www.acl.gov/.

Affect, Politics of

The feelings, the emotional realities, and movements that pervade experiences of living. Spinoza posits that affect does not reside statically in the individual; rather affect exists collaboratively and has "potentia," which extends feeling into action. This grants the individual a capacity "to be affected" (Ruddick, 2010, p. 24).

Older people's affect becomes simplified and reduced through stereotyped tropes as: childish, crotchety, grumpy, dowdy, confused, bewildered, wordy, tired, and (ironically) scornful. Stereotypes and labels of neuroses collapse opportunities for solidarity and empathic connection, yet feelings can function as sites of resistance. Making space for abject effects can counter oppressive forces which minimize, silence, obscure, or retaliate against them. Critical Theory problematizes the suppression, repression, oppression and depression of emotion. The relationship between oppression and depression is complex and illuminates the ways in which political forces can influence the individual psyche. Which emotions are not welcome, allowed, or permitted? Can policy-makers feel or "know" the impact of their policies?

How would you feel if someone rolled their eyes as you asked how to use the computer? How would you feel if someone said you were greedy and yet you couldn't afford to buy food?

The following are affective states, contextualized and problematized:

1) *Boredom*: Ascribed to an aging person as a causality of being unimportant, perhaps the conclusion of cognitive failure: inability to think and remember. But how stimulating is life in an 8x10 nursing home room that you can rarely leave? Confined to the same limited routine every day will almost certainly not be exciting. Yet boredom can also function as a site of resistance in a capitalistic culture where consumers are expected to buy into the fascination and enchantment of a public spectacle like the American Dream.

2) *Despair*: Disempowerment and a sense of helplessness, impotence, and weakness. An emotional paralysis. Abjection and exclusion produce despair. In terms of social policy, this could be the feeling of being trapped under (or without) a safety net, instead of supported by it.

3) *Anger*: Is only socially acceptable conditionally. The marginalized cannot show anger without repercussions. Women cannot appear angry and hang onto the security of a man who is going to support them. Those who exhibit anger are often resented for "disturbing the peace" and for violating social norms.

4) *Hope*: We talk about disadvantaged people being robbed of hope. Can hope be commodified and sold? Where does it generate? How is hope a cornerstone of resilience? Castells (2015) speaks of networks organizing around outrage and hope.

5) *Compassion*: Self-esteem builds out of compassion for the self, a belief that one is worthy. A (symbolic) interactionism of seeing others as one sees one's self.

See also: Abjection, Empathy, Framing, Interactional Ritual Chains, Networks, Social Movement Theory

Further Reading

Castells, M. (2015). *Networks of outrage and hope: Social movements in the internet age* (2nd edition). Malden, MA: Polity Press.

Ruddick, S. (2010). The politics of affect: Spinoza in the work of Negri and Deleuze. *Theory, Culture & Society, 27*(4): 21–45.

Affordable Care Act (ACA/Obamacare)

The Patient Protection and Affordable Care Act (PPACA), often called the ACA or Obamacare, is a United States federal statute enacted by Congress and signed by President Barack Obama on March 23, 2010. The bill, one of the first major achievements of Obama's first term, expands Medicaid coverage and requires most individuals to procure health insurance coverage for themselves and their dependents, or potentially to pay a penalty for noncompliance. By requiring insurance of most adults, of healthy and less healthy statuses, the law spreads financial risk among a larger pool of individuals, enabling lower cost insurance premiums, aided by government supports, for those who could not afford health insurance previously.

The ACA immediately became a partisan rallying tool. GOP lawmakers instantly attacked the constitutionality of federal regulations and standards for the private market. On June 28, 2012 the Supreme Court rendered a final decision to uphold the health care law, but gave states the option to refuse the ACA Medicaid provisions. Some 19 states refused the ACA Medicaid expansion, leaving millions of their poorest uninsured.

Specifics and Variances

The Act expands Medicaid coverage eligibility requirements to 138 percent of the federal poverty level in states which have agreed to expand coverage. In contrast to previous law, the Act extends the age of young adult coverage on family health plans to 26 years of age, and requires insurers to justify rate increases greater than 10 percent before they may take effect. The ACA prohibits insurers from discriminating based on pre-existing conditions. It also includes: (a) requirements to offer premium assistance for employer-sponsored insurance; (b) Medicaid coverage for former foster care children; (c) payments to territories (Guam and Puerto Rico); (d) adjustments for States recovering from major disasters, and (e) protections for Native American Indians and Alaska Natives. Most enrollees in the health care exchanges (>80 percent) receive a subsidy from the federal government to offset the cost of their premiums.

For Medicare beneficiaries, the ACA provides new preventive health benefits, although age rating was retained, meaning that older persons may be charged more than younger persons for additional coverage they may seek. The Medicare Trust Fund balance will be improved over 10 years, while Medicare cost reductions helped to finance the ACA. Programs for dual eligibles (Medicare and Medicaid dual beneficiaries) via waivers and demonstrations were added, as were provisions to close the Medicare Part D coverage gap ("donut hole") through which elders with high drug costs each year eventually pay 100 percent of their prescription drug costs.

From a critical perspective the ACA is a patchwork of neoliberal health reform based on maintaining the central role of commercial health insurers. It includes unequally tiered benefits packages based on ability to purchase. A package of minimum essential services provides far less financial protection than more expensive plans. Various metals – bronze, silver, gold, platinum – name the tiers of coverage, where bronze represents the lowest tier (covering 60 percent of in-network health care expenses) and platinum the highest (90 percent). Individual and family premiums cost the most under the most valuable metal, and out-of-pocket copayments are lowest. Because the actuarial calculations by insurance companies are based on yearly payouts for services for beneficiaries at a specific tier, their out-of-pocket premiums, deductibles, and copays may rapidly rise by tier. The "value" of coverage in a tier is strictly an actuarial determination based on financial calculations and accounting that attempt to gauge the percentage of medical costs that an individual would have to pay themselves. Tiered benefit approaches to services and medications have also been instituted within managed care programs and prescription drugs under Medicare and Medicaid (Waitzkin, 2011; Dutta, 2015).

The Public Option

This was proposed, but dropped from the final bill, and would have made a public federal option available to anyone who wanted to buy coverage under the ACA. This would permit the government to compete against private insurance companies. Such an option is consistent with the market ideology that competition drives down costs, but GOP lawmakers and Independent Senator Joe Lieberman demanded its removal, threatening a filibuster of the ACA. Conservatives claimed this was "unfair competition" (allowing a Medicare option) that would hurt private companies, but 62 percent of Americans supported the public option (Kaiser Health Tracking Poll, 2017).

The lack of a public option strengthened the privatization monopoly in health insurance coverage via the ACA as a private model, funded by government subsidy. Forty percent of all US healthcare costs were already funded by government before the ACA. Under the ACA, private insurers and other stakeholders in the medical industrial complex exploit multiple subsidies (e.g.,

employer tax write-offs and the infusion of 21 million newly insured "customers"). Other countries (Switzerland, Japan, and Germany to name a few) use a model similar to the ACA, sometimes called the Bismarck System. However, unlike the United States, insurance providers are operated as non-profits in these systems and costs are directly regulated to ensure equitable treatment for everyone.

In 2017, Nevada considered enacting a public option that would have allowed residents to buy into the State's Medicaid program, but the Governor, Brian Sandoval, vetoed the bill after it passed the State's legislature (Montero, 2017).

TrumpCare and Repeal and Replace Models

Congressional Republicans and President Trump sought repeal of the Affordable Care Act almost immediately after Trump was inaugurated. Key targets for repeal have been the pre-existing condition protections for individuals, the "essential health benefits" (and with it, women's reproductive health benefits), "community rating", limitations on age rating, the individual mandate, and the Medicaid expansion. Under the Freedom Caucus proposed repeal (ObamaCare 2.0, April 2017), states would be allowed to waiver out of most or all of these requirements. While the individual mandate is unpopular, it is necessary to create a large risk pool that brings down overall costs. Without this mandate, it is extremely difficult to pay for and justify the popular portions of the law.

Popular parts of the ACA (e.g., covering children up to age 26 and pre-existing conditions, limitations on age rating) all rely on the individual mandate and subsidies to bring as many people into the risk pool as possible (Wynne, 2016). Virtually all health care economists on the Right and Left agree that the largest possible (universal) *risk pool* is essential for health insurance to be affordable/available for purchase in a private market (Wynne, 2016).

Republican proposals to replace the ACA are predicated on the idea of ensuring a higher degree of choice for individuals. However, without the subsidies and individual mandate, costs for individuals to buy health insurance will necessarily be higher. Similarly, without protections for pre-existing conditions, limits on age rating, and required essential health benefits, the quality and actuarial value of insurance decreases to such an extent that choice between plans becomes relatively meaningless.

Author reflections and critical questions: ACA options for coverage are predicated on economic means-qualifying and self-assessed affordable "choice" in coverage by individual consumer "price". Cost and access are highly significant for the near-elderly, those in their fifties and sixties pre-Medicare age. The variability in people's ability to afford the costs can produce serious inequalities in coverage according to ability to pay. Bronze, Silver, Gold and Platinum Plans. *What is this? The Olympic-Jewelers of Health Care Coverage?* The tiered coverage named after increasingly precious metals immediately announces the differing valuation and worth. The contradiction is that the ACA does not ensure equal protection to all who are covered, although the "essential health benefits" protection is crucial. (*Note*: Removing this provision is central for the proponents of ACA Reform and Replace, promoting states' rights.)

ACA repeal and replace actions promised and proposed by President Trump and the GOP-dominated Congress raised major alarm for older and near-old persons, particularly those disadvantaged by race, ethnicity, class, gender, older age, (dis)ability, and pre-existing health conditions. Pernicious attacks and cuts to Social Security, Medicare, and Medicaid will compound inequality.

The emergency Bipartisan Budget Act (BBA) of 2018 provided protection and funding for some programs that ACA

Repeal could end. In the rush to prevent a government shutdown, BBA 2018 health care provisions included changes to Medicare programs and funding for others that support low-income older adults, dual eligibles, people with disabilities and their families (see Legislative Appendix, The BBA 2018, Justice in Aging). The fate of the ACA is uncertain with a new House Democratic majority leading in the 116th Congress commencing in January 2019 while the GOP retains Senate majority.

See also: Age Rating, Cross-national Comparisons, Insurance/Reinsurance, Medical Industrial Complex, Medicare, Medicaid, Neoliberalism, Social Security, Poverty Threshold

Further Reading

Community Catalyst. Retrieved from www.communitycatalyst.org/.

Center for Consumer Engagement in Health Innovation. Retrieved from www.healthinnovation.org/,

Dutta, M. J. (2015). *Neoliberal health organizing*. Walnut Creek, CA: Left Coast Press.

Gabler, N. (2017). Forget fascism, it's anarchy we have to worry about. Retrieved from http://billmoyers.com/story/forget-fascism-anarchy-we-have-to-worry-about/.

Justice in Aging. Retrieved from www.justiceinaging.org/.

Kaiser Health Tracking Poll: The public's views on the ACA. (2017). Retrieved from http://kff.org/interactive/kaiser-health-tracking-poll-the-publics-views-on-the-aca/#?response=Favorable--Unfavorable&aRange=twoYear.

Montero, D. (2017). Nevada governor vetoes Medicaid-for-all bill. *Los Angeles Times (Online)*, June 17. Retrieved from www.latimes.com/nation/la-na-nevada-medicaid-2017-story.html.

Waitzkin, H. (2011). *Medicine and public health at the end of empire*. Boulder, CO: Paradigm.

Wynne, B. (2016, December 7). Five reasons the ACA won't be repealed. *Health Affairs Blog*, December 7. Retrieved from http://healthaffairs.org/blog/2016/12/07/five-reasons-the-aca-wont-be-repealed/.

Age/Aging

Describes an accumulation of experience. It's a complex and highly politicized identity, constructed socially through everyday interactions, cultural norms, and age-based restrictions on social insurance.

Mainstream (and medical) understandings of age are largely chronological in terms of years of life following birth, associated with stages of development throughout the life course (including infancy, childhood, adolescence, and gradations of adulthood and old age/elderhood). Ideologically, concepts of youth, health, and beauty become constellated as visible markers of aging as a process to manage.

Third and Fourth Age

Refers to specific later life course stages. The third age is the life course stage after retirement and before disability (generally framed as the ages between 65 and 80). The fourth age refers to aging after the onset of disability (aged approximately 80+).

The concepts of the third and fourth age may reflect and collapse the liminality or gradations of disability, marginalization, and impairment that occur non-linearly through the life course. The idea of the third age proposes a liminal fantasy land between work and death. The concept of the fourth age is proposed as the final chapter, which functionalist theories have always located as the process of decline. This focus on decline is part of the abjection of old age, and it veers away from any recognition of growth or empowerment.

Critical discourse can examine the dynamics of age and the positive or negative traits and experiences associated by each. Critical gerontology problematizes popular conceptualizations such as chronology to define age, as chronological age erases distinctions between generations, failing to recognize persons through diverse, heterogeneous attributes, such as race, class, gender, and ability.

See also: Abjection, Ableism/TABS, Anti-aging, Liminality, Retirement, Youth

Further Reading

Antonucci, T. C., Ajrouch, K. J., & Birditt, K. (2006). Social relations in the third age: Assessing strengths and challenges using the convoy model. *Annual Review of Gerontology & Geriatrics, 26*: 193–210.

Carr, D. C. & Komp, K. S. (2011). *Gerontology in the era of the third age: Implications and next steps*. New York: Springer.

Gilleard, C. & Higgs, P. (2010). Aging without agency: Theorizing the fourth age. *Aging & Mental Health, 14*(2): 121–128.

Gilleard, C. & Higgs, P. (2015). Social death and the moral identity of the fourth age. *Contemporary Social Science, 10*(3): 262–271.

Higgs, P. & Gilleard, C. (2015). *Rethinking old age: Theorising the fourth age*. London: Palgrave.

Neugarten, B. L. & Neugarten, D. A. (1996). *The meanings of age: Selected papers of Bernice L. Neugarten*. Chicago, IL: University of Chicago Press.

Age Discrimination in Employment Act (ADEA)

This Act was enacted in 1967 to prevent discrimination by age (40 and over) in hiring and to protect employment based on capacity rather than on age. This encompasses the term, condition, or privilege of employment, including layoff, compensation, promotion, job assignments, benefits, and training. The protections apply to private employers with more than 20 employees, all levels of government, union organizations, and employment agencies.

The Older Workers Benefit Protection Act of 1990 (OWBPA) amended the ADEA to specifically prohibit employers from denying benefits to older employees. Employers are permitted to coordinate retiree health benefit plans with eligibility for Medicare or a comparable State-sponsored health benefit.

Complaints may be filed with the U.S. Equal Employment Opportunity Commission (EEOC), whose vision is "Justice and equality in the workplace," and its mission is to "Stop and remedy unlawful employment discrimination." The EEOC:

> is responsible for enforcing federal laws that make it illegal to discriminate against a job applicant or an employee because of the person's race, color, religion, sex (including pregnancy, gender identity, and sexual orientation), national origin, age (40 or older), disability or genetic information. It is also illegal to discriminate against a person because the person complained about discrimination, filed a charge of discrimination, or participated in an employment discrimination investigation or lawsuit.
>
> (info@eeoc.gov. Retrieved November 9, 2017)

Related EEOC Initiatives are (website as of November 9, 2017):

- E-RACE is designed to improve the EEOC's efforts to ensure workplaces are free of race and color discrimination. Specifically, the EEOC will identify issues, criteria and barriers that contribute to race and color discrimination, explore strategies to improve the administrative processing and the litigation of race and color discrimination claims, and enhance public awareness of race and color discrimination in employment (www.eeoc.gov/eeoc/initiatives/e-race/index.cfm).
- LEAD (Leadership for the Employment of Americans with Disabilities) is to address the declining number of employees with targeted disabilities in the federal workforce. The goal for this initiative is to significantly increase the population of individuals with severe disabilities employed by the federal government (www.eeoc.gov/eeoc/initiatives/lead/index.cfm).
- Youth@Work is a national education and outreach campaign to promote equal employment opportunity for America's next generation of workers (www.eeoc.gov/eeoc/initiatives/youth/index.cfm).

In practice, where the EEOC is not able to resolve complaints, the ADEA has had a checkered career in US courts. Some of these have significantly narrowed the coverage protections, leaving the aggrieved believing the law is substantially unenforceable.

See also: Ageism, Civil Rights Movement/ Civil Rights Act, Discrimination, Equality, Watch Dogs/Watch Bitches

Further Reading

EEOC. www.info@eeoc.gov. Quotes and data accessed November 9, 2017.

Harootyan, B. & Sarmiento, T. (2011). The future for older workers: Good news or bad? *Public Policy and Aging Report*, *21*(1), 3–10. Retrieved from https://doi.org/10.1093/ppar/21.1.3.

Macnicol, J. (2012). Action against age discrimination: US and UK comparisons. *Public Policy & Aging Report*, *22*(3): 21–24.

Age Rating

The practice of treating or charging people differentially according to their chronological age for insurance (commercial and social/public) products and markets.

1) The age rating inequity was initially limited by the ACA, which mandated that health insurance rates for older persons may not vary by more than a 3:1 ratio for similar individuals. This is rationalized by actuarial statistics differentiating health costs by age, but it has the effect of cost discrimination by age, with older persons being charged three times more that younger (non-older) persons. Such "risk aversion" or "risk selection" is justified under the logic of private insurance underwriting. Yet research affirms that charging more for those who need (and use) one or another type of care more (age rating or gender rating) is a major contributing factor to vulnerability and cumulative disadvantage. How much money (and for whom) does it save to put by law a higher burden of costs on older persons? On women who have different reproductive care needs than men? Age rating increases the cost of care (out of pocket) for older adults, especially for those on middle or lower incomes. Costs are a barrier to access, and a particular difficulty for lower- and middle-income populations, because housing, transportation, and basic survival needs must be met before purchasing health care insurance. Increasing the age rating ratio, up to 5:1 was proposed in the Republican legislation to repeal the ACA.

2) Age rating is permitted and operative in private long-term care (LTC) insurance "underwriting" (a term that means insurers are allowed to charge consumers the costs of the actuarial risk) based on the age, sex, and health conditions of the purchaser. For example, those under certain ages – say, ages 50 or 55, male or female – as purchasers of insurance may do so for a fraction of the cost for those

aged 60 or 65 and older. But if you have diabetes, high blood pressure, cancer, or heart problems (yourself or in your family), you may be denied (unable to purchase) private LTC insurance at any price. The costs are underwritten at actuarially adjusted rates which are sold at differential costs at the age of the purchaser, as well as where you live and other "market" characteristics. LTC costs and access may change insofar as they apply across the board to particular classes of insured. Private insurers have rate negotiability privileges, pending projected and experience-rated costs of care and certain characteristics of potential purchasers (e.g., pre-existing health conditions, and other characteristics like having a uterus). Notably, many private insurers are exiting the LTC market, given political, economic, actuarial uncertainties, and the low volume of purchasers.

See also: Cumulative Advantage/Disadvantage, Gender Rating

Ageism

A form of discrimination and prejudice, which limits the value of a person through definitions and stereotypes of old age. These include views of older adults as greedy geezers, ugly, out of touch, weak, and worthless. This bigotry justifies denying human rights such as access to needed life resources and participation in civil society. Robert Butler and Maggie Kuhn coined the term "ageism" in the 1970s.

> Ageism is the notion that people become inferior because they have lived a specified number of years.
>
> Maggie Kuhn, Co-founder of the
> Gray Panthers (Hessell, 1977, p. 13)

Ideologically: Ageism bolsters an image of elders as undeserving of well-earned benefits, an effect which can accumulate across many generations of a family.

Structurally: Ageism influences agenda setting, policy formation, policy implementation, and access to public resources.

Physically: Ageism in motion occurs as older persons are visibly seen and depicted as dependent and passive, incapable of mobilizing for social change (they become depoliticized, lacking power and *potential*). Dependence is ascribed only to them and is not recognized as a part of social interdependence.

See also: Abjection, Age Rating, Consciousness Raising, Ideology, Social Construction of Reality

Further Reading

Applewhite, A. (2016). *This chair rocks: A manifesto against ageism*. New York: Networked Books.

Butler, R. N. (1975). *Why survive? Being old in America*. New York: Harper & Row.

Gullette, M. M. (2011). *Agewise: Fighting the new ageism in America*. Chicago, IL: University of Chicago Press.

Hessell, D. T. (1977). *Maggie Kuhn on aging: A dialogue*. Philadelphia, PA: Westminster Press.

Polivka, L. & Estes, C. L. (2009). The economic meltdown and old age politics. *Generations*, *33*(3): 56.

Agency

The ability to act on opportunity, established through individual and collective capacities to enjoy social freedom.

"It is the power to act, not just react" against the omnipotence of the powerful in mobilizing for social change (Dandaneau, 2001, p. 58). Power, as explored throughout this text, is bound and constructed through social relations. Agency is the exercise of the human potential of consciousness to abide by or resist the power of structures comprised through networks.

Revolutionary Human Subject

Enables oneself and others to act as diverse moral agents. In postmodern society, "the future is determined by acts of human will, but within concrete cultural and historical conditions: human subjects act, 'but not in circumstances of their own choosing'" (Leonard, 1997, p 178). A profound question is what is the "possibility of a relatively autonomous subject" because global capitalism "subjugates the individual to a mass culture in which desire is commodified," with "the subordination of nature and the individual subject to the logic of accumulation" (Jameson on the "cultural logic of late capitalism," in Leonard, 1997, p. 46)?

Human agency resides in the "interplay of power and freedom's refusal to submit" (Foucault, 1983, pp. 221–222) and in "the possibility of resistance to dominating power" (Leonard, 1997, p. 47). "The constitution of the revolutionary human subject is historically specific and in the present, related to the resistance of the forces pressing for the homogenization of the dominant [white] culture" (Leonard, 1997, p. 45). It is essential to examine and interrogate the micro processes of power relations. One formulation is that "Human beings make society through their own praxis" (Collins, 1988, p. 80).

In *On tyranny* (2017), Snyder posits that the individual has potentially more power at the moment when a regime shifts toward authoritarianism. Authoritarians rely on a very particular kind of support, or "consent," as Snyder puts it. Individuals can withdraw this support if they are aware of the moment of opportunity and believe in their ability to bring about change. Yet the moment of possibility for change can diminish as time goes on and an authoritarian regime progresses: freedoms such as speech and assembly are increasingly restricted.

Critical gerontological interventions by human agents are exemplified in the lives and legacy of two women, each of whom mobilized a powerful social movement that empowered the agency and social consciousness of many individuals: Maggie Kuhn (co-founder of the Gray Panthers) and Tish Summers (co-founder of Displaced Homemakers and the Older Women's League). Today, individual and collective agency is demonstrated by those taking risks by speaking out and participating on the front and back stages of Black Lives Matter, a justice movement supported by more than one million Americans.

See also: Affect, Authoritarianism, Black Lives Matter, Gray Panthers, Human Rights, Interaction Ritual Chains, Maggie Kuhn, Networks, Praxis, Resistance, Social Movements, United States Constitution

Further Reading

Bandura, A. (2000). Exercise of human agency through collective efficacy. *Current Directions in Psychological Science*, 9(3): 75–78.

Collins, R. (1988). *Theoretical sociology*. San Diego, CA: Harcourt Brace Jovanovich.

Dandaneau, S. P. (2001). *Taking it big*. Thousand Oaks, CA: Pine Forge Press.

Foucault, M. (1983). The subject and power. Afterword to H. Dreyfus & P. Rabinow (Eds.), *Michel Foucault: Beyond structuralism and hermeneutics* (pp. 208–264). New York: Routledge.

Leonard, P. (1997). *Postmodern welfare: Reconstructing an emancipatory project*. London: Sage.

Snyder, T. (2017). *On tyranny*. New York: Penguin Random House.

Aging Enterprise

A term coined by Estes (1979) to describe the congeries of stakeholders, professionals, politicians, governments, scientists, industries, trade associations, and lobbyists that benefit from old age being defined as a problem to be dealt with by experts and served by corporate interests. Transforming the health needs of aging persons into commodities for specific economic markets has produced the aging enterprise which supports a highly profitable, technological, pharmaceutically intensive, and specialist-driven approach for treating individual symptoms as presented by older persons who are labeled "consumers" and "customers." The enterprise, comprising well-meaning professionals, scholars, and service workers that serve the aged, also includes nurses, physicians, pharmacists, hospitals, nursing homes, the Social Security Administration (SSA), the Administration on Aging (AoA), state and regional agencies on aging, Congressional committees on aging, and the aging network of home- and community-based agencies spawned under the Older Americans Act.

These numerous organizations and programs have been fueled by age-segregated policies, and services have singled out and isolated the aging population as a problem and burden to society. This selection process stigmatizes and separates the old from the rest of society, promoting policy and practice efforts to integrate services across different funding streams such as Medicare, Medicaid, the ACA, and programs and services of the Administration for Community Living/ACL and the Older Americans Act. The Aging Enterprise is a large component of the gargantuan medical industrial complex (MIC), which commodifies and exploits the illnesses of old and young alike.

See also: Affordable Care Act, Ageism, Financialization, MIC, Medicaid, Medical

Industrial Complex, Medicare, Neoliberalism, Older Americans Act, Structured Dependency Theory

Further Reading

Estes, C. L. (1979). *The aging enterprise: A critical examination of social policies and services for the aged*. San Francisco, CA: Jossey-Bass.

Estes, C. L. (1993). The aging enterprise revisited. *The Gerontologist, 33*(3): 292.

Aging in Community/ Aging in Place

Entails continuing to live and grow older within the community in which one lives. Relocating to retirement zones or to remote assisted living facilities often removes an aging individual from social networks and cultural ties to place. Aging in community is frequently associated with social policies and ideals, such as "aging in place" or "age-friendly" efforts. The term "aging in place" refers specifically to being able to remain in one's own home and community safely and independently regardless of age, income, or ability level. "Age-friendly" is a global effort to transform cities and communities into places where all residents can grow up and grow old, with a focus on eight domains: housing, transportation, outdoor spaces and buildings, community support and health services, communication and information, civic participation and employment, respect and social inclusion, and social participation.

Critical gerontology may examine how social policies and ideals for aging in community, such as "aging in place" and "age-friendly" efforts, are on the rise, but in the context of the political economy of urban change, such as economic recession, contraction of the welfare state, austerity policies, gentrification and ownership problems,

migration of people and capital, and the intensification of global competition (Buffel, Handler, & Phillipson, 2018; Stafford, 2018; Torres, 2018). Critical gerontology may also challenge how "aging in place" and "age-friendly" efforts are parts of a commercially promoted initiative of healthy aging, commodifying experiences through technoscientific interventions, such as architecture and design (Yeh, 2015; Yeh et al., 2016; see chart below). Praxis toward acommunity gerontology (Greenfield et al., 2018 forthcoming), a focus on urban management, and embedding efforts within a radical public policy agenda are pivotal for aging in community (Buffel, Handler, & Phillipson, 2018; Phillipson, 2015).

See also: Climate Change, Ecologies, Gentrification, Healthy Aging/Active Aging, Housing

Further Reading

Becker, G. (2003). Meanings of place and displacement in three groups of older immigrants. *Journal of Aging Studies, 17,* 129–149.

Black, K. & Hyer, K. (2016). From aging in community to age-friendly community: Translating applied research into practice. *The International Journal of Aging and Society, 6*(4): 59–71.

Buffel, T., Handler, S., & Phillipson, C. (Eds.). (2018). *Age-friendly cities and communities: A global perspective*. Bristol: Policy Press.

Caro, F. G. & Fitzgerald, K. G. (Eds.). (2016). *International perspectives on age-friendly cities*. New York: Routledge.

Golant, S. (2015). *Aging in the right place*. Baltimore, MD: Health Professionals Press.

Greenfield, E. A., Black, K., Buffel, T., & Yeh, J. (2018). Community gerontology: A framework for research, policy, and practice on communities and aging. *The Gerontologist*, gny089, https://doi.org/10.1093/geront/gny089.

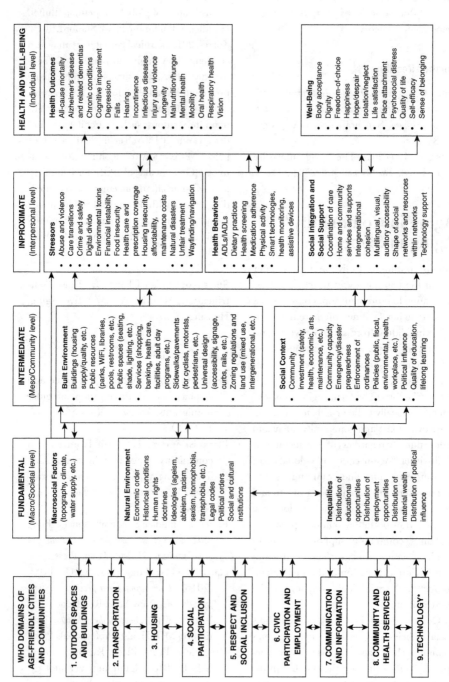

Figure A1 Building Inclusion

Source: Yeh et al. (2016, pp. 1947–1949).

Greenfield, E. A., Oberlink, M., Scharlach, A. E., Neal, M. B., & Stafford, P. B. (2015). Age-friendly community initiatives: Conceptual issues and key questions. *The Gerontologist, 55*(2), 191–198.

Phillipson, C. (2015). Developing age-friendly urban communities: Critical issues for public policy. *Public Policy and Aging Report, 25*(1), 4–8.

Scharlach, A. E. & Lehning, A. J. (2016). *Creating aging-friendly communities.* New York: Oxford University Press.

Stafford, P. (2018). *The global age-friendly community movement: A critical appraisal.* New York: Berghahn.

Torres, S. (2018). Aging in places. In C. Wellin (Ed.), *Critical gerontology comes of age: Advances in research and theory for a new century* (pp. 151–163). New York: Routledge/Taylor & Francis.

Torres-Gil, F. & Hofland, B. (2012). "Vulnerable populations." In H. Cisneros, M. Dyer-Chamberlain, & J. Hickie (Eds.), *Independent for life: Homes and neighborhoods for an aging America* (pp. 221–232). Austin, TX: University of Austin Press.

Webster, N. J., Ajrouch, K. J., & Antonucci, T. C. (2013). Living healthier, living longer: The benefits of residing in community. *Generations, 37*(4), 28.

World Health Organization, Age-friendly world. Retrieved from www.who.int/ageing/age-friendly-world/en/.

Yeh, J. C. (2015). "The lure of restoration: Transforming buildings and bodies for ever-longer life." In A-L. Müller & W. Reichmann (Eds.), *Architecture, materiality, and society: Connecting sociology of architecture with science and technology studies* (pp. 119–144). New York: Palgrave Macmillan.

Yeh, J. C., Walsh, J., Spensley, C., & Wallhagen, M. (2016). Building inclusion: Toward an aging- and disability-friendly city. *American Journal of Public Health, 106*(11), 1947–1949.

Yen, I. H., Shim, J. K., Martinez, A. D., & Barker, J. C. (2012). Older people and social connectedness: How place and activities keep people engaged. *Journal of Aging Residents, 139523,* 1–10.

Alienation

Absence of belonging or connectedness, including the act of forcing a person away from integration and personal value, through rejection, denial, or separation. The following include theoretic frameworks and dimensions of alienation:

1) Marx spoke of alienation of labor, in which an institution or process creates something (or a fragmented piece of it) that the worker involved in production would never own or enjoy, and conceivably would neither be owned nor enjoyed by members of one's family or community. The worker does not know how the products of her or his time, focus, and energy manifest and matter to self or others. In a sense one is controlled by the work and not in control of the product, whether it be material or ideal (from the mind). There is little choice of how to create and the methods of production are not determined by the worker.

2) Durkheim (1897/1951) extended this analysis as part of his formulations on suicide and "anomie," the dislocation from societal values as a result of individualism (in the industrial era) and the futility of striving.

3) Stereotyping may be understood as an act of alienation. It obscures value by simplification and constriction, as it reduces the complexity and nuances of identity and produces an intersubjective dislocation of the self or personhood.

4) Alienation functions in xenophobia and nativism: where belonging becomes contingent upon officially sanctioned, State-granted citizenship, or in skin color, and/or birthplace.

5) Knowledge can also function as a form of alienation, where thinkers do not try to change the world but only to know it (Lefebvre, in Collins, 1988, p. 104).

An important set of questions for critical gerontology include how policy and practice shape geographic realities that alienate elders from their communities: forcing them to relocate or enter into institutions where their community participation may be halted or severely restricted.

Alienation may also be understood through interaction and intersubjectivity. Someone listening to the struggles of older adults' realities and who responds with "That's not my problem" engages in operational alienation. This example is also an alienation from the self, as a younger individual fails to understand that he or she, too, will eventually face the same or similar struggles.

Many/most marginalized people experience a loss or lack of self-esteem. This doubt in self-worth is a profound experience of internalized alienation.

See also: Abjection, Internalization/Internalized Oppression, Oppression, Xenophobia

Further Reading

Collins, R. (1988). *Theoretical sociology.* San Diego, CA: Harcourt Brace Jovanovich.

Durkheim, E. (1951). *Suicide: A study in sociology* (trans. J. A. Spaulding & G. Simpson). Glencoe, IL: Free Press. (Originally published 1897.)

Allostatic Load

Measures the "wear and tear" on the body due to chronic stress and everyday living, including high blood pressure, inflammation, and other diseases (McEwen & Stellar, 1993).

Critical implications include exposure to stress due to insecurity and inequality experienced in and through oppressive systems across the lifespan and life space. Allostatic load relates to Cumulative Disadvantage/Advantage Theory in that it helps to reveal how successive negative forces can have an outsized impact over the course of a lifetime.

See also: Cumulative Advantage/Disadvantage, Gene–Environment, Life Course Perspective/Theory, Racism, Sexism, Stereotype Threat

Further Reading

Adler, N. E., Boyce, W. T., Chesney, M. A., Folkman, S., & Syme, S. L. (1993). Socioeconomic inequalities in health: No easy solution. *Journal of the American Medical Association, 269*(24), 3140–3145.

Gruenewald, T. L., Karlamangla, A. S., Hu, P., Stein-Merkin, S., Crandall, C., Koretz, B., & Seeman, T. E. (2012). History of socioeconomic disadvantage and allostatic load in later life. *Social Science & Medicine, 74*(1), 75–83.

Levine, M., Cole, S., Weir, D., & Crimmins, E. (2015). Childhood and later life stressors and increased inflammatory gene expression at older ages. *Social Science and Medicine, 130*, 16–22. NIHMSID 672793.

Lynch, J. W., Kaplan, G. A., & Shema, S. J. (1997). Cumulative impact of sustained economic hardship on physical, cognitive, psychological, and social functioning. *The New England Journal of Medicine, 337*(26), 1889–1895.

McEwen, B. S., & Stellar, E. (1993). Stress and the individual: Mechanisms leading to disease. *Archives of Internal Medicine, 153*(18), 2093–2101.

Alt-Right

A new name for pre-existing (but covert and in many cases anonymous) reactionary conservative movements, primarily in digital spaces, that offers an extreme alternative to established right-wing groups and mainstream conservatism.

These groups are loosely organized around outrage and cynicism, geared toward attacking sensitivities for the "politically correct," opposing multiculturalism, feminism, globalism, and integration. It involves code words for racial slurs and internet lingo to ridicule social movements and social justice. Often provoking backlash and censorship from the Left, the Alt-Right revels in "trolling" liberals by boldly displaying racism and misogyny, while claiming the freedom to discriminate and articulate hate. The movement mocks "safe spaces" and "trigger-warnings" which many college campuses promote as necessary for inclusive learning. Alt-right groups typically embrace various aspects of white supremacy and ethnonationalism.

We include the term here because it represents the shifting ideological frameworks and organizing that appear on social media. Their mocking tugs at discursive threads by promoting new oppositional voices, threatening actors on the Left, women, religious minorities, and people of color.

See also: Fascism, People of Color, Trolling, War on Women

Alzheimer's Disease (AD)

Affects the brain and degrades cognitive function and memory. Estimates on/of the prevalence of Alzheimer's in society differ significantly depending on the source and on the definition of cognitive impairments that are included under Alzheimer's. In particular, Mild Cognitive Impairment diagnoses may or may not develop into a more specific diagnosis of Alzheimer's, but there is often a "jumping-the-gun," a quick and fearful leap. A diagnosis of AD is equivalent to a death sentence (Beard, 2016), in which the privileges of interdependent social relationships may be eliminated or restricted. It may be

tantamount to a loss of "personhood, maybe even a loss of humanity" (Beard, 2016; Beard & Fox, 2008).

A critical perspective on AD locates the construction of the "disease" in the crisis constructions of old age and aging that bolsters the medicalization, commodification, and aging enterprise of brain health-related sciences, professions, services, and industries. Alzheimer's is frequently framed not only as a crisis of public health but also as an impending demographic disaster as an aging population leads to increased prevalence of the disease (Chaufan et al., 2012).

The Alzheimer's Movement

The Alzheimer's Movement is comprised of both coordinated and fragmented social and political efforts to study and eradicate Alzheimer's Disease (AD), diagnose and treat it, to support individuals, families, and communities, and to capitalize on the disease for economic, political, and social gains that may be realized. In other words, measures to improve lives can have ulterior motives and effects.

"The Alzheimerization of aging" (Adelman, 1998) denotes the emphasis (if not the domination) of Alzheimer's disease as one of the main NIH/NIA research priorities, overpowering the "basic science" investigator-initiated open federal funding power structures. The success of the Alzheimer's Movement is seen in the crisis construction of the disease; Congressional designation of AD studies and clinical trials; wide adoption among media, the public, Congress, university scientists, and biomedical industries; and echoed by trade groups of professionals and providers. Biological science critics argue that research on aging has been taken over (and conflated with) research on AD.

Fundamental in the process of the Alzheimerization of aging has been the redesignation of senility as a qualifier for an

Alzheimer's diagnosis. In the 1980s Dr. Robert Katzman spearheaded an effort to relabel the vast majority of cases of senile dementia as Alzheimer's (Chaufan et al., 2012). This relabeling led to Alzheimer's rates that were shockingly high, helping the emerging crisis construction of the disease. The advocacy groups that coalesced around the disease, many of them formed, in part, out of previous dementia advocacy groups, struggled initially to determine where to focus their efforts, on biomedical research or public assistance for families and individuals. The vast majority of resources have been funneled into research, through the NIH/NIA (Chaufan et al., 2012).

The fear of memory loss and cognitive impairment is widespread. A 2012 poll, by the Marist Institute, found that Alzheimer's is the most feared disease among Americans (O'Neill, 2012). Some of this fear has undoubtedly resulted from mislabeling and imprecision in the science of AD.

See also: Medical Industrial Complex, Social Movements, Statistical Panic

Further Reading

Adelman, R. C. (1998). The Alzheimerization of aging: A brief update. *Experimental Gerontology*, *33*(1), 155–157.

Beard, R. L. (2016). *Living with Alzheimer's: Managing memory loss, identity, and illness.* New York: New York University Press.

Beard, R. L. & Fox, P. J. (2008). Resisting social disenfranchisement: Negotiating collective identities and everyday life with memory loss. *Social Science & Medicine*, *66*(7), 1509–1520.

Behuniak, S. M. (2011). The living dead? The construction of people with Alzheimer's disease as zombies. *Aging and Society: An Interdisciplinary Journal*, *31*, 70–92.

Bredesen, D. (2017). *The end of Alzheimer's: The first program to prevent and reverse cognitive decline.* New York: Penguin.

Chaufan, C., Hollister, B., Nazareno, J., & Fox, P. (2012). Medical ideology as a double-edged sword: The politics of cure and care in the making of Alzheimer's disease. *Social Science & Medicine*, *74*(5), 788–795.

Flatt, J., Johnson, J., & Mack, A. (2018). Dementia prevalence among sexual minority older adults. *Alzheimer's and Dementia*, *14*(7 supplement), P577–P578.

Hollister, B., Flatt, J. D., & Chapman, S. A. (2018). Dementia-capable care coordination in duals demonstration programs: Workforce needs, promising practices, and policy. *The Gerontologist*, 58(4), 768–778.

Latest Alzheimer's facts and figures. (2013). Retrieved from www.alz.org/facts/overview.asp.

O'Neill, S. (2012). Alzheimer's is top health fear of most Americans. *Southern California Public Radio: News*, November 14. Retrieved from www.scpr.org/news/2012/11/14/34931/do-you-fear-alzheimers-many-americans-do-poll-says/.

Rice, D., Fox, P., Max, W., Webber, P. A., Hauck, W. W., Lindeman, D. A., & Segura, E. (1993). The economic burden of Alzheimer's disease care. *Health Affairs*, *12*(2), 164–176.

Ambiguity

Uncertainty, inexactness; open to interpretation and often not clearly contextualized.

Intentional Ambiguity

Policy or action that denotes legislative and administrative mandates that are deliberately vague and nonspecific. "Intentional ambiguity obviates the necessity for making value decisions explicit, and permits multiple interpretations," and it is handy:

[W]hen (1) there is little apparent national consensus on the nature of the problem to be addressed, the goals to be achieved, or the methods to be used in implementing policies; (2) suggested alternative policies are . . . politically controversial, making it risky to establish an unambiguous policy choice; or (3) a measure passed by one political party is then implemented during the administration of another party with differing policies and priorities.

(Estes, 1979, p. 66)

Intentional ambiguity is now embedded in the dizzyingly stratified maze of Medicare policy and coverage, the many-fold options (and attendant penalties or incentives) in qualifying for and collecting Social Security, Medicaid, and other benefits. Intentional ambiguity facilitates "window and door opening" during turbulent historical moments such as the Trump-led repeal of the Affordable Care Act (ACA), and the power plays in Washington, DC, gridlock that may produce government shutdowns, and other potentially calamitous results for people.

Those who are most powerless in the situations created by ambiguous mandates are a program's clientele (potential and actual) and advocates, who possess the least means to redress program faults (or perhaps class action legal cases) because there are few clear expectations of required benefits and uniformity of definitions and standards against which to measure performance. The wide range of choices about required activities (e.g., even women's mandated health coverage under the ACA), how such requirements are to be carried out, and what is to be accomplished, escapes legislative specificity that would ensure public accountability. Ambiguity facilitates complexity and tends to assure that nothing more drastic will occur universally (e.g., economic redistribution or equal treatment by gender or race across the board) will be accomplished. Ambiguity contributes to the maintenance of the existing social order.

The Older Americans Act (OAA) is replete with ambiguous mandates and widespread state and intra-state discretion, including suggestions that the OAA address the special needs of low-income and minority older persons. Indeed, the issues of block granting and states' rights pervade welfare programs such as Temporary Assistance for Needy Family (TANF), Supplemental Nutrition Assistance Program (SNAP or more popularly known as Food Stamps), and Supplemental Security Income (SSI). Ambiguity in policy and implementation may maintain institutional practices of discrimination and favoritism by race, ethnicity, class, gender. ability, and age. The assertion of block grants and states' rights tends to work against extending universal and uniform rights and protections nationally, including voting rights. Ambiguity and new federalism arguably favor the increasingly dominant corporate power networks across social policy domains.

See also: Affordable Care Act, Block Grants, Framing, New Federalism

Further Reading

Estes, C. L. (1979). *The aging enterprise* (pp. 65–72). San Francisco, CA: Jossey-Bass.

Estes, C. L. & Newcomer, R. J. (1983). *Fiscal austerity and aging: Shifting government responsibility for the elderly*. Beverly Hills, CA: Sage.

Americans with Disabilities Act (ADA)

A policy enacted in 1990 that defines the rights of and grants protections to disabled Americans. These include equal employment opportunities, access to public accommodations and commercial facilities (including the use of service animals), and telecommunication supports.

This legislation has been referred to as a "second-generation civil rights statute."

See also: Ableism/TABS, Choice, Commodification, Disability, Medicaid, Medical Industrial Complex, Medicare, Older Americans Act, Resistance, Social Security Disability Insurance, Supplemental Security Insurance

Further Reading

Burgdorf Jr., R. L. (1991). The Americans with Disabilities Act: Analysis and implications of a second-generation civil rights statute. *Harvard Civil Rights/Civil Liberties Review, 26*: 413.

Krieger, L. H. (Ed.). (2010). *Backlash against the ADA: Reinterpreting disability rights.* Michigan, OH: University of Michigan Press.

www.ada.gov/.

Anti-aging

Frames aging as a degenerative process to be controlled, prevented, and avoided. It is concerned with multi-level efforts to extend life expectancy, enhance healthy aging, and improve and extend quality of life years (see Quality-adjusted Life Years), cognition, and respect.

Anti-aging is an ideology and a set of micro, meso, and macro forces related to many concepts in this book such as plasticity, resilience, telomeres, productive aging, ageism, gene–environment, biomedicalization, capitalism, the State, NIH, the MIC, PHARMA, globalization, life course experience, oppressions, racism, sexism, and cumulative dis/advantages.

Justice/injustice, suffering, and micro aggressions may be illuminated within the critical theoretical lens on anti-aging and the knowledges it produces. (The cosmetic surgery empire lives off the abhorrence of

aging, a perverse form of anti-aging across all ages, genders, and sexuality.)

In Silicon Valley, tech giants have founded numerous research and development companies (e.g., Google's Calico) looking for death-defying synthetic biological interventions. Big capital collides with anti-aging research. Both Jeff Bezos (CEO/founder of Amazon) and Peter Theil (conservative venture capitalist and co-founder of PayPal, who ruined Gawker Media for outing him as a gay conservative) invested in Unity Biotechnology in 2016.

Anti-aging therapies include gene manipulation, 3D printed organs, and infusions of enzymes to prevent senescence (cell death). Tad Friend for *The New Yorker* reports that masculinism pervades how the biotech moguls court venture capitalists. He posits that, ironically, the most proven way of extending a man's life is suppression of testosterone, which has historically been achieved via castration; yet it seems the male hero's quest to win the battle against death.

Aging A–Z contains the key elements required for a political economy of anti-aging from a critical perspective at the micro, meso, and macro levels. The critical theoretical foundations surrounding health disparities, inequality, necropolitics – located alongside research about epigenetics, gene–environment and telomeres – provides opportunities for readers to problematize the complexity of the anti-aging industry.

See also: Ageism, Biomedicalization, Medical Industrial Complex, Quality-adjusted Life Years

Further Reading

Friend, T. (2017). Silicon Valley's quest to live forever. *The New Yorker*, April 3. Retrieved from www.newyorker.com/magazine/2017/04/03/silicon-valleys-quest-to-live-forever.

Joyce, K. & Mamo, L. (2006). Graying the cyborg: New directions in feminist analyses of aging, science and technology. In T. M. Calasanti and K. F. Slevin (Eds.), *Age matters: Realigning feminist thinking* (pp. 99–122). New York: Routledge.

Katz, S. & Marshall, B. (2003). New sex for old age: Lifestyle, consumerism, and the ethics of aging well. *Journal of Aging Studies, 17*, 3–16.

Kaufman, S. R. (2010). Making longevity in an aging society: Linking Medicare policy and the new ethical field. *Perspectives in Biology and Medicine, 53*(3), 407–424.

Kaufman, S. R., Shim, J. K., & Russ, A. J. (2006). Old age, life extension, and the character of medical choice. *Journal of Gerontology Series B; Psychology and Social Sciences, 61*(4), S175–S184.

Shim, J. K., Russ, A. J., & Kaufman, S. R. (2006). Risk, life extension and the pursuit of medical possibility. *Sociology of Health and Illness, 28*(4), 479–502.

Vincent, J. (2006). Anti-ageing science and the future of old age. In J. A. Vincent, C. Phillipson, & M. Downs (Eds.), *The futures of old age* (pp. 192–200). Thousand Oaks, CA: Sage.

Art as Resistance

Promotes the idea that creative expression is a vehicle of emancipation and a method of resisting repressive political and social forces.

- Murals portray a cultural history that gentrification and urban development threaten to erase or obscure a people's voice.

Julene Johnson (2013) explores how older adults use choral song. She writes:

We have so much to learn about how the arts impact human development. We need to better understand the basic mechanisms involved in the positive effect of music on the health and well-being of elders. We do know that choral singing can be a demanding activity that involves a combination of physical, emotional, cognitive, and social elements.

Further Reading

Johnson, J. K. (2013). The effects of singing on older adults. *Art Works Blog*, February 15. National Endowment for the Arts. Retrieved from www.arts.gov/art-works/2013/effects-singing-older-adults.

Johnson, J. K., Stewart, A. L., & Acree, M. (2018). A community choir intervention to promote well-being among diverse older adults: Results from the community of voices trial. *The Journals of Gerontology Series B:* gby132, https://doi.org/10.1093/geronb/gby132.

Austerity

An economic ideology and policy predicated on the belief that scarcity of resources should govern public policy. Austerity purports to reduce or eliminate public deficits and debt by reducing spending on social programs and other financial commitments of the State, often shifting subsidies and services to the private, for-profit sector.

Internationally, following the 2008 financial crisis, governments imposed austerity to rein in public spending, led by the IMF and the largest banks. Across the European Union, countries sought to decrease their debt in response to shrinking GDP and high unemployment. This approach has been relatively ineffective, as increased austerity has not correlated with rapid economic recovery, while debt reductions are small compared to the spending cuts made. Government expenditures do not exist in a vacuum. State spending, itself, contributes to GDP and employment. Cuts in the former do not automatically lead to reductions in the latter (De Grauwe & Ji, 2013). Social consequences include destabilizing social lives and causing human misery for many.

In the United States, austerity is the ideology and solution to the crises espoused by the political right wing and by moderates. Groups like the Committee for a Responsible Federal Budget (CRFB) tirelessly analyze and advocate budget and service cuts, fueled by an endless stream of private financial and business interests and politically active members of the super-wealthy class. CRFB has spawned discourse and subsidiaries to campaign against public debt. Fix the Debt, one such subsidiary, acts as an ardent proponent for "corporate welfare" by cutting social spending and promoting generous corporate tax cuts and loopholes for wealthy executives (Anderson & Klinger, 2012).

A critical lens tells us that austerity is the product of an artificial crisis, constructed for economic and political interests. Debt is everywhere and affects everyone. The point at which it traverses from helpful to harmful, in an aggregate sense, may be entirely subjective. The Reagan Administration promoted the idea of a large-scale crisis of spending and debt (Estes & Newcomer, 1983). This socially constructed state of economic crisis continues to this day, since Reagan has become sacrosanct in conservative circles still basking in the glow of massive tax cuts and increased federal subsidies to private industry.

Today, claims of crisis (however produced) provide the rationale for sustained ideological attacks and deficit crisis rhetoric intended to reduce welfare state commitments to the American public. This "debt crisis" is often blamed on older US citizens who had nothing to do with it. The solution most often proposed is to cut the only program that has not contributed to the deficit, namely Social Security (Altman, 2017). The entrenchment of the deficit crisis frame on both the political Right and the political Left reflects the strength of adherents to market

fundamentalism, who are unalterably opposed to domestic spending on the social safety net (Mendoza, 2015).

Through the lens of aging, Ghilarducci (2013) describes the downside of austerity political economy as being a distortion of the natural common economic interests between generations, which results in "false intergenerational warfare" (p. 953). The austerity discourse sows fear and distrust between generations instead of promoting learning and cooperation, which are essential in establishing solidarity.

A noteworthy contradiction is that the 2017 Tax Cut and Jobs Act scored a $1.7 trillion federal deficit by the Congressional Budget Office, while the GOP touted that the tax cuts (mostly for corporations and the wealthy) would produce GDP growth sufficient to make much of that deficit go away. One joke was that it should be called the Cut, Cut, Cut, Cut Act (as Trump suggested) or the Leona Helmsley Tax Act (as some progressives suggested). For aging policy, the elderly, and the middle aged, and the middle class, it is clear that "deficits" are (and will continue to be) used as the rationale for reducing Social Security, Medicare, and Medicaid benefits.

See also: Capitalism, Crisis, Debt, Deficit Crisis Frame, Economics, Solidarity

Further Reading

Altman, N. (2017). Wall Street's 'solution' to every problem: Cut Social Security. *HuffPost*, April 27. Retrieved from www.huffingtonpost.com/entry/wall-streets-solution-to-every-problem-cut-social_us_5900d878e4b0768c2682e21b.

Anderson, S. & Klinger, S. (2012). *The CEO campaign to 'fix' the debt: A Trojan horse for massive corporate tax breaks*. Washington, DC: Institute for Policy Studies.

Brown, W. (2015). *Undoing the demos* (1st edition). Cambridge, MA: MIT Press.

De Grauwe, P. & Ji, Y. (2013). Panic-driven austerity in the eurozone and its implications. Retrieved from http://voxeu.org/article/panic-driven-austerity-eurozone-and-its-implications.

Estes, C. L. & Newcomer, R. J. (1983). *Fiscal austerity and aging: Shifting government responsibility for the elderly*. Beverly Hills, CA: Sage.

Ghilarducci, T. (2013). Austerity distorts the common economic interests between generations. *Social Research*, *80*(3), 953–976. Retrieved from www.jstor.org/stable/24385699.

Mendoza, K-A. (2015). *Austerity: The demolition of the welfare state and the rise of the zombie economy*. Oxford: New Internationalist Publishing.

Authoritarianism

Characterized by governments and regimes which restrict political freedoms and their citizens' orientation. Authoritarianism does not belong to the Right or the Left, but rather describes the behaviors of leaders and followers as dimensions of personality (Adorno et al., 1950).

At the core of the authoritarian personality is an intolerance of difference. This includes aggression toward the Other, articulated through racism, sexism, xenophobia, ageism, and ableism. Fear mobilizes a group of people toward exclusionary behaviors and obedience to central authority (holding all power, embodying privilege). Altemeyer (1988) says that this fear is socially conditioned, and that it can be scaled and measured.

MacWilliams (2016) writes about how Donald Trump "activated" his base, tapping into the fears of his followers and offering them representation of their ideas in mainstream politics: birtherism, advocacy for the "forgotten man," extreme anti-immigrant sentiment, Islamophobia, and regressive views on gender.

See also: Civil (Dis)obedience, Demagogue, Domination, Fascism, Networks, Power, State, Violence

Further Reading

Adorno, T. W., Frenkel-Brunswik, E., Levinson, D. J., & Sanford, R. N. (1950). *The authoritarian personality*. New York: Harpers.

Altemeyer, B. (1988). *Enemies of freedom: Understanding right-wing authoritarianism*. San Francisco, CA: Jossey-Bass.

MacWilliams, M. C. (2016). *The rise of Trump: America's authoritarian spring*. Amherst, MA: Amherst College Press.

B

Baby Boomers

The population cohort born between 1946 and 1964 comprising approximately 76 million individuals.

Rarely esteemed, the "baby boom" generation is often disparaged as an intractable burden on all those born after this period. A book by Peter Peterson (2000) entitled *Gray dawn: How the coming age wave will transform America – and the world* imagines a future overloaded by millions who drain social institutions and sink the economy. Terms employed to describe the demography of aging such as "gray dawn" and "silver tsunami" (another popular metaphor; *see* labeling) advance a statistical panic. Hype, memeification, and hyperbole hysterically portray the 'baby boom' as a force that kills our society and blots out the promise of opportunity for all of humankind to follow.

Increasing life expectancy, popularly celebrated by modern medicine and public health institutions, becomes a liability in the face of the "baby boomer" discourse. The rant of unsustainability – of runaway budgets, of insolvent institutions – frames the "baby boomers" as a threat to the American Dream, echoing the chorus of austerity hawks who label older adults as "greedy geezers" – those who want support but can no longer contribute. This fear advances the rationalization and justification for neoliberalism, quashing the safety net, and dismantling social insurance programs. These politicized images of baby boomers have been an operating rationale among opponents of the welfare state to "take back" the New Deal and reduce social insurance, like Social Security and Medicare

The critical perspective – that interdependence is not a liability, but rather a social reality to be valued – challenges the dominant ideology of individual responsibility.

See also: Austerity, Crisis, Debt, Demography, Discourse, Framing, Ideology, Labelling, Neoliberalism, Statistical Panic, Welfare State

Further Reading

Estes, C. L., Biggs, S., & Phillipson, C. (2003). Productivity and aging. In C. L. Estes, S. Biggs, & C. Phillipson (Eds.), *Social theory, social policy and ageing: A critical introduction, critical perspectives* (pp. 62–78). London: McGraw-Hill Education.

Kleyman, P. (2017). The myth of anti-aging: Media hype and the myth of the ageless baby boomer. *Generations: Journal of the American Society on Aging, 41*(2/1), 41–47.

Morrow-Howell, N., Hinterlong, J., & Sherraden, M. (2003). *Productive aging: Concepts and challenges.* Baltimore, MD: Johns Hopkins University Press. Retrieved from

http://muse.jhu.edu/books/978080
1876578.

Peterson, P. G. (2000). *Gray dawn: How the
coming age wave will transform America – and
the world*. New York: Three Rivers Press.

Big Data

Large, complex sets of data collected over
time that may reveal trends and developments over ever-expanding time and space
dimensions. Meta-analyses combining multiple datasets and graphics technology and
capabilities permit future projections and
predictions. Combined big data resources
may illustrate the interactions between phenomena (measured as variables) such as
race, class, gender, and health with phenomena such as institutional racism and sexism
measured and factored in. The aggregation
of such data and its availability and accessibility is a relatively new phenomenon. The
NIA provides millions of dollars in funding
to analyze the data now available. This
model departs from past studies which
required primary data collection (through
participants). Research.gov and data.gov
provide public access to large datasets, and
many local and state governments have
similar data-sharing platforms.

The advancement of scientific knowledge has been taken for granted as a core
responsibility of the State. However, a large
anti-science movement has grown in tandem with the increasing science in support
of a green earth and green economy (see
Climate Change). Anti-science interests
have enveloped the conservative Right,
advancing their agenda of bringing back
coal and drilling for oil and gas in the name
of economic growth (and as a political strategy to win voters by exploiting the desperation of economically depressed areas such
as Appalachia). The Trump presidency
installed cabinet members who are adherents of EPA abolishment and who deny the
scientific consensus on climate change. The
Trump government's support for gag rules
and the suppression (if not the disappearance) of big data drew concern and fear
from the academic and activist communities. Scientists around the globe and the
public expressed this via multiple modalities (e.g., the 2017 March for Science in
the capitol and 500+ communities worldwide). Principles of the Science March
included: science that serves the common
good; evidence-based policy and regulations in the public interest; cutting-edge science education; diversity and inclusion in
STEM; open, honest science and inclusive
public outreach; and funding for scientific
research and its applications.

In gerontological and geriatric research
and policy, there are major advances in the
collection and availability of big data and
ever-newer models and analytics of income,
health, social networks, and life expectancy
utilizing the NIA-funded Health and Retirement Survey (HRS) and multiple federally
funded longitudinal studies. Many of these
now reside in university research centers
with vast public use access. Biodemography
and gene–environment work is being integrated into social, behavioral, and policy sciences. These developments open up major
opportunities for critical scholarship on
aging and aging policy in relation to under-
studied and under-conceptualized alternative frameworks, including examining the
macro-institutional measures of racism and
sexism and the manifestations of oppression, exploitation, and human suffering. Big
data examples exist throughout *A–Z*, demonstrating inequalities in life expectancy,
health, and retirement security.

Big data tracking marginalized populations is key in holding a collective memory of disparity in the wake of historical
trauma. As an example, data collected for
Holocaust survivors, both for first generation and subsequent generations, provides

opportunities for analyzing ties within networks (Blanke & Prescott, 2016). The European Holocaust Research Infrastructure (EHRI) "investigates, collects and integrates Holocaust material from archives across Europe [linking] the material in archives into virtual collections [illustrating] how the linking, identification and cross-referencing of records which characterizes big data is also at the heart of much traditional historical research" (Blanke & Prescott, 2016, p. 195).

The Administration for Community Living (ACL) proposes to erase lesbian, gay, bisexual, and transgender (LGBT) older adults from the National Survey of Older American Act Participants (NSOAAP). This survey provides critical data on whether federally funded aging programs like meals on wheels, family caregiver support, adult day care, and senior centers reach all older adults, including LGBT older adults. This disrupts grant proposals, delivery modules, and program structuring which relies heavily on such data; and at its core such an erasure communicates an ideology of unworthiness and exclusion.

Two *aging policy examples* include the measuring of the "economic stimulus" provided by Social Security, and the distributional consequences (negative and positive) of proposed policy changes in the US State (such as raising the Medicare eligibility age from 65 to 67). Arno, Maroko, & Estes (2017) projected the changes in the proportion of uninsured elders under the proposed raise in Medicare eligibility age, finding that there would be skyrocketing increases in the percentage of uninsured persons aged 65 to 67 for men and women and across all racial and ethnic groups. This big data simulation model uses Medicare claims and administrative data, the Medicare Current Beneficiary Survey (MCBS), the Health and Retirement Study (HRS), Medicare Trustees' Reports, census data, National Health Expenditure projections of the CMS Office

of the Actuary, the Medical Expenditure Panel Survey, and the Current Population Survey (Arno, Actuarial Research Corporation, 2017).

Author's Reflection

In the 1980s, President Reagan decimated the research and evaluation capacity of SSA, weakening the analytic capability of the SSA to ascertain the distributional consequences of major policy changes in the program. When President George W. Bush initiated his 2005 privatization of Social Security tour, my graduate students and I co-founded "Students for Social Security" and "Concerned Scientists in Aging," each with a mission of education, public information, and dialogue via listservs and bibliographic resources by websites and social media. Students and faculty held "teach-ins" on campuses in the San Francisco Bay Area and joined forces nationally with student organizations, and published articles for student newspapers. Conservative think tanks like Heritage, Cato, and Concord Coalition were weaponizing messaging and data against Social Security and Medicare. We understood then, as now, that open access to information and science in the public interest is a cornerstone of a democratic society.

A different and concerning problem of big data has arisen with the evidence of Russian interference in the 2016 US presidential elections through trolling, advertising, hacking, and unchecked uses of Facebook, Twitter, and other trending social media networks that misinformed hundreds of millions of voters. Big data and big money go together, raising profound questions surrounding the perils for democracy (Sachs, 2017). Billions in private profits were made by US social media as their aggregated data on social media users enabled actors to target misinformation to the most receptive and critical.

See also: Authoritarianism, Climate Change, Gene–Environment, Memory, Methodologies, Networks, Social Insurance, Trauma

Further Reading

Arno, P. S. (2017). *Impact of raising eligibility age of Medicare*. National Committee to Preserve Social Security and Medicare Foundation.

Arno, P. S., Maroko, A., & Estes, C. (2017). Social security: The nation's biggest (hidden) economic stimulus. *American Society on Aging Conference at Chicago*, March 23.

Blanke, T. & Prescott, A. (2016). Dealing with big data. *Computing Research Repository*. Retrieved from http://arxiv.org/abs/1605.06354.

Sachs, J. D. (2017). Big data and big money have subverted our democracy. *The Boston Globe*, November 3.

Bioethics

Concerns emerging issues in medical and biological science. Topics include health and health care (access, gene mapping, privacy), reproductive rights and capabilities (i.e., cloning, surrogacy, eugenics), and euthanasia (forced and voluntary).

Particularly as gene-manipulation therapies advance, questions of ethics arise about social engineering and the consequences of potentially extending lifespans and promoting new functional standards. Advances in biomedical science do not necessarily elevate everyone in society uniformly. In fact, advancements often create opportunities for new inequalities to emerge and existing inequalities to deepen. Questions of ownership and profit of such life-altering and structuring medicines have given rise to much debate in the public sphere. Controversy pervades discussions of when life begins and how it should end. The *Huffington Post*'s website features news articles on developments and controversies, as well as opinion pieces from bioethicists.

Critical gerontology can problematize theoretical models such as in "Justice between age groups: An objection to the Prudential Lifespan Approach," in which Jecker (2013) examines models that allocate or ration health care based on age. She argues against the Prudential Lifespan Approach which proposes that it is sometimes prudent to prefer a health care plan that distributes fewer services to those in old age in exchange for more services earlier in life. Jecker argues instead for a capabilities approach proposed by Nussbaum (2006):

> The capabilities approach does not create outliers of those who lack cognitive capacities. Moreover, it pays close attention to the social determinants of health by considering whether or not people can convert resources into functioning and capabilities. Finally, it recognizes the equal worth and dignity of all human beings. When we reflect upon what we owe each other, the capabilities approach does not focus on autonomy and choice, but instead recognizes the vulnerability and dependency that each of us experience at different stages of life. By affirming the equal dignity of all human beings, the capabilities approach affirms the duty to support human dignity across the life span.
>
> (Jecker, 2013, p. 13)

See also: Age Rating, Anti-aging, Death, Ethics, Gender Rating, Necropolitics

Further Reading

Estes, C. L., Kelly, S. E., & Binney, E. (1996). Bioethics in a disposable society: Healthcare and the intergenerational state. In: Walters, J. W. (Ed.), *Ethics and ageing* (pp. 95–119), Chicago: University of Illinois Press. www.huffingtonpost.com/topic/bioethics.

Jecker, N. S. (2013). Justice between age groups: An objection to the Prudential Lifespan Approach. *American Journal of Bioethics, 13*(8), 3–15.

Jennings, B. (Ed.). (2014). *Encyclopedia of bioethics* (4th edition). New York: Cengage.

Marshall, P. & Koenig, B. (2004). Accounting for culture in a globalized bioethics. *The Journal of Law, Medicine & Ethics, 32*(2), 252–266.

Nussbaum, M. (2006). *Frontiers of justice*. Cambridge, MA: Harvard University Press.

Biomedicalization

Occurs through the aggregation and advancement of medical and biological knowledges to understand phenomena (for our purposes aging; e.g., through disease, mortality, cellular function). It privileges this way of knowing (empirical, functionalism) aging over other ways of knowing, such as social, cultural, economic, and political treatment and experiences of old age and aging.

The biomedical model is the hegemonic "institutionalized thought structure" (Warren, Rose, & Bergunder, 1974) of the field, despite increasing evidence of the importance of social, behavioral, and environmental factors in explaining health and aging. The study of aging has been biomedicalized through research funding (the NIH, venture capital, and elite universities), which advances through the support of money and prestige. The academies of science often neglect developing or recognizing knowledge that is not foreseeably profitable (i.e., subjugated stories, marginalized populations, and learning which challenges dominant paradigms and social conditions).

The dominance of the biomedical model emphasizes a "more sophisticated diagnosis, pursuit of underlying mechanisms, therapeutic intervention or prevention [and identification of] . . . modifiable biological markers" (Adelman, 1998). This influences everything else – other research, policy-making, and gerontological study as they are defined and evaluated in terms of power, economics, and culture. The biomedical model must be distinguished separately from either a biological or scientific model, although it incorporates elements of both. The relationship between the biomedical model, as constructed and controlled by the biological sciences and medicine, is problematic for its incompleteness and partial lens.

Estes and Binney (1989) identify four dimensions of thinking about aging as a medical problem: (1) the scientific (or consequences for the overall shaping of the discipline and knowledge base), (2) the professional (consequences for the various related professions, including status, training, and work organization), (3) the policy arena (impact on public policy formation, including research and training), and (4) the lay or public perceptions and understanding and their consequences.

Equating old age with illness and inevitable biomedical decline has encouraged society (and elders themselves) to think about aging as pathological or abnormal. *You lose yourself as you become your diagnosis, likely named after a man who discovered it.* Old age is framed as something to be combatted, resisted, aided, and abetted by the flourishing anti-aging industries. It is thus a major ideology in support of ageism in health care (and society more generally). The surge in "body surveillance" and the personal responsibility crusade promotes the healthy, positive, successful, and productive aging discourse, as it also denies by neglect our understanding of the injuries of inequality.

Science and technology studies (STS) are now oriented to the high-stakes gene–environment discourse. Biomedicalization is being replayed in real-time power struggles over the social construction and control of the fields engaged in the gene–environment and human social genetics development. There are major stakes for those with the most to gain: in venture capital, the National Institute for Health, biomedical industries, Big Pharma (the pharmaceutical industrial network of research, medicine, and lobbying), the university industrial complex, and, especially so, for the scientific disciplines and professions. In this way biomedicalization advances the financialization of aging and the dominant resource control by the practice of medicine. It accords a preference for geriatrics over gerontology in the competitive science of aging and its practice and policy.

See also: Aging Enterprise, Functionalism, Gene–Environment, Knowledges, Medical Industrial Complex

Further Reading

Adelman, R. C. (1998). The Alzheimerization of aging: A brief update. *Experimental Gerontology, 33*(1), 155–157.

Clarke, A. E., Mamo, L., Fosket, J. R., Fishman, J. R., & Shim, J. K. (2010). *Biomedicalization: Technoscience, health, and illness in the US.* Durham, NC: Duke University Press.

Clarke, A. E., Shim, J. K., Mamo, L., Fosket, J. R., & Fishman, J. R. (2003). Biomedicalization: Technoscientific transformations of health, illness, and U.S. biomedicine. *American Sociological Review, 68*(2), 161–194.

Conrad, P. (1992). Medicalization and social control. *Annual Review of Sociology, 18*(1), 209–232.

Estes, C. L. & Binney, E. A. (1989). The biomedicalization of aging: Dangers and dilemmas. *The Gerontologist, 29*(5), 587–596. doi:10.1093/geront/29.5.587.

Warren, R. L., Rose, S. M., & Bergunder, A. F (1974). *The Structure of Urban Reform.* Lexington, Mass.: D.C. Heath.

Blacklands

Jacquelyne Johnson Jackson's term for the outskirts and hinterlands of scholarship where marginalized voices are forced out.

Blacklands locates study that is far outside of the mainstream of the academy, out in the swampy areas of thinking where no one wants to build. This is scholarship that gets abandoned or forgotten, especially by the dominant/institutional white literature. When ethnogerontology theorizes about black populations, it often does so divorced from the rich history of black gerontologists: this is "epistemological oppression."

See also: Epistemology, Ethnogerontology/Ethnogeriatrics, Gray Gray Literature, Liminality, Resistance, Spheres (Counterpublic, Subaltern)

Further Reading

Jackson, J. J. (1971a). The blacklands of gerontology. *The International Journal of Aging and Human Development, 2*(3), 156–171.

Jackson, J. J. (1971b). National goals and priorities in the social welfare of the aging. *The Gerontologist, 11*(1), 88–94.

Jackson, J. J. (1971c). Negro aged: Toward needed research in social gerontology. *The Gerontologist, 11*(1), Suppl: 52–Suppl: 57.

Black Lives Matter (BLM)

A social movement that began in 2013 and expanded in response to the continued killings of black men and women by police officers.

Three queer black women, Alicia Garza, Patrisse Cullors and Opal Tometi, created #BlackLivesMatter in response to the discourse about Trayvon Martin's death at the hands of George Zimmerman. The unarmed 17-year-old who was killed seemed to be under more scrutiny for what he was wearing and how he was walking than his killer. Subsequently there have been numerous appropriations of the struggle for entertainment and news value.

The movement stands as an inclusive and explicitly intergenerational struggle for black lives, regardless of gender expression, perceived sexual orientation, ability and disability, economic status, religious belief or disbelief, and citizenship status or location. Campaign Zero is an important BLM effort that has collected data and is developing policy aimed at reducing police violence while supporting the movement.

We include BLM in *Aging A–Z* because the movement commands attention to the trauma of racial violence and intergenerational legacies of the trauma that informs the lived experience of aging. There is also a huge literature on inequality and disparities on black aging: the effects of racism in patterns of aging and cumulative disadvantage.

See also: Blacklands, Critical Realism, Morality, Racial Wealth Gap, Racism, Resistance, Social Movements, Violence, Zeitgeist

Further Reading

http://blacklivesmatter.com.

Rockeymoore, M. (2016)). Black lives, white silence and the second reconstruction. *Huffington Post*, July 30.

Block Grants

A funding mechanism for federal, state, and local programs to merge funding into a packaged block, calculated by federal formulas to (theoretically) assess the needs for the program.

In *The aging enterprise* (1979), *Fiscal austerity & aging* (1983), and *The crisis in long term care* (1993), Estes and colleagues detail the pitfalls and promise for aging services under policies of New Federalism, devolution, and block granting, though, as they relate to the Older Americans Act, the Social Services Block grant, home and community-based care, and long-term care.

The topic of block grants has major implications for many citizens, including older adults. Beginning in the Nixon presidency, a number of programs have been converted to block grants, on the rationale that they provide states and localities with increased flexibility and local control. Fiscal hawks have steadily *starved* social programs via cuts at the state level. Of the 13 major housing, health, and social services block grants, all but 3 have experienced funding cuts, in inflation-adjusted terms, since their inception. The total funding for major block grants has fallen a collective 23 percent since inception (Shapiro et al., 2016). Block grants undermine the more universal fundamental structure and content of federal programs. Such decentralized (conglomerated) programs obscure their individual respective program's identity, salience, and support.

The Trump Administration and GOP Congress sought enormous Medicaid cuts and block grant reform (including a $800 billion cut proposed in May 2017 in the House AHCA Repeal/Replace bill). With undivided Republican control of government, block grants could change Medicaid from its uncapped funding to a severely capped and strapped program. Notably, block grants unleash major opportunities for states to radically alter eligibility, program content, benefits, and funding. State discretion invites the battles and dreadful politics over the willingness of individual states to tax and/or spend. Control over social supports is central to states' rights. The future of Medicaid block grants, and coverage rests on the fate of ACA Repeal and Replace. In any case, Medicaid will be amerced with rising medical costs and the uncertainty of sudden changes in the Medicaid-eligible population (Luthra, 2017). We know that significantly limited state funding in the past has led states to drastically deny coverage, sometimes disqualifying children entirely, or simply limiting the services only for care in life-threatening situations (Nikpay & Goodman-Bacon, 2017).

The devolution of power and authority to the states not only decentralizes control;

it also decentralizes the work and resources required to advocate for policy change. Voices across state lines build a critical mass and have more power to appeal to federal and executive powers, but these struggles become fragmented on a state-by-state basis (such as reproductive rights). The decision-making is transferred to the obscure reaches of state and local government where private interests and lobbyists wield enormous power and where public accountability and transparency are rare.

See also: Austerity, Devolution, States' Rights

Further Reading

Luthra, S. (2017). Everything you need to know about block grants the heart of GOP's Medicaid plans. *Kaiser Health News,* January 24. Retrieved from http://khn.org/news/block-grants-medicaid-faq/.

Nikpay, S. S. & Goodman-Bacon, A. J. (2017). Per capita caps in Medicaid – lessons from the past. *The New England Journal of Medicine, 376*(11), 1005.

Shapiro, I., Dasilva, B., Reich, D., & Kogan, R. (2016). *Funding for housing, health, and social services block grants has fallen markedly over time.* Washington, DC: Center on Budget and Policy Priorities.

Boost Social Security

The campaign to protect and expand Social Security in the face of repeated and sustained assaults by free market ideologues and activists to undermine the program.

From the inception of the Reagan presidency in 1981, an ideological war has been waged against Social Security and the social insurance principles within which it historically resides (see Leninist Strategy). A 1983 Federal Commission made policy changes to shore up trust funds, which included raising the normal retirement age of 65 to 67, abolishing college benefit coverage for Social Security-dependent children, and shaving the minimum benefit levels. George H. W. Bush essentially stayed the course. President Bill Clinton then opened earnest debate on Social Security privatization options via his sponsorship of three different commissions to examine the issue. All three commissions included individual accounts and varying degrees of privatization in their proposals.

After being re-elected in 2004, President G. W. Bush set his sights on Social Security privatization as his main priority, with a 60-city, 60-day campaign. Social Security advocates mobilized public demonstrations that put the Bush's privatization plans on ice (Estes, 2017). The Boost Social Security campaign was initiated by the National Committee to Preserve Social Security & Medicare (NCPSSM) in 2005. In 2010, as conservative think tanks and fix-the-debt hawks circled, the organizational and coalitional base beat off the Social Security benefit cuts proposed by a near-majority of President Obama's Simpson-Bowles Fiscal Commission.

During Obama's second term the Boost Social Security (NCPSSM, 2005 to the present) and the expand Social Security Campaign (SSW, SSC) aligned with leaders of Democratic Congressional Caucuses promoting the "expand Social Security" wing. Consensus rose in the Democratic House and Senate, signaled by bills introduced in the 113th and 114th Congress, aimed at protecting and extending Social Security (*see* Legislative Appendix). In the run-up to the 2016 election, Obama finally abandoned his Social Security "grand bargain – get a compromise" stance and his efforts to come to an agreement with Republicans on benefits reductions. He averred that folks need improvements in Social Security.

Both 2016 Democratic presidential candidates proclaimed their support for Social

Security, with Senator Bernie Sanders in the lead, followed by Hillary Clinton's support for the most progressive Social Security platform since Franklin D. Roosevelt. Trump was the only Republican candidate to say that Social Security and Medicare were safe, which was at odds with his party platform clearly stating their "cut and reform" position. As Trump embarked on his first term, many expected Republican control of Congress to cut Social Security and Medicare, with efforts to privatize both programs and raise the eligibility age (proposals introduced on both).

The US's largest trade group of elders, the AARP, has responded often by holding organized "conversations" and by pressing policy-makers to make "decisions." Pro-social insurance advocates privately worry that this stance is weak if not unhelpful in the Trump presidency run and since. AARP has declined to join the major national coalition for expanding Social Security known as Social Security Works, although most of the national aging advocacy groups and others have done so.

Post Trump's election, a series of resistance movements have flowered in opposition to Cabinet appointees and the pledges and steps toward taking down the "Administrative State Apparatus." Old and new alliances have developed and the Boost Social Security campaign has been expanded in new forms (e.g., Medicare for All). In 2017 (115th Congress), multiple Congressional resolutions and bills have been introduced to protect, improve, and expand Social Security, Medicare, Medicaid, and the ACA. The successful passage of tax reform in 2017 created trillions in deficits that will heat up forces seeking to cut all such programs through block granting Medicaid.

See also: Leninist Strategy

Further Reading

Estes, C. L. (2011). Crises in old age policy. In R. A. Settersten Jr. & J. L. Angel (Eds.), *Handbook of sociology of aging* (pp. 297–320). New York: Springer.

Estes, C. L. (2017). Older US women's economic security, health and empowerment: The fight against opponents of social security, Medicare and Medicaid. In S. L. Dworkin, M. Gandhi, & P. Passano (Eds.), *Women's empowerment and global health* (pp. 232–250). Berkeley, CA: University of California Press.

http://strengthensocialsecurity.org. Social Security Works (SSW & SSS Campaign).

www.entitledtoknow.

www.NCPSSM.org.

C

Capitalism

An economic system in which individuals trade and utilize property for profit. Profit is "forever renewed . . . by means of continuous, rational, capitalistic enterprise," and is described as "the most fateful force in our modern life" (Agevall & Swedberg, 2016, p. 27).

A property-based regime increases inequality and the immiseration of people through the exploitation of labor. Such a system is predicated on the ideology of individualism rather than collectivism. This "responsibilizes" older people to have their own needs met, irrespective of ability or structural barriers to access to care and to the essential resources necessary to ensure and enforce that access.

Wallerstein (1974, 1980) identifies three key features of the capitalist system's survival: continued growth of markets, production capacity, and the labor force; the nation-state's assistance in meeting the incurred costs of environmental cleanup and "sustainable" resource accumulation; and the security and strength of the nation-state to stabilize markets and lend power to trade negotiations (borders, citizenship and labor restrictions, and tariffs and sanctions for importing and exporting).

Foster and Clark (2018) argue that family, gender, and reproductive labor are barriers to and sources of crisis in capital accumulation. Two additional broad categories of barriers must be managed and controlled for the capitalist system to prosper: nature, ecology, and the planet; and the nation-state, imperialism and ethnicity (Foster & Clark, 2018). Fraser and Jaeggi (2018) discuss how institutional separations in understandings of the reproduction of capitalism through dimensions of polity and ecology obscure alternatives from the Left. Psychoanalytic Social Theory, as developed in our text, and theories of colonialism provide frameworks for thinking of institutional splits and dissociative mechanisms that de-historicize and deny more holistic syntheses of these perspectives on polity, humanity, and ecology – as well as perspectives on internalized oppression and the blindness of privilege.

Dilemmas and contradictions of capitalism, under pervasive corporate and financial globalism, include cataclysmic levels of inequality between the top 1 percent and the 99 percent, indicated on one level by the gaping chasm between the robust and rising US Gross Domestic Product growth that has far outpaced stagnant, and even declining, wages over the past three decades. The Council of Economic Advisors (2016) attributes this disparity, in part, to the Labor Market Monopsony, a market condition in which there is only one buyer. Corporations exert labor market power, allowing them to determine wages, a powerful position strengthened by outsourcing jobs, by unemployment and underemployment, and by weakened unionization. The results are lower wages and profit redistribution from workers to employers.

The impoverishment of workers registers in aging policy on multiple fronts:

- decline in full-time employment reduces contributions to Social Security and Medicare, as paid through payroll tax by both employee and employer;
- stagnation and low wages, which depresses the amount of contributions that workers and their employers make to the Social Security Trust Fund, determining future benefits;
- job outsourcing and US job losses contribute to workers taking earlier retirements (i.e., with lower benefits for workers, and earlier withdrawals from the Social Security Social Insurance program);
- forcing some younger workers who become unemployed or underemployed to take Social Security Disability (SSD) benefits, when otherwise they might have stayed employed;
- reducing household income, perhaps spending savings, and accelerating the unaffordability of health insurance, leaving individuals and families vulnerable to today's cascading out-of-pocket medical care costs.

Thus, the social costs of capitalism are disproportionately borne by those of a marginalized class, gender, race, ethnicity, (dis)ability, and age, while the profits and benefits of capitalism accrue to the privileged few. Everything is connected: the risks and uncertainty of global finance capitalism and its destructive wake are why Social Security and social insurance have been and remain the most important anti-poverty programs. These programs provide a degree of security that is desperately necessary for most individuals. They correct to at least a modest extent the ruthless exploitation that characterizes modern-day capitalism and the reckless disregard for the collective good that pervades American politics.

See also: Colonialisms, Commodification, Ecologies, Inequality, Precarity, Privilege, Psychoanalytic Social Theory

Further Reading

Agevall, O. & Swedberg, R. (2016). *The Max Weber dictionary: Key words and central concepts*. Redwood City, CA: Stanford University Press.

Council of Economic Advisors. (2016). *Labor market monopsony: Trends, consequences, and policy responses* (October). Washington, DC: Council of Economic Advisors.

Foster, J.B. & Clark, B. (2018). Women, nature & capital in the industrial revolution. *Monthly Review, 69*(8), 1–24.

Fraser, N. & Jaeggi, R. (2018). *Capitalism: A conversation in critical theory*. New York: John Wiley & Sons.

Piketty, T. (2014). *Capital in the twenty-first century*. Cambridge, MA: The Belknap Press of Harvard University Press.

Streeck, W. (2016). *How will capitalism end?* London: Verso.

Wallerstein, I. (1974). *The modern world system, Vol. I: Capitalist agriculture and the origins of the European world economy in the sixteenth century*. New York: Academic Press.

Wallerstein, I. (1980). *The modern world system, Vol. II: Mercantilism and the consolidation of the European world-economy, 1600–1750*. New York: Academic Press.

Williams, E. (1944). *Capitalism and slavery*. Chapel Hill, NC: University of North Carolina Press.

Caregiving/Caregivers

Caregiving provides support to dependent individuals, which may be formal (paid), informal (unpaid), or a mixture of the two.

Former First Lady Rosalynn Carter testified before the Senate Special Committee on Aging (2011) that: "there are only four kinds of people in the world: those who have been caregivers, those who are currently caregivers, those who will be caregivers and those who will need caregivers."

It is well documented that unpaid informal caregivers (family members, volunteers) provide 80 percent or more of long-term care and support for the elderly, and that there are significant physical, mental health, and economic sacrifices that such care workers endure. For informal (unpaid) care workers, the consequences sometimes become a matter of life and death. Pioneering research by Len Pearlin and colleagues (1990) reveals the stress of caregiving, highlighting "proliferation" as a key process in which stressors in one area of life accumulate across others (see Chiraboga et al., 2017).

There is a vast underestimation of the costs of unpaid caregiving in the US and the contribution of unpaid caregivers to the economy. Neoclassical and mainstream economics accords little attention in national assessments to the unpaid workforce. Among gerontologists and elderly care specialists, attention given to this issue is evident primarily in long-term care. Even then, the accumulated "social" costs (individual and societal), if analyzed at all, are under-reported. Peter Arno and his colleagues (2011) calculate the costs of a double jeopardy for baby boomers. They measure the costs of caring for aging parents and the economic value of youth caregiving. In dollar terms alone, "the total estimated aggregate lost wages, pension and Social Security benefits of these caregivers of parents is nearly $3 trillion" (Arno, Viola, & Shi, 2011). Little analysis covers the race and ethnic dimensions of this work, but the Institute for Women's Policy Research (see IWPR, 2016) shows that an overwhelming majority, 61 percent, of all black mothers are single moms raising children on their own.

Paid home care workers generally work without benefits and on low pay. It was only in 2016 that the Department of Labor granted home care workers access to a status above "babysitter" by granting the right to overtime pay, a decision upheld by the US Supreme Court. President Trump's Secretary of Labor has discretion in implementing this DOL ruling, which suggests the ongoing precarity of these policies and standards. Regulatory and cost-saving measures pressure institutions, which impacts caregivers and dehumanizes care – especially as the welfare and dignity of both caregiver and care receiver are wedded to the material support they receive.

Richard Schulz, in a report of the National Academies (2016), called for a National Family Caregiver Strategy for the Secretaries of Health and Human Services, collaborating with Secretaries of Labor and Veterans' Affairs. Access to family caregivers, and long-term care in general, is severely lacking in the United States. There is a pressing need to motivate, train, and engage caregivers in elder care, and to enact policies (economic and other) to support working caregivers. Coverage or compensation for these costs has not been included in federal attempts to pass long-term care policy. Financial and/or programmatic policy support for family caregivers is limited to none. The lack of childcare for family caregivers subject to this double jeopardy is well known and although lamented, remains costly and scarce. Public elder care services are mainly information and referral sources funded by the Older Americans Act, and when funded are again scarce, costly, and mostly privatized under corporate care.

See also: Care Penalty, Cumulative Advantage/Disadvantage, Long-term Care/LTSS, Precarity, Reproduction, Zero Years

Further Reading

Accius, J. (2017). *Breaking stereotypes: Spotlight on male family caregivers*. AARP Public Policy Institute, March 26. Retrieved from www.aarp.org/ppi/info-2017/breaking-stereotypes-spotlight-on-male-family-caregivers.html.

Anderson, J. (2016). *Breadwinner mothers by race/ethnicity and state.* Institute for Women's Policy Research.

Anderson, J. G. & Flatt, J. (2018). Characteristics of LGBT caregivers of older adults: Results from the National Caregiving in the U.S. 2015 survey. *Journal of Gay and Lesbian Social Services, 30*(2), 103–116.

Arno, P. S., Viola, D., & Shi, Q. (2011). *The MetLife study of caregiving costs to working caregivers: Double jeopardy for baby boomers caring for their parents.* Hartford, CT: MetLife Mature Market Institute.

Ciscel, D. H. & Heath, J. A. (2001). To market, to market: Imperial capitalism's destruction of social capital and the family. *Review of Radical Political Economics, 33*(4), 401–414.

Eden, J. (2016). *Families caring for an aging America.* Washington, DC: National Academies of Sciences, Engineering, and Medicine.

Folbre, N. (1994). *Who pays for the kids?* (1st edition). London: Routledge.

Glenn, E. N. (2010) *Forced to care: Coercion and caregiving in America.* Cambridge, MA: Harvard University Press.

Institute for Women's Policy Research. (2016). Washington, DC: IWPR.

Montgomery, R. J., Kwak, H., & Kosloski, K. D. (2016). Theories guiding support services for family caregivers. In V. L. Bengtson & R. Settersten Jr. (Eds.), *Handbook of theories of aging* (3rd edition) (pp. 443–462). New York: Springer.

Pearlin, L. I., Mullan, J. T., Semple, S. J., & Skaff, M. M. (1990). Caregiving and the stress process: An overview of concepts and their measures. *The Gerontologist, 30*(5), 583–594.

Poo, A.-J. (2015). *The Age of Dignity: Preparing for the elder boom in a changing America.* New York: The New Press.

Poo, A.-J. (2017). Caregiving in America: Supporting families, strengthening the workforce. *Generations, 40*(4), 87–93.

Schulz, R. and Eden, J. (2016). *Families caring for an aging America.* Washington, DC: National Academies of Sciences, Engineering, and Medicine.

Viola, D., Arno, P., Siskowski, C., Cohen, D., & Gusmano, M. (2012). The economic value of youth caregiving in the United States. *Relational Child and Youth Care Practice, 25*(2), 10.

Caring Across Generations: https://caringacross.org/.

National Domestic Workers Alliance: www.domesticworkers.org/.

Older Americans Act, Administration for Community Living (2017) websites:

- Eldercare Locator website: https://eldercare.acl.gov/Public/Index.aspx.
- ARCH National Respite Network and Resource Center: https://archrespite.org/respitelocator.
- Aging and Disability Resource Center (ADRC): www.adrc-tae.acl.gov/tiki-index.php?page=ADRCLocator.
- National Family Caregiver Support Program: www.acl.gov/AoA_Programs/HCLTC/Caregiver/.
- Lifespan Respite Care Program: www.acl.gov/Programs/CIP/OCASD/Lifespan Respite/index.aspx.
- Alzheimer's Disease Supportive Services Program: www.acl.gov/grants/alzheimers-disease-supportive-services-program-adssp-creating-and-sustaining-dementia.

Care Penalty

The cost that women bear because of their responsibilities and time spent in reproducing and nurturing the human species through pregnancy, maternity, birthing, nurturing, caregiving, educating, housing, and feeding children through decades of work, for which there is little or no financial remuneration or recognition. Public policy and programs such as Social Security do not ensure childcare as a state-supported right.

Monetarily, the care penalty for young women today is more than $1 million. For women who are on the front line of providing "free" family caregiving for children, parents, in-laws, siblings, and grandchildren, the costs are more than financial: they include physical health, mental health, and life expectancy, all of which can be adversely affected. Those who are the most disadvantaged by class, race, ethnicity, gender, marital status, and educational attainment are even more likely to experience care penalties.

Caregiving and the care penalty reflect and refract the glass ceiling imposed through ideology, social norms, and unending conflict on the cultural, social, political, and economic levels. In critical voice, caregiving must be understood as a social good (bringing the generations into being and bringing the next generations and society forward), yet caregiving is described (in economists' terms) as an *individual choice, as if it were a preference freely chosen*. Evelyn Nakano Glenn (2010) refutes the choice thesis by demonstrating that caregiving is rooted in coercion, straining women of color and lower class white women. Women's disadvantage in care work magnifies inequality.

In critical feminist thought, caregiving roles, norms, and responsibilities are understood as (1) expectations laced with power and moral judgment for deviants; (2) as benefits for business and profits, and (3) as informalization of an economic sector (e.g., work transferred from paid, medical care to the informal sector of unpaid or low-paid, largely female caregivers who receive little or no monetary compensation and negligible publicly provided benefits). Feminist economists criticize mainstream economics for valuing the costs and benefits of production in ways that ignore the economic benefits of reproduction:

- birthing the next generation;
- family care work, nurturance, socialization, and the costs of preparing future generations for the economy;

- care for all sexes and multiple generations, often until there is no one to care for the oldest female caregivers.

The following book titles on women's care work offer social commentary:

- *Counting for nothing: What men value and what women are worth* (Marilyn Waring, 1999, 2004).
- *Never done: A history of American housework* (Susan Strasser, 1982).
- *Women's paid and unpaid labor* (Nona Glazer, 1993).
- *Forced to care: Coercion and caregiving in America* (Evelyn Nakano Glenn, 2010).
- *For giving: A feminist criticism of exchange* (Genevieve Vaughan, 1995).
- *Market friendly or family friendly? The state and gender inequality in old age* (Madonna Harrington Meyer & Pamela Herd, 2007).
- *Regulating the lives of women* (Mimi Abramovitz, 1988).
- *Talking back: Thinking feminist. Thinking black* (bell hooks, 1989).
- *The declining significance of gender?* (Francine D. Blau, Mary C. Brinton, & David B. Grusky (Eds.), 2006).

See also: Caregiving/Caregivers, Reproduction, Zero Years

Further Reading

Abendroth, A. K., Huffman, M. L., & Treas, J. (2014). The parity penalty in life course perspective: Motherhood and occupational status in 13 European countries. *American Sociological Review, 79*(5), 993–1014.

Estes, C. L., Biggs, S., & Phillipson, C. (2003/2009). Feminist perspectives and old age policy. In Estes, C. L., Biggs, S., & Phillipson, C., *Social theory, social policy and Ageing: A critical introduction* (pp. 44–62). Maidenhead, Berks: Open University Press.

Folbre, N. (2001). *The invisible heart.* New York: New Press.

Folbre, N. (2012). *For love or money.* New York: Russell Sage Foundation.

Glenn, E. N. (2010). *Forced to care: Coercion and caregiving in America.* Cambridge, MA: Harvard University Press.

Heymann, J., Earle, A., & Hayes, J. (2008). *The work, family, and equity index: How does the United States measure up?* McGill University, Institute for Health and Social Policy.

Schulz, R. & Beach, S. R. (1999). Caregiving as a risk factor for mortality: The caregiver health effects study. *Journal of the American Medical Association, 282*(23), 2215–2219.

Schultz, R. & Eden, J. (2016). *Families caring for an aging America.* Washington, DC: National Academies of Sciences, Engineering, and Medicine. Washington, DC: The National Academies Press.

Children

Young people between birth and adulthood who depend on a parent or guardian. The definition varies depending on context and can be variously biological or legal.

Social Security is often described as a family values program that is not only intergenerational but also multi-generational. The earned benefits that beneficiaries and their family members receive lift millions of kids out of poverty. It is one of the largest anti-poverty programs for children.

Children under the age of 18 are Social Security (SS) monetary beneficiaries in two ways: (1) as *direct child beneficiaries*, eligible because of (a) being a child survivor following the death of a parent covered by SS (e.g., the 2000+ children of workers who died in the 9/11 terrorist attack or in Iraq); (b) the child of a disabled parent, and (c) the child of retired parents; and (2) as *indirect child beneficiaries* who live in households with one or more family members receiving Social Security (e.g., a grandparent raising a grandchild). Two-thirds of indirect child beneficiaries live in multi-generational households, a living arrangement that is growing rapidly. The number of indirect child beneficiaries has risen from 2.2 million to 3.2 million, while the number of direct beneficiaries has remained stable. Overall, the child beneficiaries of Social Security approximate 6.4 million (data for 2001 to 2014, Center for Global Policy Solutions, 2016).

Social Security benefits children of color significantly. Without Social Security benefits (direct or indirect) the following would be in poverty: 58% of black children, 45% of Latino children, 39% of white children, and 29% of Asian and other racial/ethnic group children (Arno & Wicks-Lim, 2016). Because there are more whites than persons of color in the total population, white children comprise the largest number of children supported by Social Security.

Even with Social Security, child poverty is a significant and pernicious problem. Contrary to individualist stereotypes, parents and grandparents are required to spend and save for their children and grandchildren. In many cases, this means "spending down" their own meager retirement resources to house, educate, and nourish their grandchildren. Around 7.8 million children live in grandparent households, of which fully 22 percent are in poverty (Arno & Wicks-Lim, 2016). This stands in direct opposition to the erroneous slur that older persons are greedy and selfish.

From a critical perspective, globalization, wage and employment stagnation, and the accelerating chasm in economic and health inequalities mean that austerity policies and declining welfare state support are bad for youth and children. Families and women are similarly negatively implicated (Ruddick, 2003).

Recommendations for boosting Social Security gained traction leading up to the 2016 election cycle and since, in opposition to Trump policy moves. Benefit improvements for children and families, people of color, women, those on low income and the disabled could be advanced via increasing minimum benefit levels, restoring the post-secondary student benefits for child dependent beneficiaries, providing a structural unemployment credit, and adding a caregiver credit in place of the current "zero years" of benefit credit under Social Security (Arno & Wicks-Lim, 2016; Rockeymoore & Lui, 2011; Estes, O'Neill, & Hartmann, 2012; Social Security Campaign/Social Security Works, 2017).

Additional critical gerontological perspectives may examine developmental and generational trauma to children and how this extends throughout the life course, as well as the social movements and resistance organized to heal communities. The high frequency of gun violence, and specifically mass shootings at schools, galvanized the 2018 intergenerational movement for gun control (Leonhardt, 2018). Especially in the United States, the number of deaths of children leads in stark contrast when compared cross-nationally with other "high-income" nations (Thakrar et al., 2018). This marker signifies a critical realist data point of an American experience of violence.

There are several functionalist ideological aspects which presume that children have resilience and a path for equality, as imposed by mainstream developmental assumptions on children from very different socioeconomic/cultural backgrounds. As Dannefer (2011) observes, these are related to mechanisms of inequality and social reproduction. Just as caregiving exhibits reduction in quality as regulatory measures cut costs, services for children (including schooling) exhibit diminished quality. These diminishments are part of the dismantling that takes place as privatization pushes into these "untapped" markets.

Child Deaths

Annual deaths per one million children, up through age 19, for select countries

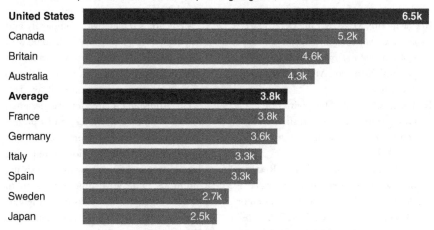

Note: Average covers 20 high-income nations that are members of the O.E.C.D.

By *The New York Times* | Source: Ashish P. Thakrar, Alexandra D. Forrest, Mitchell G. Maltenfort, and Christopher B. Forrest

Figure C1 Child Deaths

See also: Boost Social Security, Care Penalty, Cross-national Comparison, Violence, Youth

Further Reading

Arno, P. & Wicks-Lim, J. (2016). *Overlooked but not forgotten: Social security lifts millions more children out of poverty*. Washington, DC: Center for Global Policy Solutions.

Dannefer, D. (2011). Age, the life course, and the sociological imagination: Prospects for theory. In L. George (Ed.), *Handbook of aging and social sciences* (7th edition) (pp. 3–16). San Diego, CA: Academic Press.

Estes, C., O'Neill, T., & Hartmann, H. (2012). *Breaking the social security glass ceiling: A proposal to modernize women's benefits*. Institute for Women's Policy Research.

Leonhardt, D. (2018). Letting American kids die, with data from "Child deaths; Annual deaths per one million children, up through age 19, for select countries." In A. P. Thakar, A. D. Forrest, M. G. Maltenfort, & C. B. Forrest, *The New York Times*, February 17. Retrieved from www.nytimes.com/2018/02/17/opinion/sunday/letting-american-kids-die.html.

Rockeymoore, M. M. & Lui, M. (2011). *Plan for a new future: The impact of social security reform on people of color*. Washington, DC: Commission to Modernize Social Security.

Ruddick, S. (2003). The politics of aging: Globalization and the restructuring of youth and childhood. *Antipode, 35*(2), 334–362.

Social Security Works. (2017). Retrieved from www.socialsecurityworks.org/.

Thakrar, A. P., Forrest, A. D., Maltenfort, M. G., & Forrest, C. B. (2018). Child mortality in the US and 19 OECD comparator nations: A 50-year time-trend analysis. *Health Affairs, 37*(1), 140–149.

A young person's guide to social security. (2016). Washington, DC: Economic Policy Institute, National Academy of Social Insurance.

Choice

Involves deciding between two or more objects, options, policies, proposals, benefit plans, or other phenomena. Usually implying a "free" choice in the American context, choice is an ideology as well as a process. For instance, choices may be between progressive or conservative perspectives, agendas, policies, or programs.

Core principles in mainstream economics are "preferences" which are presented as rational choices *as if* an individual's actual preference is free from coercive or repressive influence. Yet, "the market" theoretically prioritizes choice of what to buy, what to risk. Choices exist at all levels of micro, meso, macro as they are made by individuals, families, organizations, institutions, communities, states, and societies. Choice is a sacred value attached to the concept of individual freedom. An economic requisite of competition and fair play is symmetry of information, in which individuals and other organizations making decisions theoretically have the information they need.

Medicare is replete with complexity and dizzying choices, many of which come with serious penalties or repercussions, which are foreclosed by inequality "as if" the ability to buy or sign up for any option really exists.

The Affordable Care Act was designed around the market, choice, and options. The ACA's daunting structure was designed to deter adverse risk selection by requiring insurers to cover persons with pre-existing conditions. The government pays them extra for covering those risks in a variety of ways. Overall, the system was intended to bring as many people into a market-based system as possible, letting private insurers do the work of expanding the risk pool.

Choice may be life and death, and the choices available to individuals are highly contentious and restricted in various ways. Decisions about women's health, women's bodies, are often more political judgments than health decisions. Even contraception is controversial, as the interests of the patriarchal males, families, churches, religious institutions, and political beliefs exert significant influence on policy and discourse. The material availability of choice is steeped in and constrained by race, ethnicity, class, sexuality and gender, ability, and age. Both availability and access to choose (e.g.., freedom from discrimination) are fraught with political, cultural, and economic struggles in which, who and what principles and policies win and lose. Choices are highly consequential.

A critical perspective calls out and investigates the stacked deck in most of the choices in our lives, families, neighborhoods, education, and job opportunities. bell hooks (2000) describes oppression as "the absence of choice." The ACA and its repeal and reform proposals threaten to abolish the federal requirement of an "essential benefits" package, including emergency care, particular aspects of women's health care, and mental health care among other requirements. The "choice" as to whether insurers would be required to cover these care benefits could be delegated to states (or ditched entirely). Frequently people do not determine what they are choosing between: opportunity to decide is often restricted, coerced, or influenced by social and structural forces and ideologies of consumerism and privatization.

See also: ACA, Agency, Capitalism, Class, Conflict, Cumulative Advantage/Disadvantage, Ideology, Individualism, Inequality, Privatization, Power

Further Reading

Fullbrook, E. (2004). *A guide to what's wrong with economics*. London: Anthem.

hooks, b. (2000). *Feminist theory: From margin to center* (2nd edn). London: Pluto Press.

Citizenship

Sanctioned and recognized membership to the State (i.e., nation). This membership requires participation for sustained protections and sense of *belonging*. The abstract and non-problematic characterization of the citizen as "universal" effectively occludes the gendered structuring of public and private spheres and the racial structuring of exclusion. The everyday worlds of people of color, women, the disabled, and the poor stretch the credulity of this version of homogeneous, undifferentiated citizenship (Estes, 2001). Somers (2008) identifies three phenomena associated with citizenship:

- Citizenship, contractualization: "A process driven by the withdrawal of the state from social and market embeddedness, accompanied by the systematic dismantling of civil, political, and social citizenship rights. In this process, statelessness is both the end and the means of exclusion" (Somers, 2008, p. 135).
- Citizenship, social: "the whole range from the right to a modicum of economic welfare and security to the right to share to the full in the social heritage and to live the life of a civilized being according to the standards prevailing in the society . . . which in turn means a claim to be accepted as full members of society, that is, as citizens" (Marshall,1950; Somers, 2008, pp. 164–167).
- Citizenship, imperiled: "marketization creates social exclusion, statelessness, and rightlessness" (Somers, 2008, p. 61): the conversion of "the ethos of a socially inclusionary citizenship to one of contractual morality . . . amount[ing] to a complete inversion: from a triadic balance of power, in which the social state

protects citizens in civil society against the exposure to the market, to one in which citizenship collapses into a dyadic instrument of unbalanced power pitting an alliance of state and market against individuals – now bereft of both state protection and membership in civil society" (Somers, 2008, p. 37).

Classic British scholar T. H. Marshall (1950) claimed that in modern society social rights are earned based on citizenship rather than on class or need. The nation-state is the arbiter of citizenship. Turner (1990) highlights the relationship between citizenship, as it is demanded from the people and as it is provided by the State, in the context of the political and economic spheres. Carey (2009) cites the contradictions that arise between federal and state legislation granting or limiting rights, the interstate variation in access to rights, and the limited scope of rights, in which certain aspects of social citizenship are supported through legally guaranteed assistance and others are not. Such federalism States' rights issues were front and center in Republican policy and regulatory power struggles. The conservative Right's war on immigrants and the resistance to these efforts from sanctuary cities, churches, and restaurants have revealed profound divisions in concepts of citizenship and the rights of non-citizens.

Critical perspectives relevant to old age and the State and aging policy attend to the relations of race, ethnicity, gender, class, (dis)ability, and age as inflected in and through citizenship. On the subject of the gendered character of citizenship (Reiger, 2000; Lister, 1997) feminist scholars (MacKinnon, 1989) challenge the historically dominant Western view that has portrayed the proverbial citizen as universal (white male) in values and interest in contrast to the "particularistic" view of the private world of home and family (female).

Significantly, in 1930 (*Klein v. Board of Tax Supervisors*, 282 U.S. 19) a form of individual rights (a form of citizenship) was conferred upon corporations. Referred to as an "artificial person," corporations have claimed and received Supreme Court blessing of many to the same rights and privileges as an individual. The constitutional protections do not extend the Fourteenth Amendment "liberty protections," but artificial persons are entitled to constitutional protections of property and life as well as equal protection. This has produced a stark power asymmetry between individual citizens and business. Corporations have access to vast resources (fiscal, political, and human capital) to claim and defend their "rights," which places the claims, defense, and infringement of the rights of the individual citizen at a distinct power disadvantage. The Hobby Lobby case, for instance, allowed the company, Hobby Lobby, to refuse to provide employee insurance coverage for contraception due to religious privilege.

Grossman and colleagues (2009) critically describe the shifting boundaries of citizenship through Social Security and Medicare policy changes.

See also: Class, Deportation, Gender, Racism, Social Insurance

Further Reading

Carey, A. C. (2009). *On the margins of citizenship*. Philadelphia, PA: Temple University Press.

Estes, C. L. (2001). Sex and gender in the political economy of aging. In C. L. Estes & Associates, *Social policy & aging: A critical perspective* (p. 119). Thousand Oaks, CA: Sage.

Grossman, B. R., Solway, E., & Hollister, B. A. (2009). One nation, interdependent: Exploring the boundaries of citizenship in the history of social security and

Medicare. In L. Rogne, C. L. Estes, B. Grossman, B. A. Hollister, & E. Solway (Eds.), *Social insurance and social justice: Social security, Medicare and the campaign against entitlements* (pp. 115–147). New York: Springer.

Lister, R. (1997). *Citizenship: Feminist perspectives.* London: Macmillan.

MacKinnon, C. A. (1989). *Toward a feminist theory of the state.* Cambridge, MA: Harvard University Press.

Marshall, T. H. (1950). *Citizenship and social class.* Cambridge: Cambridge University Press.

Reiger, K. (2000). Reconceiving citizenship. *Feminist Theory, 1*(3), 309–327.

Somers, M. R. (2008). *Genealogies of citizenship.* Cambridge: Cambridge University Press.

Turner, B. S. (1990). Outline of a theory of citizenship. *Sociology, 24*(2), 189.

Civil (Dis)obedience

The deliberate breaking of laws or commands as an act of protest. The concept is an old one; though by most accounts the modern American concept of the term starts with Henry David Thoreau's essay, *Resistance to civil government: Civil disobedience.* The central point is the idea that the citizen is complicit in the actions of the nation. This produces a responsibility for the citizen to resist laws and actions by the government that she or he deems unjust. Thoreau was inspired by his personal opposition to the US government over the issues of slavery and the Mexican American War.

The ideas outlined by Thoreau have been put into action many times. Martin Luther King Jr., Mohandas Gandhi, John F. Kennedy, and many others cited Thoreau as a significant influence. Civil disobedience is and has been practiced by a wide variety of groups in the United States. The Trump era and social media opened up new venues for renewed rounds of consciousness

raising and mobilizing against institutional barriers of race, ethnicity, class, gender, ability, and age. The emancipatory historian and activist Howard Zinn says it best:

> As soon as you say the topic is civil disobedience, you are saying our problem is civil disobedience. That is not our problem. Our problem is civil obedience. Our problem is the numbers of people all over the world who have obeyed the dictates of the leaders of their government and have gone to war, and millions have been killed because of this obedience. Our problem is that people are obedient all over the world, in the face of poverty and starvation and stupidity, and war, and cruelty.
> – from *Uncommon sense: From the writings of Howard Zinn,* selected and introduced by Dean Birkenkamp and Wanda Rhudy (Paradigm, 2009/2016)

See also: Authoritarianism, Black Lives Matter, Discourse, Maggie Kuhn, Resistance, Social Movements, Solidarity

Further Reading

Thoreau, H. D. (2016). *Resistance to civil government: Civil disobedience.* Calgary, Canada: Broadview Press.

Zinn, H., Birkenkamp, D., & Rhudy, W. (2016). *Uncommon sense: From the writings of Howard Zinn.* Abingdon, Oxon: Routledge. (Original work published 2009 by Paradigm.)

Civil Rights Movement/ Civil Rights Act

A social movement in the United States that sought to promote and guarantee the rights of African Americans and bring an end to racial segregation. The movement secured an impressive array of victories over the course of the 1950s and 1960s through sustained campaigns of civil action, including boycotts, civil disobedience, marches, rallies, and widespread organizing efforts.

The Civil Rights Movement of the 1950s and 1960s represents a particularly productive and turbulent period in a movement that stretches back to the abolition of slavery and reaches forward to modern protest movements. Local and national activists and organizations came together to push for civil rights reforms on the national level and within their communities. Some of the most prominent protests and other actions include the Montgomery Bus Boycott, The Selma to Montgomery Marches, The March on Washington, The Greensboro Sit-ins, The Freedom Rides, and many more. Many important activists emerged as leaders of the movement, the most prominent being Martin Luther King Jr., yet a variety of groups contributed to various actions and advocacy efforts.

The Civil Rights Movement made many radical aims and employed rhetoric that included Marxist and radical liberation elements. However, the radical tendencies of various leaders and organizations have been largely ignored by mainstream history, just as much of the media ignored them at the time while other radicals were marginalized. The result of this is a retrospective view of the movement as rooted in a specific time and place and as having come and gone, achieving successes then fading. The reality is much more complicated.

Toward the end of the 1960s public opinion began to turn on the Civil Rights Movement. Conflict over the Vietnam War and other counter-culture movements reached a high-point as conservative forces joined under the banner of the New Right. Civil rights was successfully used as a wedge to turn the South reliably Republican and to convert white Southerners to the growing neoconservative consensus within the Republican Party. Rather than fight civil rights directly, conservatives instead contended that the movement had achieved its goals and that further change was unnecessary. This helped usher in an era defined by implicit, structural racism rather than explicit racism, though explicit violence continued.

The high-profile legislative victories of this period include the Civil Rights Act, the Voting Rights Act, and the Fair Housing Act. Legal advocates, often led by the NAACP, also won a variety of legal battles during this time, the most important being *Brown v. Board of Education*, in which the Supreme Court ruled segregated schools unconstitutional.

Civil Rights Act (1964)

Outlaws discrimination based on race, ethnicity, religion, national origin, and sex. Though the law came about during the height of the Civil Rights Movement its scope is extremely broad and includes protections for women, religious minorities, and immigrants, in addition to African Americans.

Voting Rights Act

Prohibits discrimination in voting based on race. The 1965 Act enforces the Fourteenth and Fifteenth Amendments to the Constitution, which respectively guarantee citizens equal rights and the right to vote.

The Voting Rights Act is divided into two parts: the General Provisions and Special Provisions. The General Provisions provide universal voting protections that apply to every county and state in the US. The Special Provisions apply to jurisdictions that have a history of discrimination in their voting laws and imposes requirements for pre-clearance, and federal approval of all laws affecting voting.

The Special Provisions were rendered effectively toothless after the Supreme Court ruled in *Shelby County v. Holder* in 2012 that the categorization of counties for pre-clearance was unconstitutional because the qualifications for pre-clearance were outdated. Implicit in this decision was the notion that voting discrimination no longer represents a significant problem in these counties. This decision ushered in a new era of voting rights infringement with voter ID laws, early voting restrictions, and polling place limitations proliferating across the country, especially in areas with large minority populations. Many of the new laws had legal challenges made against them and some have been struck down, but discriminatory intent can be very difficult to prove in court (Berman, 2015).

In 2017, US Congressman John Lewis, who had been severely beaten by police in the civil rights struggles, led a historic first "sit-in" by Democrats on the floor of the US House of Representatives (with some Senators joining). This protest was against President Trump and GOP intransigence over the rights of all peoples.

Fair Housing Act (1968)

Technically a provision of the Civil Rights Act, the Fair Housing Act was enacted to protect minorities from housing discrimination. Like much of the rest of the Civil Rights Act the Fair Housing Act applies to many groups, including older Americans.

The Act specifically prohibits discrimination in the process of selling or renting a property or in the process of advertising a property for sale or rent. It has encountered problems with enforcement and relies primarily on individual reports of misconduct to function.

See also: Age Discrimination in Employment Act, Black Lives Matter, Racism, Resistance, Social Movements

Further Reading

Berman, A. (2015). *Give us the ballot*. New York: Farrar, Straus, and Giroux.

Lewis, J., Aydin, A., & Powell, N. (2015). *March*. Marietta, GA: Top Shelf Productions.

Class

A socioeconomic categorization reflecting divisions in the order of society and the individuals within it. Class may be defined purely by wealth, by types of occupation, or by other social characteristics. Within the framework of critical political economy, class is not static; nor is it one simple measure. The concept reflects and inflects (in individuals) what is a larger totality, especially dimensions of power that invoke economic privilege and how this relates to the political, social, and cultural dimensions of society.

Consistent with perspectives grounded in the critical political economy of aging, class analysis points to power, and the structure that gives people effective control over economic resources and the ability to accumulate them. Capital, the State (in its many forms), and the public are engaged in power struggles and conflict.

Critical perspectives on social class and aging policy may be understood on three theoretical and analytical levels: (1) class as individual attributes across life course development; (2) class as cumulative advantage and disadvantage, and (3) class as domination and exploitation. Each level links primarily to economic differences that are relevant to power, policy, and aging.

(1) Class as individual attributes. A central concern is to understand how people acquire the attributes that locate them in one class or another; the processes by which people acquire cultural, motivational, and educational resources that

reflect their class location and channeling to occupations in the labor market; and the class character of family settings or their "class background." This work is linked to scholarship on social stratification. In gerontology, it tracks closely with the influential strands of social psychology, life course, and human development perspectives.

(2) Class as related to Cumulative Advantage and Disadvantage (CDA). In the late 1980s, the phenomenon of increasing inequality with age was observed by US sociologists (Dannefer, 1987; Crystal & Shea, 1990, O'Rand, 1996). The social processes producing such age-based inequalities are robust and identifiable (Dannefer, 1987, 1988), and serve as an important corrective to the tendency of some researchers to treat such patterns as originating from "individual differences." The pattern of increasing inequality with age in the USA has been replicated numerous times, and has been extended to other domains, notably health, where class differences are shown to be a basis for increasing health disparities over the life course (Dannefer, 2003; Ross & Wu, 1995). The CDA perspective is consistent with the work of social epidemiologists (e.g., Len Syme and Lisa Berkman, and psychologist Nancy Adler and colleagues (1999) in the US, UK, and Canada, following Townsend (1979), and including Marmot, Wilkinson, Williamson, and McEwen. Class on this second level has been described by State and class theorists Charles Tilly (1998) and Erik Olin Wright (2015) as a form of "opportunity hoarding" that represents "social closure." Hoarding as class process is advanced in Reeves' (2018) investigation of the upper middle class in America.

(3) Class as exploitation and domination. A third level of class analysis related to policy and aging examines exploitation and domination. "'Domination' refers to the ability to control the activities of others. 'Exploitation' refers to the acquisition of economic benefits from the laboring activities of those who are dominated. All exploitation implies some kind of domination, but not all domination involves exploitation" (Wright, 2015, p. 9). "Exploitation defines a structure of interdependent interests in which advancing the interests of exploiters depends on their capacity to impose deprivations on the exploited" (Wright, 1999). Property and ownership of the means of production (in all its contemporary forms) remain central in this third analytic level and measurement of class. Those with property and ownership exercise power to the fullest extent possible to control access to jobs, wages, benefits, and the structure of work. Ownership also confers unique control over corporate behavior and resource distribution. Corporate power and economic concentration through globalization, financialization, and trade agreements have elevated the significance of this third level of class forces with consequences for vast swathes of populations and geopolitics. Economic and political systems become inseparable, bolstered by cultural forces (e.g., ideology and religion) which seemingly justify the inequalities imposed through State policy.

This simple, rather formulaic three-level approach to theory and research regarding social class is variously measurable and significant for understanding the origins, processes, and effects of inequalities for the health and well-being of older persons and populations. However, these levels, as presented, are incomplete to the extent that they are not also focused on core complexities in how class operates by, in, and through race, ethnicity, gender, (dis)ability, and age. Intersectionality is a concept that acknowledges the interweaving of multiple dimensions on class location and outcomes in terms of power, wealth, and health disparities.

With regard to social class and age and aging, the meso and macro level of scholarship on the political economy of aging has been largely subsumed under "inequities," with most of the advances being at and within the cohort level, across the life course. "Inequality" is the primary concept used in US gerontology and health services studies. This is consistent with a long-honored tension in the USA to deny or minimize the term "social class." Postmodernist theories and research, emphasizing the local and the specific, have been significant (positively and negatively) in challenging the existence of universal macro forces. There is a postmodern and public aversion to recognizing and naming "class" as a reality in US life and politics. Many pretend that the US is not a class society, reluctant to explicitly acknowledge the reality of prejudicial class warfare, as well as race and gender wars for equality. Word preference for socioeconomic "disparity" or "diversity" can downgrade or obfuscate the material realities of class. In contrast, critical scholars across a broad spectrum of disciplines produce analyses of class and capitalism at large macro-structural levels that are highly relevant to old age and aging, and the policies that facilitate gross inequalities (e.g., through globalization, ecological degradation, diaspora of many peoples, precarity, nativism, and violence) through institutional formations that shape human lives.

More directly related to social class and aging, Estes, Swan, and Gerard (1982) speak to "class" theory and research and its grounding in policy. The scholarship on austerity, neoliberalism, globalization, State policy, privatization, commodification, and crisis over the past three decades is an ongoing socio-historical narrative of the forces of class, dispossession (Estes &

Phillipson, 2002; Harvey, 2005; Polivka & Estes, 2009), and forms of institutionalized harms to the most vulnerable among the elderly. It is the bottom line in the attacks and power struggles over fiscal cuts and reform of Social Security and Medicare and the Repeal of the Affordable Care Act (Estes, 2011). *What does class have to do with aging policy? EVERYTHING!*

Max Weber informs us that class has an impact on the long-term "life chances" of members of society. Karl Marx points to class as a force for human liberation and social change. Aging policy and politics reflect the meaning and measure of class on all three levels of conceptualization and analysis, with attention to the importance of intersectionality as noted above. The reproduction of class-based advantages and disadvantages is lodged (and fought) in and through power struggles culminating in social structural arrangements (e.g., families, public and higher education), practices, policies, and ideologies that are inflected within social conflicts in the capitalist state and society.

See also: Austerity, Cumulative Advantage/Disadvantage, Domination, Exploitation, Globalization, Inequality, Institutions, Intersectionality, The State

Further Reading

Adler, N. E. (1999). Socioeconomic status and health in industrial nations. *Annals of the New York Academy of Medicine*, 896.

Crystal, S. & Shea, D. (1990). Cumulative advantage, cumulative disadvantage, and inequality among elderly people. *The Gerontologist*, *30*(4), 437–443. doi:10.1093/geront/30.4.437.

Dannefer, D. (1987). Aging as intracohort differentiation: Accentuation, the Matthew effect, and the life course. *Sociological Forum*, *2*(2), 211–236. doi:10.1007/BF01124164.

Dannefer, D. & Huang, W. (2017). Precarity, inequality and the problem of agency in the study of the life course. *Innovations in Aging 1*(3), https://doi.org/10.1093/geroni/igx027.

Estes, C. L. (2011). Crises in old age policy. In R. A. Settersten Jr. & J. L. Angel (Eds.), *Handbook of sociology of aging* (pp. 297–320). New York: Springer.

Estes, C. L., Swan, J. H., & Gerard, L. E. (1982). Dominant and competing paradigms in gerontology: Towards a political economy of ageing. *Ageing and Society, 2*(2), 151–164.

Estes, C. L., Zones, G. J., & Swan, J. (1984). An era of crisis: The class basis of sacrifice. In *Political economy, health, and aging* (pp. 92–100). Boston, MA: Little Brown.

Harvey, D. (2005). *A brief history of neoliberalism*. Oxford: Oxford University Press.

Lukács, G. & San Juan, E. (1973). *Marxism and human liberation*. New York: Dell Publishing.

O'Rand, A. M. (1996). The precious and the precocious: Understanding cumulative disadvantage and cumulative advantage over the life course. *The Gerontologist, 36*(2), 230.

Phillipson, C. (2013). Ageing and class in a globalised world. In M. Formosa & P. Higgs (Eds.), *Social class in later life*. Bristol: Policy Press.

Polivka, L. & Estes, C. L. (2009). The economic meltdown and old age politics. *Generations, 33*(3), 56.

Reeves, R. V. (2018). *Dream hoarders: How the American upper middle class is leaving everyone else in the dust, why that is a problem, and what to do about it*. Washington, DC: Brookings Institution Press.

Ross, C. E. & Wu, C. (1995). The links between education and health. *American Sociological Review, 60*(5), 719–745.

Tilly, C. (1998). *Durable inequality*. Berkeley, CA: University of California Press.

Townsend, P. (1979). *Poverty in the United Kingdom*. Berkeley, CA: University of California Press.

Weber, M. (1958). Class, status and party. In H. H. Gerth & C. W. Mills (Eds.), *Max weber: Essays in sociology* (pp. 180–195). New York: Oxford University Press.

Weber, M. (1968). *Economy and society: An interpretative sociology*. New York: Bedminster.

Wright, E. O. (1999, July). Foundations of class analysis: A Marxist perspective. In *Annual Meeting of the American Sociological Association, Chicago*, July, 1–21. Retrieved from www.ssc.wisc.edu/~wright/Foundations.pdf.

Wright, E. O. (2015). *From grand paradigm battles to pragmatist realism: Towards an integrated class analysis. Understanding class* (pp. 1–18). New York: Verso.

Climate Change

Large-scale and long-term change in the environment caused primarily by human activity. Backed by extensive research and evidence, scientists have demonstrated that we are currently in, or are closely approaching, the Anthropocene, a name for a geological epoch beginning at the time when human activities began to have a substantial global effect on the Earth's ecosystems, including non-humans (Gabardi, 2018).

Increasing destabilization of the environment due to pollution, commercial trade, population growth, and industrial development threatens ecological balance and the life of all species. Climate-disasters (from fire, drought, floods) affect disadvantaged and marginalized communities disproportionately, since governmental aid, recovery efforts, and relocation opportunities are not shared or utilized equally.

In the meantime, a conservative, anti-science campaign by climate-change deniers helped elect Donald Trump, who withdrew from the Paris Climate Accord, which all other nations view as vital to saving the planet. Trump and other Republicans enacted other policies that threaten the future of all peoples, all ages, and all living things in the ecosystem.

Imagine how a 90-year-old African American woman living in the Lower 9th Ward during Hurricane Katrina envisioned her rescue and rebuilding? Did the result look anything like the rebuilding of white and gentrified neighborhoods in the years following the hurricane? Though wealthy neighborhoods in New Orleans recovered most of their pre-Katrina population, many poor neighborhoods have seen little improvement (Martinez, Eads, & Groskopf, 2015). Since 2000, New Orleans has lost 95,625 African American residents, compared to 6811 white residents (Data Center, 2019). This is but one example of inequality due to climate disasters, while many other swathes of coastal land are increasingly susceptible to rising ocean levels that inflict more damage upon vulnerable communities.

Older adults living independently suffer disproportionately during heatwaves, a more common occurrence as cities experience record-setting temperatures. A significant body of research in medicine and sociology shows that elderly city residents living alone are the single most likely group to die or need emergency medical assistance during summer heatwaves (Portacolone, 2015).

Climate change is a politically divided and inconsistently recognized phenomenon. Scientists and many policy-makers warn about the hastening change and impending costs of ignoring climate change, yet many conservatives deny any connection between climate change and pollution (thus positing that deregulation of pollution is not necessary and justifying non-participation in global initiatives such as The Paris Climate Accord). *The New York Times* editorial board notes the Trump Administration's erasure and rebranding (framing) of climate change:

> Even the official vocabulary of global warming has changed, as if the problem can be made to evaporate by describing

it in more benign terms. At the Department of Agriculture, staff members are encouraged to use words like "weather extremes" in lieu of "climate change," and "build soil organic matter, increase nutrient use efficiency" instead of "reduce greenhouse gases." The Department of Energy has scrubbed the words "clean energy" and "new energy" from its websites, and has cut links to clean or renewable energy initiatives and programs, according to the Environmental Data & Governance Initiative, which monitors federal websites.

At the E.P.A., a former Trump campaign assistant named John Konkus aims to eliminate the "double C-word," meaning "climate change," from the agency's research grant solicitations, and he views every application for research money through a similar lens. The E.P.A. is even considering editing out climate change-related exhibits in a museum depicting the agency's history.

The EPA has historically had a staff person responsible for policies affecting the aged and a related public information initiative. In 2017 the Trump Administration terminated this position.

See also: Commons, Framing, Gentrification, Housing, Knowledges

Further Reading

Gabardi, W. (2018). *The next social contract: Animals, the anthropocene and bipolitics*. Philadelphia, PA: Temple University Press.

Martinez, P., Eads, D., & Groskopf, C. (2015). Post-Katrina New Orleans smaller, but population growth rates back on track. *NPR*, August 19. Retrieved from www.npr.org/2015/08/19/429353601/post-katrina-new-orleans-smaller-but-population-growth-rates-back-on-track.

New York Times Editorial Board. (2017). President Trump's war on science. *The New York Times*, September 9. Retrieved from www.nytimes.com/2017/09/09/opinion/sunday/trump-epa-pruitt-science.html?mcubz=3&_r=0.

Portacolone, E. (2015). Older Americans living alone. *Journal of Contemporary Ethnography*, *44*(3), 280–305.

Who lives in New Orleans and metro parishes now? (2019). June 30. Retrieved from www.datacenterresearch.org/data-resources/who-lives-in-new-orleans-now/.

Coalitions

Groups and organizational alliances working toward a common mission and actions by combining and sharing resources. Instead of duplicating efforts and competing for scarce resources, these collectives aim to harvest collaborative prospects for achieving mutual aims. There are successes and failures of coalitions, which shape structural outcomes and the promises of social movements.

Beamish and Luebbers (2009) describe the important role of coalitional alliances as "bridging processes" in the development of movements for social change. Cross-movement coalitions extend the viability and capacity to promote social change through (1) cause affirmation, (2) co-development of cross movement commitments, (3) strategic development, and (4) exclusion, which clarifies rules and roles for participation.

For aging, one the most established and active coalitions is the Leadership Council of Aging Organizations (LCAO), a nonpartisan national coalition of 70 national non-profit organizations committed to the well-being of America's older population and to representing their interests in public policy. The membership of LCAO represents more than 50 million older Americans. It meets monthly and has active committees that review and adopt policy positions. Over nearly 40 years, LCAO member organizations and the coalition itself have guided and supported the development and expansion of social insurance and other federal and State programs under both Republican and Democratic administrations. LCAO has established statements of principles on big policy issues such as Social Security, health care, and the federal budget.

Advocacy coalitions have emerged in response to austerity politics and persistent attacks on Social Security and Medicare. Social Security Works (SSW) with its Strengthen Social Security Campaign (SSSC) is an active national coalition of social insurance proponents (Altman & Kingson, 2015). With funding from a private foundation, the Alliance for Retired Americans (ARA), many advocates benefit from the SSW's technical assistance, polling, message development, and campaign staff.

Communities of color are engaged via policy think tanks and member organizations, including the Center for Global Policy Solutions (CGPS), POLICY LINK, Urban League, and the National Association of Colored People. CGPS has taken a lead on Social Security, the racial wealth gap, racial health disparities, and the inclusion revolution. The coalitional work of the Tri Caucus is significant (see Congressional Caucus). Trump resistance agents have been fortified by the efforts of Senators Sanders and Warren and the Senate and House Democratic opposition. Campaign Zero of Black Lives Matter, and anti-deportation resisters have leveraged links to millions on the Web, ushering in new waves of likely coalitional formations.

Cross-movement coalitions of resistance offer an untapped and unfolding power source in working against oppression across a rainbow cast of intersectionalities, social policy constituencies, and problems. However, it must be noted that marginalized groups often draw necessary limits of who and how one can join as coalitional allies. Exclusion, mentioned before by Beamish and Luebbers (2009), clarifies the rules and roles so that they are not mangled or subsumed by dominant interests. White progressives often employ the lens of intersectionality to claim (and romanticize) a racial harmony that does not exist, as people of color's voices and concerns are dismissed or managed.

See also: Congressional Caucus, Interaction Ritual Chains, People of Color, Social Movements

Further Reading

Altman, N. & Kingson, E. (2015). *Social Security works! Why Social Security isn't going broke and how expanding it will help us all.* New York: The New Press.

Beamish, T. D. & Luebbers, A. J. (2009). Alliance building across social movements: Bridging difference in a peace and justice coalition. *Social Problems, 56*(4), 647–676.

Code Switch

Entails alternating between types of speech. Often one type of speech comes with more legitimacy and recognition by those with power (e.g., academic elite and those with class privilege), and the other with associations of home, community, and culture. Code switching describes how one might use Yiddish, patois, or Ebonics within familiar circles and switch to standard English in other spaces.

Recognizing code switching acknowledges power. Clinicians, researchers, and academics have opportunities to encourage themselves and others to confront the limits of standardized discourse – and to celebrate the diversity of voices and expressions. Not everything can be or should be put into "professionalized" speech or text. Hybrid

dialects and subaltern/regional linguistic codes offer opportunities for discursive widening and the articulation of community values. At the core of code switching is an experience of navigating identity through voice.

See also: Discourse, Rhetoric

Cognitive Liberation

Occurs the moment when participating activists believe that collective social change will succeed (McAdam, Tarrow, & Tilly, 2003). It has been advanced as a crucial component of colonized people's healing and emancipation through reclaiming fractured epistemologies (epistemicide).

Relevant classical theoretical concepts are the Looking Glass Self (Cooley), Self-Fulfilling Prophecy, and the power of the definition of a situation, each denoting the power of symbolic interaction among participants in affecting self-esteem and motivating action. Cognitive liberation signals a freedom in thought, which is a freedom in experience. This occurs when one identifies and shucks stereotypes which threaten the fullness of one's humanity.

See also: Agency, Emancipatory, Epistemologies, Framing, Interactionism, Interaction Ritual Chains, Stereotype Threat

Further Reading

McAdam, D., Tarrow, S., & Tilly, C. (2003). Dynamics of contention. *Social Movement Studies, 2*(1), 99–102.

Collective Impact

A goal or mission of a group of agents and organizations from different spaces, locations, or sectors toward a common agenda for solving a social problem. A *collective* is a group of individuals who unite to support each other.

Efforts to achieve collective impact are best employed for problems that are complex and systemic rather than technical in nature. There are five conditions of collective impact success measurement:

1. *Common agenda*: All participants share a vision for change that includes a common understanding of the problem and a joint approach to solving the problem through agreed-upon actions.
2. *Shared measurement*: All participating organizations agree on the ways in which success will be measured and reported, with a short-list of common indicators identified and used for learning and improvement.
3. *Mutually reinforcing activities*: A diverse group of stakeholders, typically across sectors, coordinate a set of differentiated activities through a mutually reinforcing plan of action.
4. *Continuous communication*: All players engage in frequent and structured open communication to build trust, assure mutual objectives, and create common motivation.
5. *Backbone support*: An independent, funded staff dedicated to the initiative provides ongoing support by guiding the initiative's vision and strategy, supporting aligned activities, establishing shared measurement practices, building public will, advancing policy, and mobilizing resources.

See also: Black Lives Matter, The Commons, Gray Panthers, Social Movements

Further Reading

Collective impact shared resources. (2017). Retrieved from http://collectiveimpact forum.org/resources/collective-impact-shared-resources.

Colonialisms

Speak to multiple forms and framings of colonization.

Colonization is the process of claiming land, establishing ownership of a territory and people. Neocolonialism is the modern, transnational process of ownership through military coercion, economic or trade sanctions (siege), or ideological domination. The violence (physical and psychic) used to establish ownership extends to educational practices and to the stratification of economy and citizenship. Indoctrination and subordination leave citizens with less power and a need to seek rights.

Neocolonialism asserts itself not only within formerly land-colonized regions but also via differentials in rights, for example, in the inscription of visitor stamps (visa status, or what one's citizenship allows with regard to the movement between former colonial and neocolonial powers). Postcolonialism is a discipline of critical study that considers the legacies of domination and exploitation from imperialism and neoliberal globalism.

In gerontology, colonialism is perpetuated by several primary factors: (1) Western biomedical and pharmaceutical companies and governments export specific ideologies of mental health and philosophies of care to other populations and countries; (2) transnational and migratory labor (caregivers, nurses) working in other countries; and (3) international educational forums and exchanges that import or export models and philosophies of care. With this awareness, aging study can employ theories of colonialism to expand an understanding of many aspects of inequality: as colonialism relates to immigrant caregivers, expat retirees enjoying higher standards of living than local populations throughout the world, health tourism, and how medical care and practice typically neglects or exploits (through rebranding and patenting) indigenous traditions.

Understanding that colonization is an active, continuing phenomenon rather than a static historical reality is a first step toward healing. Driskill (2015, p. 57) suggests, "Decolonization is learned through embodied practices that restore cultural memory to our bodies and communities. Colonization and genocide in the Americas and elsewhere depended on the destruction of cultural memory through attacks on indigenous rhetorical practices." Older adults possessing cultural memory can act as elders of the tribe most effectively when they are given resources and support.

See also: Globalization, Memory, Neoliberalism, Xenophobia

Further Reading

Driskill, Q. (2015). Decolonial skillshares: Indigenous rhetorics as radical practice. In K. Lisa, J. R. Anderson, & G. Rose (Eds.), *Survivance, sovereignty, and story: Teaching American Indian rhetorics* (pp. 57–78). Logan, UT: Utah State University Press.

Fanon, F. (1963). *The wretched of the Earth* (trans. R. Philcox). New York: Grove Press.

Commodification

Describes the process by which human and social experience, including needs (like health care) and even relationships, identities, and emotional states, become marketized.

Commodities may be sold, often for profit, and become the capital for local or global companies and/or governments (increasingly harder to distinguish between the two) which reap the surplus value of commercialization, proprietarization, and monetization.

De-commodification requires a radical act of reimaging something as shared and essential. Esping-Andersen (1990) describes the de-commodification of labor as a

situation in which "a service is rendered as a matter of right, and when a person can maintain a livelihood without reliance on the market" (p. 22). He notes that elements of the welfare state that provide support based on need solidify labor's commodification.

The continuing and growing influence of the medical engineering model of health has contributed to the commodification of old age and aging over the past century. This is reflected in the shift in the mode of production of medical goods and services from an orientation of fulfilling human needs to a mode of medical production oriented toward monetary exchange and corporate profit. This is part of a larger trend in which commodification entails the diminution of human needs. Companies and governments build wealth by shifting the mission from service-providing to profit-making: touted as the health of the market, this supersedes human need. Commodification diminishes the consideration of social needs and the "right" of the elderly to health and health care (Estes & Associates, 2001).

See also: Capitalism, The Market, Neoliberalism, Privatization

Further Reading

Esping-Andersen, G. (1990). *The three worlds of welfare capitalism*. Cambridge: Polity Press.

Estes, C. L. (1979). *The aging enterprise: A critical examination of social policies and services for the aged*. San Francisco, CA: Jossey-Bass.

Estes, C. L. & Associates. (2001). *Social policy & aging: A critical perspective*. Thousand Oaks, CA: Sage.

Commons, The

Announces shared rights of all human beings to air, water, space – even a right to have rights – with no requirement of possessing wealth to gain access. The violation of the commons is its opposite. Enclosing open spaces and granting land titles to individuals or corporations circumscribes and disallows access to common lands and rights. Our concern is the loss of the concept of the commons. Its continuing denigration as a human right to very basic elements (the air we breathe) points to the vigilance citizens must exercise to safeguard the concept of the commons as a human right. The commons pertain not only to land and basic life elements but also in other forms of opportunity and sustenance like intellectual and social capital – a sense of belonging and participation.

To fully appreciate the significance of the commons and the threats to its survival, we need to go big. Globalization is clearly implicated in terms of the protection, control, ownership, and profits of natural resources of air, water, and public lands, and open seas and oceans. These and other natural resources, including wildlife and plants, are not inexhaustible; they are essential elements of the Earth's biosphere that affect the climate system. As such, the Earth's biosphere does "not belong to any particular country or individual and are therefore held in common" (Lowes, 2006, p. 104; Global Commons Institute: www.gci.org.uk). "The tragedy of the commons" describes the phenomena by which collective resources, if not properly managed, will be exploited to the point of depletion. Intervention on the part of the State or stakeholders is necessary to ensure that any common good remains stable.

Borders and geopolitical territories undermine the concept of the commons, determining who has access to resources and protections. What does it mean that the people who live in areas which regulate pollution purchase commodities from areas polluted by the production of those very commodities? And how can an American's retirement to the Global South be considered acceptable expatriation (even an adventurous luxury), while movement across borders for safety labels one an alien threat to domestic resources?

Hardin (1968), in one of the most cited articles in the social sciences, makes a persuasive case that the world has a class of problems which have no technical solutions. They require a fundamental extension to solutions found in morality. Morality contrasts with the near-universal assumption by experts that the answer is technical, defined as one that requires a change only in the techniques of the natural sciences, demanding little or nothing in the way of change in human values. The work of Elinor Ostrom (2015) won her the Nobel Prize for analyzing common resource management, and the identification of recurring institutional structures that facilitate successful common ownership.

The activist organization Demos, working jointly with Americans United for a Fair Economy, initiated a program on Inequality and the Common Good to document the dangers of increasing privatization and inequality for democracy, the economy, and civic life. The Amsterdam Declaration on Social Quality was adopted for the European Union (EU) to commit to preserving the unique nature of the Western European model in its "social dimension." Brexit, the divorce of Britain from the EU, is seen as a symbol of xenophobia and the potential spread of populist fascism. As the Comité des Sages (1996) stated, "Europe will be a Europe for everyone, for all its citizens, or it will be nothing" (Walker & Corbett, 2017).

See also: Morality, Social

Further Reading

Collins, C. & Muhammad, D. (2007). Race, wealth and the commons. *Poverty & Race, 16*(3), 3–7.

Demos & Americans United for a Fair Economy. *Inequality and the common good.*

Washington, DC and Boston, MA: Demos and Americans United for a Fair Economy.

Global Commons Institute: www.gci.org.uk.

Hardin, G. (1968). The tragedy of the commons. *Science*, *162*(3859), 1243–1248. Retrieved from http://science.sciencemag.org/content/162/3859/1243.

Lowes, D. E. (2006). *The anti-capitalist dictionary: Movements, histories and motivations.* New York: Zed Books. (pp. 104–105).

Ostrom, E. (2015). *Governing the commons* (Canto Classics edition). Cambridge: Cambridge University Press.

Response to "Tragedy of the commons" thesis: www.infoshop.org/faq/sec16.htm.

Walker, A. & Corbett, S. (2017). *The post Brexit declaration on social quality in Europe.* International Association on Social Quality, March 8, p. 8.

Complicit

Means "choosing to be involved in an illegal or questionable act, especially with others; having partnership or involvement in wrongdoing. Or, put simply, it means being, at some level, responsible for something . . . even if indirectly" (Dictionary.com, 2017).

Complicit is Dictionary.com's *Word of the Year*, which they write:

> is as much about what is visible as it is about what is not. It's a word that reminds us that even inaction is a type of action. The silent acceptance of wrongdoing is how we've gotten to this point. We must not let this continue to be the norm. If we do, then we are all complicit.

The word *complicit* has sprung up in conversations this year about those who speak out against powerful figures and institutions, and about those who stay silent as this relates to climate change, sexual assault, social media, and political advertising. As we look at the cultural and political landscape, we ask: "What does it mean to be complicit in 2017?" How does this concept relate to privilege and subject positioning within systems of oppression?

A political economy of aging perspective calls attention to processes and structures in our society, communities, and gerontological practices that are directly or indirectly complicit in serious forms of discrimination such as ageism, classism, racism, and sexism. Complicity allows abuses of power to root and remain in our health and aging policy. Examples of policies in the US that are complicit in inequality reveal themselves in what they do not feature; that is, they lack universal health care and the right to shelter through housing. Complicity extends to standing by (i.e., the bystander effect) as institutions such as the State Department, the Environmental Protection Agency, the Department of Food, Drug and Agriculture, the National Park Service, and the Education Department are gutted, dismantled, and stacked with conservative bureaucrats.

See also: Ageism, Authoritarianism, Climate Change, Demagogue, Fascism, Housing, Inequality, Oppression, Power, Privilege, Racism, Sexism

Further Reading

Dictionary.com. (2017). #complicit.

Conflict Theory and Consensus Theory

Two opposing theories of social order and social change pivotal to decision- and policy-making structures. The rendering here of conflict and consensus theory reflects its formation during the social movements of the 1960s alongside the political economy of aging. Today these theories have become much more nuanced and complex.

Conflict Theory

The *conflict perspective* is a central theoretical tenet of critical perspectives on aging policy. Conflict theory posits that society, the social order, and its institutions are produced and held together as a result of power struggles and conflicts between different groups (e.g., race, ethnicity, class, gender) and the relative strength of their interests. The outcomes of conflicts and power struggles are profoundly consequential for how society is ordered, laws are designed, resources are distributed, and inequalities and even identities are constructed, contested, reproduced, maintained, or changed. Critical perspectives posit that society and its major institutions are produced, shaped, and held together (or reproduced) by "constraint" and "soft and hard forms of coercion" (Collins, 1988, p. 118). The conflict perspective is distinctly oppositional to the consensus theoretical perspective of structural functionalism which posits that society is structured because we have consensus (generally agree) with how things are organized, functioning, and operating (i.e., the status quo).

Notably, conflict theory is a theory of change. Conflict theory is a theory of power, dominance, and resistance. The relentless and vicious struggles of conservative oppositional forces against social insurance, Social Security, Medicare, Medicaid, the Affordable Care Act, and public long-term care (e.g., the CLASS Act) illustrate just that. These conflicts embody dynamic and dialectical processes – the outcome of which spurs other continuing rounds of political struggles, wins, and losses. Key issues include how the State and civil society work within and on behalf of the US capitalist economic system and economic globalization, in the midst of anti-human rights campaigns, global warming, and the rising tide of vulnerable peoples everywhere.

Power conflicts persist in the struggles over US public policy about aging across the life course. Examples include the partisan, political, ideological, and economic battles between proponents and opponents of privatizing and dismantling Social Security and Medicare. Struggles for identity rights and equality, by race, ethnicity, gender, and sexuality; for a living wage; for the right to a job; and rights to housing and food security have been fought for many decades. Social movements seek change about conflicting values and ideologies, economic stakes, political control, and the preservation or obliteration of cultural heritage and communities.

In the critical political economy framework, conflict is animated through the aggregation and exercise of power resources and relations. Winners and losers differentially shape (and reap benefits of) the policy and distributional agendas of various governmental sectors, for example, Departments of Education, Housing and Urban Development, and Health and Human Services. The forces, tensions, and struggles unleashed by neoliberalism, globalization, hypercapitalism, wars, immigration, unemployment, and migration in the developed and developing worlds are significant for social policy and aging. The Reagan presidency ushered in massive tax cuts and policy shifts, laying the ground for discrimination, exacerbating class inequalities, sexism, racism and ethnic discrimination, ableism, nativism, and ageism. The rising demographics of older adults are used as a political battering ram (*see* Statistical Panic) to rationalize the dismantling of Social Security and Medicare and other safety net programs.

Consensus Theory

The conflict perspective of the political economy of aging may be contrasted with consensus theoretical perspectives of structural functionalism, which in Parsons' rendering contends that society is structured in the way it is because there is broad societal agreement (consensus) regarding how things are organized, functioning, and operating. Consensus theories support the status quo, while conflict theory seeks social change favoring less discrimination and inequality.

Consensus theory argues that the structure and rewards of US society result from ("happy") accommodation and consensus between and among disparate groups and interests. This is a "pluralist" theory that has been rejected by critical theorists, as it does not attend to the dominance and unequal balance of power between ruling and subject classes and identities in society.

Consensus theorists are attentive to social integration and social order that maintains stability in society (and US policy on aging) depends on agreement between and among diverse interests and sectors of society. According to this theory, the current structure of society is organized around a unitary or homogeneous set of values. The influential theory proponents of consensus models in US sociology are Talcott Parsons and his contemporary adherents, who have argued that inequalities are legitimate (and merited) because they are necessary in order to assure that disparate functions of society are performed efficiently and the social order remains stable. The strength of the consensus perspective is reflected in its consistency with the dominant ideology of pluralism in political science and market fundamentalism. It may also be seen in theories of age and development (e.g., in Cumming and Henry's disengagement theory of aging or in Baltes' S-O-C model) which assume social consensus by rendering invisible the entire realm of power and the defining and shaping of individuals to fit institutionally established imperatives. The co-optation of theories of age and development in service of functionalist ideology, even when it goes against human interests, Dannefer (2011) identifies as the "*functional–developmental nexus.*"

Today, conflict theory, within the broader critical theory tradition, draws upon and reworks Marxian and Neo-Marxian perspectives as well as Weberian, Frankfurt School, Gramscian, and other New Left perspectives. In the political economy of aging policy, conflict, power accumulation, and struggles are a core theoretical premise (Estes, 1979, 2016).

See also: Disengagement, Functionalism, Statistical Panic

Further Reading

Collins, R. (1988). Conflict and social change. In *Theoretical sociology* (pp. 118–153). San Diego, CA: Harcourt Brace Jovanovich.

Dannefer, D. (2011). Age, the life course, and the sociological imagination: Prospects for theory. In Linda George (Eds.), *Handbook of aging and social sciences* (7th edition) (pp. 3–16). San Diego, CA: Academic Press.

Estes, C. L. (1979). *The aging enterprise: A critical examination of social policies and services for the aged*. San Francisco, CA: Jossey-Bass.

Estes, C. L., with DiCarlo, N. R. (2016). Social movements and social knowledges: Gerontological theory in research, policy and practice. In V. L. Bengston & R. Settersten Jr. (Eds.), *Handbook of theories of aging* (pp. 87–106). New York: Springer.

Gouldner, A. W. (1970) *The coming crisis of Western sociology*. New York: Basic Books.

Parsons, T. (1951). *The social system*. Glencoe, IL: Free Press.

Rex, J. (1961). Theory of social conflict and change. In *Key problems of sociological theory* (pp. 115–135). New York: NYL Humanities Press.

Congressional Caucus

A group of Congress members who work together on shared policy preferences. Common ground is based on ideology, party, race, industry, and much more. Congressional Caucuses and their membership are constantly shifting, with new groups emerging and old groups fading away.

Progressives between 2005 and 2016 have mobilized in favor of Social Security, its protection, and improvement. Among the proponents are the Ranking (minority party) Congressional organizers and leaders of House and Senate Caucuses. Most active in the Social Security struggles have been the Progressive Caucus, the Black, Hispanic, Asian-Pacific Islander Caucuses (and their coalitional Tri-Caucus), the Women's Caucus, the Democratic Women's Working Group, the Democratic House Aging Caucus, and a LGBT Caucus. Supporting Social Security, Caucus leaders and staff work from the inside of Congress and with outside groups in the "Washington DC Beltway" – think tanks, coalitions, policy wonks, and social media groups which provide instant data and messaging that support Social Security essential for economic and health security.

The most prominent Caucus within the Republican Party is the Freedom Caucus, a group of extremely conservative House Members that grew out of the very conservative but larger Republican Study Committee. The Freedom Caucus does not disclose the names of its members. Members may choose to identify themselves; otherwise it is generally difficult to know exactly how large the Freedom Caucus is. The Caucus consistently opposes virtually every form of government social spending, while it supports defense spending and seeks to abolish most business and environmental regulation.

Congressional mid-terms in 2018 produced a Democratic House majority, opening Caucus windows wide on both sides as Dems gained a 40-seat majority.

See also: Boost Social Security, Coalitions, Fix the Debt, Framing, Resistance.

Consciousness Raising

The process of expanding perception and understanding of the world, often through collaborative exploration and interrogation of common norms and biases. It describes the process of liberation, or coming into contact with previously repressed or denied thoughts and feelings, especially with regard to experiences of oppressing and being oppressed.

Consciousness raising happens within communities through dialogue with others who together gather and chart instances of abuse, coercion, and dehumanization. Consciousness raising and it processes, including its narratives, are typically not valued or are actively suppressed by dominant powers. In fact they have transformative potential to upset and destabilize the comfortable positions of those in power. "Critical consciousness" is the primary tool of pedagogy proposed by Freire. It is the final stage in growth of consciousness (Freire, 1998, p. 79). It is "a way of reading how society works . . . to understand better the problem of interests, the question of power. How to get power, what it means not to have power. Finally, conscientizing implies a deeper reading of reality" (p. 9).

The mentorship of Maggie Kuhn advocated for intergenerational consciousness raising and was modeled as such. "Elders of the tribe" (Maggie's term) carry the progress and journey of their consciousness raising to younger generations. Without progressive elders a young generation is distorted and alone in a landscape where social problems feel more absolute, timeless, and impenetrable. Dorothy Smith in *Writing the social* (1999), accentuates Marx's point that consciousness functions over and independent of individuals. Smith applies this idea to the relations of ruling that in the everyday and everynight lives of women become their consciousness.

Feminist circles held consciousness raising workshops and created spaces in which small supportive groups in women-only meetings discussed their experiences. The women's health movement organized groups where, for the first time, women looked at their own vaginas (encouraged by the classic book, *Our bodies ourselves*). Without consciousness as an integral part of knowledge(s), people lose connection to each other and to the means of advancing themselves. One way that consciousness of women has been suppressed is through mainstream culture's ritual shaming of their bodies, depicting women's bodies as being too much, ruined, or not working. Women learn that their bodies must be tamed, ready for sex (but without the stigma of experience), and able to reproduce. This fosters a false consciousness which, in a critical lens, may be directly or indirectly linked to ideology and domination: as those in power manipulate perceptions to hide oppressive relations and the violence and disparity engendered.

Social movements require consciousness and affiliations in their development. Groups provide space and co-presence through interaction ritual chains that are not just energy building, but areas for emotional development. Progressive social policy and lawmaking may also serve as eruptive/interruptive and/or disruptive events, signaling where a culture is and what is possible. Title IX's expansion first to include protection for women, and recently for trans peoples, not only signifies a new marker and shift in what has normally been said; it also demands that the reign of tradition – the doxa – be resisted. Consciousness raising requires opening up awareness to the intersectional forces of oppression, and to many social realms, including spatial, formulate and constellate experiences of marginalization and voicelessness. What spaces might exist for consciousness raising with regard to aging? Who would be invited to participate? Where does the power of the oppressor lie with regard to age, race, ethnicity, class, and gender? What age and subject positioning is the most powerful?

See also: Cognitive Liberation, Doxa, Empowerment, Feminism, Generation, Generational and Intergenerational Consciousness, Ideology, Interaction Ritual Chains, Levels of Analysis, Maggie Kuhn, Power, Privilege

Further Reading

Freire, P. (1998). *Pedagogy of freedom*. Lanham, MD: Rowman & Littlefield.

Smith, D. E. (1999). *Writing the social*. Toronto, ON: University of Toronto Press. (Originally published 1978.)

Contradiction

Exists when beliefs or statements negate or oppose each other through dissonant values, factual inconsistencies, and logical fallacies such as presumptive relativism or equivalencies. For our purposes, contradiction is not so much about challenging power (or the status quo), but rather when dominant interests contradict the will of the people, through lies and hypocrisy.

One of the victories of the Right has been selling to the public the idea that the growth of capitalism (the increased robustness of markets) is equivalent and necessary to a robust democracy, when in fact capitalism and democracy are often at odds. Democracy is based on one person having a vote, yet capitalism is based on who owns the most. Campaign financing, in light of the *Citizens United v. US* ruling, provides an opportunity to unmask the inconsistency of representative power. How can these competing bases reconcile their differences, and do they try?

One contradiction posited by classical economics is that regulation or constraints on capital and capital markets will by definition be negative for "the economy." Constraints on capital are defined by classical economists to include labor practices and corporate decisions about where to invest, or whether to escape US taxes (while using US intellectual resources and labor), and

The logic of capitalism requires the inexhaustible search for profits, the accumulation of private property and wealth and, with it, social inequality. Closed instead of open (J. P. Thompson, enclosure movement); boundaries of inside and outside. Exploitation, immiseration, and greed – accompany ideologies of "we deserve it because we worked for it" and "survival of the fittest." These are central to the Protestant ethic and the spirits of capitalism.	The logic of democracy is that everyone is part of the social whole. Society and its opportunities are open versus closed. One person one vote. Inclusion, not exclusion. The right to a voice with guaranteed and equal access to all means to vote and speak, regardless of class, ethnicity, race, gender, sexuality, (dis)ability, education, or property. The importance of the commons and the commitment to the public good underlie democratic values.

whether to bear the costs of industrial pollution, health, and safety. Theory coexists with the reality that "American democracy has never been truly consolidated . . . key elements remain unrealized or vulnerable; others have been exploited for antidemocratic ends" (Wolin, 2008, p. xix).

For aging, several contradictions exist in the discrepancies of valuing older adults. They are simultaneously theoretically to be respected for their wisdom, yet cost controlled because they are not "adding to the economy." They are supposed to be active and healthy, but the financialization of their care, especially medical, encourages reliance on medication and intervention to extend life by any means at whatever cost. Are they a precious resource or a market to exploit? They are both.

See also: Capitalism, Citizenship, Class, Commodification, Democracy, The Market, Privatization

Further Reading

Dean, K. (2003). *Capitalism and citizenship.* London: Routledge.

L. Estes & Associates (2001). *Social policy and aging: A critical perspective.* Thousand Oaks, CA: Sage.

Myles, J. (1984). *Old age in the welfare state.* Boston, MA: Little Brown.

Wolin, S. S. (2008). *Democracy incorporated: Managed democracy and the specter of inverted totalitarianism.* Princeton, NJ: Princeton University Press.

Co-presence

Results when people come together and allow space for alterity (difference or otherness). The generative potential in praxis, self-reflection, and knowledge of the self happens through contact with an "other." Co-presence is a gathering and a fostering of a tolerant dwelling space. It's inviting or answering the invitation to intersubjectivity. Co-presence is what Martin Buber (1923/1970) refers to as an "I-You," it's open and dynamic, and distinct from the relationship with an object or group which is static (an "I-It").

Co-presence is a tenet of social movement theory, seen as essential to building consciousness and emotional energy that motivates engagement and what engagement produces (Durkheim, 1912/1965; Goffman, 1963; Collins, 2004). Symbolic interaction, in Herbert Blumer and George Herbert Mead's social theories is essential to the identity of the self, and that identity is shaped by the social co-presence that occurs in interactions. We become who we are in relation to others; not only how we are perceived, but also how we care and are cared for.

The viral nature of the internet and social media create vast new possibilities for a meeting of the minds – and for mobilization. What is new in the digital world generally is that physical face-to-face presence is extended by Facebook, SnapChat, Youtube, Twitter, and the wealth of other options to connect and diversify what we know, what we think, what we look like, and who we are. These direct communications stir identity formation that determines the emotions, motivations, and actions we undertake.

On the Right, Breitbart and other right-wing websites have raised internet and social media co-presence to a new level. On the Left, there are several websites and organizations such as MoveOn.org and the Daily Kos. Net Roots Nation exemplifies an organization of progressive thinkers and doers who extend their access and knowledge through varied forms and techniques of co-presence. Similarly, Google Groups in Social Insurance, a 300-person (closed) network of intellectuals, policy wonks, and advocates for social insurance, daily correspond about and respond to the positions of leading corporate media, think tanks (Right and Left), policy-makers, and elected officials.

See also: Digital Spheres, Interaction Ritual Chains, Intergenerational Intersubjectivity, Psychoanalytic Social Theory, Social Movement Theory

Further Reading

Buber, M. (1970). *I and thou* (trans. W. Kaufmann). New York: Charles Scribner's Sons. (Originally published 1923.)

Collins, R. (2004). *Interaction ritual chains.* Princeton, NJ: Princeton University Press.

Durkheim, E. (1912/1965). *The elementary forms of religious life.* New York: The Free Press.

Goffman, E. (1963). *Behavior in public places: Notes on the social organization of gatherings.* New York: The Free Press.

Cost of Living Adjustment (COLA)

In theory, the change in financial support required to maintain a standard of living.

Automatic COLAs for Social Security benefits were enacted in the 1970s; it is based on the general price increases of urban wage earners and clerical workers (the CPI-W). The COLA's purpose is to offset additional expenses each year resulting from general inflation. Historically, the proposed cost-of-living-adjustment (COLA) only accounts for general inflation. It applies to generalized economic data for the entire country, while it neglects to factor in locally varied costs such as housing, and the accelerating expenses older adults face.

An analysis of the costs of structural inequality would show that the typical 0.3 percent COLA fails to adequately reflect the actual costs seniors live with – food insecurity, transportation challenges, the spiraling expenses of privatized Medicare plans and out-of-pocket medical and supplemental insurance costs – none of which is specifically reflected in the Social Security COLA. In 1982, the Consumer Price Index for the Elderly (CPI-E) was developed but was never incorporated into supplemental income for Social Security/disability (SSI/SSDI) to reflect spending patterns of consumers aged 62 and older and incorporating health expenditures, for which elders have higher costs than younger consumers.

A "Chained CPI" works differently from the current method of the "Consumer Price Index for Urban Wage Earners and Clerical Workers" (CPI-W) in that it allows for substitution, rather than the inclusion, of expensive goods as costs rise. This means that estimated costs rise far more slowly, justifying the minimal increments of the COLA. Under the Chained CPI the COLA amount is reduced. While the short-term effect of using this method is initially minimal, the amount of the COLA losses compounds, resulting in extensive long-term COLA reductions that will be harmful to beneficiaries who are most dependent on Social Security for their primary or major income source, as benefits would fall in the long run. This is a more sophisticated (tricky) way to "pre-embezzle" from the benefits which people have earned and expect to receive.

See also: Fix the Debt

Further Reading

www.ssa.gov/news/cola/.

Crisis

Conveys a situation and/or time of intense difficulty, uncertainty, and trauma. Sheldon Wolin (1969) observes that "crises in the world" create urgency for "epic theory" in which "problems-in-the-world" take precedence over "problems-in-a-theory."

Crises are "moments of truth" that signify "the restructuring of social relationships that occur when new power centers confront existing structures of domination: the outcome is generally unknown and existing institutions and social practices can no longer be taken for granted" (O'Connor, 1987, pp. 54–55). Pre-existing relationships and meanings can no longer be assumed.

Critical scholars such as Habermas, Offe, and Keane weave together individual and system level crisis theories in ways that implicate political, economic, and sociocultural realms, including self and personality. O'Connor posits "that modern economic, social, political, and cultural crises interpenetrate one another in ways which transform them into different dimensions of the same historical process . . . [and] the modern crisis becomes one 'general crisis'" (1987, pp. 11, 54).

From a Marxist perspective, "crisis" denotes "interruptions in the process of capital accumulation and economic growth." Specific crises are distinct. Some are deeper structural crises; they are "moments in the development of global capitalism" (Panitch, Albo, & Chibber, 2010, p. 4). Neoclassical economics generally defines crisis and crisis tendencies in measures like Gross National Product Growth, profits, and capital accumulation.

Perspectives on aging crises span the topics of individual and human development, the family, demography and population, health, health disparities, health costs and social inequalities, and national and global economics of aging, among others.

The theme of crisis is a central motif resonating throughout conservative politics from Reagan onward. Crisis is an integral part of austerity discourse, the threatened defunding and dismantling of social insurance programs, and the devolution of federal power.

Aging policy is a key element of the schema of crisis definition and the resulting outcomes. Understanding the contemporary welfare state requires theoretical and empirical attention to crisis construction and crisis management by the State and the role of other interests in the economic, political, and civil sectors of society. The "Reagan Revolution" illuminated the tensions within and among the State (government and its institutions), the corporate and financial sectors (and the fractions of capital therein), and labor, in working through the crisis tendencies associated with capitalism.

Since the rebirth and ideological dominance of market fundamentalism beginning in the 1980s, crisis tendencies persist and are deeply contested in the legitimacy of the State, capital, and democracy itself. These crises of the "social versus the individual" are deeply exacerbated throughout the Trump presidency.

With financial globalism, deficit politics – and austerity ideology discourse – engage in "word wars" against progressive alternatives, including universal health care or other policy measures to correct economic and health inequality. The power of campaigns to repeal

"Obamacare" and the imagined conservative mythologies of "death panels" immediately collapses public perception of possibility. Social Security has been cast by some conservatives as a Ponzi scheme – as if it were a corrupt and duplicitous machine. This discourse reflects a similar duplicity to that of Wall Street profiteers who promote "wealth management," while their management protects inequality in the market. As Teresa Ghilarducci has shown with 401(k) plans, financial advisors have driven more people away from public pensions into privatization, a system of management fees and market manipulation. Prior to the 2016 presidential election, AARP sponsored a television ad saying, "Our next president needs to take action on Social Security, or future generations could lose up to $10,000 a year." Yet some critical scholars challenge AARP's fanning of the crisis rhetoric while failing to suggest alternatives that would support or expand Social Security. Financial panic short-circuits the needed focus on solutions to Social Security's financial condition. Republicans support raising the retirement age, which could favor white-collar workers and disproportionately affect populations who do physical labor and have less access to company pension plans. Options like increasing the minimum wage, legalizing more immigrant workers, and scrapping the cap on Social Security contributions (only levied on the first $128,500 of income) would secure more funding and promote equal distribution of responsibility and resources.

See also: Capitalism, Debt/Fix the Debt, Deficit Crisis Framing, Dispossession, Neoliberalism, Privatization

Further Reading

Estes, C. L. (2011). Crisis and old age policy. In R. A. Settersten Jr. & J. L. Angel (Eds.), *Handbook of sociology of aging* (pp. 297–320). New York: Springer.

Estes, C. L., Swan, J. H., & Associates. (1993). *The long-term care crisis: Elders trapped in the no care zone.* Thousand Oaks, CA: Sage.

Ghilarducci, T. (2013). Austerity distorts the common economic interests between generations. *Social Research, 80*(3), 953–976.

O'Connor, J. (1987). *The meaning of crisis: A theoretical introduction.* Oxford: Blackwell.

Panitch, L. & Gindin, S. (2011). Capitalist crises and the crisis this time. *Journal of Economics of Shanghai School, 9*(4), 164–179.

Panitch, L., Albo, G., & Chibber, V. (Eds.). (2010). *Socialist Register: The crisis this time.* New York: Merlin Press, p. 4.

White, J. (2003). *False alarm: Why the greatest threat to Social Security and Medicare is the campaign to save them.* Baltimore, MD: Johns Hopkins University Press.

Wolin, S. S. (1969). Political theory as a vocation. *The American Political Science Review, 63*(4), 1062–1082.

Critical Realism

Attempts to observe and locate objective realities.

Critical Realism (CR) depicts the interplay between natural and social worlds and speaks to material need. It is a combination of Roy Bhaskar's approach to transcendental realism and critical naturalism. CR locates causal relationships at the level of events, while questioning the "natural" order and critiquing positivism or what Dannefer identifies as microfication. This approach is more popular and established in the UK, where there is a membership association, journal, and annual meeting devoted to this scholarly movement.

Offe (1985, p. 90) defines realism as describing any ideology that seeks to ground itself in an objective concept of reality. He states that the ability to change and to progress in response to social and political progress is critical to any type of realism.

Critical realist social epidemiology means going beyond the "observed" by abandoning philosopher Hume's notion of causality and adopting a realist philosophy to measure the "unobserved." This requires developing measurement models for abstract latent concepts (e.g., social inclusion and exclusion, institutional racism and sexism, social justice). One application is the model of systemic racism, which is "concrete material social reality . . . embedded in all major institutions" (Elias & Feagin, 2016, p. 258). Likewise, one can observe the multiple forms of institutional sexism in US social policy. CR accords theoretical and empirical openness to the symbolic and material bases of social injustice.

Microaggressions via acts of oppression, dehumanization, and exploitation (Dover, 2016), are taken as measurable theoretical realities to be investigated.

In aging, CR would suggest research on the effects of such phenomena as the material immiseration and social abjection of populations and marginalized individuals and groups. Examples would include how the continued trauma of social exclusion and the deprivation of economic and health security restrict or enrich experiences of old age and aging, and how these may be reinforced or ameliorated through social policy or social change. Critical Realism is reflected in recent gene–environment research that identifies the physical changes in DNA that result from exposure to toxic triggers associated with psychological, racial, ethnic, gender, class, and neighborhood stresses. These stresses show up in maternal depression, which in turn impact infant and child development in other determinants of late life health and illness (Bhaskar & Hartwig, 2010, p. 261).

See also: Abjection, Ageism, Cumulative Advantage/Disadvantage, Event, Exploitation, Feminism, Human Rights, Immiseration, Microaggressions, Oppression, Political Economy, Racism, Social Constructions of Reality, Trauma

Further Reading

Bhaskar, R. & Hartwig, M. (2010). *The formation of critical realism* (1st edition). London: Routledge.

Dover, M. A. (2016). The moment of microaggression: The experience of acts of oppression, dehumanization, and exploitation. *Journal of Human Behavior in the Social Environment, 26*(7–8), 575–586.

Elias, S. & Feagin, J. R. (2016). *Racial theories in social science.* New York: Taylor and Francis.

Graeber, D. (2001). *Toward an anthropological theory of value.* Basingstoke: Palgrave.

Hartwig, M. (Ed.). (2007). *Dictionary of critical realism.* London: Routledge.

Kontos, P. C., Miller, K.-L., Mitchell, G. J., & Cott, C.A. (2010). Dementia care at the intersection of regulation and reflexivity: A critical realist perspective. *Journal of Gerontology: Social Sciences, 66B*(1), 119–128.

Naess, P., & Price, L. (2016). Crisis system; a critical realist and environmental critique of economics and the economy. London: Routledge.

Offe, C. (1985). *Disorganized capitalism.* Cambridge, MA: Polity Press.

Critical Theory

Defines various theoretical approaches that challenge basic assumptions of mainstream positions, especially those of classical theories based on the dominant paradigms of positivism, functionalism, pluralism, heteronormativity, patriarchy, and racism.

These classical theories have guided modern "normal science" and provided disciplinary grounding for the intellectual mainstream of the social, behavioral, and policy sciences. World War II launched the Frankfurt School from Germany, comprised of social scholars critical of power and the presumed authority of the classical sciences. Postmodernism contributes to critical theory through the reimagining of science and taking positions against the grain of white sociology, stratification/classism, racism, sexism, colonialism, disability, sexualities, and hybridities and intersectionalities.

This work has enriched critical theory scholarship and its excavation of subaltern knowledges. The mission of critical theory is interrogating the *material* within diverse spaces, identities, and knowledges. Although there are many variant perspectives, critical scholars generally reject radical relativism and solipsism (the view that the self is all that can be known to exist) of some "strict postmodernist views. . . . If we can achieve neither reliably objective knowledge of existing social reality nor generally applicable norms and values," then there is no possibility of any "significant contribution to social and political emancipation" (West, 2013, ch. 9). There are knowledges (provisional truths) in multiple perspectives, experiences, and voices.

Critical scholars do not have to adopt "totalizing theories and universal normative frameworks" to be committed to social justice and material equality. Gramsci's life's work tells us that it is not possible to live without a philosophy of life, without some assumptions and values. In our view it is "the task of the critical theorist to engage with actually existing theories and values of agents . . . [with] critical reflection and investigation" (West, 2013). Material and monetary reality exist in our daily lives, as do socially structured forms of power, structure, ideology, and democracy. It is incumbent upon us to investigate attacks on democracy as a "particular structure of open and fair communication" and ideology. as it "restricts or limits such processes of communication and undermines the conditions of success within them" (Bohman, 2005).

See also: Authoritarianism, Critical Realism, Democracy, Ideology, Knowledges, Oppression, Postmodernism, Power, Theories of Aging

Further Reading

Bohman, J. (2005). Critical theory. In E. N. Zalta (Ed.), *The Stanford encyclopedia of philosophy*. Stanford, CA: Stanford University Press.

West, D. (2013). *Social movements in global politics*. Cambridge, MA: Polity Press.

Crone

A term historically characterized as an old woman, ugly, a hag, and likely a witch (Bullough, 1973; Daly, 1978; Walker, 1985). Her archetype was said to possess foreboding and mysterious female (hence threatening) powers.

The crone and the witch were intertwined in dubious light. She could be cast in a derogatory sense for her words, her (lack of) intellect, and the spells that she could visit upon others. Four centuries of the European Inquisition subjected women healers and carers to being reviled, declared heretics, and a witch, being shorn of all hair and clothes on her body, being caged with her head locked in a "scolding bridle" with nails through her tongue and cheeks. By 1375, the Catholic Church had declared war on village wise-women (*medwyf*) and female healers who ministered to "matters pertaining to women," "mysteries, sexuality and reproduction" (Kramer & Sprenger, 1971, p. 66). Leaders of the Church and commerce were in control of the resources and the power of the word. Walker contends, more ominously, the coexistence of the death fear and mother dependence resided in the "fear of abandonment by the life-giving maternal figure." This had to be controlled and managed. Laws of the Church took away most of women's roles and words, all but those of the mother and subservience. Nuns were forbidden from the "mad" offense of discussing theological matters among themselves. The fathers controlled that. It meant that women were cut off from their own direct experience of spiritual vision, and any knowledge of "their Goddess-given moral codes."

The witch-hunts left a lasting effect. Ehrenreich and English (1973) bring it forward in their classic treatise, *Witches, midwives, & nurses*.

An aspect of the female has ever since been associated with the witch, and an aura of contamination has remained – especially around the midwife and other women healers. This early and devastating exclusion of women from independent healing roles was a violent precedent and a warning, as Ehrenreich and English (1973, p. 1) observe:

> For centuries women were doctors without degrees, barred from books and lectures, learning from each other, and passing on experience from neighbor to neighbor and mother to daughter. They were called "wise women" by the people, witches or charlatans by the authorities. Medicine is part of our heritage as women, our history, our birthright. . . . We are told that our subservience is biologically ordained: women are inherently nurse-like and not doctor-like.

The demonization of women healers is linked with male power and its monopolization and sexism through science, medicine, and the American health empire.

The Feminist Movement gained momentum in the 1960s, followed closely by the Women's Health Movement and the Women's Health Collective, Our Bodies, Ourselves. Women registered their revulsion and rejection of men's right to control women's bodies, women's knowledge, decisions, science, and health. It was and still is about power, control, and the hegemonic dominion and dominance of white male elites and their instruments of the corporation (as "artificial person"), the religious Right, and State power.

Back to aging: Phyllis Chesler (1972) in *Women and madness*, observes that women's madness was and is "about repression, denial and punishment of wisdom among 'older women.'" Mary Daly contends that Crones are "The great Hags of history. . . . They are the Survivors of the perpetual witch-craze of patriarchy, the Survivors of The Burning Times" (Daly, 1978, p. 16). "Witchraft mania" is "man's inhumanity to woman" for "women living free of male-control: self-supporting single women or widows" (Walker, 1985, p. 133).

In *Critical feminist lens on aging*, the Crone is re-envisioned as a woman of *Age, wisdom and power* (Walker, 1985). This rendering of the crone relates to "Crown" and

> the power of the ancient tribal matriarch who made the moral and legal decisions for her subjects and descendants. . . . As embodiment of wisdom. . . . She . . . established the first cyclic system of perpetual becoming, whereby every temporary living form in the universe blends eventually into every other form, nothing is unrelated, and there can be no hierarchy of better or worse, "We and They". It was a philosophical system profoundly opposed to the ones devised by men.
>
> (Walker, 1985, p. 14)

Walker offers the position that the crone, as "The Old Woman, who acknowledges no master, may be our best guide in this long, dark, labyrinthine spiritual journey" (Walker, 1985, p. 14). The work of Clarissa Pinkola Estes lifts and brings the healing forward in *Women who run with the wolves* (1992) and *The dangerous old woman* (1996). She tells myths and stories about the dangerous wise old archetype and a knowing of the soul. Maggie Kuhn embodied the power, strength, passion, and outrage of the crone.

Recent literature on the crone affirms movement across women's herstory from the archetypal figure of a menacing, terrifying non-human old witch (benignly called a fable, a folklore) to a much more positive wise woman, women speaking out for themselves individually and collectively (Sollee, 2017), including the online Tech Witch. It is a welcomed reprieve (albeit mild) for the millions of angry, irreparably violated, and materially injured old women. The cry that "It's a man's world" still exists even in the unveiling of sexual harassment in the #MeToo disclosures (*see* War on Women). Patriarchal inequality plays out (in the pay especially) in the helping professions traditionally considered "women's work,"where nurses, teachers, and social workers receive less recognition, legitimacy, and authority for their knowledge and expertise.

We, the author and collaborator of *Aging A–Z* (DiCarlo and Estes, and friends), have opened an invitation to and the founding of The CRONE Institute. The CRONE Institute is the Center for Respecting Our Noetic Equality; as a website it is a space and place for gray gray literature, crone chronicles, and more.

See also: Ageism, Feminism/Feminist, Maggie Kuhn, Sexism, War on Women

Further Reading

Bullough, V. L. (1973). *The subordinate sex.* Chicago: University of Illinois Press.

Chesler, P. (1972). *Women and madness.* Garden City, NY: Doubleday.

Daly, M. (1978). *Gyn/ecology:The metaethics of radical feminism.* Boston, MA: Beacon Press.

Ehrenreich, B. & English, D. (1973). *Witches, midwives & nurses.* New York: Feminist Press.

Estes, C. P. (1992). *Women who run with the wolves.* New York: Ballantine.

Estes, C. P. (1996). *The dangerous old woman. Myths and stories of the wise women archetype.* Loisville, CO: Sounds True Audio Book.

Kramarae, C. & Treichler, P. A. (1985). *Amazons, bluestockings & crones: A feminist dictionary.* London: Pandora Press.

Kramer, H. & Sprenger, J. (1971). *Malleus maleficarum.* New York: Dover Press.

Ruzek, S. B. (2004). How might the women's health movement shape national agendas on women and aging? *Women's Health Issues, 14,* 112–114, 2004.

Sollee, K. J. (2017). *Witches, sluts, feminists: Conjuring the sex positive.* Berkeley, CA: ThreeL Media.

Walker, B. G. (1985). *The crone: Woman of age, wisdom and power.* San Francisco, CA: Harper & Row.

www.croneinstitute.org.

Cross-national Comparisons

Examine variables in social conditions and policies, identifying difference in approaches and outcomes across nations. Such comparisons indicate strengths and weaknesses, and these can serve as guiding examples of what is possible under specific conditions. These studies include analyses of aging, income inequality, disability support, health insurance coverage, health outcomes, attitudes, and even affects such as loneliness (de Jong-Gierveld & Havens, 2004).

For example, analysis by Benjamin Veghte of OECD Social Expenditure Database (Altman & Kingson, 2015, p. 127) compares the spending of various nations on retirement, disability, and survivor protection.

For critical gerontologists and policymakers, cross-national comparisons can reveal myths about the limits of what is possible and stir the gerontological imagination. To "buff up" one's cross-national analysis, special attention to globalization, neocolonialism, and imperialism can add a critical dimension about power, resources, and unmeasured "invisibilized" populations that are not included (such as indigenous peoples).

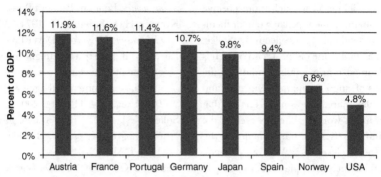

Many Nations Spend Much More than the USA on Retirement, Disability, and Survivor Protection

Source: Analysis by Benjamin W. Veghte of OECD Social Expenditure Database.

Note: All data are for 2009 (most recent comparative data available). All countries compared have similar, defined-benefit pension systems. Private systems are excluded, as are targeted social assistance programs. To increase data comparability, only half of spending was counted for program components in other countries that cover all government employees (and only a quarter of spending on those that cover a combination of government employees and members of the military/veterans), as only roughly half (a quarter) of such spending in the USA is Social Security spending.

Figure C2 Retirement Spending

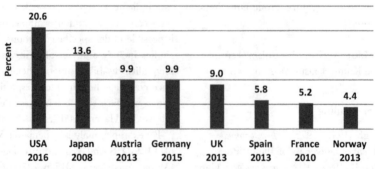

Percent of the Elderly Population with Income less than 50% of the Median Income by Country (most recent year available)

Source: LIS Tabulator, Inequality and Poverty Key Figures

Figure C3 Elderly Income Level

See also: Colonialisms, Globalization, Methodologies, Welfare State

Further Reading

Altman, N. J. and Kingson, E. R. (2015). *Social Security works! Why Social Security isn't going broke and how expanding it will help us all.* New York: The New Press.

de Jong Gierveld, J. & Havens, B. (2004). Cross-national comparisons of social isolation and loneliness: Introduction and overview. *Canadian Journal on Aging/Revue Canadienne Du Vieillissement, 23*(2), 109–113.

Dykstra, P. A. (2018). Cross-national differences in intergenerational family relations: The influence of public policy arrangements. *Innovation in Aging, 2*(1), igx032.

Culture

Reflected in social formations, traditions, and histories of peoples.

Rituals and symbols manifest culture in social solidarity and social organization – the substance of social structure. Culture is embedded in religious beliefs, practices, and hierarchies. Cultural groups may be based on national, ethnic, locational, ideational, or almost any other identifying human characteristic. Politics, power, ideology, and identity are expressed in culture. Group consciousness, social status, collective representations, and language and speech cultural codes that signal exclusion and inclusion. As W. E. B. Du Bois (1903/2007) observed of cultural definitions of African Americans in the Antebellum South, "withal slavery, which so far as human aspiration and desert were concerned, classed the black man and the ox together" (quoted in Berger, 2010, p. 69).

Cultural studies are a core component of critical thought, a foundation of research and writing on old age and aging policy (Estes, Linkins, & Binney, 2001, pp. 38–39). The field of cultural studies has been characterized as "a dissenting movement" that "helps to understand the mechanisms of cultural power . . . and the means to resist them" (Sardar & Van Loon, 1997, p, 170). In the words of Sardar and Van Loon (1997, pp. 170–171), cultural studies:

(1) aim to examine its subject matter in terms of *cultural practices* and their *relation to power*. Its constant goal is to expose power relationships and to examine how these relationships shape cultural practices . . .;
(2) [seek] to analyze the *social and political context* within which [culture] manifests itself . . . [and]
(3) commit . . . to a *moral evaluation* of modern society and to a *radical line of*
(4) *political action.*

Although the cultural studies field comprises various theoretical and methodological perspectives, its tradition is one of social reconstruction by political involvement; that is, to understand and change structures of dominance. Sociologist Max Weber theorized that the cultural domain was one of the three key sources of power, while Neo-Marxist Antonio Gramsci wrote that culture is where struggles for ideological hegemony occur.

Postmodernism and the multinational corporate fantasy of the "global village" complicates defining culture as a singular, stable entity. What is meant by culture today? It is used interchangeably with ethos to describe perceptions of attitudes and trends in what has become known as "culture at large."

The cultural turn, which occurred across the social sciences and humanities in the late twentieth century, "has recast aging studies, widening its theoretical and substantive scope, taking it into new territory intellectually and politically" (Twigg & Martin, 2011, p. 353). A major question for critical gerontologists is how a culture values or supports people across the life cycle, especially as they age. Is saving the young a greater value than saving the old? Does "intergenerational trade-off ideology" reflect majority public opinion or values? Or is it markets over human beings? Does this trade-off seem disproportionate or justified to people? And to whom? What do people mean when they say, "respecting elders?" What kind of engagement does this entail? How do people view death? Is it seen as something to fight against, to succumb to out of sacrifice or resignation, or is it acceptable to actively seek death in the face of chronic illness and disability?

Such questions are not uniformly answered; they are shaped in social discourse where cultural beliefs and values are negotiated, fought over, and enforced. They appear in social movements and bloody wars, in protests and in contestations over the answers. News media and scandals stir these debates.

Anti-multicultural sentiments animate the Alt-Right and white nationalism, placing them front and center in US politics and policy in ways that are likely to be pivotal in generational and intergenerational results of aging politics and policy. Countering right-wing perspectives, cultural studies was built, in part, upon Max Weber's influential work on the protestant ethic and the spirit of capitalism, and on Emile Durkheim's pioneering writing on the sacred and secular ritual requisites of social solidarity. Randall Collins' (2004) radical micro-sociology depicts the use of emotional, moral, and symbolic mobilization and rituals *as weapons* that produce charged emotional energy (EE) and group solidarity.

Successful resistance campaigns invoke, maintain, and advance cultural identity and symbols (Edelman, 1964) via consciousness raising, shared missions, and member recruitment and retention. For the past three decades, proponents and defenders of social insurance have organized to compete against the richly resourced deficit hawks and privatizers of Social Security and Medicare. Tracking, participating, enduring, and learning to be effective in the culture of resistance are essential labors for those committed to *critical aging policy* in the currently volatile climate of rising inequalities, infractions against democracy, and fraying human rights.

See also: Co-presence, Discourse, Interaction Ritual Chains, Resistance, Social Movements, Symbolic, Zeitgeist

Further Reading

Berger, A. A. (2010). *Cultural theorist's book of quotations*. Walnut Creek, CA: Left Coast Press.

Blaikie, A. (1999). *Ageing and popular culture.* New York: Cambridge University Press.

Collins, R. (2004). *Interaction ritual chains.* Princeton, NJ: Princeton University Press.

Du Bois, W. E. B. (2007). *The souls of black folk.* New York: Cosimo Classics. (Originally published 1903.)

Edelman, M. J. (1964). *The symbolic uses of politics.* Urbana: University of Illinois Press.

Estes, C. L., Linkins, K. W., & Binney, E. A. (2001). Critical perspectives on aging. In C. Estes & Associates (Eds.). (2001). *Social policy & aging: A critical perspective* (pp. 38–39). Thousand Oaks, CA: Sage.

Gilleard, C. & Higgs, P. (2000). *Cultures of ageing: Self, citizen, and the body.* London: Routledge.

Katz, S. (2005). *Cultural aging: Life course, lifestyle, and senior worlds.* Ontario, Canada: Toronto Press.

Sardar, Z. & Van Loon, B. (1997). *Cultural studies for beginners.* Trumpington: Icon Books.

Shim, J. (2010). Cultural health capital: A theoretical approach to understanding health care interactions and the dynamics of unequal treatment. *Journal of Health and Social Behavior, 51*(1), 1–15.

Twigg, J. & Martin, W. (2011). The challenge of cultural gerontology. *The Gerontologist, 55*(3), 353–359.

Twigg, J. & Martin, W. (Eds.). (2015). *The Routledge handbook of cultural gerontology.* London: Routledge.

Cumulative Advantage/ Disadvantage

Theory offers a lens to analyze socioeconomic stratification across the life course and its effects. This pattern of inequality is often seen as reflecting a lifelong, cohort-based process of *cumulative dis/advantage (CDA)*, defined by Dannefer (2003) as "the systemic tendency for inter-individual divergence to increase with the passage of time" (p. 327).

A pattern of increasing inequality with age in the USA and other countries has been demonstrated numerous times. The research has been replicated and extended to other domains, notably health, where class differences are found to be a basis for increasing health disparities over the life course (Dannefer, 2003; Ross & Wu, 1995). As Dannefer observes, dynamics of power and ideology that produce CDA also occur as a regular part of micro-interaction (Dannefer, 2009).

As Dannefer (2017) observes, this pattern is a:

> tendency toward increasing inequality with age. . . . Aging is something that occurs, not just within people, but also between them, as the dynamics of everyday life interaction tend to generate inequality among age peers. . . . [It is] biographical, where inequality generation is constantly occurring among age peers, making it a patterned feature of aging within each succeeding cohort of individuals.

The social processes that regulate CDA over the life course are socially modifiable. Historical comparisons (e.g., Crystal, Shea, & Reyes, 2016) and cross-societal comparative analyses (Kelley-Moore & Lin, 2011) showcase this modifiability and demonstrate that interventions in public policy can make a material impact.

Given that CDA theory and research defines the problem as a lifetime of risks or benefits that accumulate, it is essential to identify problems and solutions that could target macro- or meso-level social processes and policy structures (e.g., the institutions of health, education, or prison) as early in life as possible. This analysis is significant for a critical political economy of aging. The links between education, income, wealth, and health are empirically well validated (Mirowsky & Ross, 2008). Changes to the

education system to ameliorate unequal opportunities are essential to ensure access and availability to quality early childcare and public education, from pre-school through high school, and after school for all, with resources to support those disadvantaged by race, class, gender, and ability. To this list we must add the availability of universal and affordable childcare.

See also: Inequality, Jeopardy, Oppression, Poverty, Precarity

Further Reading

Beard, R. L. & Williamson, J. B. (2016). Frames matter: Aging policies and social disparities. *Public Policy & Aging Report*, *26*(2), 48–52.

Crystal, S. (1982). *America's old age crisis*. New York: Basic Books.

Crystal, S. & Shea, D. (1990). Cumulative advantage, cumulative disadvantage, and inequality among elderly people. *The Gerontologist*, *30*(4), 437–443.

Crystal, S., Shea, D. G., & Reyes, A. M. (2016). Cumulative advantage, cumulative disadvantage, and evolving patterns of late-life inequality. *The Gerontologist*, *57*(5), 910–920.

Dannefer, D. (1987). Aging as intracohort differentiation: Accentuation, the Matthew effect, and the life course. *Sociological Forum*, *2*(2), 211–236.

Dannefer, D. (1988). What's in a name? An account of the neglect of variability in the study of aging. In V. L. Bengston & J. E. Birren (Eds.), *Emergent theories of aging* (pp. 356–384). New York: Springer.

Dannefer, D. (2003). Cumulative advantage/disadvantage and the life course: Cross-fertilizing age and social science theory. *The Journals of Gerontology Series B: Psychological Sciences and Social Sciences*, *58*(6), 327.

Dannefer, D. (2009). Stability, homogeneity, agency: Cumulative dis/advantage and problems of theory. *Swiss Journal of Sociology, 35*(2), 193–210.

Dannefer, D. (2017). History, biography, and age: Three levels of inequality. Keynote lecture. *International Association of Gerontology and Geriatrics (IAGG)*, San Francisco, CA, July.

Dannifer, D. (2020). *Age and the research of sociological imagination; power, ideology, and life course.* New York: Routledge.

Dannefer, D. & Maddox, G. L. (1988). Differential gerontology and the stratified life course: Conceptual and methodological issues. In P. Lawton & G. Maddox (Eds.), *Annual review of gerontology & geriatrics* (Vol. 8, pp. 3–36). New York: Springer.

Ferraro, K. F. & Morton, P. M. (2018). What do we mean by accumulation? Advancing conceptual precision for a core idea in gerontology. *The Journal of Gerontology: Series B, 73*(2), 269–278.

Ferraro, K. F. & Shippee, T. P. (2009). Aging and cumulative inequality: How does inequality get under the skin? *The Gerontologist, 49*(3), 333–343.

Kelley-Moore, J. A. & Lin, J. (2011). Widening the view: Capturing "unobserved" heterogeneity in studies of age and the life course. In *Handbook of sociology of aging, 2011* (pp. 51–68). New York: Springer.

Mirowsky, J. & Ross, C. E. (2008). Education and self-rated health: Cumulative advantage and its rising importance. *Research on Aging, 30*(1), 93–122.

O'Rand, A. M. (2016). Long, broad, & deep: Theoretical approaches in aging and inequality. In V. L. Bengston & R. Settersten Jr. (Eds.), *Handbook of theories of aging* (pp. 365–380). New York: Springer.

Ross, C. E., & Wu, C. (1995). The links between education and health. *American Sociological Review, 60*(5), 719–745.

D

Death

The end of life, yet it has different frames and meanings.

In the USA, death is often understood as the inevitable conclusion to the aging process or the outcome of an event such as illness or trauma. The dominant paradigm for medical interventions frames death as something to prevent or avoid; in contrast, palliative care and hospice focus on how medicine and social support may improve the dying process and relieve pain. The "right to die" is currently debated in many states, while the physician protocols for assisting suicide continue to be debated in states that have legalized assisted suicide, among them Oregon (1994), Washington (2008), Vermont (2013), and California (2015).

Critical perspectives on death often focus on the economic incentives that determine care plans for dying people (what insurance will cover, what hospitals spend, what it costs people and their families). Critical gerontology can also interrogate lifespan inequality and grievability, questioning how some people receive more or less care throughout the course of their lives and how society registers attention and concern for death across intersections of race, gender, sexuality, citizenship, age, and ability.

In a similar vein, critical gerontology can also locate social aspects of mortality, focusing on how meaning and ceremony vary cross-culturally, or how colonialism and war destroy bodies and culture. Practitioners point to the process called *life review*, when, at the end of life, dying people tend to reminisce in an attempt to integrate life lessons and achieve peace (Butler, 1963).

See also: Grievability, Necropolitics

Further Reading

Butler, R. N. (1963). The life review: An interpretation of reminiscence in the aged. *Psychiatry*, *26*(1), 65.

Debt

Capital owed. It occurs when expenditures exceed revenues and comes with ideological values of irresponsibility, failure, shame, and blame. In German the word is *Schulden*, which means guilt.

A critical perspective is offered by David Harvey: "Debt is a claim on future labor. Your future is foreclosed!" (Harvey on *Intercepted*, in Scahill, 2018).

A. *"Fix the Debt"*

The mantra of the Right and the opponents of entitlements and social insurance programs (Social Security, Medicare, Medicaid) or any social welfare provided by government rather than in a profit-generating corporate context. "Austerity politics" frames our understanding of health and economic rights as unafford-able/unsustainable; a tenant reflected is the larger political economy of American society. Along with austerity politics comes the social construction of the preservation of our economic system and way of life as requiring necessary sacrifice. The question is who sacrifices what, and are these sacrifices visible/recognized? Murray Edelman in his book *Words that succeed, policies that fail* illustrates that such calls for sacrifice are almost always unequally borne on the backs of vulnerable populations (those without the power to refuse the sacrifice).

Globalization and its paramount need to protect the interests of the nation state provides rationale for austerity politics; however, neoliberalism is the end goal of the power brokers (heads of state and those who manage multinational corporations). Neoliberal ideology holds that nations with less debt or who own other nations' debts have more power. Competition under globalization promotes the rationale for "fixing the debt," because debt is construed as weakness. International policy built on this ideology calls for borrowing nations to open up their markets and requires them to simultaneously abandon their national health plans and public education programs, so as to capitalize on corporate ownership of the commons. Ultimately, the austerity discourse is used to stoke anti-government sentiments and nullify the State's authority to regulate markets.

Proponents of austerity and mantras like "fix the debt" often couch their policy solutions in the frame of increasing economic growth and prosperity. One of the main culprits in this narrative is older Americans who are portrayed as dragging the economy down. A 2017 report from the Committee for a Responsible Federal Budget specifically states that "The aging population is the biggest driver of slower growth. It is responsible for three-quarters of the decline in projected labor force participation and may also be partially responsible for a slowdown in capital and productivity growth" (CRFB, 2017). CRFB specifically views older Americans as one of the primary barriers to achieving 3 percent growth moving forward. To make up for our aging society they suggest that we eliminate a variety of social programs and curtail others. One of their primary suggestions is to raise the eligibility age of Social Security; another is to repeal the Affordable Care Act. In both cases, capital growth (one definition but not the only definition of economic growth) would come at the cost of individuals' financial and physical well-being.

Americans for Tax Fairness (ATF) is a coalition of 425 endorsing organizations united in support of a fair tax system that works for all Americans. ATF has organized resistance to the recent Republican tax reform bill, which, they argue, are tax cuts for the wealthy and corporations. Seniors and the aging community are ground zero in this fight because they have the most to lose. The services which elders rely upon are targeted for elimination and reduction in order to "pay for" big tax cuts for the wealthy and corporations. Tangible examples are the proposed trillions in Medicaid cuts, and billions in Medicare cuts, including the elimination of the Medicare Health Insurance Counseling Program in the budgets of the 2018 fiscal year proposed by the President, House, and Senate.

B. *Deficit Crisis Frame*

The dominant frame for health care reform in the USA is one of constraint and competition: (1) the deficit determines how much we can allocate to reform (constraint), and (2) promoting market competition (e.g., private sector health insurance) is touted as key to regaining national economic predominance. There is a conflation of whatever is understood as wrong in society with fixing the debt.

The deficit hawks insist that State subsidies to private insurers through part D (the Medicare Industrial Complex, as coined by Bruce Vladeck) is a necessary economic component of health care. However, the facts contradict this "cost saving" measure; Part D is an ineffective cost control method for the State; managed care, in fact, costs 15 to 40 percent more than the public option. This goes largely unquestioned because the government is seen as responsible for national debt and cannot be trusted. The demographic "tsunami" of aging people rising to cost the State more becomes the enemy while the laissez-faire economic model says that unregulated markets can fix everything: that it will adjust to handle the rising tide through false claims that it will fairly decide how to take care of this population. Yet, unregulated markets have no incentive to cover marginalized populations. Coverage, security, and protection are only promised for the powerful.

A second component of the laissez-faire market is to forbid raising tax revenue so as to "free" the market even more. Incentivize financial investing by taking away the governmental costs that support entitlements. It is freedom of the market over freedom of the people. Austerity politics and the laissez-faire market are antithetical to any rights-based perspective. Individual debt is seen as individual fault, which ignores the structural foundations of debt and lending and the need for social insurance.

C. *The People's Budget*
An analysis by the Progressive Congressional Caucus that frames and analyzes the federal budget and deficit in terms of the public interest and the values of the people of the USA (Blair, 2017). It proposes a detailed, alternative US budget that addresses egregious overspending on the top 1 percent of society and the military. The People's Budget contains US State investments in infrastructure, jobs, and human lives. Justice, fairness, and the reduction of inequality are the priorities. The 2018 People's Budget seeks "a fair shot at the American Dream" by focusing on infrastructure spending, education, and wage growth to increase opportunities for all for safety and prosperity.

Note on Congressional Tax Reform: Trillions in deficits and subsidies for corporations and the top 1 percent are front loaded, while cuts to Medicare and Medicaid are assured. With a Republican-led Senate (and both Houses of Congress in 2017/2018), cuts to Social Security and Medicare become increasingly likely. "Fix the debt" is revealed as a shallow ideology that contradicts US spending and revenue plans that advantage the few at a high cost to the many.

D. *Debt and Inequality*
Scholars and activists demonstrate the correlations between debt, credit, and inequality. Dwyer (2018) employs a relational approach to identify the political economy of debt and credit – to understand the distribution, regulation, and control over social and economic resources. She identifies the role of the State in structuring credit markets to include or exclude, "[producing] winners and losers" (p. 240). Critical gerontology highlights the antagonistic and cumulative effects of debt for older and marginalized peoples.

See also: Austerity, Capitalism, Cumulative Advantage/Disadvantage, Inequality, Jeopardy, State

Further Reading

Blair, H. (2017). *The People's Budget, 2018; A roadmap for resistance*. Analysis by the Economic Policy Institute (May 7). Washington, DC: EPI.

CRFB. (2017). How fast can America grow? Retrieved from www.crfb.org/papers/how-fast-can-america-grow.

Dwyer, R. E. (2018). Credit, debt, and inequality. *Annual Review of Sociology, 44*(7), 237–261.

Edelman, M. J. (1977). *Political language*. New York: Academic Press.

Scahill, J. (Producer). (2018). Leading Marxist scholar David Harvey on Trump, Wall Street, and debt peonage. *Intercepted* [Audio Podcast], January 21. Retrieved from https://theintercept.com/podcasts/.

www.americansfortaxfairness.org.

Delirium

Confusion and cognitive disturbance, conventionally defined as a geriatric syndrome but radically energized by a critical perspective.

Derrida writes of delirium as a psychic dislocation that occurs when one is called to a place where one cannot dwell in his theorizing of German Jews who remained in Nazi Germany. Derrida's definition proposes that there are delusions of being or coming home when, in reality, one is in unfamiliar and unsafe terrain. Critical theoretical perspectives can problematize medical discourse of delirium (which is focused primarily on disoriented and confused older adults with low oxygen levels in hospitals and the burden placed on families and staff) by questioning the implications of structural barriers for aging people and how they contribute to disorientation. How does unpredictability in care and coverage result in confusion and feelings of not belonging?

Employing the critical framework of delirium to understand the general population also deepens connections made by younger populations as to the experiences of older adults. For example, using Derrida's definition of a dislocation, we might think of how delirium functions in elections such as in the UK's passing of Brexit and the election of Donald Trump. Immediately following these events there was widespread shock among liberals and progressives. Persons of color were less surprised, pointing to the strength and legacy of White Supremacy in America. While the words "Make America Great Again" call out indiscriminately, the words conjure up and impart different meanings and are anything but unifying. American exceptionalism, the ideological framing of the country's inherent goodness and superior ability as a powerful nation, may be understood as an ideology of delirium – where power and moralism threaten the humility and sanity required for collaboration and coalitions.

Psychoanalytic social theory, as defined later, also serves as a framework for thinking about psychic events within a social context. This offers opportunities to question how conditions diagnostically relegated to certain populations can speak to disturbances in the larger culture (e.g., Freud's investigations of hysteria). Critical gerontologists could imagine how responses to medical events of delirium and dementia (specifically Alzheimer's Disease) might relate to crises and cultural memory (DiCarlo, 2016). How do we as a collective culture preserve or deny memory as it relates to violence, loss, and trauma?

See also: Alzheimer's Disease, Coalitions, Crisis, Geriatric Syndromes, Memory, Necropolitics, Psychoanalytic Social Theory, Statistical Panic

Further Reading

DiCarlo, N. (2016). Reimagining delirium: Social and psychic breakdown of habitus and dwelling place. Abstract in *The Gerontologist, 56,* 224. Presented at the Gerontological Society of America,

November 16–20. Oxford: Oxford University Press.

Demagogue

A political leader who panders to popular prejudices to achieve and sustain power.

Demagogues come in all shapes and sizes and exist on all points of the political spectrum.

> Democracy has two chief values, liberty and equality. In most conceptions of liberty, demagoguery is allowed in a democracy. Controversial speech is still free speech. The problem of demagoguery lies not in its conflict with freedom, but with the democratic value of equality.
>
> (Stanley & Justice, 2016, p. 36)

The strength of a democracy is defined not by the presence of demagogues and populism but rather by the ways in which these impulses and desires of populace organize and balance as a polity.

In the modern context, the term is primarily linked to populism which has been on the rise across Europe and the United States. Donald Trump and Marine Le Pen, the two main standard bearers of nationalistic populism, may both be described as demagogues. They both position themselves strategically with their voters and against the "establishment," and both use racialized appeals to take advantage of voters' prejudices.

A demagogue can extend control through a network of surrogates who adopt a message, promote the platform, or intentionally confound (*see* "gas lighting" in Propaganda).

See also: Fascism, Propaganda, Rhetoric

Further Reading

Snyder, T. (2017). *On tyranny: Twenty lessons from the twentieth century*. New York: Tim Duggan Books.

Stanley, J. & Justice, B. (2016). Teaching in the time of Trump. *Social Education*, January 1, *80*, 36.

Dementia

A general term for conditions regarding neuro-cognitive decline and memory loss, often lumped into what has been disparagingly called "senility."

This includes changes in thinking, ability to recall words, emotional lability (quickly changing emotions), as well as physical changes regarding coordination and mobility. Alzheimer's Disease makes up the majority of dementia diagnoses. Strokes (especially small successive strokes) result in vascular dementia, and people with Parkinson's Disease develop dementia, on average, ten years from their diagnosis. Some 5 to 8 percent of older adults (aged 60) have some form of dementia, and the number of adults living with dementia is expected to grow to 82 million by 2030 (WHO, 2017).

It appears that education stimulates brain growth and is a protective factor signaling the potential stratification of risk for dementia. This may be one way that inequalities get perpetuated – not just gene–environment or exposure to environment harms, but brain environment and opportunity. A separate critical point concerns critique of the diagnosis of Alzheimer's and dementia as socially constructed (Chaufan et al., 2012; Beard & Fox, 2008; Shabahangi et al., 2009). It is still the case that in postmortem examinations, many diagnosed with Alzheimer's Disease lack its putative symptoms and conditions, while many who do not have symptoms have those conditions (plaques and tangles).

Drug therapies exist to slow the progression of dementia-related diseases; however, there are currently no cures. There is much research (and funding) into learning about the neurobiology of dementia, as well as a burgeoning attempt from social science to understand the social impacts of dementia. The social research investigates many dimensions: social isolation, support networks, caregiving, and economic impacts. There is also an opportunity to explore the concept of selfhood: What is remembered and recognized especially in the context of culture, love, and pleasure?

Many social service agencies for older adults now feature "adult day care" units for individuals with memory loss. Some feature cafés or markets where people need not recall the details of who they are, in order to participate and engage with those around them. Social workers facilitate these environments. Similarly, psychotherapists can employ non-verbal modalities such as sand tray therapy in their work with older adults, providing opportunities to demonstrate associations and express their emotional realities of living with unfamiliarity and their desire to belong.

See also: Alzheimer's Disease, Memory

Further Reading

Beard, R. L. & Fox, P. (2008). Resisting social disenfranchisement: Negotiating collective identities and everyday life with memory loss. *Social Science & Medicine, 66*(7), 1509–1520.

Chaufan, C., Hollister, B., Nazareno, J., & Fox, P. (2012). Medical ideology as a double-edge sword: The politics of cure and care in the making of Alzheimer's disease. *Social Science & Medicine, 74*(5), 788–795.

Hollister, B., Flatt, J. D., & Chapman, S. A. (2018). Dementia-capable care coordination in duals demonstration programs: Workforce needs, promising practices, and policy. *The Gerontologist, 58*(4), 768–778.

Kontos, P. & Martin, W. (2013). Embodiment and dementia: Exploring critical narratives of selfhood, surveillance, and dementia care. *Dementia, 12*(3), 288–302.

Leibing, A. & Cohen, L. (2018). *Thinking about dementia: Culture, loss, and the anthropology of senility.* New Brunswick, NJ: Rutgers University Press.

Shabahangi, N., Faustman, G., Thai, J. N., & Fox, P. (2009). Some observations on the social consequences of forgetfulness and Alzheimer's disease: A call for attitudinal expansion. *Journal of Aging, Humanities, and the Arts, 3*(1), 38–52.

World Health Organization. (2017). Dementia Fact Sheet, December. Retrieved from www.who.int/mediacentre/factsheets/fs362/en/.

Democracy

A form of governing by and for the people, opening instead of closing channels of recognition and representation. Current threats to democracy include voter registration initiatives designed to suppress the voting rights of particular (often marginalized) populations; and gerrymandering (the redrawing/redistricting of the electoral map to sway representative power). Recent elections, including the 2018 mid-terms, starkly reveal the perils and promise in securing the vote for all and the unrelenting action and vigilance of the powerful and devious who seek to disenfranchise the American voter, by almost any means necessary.

Richard Flacks, in *Making history: The American Left and the American mind* (1988), argues that democracy necessarily arises from "history-making" by ordinary people. Democratic progress sometimes necessitates actions that do not fit into a person's short-term interests, or the short-term interests of those around them. There is an implicit cost to progress; sacrifices have to be made in the service of long-term goals.

Sheldon Wolin (2008, pp. 159–183) shows how "intellectual elites" worked against democracy. He also describes the counter-revolution of "new conservatism" under President Reagan that "deliberately" promoted inegalitarianism. "By reducing or eliminating programs that had helped to empower the Many, inegalitarianinism reinforced a structure which combined state and corporate power" (Wolin, 2008, pp. x–xi).

Our public institutions fail to represent the will of the people in a way that ignores the critical salience of income, wealth, property, race, ethnicity, class, ability, gender, and age. Trump and the Congressional vanguard have been at odds with public opinion about Social Security policy, Medicare, Medicaid, and the ACA. Foot dragging on safeguards of the Voting Rights Act and on the Federal Election Commission allows State legislatures to impose tactics to prevent voters from expressing their will via the ballot-box.

Critical gerontologists need to be concerned with the role, presence, and agency of older people as advisors and actors in political processes. Social exclusion limits the franchise, including older adults' opportunities to frame and meaningfully intervene in policy debates and outcomes. Power elites and their disregard of the underrepresented are emblematic of the brewing crisis of democracy in the USA. These processes call into question the legitimacy of governance and foster distrust in the State and society.

See also: Ageism, Agency, Contradictions, Crisis, Goal Displacement, Human Rights, Legitimacy, Socialism

Further Reading

Berman, A. (2010). *Herding donkeys*. New York: Farrar, Straus, and Giroux.

Estes, C. L. (2011). Crises in old age policy. In R. A. Settersten Jr. & J. L. Angel (Eds.), *Handbook of sociology of aging* (pp. 297–320). New York: Springer.

Flacks, R. (1988). *Making history: The American Left and the American mind*. New York: Columbia University Press.

Ginsberg, B., Lowi, T. J., Weir, M., & Tolbert, C. J. (2017). *We the people: An introduction to American politics* (11th core edn). New York: W.W. Norton & Co.

Hersh, E. D. (2015). *Hacking the electorate*. New York: Cambridge University Press.

Powell, L. F. (1971). Powell Memorandum: Attack on American Free Enterprise System. In *Lewis F. Powell, Jr. Papers, Powell Archives*, August 23. Washington and Lee University School of Law. Retrieved from http://law2.wlu.edu/powellarchives/page.asp?pageid=1251.

Wolin, S. S. (2008). *Democracy incorporated: Managed democracy and the specter of inverted totalitarianism*. Princeton, NJ: Princeton University Press.

Demography/ Demographics

A field of statistical study that examines compositions, characteristics, and population projections, including analyses by fertility, and morbidity and mortality and migration across cohorts and populations over time. These are inflected in gender, race, culture, and ethnicity.

The field of demographic sciences is an invaluable source of information relative to aging and the aging society and detailed population characteristics, issues, and trends. One critical question animating the field has been *Is demography destiny?* (Friedland & Summer, 2005). Because much focus is on populations of *individuals*, demographers generally pay limited attention to social structures and processes and their impact on individual lives. Yet there are many factors and forces that play into and work in relation to how demographic shifts change policy and society. Critical gerontological perspectives examine the empirical constructions of demographic labeling (abjectification/othering) as well as their links to definitions of crisis (e.g., deficit framing). The demographics of aging are often portrayed in fearful negative terms rather than as a triumph. On the negative side, "apocalyptic demography" is a concept coined by Robertson (1997); others are "silver tsunami," "grey dawn," and "demographic apocalypse."

During the Reagan/Clinton administrations, some actuaries (i.e., Anna Rappaport) voiced their skepticism about the creative measures devised and used by demographers and actuaries called "infinite horizon" budgeting that calculates data across centuries (essentially forever). The concept appeared during the 2005 G. W. Bush Social Security privatization political fight in support of arguments that universal public Social Security is unsustainable – if data are calculated as far as the eye can see and beyond. Canons of statistical inference and validity are stretched in credulity over such elongated time periods; yet, this concept is still employed in political debates as needed. A related concern, given the urgency for accurate demographic projections, is the 2017 resignation of the director of the US Census Bureau in response to the Trump Administration's budget cuts and targeted areas of politically inspired tinkering with technical program decisions, samples, measurement, and statistics.

See also: Framing, Statistical Panic

Further Reading

Choi, H. J. & Schoeni, R. (2017). *Health of Americans who must work longer to reach social security retirement age.* Ann Arbor, MI: University of Michigan Press.

Friedland, R. B. & Summer, L. (2005). *Is demography destiny, revisited.* Washington, DC: Center on an Aging Society. Georgetown University, March.

Robertson, A. (1997). Beyond apocalyptic demography: Towards a moral economy of interdependence. *Ageing and Society, 17*(4), 425–446.

Society of Actuaries/SOA. (2016). Age wise. Retrieved from www.soa.org/research/research-projects/pension/default.aspx.

Steverman, B. (2017). Americans are retiring later, dying sooner and sicker in-between. Bloomberg, October 23.

Dependency and Dependency Ratio

A matter of both *social* definition and *self-* definition. State policy reflects society's and the medical profession's classification and treatment of an individual or group as dependent. Dependency describes a relationship in which one person relies on another person or source to meet some or all of their needs, such as a parent with an infant or child. Dependency is also a matter of self-definition, of seeing oneself as helpless, powerless, or needy (van den Huevel & Munnichs, 1976; Collins, Estes, & Bradsher, 2001). Dependence is a highly politicized and ideologically charged concept often employed in negative narratives of burden, indebtedness, and scarcity and even as a threat to the sustainability of a person, family, corporation, or larger community, society, or the nation-state.

Dependency is commonly defined in the literature as a function of individual lifetime choices about education, work skills, occupation, savings, and economic resources (Clark & Spengler, 1980). Yet this says little about social conditions leading to dependency and even less about the social production of dependency across generations. Although negative connotations of dependency are deeply rooted in the national psyche of the USA, the social phenomenon of dependency is neither stable nor desirable. Mutual dependence (interdependence) is essential in the formation and maintenance of human relationships, and a functioning community or "civilized society."

Dependency Ratio

Statisticians and actuaries, business professionals who measure and manage risk and uncertainty for corporations or governments, calculate a society's dependency ratios using demographic patterns and projections. One major purpose is to estimate the costs of economic dependency for retirement and medical insurance, caregiving and other societal institutional needs and demands. Countries with lower dependency ratios are said to have relatively more resources freed up for economic development. This is according to the dominant economic logic of global agencies such as the UN, and shared by international financial elites and their institutions (e.g., World Bank, International Monetary Fund).

Different dependency ratios may produce different answers to the larger question of whether there is an economic destiny in dependency, as measured by age ratios in the population throughout the globe. Different dependency ratios produce different answers. The most used dependency ratio is the Total Dependency Ratio in ratio to those *not* participating in the labor force (children and elders combined) to those persons of working age (i.e., 15 to 64 years of age). Opponents of social insurance use the Total Dependency Ratio – political and rhetorical strategy – to proclaim a fairness crisis to young people and the unsustainability of Social Security. In this case, negative fears are contingent upon the size of the working population and their willingness and capacity (productivity and price/tax structure) to provide for "non-workers." This rebuttal enrages those who subscribe to the bootstrap ideology of self-dependence and ascendance. Other types of dependency ratios include the old-age dependency ratio (number of people older than 64 per 100 people of working age, i.e. ages 15 to 64); and child dependency ratios (number of children younger than age 15 per 100 people of working age) (Pew Research Center, UN, 2013).

Walker (1980) underscores the point that many complex social, political, and economic forces contribute to the production of dependency by age (rather than its reduction).

Myles (1984) concurs: "Old age and 'old people' as we now know them are an effect, not a cause of the welfare state." Dependency is an inherently social product (Estes, 1979) that profoundly affects and reflects public policy. For example, without Social Security, older persons as an age category would be impoverished, not because of lack of planning, but because the economy is organized according to differential rewards for productive labor, from which elders are generally and systematically excluded via retirement. Similarly, without Medicare, a much larger segment of the older population would be more economically and/or physically dependent because of their full exposure to the unaffordability of medical care. The dominant "Discourse of Dependency" replaced the earlier "Discourse of Deprivation" as the rationale undergirding welfare state policy (Medvetz, 2012). The shift in discourse has contributed to attacks on the welfare state and the poor as evidenced by the 1993 Welfare Reform Act (TANF) and the hateful myth of welfare queens in pink cadillacs.

A major factor that may reduce the old-age dependency ratio is immigration policy. Immigrant births were 87.8 per 1000 immigrant women in the USA compared to 58.9 births to native-born US women (Livingston & Cohen, 2012, in Pew Research Center, UN, 2013). Notably Australia and Canada have adopted immigration policies in order to sustain population growth (Passel & Cohen, 2008, in Pew Research Center, UN, 2013).

See also: Aging Enterprise, Aging in the Community, Generational Equity, Immigration

Further Reading

Clark, R. L. & Spengler, J. J. (1980). Dependency ratios. *Research in Population Economics*, 2, 63–76. Retrieved from

www.econis.eu/PPNSET?PPN=3852
61543.

Collins, C. A., Estes, C. L., & Bradsher, J. E.
(2001). Inequality and aging: The creation of dependency. In C. L. Estes &
Associates, *Social policy & aging: A critical
perspective* (pp. 137–164). Thousand Oaks,
CA: Sage.

Estes, C. L. (1979). *The aging enterprise: A critical examination of social policies and services for
the aged.* San Francisco, CA: Jossey-Bass.

Hardy, M. & Hazelrigg, L. (2007). *Pension
puzzles: Social security and the great debate.*
New York: Russell Sage Foundation.

Medvetz, T. (2012). *Think tanks in America.*
Chicago, IL: University of Chicago Press.

Myles, J. (1984). *Old age in the welfare state.*
Boston, MA: Little Brown.

Pew Research Center report data source.
(2013). Global population estimates by
age: 1950–2050. United Nations, Department of Economic & Social Affairs,
World Population Prospects: 2012. Revi-
sion, June 2013. Retrieved from http://
esa.org/unpd/wpp/index/htm.

van den Heuvel, J. A. & Munnichs, J. M.
(1976). *Dependency or interdependency in old
age.* New York: Springer.

Walker, A. (1980). The social creation of
poverty and dependency in old age. *Journal of Social Policy, 9*(1), 49–75. Retrieved
from www.econis.eu/PPNSET?PPN=
492672040.

Deportation

To forcibly expel people from a country,
often making non-citizens of a host country
return to their country of origin.

Deportees in waiting are detained in
detention centers (which may be jails or cor-
rectional facilities) across the USA, many of
which are run by private prison companies.
Older persons are among those deported,
and these people often face challenges due
to their health and ability. Advocates and
legal resources are only available to some

under limited guaranteed legal rights.
Detention centers for deportees are often
run by private contractors, who do less to
ensure rights and well-being.

Deportation exemplifies a rupture in the
life course and often presents intergenerational ruptures for families: people separated from their communities and families,
their contributions disregarded. For practitioners, awareness of and respect for the
many and varied inflections of pain and
trauma that deportation exerts on individuals, families, and communities can inform
and deepen the level of care provided. The
Trump Administration questioned the criteria for asylum, discarding political refugees
as well as all undocumented immigrants.
Along with separating children from their
parents in deportation centers, these admin-
istrate moves signaled that the United States
did not welcome or accept responsibility for
people deemed outsiders.

See also: Alienation, Citizenship, Immigration, Nativism, Prison Industrial Complex, Right to Have Rights, Statelessness,
Xenophobia

Further Reading

Quenenmoen, M. (2016). Caught in the
deportation machine: Elders, family separation, and immigration reform. Retrieved
from www.nhcoa.org/caught-in-the-
deportation-machine-elders-family-
separation-and-immigration-reform/.

Desire

A feeling related to the act of accumulation,
connection, possession, and recognition.
The effect of desire features a longing, as
well as the desperation of need and necessity. French psychoanalyst Lacan theorized
desire in relation to "lack." Desire is part of
the drive to fill an absence, and it is constructed only in relation to absence/lack.

Lack is a key component in driving consumer behavior, scarcity panic, and the State's constructions of crisis.

Gerontology and social science, grounded in human rights perspectives and critical realism, largely focus on theories of need. Expanding this focus to include theories of desire, as psychic realities that pertain to alienation and belonging (very much situated in markets of capital), can invigorate philosophies of living.

See also: Affect (Politics of), Capitalism, Crisis, Psychoanalytic Social Theory, Scarcity, Spirits of Capitalism, Theories of Need

Further Reading

Lichtman, R. (1982). *The production of desire: The integration of psychoanalysis into Marxist theory*. New York: The Free Press.

Devolution

Describes the shift of power (and financial responsibility) from an upper level (federal) government to a lower one (state and local governments).

Devolution is intended to permit state and local discretion. It contributes to the considerable variations and inequalities in social insurance programs throughout states and local sectors. With less federal oversight, communities can centralize and reapportion access to resources. Devolution tends to benefit wealthy municipalities and states, as well as those with wealth in poor municipalities, as they become the decisionmakers. Those with the most decide how to spend these funds or how to privatize tiers of care/support as benefits them.

Similar inequalities may be seen in education, where local taxes determine the resources available to schools, and local school boards dictate subject matter and staffing decisions. This results in schools of very different qualities in different districts and may contort the content of curriculum in ways that result in different educational opportunities and outcomes.

Distributions are distorted by how power articulates itself at different agency levels and the varying commitment of those bodies of power to promoting and protecting equality. Devolution of federal control has been the continuing goal of "states' rights," which sprang forward to resist federal pressures for racial integration. Devolution is central to legitimating the rights of state and local government (or "no government") to attend/interpret, reject, and subvert national understandings and policies designed to address social justice and civil rights. In this way devolution may be seen as subverting national consensus and the federal system more generally as it seeks to usurp federal roles and rights. In 2010 states debated and self-selected how to receive and employ federal subsidies for Medicaid; and in 2017 and 2018 trans-rights and workplace protections for marginalized sexualities were centers of the devolution debate.

Example

The Older Americans Act of 1973 features amendments that created state and local bureaucratic bodies to implement federal funds for local/community organizations. This leads to younger people telling older people what to do via the velvet glove of social control (e.g., oversimplifying the issues by funding senior centers as the primary solution to old age). This sends a message that age-rights activist Maggie Kuhn identified as tantamount to "get in your playpen and stay there."

See also: Austerity, Block Grants, Dispossession, Neoliberalism, Power, Reform/Deform, States' Rights

Further Reading

Estes, C. L. & Linkins, K. W. (1997). Devolution and aging policy: Racing to the bottom in long-term care. *International Journal of Health Services*, *27*(3), 427–442.

Estes, C. L. & Newcomer, R. J. (1983). *Fiscal austerity and aging: Shifting government responsibility for the elderly*. Beverly Hills, CA: Sage.

Shapiro, I. (2015). Block grant funding falls significantly over time, data show. Retrieved from www.cbpp.org/blog/block-grant-funding-falls-significantly-over-time-data-show.

Dialectical

A process in which tension is held between antagonistic elements (i.e., cruel/caring, insider/outsider, domination/oppression). The theory posits that reality is never completed until everything has been exposed to what its potential might become.

Dialectical processes, according to Hegel, are in society, history, and struggle: thesis, antithesis, and synthesis. The dialectic is turned into its opposite reasoning through juxtaposing seemingly opposite sides and examining their unity, disunity, and polemics. Such discursive processes are found in the dialectics of the Church versus the State, which resulted in the accommodation of both Church and State through morals and law. Other examples, historic and evolving, may be located in class (superior and subordinate, owner versus worker), in race and ethnicity (white colonists/colonialists versus indigenous and enslaved peoples), and in gender (patriarchy versus women as full human beings). In *aging policy*, dialectical tensions may be examined through: young and old; able-bodied and disabled-bodied; happy and sad; love and hate; healthy and sick, and through class, race, ethnicity, ability, gender, sexualities and their relative cumulative dis/advantages in historical time and space, and in generation and cohort.

See also: Contradiction, Power, Praxis

Further Reading

Dannefer, D., Stein, P., Siders, R., & Patterson, R. S. (2008). Is that all there is? The concept of care and the dialectic of critique. *Journal of Aging Studies*, *22*(2), 101–108.

Digital Sphere

Operates on multiple fronts incorporating (1) social media networks and all communications technologies they open up that accelerate daily life, visualization, consciousness raising, mobilization, protest, rage, instant and constant video streaming, messages, contacts, and fake and hate discourse; (2) corporate and government surveillance (and cooperative surveillance), cyber security, cyber wars, encryption, hacking, leaking, terrorism; and (3) constitutional freedoms of expression, right to know, right to privacy, and more.

From a critical perspective, the advent of digital technologies and social media (aka "the merchants of attention – Google, Facebook, Twitter, Apple, etc.") has given rise to what Akhtar (2017) calls the "attention-finance complex."

> The attention-finance complex has given us devices to which we are tethered by more than compulsion. Our pleasure principle – long prey to the manipulations of capitalism – has been turned against us, irretrievably yoked to ends that are not ours, ends we cannot fully comprehend.

> Transformed into economic subjects, our humanity is being redefined; we are valuable only insofar as our economic behavior can be predicted and monetized. Indeed, the technology has enabled the very movements of our mind to become a steady stream of revenue to someone, somewhere.

> Somehow we are sold the story that this narrowing of the world into streams of

monetized information is actually about liberation. That it represents a new era in human communication. The triumph of democracy. A victory over centralized power.

In terms of the manipulations of capitalism in relationship to selfhood, an industrial-era adage may have been "You are what you produce." In today's post-industrial digital sphere, an adage could be "You are what you consume." Our consumption is performed by our participation in the digital sphere – this is the content we share about ourselves, such as pithy texts, pictures, videos, or GIFs of our daily mood, our outfits of the day, the meals we eat, who we hang out with, the places we visit, the brands we like, the news we read, our political views, etc. The objective of our consumption comes in the form of gaining likes, shares, and followers. Those with many followers are known as "influencers."

The "influencer economy" is "a budding market" where "advertisers now lavish billions of dollars a year on sponsorship deals. The more people influencers reach, the more money they make" (Confessore et al., 2018). This digital influencer economy has also led to a growth in fake social media accounts, known as bots, that are bought and sold to inflate perceptions of having many followers. Where popularity translates to influence, and influence translates to mainstream attention, and mainstream attention translates to power, the practice of manipulating social media is becoming increasingly common, and is altering many aspects of social life in positive and negative ways.

For instance, the digital sphere and social media networks are used to construct the cultural identity of a particular community (e.g., Black Twitter) by offering a space where members of the community can focus on issues of interest to them. The digital sphere and social media networks are also used to promote political agendas and social change

by blending activism and hacking, known as hactivism (a portmanteau of hack and activism), and may be used for trolling (i.e., people who intend to inflame or provoke outrage by saying hyperbolic vile things). Increasingly, the digital sphere is a space flooded with information promoted by social actors pushing to gain public influence, thus making it ever more difficult to identify legitimate sources of information and constructions of reality (e.g., Fake News, Russian interference, bots of divisiveness, Wikileaks).

For example, Anonymous is a broad, highly decentralized digital network of hacktivist resistance that contains a mix of actors, motives, and methods. The movement involves accessing restricted data and exposing corruption and individuals involved in unethical activities. Identifying who these hacktivist players are, what motivates their participation, and understanding their threats and actions is often difficult. Some threaten to cause problems for those speaking in a way they consider hateful or dangerous (e.g., releasing a video telling presidential candidate Donald Trump to watch what he says regarding Muslims and immigration). In addition, some have shut down Twitter accounts linked to terror networks (Isis and Al Qaeda had 30,000 accounts disabled), thus controlling who has access to the digital realm. Anonymous hactivists have also exhibited a watchdog vigilantism – shutting down websites, leaking unreleased memos, or leaking addresses of police officers who shot or killed unarmed black men. Anonymous has been criticized by law enforcement for its methods, which often eschew legal restrictions. There is some question as to the identities and motives of actors within the movement, some of whom may be professional criminals. Anonymous is a powerful social actor. While we do not know of any instances where *hacktivism* aimed to advance aging rights, we can imagine such an intersection (e.g., in exposing the labor abuses and tax returns of wealthy politicians who threaten the social safety net with deregulation and cuts).

To help sift through the information glut of the digital sphere – the streams of content on social media – hashtags (#) are used to categorize and raise visibility of the content we want to see or are being told to see. Social media networks are underpinned by algorithmic codes designed to show us content that is in close alignment with our interests, beliefs, and viewpoints, or content that is "trending" due to its popularity of being shared and re-shared on social media. "The world of social media has become a de facto public square. Much of our politics and business is conducted there, yet it remains in many ways a kind of 'Wild West' (Winstead, 2018).

As social media grows as a dominant form of communication and participation in society, some may say, "If it is not on Twitter or Facebook, it didn't happen." Others may say, "Snapchat is it." Regardless, "Meme is everything." A meme is a virally transmitted cultural symbol or social idea. Memeification requires participation, action, and even innovation, which acknowledges our humanity and has social implications.

For instance, there is a rising awareness of the digital dehumanization caused by social media. Because the digital sphere can be a place devoid of emotion, there are digital accessories available that allow us to summon ways to emphasize how we feel, such as through memes, emojis, styles of text formatting, and animated GIFs. A growing concern of this is with "digital blackface," the use of online imagined black English and the recurring use of black people as reaction GIFs intended to perform emotive commentary (Jackson, 2014; Hess, 2017; Abreu, n.d.). According to Jackson (2014), digital blackface is "the odd and all-too-prevalent practice of white and non-Black people making anonymous claims to a Black identity through contemporary mediums such as social media." It is the way in which memeification and the digital sphere has

appropriated black people and black culture, turning them into products for consumption with little interest paid to their full humanity. Even something as seemingly benign as affective expression in the digital sphere is complicated by structural racism, "an old structure that keeps encoding itself into new technology" (Hess, 2017).

Another trend within the digital sphere is the rise of self-tracking devices in the form of wearable, wireless, and "smart" technologies (e.g., watches, tablet computers, or tiny sensors incorporated into everyday items such as a toothbrush). The confluence of the medical industrial complex and self-tracking devices with the capability of collecting, measuring, computing, and displaying vital, bodily data has given rise to the "quantified self," which is, essentially, self-knowledge through numbers. The quantified self incorporates technology into data acquisition on aspects of a person's daily life in terms of inputs (e.g., food consumed, quality of the surrounding air), states (e.g., mood, arousal, blood oxygen levels), and performance (mental and physical). It constructs the body/self as a machine-like entity that can be measured, quantified, and even biohacked.

Deborah Lupton (2012) provides critiques to the quantified self. One critique views the quantified self as a means of attempting to contain risk, to control the vagaries of fate to some extent.

In relation to health matters, self-tracking offers users of such technologies a strategy by which they feel as if they can gather data upon their health indicators as a means of avoiding illness and disease. The self-knowledge that is viewed as emerging from the minutiae of data recording a myriad of aspects of the body is a psychological salve to the fear of bodily degeneration.

Another critique views self-tracking as "one of many heterogeneous strategies and discourses that position the neoliberal self as a responsible citizen, willing and able to take care of her or his self-interest and welfare." A third critique views digital technologies as reinforcing a surveillance society because it increasingly monitors and measures individuals, and even allows people to broadcast their "numbers" to many others via social media platforms for further attention, acceptance, or scrutiny.

While the digital sphere is a frontier with potential to be used for social change and health benefits, there is a politics of the digital sphere as well. The algorithms and numbers used are not neutral, despite the accepted concept of them as objective and devoid of value judgments, assumptions, and meanings. Algorithms and quantification are always implicated in social relationships and power dynamics that affect ways of seeing/knowing. For instance, Buolamwini (2016), a black technologist, describes how the algorithmic bias of social robots to perform facial recognition is skewed toward perceiving white facial features.

Today, corporations and the government collect unprecedented amounts of data about us and parse that data to benefit their purposes. Algorithms are used to sort data to assess the worthiness of individuals for public benefits, jobs, loans, insurance, and for suspicion in the criminal justice system. This mining of data to rate and rank individuals is what Citron and Pasquale (2014) call a "scored society." While the rich are not exempt from these algorithms, the poor and working class are the most endangered by them. Machine learning and predictive policing algorithms tend to advantage the already advantaged and marginalize the already marginalized.

Eubanks (2017) explores how algorithmic automation has played out in America's welfare system by investigating three examples where algorithms replaced or augmented human decision-making in public assistance – Indiana's automated Medicaid eligibility process; Los Angeles' coordinated entry system for the homeless; and Allegheny County, Pennsylvania's predictive algorithm for assessing childhood risk of abuse and neglect. She found that algorithmic automation has two principal effects: (1) it undermines poor people's right to self-determination, and (2) it abstracts questions of political morality into questions of efficiency. In this way, the poor become "managed," rather than focusing attention toward the eradication of poverty. Eubanks (2017) calls this "automating inequality."

To help fight bias in algorithms, Buolamwini founded the Algorithmic Justice League and seeks to raise awareness of what she calls the "coded gaze." Just as the male gaze sees the world as a place made for men's pleasure, the "coded gaze" sees the world according to the data on which its creators trained it, which tends to skew toward the dominant, normative, and status quo.

See also: Affect, Big Data, Biomedicalization, Co-presence, Inequality, Media Watch, Neoliberalism, Resistance, Social Movements, Spheres, Trolling, Tweetstorm

Further Reading/Web Browsing/ Participatory Media

#campaignzero
#BlackLivesMatter
#heretostay
#inclusionrevolution
#lastrealindians
#undocumentedandunafraid
#SayHerName
#staywoke
#MeToo

Algorithmic Justice League: www.ajlunited. org/
Quantified Self: http://quantifiedself.com/

Abreu, M. A. (n.d.) Imagined Black English. Arachne Webzine. Retrieved from http://arachne.cc/issues/01/online-imagined_manuel-arturo-abreu.html.

Akhtar, A. (2017). One mind, one heart, one body. *The New York Times*, December 31. Retrieved from www.nytimes.com/2017/12/29/theater/ayad-akhtar-steinberg-award-digital-dehumanization-live-theater.html.

Bergal, J. (2017, January 10). Hactivists launch more cyberattacks against local, state governments. PBS Newshour, January 10. Retrieved from www.pbs.org/newshour/nation/hacktivists-launch-cyberattacks-local-state-governments.

Buolamwini, J. (2016). How I'm fighting bias in algorithms. TEDXBeaconStreet, November. Retrieved from www.ted.com/talks/joy_buolamwini_how_i_m_fighting_bias_in_algorithms.

Citron, D. K. & Pasquale, F. (2014). The scored society: Due process for automated predictions. *Washington Law Review*, 89(1), 1–33.

Confessore, N., Dance, G. J. X., Harris, R., & Hansen, M. (2018). The follower factory. *The New York Times*, January 27. Retrieved from www.nytimes.com/interactive/2018/01/27/technology/social-media-bots.html.

Eubanks, V. (2017). *Automating inequality: How high-tech tools profile, police, and punish the poor*. New York: St. Martin's Press.

Froomkin, D. & McLaughlin, J. (2015). Comey calls on tech companies offering end-to-end encryption to reconsider "their business model". The Intercept, December 9. Retrieved from https://theintercept.com/2015/12/09/comey-calls-on-tech-companies-offering-end-to-end-encryption-to-reconsider-their-business-model/.

Hess, A. (2017). The white internet's love affair with digital blackface. *The New York Times*, November 28. Retrieved from www.nytimes.com/video/arts/100000005615988/the-white-internets-love-affair-with-digital-blackface.html.

Jackson, L. M. (2014) Memes and Misogynoir. The Awl. Retrieved from www.theawl.com/2014/08/memes-and-misogynoir/.

Jackson, L. M. (2017). We need to talk about digital blackface in reaction GIFs. In Teen Vogue, August 2. Retrieved from www.teenvogue.com/story/digital-black face-reaction-gifs.

Joyce, K. & Loe, M. (2010). *Technogenarians: Studying health and illness through an ageing, science, and technology lens*. Malden, MA: Blackwell.

Lupton, D. (2012, November 4). The quantified self movement: Some sociological perspectives. Blog post on The Sociological Life, November 4. Retrieved from https://simplysociology.wordpress.com/2012/11/04/the-quantitative-self-movement-some-sociological-perspectives/.

Winstead, E. (2018, January 27). Faked: The headquarters. The followers. The influence? *The New York Times*, January 27. Retrieved from www.nytimes.com/2018/01/27/insider/twitter-buy-followers-bots-investigation-devumi.html.

Disability

Physical or mental limitation or disadvantage. The UN World Health Organization (WHO, 2018) estimates that 15 percent of the world's population have disabilities.

The WHO disability definition includes activity limitations, impairments, participation restrictions, and interactions encompassing "features of a person's body and features of the society." The Centers for Disease Control/CDC estimates that the disabled account for one in five US adults – around 56 million people, "the largest minority group," with labeling and diagnostic categories multiplying (Garland-Thomson, 2016). Most Americans will experience disability, often going in and out of disability status during the life course.

A critical political economy perspective on disability policy is sharply rendered in Marta Russell's treatise, *Beyond ramps* (1998).

What do you do with those defined as "unproductive" as "not exploitable for profit" (Russell, 1998)? Commodify disability, of course: first, through nursing home incarceration, via Medicaid and subsidies to for-profit facilities, and then Medicaid waivers for personal care providers, through "Unenforceable Civil Rights" through The Americans with Disability Act of 1990.

The Independent Living Movement was galvanized by Ed Roberts' refusal to be housed in the Infirmary (his "dormitory") at the University of California, Berkeley. The movement set off decades of consciousness-raising and empowerment confrontations orchestrated by the younger disabled. Unwilling to be "fed," institutionalized, dependent, and controlled, they confronted the implacable institutional barriers. They demanded accessibility via sidewalk "cutouts," public transportation such as kneeling buses, ramps and elevators in public spaces, and the ability to hire and fire their own personal care workers (the model and practice of In-Home Supportive Services/ IHSS, CA policy).

Notable advocacy strategies and battles for rights of the (dis)abled were fought in and on local institutions, community, and state spaces. The young resisted their discredited identity and stigma of disability as they whirred by in their wheelchairs, mobilizing, sitting in on the ground. Advocacy and action on public policy included ADAPT (Americans Disabled for Attendant Programs Today), and the World Institute on Disability/WID. "Crip" was proposed as a radical, inclusive term to reclaim disability identity. Crip Power and Mad Pride, a movement to de-pathologize mental illness (and those maligned as mad, nutty, psycho), empowered consciousness raising and dignity of voice. This approach to civil rights distinctly contrasted with the work of advocates for the elderly, which operated from a national perch of the Older Americans Act (OAA). The OAA established state and local agencies that trained and marshalled younger would-be

gerontologists. This gerontological cadre became the self-appointed "experts" of what the old "needed." The resistance means the most when it rises from the oppressed.

Deborah Stone in *The disabled state* (1984) proposes that disability is a movable social boundary. She identifies that the trend toward the medicalization of social problems has increased the diversity of definitions of disability in public programs. She argues that disability is far from an objective medical notion – it is an administrative category that entitles its members to social aid. Society's definition of disability embodies a society's basic notions of justice, and the definitions of disability can be expanded or contracted by politicians, interest groups, and bureaucratic agencies. Stone posits that the increase in visibility and services (via medicalization) has fueled the political backlash against the disabled. Definitions of disability in public programs are part of battles between those seeking to expand need-based justice and those seeking to preserve work-based distribution. This illustrates how the category of disability acts as a restrictive mechanism in the face of constant pressures for expansion.

Note: Consumer Protection Agency Director and Budget Director Mick Mulvaney openly bragged that he tricked Trump into violating his campaign promise not to cut Social Security. He persuaded Trump that the SSDI program is not really part of Social Security (Yglesias, 2017; Jilani, 2017). This exemplifies the devaluing of disability as undeserving of accommodation or care, thus making disability a liability for members of society.

See also: Ableism/TABS, Americans with Disabilities Act, Commodification, Medical Industrial Complex, Supplemental Security Income/SSI

Further Reading

Ben-Moshe, L., Chapman, C., & Carey, A. (Eds.). (2014). *Disability incarcerated:*

Imprisonment and disability in the United States and Canada. New York: Palgrave Macmillan.

Charlton, J. I. (1998). *Nothing about us without us.* Berkeley, CA: University of California Press.

Conner, D. J., Ferri, B. A., & Annamma, S. A. (Eds.). (2016). *DisCrit: Disability studies and critical race theory in education.* New York: Columbia University Press.

Disability and health data system. (2016). August 19. Retrieved from https://dhds.cdc.gov/.

Garland-Thomson, R. (2016). Becoming disabled. *The New York Times,* August 21. Retrieved from www.nytimes.com/2016/08/21/opinion/sunday/becoming-disabled.html.

Jilani, Z. (2017). Trump budget director takes aim at "wasteful" Social Security program that helps disabled Americans. March 20. Retrieved from https://the intercept.com/2017/03/20/trump-budget-director-takes-aim-at-wasteful-social-security-program-that-helps-disabled-americans/.

Russell, M. (1998). *Beyond ramps: Disability at the end of the social contract: A warning from an uppity crip.* Monroe, ME: Common Courage Press.

Stone, D. A. (1984). *The disabled state.* Philadelphia, PA: Temple University Press.

World Health Organization. (2018). Jan 8. Disability and health. Retrieved from https://www.who.int/news-room/fact-sheets/detail/disability-and-health

World Report on Disability. (2011). Geneva, Switzerland: World Health Organization.

Yglesias, M. (2017). Mick Mulvaney brags that he tricked Trump into proposing Social Security cuts: An extraordinary story from the OMB director. September 1. Retrieved from www.vox.com/policy-and-politics/2017/9/1/16243288/mick-mulvaney-social-security.

Discourse

Includes the words that structure conversation, statements, stories, tropes, meanings, and ideologies. Race, ethnicity, class, and gender are deeply inscribed in all manner of discourse and debate, including whether the voice is allowed, recognized, and heard. Inclusion and exclusion pervade discourse.

Political Discourse Theory (PDT)

Political discourse theory is an approach focused on the discourse of debates, speeches, and hearings. PDT assesses power and strategy, identifying actors in the context of events (i.e., political upsets, social movements). Key concepts include: "hegemony, antagonism, empty signifier, dislocation, identity, articulation, nodal points, and logics of equivalence and difference" (Dellagnelo, Böhm, & Mendonça, 2014, p. 143). PDT looks, for example, at the political positioning of most journalistic questioning and how it mainstreams and marginalizes alternative (subordinate) discourses. PDT illuminates the micro-politics of legitimacy, conformity, and social stability – or alternatively, contingent legitimation or delegitimation (Clayman, 2017).

See also: Methodologies, Social Construction of Reality, Social Movements

Further Reading

Clayman, S. E. (2017). The micropolitics of legitimacy. *Social Psychology Quarterly, 80*(1), 41–64.

Communicating with older adults. Retrieved from www.geron.org/publications/communicating-with-older-adults.

Dellagnelo, E. H. L., Böhm, S., & Mendonça, P. M. E. de. (2014). Organizing resistance movements: Contribution of the political discourse theory. *Revista De Administração De Empresas, 54*(2), 141–153.

Hindman, M. (2008). *The myth of digital democracy* (1st edition). Princeton, NJ: Princeton University Press.

Keller, R. (2011). The sociology of knowledge approach to discourse (SKAD). *Human Studies*, *34*(1), 43–65.

Polzer, J. & Power, E. M. (2016). *Neoliberal governance and health: Duties, risks, and vulnerabilities*. Montreal, Canada: MQUP.

Discrimination

Involves exclusionary practices of denying resources or opportunities based on race, gender, ethnicity, national identity, class, sexual orientation, or age. Discrimination is part and parcel to marginalization and the creation of "minority status."

In the realm of legal analysis, the primary distinction is between de facto and *de jure* discrimination, generally used in the examination of segregation allegations and court cases. De facto discrimination describes discrimination that occurs primarily due to social factors (e.g., sexism, classism, and racism) while *de jure* discrimination describes discrimination that is instituted by law or caused by the government (e.g., Jim Crow laws). Discrimination by law is illegal in many forms, though some groups are vulnerable, as they lack explicit protections and it is very difficult to challenge the de facto realm, which is maintained through laws that benefit groups in power disproportionately (or are disproportionately employed in areas such as real estate, tax, employment, and drug law).

Housing Discrimination

Primarily manifests in two forms: non-exclusionary practices and exclusionary practices. Non-exclusionary practices occur within a pre-existing housing arrangement that can involve any kind of harmful or unequal treatment on the basis of race, gender, or age. In a comprehensive study by the Fair Housing Centers of Michigan (FHCM)

in 2007, results showed that almost 30 percent of the same-sex couples participating in the study were subject to higher rental rates or otherwise discouraged to rent. Both of these practices are forms of non-exclusionary housing discrimination.

Exclusionary housing discrimination occurs when a family or individual is disallowed from obtaining housing or to enter into a housing arrangement due to their race, age, or gender. Such practices were commonplace and legal in many regions, until the passage of the national Fair Housing Act. The legacy of these practices is still visible in the United States in the form of housing segregation. Though these practices have been outlawed, they persist, as they tend to affect communities with very little access to legal resources, and because discrimination can be hard to prosecute in court. A study by the US Department of Housing and Urban Development found that:

> the greatest share of discrimination for Hispanic and African American home seekers can still be attributed to being told units are unavailable when they are available to non-Hispanic whites and being shown and told about less units than a comparable non-minority.
>
> (HUD, 2005).

Age Discrimination

The Federal Fair Housing Acts do not expressly ban discrimination based on age. Nevertheless, it is forbidden under the broader prohibition against discrimination on the basis of familial status.

A landlord cannot refuse to rent to an older person, or impose special terms and conditions on the tenancy, unless these same standards are applied to everyone else. If you have excellent references and credit history, a landlord has no legal basis for refusing you, even if you are 85 and rely to some degree on the regular assistance of a nearby adult child or friend. However, if your current landlord reveals that you suffer from advanced senility, to the point that you often wander into the wrong apartment, frequently forget to pay the rent, or are unable to undertake basic housekeeping chores, the prospective landlord can refuse to rent based on this age-neutral evidence that you are not likely to be a stable, reliable tenant.

In most cases, the strength of protections is highly dependent on the accessibility for recourse on the part of tenants. The legal system is complicated and can be costly, producing structural disadvantages for the elderly.

Critical Reflection

Discrimination is the antithesis of equality or the justice advocated for in equity; and it is more than a matter of legality or access to markets. It is also in the interpersonal and everyday experiences of people treating each other with dignity and respect or as only worth what their incarceration can earn for stockholders. These are situational and structural, the psychic toll – the trauma – accruing over time. For transgender people, access to labor and health rights are a constant struggle against the ideological hegemony of cisgendered policy that reifies gender binaries.

See also: Age Discrimination in Employment Act, Civil Rights Movement/Civil Rights Act, Empathy, Epistemology, Exploitation, Gender, Microaggressions, Oppression, Prison Industrial Complex, Racism, Stereotype Threat, War on Women, Watch Dogs/Watch Bitches

Further Reading

Bonastia, C. (2006). *Knocking on the door*. Princeton, NJ: Princeton University Press.

Desmond, M. (2016). *Evicted* (1st edition). New York: Crown Publishers.

HUD. (2005). *Discrimination in metropolitan housing markets: National results from phase 1, phase 2, and phase 3 of the housing discrimination study*. Office of Policy Development and Research, U.S. Department of Housing and Urban Development.

Sexual orientation and housing discrimination in Michigan. (2007). Ann Arbor, MI: Fair Housing Center of Southeastern Michigan. Retrieved from www.fhcmichigan.org/images/Arcus_web1.pdf.

Disengagement

Posits that old age is a period in which an individual and society simultaneously and mutually separate from each other.

Disengagement theory assesses the aging process in terms of the biological breakdown of the individual, or the loss of dependency and self, over the course of time. This theory views disengagement as a natural, universal, and normal part of life's trajectory. Aging, from this perspective, is "functional" because it is beneficial for both the individual and society for disengagement to take place because it minimizes the disruption caused by a person's gradual, inevitable, and eventual death (Cumming & Henry, 1961; Estes, Swan, & Gerard, 1982; Estes, Linkins, & Binney, 2001).

This theory is now widely criticized as being based on samples of white middle class in middle America and thus not universally or globally generalizable. Further, it reflects and promotes stereotypes of older age as a state of decline and as persons to be shunned. Critical scholars continue to locate the ways in which lawmakers and institutions (especially for retirement and long-term care services) encode disengagement into social policy (e.g., through nursing home institutionalization).

See also: Conflict Theory and Consensus Theory, Culture, Functionalism, Rationalization

Further Reading

Cumming, E. & Henry, W. E. (1961). *Growing old: The process of disengagement*. New York: Basic Books.

Estes, C. L., Linkins, K. W., & Binney, E. A. (2001). Critical perspectives on aging. In C. L. Estes & Associates. (2001), *Social policy & aging: A critical perspective* (pp. 38–39). Thousand Oaks, CA: Sage.

Estes, C. L., Swan, J. H., & Gerard, L. E. (1982). Dominant and competing paradigms in gerontology: Towards a political economy of ageing. *Ageing and Society*, 2(2), 151–164.

Hochschild, A. R. (1975). Disengagement theory: A critique and proposal. *American Sociological Review*, 553–569.

Dispossession

The shifting of power and accumulation of wealth through deprivation, robbery of resources, and environmental transformations. This concept is presented by Marxist geographer David Harvey.

Harvey argues that "Capitalism internalizes cannibalistic as well as predatory and fraudulent practices" (Harvey, 2004, p. 76). Capitalism, since the 1970s under neoliberalism, has not been effective at generating high levels of growth. Therefore, the wealth that has accumulated in the upper classes has not come out of growth, but out of accumulation by dispossession. The dynamics of accumulation by dispossession are exemplified by the credit system. For example, in the United States, the subprime mortgage crisis between 2007 and 2010 caused many people to lose their homes. The foreclosures were a massive dispossession that infected the whole financial system. However, sectors of the population that were particularly affected were relatively poor people, African American and Latino people, and people concentrated in poorer zones of most cities. While many of these owners lost the asset of their home, bankers, investors, and financiers took possession of property for resale and kept their remunerations.

While accumulation by dispossession is present in any historical period, "it picks up strongly when the crises of overaccumulation occur in expanded reproduction, when there seems to be no other exit except devaluation" (Harvey, 2004, p. 76). The mechanisms of dispossession have resurged since the 1970s. Harvey (2005) identifies four elements of accumulation by dispossession:

1. Privatization of public resources and services to create new opportunities in areas once protected from the "calculus of profitability," the "reversion of common property rights won through years of hard class struggle," and the "transfer of assets from the public and popular realms to the private and class privileged domains" (Harvey, 2005, p. 153). Examples include shifts of funding from public schools to private charter schools or the privatization of public pensions and health care.

2. Increasing financialization of economies across the world (speculation, predation, and fraud), such as stock promotions, asset stripping through mergers and acquisitions or by credit and stock manipulation, such as decimating and raiding pension funds by stock and corporate collapses.

3. Management and manipulation of crises, such as destabilizing, control of international economies, and structural adjustment programs administered by the International Monetary Fund or World Bank.

4. State redistributions, tax reductions on the rich, and capital income which serve as the rationale for privatization of public programs.

Harvey argues that successive waves of accumulation by dispossession is a hallmark of US-centered imperialism. It has sparked resentment, generating a worldwide anti-globalization movement and active resistance to US hegemony by formerly pliant subordinate countries, particularly in Asia, and now in Europe. Harvey sees this trend deepening, which could transition the US out, and Asia in, as the hegemonic center of global power. There are a variety of forces that could easily tip the balance in one direction or another. The only certainty is that we are currently amid a major transition in how the global system works.

Harvey is interested in knowing *which form of class struggle is going to be at the heart of any kind of revolutionary movement*. He contends that within contemporary society, a movement can be built among the dispossessed – people who have lost their assets, rights, and dignity, through accumulation by dispossession. He argues that the political struggles against accumulation by dispossession are just as important as any traditional proletarian movements. However, the class struggles provoked by dispossession are of a radically different nature from traditional proletarian struggles upon which the future of socialism was supposed to rest. Harvey (2004, p. 83) asserts that:

> The unities beginning to emerge around these different vectors of struggle are vital to nurture, for within them we can discern the lineaments of an entirely different, non-imperialistic, form of globalization that emphasizes social well-being and humanitarian goals coupled with creative forms of uneven geographical development, rather than the glorification of money power, stock market values and the incessant accumulation of capital across the variegated spaces of the global economy by whatever means, but always ending up heavily concentrated in a few spaces of extraordinary wealth.

See also: Exploitation, Neoliberalism, Socialism

Further Reading

Harvey, D. (2004). The 'new' imperialism: Accumulation by dispossession. *Socialist Reader*, 40, 63–87.

Harvey, D. (2005). *A brief history of neoliberalism*. New York: Oxford University Press.

Disruption

A radical or significant change to an institution, economy, society, or lived experience.

In a critical context it refers to the disruption of domination. This might involve an interruption of the downward flow of power, which could entail revaluing labor and labor interests, the redistribution of wealth or resources, and the emergence of previously silenced voices.

In contrast, the politics of the Trump White House and the GOP exemplify the meaning of disruption of domination by the Right, as the far-right pursued policies designed to deconstruct what President Trump's former chief strategist, Steve Bannon, calls the "Administrative State."

Disruption is also a prominent concept in business, especially in tech. It is part of an ethos of creative destruction that can produce breakthroughs but can also undermine legal protections as well as consumer and labor well-being. Google, Amazon, and Apple announce their plans to enter into the field of health care and "disrupt" the status quo. While private companies find innovative ways to enter the market, the questions of equity are absent from the discourse of affordability and access.

In the psychic realm, at the deeply personal level, disruption occurs with major health events, particularly in old age. Becker (1993) is one of the few scholars to study life course disruption in old age and its implications for gerontological theory, research, and practice. Disruption and precarity are each concepts that require renewed focus in gerontological and geriatric work. Life course research and theory has focused primarily on continuities. The effects on the aging of discontinuities in life events remain empirically under-conceptualized and relatively unexamined.

See also: Black Lives Matter, Event, Precarity, Social Movements, Subversive, Transgressive

Further Reading

Becker, G. (1993). Continuity after a stroke: Implications of life-course disruption in Old Age. *The Gerontologist*. *33*(2), 148–158.

Domination

"[T]he probability that a command with a given specific content will be obeyed by a given group of persons" (Weber, 1922/1968, p. 53). "[W]ithout exception every sphere of social action is profoundly influenced by structures of domination" (Weber, 1922/1968, p. 941).

Max Weber's three forms of legitimate domination are Traditional, Charismatic, and Legal (usually a combination). In the capitalist United States "Economic Dominance" and "Dominant Ideologies" are central components of domination. They explain the likelihood that a command within a given organization or society will be obeyed. Domination is distinguished from "power/Macht" which is the capacity of a social actor to impose his or her will upon others despite resistance from them. Other forms include domination by "virtue of authority" and economic forms of domination are to be distinguished.

Within a traditional critical perspective, dominated people are considered compromised as to their social development, individuality or singularity, and psychic integrity; stunted by a lack of opportunity and pervaded by a sense of inferiority and subservience. The dominant are defined as the incarnation of achieved human nature. Violence and safety are the purview of the dominant, as specified by law and executed through the State. Those deputized by law carry an expectation to be safe from violence from oppressed people, but may exercise impunity in perpetrating violence on those over whom they are dominant. Dominated persons or groups often face barriers in the freedom to take effective action because of this sanctioned retaliation from the dominating. Domination is about control and restriction of access to freedom and risk. Domination is also about control and restriction of access to resources and movement through time and space.

Critical gerontological perspectives might look at institutional barriers to higher education (e.g., tuition, fees, timing, debt, and performance standards) that limit participation. One can observe a classroom and ask who is there and who is not there; likewise, in their professional bodies, in their syllabi.

On macro-situational levels, those who are dominant are the political and economic leaders and the individuals and organizations of big capital (and their capture of little capital). On the institutional level guided by the Older Americans Act, elder care professionals construct and maintain the existing aging network, including state and regional agencies and increasingly for-profit service providers that dominate the definition of issues, the policy agenda, and its implementation. In academia and the sciences, it is in the elite and hierarchical individual and institutional identities, scientific standing and funding.

See also: Affect (Politics of), Colonialisms, Exploitation, Hegemony, Ideology, Levels of Analysis, Oppression, Power, Racism, Sexism, Violence, War

Further Reading

Agevall, O. & Swedberg, R. (2016). *The Max Weber dictionary: Key words and central concepts*. Redwood City, CA: Stanford University Press.

Estes, C. L. (1979). *The aging enterprise: A critical examination of social policies and services for the aged*. San Francisco, CA: Jossey-Bass.

Weber, M. (1968). *Economy and society: An interpretative sociology*. New York: Bedminster. (Originally published 1922.)

Wright, E. O. (2001). Foundations of class analysis. In J. Baxter & M. Western (Eds.), *Reconfigurations of class and gender* (pp. 25–27). Redwood City, CA: Stanford University Press.

Doxa

The prevailing ideology which renders things normal and ordinary. People are largely unconscious that there are realities outside of this realm.

Bourdieu (1977) writes that doxa is what is taken for granted as natural and self-evident, the reified fabric of the social order. These are things that seem so natural and ordinary that they go unquestioned. *Doxa* comes from the Greek word for public opinion or common belief, and was also used in Hebrew as "glory" and as *orthodoxy* to identify "true belief." Plato framed "doxa" as opposite to knowledge or "episteme." It is inherited ideology, not lived experience.

It is a central task of critical gerontology to examine unquestioned beliefs which render invisible the very factors that govern everyday social life, individual development, and collective experience. This thinking has been essential in subverting stereotypes about aging (redefining it as something more than just an experience of decline and withdrawal) as well as maintaining structures of inequality. In addition, scholars and activists can interrogate the "climates" of debt crisis and austerity, rejecting the notion that budget-slashing is the only way for economic systems to survive.

See also: Abjection, Ageism, Austerity, Capitalism, Crisis, Debt, Discourse, Framing, Ideology, Psychoanalytic Social Theory, TINA

Further Reading

Bourdieu, P. (1977). *Outline of a theory of practice* (trans. R. Nice). Cambridge: Cambridge University Press.

E

Ecologies

Harmonious systems, balanced and responsive. Ecology refers to an interconnected environment of existence and coexistence; it denotes a model or study of environment, interplay, and coexistence within a system. Ecological models may speak to open and closed networks, evolutionary functions of cultural values or mores. Mainstream models have been criticized for not taking into account structural forces of domination and oppression.

In considering causal processes, ecological frameworks sometimes examine dynamics in a linear way, failing to appreciate the complexity inherent in every search for meaning. Ecological models value historicity but often focus on very literal developmental moments throughout the lifespan. The cause and effect of larger trends, such as feudalism, industrialization and post-industrialization, are generally ignored. Apart from these trends toward chronological and historical blind spots, ecological models can encourage critical thinking about the ways in which objects and people are arranged physically within a given space. Urban design, infrastructure, and building design can be seen through a more critical lens by incorporating ecology.

Critical ecology is a complex project, buffeted by anti-science skeptics and formidable big oil, gas, and coal adversaries against Earth Day and the cross-movement issues, including Green politics and meaningful climate change action and policy to stem and reverse greenhouse gas accumulation in the near and far term. These are nature-imposed conditions of human existence.

O'Connor (1998) observes that ecological crises produce "integrity" difficulties for both the natural and social worlds, with "an exponential increase in environmental/ecological and social/political problems of all kinds." He contends "that radical green (and green radical) movements today are born from what is arguably *the* basic contradiction of world capitalism": the weakening of both "national capitalist interests and national labor" in the face of the acceleration of "an international ruling class and the rudiments of an international political elite and capitalist state. . . . They have delegitimated and partially defanged national states once capable of effective social and environmental/economic regulation" (O'Connor, 1998, pp. xii and xiii).

Magdoff and Williams (2017) declare "the social and ecological planetary emergency" (p. 25) in terms of capitalism versus the biosphere and capitalism's effect on people (pp. 75–150). They pronounce "equality as a biological fact" (p. 197) and propose "ecological approaches to fulfilling human needs" (p. 247). Sustainable human development requires us to maintain the Earth for future generations. Human existence requires the protection and extension of our natural ecological resources. Human, animal, plant, and global health are *one* in the livable universe required for the development of human freedom and potential.

Aging and the life course, life expectancy, and cumulative advantage and disadvantage are each directly and indirectly implicated in the larger scheme of ecological concerns. Public health epidemiology (U.S. DHHS, 2000) addresses elements of "eco-epidemiology," "social ecological," and "ecosocial," considerations in the broader historical, social, economic, political, and environmental context. Lawton's environmental gerontology demonstrates that the physical environment is profoundly influential, particularly in "individual competency" in old age – and that, just as important, the demands or "press" of environments and personal competencies are objectively measurable (Wahl, Iwarsson, & Oswald, 2012).

See also: Aging in Community, Cumulative Advantage/Disadvantage, Human Rights, Life Expectancy, The Social, Theories of Aging, Theories of Need

Further Reading

Capitalism Nature Socialism: A Journal on Socialist Ecology. Retrieved from http://environment-ecology.com/journals/411-capitalism-nature-socialism-a-journal-of-socialist-ecology.html.

Chitewere, T., Shim, J. K., Barker, J. C., & Yen, I. H. (2017). How neighborhoods influence health: Lessons to be learned from the application of political ecology. *Health & Place, 45,* 117–123.

Klein, N. (2014). *This changes everything*. New York: Simon & Schuster.

Magdoff, F. & Williams, C. (2017). *Creating an ecological society: Toward a revolutionary transformation*. New York: Monthly Review Press.

O'Connor, J. (1998). *Natural causes: Essays in ecological Marxism*. New York: Guilford Press.

U.S. Department of Health and Human Services. (2000). *Healthy people 2010*. Washington, DC: U.S. DHHS.

Wahl, H-W., Iwarsson, S., & Oswald, F. (2012). Aging well and the environment: Toward an integrative model and research agenda for the future. *The Gerontologist, 52*(3), 306–316.

Economics

Studies systems of capital and power, which include exchange networks and processes of financialization/monetization (turning things into money).

1. *Laissez-faire Economics*

   Classical economics says that the State should not regulate markets; unfettered markets are "healthy" and "grow." This is used to justify the neoliberal ideology of privatization, which promotes minimal regulations and few protections. Mainstream neoclassical economics is characterized by what Naess and colleagues (2016) identify as significant and profound commodification of human needs, culture, and virtually every other aspect of society.

   In addition, there are the Keynesian model and Marxist model – with critiques and scholarship (in aging as well) from the feminists, anti-racists, the Greens, and a host of models of socialist economies (including Soviet and Chinese).

2. *Heterodox Economics*

   Though neoclassical economics and Keynesian macro-economic theory are the most dominant schools of thought across the discipline, many other frameworks exist. *Heterodox schools of Economic Thought* reject many of the central tenets of mainstream economics as well as its goals and metrics. There is significant diversity of thought among heterodox economists, though in general they seek to remedy the limitations of mainstream economic thought by examining phenomena and outcomes that are ignored by the mainstream. Marxian economics is one of the oldest and most prominent schools of heterodox economics, emphasizing the role of capital, issues of economic evolution, the value of labor, and the dynamics of class, including the relationship between capital and labor.

3. *Feminist Economics*

Patriarchy, social reproduction, and the gendered division of labor provide a framework for examining gendered inequality. This includes the wage gap, the wealth gap, the caregiving penalty, sex discrimination, the devaluations of predominantly female-led occupations (e.g., education, care work), white feminism, and economics for women of color.

4. *Racial/Ethnic/Anti-colonialist Economics*

Slavery, exploitation, and expropriation of peoples, lands, and lives are inscribed in inequality and multiple forms of individual, group, and institutionalized oppression. The racial wealth gap, the racial wage gap, the education gap, the racial and economic life-expectancy gap, and the access to private pensions gap speak to economics of closure, discrimination, and cumulative disadvantage at all ages, particularly for survivors in old age.

5. *The Economics of Inequality*

Recently, economists have drawn increased attention to the problem of global wealth inequality. In his book, *Capital in the twenty-first century* (2014), Piketty outlines the mechanisms that have produced the extreme level of wealth inequality which has become a hallmark of the economic landscape in the twenty-first century. Piketty explains

that capital, and the investments it allows for the wealthy, increases much faster than wages or the economy as a whole grow. This creates a structural bias in the global economy toward the wealthy. Christensen (2017) provides comparative case studies showing that the adoption of preferential market-oriented tax policies is related to neoclassically trained economists occupying powerful positions in states around the world.

See also: Capitalism, The Market, Political Economy

Further Reading

Anderson, E. (1990). The ethical limitations of the market. *Economics and Philosophy*, 6(2), 179–205.

Christensen, J. (2017). *The power of economists within the state*. Stanford, CA: Stanford University Press.

Collins, C. & Wright, M. (2007). *The moral measure of the economy*. Maryknoll, UK: Orbis Books.

English, A. & Hegewisch, A. (2008). *Still a man's labor market: The long-term earnings gap*. Washington, DC: Institute for Women's Policy Research.

Folbre, N. (2009). *Greed, lust and gender*. Oxford: Oxford University Press.

Held, V. (1990). Feminist transformations of moral theory. *Philosophy and Phenomenological Research*, 50, 321–344.

IWPR. (n.d.). *Pay equity and discrimination*. Washington, DC: Institute for Women's Policy Research. Retrieved from https://iwpr.org/issue/employment-education-economic-change/pay-equity-discrimination/.

Jo, T. & Lee, F. (2015). *Marx, Veblen, and the foundations of heterodox economics*. London: Routledge.

Jo, T. & Todorova, Z. (2015). *Advancing the frontiers of heterodox economics*. London: Routledge.

Naess, P., Price, L., Hoyer, K. G., & Naess, P. (2016). *Crisis system*. London: Routledge.

O'Hara, P. A. (1999). *Encyclopedia of political economy*. London: Routledge.

Piketty, T. (2014). *Capital in the twenty-first century*. Cambridge, MA: The Belknap Press of Harvard University Press.

Ruffins, P. (1996). Black economists: An "elite clan of warrior intellectuals". *Black Issues in Higher Education, 13*(19), 18–24.

Yonay, Y. P. (1998). *The struggle over the soul of economics: Institutionalist and neoclassical economists in America between the wars*. Princeton, NJ: Princeton University Press.

Education

The process of transmitting and growing knowledge, extended through opportunity and recognition.

The all-encompassing privatization movement within conservative politics has and continues to have a serious impact on public and private education policy. The selection, by President Trump, of Betsy DeVos as Secretary of Education, marked both a fundamental change in and a culmination of years of activism seeking to undermine public schools. DeVos was a noted proponent of "school choice" and vouchers, both of which are used by conservatives to redirect federal and state funding from traditional public schools to the private sector and religious institutions.

Within the field of higher education, privatization has manifested itself primarily in the form of for-profit institutions. Under President Obama, the Department of Education made significant efforts to curb the excesses of the for-profit education sector and leveraged federal grants and loan programs to force changes within the industry via the "gainful employment" rule that gave the federal government the ability to withhold aid and loans for institutions whose graduates failed to find employment and pay off loans. With the change of adminis-

tration many of these policy initiatives were in jeopardy as the Trump Administration signaled a much more favorable attitude toward for-profit institutions.

Critical reflection: is there a contradiction in learning/teaching at for-profit institutions about emancipatory knowledge and the undergirding ideologies and economic structures of higher education? Since markets of and competition for healthy aging drive consumption by older persons, tensions mount between education and credentialing in the proprietary versus public and non-profit sectors. Turf (and patent) battles within blurred university-corporate labs entities and campuses compete to define who "owns" and "controls" aging and medical breakthroughs through the discourse and practice of discovery in areas such as precision medicine. These challenges reflect the relative prestige and resource disparities between *gerontology* and *geriatrics* and who has scientific access via funding and academic recognition to define the fields, paradigms, research questions, protocols, and access to scientific scholar networks and top-ranked publications.

See also: Consciousness Raising, Human Rights, Knowledges, Pedagogy, Privatization, Policy

Emancipatory

Delineates the potential and capacity to liberate and free from restraint. It is a form of extrication from the uncomfortable, the unacceptable, and the unjust. Emancipatory frameworks are integral to social movements combatting all forms of oppression whether on the basis of class, race, gender, ability, heritage, age, or other concerns.

Emancipatory education, learning, teaching, research, practice, and action are arenas dedicated to informing and facilitating the labor and mobilization required to overcome social exclusion, discrimination, oppression, and inequalities. "Emancipatory research commits to producing knowledge to reflect and benefit disadvantaged peoples. It builds off of many streams of critical theory such as feminist, disability, race and gender theory" (Noel, 2016).

Emancipatory social movements such as the civil rights and feminist struggles of the 1960s undertook the oppositional and radical questioning and bold confrontation of hierarchies of authority and power, their practices, values, and deleterious effects on individuals, groups, communities, and society. Courageous and bloody organizing, demonstrating, and protesting forged the emancipatory expansion of the franchise for black Americans (although it is again under siege in recent and current US elections). Freire's liberation theory and praxis (1970) inspires emancipatory practice, learning, and resistance to this day.

A Critical Gerontological Perspective

Values of equality and justice are touchstones of emancipation. Leonard (1997) suggests that collective resistance and emancipatory welfare building are two pathways forward when the targets of social change seek to address repressive professional power, the commodification of culture, the manufacture of desire, and the global market.

The 2017 and 2018 Presidential and Congressional actions to repeal the ACA (ObamaCare) and enact sweeping tax reform favoring corporations and the rich have fueled multiple progressive resistance movements to save vital social insurance programs for elders, the disabled, and children (e.g., Medicare, Medicaid, Social Security, Supplemental Security Income, and long-term care). On a daily basis, social and mainstream media unveil spectacles of truth, lies, and hate. Political, cultural, and economic fighting has altered the fabric of US society, challenging our state institutions, democracy, and the security of our daily existence. The pain and suffering is a seed-bed for individual and collective struggles toward emancipation.

See also: Agency, Cognitive Liberation, Epistemology, Feminism, Pedagogy, Resistance, Social Movements

Further Reading

Freire, P. (1970). *Pedagogy of the oppressed.* New York: Herder & Herder.

Leonard, P. (1997). *Postmodern welfare: Reconstructing an emancipatory project.* Thousand Oaks, CA: Sage.

Noel, L. (2016). Promoting an emancipatory research paradigm in Design Education and Practice. *Proceedings of DRS 2016, Design Research Society 50th Anniversary Conference.* Brighton, UK, June 27–30.

Embodiment

The manifestation of knowing and feeling, located through one's physical body.

Language of the body illustrates how we identify and relate social phenomena and our experiences in cultural and social spheres to embodiment. Social insurance programs are discussed as being "bloated" or needing to be "gutted." Limitations and constraints can "blind" and "cripple." Elaborating on stereotype threat, Levy (2009) proposes Stereotype Embodiment Theory (SET) to explain how the stress of negative stereotypes affects health and the internalization of these beliefs inform health behaviors. The psychiatrist and researcher Bessel Van der Kolk (2014) explores post-traumatic stress in his book *The body keeps the score.* The science of gene–environment and intergenerational coding of trauma returns the focus on the body to the foreground.

Critical Connection

The political, economic, and sociocultural dimensions of old age oppression manifest in the bodily, lived experience. These are dis-abling. Medicare fails to provide hearing aids, glasses, and dentistry. The fairytale of *Little Red Riding Hood* comes to mind, where it is remark-able that granny possesses big eyes, ears, and teeth. It is time to reimagine an equipped aging person entitled to health insurance cov-erage for ears, eyes, and teeth – not as the big bad wolf, but as a whole and valued person.

See also: Epigenetics, Gene–Environment, Stress, Telomeres

Further Reading

Gilleard, C. & Higgs, P. (1998). Ageing and the limiting conditions of the body. *Socio-logical Research Online*, *3*(4). Retrieved from www.socresonline.org.uk/3/4/4.html.

Gilleard, C. & Higgs, P. (2014). *Ageing, corpo-reality and embodiment*. London: Anthem Press.

Levy, B. (2009). Stereotype embodiment: A psychosocial approach to aging. *Current Directions in Psychological Science*, *18*(6), 332–336.

Van der Kolk, B. (2014). *The body keeps the score: Brain, mind, and body in the healing of trauma*. New York: Viking.

Emotional Energy (EE)

The excitement and investment arising in interactions of individuals and others that may precipitate one's allying with or being drawn into a collective movement.

With attribution to Durkheim, Goffman, and symbolic interactionists, Collins theo-rizes interaction ritual chains as a form of cultural process in which people lose or gain emotional energy (EE) and the motivation to participate. "EE is an empirical variable" observed in power and status rituals (Collins, 2004, pp. 112, 115, 133). *Power rituals* dem-onstrate asymmetric relations between order-givers and order-takers. *Status rituals* bring forward the sense of belonging,

inclusion, or exclusion. Empirically, EE is the flow from one's consciousness and one's bodily sensations, reflecting a "continuum from enthusiasm, confidence and initiative at the high end, down to passivity and depres-sion at the low end" (p. 134). Occurring with EE are processes of "collective entrainment" and "collective effervescence." Inequalities in EE enable "energy stars" in using and accumulating power over others, thereby attaining dominance and legitimacy. These processes may become part of a vicious cycle in which those who are most disadvantaged in society are less able to engage in political action. It is significant that organizing and advocating politically are actions that come with aggregating emotional wins and losses that are akin to an electric charge. This relates to *potentia* (Spinoza, 1670, republished 2004) and the politics of affect.

See also: Consciousness Raising, Co-presence, Culture, Empowerment, Resis-tance, Social Movement Theory

Further Reading

Collins, R. (2004). *Interaction ritual chains*. Princeton, NJ: Princeton University Press.

Durkheim E. (1912/1965). *The elementary forms of religious life*. New York: Free Press.

Goffman, E. (1955/1967). On face work: An analysis of ritual elements in social interaction. *Psychiatry*, *18*, 213–231. Reprinted in Goffman (1967). *Interaction ritual*. New York: Doubleday.

Spinoza, B. de. (2004). *A theologico-political treatise and a political treatise*. New York: Dover Publications. (Originally pub-lished 1670.)

Empathy

The ability to feel and respond to others' suf-fering and experience. It requires recognition and willingness to enter into intimate experi-ences of vulnerability through solidarity.

Social relations and human contact including physical touching, as well as presence and communication, are central to human development and well-being.

Lack of empathy is often a casualty of competition, scarcity, and segregation. Abjection and devaluing of alterity limit empathic knowing and seeing of the Other. Oppressor and oppressed are split through failures to empathically connect.

Racism can have a distinct negative impact on empathy:

racial oppression not only severely distorts human relationships but also desensitizes the minds of those involved in oppressing others. Racial oppression requires and stimulates in the oppressors a lack of recognition of the full humanity of the exploited and racialized others.
(Feagin, 2006, pp. 27–28)

The same claim can be made for other (and often intersecting) forms of discrimination such as ableism and ageism. In any exploration or theorization of empathy, the dialectic tension between sociopathy and cruelty must be addressed, as well as the role of the unconscious and the phenomenon of "cognitive dissonance" between proclaimed values and expressed violence.

See also: Co-presence, Intergenerational Subjectivity

Further Reading

Feagin, J. R. (2006). *Systemic racism*. New York: Routledge.

Feagin, J. R. & Hernan, V. (2000). *White racism: The basics*. New York: Routledge.

Empowerment

Develops the potential to think and act, to reclaim a voice silenced, and to connect deeply with a sense of dignity. It involves seizing, realizing, or seeking power of recognition and more for an individual, group, or cause.

Empowerment operates through multiple dimensions: intrapersonal and interactional (Speer, 2000); it is influenced by interactions between an individual (his or her attributes) and the features and forces of his or her social settings and conditions (cultural, economic, and political). The health and economic security of individuals, groups, and collectivities both requires and reproduces their empowerment (and its opposite, disempowerment). Research confirms that powerlessness is associated with negative health risks. Empowerment, efficacy, and the sense of personal control enhance health. Disempowerment forces are reflected in treatment disparities (systemic and individual) by race, ethnicity, sex and gender, and how policy defines and treats women's and men's needs, respectively. As legal struggles over the ACA illustrate, men's health issues tend to be defined as medical problems while women's health issues tend to be defined as political problems. Class, racial, and ethnic differences also matter, as do disabilities.

Persons and communities taking back and asserting power that has been co-opted or denied by dominant groups accords a form of empowerment. In order to contest and subvert dominant paradigms, oppressed groups must attain an understanding of their oppressed status and the coercive mechanisms that oppressive entities employ. This is consciousness raising. With cycles of action with reflection (praxis), change becomes increasingly viable, although still faced with coercive threat from dominant oppressive forces. Such transformations of consciousness produce recognition of the self (unifying political and personal selves). This is integral to feminist, anti-ableist and anti-racist resistance.

If everyday life is increasingly fragmented [and situational] the notions of oppression and justice are either effaced or atomized into oblivion.

(Charlton, 1998, p. 177)

We cannot draw equivalencies between oppressive forces, but we can explore the relative suffering and inequality, and how power structures and players promote these phenomena through networks of power and resistance.

Studies of empowerment education delineate pathways to health through organizational and community capacity-building and leadership. These efforts enhance control and beliefs in the ability to change one's own life (Miller, Chen, & Parker, 2011). Sánchez-Jankowski's (2008) research on social change and resilience in poor neighborhoods shows how communities can be supportive of their residents and creative in solving problems.

How to get to empowerment is an important question to acknowledge/explore. It seems that strategies of empowerment are very different than the factors/reasons people are disempowered, which is embedded in structures of, for example, racism and patriarchy and privilege. For this reason, our text explores concepts of co-presence, resistance, and social movements.

Example

The Office of Employment Opportunity, President Lyndon Baines Johnson's 1960s Poverty Program, empowered local councils of people in poverty to define interventions that could reduce poverty. This was an enormous social engineering experiment. This collaboration and responsiveness between federal and local levels is distinctly different from the policies of devolution and states' rights policies subsequently promoted by Presidents Nixon, Reagan, and Trump that undermine the pursuit of concerted national universal federal goals.

See also: Agency, Consciousness Raising, Co-presence, Devolution, Intersectionality,

Oppression, Power, Praxis, Resistance, Social Movements, States' Rights

Further Reading

Bottomore, T. B. (1983). *A dictionary of Marxist thought*. Cambridge, MA: Harvard University Press.

Charlton, J. I. (1998). *Nothing about us without us*. Berkeley, CA: University of California Press.

Miller, G. E., Chen, E., & Parker, K. J. (2011). Psychological stress in childhood and susceptibility to the chronic diseases of aging: Moving toward a model of behavioral and biological mechanisms. *Psychological Bulletin, 137*(6), 959–997.

Sánchez-Jankowski, M. (2008). *Cracks in the pavement*. Berkeley, CA: University of California Press.

Speer, P. W. (2000). Intrapersonal and interactional empowerment: Implications for theory. *Journal of Community Psychology, 28*(1), 457–472.

Entitlement

Refers to a right or benefit granted by law or regulation at some level of authority (governmental and/or nongovernmental).

The Congressional Budget Office (2016, p. 8) defines entitlement as:

A legal obligation of the federal government to make payments to a person, group of people, business, unit of government, or similar entity that meets the eligibility criteria set in law and for which the budget authority is not provided in advance in an appropriation act. Spending for entitlement programs is controlled through those programs' eligibility criteria and benefit or payment rules. The best-known entitlements are the government's major benefit programs, such as Social Security and Medicare.

By this definition, entitlements include retirement benefits, disability and workers' compensation protections, Social Security, survivors' benefits, and Medicare and Medicaid. Entitlement has long been derided by the Right as an excessive indulgence of the State's charity that ultimately encourages laziness and poor planning. Political, economic, and cultural attacks on entitlements have shifted the dialogue around social insurance, particularly Social Security, to such a degree that proponents of these programs have adopted the phrase "earned benefit" in preference to the term "entitlement." Quadagno (1996) writes of the particular attack against Social Security. In 2018 entitlement is still touted as a conservative's "dirty word" to characterize beneficiaries as people getting resources they do not deserve. The Right's success in re-framing the word "entitlement" as politically toxic exemplifies a loss in the messaging battle for the Left in its own self-censoring use of the historically and symbolically important concept of deservingness (Nunberg, 2006). Thus, in aging policy, the concept of entitlement is not only at the center of highly politicized discourse, but also loaded with negative ramifications for marginalized and disadvantaged peoples and, paradoxically, even for middle-class whites.

See also: Medicaid, Medicare, Social Security

Further Reading

Congressional Budget Office. (2016). Glossary, July. Retrieved from www.cbo.gov/publication/42904.

Nunberg. G. (2006). *Talking right: How conservatives turned liberalism into a tax-raising, latte-drinking, sushi-eating, Volvo-driving, New York Times-reading, body-piercing, Hollywood-loving, left-wing freak show.* New York: Public Affairs.

Quadagno, J. (1996). Social security and the myth of the entitlement "Crisis". *The Gerontologist, 36*(3), 391–399.

Environmental Protection Agency (EPA)

Created in 1970 by President Nixon to consolidate the various federal programs devoted to environmental monitoring and protection.

The EPA has authority to ensure the safety of water, air, soil, and wildlife based on various pieces of legislation. Historically, legislation on the topic follows a familiar pattern. An environmental problem becomes hazardous to public health and public pressure spurs action from Congress. The problem often improves but lasting effects are left to the EPA to monitor and clean up. In theory, private firms bear financial liability for their pollution, depending on how serious it is. However, it can be hard to prove liability and most individuals do not have the legal resources necessary to make a claim.

Environmental protection and pollution have many impacts on communities. Poor communities are far more likely to be exposed to hazardous waste either because of deliberate dumping or a lack of resources for cleanup. By passing laws requiring the EPA to protect human health and the environment (e.g., the Clean Air and Water Acts), Congress recognized the importance of protecting our most vulnerable populations, the young and the old, from environmental hazards.

The EPA is not omniscient or omnipresent and relies on state groups and nonprofits for reporting and identification of problems. As in all things, state agencies have varying levels of capacities and resources and many hazards fall through the cracks. A good example of this is Flint Michigan Water Crisis in which the EPA delayed action for months, as it incorrectly believed it lacked the authority to intervene without approval from the State of Michigan. Meanwhile the state regulators did little to nothing despite being aware of heavy levels of lead in the water. Under the Trump Administration the EPA itself has been disrupted as part of the larger plan to take down this central element of the administrative state apparatus.

From 2002 until it was wiped from the Web in 2017, the EPA established and led a specific initiative on aging led by gerontologist, Kathy Sykes. The EPA has also participated in the Interagency Forum on Aging Statistics. Its future is uncertain, as the fate of the 2020 Census has become politicized and possibly endangered.

Nevertheless, it is empirically demonstrated that older persons are particularly vulnerable to environmental weather events and hazards (Klinenberg, 2002; Portacolone, 2014). Public health research suggests that environmental toxins disproportionately compromise the health of the older population. As the population ages, it is crucial that we understand how environmental hazards affect those with chronic conditions, compromised immune systems, and diminished capacity to respond to these threats.

We must also address climate change that threatens this and future generations and the survival of planet Earth. In addition to environmental hazards, both man-made and naturally occurring in the air, soil, and water, climate change now presents the greatest public health threat facing our world. If we care about promoting public health and ensuring we can breathe clean air and drink clean water, it is essential that we work for a safe and healthy environment, and reduce and adapt to the impacts of climate change that will be with us for decades.

See also: Big Data, Climate Change, The Commons, Ecologies, Gene–Environment

Further Reading

Flint Water Advisory Task Force final report. (2016). Office of Governor Rick Snyder. Retrieved from www.michigan.gov/documents/snyder/FWATF_FINAL_REPORT_21March2016_517805_7.pdf.

Frumkin, H., Fried, L., & Moody, R. (2012). Aging, climate change, and legacy thinking. *American Journal of Public Health, 102*(8), 1434–1438.

Hunter, R. H., Sykes, K., & Lowman, S. G. (2011). Environmental and policy change to support healthy aging. *Journal of Aging & Social Policy, 23*(4), 354–371.

Klinenberg, E. (2002). *Heat wave: A social autopsy of disaster in Chicago.* Chicago, IL: University of Chicago Press.

Portacolone, E. (2014). Older Americans living alone: The influence of resources and intergenerational integration on inequality. *Journal of Contemporary Ethnography, 44*(3), 230–305.

Schettler, T. (n.d.). Dementia slows down: An unanticipated benefit of environmental policies? Science and Environmental Health Network. Retrieved from http://sehn.org/dementia-slows-down-an-unanticipated-benefit/.

Sykes, K. (2005). A healthy environment for older adults: The aging initiative of the Environmental Protection Agency. *Generation, 2*(5), 65–69.

Sykes, K. & Pillemer, K. (2009/2010). The intersection of aging and the environment. *Generations, 33*(4), 6–9.

Sykes, K. E. & Robinson, K. N. (2014). Making the right moves: Promoting smart growth and active aging in communities. *Journal of Aging & Social Policy, 26*(1–2), 166–180. doi:10.1080/08959420.2014.854648.

Sykes, K., Moya, J., Penalva-Arana, C., Phillips, L., & Gilbert, S. (2015). Aging: Characteristics, exposure factors, epigenetics, and assessment of health risks of older adults. In A. M. Fan, G. Alexeef, & E. Khan (Eds.), *Toxicology and risk assessment* (pp. 1029–1041). Boca Raton, FL: Taylor & Francis Group.

Epigenetics

A field that bridges genetic and environmental factors. It studies heritable changes in gene expression (active versus inactive genes) that does not involve changes to the underlying DNA sequence.

DNA methylation is an epigenetic mechanism used by cells to control gene expression. A number of mechanisms exist to control gene expression in eukaryotes, but DNA methylation is a commonly used epigenetic signaling tool that can fix genes in the "off" position.

Epigenetics is part of the science of senescence and anti-aging research which aims to change gene expression in order to prevent aging, cell degradation, and death (which may be seen as all the same through the biomedical lens). Ethics and social investigations raise questions about the meaning of such power, disparities it exacerbates or potentially addresses, and long-term consequences. Catherine Bliss (2018) cautions that sociogenomics, a discipline which seeks to link genetics and behavior, in many ways fits into the paradigms of positivism and eugenics: generalizing and assuming an essentialism to complex factors mired in forces of inequality and attendant trauma.

See also: Anti-aging, Biomedicalization, Ethics, Gene–Environment, Life course Perspective, Telomeres

Further Reading

Bliss, C. (2018). *Social by nature: The promise and peril of sociogenomics.* Stanford, CA: Stanford University Press.

Brunet, A. & Berger, S. L. (2014). Epigenetics of aging and aging-related disease. *The Journals of Gerontology Series A: Biomedical Sciences and Medical Sciences, 69*(Suppl.1), S17–S20.

Christiansen, L., Lenart, A., Tan, Q., Vaupel, J. W., Aviv, A., McGue, M., &

Christensen, K. (2016). DNA methylation age is associated with mortality in a longitudinal Danish twin study. *Aging Cell, 15*(1), 149–154.

Kahn, A. & Fraga, M. F. (2009). Epigenetics and aging: Status, challenges, and needs for the future. *The Journals of Gerontology Series A: Biomedical Sciences and Medical Sciences, 64*(2), 195–198.

Epistemology

Describes ways of knowing and coming into knowledge. *Episteme* is firsthand knowledge, embodied and lived. It is in direct opposition to doxa, which is belief or faith handed down through indoctrination and mythology. Epistemology is what we understand, what we have experienced. It includes the study of knowledge, but it is rooted in more: the experiential, the intergenerationally transmitted, and the reclaimed ways of knowing.

A feminist perspective on aging and old-age policy requires critical reflexivity and a feminist epistemology (de Beauvoir, 1970; Haraway, 1988; Smith, 1990; Harding, 1986; Collins, 2000). Scholars engaged in the gerontological imagination and production of knowledge about aging (Estes, 1979, 1991 Estes & Associates, 2001; Estes, Binney, & Culbertson, 1992) are compelled to work outside the frame of "patriarchal thought" (Lerner, 1986, p. 228), which means "accepting . . . our [women's] knowledge as valid," while exhibiting "intellectual courage" in pushing beyond mainstream and masculinist social science and methods. Harding's (1986) clarion call is for feminist standpoint theory and feminist epistemology to "enable one to appropriate and redefine objectivity" (p. 119);. "The perspective from women's everyday activity is scientifically preferable to the perspective available only from the 'ruling' activities of men in the dominant groups" (Harding, 1986, p. 128).

Maggie Kuhn and the Gray Panthers offered a similar scathing critique of gerontologists for objectifying older people through research with little regard for the reality of their lives (Estes & Portacolone, 2009).

Race and ethnicity scholars have taken the lead in demanding attention to the epistemic oppression of being treated/discriminated against as a person of color, as mixed race, as "other," stranger, and as "alien" (Du Bois, 1903/1999; Crenshaw, 1989; Cho et al., 2013). Boaventura de Sousa Santos (2015) coined the term *epistemicide* to describe the colonial destruction of indigenous knowledges and experience.

See also: Ethnicity, Generational and Intergenerational Consciousness, Intersectionality, Racism, Standpoint Theories

Further Reading

Andermahr, S., Lovell, T., & Wolkowitz, C. (2000). "Epistemology." *A glossary of feminist theory*. London: Arnold.

Cho, S., Williams, K., Crenshaw, K.W., & McCall, L. (2013). Toward a field of intersectionality studies: Theory, application, and praxis. *Signs, 38*(4),785–810.

Collins, P. H. (2000). *Black feminist thought* (2nd edition, revised 10th anniversary edition). New York: Routledge.

Collins, P. H. (2009). Foreword: Emerging intersections – Building knowledge and transforming institutions. In B. T. Dill and R. E. Zambrana (Eds.), *Emerging intersections: Race, class and gender in theory, policy and practice* (pp. vii–xvii). New Brunswick, NJ: Rutgers University Press.

Crenshaw, K. W. (1989). Demarginalizing the intersection of race and sex: A black feminist critique of antidiscrimination doctrine, feminist theory and antiracist politics. *University of Chicago Legal Forum, 140*,139–167.

de Beauvoir, S. (1970). *The coming of age.* New York: W. W. Norton.

de Sousa Santos, B. (2015). *Epistemologies of the South: Justice against epistemicide.* New York: Routledge.

Deleuze, G. & Guattari, F. (1990). What is a minor literature? In R. Ferguson, M. Gever, T. T. Minh-ha, & C. West, *Out there: Marginalization and contemporary culture* (pp. 59–62). Cambridge, MA: MIT Press.

Du Bois, W. E. B. (1903/1999). Double-consciousness and the Veil. In C. Lemert (Ed.), *Social theory: The multicultural and classic readings* (pp. 162–168). Boulder, CO: Westview Press.

Estes, C. L. (1979). *The aging enterprise: A critical examination of social policies and services for the aged.* San Francisco, CA: Jossey-Bass.

Estes, C. L. (1991). The Reagan legacy: Privatization, the welfare state and aging in the 1990s. In J. Myles & U. S. Quadagno (Eds.), *States, labor markets and the future of old age policy*, (pp. 49–93). Philadelphia, PA: Temple University Press.

Estes, C. & Portacolone, E. (2009). Maggie Kuhn: Social theorist of radical gerontology. *International Journal of Sociology and Social Policy, 29*(1/2), 15–26.

Estes, C. L. & Associates. (2001). *Social policy & aging: A critical perspective.* Thousand Oaks, CA: Sage.

Estes, C. L., Binney, E. A., & Culbertson, R. A. (1992). The gerontological imagination: Social influences on the development of gerontology, 1945–present. *The International Journal of Aging and Human Development, 35*(1), 49–65.

Haraway, D. J. (1988). Situated knowledges: The science question in feminism as a site of discourse on the privilege of partial perspective. *Feminist Studies, 14*(3), 575–599.

Harding, S. (1986). The science question in feminism. Ithaca, NY: Cornell University Press.

Harding, S. (1996). Standpoint epistemology (a feminist version): How social disadvantage creates epistemic advantage. *Social Theory and Sociology: The Classics and Beyond*, 146–160.

Lerner, G. (1986). *The creation of patriarchy.* New York: Oxford University Press.

Minkler, M. & Estes, C. L. (Eds.). (1991). *Critical perspectives on aging.* Amityville, NY: Baywood.

Smith, K. K. (1990). Notes from the epistemological corner: The role of projection in the creation of social knowledge. *The Journal of Applied Behavioral Science, 26*(1), 119–127.

Equality

A cornerstone of theories of justice. Equality reflects the normative principle of egalitarianism. Equality necessitates human development in the fullest sense of that concept, grounded in mutuality and respect. Struggles for racial and gender equality, LGBTQ advocates for anti-oppressive, and anti-discriminatory environments are grounded in the principles of equality and fundamental fairness. Non-discrimination provisions in hiring and "equal work, equal pay" are steps toward equality for women, the disabled, and the aging. The Western philosophy of liberalism has embraced policies to promote equality via shared access to opportunity and resources (Turner, 2006), sometimes in the form of explicit and compensatory affirmative action (albeit contested).

It means being equal as defined under the Constitution.

Two specific policies mandating equality under the Civil Rights Act are:

1. The Fair Housing Act (Title VIII of the Civil Rights Act of 1968), which outlaws discrimination based on race, color, religion, or national origin in the sale or rental of a dwelling.
2. The Equal Employment Opportunity Commission and the Department of Labor which is designated to monitor violations as framed by Title VII of the Civil Rights Act of 1964. This federal law prohibits employers from discriminating against employees on the basis of sex, race, color, national origin, and religion. EEOC interprets and enforces Title VII's prohibition of sex discrimination as forbidding any employment discrimination based on gender identity or sexual orientation. These protections apply regardless of any contrary state or local laws.

"Separate is not equal" was the landmark Supreme Court ruling that racially segregated public schools are unconstitutional (*Brown v. Board of Education*). Upheaval, foot dragging, resistance of public officials, and federal and state police actions ensued along with decades of "bussing," changes to public education taxing and distribution policies, white flight to the suburbs, and charter schools. Conflicts over the Americans for Disabilities Act and the Affordable Care Act are other examples that directly affect older persons. Medicare was designed to provide equality of access and basic services in hospital care and physician services. Major incursions against the principles of universality are loaded into US Medicare, Medicaid, and health and tax "reform."

Against ageism The Age Discrimination in Employment Act is to protect work opportunity and fairness in treatment regardless of age; and The Older Workers Benefit Protection Act of 1990 (OWBPA).

A Critical Perspective

Equality is philosophically in tension with systems that thrive on inequality and "creative destruction" as markets do. The status quo of capitalism is competition and private wealth accumulation as the end goal. Countless court cases challenge the right to equality as legislated and implemented, based on differing interpretations of the US Constitution (e.g., Freedom of Religion and Free Speech). Extensive legal actions, appeals, and stays in court opinions may delay or impede key equality provisions of the law, or the opposite: to impose conditions granting selected equality provisions, while striking down others. Three hotly contested Supreme Court rulings that stack the deck against equality, fairness, and "one person one vote" promised by the US Constitution are: (1) "Citizens United" that equates money with free speech; (2) the elimination of Voting Rights Act provisions that required Department of Justice pre-approval of voter registration changes in states previously convicted of voter suppression; and (3) the "Hobby Lobby" case allowing a particular class of corporate owners and (later) religious entities to deny women reproductive health insurance coverage as required by the ACA (in violation of the separation of Church and State as well as women's equal right to health care that is guaranteed to men).

The unmet promise of equality (2018) revisits the shocking inequality in which half of the American poor are in extreme poverty, meaning that they have half of the income of those barely surviving at the poverty level. This report chronicles the "backsliding" in progress on each of the five indicators of inequality identified by the forerunner 1960 Kerner Commission: (1) the economic playing field; (2) jobs; (3) education; (4) housing; and (5) the justice system.

See also: Ageism, Contradiction, Cumulative Advantage/Disadvantage, Human Rights, Inequality, Justice, Poverty

Further Reading

Harris, F. & Curtis, A. (2018). The unmet promise of equality. Opinion/OpEd. *The New York Times*, February 28.

Turner, B. S. (2006). Equality. In B. S. Turner (Ed.), *The Cambridge dictionary of sociology* (pp. 171–173). New York: Cambridge University Press.

Equity

Describes the distribution of resources between parties and the fundamental fairness or unfairness of that relationship. It is distinct from equality, which focuses primarily on consistent across-the-board treatment to all, in that equity recognizes disparities and concerns itself more with the necessary redistribution of providing more to those who have less.

Health equity refers specifically to differences of health and health care across groups and the examination of the causes of disparate treatment and outcomes. Gender, race, social class, occupational status, and sociogeographic location each contribute to inequitable health among different social groups. A high level of societal inequality is correlated with poorer national health (Peter, 2001; Nelson, Smedley, & Stith, 2002; Wilkinson, 1996).

The relationship of benefits and contributions between generations and questions of generational equity are ideologically politicized. Attias-Donfut and Arber, in *The myth of generational conflict*, write, "The problem of equity between the generations is part of a more general problem of social inequality within society" (Attias-Donfut & Arber, 2000, p. 7). They describe three components of *intergenerational* equity:

- The allocations of social spending at any given moment between younger and older people. . . .
- The just treatment of successive cohorts – that is ensuring that the rights of future generations to levels of retirement pensions are equivalent to those of today's older generation. . . .
- The right of just returns, applicable to the same cohort, for the efforts they have made during their lifetime.

(Attias-Donfut & Arber, 2000, pp. 6–7)

Example

The issue of equity arises when considering what is fair in terms of payments into and returns that may be realized from Social Security. The deficit rant of fiscal conservatives is compatible with the argument advanced by the opponents of Social Security who claim that elders are getting *more* than their fair generational share of benefits from the program (Williamson, Watts-Roy, & Kingson, 1999). This argument gives no attention to the regressive tax rate paid into Social Security (inequity in percent with a higher tax rate paid by low earners versus high earners due to the US tax cap on wage income). Social insurance/Social Security opponents (privatizers) discount the need for income adequacy during old age and disability for beneficiaries to sustain a habitable living standard. Fully 20 percent of all retirees, 40 percent of retired African Americans, 41 percent of retired Hispanics, and 28 percent of Pacific islanders rely on Social Security for all of their income (Apfel & Graetz, 2005).

See also: Intergenerational Contract, Social Insurance, Social Security

Further Reading

Apfel, K. S. & Graetz, M. J. (Eds.). (2005). *Uncharted waters: Paying benefits from individual accounts in federal retirement policy*. Washington, DC: Brookings Institution and National Academy of Social Insurance.

Attias-Donfut, C. & Arber, S. (2000). Equity and solidarity across the generations. In S. Arber & C. Attias-Donfut (Eds.), *The myth of generational conflict: The family and state in ageing societies* (pp. 1–21). London: Routledge.

Nelson, A. R., Smedley, B. D., & Stith, A. Y. (2002). *Unequal treatment: Confronting racial and ethnic disparities in healthcare*. Washington, DC: National Academy Press.

Peter, F. (2001). Health equity and social justice. *Journal of Applied Philosophy*, *18*(2), 159–170.

Wilkinson, R. G. (1996). *Unhealthy societies*. London: Routledge.

Williamson, J., Watts-Roy, D. M., & Kingson, E. R. (1999). *The generational equity debate*. New York: Columbia University Press.

Essentialism

The tendency to reduce a complex reality to a simple formulation that takes on the form of a normative expectation. This occurs in limiting identities or social problems to categorically narrowly or rigidly defined classifications and boundaries. Essentialism is critiqued for its use in promoting functionalist perspectives that define health in opposition to disability, as well as framing aging as either a weakening or a strengthening. Proclaiming essential qualities or conditions fails to recognize, examine, or understand the nuance and diversity, inevitably reifying the social phenomena and the social order.

See also: Functionalism, Myth, Positivism, Postmodernism

Ethics

A discipline of discernment, the always contested code of right and wrong, focuses on how the use of power and influence hurts or helps others.

The field of ethics keeps evolving along with innovation and emergent problems of society; spanning decisions about human cloning to the (re)distribution of resources. However, the majority of ethics discussions focus on the elite power brokers, which neglects the ethics of the proletariat (working class), whistleblowing, and the power in labor organizing.

In critical gerontology dimensions of ethics include: adequate and comprehensive coverage provided by the social safety net; right-to-die legislation; fair labor practices, and equal pay (equality). Contentious problems in ethics surround the (de)valuing and discriminatory practices and institutional barriers against those marginalized by race, ethnicity, gender, (dis)ability, social class, age, children, immigrant status, and indigenous peoples.

See also: Bioethics, Justice, Necropolitics, Right to Have Rights

Further Reading

Holstein, M. B., Parks, J., & Waymack, M. (2010). *Ethics, aging, and society: The critical turn*. New York: Springer.

Wilber, C. K. (2004). Teaching economics as if ethics mattered. In E. Fullbrook (Ed.), *A guide to what's wrong with economics* (pp. 147–157). London: Anthem Press.

Ethnicity

Part of an identity potentially rooted in culture, language, and genetic similarity exhibited from a geographic region, tribe, and/or nationality.

Like any experience of identity, it is more complicated than any uniform definition or approach. Ethnicity is socially constructed, with no firm biological basis. It may be understood as belonging to a group, primarily by birth, and constructed through the sharing of traditions and affiliation. There is often a sameness in appearance with physical norms, fashions and style of dress, frequently traditions of food, and rituals of celebration and mourning. Nationality does not explicitly define ethnicity but can speak to ethnicity in the context of migration in location and time.

The concept differs from popular concepts of race, especially in the USA where the binaries of white and black collapse understandings of differences, cultures, heritages, and ancestral roots. Defining ethnicity is highly contentious, as the differences located and proclaimed have often been central in genocides and conflict. Marginalized ethnic groups face many pressures to conform or hide their difference through processes of assimilation.

Postmodernity and recently, ethnicity is complicated by (1) world wars, (2) mass migrations, (3) the global market, (4) the war on terror, and (5) shifting and uncertain world politics accentuated by Trump, the EU, the Middle East, Russia, and elsewhere.

There is an exportation of cultural values of xenophilic participation in culture and ethnicity, where standards of beauty, style, dress, speech, manner, and tradition find themselves taken up by "outsiders." This may be understood as blepharoplasty (double-eyelid surgery) in Asia in response to Hollywood ideals of beauty, the commodification of Día de Muertos in California, or the pub crawl on St. Patrick's Day.

Ethnomethodologists and critical gerontologists stress the importance of responding to and reflecting heterogeneity in aging populations, and we can also consider how ethnicity and status are implicated in precariousness and grievability. It is also central to understanding citizenship dynamically, including an awareness of loss and the silencing of identity and conformity as vehicles for participation.

Nicholas' Reflection

I'm adrift in a search for ethnic identity. Assimilation and loss of native tongues have made me as a fourth-ish generation American very confused. Italian and Sicilian mean very different things in terms of dialect, cuisine, and access to resources, but because of my last name, they are often identified and questioned, which obscures maternal Scotch-Irish and German ancestry. None of these were central to my upbringing in suburban Appalachia or my exodus from that place. These dislocations from ethnicities and place, as well as my generic American accent are part of how effectively hegemonic whiteness flattened and collapsed difference in my roots. To clarify: I sense the erasure of my ethnicity as part of my white American identity, and this is part of the settler colonial project – how in 100 years my family could lose connections from across an ocean.

The phenomenon of whiteness as a process of progressive erasure holds implications for "the intergenerational" – an alienation from mother tongues and disconnection from culture, and also the ability to integrate an understanding of community and belonging outside of postcolonial paradigms of competition and dominance. Whiteness is doubly grounded in epistemic violence, as colonial projects have sought to destroy the knowledges of those colonized – this is called "epistimicide."

See also: Colonialisms, Culture, Epistemology

Further Reading

Schaefer, R. T. (2008). *Encyclopedia of race, ethnicity, and society.* Thousand Oaks, CA: Sage.

Ethnogerontology/ Ethnogeriatrics

Includes the research and study of aging populations with awareness of the heterogeneity of factors constructing identity.

Race, sex, gender, sexuality, religion, ethnicity, nationality, and race inform the cultural and historical components of identity which have often struggled for visibility and legitimacy in gerontological theory and practice. Factors concerning social security and mobility (such as income, health, family support) contribute to the marginalization that minority communities often face (Markides & Miranda, 1997). Respecting the nuanced confluences of cultural identity and sociopolitical realities prevents the conflation of the two; avoiding pitfalls of

essentialism in which ethnic, cultural, or racial identity becomes synonymous with deprivation and illness.

In addition, ethnogerontologists like Jacquelyne Johnson Jackson (1988) argue for diversity in the professional field, challenging the predominance of white scholars studying minority populations. Cathy Tashiro (2013) sheds light on mixed-race older Americans, calling attention to a growing transformation in US society.

Ethnogeriatriacs emphasizes the importance of studying the ways in which different ethnic groups face distinct health challenges and threats as they age. The increasing diversity of the aged population in the United States poses many challenges to a field that has traditionally focused most on health and aging for white Americans.

Research Example

One example of ethnogerontological research is Elliott and Di Minno's (2006) article investigating how clinicians failed to understand older Chinese patients' perspective; ignorance and misrecognition of cultural difference at a dementia clinic compromised diagnosis and referral.

See also: Blacklands, Epistemology, Jeopardy, Microaggressions, Racism, Stereotype Threat

Further Reading

Crewe, S. E. (2005). Ethnogerontology. *Journal of Gerontological Social Work, 43*(4), 45–58.

Cruz-Oliver, D. M. & Cummings-Vaughn, L. (2017). *Ethnogeriatrics.* Switzerland: Springer.

Elliott, K. & Di Minno, M. (2006). Unruly grandmothers, ghosts and ancestors: Chinese elders and the importance of culture in dementia evaluations. *Journal of Cross-cultural Gerontology, 21*(3), 157–177.

Jackson, J. J. (1988). Aging black women and public policies. *The Black Scholar*, *19*(3), 31.

Markides, K. S. & Miranda, M. R. (1997). *Minorities, aging and health*. Thousand Oaks, CA: Sage.

Tashiro, C. J. (2013). *Standing on both feet: Voices of older mixed-race Americans*. New York: Routledge.

Event

Describes an occasion or happening, notable as a disruption from the usual. It is not merely an episode but breaks significantly from the succession of the ordinary. It exists as a thing located in time and space to be analyzed. It exposes doxa.

Critical theory locates historical traumas like the Holocaust and social movements (such as those in the 1960s for Civil Rights) as disturbances of established beliefs in what is possible or worthy. Lacan (1997) marked this by the intensity of change and the responses to it. Deleuze (1998) theorizes this as an opportunity to realize truth.

Event history analysis is a highly regarded methodological resource in aging studies used to study the frequency of behaviors or exposure to risk calculated through occurrence. Traumatic events are studied in life course research. The gerontological utilization of event history analysis features primarily on functional deficits and losses: medical events, losses of kin, and decline; however, it may also be used to analyze events across the lifespan, including joblessness, economic events experienced as cohorts, and exposure to violence. Event history analysis can illustrate the welfare state's adequacy or inadequacy in responding to deleterious social events, providing an additional framework for cumulative disadvantage to understand how macro-factors relate to recovery and resiliency (a departure from the ever-growing focus on resilience at the genetic level).

From a critical perspective, in 2017 and 2018 there was a sense of collective trauma in living through Trump's volatile and radical departure from the norms of the US Presidency. For aging policy and the life course, key questions concern whether (and if so, how) the emerging resistances will evolve and take root. Will the movements that emerged, and movements on the Left in general, unite or motivate particular cohorts of individuals and identities (groups and coalitions); will they form the basis of a collective ideology, and what is the future of emerging intellectual movements to take back the welfare state (Edmunds & Turner, 2002) and the Left (Domhoff, 2017)?

See also: Doxa, Memory, Power, The Left, The Social

Further Reading

Deleuze, G. (1998). *Essays critical and clinical* (trans. M. A. Greco & D. W. Smith). New York: Verso.

Domhoff, W. G. (2017). Can corporate power be controlled? Steps toward a constructive liberal–left alliance. Retrieved from www2.ucsc.edu/whorulesamerica/change/liberal_left_alliance.html.

Edmunds, J. & Turner, B. S. (2002). *Generational consciousness, narrative, and politics*. Lanham, MD: Rowman & Littlefield.

Lacan, J. (1997). *Écrits*. London: Routledge.

Tekle, F. B. & Vermunt, J. K. (2012). Event history analysis. In H. Cooper (Ed.), *The APA handbook of research methods in psychology* (Vol. 3, pp. 267–290). Washington, DC: American Psychological Association.

Exploitation

Occurs when an individual (or a system, institution) takes advantage of the labor or resources of another individual, group, or class of persons. Exploitation occurs based on the unequal possession of power and resources in the terms of an exchange (Hahnel, 2006).

"Exploitation defines a structure of interdependent interests in which advancing the interests of exploiters depends on their capacity to impose deprivations on the exploited" (Wright, 2001, p. 25). There is a "stronger antagonism of interests than simple competition," and it is a source of conflict among superordinates and subordinates in the labor market and individual enterprises. "Exploitation and domination identify ways in which these relations are oppressive and create harms, not simply inequalities" (Wright, 2001, p. 27).

Because of ageist beliefs regarding older people's low use value (in retirement or as dependent), it may be difficult for many to conceive of exploitation occurring outside the realms of elder abuse. However, if we hold a critical lens to the ways in which the medical industrial complex profits from disease models of aging or we consider predatory lending practices (as seen especially in those marketed toward older widowed women of color; *see* Housing), we may locate levels of exploitation threatening older adults.

See also: Capitalism, Class, Domination, Housing, Immiseration, Microaggression, Oppression, Power, White Supremacy

Further Reading

Hahnel, R. (2006). Exploitation. *Review of Radical Political Economics*, *38*(2), 175–192. Retrieved from www.econis.eu/PPNSET?PPN=514688521.

Wright, E. O. (2001). Foundations of class analysis: A Marxist perspective. In M. Western & J. Baxter (Eds.), *Reconfigurations of class and gender* (pp. 14–27). Stanford, CA: Stanford University Press.

F

Family

A social unit of related people which exists in several dimensions and structures. This may include shared household, heredity, and kinship ties. Definitions and ideology of what constitutes family change cross-culturally and over time.

In the USA and Western industrialized nations, the prevailing model for decades touted as the ideal was the "nuclear family." It was said to consist of two parents (married male and female) and two children (ideally boy and girl). Heterosexist gender roles divide labor into father: earner; mother: nurturer; and children: learners/future workers. Social insurance policies conform to these standards and center around one member of the married couple household being the primary earner or "breadwinner." This formulation of the family is largely a normative and mainstream white portrayal that favors the reproduction of stratified divisions of labor and worth in relation to socially sanctioned roles and the economics and policies related to them. Race, ethnicity, gender, class, (dis)ability, and age relations and discriminations are undisturbed.

In its present form, extended family includes grandparents, cousins, aunts, and uncles. These people may step into "immediate" families to provide care work or financial support. Increasingly, grandparents participate directly in raising children (Wiltz, 2016). Marital status, being a single parent (particularly a single mom), is becoming a much more common family form. It is the dominant form for mothers of color. Fully 62 percent of single black mothers are breadwinners (IWPR, 2016). The negative economic and health consequences are compounded by the decline of safety net and welfare state programs.

In feminist work, the public and private denote spaces into which men and women are allocated roles, responsibilities, and respective freedoms, or lack thereof. White men are privileged in the public spaces with work, voice, and command over the economic and political realms, while white women are assigned the more docile and less visible private spaces of home, family servitude of the father/dad, and social reproduction through childbearing and caregiving. As private space, home and family worlds are off-limits to the intrusion of public policy, guaranteeing undisturbed male power and privilege as "the law" in the household.

This portrayal is the nuclear family primarily of mainstream white America and Western European nations, characteristic of white families. It rendered invisible individuals and families of color, the enslaved and indigenous peoples, for whom family bonding over historical periods was impeded or not permitted.

The nuclear family divisions of labor in public and private roles were venerated as functional for society and the individual, according to lead US sociologists Talcott Parsons and Robert Bales (1956). The functionalist perspective on "family" saw it as a central site of the social reproduction of dominant values and the requisite preservation of the status quo. Feminist scholars from the 1970s to the present have critically appraised this normative ideal model as oppressive and ideologically stacked against women and girls, their human development, and social justice. Race, ethnicity, class, gender, ability, age, sexuality and marital and immigrant status are strongly implicated.

One bright spot is the Supreme Court's ruling in *Obergefell v. Hodges*, that same-sex couples could marry and receive equal protections and benefits under the law. This extended Social Security benefits. As the Social Security Administration's website for same-sex couples reads:

> Your marital status is important for your retirement, survivor, and disability programs because you or your spouse could be entitled to benefits or a higher benefit amount based on the relationship to a worker. Children or stepchildren could also be entitled to benefits. For some surviving spouses, divorced spouses, and adults disabled during childhood, benefits could end if they marry.
> (Social Security Administration, 2017).

See also: Housing, Kinship, Queer, Reproduction, Solidarity

Further Reading

Bengtson, V. L. (2001). Beyond the nuclear family: The increasing importance of multigenerational bonds. *Journal of Marriage and Family*, *63*(1), 1–16.

D'Entreves, M. & Vogel, U. (Eds.). (2000). *Public and private: Legal, political, and philosophical perspectives*. London: Routledge.

Harrington Meyer, M. & Herd, P. (2007). *Market friendly or family friendly?* New York: Russell Sage Foundation.

Institute for Women's Policy Research/ IWPR. (2016). *Breadwinner mothers by race/ethnicity and state Q. 054*. Washington, DC: Institute for Women's Policy Research. Retrieved from https://iwpr.org/wp-content/uploads/wpallimport/files/iwpr-export/ . . . /Q054.pdf.

Landes, J. (Ed.). (1998). *Feminism, the public and the private*. Oxford: Oxford University Press.

Lehr, V. (1999). *Queer family values*. Philadelphia, PA: Temple University Press.

Maugans, J. E. (1994). *Aging parents, ambivalent baby boomers: A critical approach to gerontology*. Dix Hills, NY: General Hall.

O'Connor, J. S., Orloff, A. S., & Shaver, S. (1999). *States, markets, families: Gender, liberalism and social policy in Australia, Canada, Great Britain and the United States*. New York: Cambridge University Press.

Parsons, T. & Bales, R. (1956). *Family socialization and interaction*. London: Routledge.

Social Security Administration. (2017). Same-sex couples. Retrieved from www.ssa.gov/people/same-sexcouples/.

Treas, J., Scott, J., & Richards, M. (Eds.). (2014). *The Wiley-Blackwell companion to sociology of families*. Oxford: John Wiley & Sons.

Wiltz, T. (2016). *Why more grandparents are raising children*. Philadelphia, PA: The Pew Charitable Trusts: Stateline.

Fascism

Describes an authoritarian system of governance characterized by complete State control of society in alliance with the private interests of elites in control of the State. Dissenters and critical voices are silenced, nationalism becomes elevated as a social value, and external and internal threats are identified to serve as scapegoats.

While Nazi Germany serves as the primary exemplar of fascism, some scholars point to fascistic tendencies and trends in many countries which proudly claim their democratic principles. These trends include police surveillance, and restriction of political expression. In the USA these include McCarthyism and the resultant House Un-American Activities Committee that framed and branded individuals and groups as un-American.

In 1980, Bertram Gross identified the collusion of big business and government working in tandem to dictate social policy in his book *Friendly fascism*. Economic dominance and coercion extend control of the fascist state by defunding/de-fanging resistance groups. If the watch bitches don't have teeth, they're much less threatening. Marxist frameworks locate capitalism and financial systems as driving forces of fascist control that are integral to destabilizing labor conditions and producing social precarity. Marxists observe the conditions that arise and may foster fascist organizing and crush nascent working-class movements. Certain conditions that arise and foster fascism are:

1. high levels of precarity;
2. the destruction of a working-class movement;
3. the social feeling surrounding debt crisis and the need for brutal measures.

Further characteristics include highly concentrated power, high levels of patriarchal pride and machismo, a flexing and fetishization of power, and xenophobic framings of outsiders as threats. Historically, fascist governments (e.g., Hitler's and Mussolini's) exhibited no compunction in destroying those with disability, queerness, and/or any qualities seen as not supporting the State (and its values).

In 2015 Dylon Matthews (for Vox News) asked fascist experts whether Donald Trump

is a fascist. The general drift is that more accurate terms include bigot, racist, islamophobe, exenophobe, "a threat to crucial values of equality and fair treatment, and a threat to the actual human beings he's targeting and demonizing" (Matthews, 2015). Vox's experts on the topic of fascism say that, technically, fascism requires that there be overt support for the revolutionary overthrow of the State's entire system of government (i.e., the rejection of the democratic process itself). Trump may be said to be "tinged with", "tampering with," or "flirting with" fascism, but they argue that he does not qualify as fascist because he does not favor overthrowing the existing constitution. Kevin Passmore, author of *Fascism: A very short introduction*, says: "For me, the point about Trump proposals is not whether or not they are 'fascist,' but whether or not they are moral."

Critical gerontology can imagine and investigate the heterogeneous experiences of aging populations as they struggle for survival under such conditions. Older bodies without use value for serving a militaristic state "tinged with" fascist tendencies may very well be discarded.

See also: Authoritarianism, Crisis, Debt, Domination, Oppression, Power, Precarity, Reactive Networks, Voicelessness, Watch Dogs/Watch Bitches, Xenophobia

Further Reading

Gross, B. M. (1980). *Friendly fascism* (2nd edition). New York: Evans.

Matthews, D. (2015). I asked 5 fascism experts whether Donald Trump is a fascist. Here's what they said. Retrieved from www.vox.com/policy-and-politics/2015/12/10/9886152/donald-trump-fascism.

Passmore, K. (2014). *Fascism: A very short introduction* (2nd edition). New York: Oxford University Press.

Feminism/Feminist

A political stance and standpoint grounded in the belief that gender should not dictate opportunity or worth. Modern feminism includes awareness of intersectionality, and an understanding that gender is located alongside and informed by other identities. Feminism is rooted in recognition and naming of male/patriarchal domination and critical examination of how that supremacy is articulated and institutionalized. Feminism entails a conscious stand against misogyny.

The experiences and situation of women are socially constructed, shaped by divisions of labor and power between men and women, the institutional configurations of family, labor market, and the State; and the normative proscriptions embodied and enacted through social roles and normalized obligations, and public policy. The constraining force of gender regimes (maintaining and reproducing status – dominant ideology, doxa, patriarchy) reside on micro, meso, and macro levels and are supported through multiple arenas of capital and the State and, differentially, across women's and men's lifespan. Cynthia Epstein (2007, p. 1) writes:

> Categorization based on sex is the most basic social divide. It is the organizational basis of most major institutions, including the division of labor in the home, the workforce, politics and religion. Globally, women's gendered roles are regarded as subordinate to men's. The gender divide enforces women's roles in reproduction and support activities and limits their autonomy. It limits their participation in decision making and highly rewarded roles, and it puts women at risk. Social, Cultural, and psychological mechanisms support the process.

This social divide is shown to produce patterned cumulative disadvantages in aging for women, particularly women of color and unmarried women. Feminist political economy of aging perspectives focuses on ideologies of gender, the gendered state, the reproduction of patriarchal power, and inequality by race, ethnicity, class, ability, and immigrant and indigenous peoples (Estes, Biggs, & Phillipson, 2003; Estes, 2018).

Wendy Brown (1995) argues that *State masculinism* asserts ownership of women as property and active or inactive participants in wealth accumulation (property rights and unpaid care are constellated here as they support the paid, presumptively male breadwinner). Caregiving and women's bodies are constructed as *natural* and *pre-political*. Bureaucratic control of women's servitude occurs mainly through processes of stigmatized means-testing (e.g., TANF, SSI, and food stamps), while women are penalized for their caregiving work in reproducing future generations to carry society forward. The deep roots and controlling power of the masculinist hold on social policy are illuminated through women's struggle for power (Beard, 2017) in the historical beginnings of Greek and Roman philosophers.

See also: Caregiving, Cognitive Liberation, Cumulative Advantage/Disadvantage, Domination, Doxa, Empowerment, Epistemology, Family, Gender, Intersectionality, Political Economy, Power, Praxis, Resistance, Sexuality, Voicelessness, War on Women, Zero Years, Zones

Further Reading

Beard, M. (2017). *Women & power: A manifesto*. New York: Liveright.

Brown, W. (1995). *States of injury*. Princeton, NJ: Princeton University Press.

Calasanti, T. (2009). Theorizing feminist gerontology, sexuality, and beyond: An intersectional approach. In V. L. Bengtson, D. Gans, N. M. Putney, & M. Silverstein

(Eds.), *Handbook of theories of aging* (pp. 471–486). New York: Springer.

Epstein, C. F. (2007). Great divides: The cultural, cognitive, and social bases of the global subordination of women. *American Sociological Review, 72*(1), 1–22.

Estes, C. L. (2018). Women's lives, women's status, women's resistance. *Generations: Journal of the American Society on Aging, 41*(4), 36–44.

Estes, C. L., Biggs, S., & Phillipson, C. (2003). Feminist perspectives in old age policy in social theory. In *Social theory, social policy and ageing* (pp. 44–62). Maidenhead, UK: Open University Press.

Gamble, S. (2000). *The Routledge critical dictionary of feminism and postfeminism.* New York: Routledge.

Hodgson-Wright, S. (2000). Early feminism. In S. Gamble (Ed.), *The Routledge critical dictionary of feminism and postfeminism* (pp. 3–15). New York: Routledge.

Joyce, K. & Mamo, L. (2006). Graying the cyborg: New directions in feminist analyses of aging, science and technology. In T. M. Calasanti & K. F. Slevin (Eds.), *Age matters: Realigning feminist thinking* (pp. 99–122). New York: Routledge.

O'Rand, A. M. (2016). Long, broad, & deep: Theoretical approaches in aging and inequality. In V. L. Bengtson & R. Settersten Jr. (Eds.), *Handbook of theories of aging* (3rd edition) (pp. 365–380). New York: Springer.

Financialization

Describes the process by which finance has come to mediate and permeate all sectors of the economy. Increasingly complex financial instruments and expanding debt have allowed finance to invade and profit from virtually every economic interaction.

The financial sector has, over the past several decades, undergone a massive expansion. This is not inherently bad, as finance provides a core set of services and functions that are important for the functioning of the economy. However, as the sector has grown these core activities have come to represent a much smaller portion of the total industry. Financial institutions have increasingly focused on markets and instruments that serve little role in generating or facilitating economic activity. Profits derive from transactions rather than from adding real value or growth. Financialization gives creditors, investment banks, and investors profits from lending. Money (and wealth) is accumulated from making money from money. It is not made from producing things or rendering services.

Hedging, the distribution of risk through diversity of assets, has become the norm, and an excuse to pursue ever more exotic products and markets that are new territories for neoliberalist and colonial extension in the name of globalization. The massive expansion of debt has allowed for many aspects of everyday life to be financialized, including car loans, mortgages, and other household debts which are all bundled and sold in complex financial instruments. Manipulations by these debt service industries were responsible for the housing bubble and the 2008 financial crisis and recession. Before and just after the crash in 2008 and 2009, average Americans lost $15 trillion in homes and assets. This followed decades of the large-scale destruction of financial regulation. The result is a world in which large banks and investment firms are able to exercise more power than ever before.

Financialization fundamentally advantages the corporations and billionaires who carve out access to ever newer market niches and products, especially when they are able to avoid rent-seeking traps used by large financial institutions. These processes have also been damaging for developing countries and markets where speculators, mostly American and European, are able to wield disproportionate power and influence over products and markets in pursuit of profits. The "products" of capital are converted into the chains of securitization of debt and the servicing of loans consumes an ever larger share of resources that could be used to promote jobs and other public goods. The Tax Cut and Jobs Act of 2017 rewards these corporate and billionaire market expansions with huge tax cuts for those at the very top and almost nothing for the bottom two-fifths of the US population.

See also: Commodification, Globalization

Food (in)Security

Describes access or lack of access to affordable, quality food. Food insecurity, along with housing, is arguably the most immediate and important problem facing the millions of Americans living in poverty, including the elderly (Lee & Frongillo Jr., 2001).

Approximately 17 percent of elders report experiencing some degree of food insecurity (Strickhouser, Wright, & Donley, 2014). Limited access to food can often be caused or compounded by limited mobility and financial resources and public resources such as food banks, delivery groups like meals on wheels, and community organizations (Arno et al., 2015). These can be particularly scarce in what have been described as "food deserts" for rural residents and within low-income areas of cities with few grocery stores.

The Primary Government program dealing with Food Insecurity is the Supplemental Nutrition Assistance Program (SNAP). SNAP provides purchasing assistance to low-income Americans through food stamps. The program serves over 42 million Americans and is a perennial target for conservatives who believe the program produces dependence and dissuades work, despite the fact that a near-majority of food stamp recipients are employed unless they are children, disabled, or elderly.

Hunger programs are embroiled in punitive politics and economics. In an "America First budget" press briefing in March 2017, White House Office of Management and Budget (OMB) Director Mick Mulvaney told the White House press corps that Donald Trump's budget cuts for meals on wheels and after-school nutrition programs was justified because those programs "aren't showing any results." Regarding meals for seniors, Mulvaney states:

Meals on wheels sounds great. That's a state decision to fund that particular portion, to take the federal money and give it to the state and say, look, we want to give you money for programs that don't work. We can't do that anymore. We can't spend money on programs just because they sound good. Meals on wheels sounds great – again, that's a state decision to fund that particular portion to. But to take the Federal money and to give it to the states and say, look, we want to give you money for programs that don't work – I can't defend that anymore. We're \$20 trillion in debt. We're going to spend money, we're going to spend a lot of money but we're not going to spend it on programs that show they deliver the promises we made to people.

As for school programs, Mulvaney states:

They're supposed to help kids who don't get fed at home get fed so they do better in school. Guess what? There's no demonstrable evidence they're actually doing that. There's no demonstrable evidence they're actually helping results, that they're helping kids do better in school, which is what – when we took your money from you to say, look, we're going to spend them on after-school programs, the way we justified it was, these programs are going to help these kids do better in school and get better jobs, and we can't prove that that's happening.

When a reporter asks if the White House budget is "hard-hearted," Mulvaney responds, "I don't think so. In fact, I think it is one of the most compassionate things we can do." His justification for the draconian cuts is to consider the needs of both taxpayers and recipients of these funds while ignoring the empirical evidence that supports the efficacy and need for these food programs. Mulvaney says:

> You're only focusing half of the equation. Right? You're focusing on recipients of the money. We're trying to focus on both the recipients and the folks who give us the money in the first place. And, I think it's fairly compassionate to go to them and say, look, we're not going to ask you for your hard-earned money anymore. A single mom of two in Detroit, give us your money. We're not going to do that anymore unless we can guarantee to you that that money is actually being used in a proper function, and I think that is about as compassionate as you can get.
>
> (Daily Kos, March 16, 2017, https://youtube/Z_Ej8g3eF0k)

As Niehaus and Faye (2018) state, "hunger politics have always been as much about the welfare of agribusiness as about the welfare of the poor." Additional degradation of the poor has been proposed for SNAP via the Farm Bill Reauthorization. OMB's Mulvaney and Trump's Agriculture Secretary suggest replacing the "cash on a card" that recipients use, instead giving SNAP recipients "America's Harvest Box," a food box of canned and shelf stable foods. Mulvaney says it will save $130 billion in ten years – getting them half-way toward the 30 percent proposed cut in the SNAP program ($213 billion) over the next decade. The distribution of America's Harvest Box would rely heavily on states and grocery stores, and remove food stamp recipients' ability to buy their own provisions, undermining their choice to make the best decisions for their families.

An additional proposal is a mandatory work requirement for food stamps. As noted above, many SNAP units are already the working poor. Based on TANF welfare reform outcomes, the new SNAP requirements are likely to drive away many families, especially single mothers and children who desperately need the nutrition assistance. Stanford University scientists report that "welfare reform encouraged employment, by drastically reducing cash assistance [and] it also pushed many children into extreme poverty," that is, living on less than $2.00 per day (Shaefer & Edin, 2018, p. 25). In 2012 they report that almost two-thirds of a million (704,000) children in SNAP assistance units (often those living with a single mother) were in extreme poverty. Shaefer and Edin also report that "1.3 million SNAP households with children reporting no source of cash income, quadrupled between 1995 and 2014." As with all means-tested programs, compliance with SNAP eligibility is monitored and costly to administer. Income verification is required every 3 to 12 months, depending on the State. SNAP fraud earns fines of up to $250,000 and prison up to 20 years, or both.

On the corporate end, many large corporations are significant beneficiaries of the SNAP program. For example, Walmart and McDonald's pay extremely low wages to their employees, so low that many are eligible for food stamps. SNAP food stamps effectively subsidize low wages and corporate profits. Food and beverage companies that dominate supermarkets also benefit from the program which directly subsidizes the purchase of their products. The administration of the electronic accounts used for food stamps is also a cash cow for corporations who receive private contracts to handle those accounts and transactions.

Another factor of food insecurity is the rise of monopoly power in the agriculture sector, which has implications for all who eat food, but it keenly affects those in rural areas and family farmers. Multinational corporations have monopolized the entire agricultural sector, from seeds to livestock, produce to dairy, genetics to chemicals, and everything in between. This inhibits the ability for independent farmers to select from multiple buyers or plant and grow what they want, which is a major driver of success. Moreover, individual farmers who are "suppliers" or "growers" under contract with large corporations are not only placed in competition with one another for scant wages, but the practice of factory-style production is harmful to the environment by putting community water supplies and waste management systems at risk, and is costly to communities by driving down local property values and destroying the tax base.

See also: Human Rights, Social Determinants of Health

Further Reading

Arno, P., Knapp, K., Russo, S., & Viola, D. (2015). Rising food insecurity and conservative policy in the US: Impact on the elderly. *World Journal of Social Science Research*, ISSN 2375–9747 (Print) ISSN 2332–5534 (Online), Vol. 2, No. 1, 2015. www.scholink.org/ojs/index.php/wjssr.

Food Research & Action Center. (2018). Working to end hunger in America. Retrieved from http://frac.org.

Lee, J. S. & Frongillo Jr., E. A. (2001). Nutritional and health consequences are associated with food insecurity among U.S. elderly persons. *Journal of Nutrition, 131,* 1503–1509.

Loundsbury, J. (2017). Scott Walker releases virulently racist food stamp ad that doubles-down on "going Trump." Blog stream reblogged by Badger State Progressive, December 27.

Niehaus, P. & Faye, M. (2018). Trump's food stamp idea is like Blue Apron had a Socialist hangover: The administration's "Harvest Box" proposal is more about the welfare of agribusiness than the poor. Politico. February 18. Retrieved from www.politico.com/magazine/story/2018/02/15/trump-food-stamps-harvest-box-blue-apron-snap-217004.

Shaefer, H. L. & Edin, K. (2018). Welfare reform and the families it left behind. In *The Next Round of Welfare Reform, Pathways* (Winter). Stanford, CA: Stanford University.

Strickhouser, S., Wright, J. D., & Donley, A. M. (2014). *Food insecurity among older adults.* Washington, DC: AARP Foundation.

Wallace, S. P., Cricel Molina, L., & Jhawar, M. (2007). *Falls, disability and food insecurity present challenges to healthy aging.* Los Angeles, CA: UCLA Center for Health Policy Research, May (Policy Brief).

Framing

George Lakoff utilizes the cognitive sciences and "the study of conceptual systems" to understand frames as "mental structures that allow human beings to understand reality – and sometimes . . . what we take to be reality" (Lakoff, 2006b, p. 25). Both of these points have been well articulated and now have the status of a truism within constructionist theory. Lakoff works on "modes of reasoning," identifying two facets of "moral and political models for reasoning about politics – conservative and liberal" (Lakoff, 1996, p. 15). Politicians seek to create "coherent political ideologies" (e.g., "strict conservative" and "strict liberal") designed to produce the situation where voters "become coherent in their views" (p. 15).

Coherency occurs when *political and moral reasoning* are linked. There are Deep Frames (moral values and principles), Surface Frames, Issue Defining Frames (used to characterize a problem, assign blame, constrain possible solutions), and Messaging Frames (Lakoff, 2006a).

Conservatives speak to their base. When progressives move to the Right, they activate and reinforce conservative values and positions. Nunberg, in *Talking right* (2006), signals that language is moving to the Right. Within three to four months, the use of Social Security privatization terms in media shifted from talking about "private accounts" to talking about "personal accounts." Simply negating the other side's frames only reinforces them.

In short, constructions of reality and frames are all about power relations and the way into the American psyche without physical bloodshed. There are two faces of power: the power expressed and the power repressed. The power to frame and the suppression of the power to frame – the most oppressed, no matter what or how they express their needs are left out of systems which produce the discursive frames. Framing *is* action (framing itself), framing *is* ideology, and as Lakoff notes, "Reframing *is* social change" (Lakoff, 2004/2014).

Identifying framing can elucidate the contradictions in how two things can be similarly worded yet framed differently. Social insurance programs are framed as in danger of bankruptcy, while multinational corporations can claim financial relief. The privatization movement has become entrenched through political struggles over the morality and affordability of social insurance and the value of collectively pooled risk versus individual responsibility. The institutionalization of a social movement encompasses both its process of formation and evolution as well as its outcomes, including the inculcation and adherence over time to value systems that become relatively stable and that both proscribe and constrain certain activities or behavior, such as the conceptualization and implementation of certain policy approaches (Jary & Jary, 2000, pp. 306–307). The privatization movement is so well entrenched that it has been defined as institutionalized (Svihula & Estes, 2009).

Framing (and examination of the power relations that accord the power of the frame) is the messaging key to intentional political strategy, especially where messages may be continuously repeated through digital channels – even by bots (robotocized non-human cyber techniques).

See also: Cognitive Liberation, Crisis, Debt, Digital Sphere, Functionalism, Insolvency, Labeling, Rhetoric, There Is No Alternative (TINA)

Further Reading

Butler, J. (2016). *Frames of war: When is life grievable?* New York: Verso.

Jary, D. & Jary, J. (2000). *Collins web-linked dictionary of sociology.* New York: Harper-Collins. (Originally published 1991.)

Lakoff, G. (1996). *Moral politics.* Chicago, IL: University of Chicago Press.

Lakoff, G. (2004/2014). *Don't think of an elephant.* (1st and 2nd editions). White River Junction, VT: Chelsea Green Publishing.

Lakoff, G. (2006a). *Simple framing: An introduction to framing and its uses in politics.* Berkeley, CA: Rockridge Institute.

Lakoff, G. (2006b). *Thinking points: Communicating our American values and vision.* New York: Farrar, Straus, & Giroux.

Nunberg, G. (2006). *Talking right.* New York: Public Affairs.

Svihula, J. & Estes, C. L. (2009). Social security privatization: The institutionalization of an ideological movement. In L. Rogne, C. L. Estes, B. R. Grossman, B. A. Hollister, & E. Solway (Eds.), *Social insurance and social justice: Social Security, Medicare and the campaign against entitlements* (pp. 217–231). New York: Springer.

Sweetland, J., Volmert, A., & O'Neil, M. (2017). *Finding the frame: An empirical approach to reframing aging and ageism.* Washington, DC: Frameworks Institute.

Freedom

The USA prides itself on being the land of the free. The Statue of Liberty symbolizes the embrace of immigrants among the huddled masses. FDR named four freedoms, among them Freedom from Fear, and Freedom from Want. The Freedom Caucus of the GOP Congress (rising since 1994), in a pique of anger, renamed "French Fries" Freedom Fries in the US House Dining Room. The US's cultural and sectarian worship of individualism enrobes itself in the idea of freedom. The National Rifle Association asserts the right of virtually all categories of Americans to be free to own guns everywhere under the hallowed veil of the Second Amendment of the US Constitution.

Lakoff (2006) dissects the battle of ideas over freedom and the radical Right's capture of the concept and reminds us that the progressive meaning of freedom in public discourse and US social policy is in serious danger of being discarded. The two different views of freedom arise from "different moral and political worldviews dividing the country."

Freedom is frequently heralded as the key principle underpinning conservative health, retirement, and tax policies. Regarding the Affordable Care Act, the freedom principle appears, not to ensure coverage but rather the freedom to purchase private insurance coverage. Without appropriate subsidies and assistance for the poor and middle class, the freedom to purchase private insurance for health care is effectively nonexistent. The same may be said for retirement insurance coverage through individually purchased commercial products.

Among the vital freedom issues that Lakoff (2014, pp. 59–73) identifies are health care, education, poverty, discrimination (race, ethnicity, gender, sexual orientation), unions and pensions, and immigration. For each there are two metaphors, one liberal and one conservative. At issue are empathy, justice, and moral values.

Pure liberty and freedom go hand in hand with bitterness. The capitalist system of the United States values individualism and yet to be truly free as an individual necessarily incurs a degree of isolation and precarity that few people could ever willingly survive. Conservatives in the United States brand themselves as the party of liberty and freedom while not actually meaningfully delivering either to their constituents. Trump-era health care, tax, and welfare reform projected to deliver more freedom to consumer taxpayers in the top 1 to 6 percent, and major corporations, while compounding the hardship and immiseration of middle-class working people and the most vulnerable at the expense of the powerful and wealthy.

A significantly more inclusive freedom is in President Franklin D. Roosevelt's four freedoms speech: Freedom from Want, Freedom of Speech and Expression, Freedom of Religion, and Freedom from Fear. These he said are worth fighting for (Roosevelt, 1941).

See also: Framing, Immiseration

Further Reading

Lakoff, G. (2006). *Whose freedom?* (1st edition). New York: Farrar, Straus, and Giroux.

Lakoff, G. (2014). *Don't think of an elephant* (2nd edition). White River Junction, VT: Chelsea Green Publishing.

Roosevelt, F. D. (1941) *State of the Union Address*. Washington, DC: The US Congress.

Functionalism

Also known as structural functionalism, a social theory which sees society as a complex system (structure) whose elements work together (function) to promote solidarity and stability. As described under the previous concept entry, Conflict and Consensus Theory, Talcott Parsons was the leading US sociologist of functionalism and Consensus Theory (*The structure of social action* (1937) and *The social system* (1951)). His intellectual standing drew significantly from his role in introducing to US scholars the early translated works of Emile Durkheim and Max Weber. Sociologists have extended, refined, and contributed to the development and resurgence of functionalism, including Robert Merton (1968) and Jeffrey Alexander (1988). Neofunctionalism (Alexander, 1988) affirms the centrality of cultural values in explaining how social systems (e.g., the firm) work and persist. The functionalist perspective is flourishing in institutional and behavioral economics, organizational and economic sociology, among other areas.

Functionalist framing of aging study and intervention has defined the aging process in terms of theories of disengagement, success, activity, and health. The classic example of structural functionalism in aging study is disengagement theory. Matilda Riley's Age Stratification Theory is the subsequent influential functionalist theory of aging. It examines the dynamic interplay between two interdependent processes: individual aging and social change (Riley, 1985, p. 371). It concentrates on (1) age as a structural feature of a changing society – as in every society both people and roles are stratified by age; and (2) individuals – as all of us grow up and grow old as members of an age-stratified society comprising individuals and cohorts of individuals, from birth to death (Riley, Johnson, & Foner, 1972). As the first leading social scientist of the National Institute on Aging (NIA), Riley mentored, collaborated, and pushed legions of students, postdocs, and established scholars in the social and behavioral sciences, also promoting NIA's support of cross-sectional and longitudinal datasets that remain foundational big data repositories today. The advance in distinguishing between *age*, *period*, and *cohort* is highly recognized in the field as a central methodological and theoretical contribution in the study of human development and aging. Yet, critics say the functionalist foundation of American gerontology was inattentive to exposing and

questioning inequality and silent in examining intra-cohort variations of injustice.

Another functionalist theory is the environmental gerontology of Powell Lawton (Lawton & Nahemow, 1973; Lawton, 1982, 1985). Lawton recognizes that age-related losses in mobility, vision, or cognitive impairment make an older adult vulnerable to demands in the environment. Environmental gerontology seeks to "exemplify the transactional nature of P–E [person–environment] relationships" (Lawton, 1985, p. 504), where personal factors are "competencies" and environmental factors are the "press." Lawton's theory for how older people react to, use, and shape their environments is a process for regaining *equilibrium* between competence and press. Environmental gerontology attempts to conceptually understand and assess the duality and joint effects of an older person *vis-à-vis* their environment at micro and macro scales. The goal is to optimize function and seek a homeostatic equilibrium between person and environmental fit (Lawton, 1982, 1985).

A larger criticism of structural functionalism has been that the theory assumes that whatever exists (even structures of oppression – a coercive institutional formation) must be requisite if not functional, for the system to maintain equilibrium. Social order, social integration, and social harmony are positive and to be achieved. There is an implicit (if not explicit) assumption of "goodness" attached to whatever is operating in the system (even inequality). Parsons functionalism heralded the positive functions of dominant American values (e.g., white male) as requisite and functional for "the social system." This position drew major criticism from the 1960s Civil Rights and other movements which questioned authority and the structural exclusion of many segments of US society. Under functionalism, the existing arrangements were lauded (as functional), while those who were outsiders excluded were labeled "deviants" and "social problems" to be managed in order to return the system to equilibrium.

Alvin Gouldner (1973) lambasted Parsons, claiming that these definitions gave legitimacy to repressive institutions and practices. Gouldner asked: Is *whatever is "functioning" (and hence normative practice), by definition, legitimate?*

Critical theoretical approaches do not assume the legitimacy of all operating systems and practices, extending this speculation to questioning the plausibility of defining a normative commitment to social justice and harm reduction. Estes, Binney, and Culbertson (1992, pp. 49–50) question the desirability of structural functionalism, noting:

> [T]he ideology of functionalism is rooted in American traditions of individualism, self-reliance, and independence, and posits that cohesion and social harmony are "natural" – in contrast to an alternate view that the status quo is explained by the dominance of some groups and ideas over others; hence, social conflict and struggle are "natural."

Alternative and critical paradigms have considered aging study in nuanced terms of intersectional identities, cumulative and dynamic processes, which exist within power relationships – struggling to articulate themselves within the context of entrenched (and very well-funded) dominant paradigms (Estes, Linkins, & Binney, 2001).

Donald Trump's presidential campaign refrain to "Make America Great Again" could be seen as his urgent call to restore the system, our society, to what it was in the good old days before the full democratic recognition of diversities by race, ethnicity, gender, class, ability, sexualities, and indigenous peoples became regarded as valued national assets.

See also: Anti-aging, Conflict Theory and Consensus Theory, Disengagement, Essentialism, Healthy Aging, Knowledges

Further Reading

Alexander, J. C. (1988). *Action and its environments: Toward a new synthesis.* New York: Columbia University Press.

Cumming, E. & Henry, W. E. (1961). *Growing old: The process of disengagement.* New York: Basic Books.

Estes, C. L., Binney, E. A., & Culbertson, R. A. (1992). The gerontological imagination: Social influences on the development of gerontology, 1945–present. *The International Journal of Aging and Human Development, 35*(1), 49–65.

Estes, C. L., Linkins, K. W., & Binney, E. A. (2001). Critical perspectives on aging. In C. L. Estes & Associates, *Social policy & aging* (pp. 23–44). Thousand Oaks, CA: Sage.

Gouldner, A. (1973). For sociology. *American Journal of Sociology, 78*(5), 1063–1093.

Lawton, M, P. (1982). Competence, environmental press, and the adaptation of older people. In M. P. Lawton, P. G. Windley, & T. O. Byerts (Eds.), *Aging and the environment: Theoretical approaches* (pp. 33–59). New York: Springer.

Lawton, M. P. (1985). The elderly in context: Perspectives from environmental psychology and gerontology. *Environment and Behavior, 17*(4), 501–519.

Lawton, M. P. & Nahemow, L. (1973). Ecology and the aging process. In C. Eisdorfer & L. Nahemow (Eds.), *The psychology of adult development and aging* (pp. 464–488). Washington, DC: American Psychological Association.

Merton, R. K. (1938). Social structure and anomie. *American Sociological Review, 3*(5), 672–682.

Merton, R. K. (1968). *Social theory and social structure.* Glencoe, IL: The Free Press.

Parsons, T. (1951). *The social system.* Glencoe, IL: The Free Press.

Parsons, T. (1975). The sick role and role of the physician reconsidered. *MMFQ Health & Society, 53*(3), 257–278.

Riley, M. W. (1985). Age strata in social systems. In R. H. Binstock and E. Shanas (Eds.), *Handbook of aging & the social sciences* (2nd edition) (pp. 369–411). New York: Van Nostrand Reinhold.

Riley, M. W., Johnson, M., & Foner, A. (1972). *Aging and society, Vol. III. A sociology of age stratification.* New York: Russell Sage Foundation.

Riley, M. W. E., Kahn, R. L. E., Foner, A. E., & Mack, K. A. (1994). *Age and structural lag: Society's failure to provide meaningful opportunities in work, family, and leisure.* New York: John Wiley & Sons.

G

Gender

Gender and sex are separate concepts. Gender and gender identities are socially constructed and, as such, they may change over time and within one person's life course as well as within a collectivity and society's historical time and space. There are dominant and competing definitions of gender, although critical feminist scholars speak of gender (and the sex/gender system) as produced and structured through power and privilege. Sex (male/female) is traditionally defined by biological, physical, and genetic characteristics of individuals, including reproductive organs. Life tables, life expectancy, and the actuarial sciences work from numbers as recorded in official birth and death certificates. The binary (M/F) widely prevails, although a larger discourse on the biological spectrum is now underway (Fausto-Sterling, 2000), which is expanding the sex binary and the conceptualization of gender.

Based on demographics alone, with older women outliving and outnumbering older men around the globe, aging has been defined as a women's and gender issue. A significant qualification is that sex-based longevity differences vary dramatically by social class, race and ethnicity, and other factors. The male–female life expectancy gap is narrowing (and even reversing) in some cases. Human lifespan is tied to individual and societal forces and risks of race,

ethnicity, income, education, and other measures of social advantage/disadvantage.

For all people, young and old, gender is an organizing principle in the economic and power relations of social institutions, of the family, the State, the market economy, and race and ethnicity as well as the experience of old and aging. The structure and distribution of resources and benefits under policy, and analyses of policy effects, flaws, and problems, necessarily draw together data based on sex and have been interpreted as a reflection on the larger social meanings and experiences of gender and sexuality.

Gender affects eligibility for, access to, and the distribution of resources to older men and women across the life course. For racial and ethnic minority women, the life chances and opportunities to be educated, to be in the paid labor force, and to receive health care are profoundly circumscribed by class of origin. For women, their reproductive responsibilities in the birthing and rearing of family and endless caregiving work across generations are pivotal. Public and private sector policies structure much of the possible and impossible. Transgender discrimination from military service and workplace protections has substantial impact on the social security and well-being of individuals and their families.

Connell describes constraining forces that reside in "gender regimes" (Connell, 1987) that are embedded and inscribed in the way in which gender relations are structured. Gender is a way in which social practice is ordered. The social relations of gender are evident in the workings of the capitalist State, the Market, and the family. The US welfare state, including the federal, state, and local institutions that comprise government, are distinctly gendered and raced. The predicament of older women is profoundly shaped by the division of power and labor between men and women, and the diverse normative, cultural, and economic proscriptions that disadvantage women, their children, and families and communities. Public policy and the institutional structures that implement gender shape work–life opportunities differentially for men and women.

Gender ideology is the ideology of familism (oriented to normative values of the family) and separate public and private spheres that are created and re-created through social practices. It is a powerful force bolstering two ideologies: (1) neoliberal ideology, and (2) neoconservative ideology.

During the period from 2016 to 2018, gender politics are intense, vigorous, vitriolic, hate-filled, and divisive. Identity politics spiral upwards during economic hard times and intensified competition under conditions of scarcity. Struggles for gender equality challenge "the most ancient of subordinations, and a subordination rooted in understandings of nature itself. . . . Liberatory reconstructions of gender struck deeply imprinted understandings" (Piven & Cloward, 1997, p. 48) (*see* Gendered State and Aging). The strong election prospects for the most qualified presidential candidate in US history, Hillary Rodham Clinton, whipped up unfathomably dirty and violent gender politics. Race was paramount, with women of color on the vanguard.

Gender work on critical aging policy has focused primarily on issues of sex and gender, formulated within, and against, the frameworks of critical feminisms, embracing race, ethnicity, and intersectionality, with limited policy work on LGBTQ aging; and virtually none on third gender and other intersubjectivities.

See also: Family, Feminism/Feminist, Sexism, Social Contract, War on Women

Further Reading

Connell, R. W. (1987). *Gender & power*. Stanford, CA: Stanford University Press.

Fausto-Sterling, A. (2000). *Sexing the body*. New York: Basic Books.

Fraser, N. (1989). *Unruly practices: Power, discourse, and gender in contemporary social theory*. Minneapolis, MN: University of Minnesota Press.

Gamble, S. (2000). *Critical dictionary of feminism and postfeminism*. New York: Routledge.

Launius, C. & Hassel, H. (2015). *Threshold concepts in women's and gender studies*. London: Routledge.

Piven, F. F. & Cloward, R. A. (1997). *The breaking of the American social compact*. New York: The New Press.

Gender Rating

Gender rating in health insurance, which results in higher premiums for young to middle-aged women and older men, was permitted before passage of the Affordable Care Act/ACA. However, states, like California, adopted legislation banning the practice following at least ten other states. Prior to ACA, Californian women buying individual health insurance policies paid as much as 39 percent more than men for similar coverage because women were determined to be more expensive to keep healthy until at least the age of 55. Later in life, older Californian men paid higher premiums than women. Gender rating was permitted only in the individual health insurance markets, not in employer-based health insurance.

Banning discrimination against pre-existing conditions under the ACA prevented health insurers from charging more for sick people. This form of "risk selection" (i.e., "risk aversion") is forbidden under the ACA. The only exception is that insurers may charge older people more than younger (i.e., *see* "Age Rating").

Under the ACA in 2014, the Supreme Court ruled that businesses have a right to their own religious beliefs by waiving the mandate of the Affordable Care Act that businesses provide contraceptive coverage in their employees' health insurance. This Hobby Lobby decision cracked a back door to denying women's equal access to health care and health insurance (through a re-imposed indirect form of gender rating and other exclusions (e.g., transgender people) from the ACA's protected coverage). The ruling under Trump's deregulations has allowed other discriminatory practices masquerading as religious beliefs. The Republican Congress's and Trump's repeal of parts of the ACA threaten destabilization of the assurance of federal policy prohibitions against health insurers charging women more than men for health care and the effective denial of women's access to reproductive care. Proposed rule changes that would effectively achieve these discriminatory practices without legislation are pending in various courts.

See also: Affordable Care Act (ACA), Age Rating, Inequality, Risk, War on Women

Gene–Environment

The social and biological reality that exerts influence on the expression of genetic material. Gene–environment studies examine the imprint of social and environmental forces on biological function, genetic makeup, DNA expression and modification, and immune function, among other biological and functional deregulation. Douthit and Marquis (2010) locate G–E interaction in "the micro-interaction of everyday experience, and its imprint on biological function at the level of life and death, in part regulated by larger social-structural arrangements imposing trajectories of cumulative advantage or disadvantage" (p. 340).

Nobel Prize winner Elizabeth Blackburn's (and co-Nobelists') discovery of telomeres and telomerase is incorporated into scientific studies of health across the lifespan. Research suggests that telomeres play a central role in aging and disease, including blindness, cancer, and cardiovascular and neurodegenerative diseases. Studies also show the impact of psychological stress and lifestyle factors on telomere length and immune function.

Biological and social models of research and theory are trending (i.e., "hot") in their focus on "biosocial interactions in the construction of late life health status" (Douthit & Marquis, 2010, pp. 329–342). Additional biomarkers and measures, developed largely by social and behavioral scientists, include: "allostatic load," which attends to stressors, assaults, negative life events, and chronic anxiety that provoke high (negative) allostatic load; and "plasticity," a term denoting that some biomarkers of aging are reversible; that disability is not permanent and stable, and that scientists need to think beyond old age as a time of decline.

Research on genetic plasticity seeks to partition independent and interdependent genetic, environmental, social and behavioral, institutional, and structural contributions to morbidity, mortality, and life course healthy aging. Various elements of "The Social" are being identified, partitioned, measured, and quantified – and found to be salient. The "Social" includes early to lifelong exposures to racism, sexism, violence, educational level, economic deprivation, and other elements tied to traumas instantiating cumulative disadvantages.

A critical perspective, consistent with Dannefer and colleagues' caution, is that there are:

> two processes by which social forces organize and regulate the effects of genes. . . . First, the social organization of genetic differences operates through

the social and cultural relevance of genetically endowed physical characteristics such as height or skin color. Second . . . the sociological possibilities . . . [of] increasing recognition in biology that gene expression and the behavior of genes themselves are responsive to the environment in ways that are consequential for individual characteristics, health and development.

(Dannefer et al., 2013)

"Human Social Genomics" examines why and how different social factors and processes (e.g., social stress, conflict, inequality, social threat, attachment) influence human gene expression that may contribute to social gradients in health. "Diverse types of social adversity evoke . . . increased expression of proinflammatory genes and decreased expression of genes involved in innate antiviral responses and antibody synthesis" (Cole, 2014).

In the NIH, medicine, labs of elite universities, venture capital, and biotech corporate circles, the race is on. Power struggles are engaged over control of the definitions, disciplines, resources, and products that attend to different sides of the equation: the social, environmental, behavioral, and structural factors – and the genetic, cell, biology side. Meloni (2016) historicizes this as "the making of the nature/nurture episteme"; it is about What is the "social"? What is the "biological"?

For critical scholarship in gerontology, this is a reappearance of the ideological, political, and economic conflicts over the biomedicalization of aging and the control of vast resources forthcoming (Estes & Binney, 1989). For critical aging policy, one question concerns whether (and what) policies and macro-structural changes, including radical redistribution efforts that research might teach us. On the practice side, supported programs offer/ensure access to protection and modify/minimize adversity exposure

(e.g., those that foster good-quality relationships, integration into the community, developmental and adaptive coping styles) (Hildon et al., 2009).

See also: Allostatic Load, Cumulative Advantage/Disadvantage, Reductionsim, The Social, Stress, Telomeres

Further Reading

Blackburn, E. H., Epel, E. S., & Lin, J. (2015). Human telomere biology: A contributory and interactive factor in aging, disease risks, and protection. *Science*, *350*(6265), 1193–1198.

Bliss, C. (2018). *Social by nature: The promise and peril of sociogenomics*. Stanford, CA: Stanford University Press.

Cole, S. W. (2014). Human social genomics. *PLoS Genetics, 10*(8), e1004601.

Dannefer, D., Douthit, K., Kelley-Moore, K., & Pendleton, N. (2013). *The social organization of genetic effects: Gene–environment interaction, neogenomics and sociological imagination*. Unpublished manuscript.

Darling, K. W., Ackerman, S. L., Hiatt, R. H., Lee, S. S., & Shim J. K. (2016). Enacting the molecular imperative: How gene–environment interaction research links bodies and environments in the postgenomic age. *Social Science and Medicine, 155*, 51–60.

Douthit, K. & Marquis, A. (2010). Biosocial interactions in the construction of late-life health status. In D. Dannefer (Ed.), *The SAGE handbook of social gerontology* (pp. 329–342). Thousand Oaks, CA: Sage.

Estes, C. L. & Binney, E. A. (1989). The biomedicalization of aging: Dangers and dilemmas. *The Gerontologist, 29*(5), 587–596.

Hagestad, G. & Dannefer, D. (2001). Concepts and theories of aging. In R. Binstock (Ed.), *Handbook of aging and the social sciences* (pp. 3–21). New York: Academic Press.

Hildon, Z., Montgomery, S. M., Blane, D., Wiggins, R. D., & Netuveli, G. (2009). Examining resilience of quality of life in the face of health-related and psychosocial adversity at older ages: What is "right" about the way we age? *The Gerontologist, 50*(1), 36–47.

Meloni, M. (2016). From boundary-work to boundary object: How biology left and re-entered the social sciences. *The Sociological Review Monographs, 64*(1), 61–78.

Generation

Defined by its members as "participation in the common destiny of its historical and social unit" (Mannheim, 1997, p. 303). A defining feature of generations is their ability to further or accelerate social change.

The question is whether and how a generation (or generation units) become(s) historical actors and how generations acquire social solidarity via shared experiences and a collective worldview. Emile Durkheim's concept of social solidarity is based on his study of rituals and the enactment of historical myths of the social group in his *Elementary forms of religious life* (1969). There is an "institutionalization of collective memory" (Halbwachs & Coser, 1992). Corsten (1999) argues that "collectively shared assumptions of a common life experience, and of a common time frame, turns into a *social fact* of itself" (p. 253).

Passive and active generations are engines of social stability and integration *and* engines of social change. Active generations exploit opportunities and resources regarding basic political and/or cultural changes (Brian S. Turner). History illuminates the real and potential oscillation between active and passive. There are active consumer generations and passive generations (Edmunds & Turner, 2002, p. 8).

Karl Mannheim's "'problem of generations' essentially a problem of social scarcity in the context of the transmission and allocation of economic, social and cultural resources over time. . . . Generation involves the structuring of resources by social cohorts through time" (Edmunds & Turner, 2002, p. 14). The question is how and when "strategic generations" arise, and with what consequences.

Katz (2017) offers a critical sociological perspective on the two concepts of life course cohort and of generation. He finds:

> conceptual gaps in life course perspective. For instance, the assumption that time based and age based experiences are interchangeable in life-course models of cohort trajectories, transitions, pathways, and strategies, can leave aside the historical conflicts and contingencies of the aging experience (see Dannefer & Kelly-Moore, 2009).
>
> (Katz, 2017, pp. 12–13)

Leonard Cain (2018) questioned the idea of prioritizing cohort over generational phenomena in social gerontology. Consistent with this view, Katz offers a "critical sociological concept of generation" in speaking of "the generational phenomena associated with Gen X [birth cohort 1965–1980] and the forging of its identity through the particular cultural politics of its time" (Katz, 2017, p. 13). Katz's point is to challenge the assumption that cohorts are "group[s] of people born in the same time and place and . . . presumed to have similar aging experiences and life trajectories" (Katz, 2017, p. 12). Andrew Achenbaum (2017) describes the summer of love for baby boomers in which "a rising generation [that] claimed its right to denounce the status quo."

Karl Mannheim's concept of generation as a social field, both within and across generations, is significant for critical gerontology. Resistances of all kinds may be linked to the daily experiences of individual and community trauma that promote precarity for virtually all peoples, particularly by race, ethnicity, class, gender, ability, age, citizenship, and nation-state.

Accius and Yeh (2017) draw attention to the racial generation gap in the USA, which has long-term implications for our nation's future. The racial generation gap is the inverse trend between younger and older age groups. "The Millennial and succeeding generations in America are not only more racially and ethnically diverse than prior generations, they are coming of age in a changed and challenging world" (Accius & Yeh, 2017, p. 101). Since today's society comprises people from distinctively different birth cohorts (e.g., the Silent Generation, Baby Boom Generation, Generation X, the Millennials, and Generation Z), these groups will think differently and have different needs and aspirations because they experience a different set of circumstances that influence their social and economic conditions as they reach old age. Accius and Yeh (2017) call for a greater investment in and a renewed commitment to our social contract because "the destinies of racially and ethnically diverse younger and older generations are intertwined" (p. 201). This includes addressing a variety of concerns seemingly unrelated, but nonetheless pertinent, to aging if current and future Americans are to grow old healthfully and successfully, with equity and dignity. Accius and Yeh (2017) write that acknowledging our increasing diversity and seeking generational unity will help us craft strong policies to meet our goals as a nation.

Whitehouse and Flippin (2017) write about aging and the generational challenges ahead, including those in the baby boom generation (1946–1964), Generation X (1965–1980) and the millennial generation (1981–1996). Calling for a move from "Diversity to Intergenerativity," Whitehouse and Flippin (2017) make an alarming statement that "we are now leaving one geological epoch, the Holocene and entering another, the Anthropocene. . . . The questions of whether our communities, civilizations, and species will survive is a relevant and responsible one to ask" (p. 7).

See also: The Commons, Generational and Intergenerational Consciousness

Further Reading

Accius, J. & Yeh, J. C. (2017). America must invest in its next generations. *Generations: Journal of the American Society on Aging, 40*(4), 101–107.

Achenbaum, W. A., Bern-Klug, M., & Rosowsky, E. (Eds.). (2017). The summer of love, the baby boomers and their arc of aging. *Generations, 41*(2/3), 4–113.

Cain, L. D. (2018). Age related phenomena: The interplay of the ameliorative and the scientific. In R. Settersten (Ed.), *Invitation to the life course: Toward new understandings of later life* (2nd edition) (pp. 295–326). New York: Routledge.

Corsten, M. (1999). The time of generations. *Time & Society, 8*(2–3), 249–272.

Durkheim, E. (1969/ 6th printing) The elementary forms of the religious life. New York: The Free Press.

Edmunds, J. & Turner, B. S. (2002). *Generations, culture and society*. Buckingham, UK: Open University Press.

Gordon, H. (2018, June 29). Millennials and activism: New strategies, identities, and coalitions. *Mobilizing Ideas*, June 29. Retrieved from https://mobilizingideas.wordpress.com/2018/06/29/millennials-and-activism-new-strategies-identities-and-coalitions/.

Halbwachs, M. & Coser, L. A. (1992). *On collective memory*. Chicago, IL: University of Chicago Press.

Hart-Brinson, P. (2018). How generational mythology misleads social movements. *Mobilizing Ideas*, June 29. Retrieved from https://mobilizingideas.wordpress.com/2018/06/29/how-generational-mythology-misleads-social-movements/.

Katz, S. (2017). Generation X: A critical sociological perspective. *Generations: Journal of the American Society on Aging, 41*(3), 12–19.

Generations defined

Post-Millennial generation
Born: 1997 and later
Age of adults in 2018: 18 to 21
Share of adult population: 5%
Share non-Hispanic white: 53%^

Millennial generation
Born: 1981 to 1996
Age in 2018: 22 to 37
Share of adult population: 28%
Share non-Hispanic white: 56%

Generation X
Born: 1965 to 1980
Age in 2018: 38 to 53
Share of adult population: 26%
Share non-Hispanic white: 61%

Baby Boom generation
Born: 1946 to 1964
Age in 2018: 54 to 72
Share of adult population: 29%
Share non-Hispanic white: 72%

Silent generation
Born: 1928 to 1945
Age in 2018: 73 to 90
Share of adult population: 11%*
Share non-Hispanic white: 79%*

Greatest generation
Born: 1901 to 1927
Age in 2018: 91 and older

^Share non-Hispanic whites are based on U.S. adults only in 2017 (e.g,, post-Millennials race/ethnicity does not include those <18).
*Since the Current Population Survey aggregates those ages 85 and older into one category, the Silent and Greatest generations can not be separately shown.
Source: Pew Research Center tabulations of the 2017 Current Population Survey Annual Social and Economic Supplement (ASEC) from the Integrated Public Use Microdata Series (IPUMS).

PEW RESEARCH CENTER

Nation's growing diversity reflected in its younger generations

% of each generation who are ...

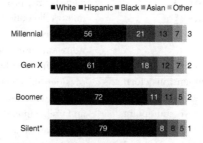

*Members of the Silent Generation were ages 72 to 89 in 2017. Since the Current Population Survey aggregates ages 85 and older, Silent and Greatest generations cannot be separately shown.
Notes: Whites, blacks. Asians, and other/multiple races include only non-Hispanics. Hispanics are of any race. Asians include Pacific Islanders. Figures may not add to 100% due to rounding.
Source: Pew Research Center tabulations of the 2017 Current Population Survey Annual Social and Economic Supplement (ASEC) from the Integrated Public Use Microdata Series (IPUMS).

PEW RESEARCH CENTER

Figure G1a, G1b Generations Defined

Source: The Pew Research Center, www.people-press.org/2018/03/01/the-generation-gap-in-american-politics/.

Mannheim, K. (1997).The problem of generations. In *Essays on the sociology of knowledge*. (pp. 286–320). London: Routledge.

Pew Research Center. (2018). The generation gap in American politics: Wide and growing divides in views of racial discrimination. March 1. Retrieved from www.people-press.org/2018/03/01/the-generation-gap-in-american-politics/.

Rogne, L., Estes, C. L. et al. (2009). *Social insurance and social justice*. New York: Springer.

Turner, B. S. (2002). Strategic generations: Historical change, literary expression, and generational politics. In J. Edmunds & B. S. Turner (Eds.). *Generational consciousness, narrative, and politics* (p. 14). Lanham, MD: Rowman & Littlefield Pub.

Whitehouse, P. J. & Flippin, C. S. (2017). From diversity to intergenerativity: Addressing the mystery and opportunities of generation X. *Generations: Journal of the American Society on Aging, 41*(3), 6–11.

Yeh, J. C., DiCarlo, N., & Estes, C. (2018). Generations can connect for empowerment: Five ways forward. *Aging Today, 39*(5), 1–3.

Generational and Intergenerational Consciousness

Denotes perceptions and viewpoints (attitudinal and meaning dimensions) formed through events across the life course. Generations develop distinctive standpoints – through experiences of fiscal collapse (e.g., Great Depression), war and their attendant losses and traumas, and technological developments (Edmunds & Turner, 2002a).

Karl Mannheim (1970) in his classic, "The problem of generations," described the role of *age groups as agents of social change*, based on the specific place and location in time of a generation, in which a "generational consciousness" may develop. He contended that a generation becomes an "actuality" when "a concrete bond is created between members of a generation by their being exposed to the social and intellectual symptoms of a process of dynamic destabilization" (Mannheim, 1970, p. 303). Traumatic and violent social events qualify.

These forms of consciousness are *not* universal, and there are subgroups and subdivisions within that may separate "generation units" within a generation.

The historical consciousness of a "generational location" occurs where there is "a cluster of opportunities or life chances that constitute the 'fate' of a generation." This is a "generation as actuality," in which "generation units" "articulate structures of knowledge or a consciousness of their situation. It produces potentiality to exercise a decisive role in historical change (Edmunds & Turner, 2002b, p. 5).

Molly Andrews, in writing "Generational consciousness, dialogue and political engagement" (in Edmunds & Turner, 2002, pp. 75–87), links Mannheim and Paolo Freire (1985: 88) concerning how shared group consciousness may be transformed into social action. Freire's concept of "conscientization" speaks to how individuals and groups become conscious of their location in the historical process. As Andrews avers, narration and dialogue (stories people tell) are means of continuity or discontinuity of generational identity.

The collective consciousness of generations and intergenerational transmissions will be marked by the events of the 2016 presidential election and what followed. Landmark events include the intentional and visible upending of historically durable democratic institutions and governmental and legal structures and practices, including the integrity of the franchise. These include the dangers of cyber hacking and the egregious Russian election interference. The presidential administration's substantial rhetoric and actions to uproot (i.e., cleanse and disband) the "administrative state apparatus" have been unpopular, according to public opinion polling, especially as Trump attacks and impedes investigations into his potential corruption and collusion. With a critical lens, the sense of a "common destiny" of the generations living have been the disempowering of our peoples and, with it, the demonization of values and practices supporting diversity, difference, equality, fairness, and democracy.

Generational Consciousness and Race

Ron Eyerman, in "Intellectuals and the construction of an African American Identity" (in Edmunds & Turner, 2002a, pp. 51–74), shows that "socially constructed, historically rooted collective memory functions to create social solidarity in the present" (p. 57). Collective memory links to Durkheim's notion of "collective consciousness" through recollections of a shared past and rituals. A related concept is W. E. B. Du Bois' "*double consciousness*" in being both African and American (1897). "Collective memory" provides individuals with "a cognitive map within which to orient present behavior" (Eyerman, in Edmunds & Turner, 2002a, p. 57).

Generational Consciousness and Women

Susan McDaniel, in "Generational consciousness of and for women" (in Edmunds & Turner, 2002a, pp. 89–109) identifies generational interconnectedness among women and changes in Generational Consciousness therein. . . . Sharp disjunctures are vivid . . . textured by historical silencing, by class and race/ethnicity. . . . and by the voice and narrative challenges.

"Women's Generational Consciousness, of themselves as women, and as generational, and for women in general, is profoundly different than men's.

"Feminism . . . can be a schism among generations of women" (McDaniel in Edmunds & Turner, 2002a, p. 105).

Gendered generations are influenced by "structures of constraint, entitlement and responsibility" in which "currencies" include *time* that, for women, may structure "inequality as much or more than the traditional masculine currencies of power . . . money and influence" (McDaniel, in Edmunds & Turner, 2002a, p. 101). Money, culture, and politics are each large currencies of import. Culture is implicated as generational groups gender their sense of identity, of belonging, of their self-definition. Also significant are "Preferences and attitudes and choices and perceptions of choices" (McDaniel, in Edmunds & Turner, 2002a, p. 101).

McDaniel's "Analytical framework of gendered generation" offers insights related to age, gender, and generational consciousness (in Edmunds & Turner, 2002a, pp. 98–99) in which:

- "Different generations embody different gender regimes."
- "Welfare State restructuring and globalization bring out . . . contradictions . . . about feminized caring as both undervalued in the global economy and the cement of social cohesion."
- "Erosion of intergenerational benefits among women is a vector of global economic change."
- "Democracy of the fortunate consolidates older men's positions at the cost of women, particularly younger women" (McDaniel, in Edmunds & Turner, 2002a, p. 99).

Gerontologist Elaine Brody reflects in *The gerontologist*, "On being very, very old: An insider's perspective" (Brody, 2010), regarding how the Great Depression influenced her understanding of poverty and the precariousness of the family. She says, "Social Security, Medicare, and subsequent legislation benefited not just old people but all generations" (p. 3). Brody shows the intersections of gender and economic pressures in research, policy, and practice, including long-term care. She was resistant to the family propaganda accompanying Ronald Reagan's New Federalism and austerity politics, saying,

> Right now, the Reagan administration is sort of cheering the family on. You know, 'Let's go back to the good old days when families did more.' Well, families did not do more in the good old days. They did less. There weren't as many elderly people, and the needs were not as great.
>
> (Brody, quoted in Hacker, 1986)

The high-profile sexual harassment scandals of powerful white media moguls against women in 2017 and 2018 and the hashtag # Me too campaign created an important space for the voices of women and girls to hear themselves and to be heard by others. These narratives are accessible and are reaching within and across generations in ways that provide openings for deepening and renewed generational and intergenerational consciousness for and bonding among women.

See also: Co-presence, Digital Spheres, Discourse, Intergenerational Intersubjectivity

Further Reading

Arber, S. & Attias-Donfut, C. (1999). *The myth of generational conflict: The family and state in ageing societies* (1st edition). London: Routledge.

Brody, E. (2010). On being very, very old: An insider's perspective. *The Gerontologist, 50*(1), 2–10.

Du Bois, W. E. B. (1897). Strivings of the Negro people. Atlantic Monthly Company.

Edmunds, J. & Turner, B. S. (2002a). *Generational consciousness, narrative, and politics.* Lanham, MD: Rowman & Littlefield.

Edmunds, J. & Turner, B. S. (2002b). *Generations, culture and society.* Buckingham, UK: Open University Press.

Freire, P. (1985). *The politics of education: Culture, power and liberation.* Santa Barbara, CA: Greenwood Publishing Group.

Hacker, K. (1986). A career of aiding the aging: Elaine Brody has spent 31 years helping people cope with growing old. *Philadelphia Inquirer,* January 8.

Mannheim, K. (1970). The problem of generations. *Psychoanalytic Review, 57*(3), 378.

O'Neill, J. (1994). *The missing child in liberal theory.* Toronto, Canada: University of Toronto Press.

Gentrification

Predominantly framed as a revival or renewal of "decayed areas" in towns, neighborhoods, and states due to the influx of wealthy residents or businesses and corporations. There are several stages to gentrification, but in general it involves the displacement of lower income residents and their neighborhoods who are bought out by developers and pushed out by landlords who plan to charge higher rents. Renting and much of real estate buying relies on credit and proof of income, so fewer people with low or fixed incomes move to the neighborhood.

Gentrification is part of the financialization of space, as there is an increase in property values through speculative investments funding renovations and new developments. This bears consequences for those without financial resources or the ability to earn money, such as older people who have experiences of cumulative disadvantage and barriers to entering the workforce (higher rates of disability, ageism). As Perry et al. (2015) write: "There is little research which relates to understanding the intersection between involuntary relocation related to gentrification and concerns of trauma in older adulthood" (p. 247). More work is needed, since gentrification has been increasingly recognized as a force and threat to older adults' physical and mental health (Smith, Lehning, & Kim, 2017) and aging in community initiatives (Buffel & Phillipson, 2016).

Gentrification is also about race, and the control of a neighborhood. White people who move to a predominantly black or brown neighborhood, lured by lower prices and attracted to new cultural offerings, soon employ the police to regulate noise and provide "safety" that disproportionately hurts established residents and begins to change the culture of the neighborhood.

See also: Aging in Community, Colonialisms, Commodification, Exploitation, Financialization, Housing, Inequality

Further Reading

Aboelata, M. J., Bennett, R., Yanez, E., Bonilla, A., & Akhavan, N. (2017). *Health development without displacement: Realizing the vision of health communities for all.* Oakland, CA: Prevention Institute.

Buffel, T. & Phillipson, C. (2016). Can global cities be "age-friendly cities"? Urban development and ageing populations. *Cities, 55*, 94–100.

Fullilove, M. T. (1996). Psychiatric implications of displacement: Contributions from the psychology of place. *The American Journal of Psychiatry, 153*(12), 1516–1523.

Fullilove, M. T. (2005). *How tearing up city neighborhoods hurts America, and what we can do about it.* New York: Random House.

Fullilove, M. T. (2013). *Urban alchemy: Restoring joy in America's sorted-out cities.* New York: New Village Press.

Fullilove, M. T. & Cantal-Dupart, M. (2016). Medicine for the city: Perspective and solidarity as tools for making urban health. *Bioethical Inquiry, 13*, 215–221. doi:10.1007/s11673-016-9713-5.

Fullilove, M. T. & Chaudhury, N. (2016). Keep the whole city in mind. *American Journal of Public Health, 106*(4), 639–641.

Fullilove, M. T. & Wallace, R. (2011). Serial forced displacement in American cities, 1916–2010. *Journal of Urban Health, 88*(3), 381–389.

Harvey, D. (2003). The right to the city. *International Journal of Urban and Regional Research, 27*(4), 939–941.

Harvey, D. (2009). *Social justice and the city.* London: University of Georgia Press.

Jacobs, J. (1961). *The death and life of great American cities.* New York: Vintage Books.

Perry, T. E., Wintermute, T., Carney, B. C., Leach, D. E., Sanford, C., & Quist, L. (2015). Senior housing at a crossroads: A case study of a university/community partnership in Detroit, Michigan. *Traumatology, 21*(3), 244–250.

Smith, R. J., Lehning, A. J., & Kim, K. (2017). Aging in place in gentrifying neighborhoods: Implications for physical and mental health. *The Gerontologist*, 26–35.

Zuk, M. & Chapple, K. (2015). Urban Displacement Project. Retrieved from www.urbandisplacement.org/.

Geographies

The places or localities where people live and events occur. These may include neighborhoods, nationalities, and ecosystems. The term *political geography* is useful in addressing the site-specific dimensions of power structures and how they relate to aging people's realities. This has direct implications for *aging in community* in the context of gentrification, welfare reform in the weakening of welfare states, and in trends of globalization.

See also: Aging in Community/Aging in Place, Climate Change, Ecologies, Gentrification, Housing

Further Reading

Andrews, G. J., Cutchin, M., McCracken, K., Phillips, D. R., & Wiles, J. (2007). Geographical gerontology: The construction of a discipline. *Social Science and Medicine, 65*(1), 151–168.

Brenner, N. (2004). *New state spaces.* Oxford: Oxford University Press.

Harper, S. & Laws, G. (1995). Rethinking the geography of ageing. *Progress in Human Geography, 19*(2), 199–221.

Harvey, D. (1973). *Social justice and the city*. London: Arnold.

Harvey, D. (1996). *Justice, nature and the geography of difference*. Malden, MA: Blackwell.

Harvey, D. (2001). *Spaces of capital: Toward a critical geography*. New York: Routledge.

Laws, G. (1993). "The land of old age": Society's changing attitudes toward urban built environments for elderly people. *Annals of the Association of American Geographers, 83*(4), 672–693.

Laws, G. (1997). Women's life courses, spatial mobility, and state policies. In J. P. Jones III, H. J. Nast, & S. Roberts (Eds.), *Threshold in feminist geography: Difference, methodology, representation* (pp. 29–46). Lanham, MD: Rowman & Littlefield.

Rowles, G. (1986). The geography of ageing and the aged: Towards an integrated perspective. *Progress in Human Geography, 10*, 511–539.

Skinner, M. W., Andrews, G. J., & Cutchin, M. P. (2018). *Geographical gerontology: Perspectives, concepts, approaches*. New York: Routledge.

Soja, E. W. (1989). *Postmodern geographies: The reassertion of space in critical social theory*. New York: Verso.

Geriatrics/Geriatric Syndromes

A subdiscipline within medicine, focused on aging and health care. The field features a number of professional organizations, conferences, and journals. It is much more part of the Medical Industrial Complex (MIC), yet geriatrics has only recently gained departmental status in a limited number of medical schools. Most often it is a subspecialty within general internal medicine. Other geriatricians (such as nurses) lack institutional status and do not generally hold departmental standing, relying on private philanthropy from organizations like the John A. Hartford and the Robert Wood Johnson Foundation. Research in the field

of geriatrics identifies and studies geriatric syndromes, which include Alzheimer's Disease, dementia, and delirium.

There are debates between gerontology and geriatrics as to which is the discipline or a subdiscipline, and they are often listed as G&G (two discrete disciplines); The American Geriatrics Society's "future vision" is stated as "Every older American will receive high-quality, person-centered care." The official journal of the Academy for Gerontology in Higher Education (AGHE) reflects both disciplines in Gerontology & Geriatrics Education.

See also: Biomedicalization

Further Reading

American Geriatrics Society. (2017). Who we are. Americangeriatrics.org. Retrieved from www.americangeriatrics.org/about_us/who_we_are/.

Estes, C. L. & Binney, E. A. (1989). The biomedicalization of aging: Dangers and dilemmas. *The Gerontologist. 29*(5), 587–596.

Estes, C. L. & Weiler, P. (1989). Health professions education for the care of the elderly. In S. Andreopoulos & J. Hogness (Eds.), *Health care for an aging society* (pp. 97–117). New York: Churchill Livingstone.

Kerin, P., Estes, C. L., & Douglass, E. (1989). Federal funding for aging education and research: A decade analysis. *The Gerontologist. 29*(5), 606–614.

Gerontological Imagination

The critical, creative potential to study and understand aging through both personal experiences and meso and macro lenses.

Estes, Binney, and Culbertson (1992) argued that gerontology was moving toward uncritical mindless empiricism, oriented and geared to medicalization and commodification. In the tradition of C. Wright Mills' "sociological imagination," the "gerontological imagination" promotes a critical reflexivity, a commitment to understanding the social forces shaping scholastic efforts and scientific interpretation. Gerontology can and must work within this tradition in order to advance the multiple disciplines relevant to old age, aging, and the life course, including policy studies.

A critical perspective may interrogate the gerontological unconscious. What has not been thought or said, but what might be dreamed or imagined. Valuable critical directions are located in the sociology of knowledges, the sociology of science and technology, and intersectionality studies that build on and extend the theoretical and empirical work illuminated by critical race, ethnicity, gender, class, (dis)ability, and inequality studies.

Radicalizing the sociological imagination, Dandaneau (2001, pp. 136–137) observes that:

a sociological imagination appropriate for our times is the conceptualization of humanity as part of the natural order . . . or, simply, as part of the structured fluidity that is nature . . . remembering that humanity is but one species of millions on a roughly 5-billion-year-old planet . . . [Meanwhile] our temporary nonidentity with nature . . . is a gap through which reason and freedom . . . moral responsibility and political imagination, ebb and flow. . . . It is this gap that provides the basis for the pursuit of a common destiny before and beyond the grave.

We must respect, reflect, and illuminate the moral basis of everyday and everynight life.

See also: Epistemology, Public Sociology, Radical, Sociology

Further Reading

Dandaneau, S. P. (2001). *Taking it big.* Thousand Oaks, CA: Pine Forge Press.

Dannefer, D. (2011). Age, the life course, and the sociological imagination: Prospects for theory. In R. Binstock & L. George (Eds.), *Handbook of aging and social sciences* (pp. 3–16). New York: Academic Press.

Estes, C. L., Binney, E. A., & Culbertson, R. A. (1992). The gerontological imagination: Social influences on the development of gerontology, 1945–present. *The International Journal of Aging and Human Development, 35*(1), 49–65.

Ferraro, K. F. (2017). *The gerontological imagination: An integrative paradigm of aging.* New York: Oxford University Press.

Mills, C. W. (2000). *The sociological imagination.* Oxford: Oxford University Press.

Globalization

Refers to linkages and the consolidation of the cultural, economic, and political realities of nation-states and peoples. It is seen in the rise of multinational corporations and multilateral institutions that negotiate financial and trade and services agreements. A key factor is that globalization represents a rise of private corporate influence in relation to public governmental power across societies.

The reach of multinational corporations and the imperial nation-states extends beyond borders and depletes national State sovereignty in central arenas. Critical gerontology examines globalization through political economies of neoliberal and neocolonial control. International trade and movement shape lived experiences of aging through the immiseration and exploitation of vulnerable populations for labor, resources, and war.

Agents of globalization participated wholeheartedly in crisis constructions of aging as a global threat to quality of life and prosperity. Led by financial, political, and military operatives of the capitalist economies, there is the World Bank (Averting the old age crisis, 1994), the Central Intelligence Agency (2001), and the Center for Strategic & International

Studies (The global retirement crisis, 2001). The International Monetary Fund (IMF) pitched in with austerity and neoliberalism policies that members of the IMF's research department (Ostry, Loungani, & Furceri, 2016) report "increased inequality" and that the growing inequality "hurts the level and sustainability of growth." Further, "as stock prices and capital returns increase, the wealthy might benefit more than [those] earning income from labor." Estes and Phillipson (2002, p. 290) write:

> Globalization has a more uneven and subtle effect on welfare spending. Governments may still resist pressure from transnational bodies such as the WTO to open their borders to accept foreign investment in health and social care, but these pressures on states are certain to restrict their ability to reproduce, expand, or otherwise improve their welfare systems. Financial globalization, while not a direct cause of the erosion of welfare states, nonetheless sets significant boundaries or restrictions around their development.

Shifting from collective nation-state responsibility to individual responsibility is the project of neoliberalism and austerity policies. Collaborating institutions, aside from multinational financial and corporate enterprises, are the World Trade Organization and the OECD and their agreements, many of which are the subject of critical analysis of the undoing of the welfare state as we know it. Vincent contends that this crisis "lies in the political failure of the nation state in the face of global capital" including the "loss of power" of nation-states (Vincent, 2003, p. 90). He connects the globalization of financial institutions to impeding State actions in mediating financial redistributions in the face of a vast expansion of privately controlled pension funds.

Global South/North

"Global South" is a term which has gained traction in speaking to the autonomy and difference of nations without vast financial wealth or military might. In postcolonial studies, this has been used to frame the North–South divide and South–South cooperation, as countries work together to resist neoliberal forces of privatization and exploitation. This departs from the labeling of the "Third World" or "developing nations" and includes countries such as Mexico, Honduras, Nicaragua, Venezuela, and Chile. This framework also distinguishes itself from "Latin America" as it considers indigeneity and non-Spanish/Hispanic identities throughout these regions.

See also: Colonialisms, Market, Neoliberalism, Political Economy, Privatization, State, Welfare State

Further Reading

Appadurai, A. (2000). Disjuncture and difference in the global cultural economy. In S. During (Ed.), *The cultural studies reader*. New York: Routledge.

Estes, C. L. & Phillipson, C. (2002). The globalization of capital, the welfare state, and old age policy. *International Journal of Health Services, 32*(2), 279–297.

Klein, N. (2002). *Fences and windows*. London: Flamingo.

Ong, A. & Collier, S. J. (Eds.). (2005). *Global assemblages: Technology, politics, and ethics as anthropological problems*. Malden, MA: Blackwell.

Ostry, J. D., Loungani, P., & Furceri, D. (2016). Neoliberalism: Oversold? *Finance and Development, 53*(2), 38–41.

Phillipson, C. (2009). Reconstructing theories of aging: The impact of globalization on critical gerontology. In V. L. Bengtson,

N. Putney, & M. Silverstein (Eds.), *Handbook of theories of aging* (2nd edition) (pp. 615–628). New York: Springer.

Powell, J. L. and Leedham, C. (2009). Post-industrial society and aging in a global world: The demographic context of social welfare. In J. Powell and C. Leedham (Eds.), *The welfare state in post-industrial society* (pp. 141–159). New York: Springer.

Vincent, J. A. (2003). *Old age.* Hove, Sussex: Psychology Press.

Goal Displacement

Part of organizational theory and explains the process of substituting goals, where the end becomes the means. Most commonly, "major goals claimed by the organization are neglected in favor of goals associated with building or maintaining the organization" (Warner & Havens, 1968).

Carroll Estes' *The aging enterprise* (1979) is a treatise on goal displacement in aging policy. The research focus is on the Older Americans Act of 1965 and the implementation of the 1973 Comprehensive Services Act. The significant goals of initial OAA enactment were followed up with a policy to establish a network of state and area agencies on aging. A central mandate was the planning, coordination, and pooling of resources to serve older persons at state and local levels. The goals of ameliorating and improving the lives of older persons were not the priority, as the meagre resources available were consumed in bureaucracy building and organizational maintenance, and expansion work. Although altruistic motives were intended, political wrangling of entities and individuals competing for power, influence, and resources displaced the ability to achieve many of the goals. Goal displacement was reflected in failed efforts to promote elder independence while treating and processing the aging via structures, professions, systems, and policies that foster old age dependency and social control. A related example is when the goals of empowering older people and their communities are displaced by (well-meaning) young gerontologist professionals who are credentialed, trained, and placed in agencies to tell elders what their needs are, and defining the solutions while reproducing and reifying their dependency. Maggie Kuhn and the Gray Panthers were early critics of this form of ageism. Frances Fox Piven and Richard Cloward, the Ehrenreichs, and others offered searing critiques of the welfare state bureaucratization and professionalization that was salient to the political economy of aging critics emerging in the late 1970s. Block grants are a contemporary example of mechanisms of goal displacement.

There are abundant complications in the task of identifying what actually is a goal, as partisan splits and maneuvers involve ambiguity and disruption. Human rights would be potentially available for recognition on a collective level as a goal; however, authoritarian sabotage to institutions of democracy and decency displace the ability for the collective to define and address this goal. In the United States, as it withdrew from the UN Human Rights Council, many progressives realized that the "goal" was not merely displaced; rather it was dismantled.

See also: Aging Enterprise, Block Grants, Dependency, Older Americans Act

Further Reading

Estes, C. L. (1973). Barriers to effective community planning for the elderly. *The Gerontologist. 13*(2), 178–183.

Estes, C. L. (1974). Community planning for the elderly: A study of goal displacement. *Journal of Gerontology, 29*(6), 684–691.

Estes, C. L. (1979). *The aging enterprise: A critical examination of programs and services for the aged.* San Francisco, CA: Jossey-Bass.

Warner, W. K. & Havens, A. E. (1968). Goal displacement and the intangibility of organizational goals. *Administrative Science Quarterly, 12*(4), 539–555.

Governance

Relates to the closeness (responsiveness) of government to people, for whom it assumes responsibility.

The World Bank (1992–1995) established a policy of good governance which required the "creation of an enabling framework of development and larger responsibilities of the private sector, reducing direct government involvement in production and commercial activity." This policy has failed to account for those at risk who formerly received protections of their rights and lands by their governing institutions, before big multinationals altered the political and economic landscape. The prerogative and expansion of private market interests in corporate development as a condition of global development loans is central to the devolution and withering of State powers as well as the privatization of formerly free or subsidized basic health and education services for the people (Polzer & Power, 2016).

See also: Globalization, Neoliberalism, Privatization, Welfare State

Further Reading

Polzer, J. & Power, E. M. (2016). *Neoliberal governance and health: Duties, risks, and vulnerabilities*. Montreal, CA: MQUP.

Gray Gray Literature

Gray literature is existing research and content that may or may not be published. Hard-to-find research data, dissertations, and personal journals fall under this category. We propose that *GRAY* gray literature registers this difficult-to-find/share information that relates to aging and activism. This literature is itself an aging body that must

resist being rewritten or eschewed in favor of "cutting-edge" new literature.

GRAY also echoes apartheid systems of knowing and not-knowing.

See also: Blacklands, Epistemology, Honky Gerontology, Liminal, Subaltern

Gray Panthers

In 1972, Maggie Kuhn co-founded the activist group, the Gray Panthers, committed to "a strong ethical-moral base in our social analysis and social strategy" (Kuhn, in Hessel, 1977, p. 123). It is a decentralized group that has chapters across the nation with variations in size and involvement across time. By 1970 there were 120 local networks across 38 states.

Agendas have focused on ending forced retirement, identifying and resisting ageist stereotypes, protecting and expanding social insurance programs, and promoting peace. In 1976, in Berkeley, California, the Panthers chapter initiated the *Over 60 Health Center* to address the needs of underserved older adults. The organization has been influential locally, nationally, and internationally (especially engaging the UN with calls for peace).

Like many radical organizations it has struggled for survival since its founding. The deaths of many founding members and the aging out of its core membership base present challenges for the future. If you need a bureaucracy to be sustaining, then the charisma of the organization suffers.

In 2015, the National Council of Gray Panthers Networks was founded as a social justice action successor to the National Gray Panthers Project fund, the former legal, tax-exempt entity that coordinated the national and international advocacy, provided leadership and support for local Gray Panthers networks, sent out action alerts, and more. The National Council of Gray Panthers Network is a truly grassroots organization of individuals who share social justice action goals, and is governed by a volunteer board of members. There is no central office fundraising millions to promote an agenda.

From a critical perspective, the vision and work on progressive issues is more needed than ever. It has challenged research and practice, demanding accountability for representation. An example is the Gray Panthers' implementation of the first media watch to document ageism in TV and radio, and fomenting hearings of the Federal Communications Commission.

See also: Maggie Kuhn, Outrageous Act of the Day

Further Reading

Hessel, D. T. (1977). *Maggie Kuhn on aging: A dialogue*. Philadelphia, PA: Westminster Press.

Kleyman, P. (1974). *Senior power: Growing old rebelliously*. San Francisco, CA: Glide Publications.

Sanjek, R. (2009). *Gray Panthers*. Philadelphia, PA: University of Pennsylvania Press.

National Council of Gray Panthers Networks. Retrieved from www.facebook.com/NationalCouncilofGrayPanthers Networks/.

Grievability

Speaks to the varied extent to which people grieve for or mourn the dead based on processes of identification and empathy.

Judith Butler's most recent work, *Frames of war: When is life grievable?*, marks the expansion of the author's already expansive theoretical corpus by employing the critical models to explore how modern warfare represents certain lives as more or less worthy of grief. The question of how grievability undergoes framing is politically pertinent. We believe that modern welfare does the same; therefore, the concept of grievability applies to people with HIV (especially sexual minorities, sex workers, and drug users), black lives, immigrants, the commons, the disabled, and older adults – anyone seen as abject or not contributing worth (often via labor). These are exacerbated through the orientation of the State toward authoritarianism, capitalism, colonialism, and fascism.

Media representations and political discourse of life put frames into operation by differentiating "the cries we can hear from those we cannot, the sights we can see from those we cannot, and likewise at the level of touch and even smell" (Butler, 2016, p. 51).

See also: Abjection, Black Lives Matter, Framing, Myth

Further Reading

Butler, J. (2016). *Frames of war: When is life grievable?* New York: Verso.

Health Disparities

Describe the preventable differences in the burden of disease, health status, and health outcomes between demographic groups. These groups may be based on racial or ethnic status, religion, social class, gender, age, or mental health; cognitive, sensory, or physical disability; sexual orientation or gender identity; immigration status, and geographic location. A focus is on social groups with historical linkages to discrimination or social exclusion.

Federal recognition of health disparities commenced with the 1987 Heckler Report and the Office of Minority Health. In 2010, the National Institutes of Health (NIH) created the National Institute of Minority Health and Health Disparities (NIMHD), formalizing the role of the elimination of health disparities in the national health agenda. The National Institute on Aging (NIA) Health Disparities Research Framework outlines four major levels of analysis for disparities research: environmental, sociocultural, behavioral, and biological. Keystone Papers are suggested for each analytic level. The NIH/NIA has invested in Resource Centers for Minority Aging Research (RCMAR) for training and mentoring current and next generation scholars from diverse ethnic and racial communities.

Policy-makers, scientists, and public health practitioners have largely adopted a social determinant of health approach to the problem, applying the definition of health disparities put forth by Margaret Whitehead of the World Health Organization (WHO). She distinguished between social conditions leading to population or group health differences that are "avoidable and unfair" such as inadequate access to essential health services or exposure to stressful living environments from social conditions that may be "unavoidable but fair" such as individual health-damaging behaviors or natural biological variation.

A long line of research on older adults confirms stark disparities among different groups of people with some demonstrating higher rates of certain diseases or health conditions than others. For instance, hypertension affects black populations at higher rates than other groups and there is a correlation between diabetes and poverty. A critical consideration for gerontology is investigating how structural inequalities – such as inadequate access to medical care, supportive services, food, housing, transportation, and exposure to stress and violence – produce and accentuate differences in morbidity and mortality across the life course, and how these inequities are transferred across generations (Fiscella and Williams, 2004).

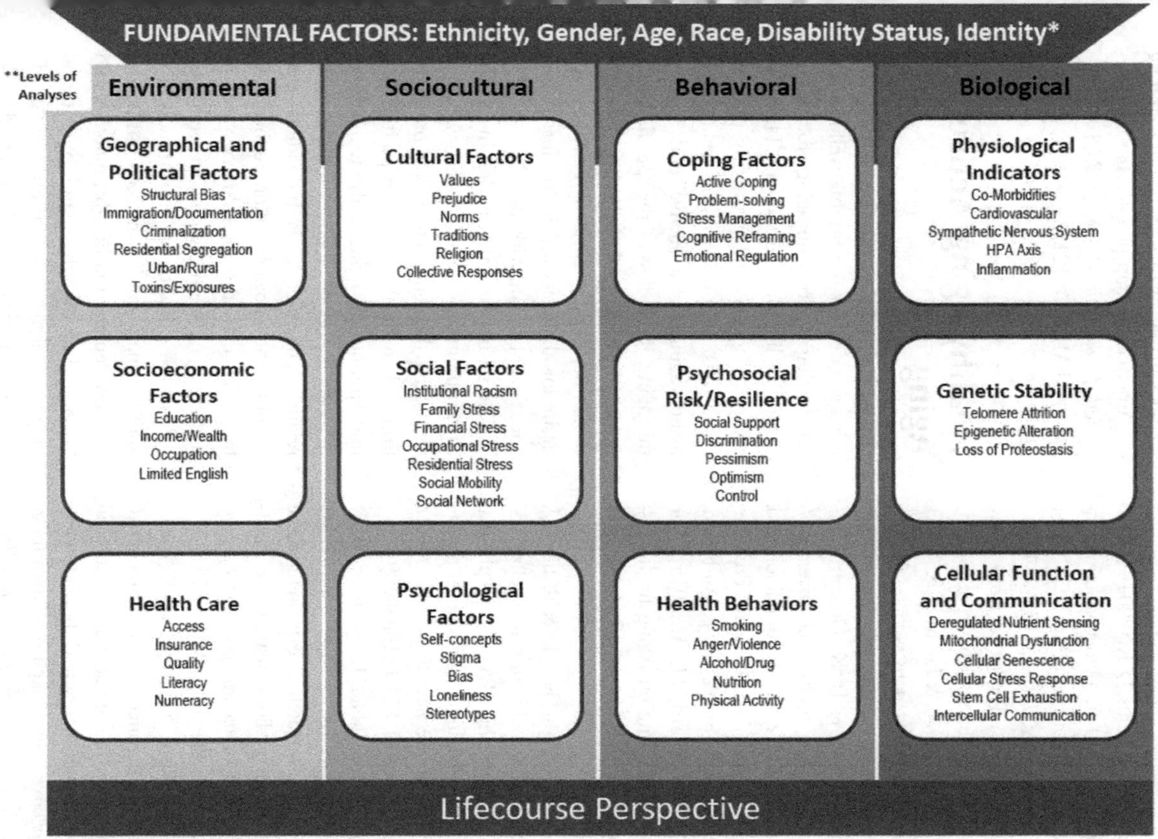

FUNDAMENTAL FACTORS: Ethnicity, Gender, Age, Race, Disability Status, Identity*

**Levels of Analyses

Environmental	Sociocultural	Behavioral	Biological

Geographical and Political Factors
Structural Bias
Immigration/Documentation
Criminalization
Residential Segregation
Urban/Rural
Toxins/Exposures

Cultural Factors
Values
Prejudice
Norms
Traditions
Religion
Collective Responses

Coping Factors
Active Coping
Problem-solving
Stress Management
Cognitive Reframing
Emotional Regulation

Physiological Indicators
Co-Morbidities
Cardiovascular
Sympathetic Nervous System
HPA Axis
Inflammation

Socioeconomic Factors
Education
Income/Wealth
Occupation
Limited English

Social Factors
Institutional Racism
Family Stress
Financial Stress
Occupational Stress
Residential Stress
Social Mobility
Social Network

Psychosocial Risk/Resilience
Social Support
Discrimination
Pessimism
Optimism
Control

Genetic Stability
Telomere Attrition
Epigenetic Alteration
Loss of Proteostasis

Health Care
Access
Insurance
Quality
Literacy
Numeracy

Psychological Factors
Self-concepts
Stigma
Bias
Loneliness
Stereotypes

Health Behaviors
Smoking
Anger/Violence
Alcohol/Drug
Nutrition
Physical Activity

Cellular Function and Communication
Deregulated Nutrient Sensing
Mitochondrial Dysfunction
Cellular Senescence
Cellular Stress Response
Stem Cell Exhaustion
Intercellular Communication

Lifecourse Perspective

* Sexual and gender minorities.

** Text within boxes represents examples of related factors.

Figure H1 NIA Health Disparities Research Framework

Source: Hill et al. (2015).

See also: Allostatic Load, Inequality, Life Expectancy

Further Reading

Fiscella, K., & Williams, D. R. (2004). Health disparities based on socioeconomic inequities: implications for urban health care. *Academic Medicine*, 79(12), 1139–1147.

Framework Papers. Retrieved from www.nia.nih.gov/research/osp/framework.

Herd, P., Robert, S. A., & House, J. S. (2011). Health disparities among older adults: Life course influences and policy solutions. In R. H. Binstock & L. K. George (Eds.), *Handbook of aging and the social sciences: A volume in handbooks of aging* (7th edition) (pp. 121–134). New York: Academic Press.

Hill, C. V., Pérez-Stable, E. J., Anderson, N. A., & Bernard, M. A. (2015). The National Institute on Aging health disparities research framework. *Ethnicity & Disease*, 25(3), 245.

Jackson, J. S., Knight, K. M., & Rafferty, J. A. (2010). Race and unhealthy behaviors: Chronic stress, the HPA axis, and physical and mental health disparities over the life course. *American Journal of Public Health*, 100(5), 933–939. PMID:19846689

Kaufman, J. S., Dolman, L., Rushani, D., & Cooper, R. S. (2015). The contribution of genomic research to explaining racial disparities in cardiovascular disease: A systematic review. *American Journal of Epidemiology*, 181(7), 464–472. PMID:25731887

Missinne, S., Neels, K., & Bracke, P. (2014). Reconsidering inequalities in preventive health care: An application of cultural health capital theory and the life-course perspective to the take-up of mammography screening. *Sociology of Health Illness*, 36(8), 1259–1275. doi: 10.1111/1467-9566.12169. PubMed PMID: 25470325.

Pérez-Stable, E. J., Nápoles-Springer, A., & Miramontes, J. M. (1997). The effects of ethnicity and language on medical outcomes of patients with hypertension or diabetes. *Medical Care*, 35(12), 1212–1219. PMID:9413309.

Whitbeck, L. B., Adams, G. W., Hoyt, D. R., & Chen, X. (2004). Conceptualizing and measuring historical trauma among American Indian people. *American Journal of Community Psychology*, 33(3–4),119–130. PMID:15212173.

Healthy Aging/Active Aging

A practical and theoretical initiative which focuses on efforts to promote wellness and functioning as part of the aging process, and quality of life for older people. There are several concepts used frequently that are extensions of, or variations related to, healthy aging, such as "active" and "successful" aging. Regardless of the specific terminology, the framing of these concepts is the same: they express an ideologically driven desire for abledness which calls for compliance from aging individuals.

The assumptions that underpin healthy aging foreground people's agency, which can lead to their engagement and participation in beneficial ways. The politics that underpin healthy aging is also wrapped up in unstable notions of power that permeate relationships on all levels. Individuals must negotiate these power relations in their daily lives. As such, the disciplinary work of healthy aging is a dichotomy wherein individuals are expected to be healthy, active, and "normal," on the one hand; otherwise they are rendered unhealthy, inactive, and "deviant," on the other hand. Such moral judgments about what constitutes a "good" or "bad" existence teem with political implications. A critical consideration for gerontology is how the promotion of healthy aging focuses the responsibility of health onto the individual and away from the State. Healthy aging tends to reinforce neoliberal discourses whereby self-care is touted as a facilitator of social action. This focus on individual health behaviors obscures how many people struggle for equal access and resources, as well as how definitions of health vary across the heterogeneous aging populations' cultures.

Active Aging

A leading term used to describe multiple international governmental organizations including the WHO, the UN, and the OECD in response to population aging. Robert Butler, the late director of the National Institute on Aging (NIH), was the single most persuasive voice in formulating and pressing for the adoption of the active aging paradigm in the USA and around the globe. For the European Union, Alan Walker has been the leading intellectual guiding the EU Roadmap designated under the framework, Active Ageing in Europe.

European Aging Research Roadmap (European Union)

Alan Walker (2018) explicitly differentiates the EU framework from the US usage of the same term: healthy aging. Comparing the different concepts that US and UK scholars employ under the same words, Walker argues that US academics tend to:

> favour "successful aging" or "productive aging" [which means] that they are speaking a different language to their European counterparts who tend to favour active ageing. In policy terms the implications of these two formulations are very different. Similarly, with the term often conjoined to active ageing. Healthy ageing . . . is an important idea and goal but it is not the same as active ageing.

Walker further contends that aging heretofore has been framed within a deficit model of ageing or a despairing demography in which the "problem" is too many older people creating demands on social protection systems. The solutions flowing from this perspective have been similarly limited: making people work longer and reducing their pension entitlements, for example. The policy of active aging marked a distinct break with the dominant deficit perspective. Instead it proffered a positive vision of later life, emphasizing the health, independence, and productivity of older people.

The WHO (2002, p. 12) has prioritized active ageing as:

> [T]he process of optimising opportunities for health, participation and security in order to enhance quality of life as people age. . . . The key environmental risk factors include both political-economic [factors] such as deprivation, low socioeconomic status, air pollution, unhealthy food production and occupational stress, and behavioural ones such as smoking, lack of exercise and poor diet.

In the EU paradigm of active aging, there is a necessary partnership of citizens and society with a State role to facilitate and motivate citizens, and where necessary provide high-quality social protection. Interrelated individual and societal strategies must link employment, health, social protection, social inclusion, transport, education, and more (housing) to be a "comprehensive active aging strategy." Walker (2018) points to the UN's "one of a society for all ages," as he suggests "taking the WHO definition a stage further," defining active aging in policy terms as a "comprehensive strategy to maximise participation and well-being as people age. It should operate simultaneously at the individual, organisational and societal levels and at all stages of the life-course."

Walker (2018) recognizes a major challenge to the EU's implementation of active aging as the:

"deep seated inequalities" both between older persons and over the life-course. These include class, gender and race. Inequalities of aging exist between different countries at similar and different levels of development. Among EU members there are life expectancy differences of 10 yrs (e.g., Denmark and Estonia), and variations among the rich and poor, and nations of the Global North and South.

Walker specifies seven principles comprising the promise of active aging:

1. Activity should consist of all meaningful pursuits contributing to well-being.
2. It is primarily a preventative concept across the whole life course.
3. It encompasses all older persons including those frail and dependent; and framed to be gender sensitive and not gender neutral (Foster & Walker, 2013).
4. Intergenerational solidarity with fairness between generations and opportunities to develop activities spanning generations.
5. It embodies rights and obligations: rights to social protection, lifelong education and training, and obligations to take advantage of them; and support for women to participate.
6. It is participative and empowering: a combination of top-down policy action and bottom-up opportunity for older people to develop their own forms of activity.
7. There is respect for national and cultural diversity.

(*Note*: all quotes are from Walker (2018), with the British spelling verbatim.)

See also: Functionalism, Globalization, Microfication, Productive Aging, Reductionism, Social Determinants of Health, Spirits of Capitalism

Further Reading

Biggs, S. (2001). Toward critical narrativity: Stories of aging in contemporary social policy. *Journal of Aging Studies, 15*, 303–316.

Estes, C. L., Phillipson, C., & Biggs, S. (2003). *Social theory, social policy and ageing: A critical introduction.* Maidenhead, Berks: McGraw Hill Education.

Foster, L. & Walker, A. (2013). Gender and active ageing in Europe. *European Journal of Ageing, 10*(1), 3–10.

Gems, D. & Partridge, L. (2013). Genetics of longevity in model organisms: Debate and paradigm shifts. *Annual Review of Physiology, 75*, 621–644.

Greenfield, E. (2015). Healthy aging and age-friendly community initiatives. *Public Policy & Aging Report, 25*(2), 43–46.

Holstein, M. (1993). Productive aging: A feminist critique. *Journal of Aging & Social Policy, 4*(3–4), 17–34.

Holstein, M. & Minkler, M. (2003). Self, society, and the "new gerontology." *The Gerontologist, 43*(6), 787–796.

Walker, A. (2018). The promise of active aging. In R. Fernández-Ballesteros, A. Benetos, & J-M. Robine (Eds.), *Cambridge handbook of successful aging* (pp. 557–569). Cambridge: Cambridge University Press.

WHO. (2002). *Active ageing: A policy framework.* Geneva: World Health Organization.

Hegemony

Derived from the Greek word *hegemon*, leader. Gramsci (1971) developed and extended the concept

to explain how liberal democracy is able to maintain the dominance of capitalist interests through the use of consent plus force . . . intellectual and moral leadership is exercised through civil society and politics, education, culture, and religion to shape perception, understanding and knowledge.

(Lowes, 2006, p. 117)

Hegemony both includes and goes beyond the concepts of "culture" as a "whole social process," that of ideology, in which a system of meanings and values is an expression or projection of a class interest (Williams, 1977, quoted in Berger, 2010, p. 95).

In capitalist societies, hegemony is key to maintaining acquiescence to the social order, as becomes the accepted common sense for most people. The media plays a pivotal role in promoting hegemonic discourses.

See also: Ideology, Power, The State

Further Reading

Berger, A. A. (2010). *The cultural theorist's book of quotations*. Walnut Creek, CA: Left Coast Press.

Gramsci, A. (1971). *Selections from the prison notebooks of Antonio Gramsci*. London: Lawrence & Wishart.

Lowes, D. E. (2006). *The anti-capitalist dictionary*. Black Point, Nova Scotia: Fernwood Publishing.

Williams, R. (1977). *Marxism and literature*. Oxford: Oxford University Press.

Heuristics

Cognitive short cuts which can lead to predictable systematic errors in reasoning.

Behavioral economists Tverksy and Kahneman (1973) developed a theory to understand how context and framing produce choice architecture and risk environment. These elements structure decision-making at the levels of intuition and reasoning.

Heuristics may lead to helpful or harmful (truthful or untruthful) actions. This is applicable to social inclusion/exclusion, financial decisions, and voting. Key concepts include: the bandwagon effect, confirmation bias, hindsight bias, illusory correlation, order effects (primacy/recency), and overconfidence. Other relevant concepts are the "representativeness heuristic" relating to stereotypes held (building on one's store of knowledge and experience); the "framing effect" (*see* Framing); the "default effect" (the tendency to go with whatever option is presented as the default, meaning that the option takes effect "if no explicit choice is made" (GSA, 2012, p. 6); the Dunning-Kruger effect, meaning the tendency of

Table H1 "Examples of Common Decision Heuristics and Biases" Table 2, p. 5, Gerontological Society of America, 2012

Heuristic or Bias	Explanation
Bandwagon Effect	Being influenced primarily by what others are doing or saying; choosing what others choose. Accepting something based solely on an increase in acceptance by others.
Confirmation Bias	The tendency to seek out, notice, and remember information that supports our pre-existing instinct or point of view, while avoiding or ignoring information that contradicts it.
Hindsight Bias	The tendency to believe, after the fact, that an event or outcome could have been predicted (the "I knew it all along" effect).
Illusory Correlation	Perceiving two events as causally related, even though the connection between them is coincidental or even nonexistent.
Order Effects (Primacy/ Recency)	The tendency to remember and be influenced more by options or facts that are presented first or last.
Overconfidence	Overestimating both how much we know and how reliably we know it.

the less experienced to perceive themselves as more skilled and effective than they are; and "availability heuristic" in which high-frequency events will be recalled better than less frequent events.

See also: Choice, Framing, Morality, Risk

Further Reading

Gerontological Society of America. (2012). *Communicating with older adults: An evidence-based review of what really works*. Retrieved from www.geron.org/publications/communicating-with-older-adults.

Tversky, A. & Kahneman, D. (1973). Availability: A heuristic for judging frequency and probability. *Cognitive Psychology*, 5(2), 207–232.

HIV/AIDS

A virus which, if left untreated, develops into a syndrome (AIDS) characterized by a severely weakened immune system. The virus emerged as a global public health crisis in the 1980s primarily in populations of MSM (men who have sex with men) as well as intravenous drug users. Thirty-five million people have died since the beginning of this epidemic. Over the past 30 years, prevention efforts have evolved to drastically reduce transmission and infection; and treatment advances have lowered the viral load of people infected with the virus, which has reduced transmissions and curbed the progression of the disease, making HIV manageable rather than a death sentence. The World Health Organization (2015) estimates that 36.7 million people currently live with HIV worldwide. However, demographics and geographic inequalities can be identified in treatment, prevention, and accompanying social services.

Social policy routinely fails these populations. In the USA this extends from the slow response by the Reagan Administration to publicly declare the crisis and the widespread discrimination toward AIDS patients to a contemporary case example of how people infected in the 1980s and have somehow managed to survive have now aged out of certain benefits and find themselves facing new precarity at age 65. They had received disability insurance (SSDI), and, as treatment advanced, extending survivors' lives beyond earlier projections, social policy has not continued to account for the many, different and unanticipated realities of this population that was not expected to age.

HIV/AIDS is an arena for critical gerontologists to examine global health disparities, the timeliness, and adaptability of social policy in responding to an epidemic, and the intersections of the Medical Industrial Complex, especially negotiations between the State and big pharmaceutical companies (such as Gilead, making billions from both treatment and prevention drugs).

The disease and response also exemplify a successful, multiple-actor, social movement. The script switch of HIV as the moral and unavoidable consequence of degenerate, dangerous sex shifted as public perception widened its awareness of how many lives were touched. It became a disease that had many faces – of children like Ryan White and straight people like Mary Fisher, who addressed the 1992 Republican National Convention.

See also: Grievability, Health Disparities, Housing, Medical Industrial Complex, Precarity, Social Security Disability Insurance (SSDI)

Further Reading

Cox, L. E. & Brennan-Ing, M. (2017). Medical, social and supportive services for older adults with HIV. In M. Brennan-Ing and R. F. DeMarco (Eds.), *HIV and AIDS: Interdisciplinary Top Gerontological Geriatry, Vol. 42* (pp. 204–221). Basel: Karger.

Epstein, S. (1998). *Impure science: AIDS, activism, and the politics of knowledge.* Berkeley, CA: University of California Press.

UNAIDS: http://aidsinfo.unaids.org.

WHO: www.who.int/gho/hiv/en/.

Home Care

The Labor Department initially passed rules that classified home care workers as companions in a class with babysitters. Eight years of struggling to reclassify this caregiving, and with a push from President Obama, home care workers finally had labor protections such as minimum wage and benefits.

The majority of home care workers are people of color. With a new Trump-appointed Secretary of Labor the fate of this reclassification of home care workers as workers rather than babysitters (with pay and overtime rules applying) was uncertain, although it had passed the Supreme Court as constitutional in late 2016.

See also: Caregiver, Long-term Care

Honky Gerontology

A term introduced by Estes at the 2015 GSA convention in Orlando, Florida. "Honky" is a derogatory term of uncertain origin for a white person (Caucasian). Members of the Black Power Movement in the 1960s suggested that this term deriding whiteness could serve as a counter to the n-word.

Estes uses "honky" to challenge whiteness and the ways in which dominant academic paradigms fail to critically interrogate its epistemological blind spots. Whiteness, as many have written (McIntosh, 1997), is largely unexamined, as recognizing disparities in privilege produces discomfort. The impetus for this is that gerontological research has struggled to describe aging phenomena for heterogeneous populations. Locating and valuing diverse and marginalized experiences of aging is a central function of critical gerontology.

See also: Blacklands, Critical Theory, Domination, Epistemology, Oppression, Outrageous Act of the Day, Privilege, Standpoint Theory, White Supremacy

Further Reading

McIntosh, P. (1997). White privilege and male privilege: A personal account coming to see correspondences through work in Women's Studies. In R. Delgado & J. Stefancic (Eds.), *Critical white studies: Looking behind the mirror* (pp. 291–299). Philadelphia, PA: Temple University Press.

Housing

Provides security and protection from outside elements. It includes space for oneself or family and belongings.

Older adults are extremely vulnerable to the rising cost of housing. If rising housing costs (and other costs of living) are factored into calculations of poverty, statistics for the "hidden poor" emerge, revealing a large population of the elderly living above the poverty line but below the Elder Economic Security Standard Index (Wallace & Padilla-Frausto, 2016).

Homelessness represents one of the ultimate failures of housing policy and has seen a significant uptick in response to the rising cost of housing nationwide. A major myth regarding homeless people is that they do not work. In reality, two-thirds do work but cannot afford housing. Gentrification (part of the commodification and financialization of space and speculated value) displaces many low-income peoples and contributes to homelessness and loss of housing in general. All White House conferences on Aging have cited access to affordable housing as a need for policy focus and intervention. The Housing for Older Persons Act (HOPA 1995) was passed in 1995 to exempt senior housing communities and facilities from the familial status clauses within the Fair Housing Act.

Many older Americans live in institutionalized housing. Skilled nursing facilities become de facto residences of many low-income older adults who have health care needs. US laws commodifying and subsidizing private ownership of long-term care facilities perpetuates this trend and undermines access to alternative types of care.

The myth that all older people own their homes is persistent and, while as many as two-thirds do, outstanding mortgages are common and many of these homes are valued at less than $70,000. This is a potential source of retirement income, but keeping up with housing repairs, accessibility modifications, and property taxes is difficult. Major waiver programs have even been developed by states to include some of these costs to be funded through various long-term programs, including OAA and the ACA, which has led to dual-eligibility pilot programs that combine Medicaid and Medicare funding.

The subprime-mortgage crisis and the subsequent Great Recession of 2008 destroyed home equity for hundreds of millions of Americans, including approximately 3.5 million older adults.

In the last several years, various states have considered using Medicaid to provide housing to the homeless. Homeless individuals are often covered by Medicaid and use significant quantities of health care, typically through emergency room services, due to the dangerous conditions they live in. Quality of life and care can be improved for these individuals by providing them with stable housing, with the bonus that it also drastically reduces costs for the State. Under the Obama Administration states were encouraged, often with generous financial incentives and grants, to develop partnerships between Medicaid services and housing agencies, and the scope of uses for Medicaid funds was left broad to encourage states to find creative solutions. Currently, California and Hawaii are both considering

using Medicaid funds to pay for housing for the homeless, and several other states have initiated partnerships between state Medicaid and housing authorities.

Meanwhile, millions are evicted each year as rents consume between 70 and 80 percent of their incomes. Desmond (2016) shows convincingly that poverty cannot be understood without understanding its inextricable links to housing. As rents and profits rise in "the business of owning the city," the crises of precarious housing and poverty mount. No age or generation is immune.

See also: Aging in Community/Aging in Place, Ecologies, Gentrification

Further Reading

Anti-eviction Mapping Project. Retrieved from www.antievictionmap.com/.

Desmond, M. (2016). *Evicted: Poverty and profit in the American city*. New York: Crown Books.

Newcomer, R., Lawton, M. P., & Byerts, T. (1986). *Housing an aging society: Issues, alternatives, and policy*. New York: Van Nostrand Reinhold.

Perry, T. E., Andersen, T. C., & Kaplan, D. B. (2014). Relocation remembered: Perspectives on senior transitions in the living environment. *The Gerontologist, 54*(1), 75–81. Retrieved from https://doi.org/10.1093/geront/gnt070.

The elder index: Research and data. Retrieved from http://healthpolicy.ucla.edu/programs/health-disparities/elder-health/elder-index-data/Pages/elder-index-data.aspx.

Trawinski, L. (2012). *Nightmare on main street: Older Americans and the mortgage market crisis*. Washington, DC: AARP Public Policy Institute.

Wallace, S. P. & Padilla-Frausto, I. (2016). *Hidden health problems among California's "hidden poor."* Los Angeles, CA: UCLA Center for Health Policy Research.

Human Rights

The freedoms and opportunities of all people, regardless of citizenship, ability, and resources.

The logic of human rights is the celebration of "human equality because we are all human, and . . . human uniqueness because none of us is the same" (Sachs, quoted in Blau & Moncada, 2015, p. 1). Human rights apply to individuals, governments, corporations, families, communities, nation-states, and the world. Rights imbue responsibilities for one another, and to "the social" as well as to the individual, including every aspect of social life: political and civil freedom, economic and social security, education, equal rights to self-determination, culture, faith, ideology, and conscience. Human rights as a principle is grounded in ancient religious and philosophical thought from Early Buddhism, Plato, and Enlightenment philosophers to the present. Human rights embody ethical principles. The idea and affirmation is that we are all equally entitled to our *human rights* without discrimination. Human rights are interrelated, interdependent, and indivisible.

A landmark document is the 1948 Universal Declaration of Human Rights (UDHR), fostered by Eleanor Roosevelt and signed by members of the UN following World War II. UDHR codifies what human rights are, embraces political and civil rights, and socioeconomic rights (the right to work, labor, and social protections), rights to education, medical care, cultural rights, and rights of the elderly. Human rights declarations aim to ensure world peace, security, human happiness, and the responsibility of nations.

Notably, there is no specific UN convention on older people, although their rights are "implicitly but not explicitly referred to" (Cox, 2015, p. 10) in the Convention on the Elimination of All Forms of Discrimination against Women (CEDAW) and other Rights Conventions, including that on Persons with Disabilities. There are UN documents (1991) on "Principles for Older Persons" on independence, participation, care, self-fulfillment, and dignity. There is a UN standing committee on rights of older persons. The Madrid International Plan of Action on Ageing (MIPAA; UN, 2002) has been endorsed by the UN General Assembly; and the Office of the High Commissioner on Human Rights (OHCHR) (2011) report identifies "inconsistent . . . [and a] lack . . . [of] legal and institutional frameworks." The OHCHR key areas include "violence against older persons and women in particular; financial exploitation; health; long term care; participation in policy-making and political life; [and] work."

A critical aging policy framework utilizes a rights-based framework in assessing the agenda, design, implementation, and outcomes of social policy in terms of how policy and regulation protect, extend (or abrogate) rights of older persons and others in society. Structural conditions as barriers to and facilitators of these rights are similarly investigated. As age is a basis for multiple layers of discrimination, policy must incorporate both consideration of rights as well as needs. Children are often framed or promoted as more deserving (a worthy investment in the future) than older people.

The USA has a checkered history, declining to support the 1948 Universal Declaration in one single treaty. All regions, including the Americas, have adopted their own human rights charters. Human Rights Watch, an organization devoted to identifying injustices, notes that the USA "rarely" ratifies human rights treaties, and, then, only with the *qualifier* that the treaty is not "self-executing," meaning that is does not apply to the USA. This is true of the conventions on the rights of women, racial minorities, the child, the disabled, and others. The Human Rights Council in 2015 gives the USA negative marks for its criminalization of the homeless, failures to guarantee access to water and sanitation, and inadequate access to housing, food, and education as major concerns and violations.

Education, in particular, is a fundamental human right and access to it is of extreme importance in guaranteeing all rights. More recently, particular focus has been given to lifelong learning and increasing access to education for individuals of all ages and all socioeconomic backgrounds.

Selected examples of US rights ratification status are instructive:

- *International Covenant on Economic, Social and Cultural Rights* (ICESCR) (1966). Part of the International Bill of Human Rights, this is the only covenant that requires governments to promote and protect such rights as health, education, social protection, and an adequate standard of living for all people. The ICESCR has been ratified by more than 150 countries. President Carter signed the Covenant in 1977, but the United States has yet to ratify it.
- *Convention on the Elimination of All Forms of Discrimination against Women* (CEDAW) (1979). The most comprehensive and detailed international agreement that seeks the advancement of women, CEDAW has been ratified by 185 countries. Although President Carter signed CEDAW in 1980, today the United States is the only industrialized country that has not ratified the treaty.
- *Convention on the Rights of the Child* (CRC) (1989). Protecting children from physical and mental abuse and hazardous work, and giving children the right to free primary education, the CRC has been ratified by 193 countries, making it one of the most widely adopted conventions. President Clinton signed the CRC in 1995 but the United States has yet to ratify it, one of only two countries in the world not to do so.
- *Rome Statute of the International Criminal Court* (ICC) (1998). The ICC conducts trials of individuals accused of genocide, war crimes, and crimes against humanity when

there is no other recourse for justice. One hundred and forty-six countries have signed the ICC, including the United States. In 2002, President Bush stated that the United States did not intend to be bound by its signature to the Rome Statute and that it had no intention of ratifying it.

- *International Convention on the Protection of the Rights of All Migrant Workers and Members of their Families* (1990). The Migrant Workers Convention protects migrant workers and their families from abuse and inhumane treatment in the countries where they work. No industrialized, migrant-receiving country, including the United States, has signed this treaty.
- *Convention on the Rights of Persons with Disabilities* (CRPD) (2006). The CRPD is the first global convention that specifically addresses the human rights of persons with disabilities. President Obama signed the treaty in 2009, but the United States has yet to ratify it.

See also: Ageism, Immigration, Inequality, Morality, Racism, Sexism

Further Reading

Blau, J. & Moncada, A. (2015). *Human rights: A primer*. Abingdon, Oxon: Routledge.

Cox, C. B. (2015). *Social policy for an aging society*. New York: Springer.

Human Rights Watch: www.hrw.org.

Moyn, S. (2012). *The last utopia: Human rights in history*. Cambridge, MA: Harvard University Press.

Moyn, S. (2018). *Not enough: Human rights in an unequal world*. Cambridge, MA: Harvard University Press.

Townsend, P. (2006). 25th volume celebration paper policies for the aged in the 21st century: More "structured dependency" or the realisation of human rights? *Ageing and Society*, *26*(2), 161–179.

The Advocates for Human Rights: www. theadvocatesforhumanrights.org.

Ideological Advocacy Coalitions

Ideological advocacy coalitions (ACF) are actors who "share a particular belief system" and demonstrate significant coordination of activity over time (Sabatier & Jenkins-Smith, 1993, p. 25). Three assumptions of the ACF are: (1) when core beliefs are in dispute in major policy controversies, the lineup of allies and opponents will tend to be stable in periods of a decade or more; (2) "[a]ctors within an advocacy coalition will show substantial consensus on issues pertaining to the policy core" (p. 32); and (3) actors from federal administrative agencies "will usually advocate more centrist positions" than other members.

Three Social Security Ideological Advocacy coalitions were empirically identified by Svihula and Estes (2007):

1. Ideological Advocacy Coalition supporting the Market, with goals of:

    *   Advancing the market
    *   Self-interest
    *   Individual equity (generational equity)
    *   Responsibility
    *   Belief in the market
    *   Market solutions
    *   Private accounts replacement for Social Security.

2. Ideological Advocacy Coalition supporting the Social Contract, with goals of:

    *   Financial security in old age
    *   Mutual protection
    *   Solidarity (generational interdependence)
    *   Belief in responsible government
    *   Government solutions
    *   Social insurance for Social Security.

3. Ideological Advocacy Coalition supporting Mixed or No ideology/values.

An in-depth analysis of Social Security Congressional testimonies (January 1, 1993 through December 31, 2003) coded the values most often expressed in Social Security testimonies across the 11-year study period (Clinton to G. W. Bush). Many values expressed were aligned with the market ideology (43%), followed by no mention of or mixed values (33%). The smallest percentage of values expressed (24%) concerning Social Security were aligned with the social contract. Conservative values not only predominated in the hearing testimonies, but were also more consistently and repeatedly expressed in their statements, compared to those that expressed social contract values. These data indicate that it is possible to analyze social policies as well as policy options as sets of values, and these as ideological models. The relative consistency (strong) coherence on one political ideological view (the market model) and the relative lack of consistency on another ideological view (the social contract model) points to the success of the Right in the first decade against Social Security and suggests difficulties ahead for the advocates of Social Security preservation and expansion. Results suggest the danger of single partisan control of Congressional hearing dockets and witnesses and its power to frame public discourse, especially in view of the 2017 trifecta of Republicans controlling the White House, Congress, and the Supreme Court.

See also: The Leninist Strategy, Social Security

Further Reading

Sabatier, P. & Jenkins-Smith, H. (1993). *Policy change and learning: An advocacy coalition approach.* Boulder, CO: Westview Press.

Svihula, J. & Estes, C. L. (2007). Social security politics: Ideology and reform. *The Journals of Gerontology Series B: Psychological Sciences and Social Sciences, 62*(2), S89.

Ideology

The framework and structure of the status quo. It is the logic that motivates the State and underpins the loyalty of its citizens. Ideologies are systems of ideas that legitimate a particular set of interests and/or social, political, and economic arrangements.

As belief systems, ideologies are worldviews competing for influence. They hold major implications for power relations. In enforcing certain definitions of a situation, they have the power to compel certain types of action while limiting others (Estes, 2001). Marx, Weber, Foucault, and Gramsci contribute to developing theories of ideology (through different perspectives on power and discourse).

Ideology is used by all political regimes to justify their position and impose their political will upon others. The contest for ideological hegemony in Gramsci's (1971) theory is about achieving and maintaining power through the means of the production, control, and deployment of ideas in broader publics rather than through overt violent coercion or revolution. All forms of communications networks, media, and internet are implicated in shaping the public consciousness, particularly as the industries providing them are increasingly integrated and concentrated across the globe. Gramsci writes that the struggle for advanced thought is the discernment between "common" and "good" sense. Critical theory provides lenses to interrogate assumptions promoted by conformity and consensus.

Ideologies structure beliefs and limit a vision of alternative futures to those with the most power to shape the reigning ideology, evidenced in dominant framing and heuristic bias (Therborn, 1980). A necessary condition of acquiescence and resignation to policy "choices" that economic and policy elites proffer (such as the privatization of the public entitlement of Social Security) is whether alternative regimes or strategies are even conceivable. The most successful ideologies have a remarkable capacity to shape public consciousness. Successful neoliberal ideology limits the vision of the "possible" to inherently pro-market solutions while neoconservative ideology limits solutions to those that impose benefits (discipline) through to the market and the traditional (patriarchal) family structure. Dominant ideologies instill a "profoundly pessimistic view of the possibilities of change" (Therborn, 1980, p. 98). In current US society, pessimism (e.g., about the sustainability of bedrock programs) is promoted through the ideological construction of the crisis surrounding the debt and deficit, entitlements, jobs, Social Security, the family, the economy, and globalization (Estes, 2001).

A *critical perspective* analyzes the power struggles over ideology and over the legitimacy of both State actions and the State itself incorporating all of government.

Legitimating and de-legitimating ideologies and practices are cultural products, and ones over which intense struggles ensue. The most powerful ideology of the Right is the natural superiority and sanctity of the market as the imperative of economic survival, and with it, the absolute requisite to obey the unfettered (chaotic) reign of international capitalism and financial markets. There is an alternative ideology grounded in the "common good" and an "inclusionary ethic of citizenship" (Somers, 2008, p. 38). This alternative is a social rights perspective that acknowledges the life course intergenerational interdependencies upon which our society is built (Twine, 1994, p. 34; Blau & Moncada, 2015).

Ideology is integral to three processes by which dominant views of social policy and aging are produced and sustained (Estes, 2001):

- The successful creation of cultural images by policy-makers, experts, and the media – for example, that the old are "greedy geezers" leaching off the young.
- The appeal to necessities of the economic system – for example, claiming that the elderly are responsible for the nation's economic problems by "busting the budget."
- The implementation of policy and the application of expertise in ways that transform conflicts over goals and means into systems of rational problem-solving.

Ideologies that are directly relevant to old age crisis, politics, and policy include: (1) market ideology, also called neoliberalism, market fundamentalism, and individualism; (2) patriarchal ideology which bolsters neoconservative ideology that imposes the traditional division of family labor of women in the social reproduction of capitalism and women's devalued, unpaid, and unending caregiving work; (3) racial ideology, an "elite color-coded ideology" and the racial

ideological frame of "colorblindness" that denies the existence of racism; and (4) the competing ideology under attack: social justice, the rights to human development, the freedom from want, the public ownership of the commons, and the social contract.

Critical work examining ideologies extends to ideological aspects of science itself. For example, in the study of human development and the life course, "universal theories" of human development, sociological theories of symbolic interactionism entrenched in functionalism, and age-based theories of aging such as disengagement theory have been shown to have ideological aspects.

The critical political economy of aging asserts that ideology and norms emerge through coercive processes of social struggle and conflict. Ideology is an essential but not the only element in the framing and disposition of State and social action, which means that the consent of the governed occurs through contentious power struggles – political, material, cultural, and ideological.

See also: Consciousness Raising, Crisis, Discourse, Doxa, Framing, Heuristic, Neoliberalism, Political Economy, Power, Resistance, The State, Theories of Aging, TINA

Further Reading

Althusser, L. (1994). Ideology and ideological state apparatuses (notes toward an investigation). In S. Žižek (Ed.), *Mapping ideology* (pp. 100–140). New York: Verso.

Blau, J. & Moncada, A. (2015). *Human rights: A primer*. Abingdon, Oxon: Routledge.

Estes, C. L. (1991). The Reagan legacy: Privatization, the welfare state, and aging in the 1990's. In J. Myles & J. Quadagno (Eds.), *States, labor markets and the future of old age policy* (pp. 59–83). Philadelphia, PA: Temple University Press.

Estes, C. L. (2001). Political economy of aging: A theoretical framework. In C. L.

Estes & Associates, *Social policy and aging: Critical perspectives* (pp. 1–22). Newbury Park, CA: Sage.

Gramsci, A. (1971). *Selections from the prison notebooks of Antonio Gramsci*. London: Lawrence & Wishart.

O'Connor, J. (1987). *The meaning of crisis: A theoretical introduction*. Oxford: Blackwell.

Sommers, M. R. (2008). *Genealoggies of citizenship: Markets, statelessness, and the right to have rights*. NY: Cambridge University Press.

Therborn, G. (1980). *What does the ruling class do when it rules?* London: Verso.

Twine, F. (1994). *Citizenship and social rights: The interdependence of self and society*. London: Sage.

Žižek, S. (Ed.). (1994). *Mapping ideology*. New York: Verso.

Immigration

The international movement of people from one country into a destination country; conditions and motivation include economic opportunity and personal freedoms, including refuge from war or persecution. US law, the Illegal Immigration Reform and Immigrant Responsibility Act of 1996 (IIRaIRA), excludes undocumented peoples from receiving (and purchasing under the ACA) health care services, as well as benefits from social insurance programs (SSI, food stamps). The REAL ID Act of 2005 introduces several restrictions and stipulates that identification must be shown to board planes, access government buildings, and open bank accounts.

A demographic "snapshot": The number of older immigrants has roughly doubled between 1990 and 2010 (Leach, 2008/2009). Older immigrants (age 65+) are more likely than their age group, non-immigrant peers to live in poverty (40% vs. 30%). They are more likely to live with family, especially if they do not speak English (Wilmoth, 2012). A majority are naturalized citizens (73%).

The racist, xenophobic political and economic debates surrounding immigration and "illegals" showcases the nativism and isolationism that pervades US culture. The stakes for all ages are real, and there is uncertainty and risk for those who are stigmatized and feared as "undocumented," "aliens," or "illegals." The repercussions extend to all members of families, many of whom are "mixed status" in their immigration and naturalization existence, especially since families with recent immigration history tend to rely on robust kinship networks of support to advance and establish themselves in new (and sometimes hostile) communities.

Policy implications: Because of the Byzantine and highly politicized immigration policy, debates, and regulations (e.g., DREAMers), older persons who are classified as undocumented or "alien" find themselves to be mostly ineligible for most US safety net programs. This situation increases precarity and exacerbates inequality of older persons in these families and communities.

Crisis myth: Opponents of Social Security, Medicaid/Medicare often incorrectly state that undocumented people take away resources from rightful beneficiaries, unduly straining the welfare state. In the past ten years the Social Security Actuary (SSA) states that undocumented immigrants have contributed $100 billion to the Social Security Trust Fund (unauthorized workers who are often using Social Security numbers that are not theirs), and none of them are collecting this. Yet still they continue to contribute approximately $12 billion a year into the system.

Further Reading

Aguila, E. & Vega, A. (2017). Social security contributions and return migration among older male Mexican immigrants. *The Gerontologist, 57*(3), 563.

Health coverage for immigrants. Retrieved from www.healthcare.gov/immigrants/.

Leach, M. (2008/2009). America's older immigrants: A profile, generations. *Journal of the American Geriatrics Society, 32*(4), 34–39.

Spotlight on SSI benefits for aliens – 2017. (2017). Retrieved from www.ssa.gov/ssi/spotlights/spot-non-citizens.htm.

Torres, S. & Cao, X. (2018). The immigrant grandparents America needs. *The New York Times*, August 20. Op-Ed.

Torres-Gil, F. & Treas, J. (2008). Immigration and aging: The nexus of complexity and promise. *Generations, 32*(4), 6.

Wilmoth, J. M. (2012). A demographic profile of older immigrants in the United States. *Public Policy and Aging Report, 22*(2), 8–11.

Immiseration

To make miserable.

It is the process of stripping away opportunity, fostering desperation. It is key in Marxist figuring of the "reserve army of labor" which drives down labor costs for owners (corporations) by driving down workers' wages and benefits (because of a desperate workforce willing to work for less).

Women have been an ersatz surplus labor force, historically ready in wartime to step out of unpaid roles into a labor force that then needs them to replace male labor. Women are the caregivers that reproduce the labor force and are the major US long-term care workforce (who work, mostly, for "free," except for the great costs to women).

Immiseration is in opposition to Franklin D. Roosevelt's Four Freedoms, specifically the "freedom from want and the freedom from fear." The condition of immiseration may be directly contrasted to the Universal Declaration of Human Rights' (UDHR) "Right to an Adequate Standard of Living" (Article 25).

See also: Capitalism, Class, Domination, Precarity, Universal Declaration of Human Rights/UDHR

Inclusion/Exclusion

Describes the phenomenon by which individuals are shut out from access to institutions, resources, or other benefits/goods.

The formation of the European Union (EU) was the occasion to affirm the significance of inclusion, social justice, and full citizenship for all as foundational in the future of the EU. Two decades ago, Alan Walker (2011) drafted and more than 1000 European academics and policy-makers signed The Amsterdam Declaration on the Social Quality of Europe. It is related to age and the aging of all peoples. The clarity of the *commitment to inclusion* in and through the EU merits this lengthy quotation, with British spelling verbatim intact:

Social quality was formulated as a potential counterweight to the . . . neoliberal hegemony of narrow economism to express the fundamental importance of social relations to all human life. It is defined as the extent to which people are able to participate in the social, economic and cultural life of their communities and countries under conditions that enhance their well-being and individual potential. To do so they must have access to life enhancing levels of socioeconomic security, experience social inclusion in all groups and organisations, live in a socially cohesive context and be empowered to reach their full potential.

[The Declaration laments] . . . the "loss of community" [which] may be interpreted as a loss of the social, and with it, the normative concepts of equality, justice and fairness. The false dichotomy between the economic and social and neoliberal reduction have prevented a clear articulation of the constitutional interdependency of the social, including the political, the cultural, the economic and the environmental. In contrast, social quality starts by defining the social: the interrelated relations of production and reproduction between people, which are constituted by a combination of processes of self-realisation and the formation of collective identities. This means that, economic relations are indivisible from wider societal relations which entail production and reproduction. The recognition of this means that the integrated approach of social quality could lead to genuine measurable inclusivity that transforms, rather than humanises, capitalism. Second, social quality is not simply an intellectual product but also has the practical goal to empower citizens in its pursuit. It proposes a political programme to change society.

(Walker & Corbett, 2017, p. 5)

In the USA, the Center for Global Policy Solutions (CGPS) has developed a Campaign for the Inclusion Revolution. The mission of CGPS as a think tank and action organization is "to drive society toward inclusion by advancing economic security, health, education, and civic success for vulnerable populations." Diversity and inclusion are not the problem, but instead, the solution. The Inclusion Revolution is with, for, and about the fundamental social, cultural, economic, and political rights of people of color, women, children and youth, older adults, and the low income group. To achieve transformative change CGPS strives to empower and build the capacity of advocates, organizations, and communities to overcome structural disadvantages to produce change in the quality of life through social justice (Rockeymoore, 2014).

See also: Inequality, Justice, Race, Racism, The Social, War on Women

Further Reading

Cann, P. & Dean, M. (2009). *Unequal ageing.* Bristol: Policy Press.

Rockeymoore, M. (2014). It's time for an inclusion revolution. *HuffPost*, July 29. Retrieved from www.huffingtonpost.com/dr-maya-rockeymoore/its-time-for-an-inclusion-revolution_b_5628904.html.

Walker, A. (2011). Social quality and welfare system sustainability. *The International Journal of Social Quality*, *1*(1), 5–18.

Walker, A. & Corbett, S. (2017). *The post Brexit declaration on social quality in Europe.* Amsterdam: International Association on Social Quality.

Individualism

A political and moral philosophy that venerates the individual self above collective systems of participation.

Ownership, as well as the sanctity of the right to private property which has historically been reserved for white male citizens, is a touchstone of American individualism. This is an ideological extension of English individualism which promoted the idea of "absolute private property" as it *excludes* any consideration "that the family and the resources were inextricably linked" (Macfarlane, 1978, p. 170).

Max Weber's classic *Protestant ethic & the spirit of capitalism* illuminates the primacy of religious individualism and Calvinism's "spirit" in motivating entire systems of social, cultural, and economic organization, bureaucracies and the asceticism, rationalization, and depersonalization that has evolved in capitalism and globalization in thought and practice today. The foundation and purposes of the American nation were built upon "Lockean individualism and liberalism," and seen as "the final stage of human progress," a "new order based on the spontaneous relationship of free and authentic personalities," and a "living faith" as the basic root of social solidarity (Arieli, 1964, p. 200, 328, 195–197; O'Connor, 1984).

Indeed, laissez-faire individualism continues as a rallying cry of neoclassical economics and market fundamentalism, held dear with religious-like fervor. James O'Connor (1984, p. 13) observes:

"American individualism" is capital's most powerful weapon of ideological domination of labor in the USA. Ideologies of individualism are stronger than racist and sexist ideologies because they are more deeply embedded in English, hence Anglo-American, economic, social, and political life. Unarguably, bonds of ethnicity, race and sex mediate the dominance of ideologies of individualism in subtle and profound ways. However, these hegemonic ideologies and their myths of the "self," private property, and natural rights "mediate back" ethnicity, race, and sex with a fateful and unconscious power which subverts or reifies "traditional" community, ethnic, and sexual identities.

The dominance of ideological individualism supports the arrogant and contentious notion that individuals are completely and solely responsible for what they become and what they accumulate in resources. It is *as if* our biology, genetics, economy, politics, and culture (including race, ethnicity, class, and gender) play little or no part in our individual life course experiences and outcomes. It is *as if* the decades of evidence-based science on the positive effects of "cumulative advantage" over those of disadvantage did not exist. It is *as if* the empirically validated effects of the social and environmental, behavioral, and structural forces are irrelevant. Whatever comprises "the social" is stripped out of meaning.

The neoliberal ideology of individualism promotes this as independence, *as it ignores the importance of interdependence.* Why do ideologues of individualism refuse to acknowledge our inextricable "interdependence"? Twine (1994) advises: "They know that,

doing so would present us with moral obligations to compensate those who bear the costs of our progress" (p. 29).

Implications for Critical Gerontology

Political attacks on universal single payer healthcare, the Affordable Care Act, and the social insurance programs of Social Security and Medicare illustrate the ideological force of individualism. The preference for individual responsibility is also reflected in the resistance to the passage of universal public long-term care and the struggles over public policy coverage of caregiving costs.

See also: Affordable Care Act (ACA), Class, Cumulative Advantage/Disadvantage, Freedom, Ideology, The Market, Medicare, Neoliberalism, Risk, the Social, Social Security

Further Reading

Arber, S. & Attias-Donfut, C. (2000). *The myth of generational conflict: The family and state in ageing societies* (1st edition). London: Routledge.

Arieli, Y. (1964). *Individualism and nationalism in American ideology* (pp. 200, 328, 195–197). Cambridge, MA: Harvard University Press.

Ginn, J., Street, D., & Arber, S. (Eds.). (2001). *Women, work, and pensions: International issues and prospects* (p. 20). Buckingham, UK: Open University Press.

Macfarlane, A. (1978). *The origins of English individualism* (p. 170). Oxford: Oxford University Press.

O'Connor, J. (1984). *Accumulation crisis.* New York: Blackwell.

Somers, M. R. (2008). *Genealogies of citizenship.* New York: Cambridge University Press.

Twine, F. (1994). *Citizenship and social rights: The interdependence of self and society.* London: Sage.

Weber, M. (1996). *Max Weber: The Protestant ethic and the spirit of capitalism. Introduction by Randall Collins, translated by Talcott Parsons* (reprinted from *Max Weber: The Protestant ethic and the spirit of capitalism. Translated by Talcott Parsons*, 1930). Los Angeles, CA: Roxbury Publishing.

Inequality

Negotiated in constellations of privilege, power, and domination/oppression. It is a force and reality, as concerns uneven valuing and rewarding, particularly with regard to the distribution of resources, status, access, and property. It is observed across sociocultural locations of age, disability, gender, sexuality, class, and race and manifested in the structural imbalances of not mutually exclusive realms of: opportunity, systemic violence, the accumulation of income and wealth, and social protection.

"Old age is being reshaped through the influence of different types of inequality, those based around differences in wealth, pension, and access to care" (Walker, Sinfield, & Walker, 2011, p. 207). Uncertain, withdrawing, and reduced access to recognition and rights through the State is producing more inequality within the US population.

Social Security plays an integral part in reducing poverty but not necessarily correcting or dismantling inequality; with age wealth inequality still increases. Still, Social Security is a vanguard of the scant resources which 22 million people depend upon to keep them out of poverty. If that income were removed it would result in many more Americans in extreme poverty. Minority communities are especially vulnerable. According to the Center on Budget & Policy Priorities (CBPP), if Social Security were removed the poverty rate among Latinos would approach 50 percent and the poverty rate for African Americans would exceed 50 percent (Romig & Sherman, 2016).

Nobel Prize economist Peter Diamond (2004, p. 22) states:

Occasionally, I run into people who believe that no one in his right mind would design a retirement income system like the one we have. Some of the details do seem far from satisfactory to me. However, looking at the big picture, this structure makes sense. Mandated savings makes sense if you think that many workers would not provide themselves a reasonable replacement rate. This is not just an issue of avoiding poverty, but one that extends quite far up the income distribution. Mandating annuitization makes sense if you think that workers do not adequately understand the value of annuities. Protection of spouses and children makes sense if you think that many workers would not do that adequately. Relating benefits to a measure of lifetime earnings surely makes sense. A progressive benefit formula makes sense to provide higher replacement rates for lower earners, in order to supplement annual income taxation as part of lifetime earnings insurance and redistribution, to offset some of the redistributive effects of uniform annuitization, and to address the low antipoverty protection for the elderly (SSI) in contrast with other advanced countries. The retirement test at some ages makes sense. Having redistributed to earlier cohorts, spreading the implied cost over the indefinite future (not fully funding Social Security) makes sense and incomplete funding contributes to risk sharing across cohorts. Relying on a mix of a smaller mandatory system than is common in Europe and voluntary private supplementation makes sense, even though the voluntary system is so incomplete in its coverage (and in need of improved regulation). This is not to say there are not other approaches that have led to systems that function reasonably well. It is just to say there is no need for radical reform in order to have a good system – just a need to put the program on a stronger financial footing while improving the benefit structure at the same time.

Income and Wealth Inequality

"The business oriented World Economic Forum identifies rising inequality as an urgent global issue," one that threatens social stability and global security (Yates, 2016, pp. 1–2). The share of national income going to the richest 1 percent in the World Wealth & Income database is highest in the USA compared to 15 other developed economies/nations and the increase in income share has risen most in the USA (1980–2014). Simultaneously wealth inequality has been on the rise.

For example, the chart below shows how Americans on different incomes will be helped or hurt by the Tax Cuts and Jobs Act of 2017, the Republican tax cuts/tax reform bill signed into law by President Donald Trump in late 2017 (Matthews, 2018).

Rising income and wealth disparities in the USA for all ages signals the nation's move from "shared prosperity" (1940s–1970s) to slow and unequal wage growth, recession, job loss, flight to global spaces (1980s to the present), and the erosion of middle-class retirement security. Scholars have also debated serious questions about adverse effects of welfare reform legislation on the poor, and the recent rise of extreme poverty in the United States; that is, the numbers of people living on $2 a day per person (Wilson, 2017).

With skyrocketing inequalities, the importance of Social Security, Medicare, and Medicaid has become critical. Aging policy and the likelihood that these programs will respond with benefit expansion is low. Stark divides in inequality of both income and wealth exist by race, ethnicity, socioeconomic status, and gender, and these divides

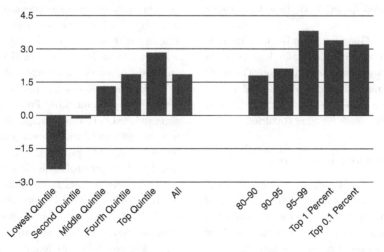

TCJA Increases Disparities in Observed After-Tax Income
Percent change in observed after-tax income, 2025

Source: Tax Policy Center, Joint Committee on Taxation, Congressional Budget Office, author's calculations.

Figure 11 Inequality

are growing. They are also reflected in gaps in life expectancy that are stunningly tracked (and increasingly evident) by income gradient. Black male Americans with less than high school education have 14.2 years' *shorter life expectancy* than college-educated white men. For white college-educated women versus black high school women, the gap in life expectancy is more than a decade (10.3 years less) (Bosworth, Burtless, & Zhang, 2016).

As is empirically verified, the rising economic disparity in life expectancy calls for improvements and increases in various levels of income support through Social Security, Supplemental Security Income, and health care coverage and access. In particular, declines and precarity in all sources of retirement security (private pensions and savings/assets) for 94 percent of the population have made the safety net programs more essential than ever (Bosworth, Burtless, & Zhang, 2016). Yet they are threatened by the Trump Administration and radical changes proposed for the US health, welfare, and retirement systems (Wilson, 2017). In a little-known study, wealth inequality of the top 1 percent directly relates to very high political participation, even in comparison with other lesser affluent Americans (with wealth of $150,000 upward) (Cook, Page, & Moskowitz, 2014).

The Gini Coefficient is one of the most used measures of inequality. It measures the equality of income distribution. The coefficient marks a steady rise in inequality in the United States over the past 50 years with varying trends for other countries.

Cumulative Inequality

Cumulative inequality is a perspective of Ferraro and Shippee (2009) who propose axioms on "systemic properties" in relation to "how individuals become stratified" and the concept of cumulative inequality:

1. Social Systems generate inequality, which is manifested over the life course through demographic and developmental processes.
2. Disadvantage increases exposure to risk, but advantage increases exposure to opportunity.
3. Life course trajectories are shaped by the accumulation of risk, available resources, and human agency.
4. The perception of life trajectories influences subsequent trajectories.
5. Cumulative inequality may lead to premature mortality; therefore, non-random selection may give the appearance of decreasing inequality in later life.

Ferraro and collaborators state that these axioms speak both to systemic levels of inequality and the potential for agency to alter or modify various dependent variable outcomes. What is posited is a "dialectic of human agency and social structure" and that resources can mitigate or accelerate favorable or unfavorable trajectories. Ferraro delineates research on "accumulation," describing two foci: the role of actor perceptions and the onset, duration, and exposure and interruptions in the life course. Ferraro (2011) points to such work as integral to gene–environment and sociogenomic studies and inequality. The pioneering work of Len Pearlin (2010) on stress and the life course is relevant to the Ferraro project, given the emphasis on individual agency and resilience. Pearlin spells out the "paradigmatic alliance" between the Stress Process Paradigm and the Life Course Paradigm, for "the ways in which social stratification generates differences in risk for psychological distress," and the role of personal agency in affecting stress management and social adjustment (Pearlin, 2010). Similarly, Pearlin's research on "linked-lives" in understanding the relations between different dimensions of caregiving and stress is highly relevant.

From a critical perspective, one of the most undeveloped (limited) aspects of cumulative inequality is the inattention to the specifics of the economic and ideological systems of capitalism, globalization, the nation-state, and other macro structures and processes for their effects on the inequalities of individual trajectories. Given that inequality is inherently a property of collectivities (Dannefer, 2017), inequality requires study well beyond the individual as the sole unit of analysis. O'Rand (2016) speaks to the dynamics of demography, economy, and policy in life course research and that aging processes and inequalities "are shaped by global forces that affect day to day lives . . . introducing new risks . . . [including the] retrenchment of social institutions . . . [and] a market ideology and a financial logic" (p. 377). The political economy of aging embraces agency, yet emphasizes that individual agency is exercised within sets of larger constraints, structures, and social struggles in the society and globe, in which power and dominance surrounding the accumulation of resources are formidable obstacles and in constant play (Estes, 2011). Research and theory must specify these factors, variables, and phenomena both within and beyond cohort frames (see Dannefer (1987) and Kelley-Moore and Lin (2011) on identifying elements of social context with increasing precision and cohort research problematics).

Diamond and colleagues (2016) speak to poverty and the global "set-up" in which "individual countries make internal decisions, and they can choose to address the underlying causes of inequality or the inequality itself or not" (p. 413). Diamond notes that we do not have a mechanism of governance to coordinate on taxation, yet also notes the importance of investments as revenues for growth. On the topic of whether richer nations have a moral obligation to help poorer ones, he says, "Sure. And by and large, they do a little bit" (p. 413), and notes Piketty's proposal for a worldwide tax on wealth. He prefers framing the issue as poverty rather than inequality, and he shies away from using the term "redistribution."

Diamond and colleagues (2016) suggest that it is better to frame questions in terms of policy issues of pre-kindergarten education, infrastructure, and to "look at taxes that fall broadly . . . not just on the top 1% or 10%" (p. 414). Diamond argues that the discussion needs to be "recast around revenues for investment in growth. . . . Public investment is the place where the government bears the responsibility directly in investing" (Diamond et al., 2016, p. 414).

See also: Austerity, Class, Cumulative Advantage/Disadvantage, Ethnicity, Food Insecurity, Gender, Globalization, Housing, Intersectionality, Neoliberalism, Poverty, Poverty Threshold, Precarity, Statelessness, War on Women

Further Reading

Abramson, C. (2015). *The end game: How inequality shapes our final years*. Cambridge, MA: Harvard University Press.

Abramson, C. M. (2016). Unequal aging: Lessons from inequality's end game. *Public Policy and Aging Report, 26*(2), 68–72.

Abramson, C. M. & Portacolone, E. (2017). What is new with old? What old age teaches us about inequality and stratification. *Sociology Compass, 11*(e12450), 1–13.

Bosworth, B., Burtless, G., & Zhang, K. (2016). *Later retirement, inequality in old age, and the growing gap in longevity between rich and poor*. Washington, DC: Brookings Institution.

Cook, F. L., Page, B. I., & Moskowitz, R. L. (2014). Political engagement by wealthy Americans. *Political Science Quarterly, 129*(3), 381–398.

Crystal, S. (2016). Late-life inequality in the second gilded age: Policy choices in a new context. *Public Policy and Aging Report, 26*(2), 42–47.

Dannefer, D. (1987). Aging as intracohort differentiation: Accentuation, the Matthew effect, and the life course. *Sociological Forum, 2*(2), 211–236.

Dannefer, D. (2017). History, biography, and age: Three levels of inequality. Keynote Lecture, *International Association of Gerontology and Geriatrics (IAGG)*. San Francisco (July).

Diamond, P. (2004). Social Security. *American Economic Review*, *94*(1), 1–24.

Diamond, P. A., Mirrlees, J. A., Ng, Y-K, & Kumar, R. (2016). Inequality: Comments, questions & answers. *Contemporary Economic Policy*. *34*(3), 412–414.

Estes, C. L. (2011). Crises in old age policy. In R. A. Settersten Jr. & J. L. Angel (Eds.), *Handbook of sociology of aging* (3rd edition) (pp. 297–320). New York: Springer.

Ferraro, K. (2011). Health and aging: Early origins, persistent inequalities? In R. A. Settersten Jr. & J. L. Angel (Eds.), *Handbook of sociology of aging* (pp. 465–475). New York: Springer.

Ferraro, K. F. & Shippee, T. P. (2009). Aging and cumulative inequality: How does inequality get under the skin? *The Gerontologist*, *49*(3), 333–343.

Kelley-Moore, J. A. & Lin, J. (2011). Widening the view: Capturing "unobserved" heterogeneity in studies of age and the life course. In R. A. Settersten Jr. & J. L. Angel (Eds.), *Handbook of sociology of aging* (pp. 51–68). New York: Springer.

Matthews, D. (2018). How the Republican tax law hurts the poor and helps the rich, in one chart. February 26. Retrieved from www.vox.com/platform/amp/policy-and-politics/2018/2/26/17044440/gop-tax-cut-tax-reform-law-chart-regressive-rich-poor-graph.

O'Rand, A. M. (2016). Long, broad, and deep: Theoretical approaches in aging and inequality. In V. L. Bengston & R. A. Settersten Jr. (Eds.), *Handbook of sociology of aging* (3rd edition) (pp. 365–380). New York: Springer.

Pearlin, L. I. (2010). The life course and the stress process: Some conceptual comparisons. *The Journals of Gerontology Series B: Psychological Sciences and Social Sciences*, *65B*(2), 207–215.

Piketty, T. & Saez, E. (2003). Income inequality in the United States, 1913–1998. *The Quarterly Journal of Economics*, *118*(1), 1–39.

Romig, K. & Sherman, A. (2016). *Social security keeps 22 million Americans out of poverty: A state-by-state analysis*. Washington, DC: Center on Budget and Policy Priorities.

Tippett, R., Jones-DeWeever, A., Rockeymoore, M., Hamilton, D., & Darity, W. (2014). *Beyond broke: Why closing the racial wealth gap is a priority for national economic security*. Washington, DC: Center for Global Policy Solutions.

Veghte, B. W. (2015). Social inequality, retirement security, and the future of social security. *Poverty & Public Policy*, *7*(2), 97–122.

Walker, A., Sinfield, A., & Walker, C. (2011). *Fighting poverty, inequality and injustice: A manifesto inspired by Peter Townsend*. Bristol: Policy Press.

Wilson, W. J. (2017). Why sociologists matter in the welfare reform debate. *Contemporary Sociology: A Journal of Reviews*, *46*(6), 627–634.

Yates, M. D. (2016). Measuring global inequality. *Monthly Review*, *68*(6), 1.

Insolvency

A term sometimes used interchangeably with "bankruptcy." This is particularly the case with aging policy, Social Security, and Medicare. In media and policy circles, the big debate on Social Security centers around the contested and socially constructed notion that Social Security is unsustainable – that it is (or will run) out of funds. The charge is that being insolvent means that these programs will not be able to pay benefits that beneficiaries have earned. The negative messaging contributes to public polling, suggesting that many young people do not believe Social Security will be there for them or for generations ahead.

Different definitions of solvency and its opposite, insolvency, are framed by various political, economic policy interests, and ideologies, often resulting in contradictory consequences. For example, the status of the SS Trust Fund may be equated with the amount of ongoing FICA (Federal Insurance Contributions Act) payments (contributions that come out of every paycheck for Social Security) against the beneficiary payments (what is paid out when an individual collects); or it may incorporate the interest payments from the general treasury on the Trust Funds it has borrowed for other purposes. Or, insolvency may be seen as what it will cost the US government to *pay back the loans borrowed* from the SS Trust Fund. Projections of future solvency and insolvency also depend on varying baseline and future assumptions of GDP growth, population, and fertility growth. Clearly important factors that will directly affect payments into and out of Social Security are economic growth, immigration, employment, unemployment, education, and whether child and eldercare policy permits caregivers to work. These factors are all forces that affect young workers and their opportunities to contribute.

In terms of aging policy, 75-year projections are required for Social Security and Medicare. The introduction of Infinite Horizon projections is another model instituted that has no time limit. Henry Aaron (2014) speaks to insolvency/solvency projections of the Congressional Budget Office (CBO), reviewing the utility of three sets of projections: long-term budget projections (1) 75-year projections for Social Security, (2) 75-year projections for Medicare, and (3) infinite-horizon generational accounts. He concludes that there is utility in the 75-year Social Security projections, although the assumptions are salient, given that Social Security was intentionally designed as a pay-as-you-go system and an infinite source of revenue via the mandatory contributions tagged to wage income. He suggests that Medicare's more accurate timeline projection is 23 years rather than

the 75-year projections, given the rapidity and fluidity of changes in medicine and medical markets. Aaron (2014, p. 1) is more skeptical about the value of infinite horizon budgeting, and states:

> All projections are based on assumptions around some set of variables and are vulnerable to error, or the variability in predictable factors, as well as uncertainty stemming from unforeseeable circumstances. Because error and uncertainty grow as the projection horizon is lengthened, in some cases, lengthening the window is not useful and can degrade decision making. . . . Infinite horizon generational account projections simply freeze the underlying variables at their value in the 75th year and extrapolate into perpetuity, providing no new information after the 75th year.

A critical political economy view: The concept of insolvency and particularly infinite horizon projections are useful for the opponents of social insurance programs like Social Security and Medicare. They confuse the public and policy-makers, and often support baseless and highly inaccurate predictions of sustainability for centuries into the future. Our present polarized paths in politics, culture, and economics in 2018, and looking forward, appear unsustainable and laden with risk of catastrophe in any one of multiple arenas (global warming Mother Earth, nuclear war obliteration, poverty beyond sustainable life).

The insolvency discourse and statistical analyses may be applied to many public and private sector programs for which profits, revenues, and benefits square off (or trade off). Diamond and Orszag (2005) suggest that Social Security will be stabilized by various tax and spending adjustments, and will gradually end the process by which the US general fund has been borrowing from payroll taxes. This requires increased revenues devoted to Social Security. Their plan, as with some other more controversial Social Security stabilization plans, relies on gradually increasing the retirement age, raising the ceiling on which people must pay Federal Insurance Contribution Act (FICA) taxes, and slowly increasing the FICA tax rate to a peak of 15 percent total from the current 12.4 percent.

From a social insurance proponents' perspective, the present Congressional and administrative line-up of opponents of Social Security, Medicare, Medicaid, and the Affordable Care Act, and the current push to enact large-scale tax cuts which will increase the federal deficit, make the likelihood of stabilizing and improving these programs far-fetched. This is especially true, given the blizzard of confusion in the public's mind, and media hype swallowing and disseminating it hook line and sinker.

See also: Actuary, Framing, Social Security

Further Reading

Aaron, H. (2014). *The economics and politics of long-term budget projections.* (Working Paper #8, December 15). Hutchins Center on Fiscal & Monetary Policy at Brookings. Retrieved from www.brookings.edu/wp-content/uploads/2016/06/15_economics_politics_longrun_budget_aaron.pdf.

Congressional Budget Office. (2016). Glossary, July. www.cbo.gov/publication/42904.

Diamond, P. A. & Orszag, P. R. (2005). Saving Social Security: The Diamond-Orszag Plan. *The Economists' Voice, 2*(1), 1–8.

Hiltzik, M. A. (2009). *The plot against Social Security: How the Bush plan is endangering our financial future.* New York: Harper Collins.

Hiltzik, M. A. (2015). Social Security trustees: Program is healthier, Congress still must act. *Los Angeles Times,* July 22. Retrieved from http://lat.ms/2zTvgZd.

Institutions

Any structure in society, organizations, groups, or entities centered on a social purpose, mission, and shared beliefs. They may be constituted as established law, formal or informal practices, customs, and traditions, and rituals that over time give a sense of social order, permanence, and stability, conveying norms and sanctions. These may be political parties or governmental branches, corporations and financial entities, religious congregations, academies and educational organizations, and other cultural, media, economic, and legal associations.

Classical sociologists Emile Durkheim and Max Weber, in different ways, argued that institutions are foundational to establishing, maintaining, and conflicting over a society's (and entities therein) social arrangements; social integration; divisions of labor; social, cultural, and economic identity (and even "spirit"), and political rankings within society. Institutions may proffer potential for real change or entrenched resistance to change. We speak of institutional racism, institutional sexism, nativism, ageism, global financial marketization, and inequalities as barriers and the contested fruits of democratic states that manifest huge gaps in life expectancy, health, and wealth. Within a constructionist perspective, we understand that our institutions are socially constructed and reproduced, but weighed in favor of dominant vested power interests with vital stakes that support, produce, and preserve the status quo. Our critical political economy lens alerts us to the vital role of power garnered through agency, discourses, ideologies, and structures of privilege, as well as the counter-resistance networks and movements required to shift the institutionalized bulwarks of subjugation and injustice.

Institutional Isomorphism

A sociological process that presses entities toward similarities in organizational forms and behavior. DiMaggio and Powell (1983) identify the import of:

1. Normative pressures that require institutions to behave in ways to establish/maintain legitimacy within the dominant field of entities (e.g., human service non-profit providers denying care in order to compete and mirror the efficiencies of for-profit business).
2. Lack of organizational identity or blurring of their mission and purpose, leading institutions to mimic others perceived as more successful in the organizational field ("mimetic/mimesis").
3. Coercive mandates by governmental authorities or societal expectations that limit the domains of institutions (e.g., President Reagan's abolishing Older Americans Act requirements that human services providers be non-profit, and replacing them with financing and computer regulations that only large national medical corporations could meet).

Such forces may explain why, as small community non-profit organizations grow, they adopt "like behavior" of large for-profit corporations in order to survive. Public sector organizations such as Community Health and Mental Health Centers have been pressed to adopt practices of institutional isomorphism on all three levels (Frumkin & Galaskiewicz, 2004). In aging services, particularly medical and health services including the aging enterprise, the once-dominant small non-profit providers have seen their comprehensive and "kinder" service missions transformed amidst their own legitimation crises, as market proponents accelerated consolidation, competition, scale, and privatization, forcing non-profits to behave more and more like (mimetic) for-profits, or more likely, to merge or "become" corporate operators (Estes, Alford, & Egan, 2001; Svihula & Estes, 2009).

Snyder (2017, p. 22), in his warnings *On tyranny*, underscores the importance of organizing (and resisting) at an institutional level:

It is institutions that help us to preserve decency. They need our help as well. Do not speak of "our institutions" unless you make them yours by acting on their behalf. Institutions do not protect themselves. They fall one after the other unless each is defended from the beginning. So choose an institution you care about − a court, a newspaper, a law, a labor union − and take its side.

Critical Distinction

Institutions are social structures which do not necessarily entrap or imprison individuals or communities. Institutionalization (physically putting people in institutions) is distinct as a method of social control similar to incarceration − especially within the gerontological canon of critical responses to poor houses and nursing homes where societies abandon the elderly to wither. Institutions on a theoretical level are foundations for community values, with robust mission statements and declarative commitments to the social good.

See also: Agency, Crisis, Legitimation, Market, Political Economy, Social Movements

Further Reading

DiMaggio, P. J., & Powell, W. W. (1983). The iron cage revisited: Institutional isomorphism and collective rationality in organizational fields. *American Sociological Review, 48*(2), 147–160.

Estes, C. L., Alford, R. R., & Egan, A. H. (2001). The transformation of the non-profit sector: Systemic crisis and the political economy of aging services. In C. L. Estes & Associates, *Social policy & aging: A critical perspective* (pp. 69–94). Thousand Oaks, CA: Sage.

Frumkin, P. & Galaskiewicz, J. (2004). Institutional isomorphism and public sector organizations. *Journal of Public Administration Research and Theory*, *14*(3), 283–307.

Snyder, T. (2017). *On tyranny*. New York: Penguin Random House.

Svihula, J. & Estes, C. L. (2009). Social security privatization: The institutionalization of an ideological movement. In L. Rogne, C. L. Estes, B. Grossman, B. Hollister, & E. Solway (Eds.), *Social insurance & social justice: Social security, Medicare, & the campaign against entitlements* (pp. 217–231). New York: Springer.

Insurance/Reinsurance

Offers protection against unanticipated loss or coverage for needed services. This coverage may include property (car and home), health, income (Unemployment Insurance, Social Security, and Disability Insurance). Private companies, the State, and employers (ESI: Employer Sponsored Insurance) offer various benefits based on qualifying employment status/history and need. For insurance benefits in old age the criteria for benefits and the cost of coverage include age rating and gender rating practices.

Critical political perspectives look at how conservative and neoliberal ideologies advance through social policy. Lobbying forces, Super PACS, and cultural values around work and worth frame the contentious struggles around who qualifies, to what extent they receive insurance benefits, and for how long this coverage extends. Unending battles for and against universal health care engulf such terrain as seen and heard about types of health insurance (see below).

Types of Health Insurance

• *Single Payer*: The government provides insurance for all residents (or citizens) and covers the cost of all health care expenses except for co-pays and co-insurance. The health care services, such as providers, may be public, private, or a combination of both.

• *Two-tier*: The government provides or mandates catastrophic or minimum insurance coverage for all residents (or citizens), while allowing the purchase of additional voluntary insurance or fee for service care when desired. In Singapore, all residents receive a catastrophic policy from the government coupled with a health savings account that they use to pay for routine care. In other countries like Ireland and Israel, the government provides a core policy which the majority of the population supplement with private insurance.

• *Insurance Mandate*: The government mandates that all citizens purchase insurance, whether from private, public, or non-profit insurers. In some cases, the insurer list is quite restrictive, while in others, a healthy private market for insurance is simply regulated and standardized by the government. In this kind of system, insurers are barred from rejecting sick individuals, and individuals are required to purchase insurance to prevent typical health care market failures from arising.

As part of the ACA, the federal government attempted to shore up and protect the private marketplaces through support of private insurers. The government offered financial support to insurers in the form of reinsurance. This meant that the federal government would step in and support insurance companies if they experienced high levels of claims. Additional risk-sharing arrangements were also put in place to encourage insurers to cover higher risk patients but these measures were somewhat half-hearted and temporary. However, there continue to be unfolding ingenious efforts to sabotage and repeal the ACA via court decisions against the insurance mandate, and those in favor of allowing states to offer non-ACA compliant skinny plans, add work requirements, and more. Possibilities also swirl around multiple renditions of "Medicare for All."

See also: Affordable Care Act (ACA), Age Rating, Gender Rating, LTSS, Medicare, Medicaid, Privatization, Social Insurance, Welfare, Workfare

Interactionism

Also called symbolic interactionism; studies relational exchanges and how these produce social reality and attach meaning. Social phenomena such as identity, self-concept, and self-awareness through taking the role of the other person and others' point of view are key.

According to George Herbert Mead (1938), persons develop a concept of self through socialization occurring through interactions. Individuals can perceive themselves through the ability to adopt, as their own, the attitudes which others press upon them. These are sources of identities by which individuals can view themselves as an object. Cooley's (1956) "looking glass self" theory posits that how others view a person may become part of the person's socialization to society and self. One's self-concept, identity, and socialization occur through interactions with and reactions of others.

In gerontology, interactionism theory posits that the experience of old age may be dependent on how others react to the old, and how the old are shaped and react back to their interactions in the social world (Estes, 1980). The social context and personal and cultural meanings are paramount. Social interactions convey symbolic meanings through individuals, families, organizations, and institutions. Social context comprises not only situational events and interactional opportunities (or lack thereof), but also structural constraints that limit the range of possible interactions, reinforcing certain lines of action while inhibiting others.

Interactionism is expressed through the power of labels, independent of inherent process of chronological years passing. Power lies in how others react to us and how we are treated (Estes, 1979), how we reflect and react back, and how we are likely to internalize these portrayals. Processes of interactionism make the attitudes of "helping" professionals working with older adults and ageism serious matters of concern. The potential formation of an "aging subculture" or "aging group consciousness" has been explored by interactionist scholars (Rose, 1964), raising questions about whether programs and services for the aging should be segregated or integrated within community, society, and policy (e.g., whether housing should be age segregated or age integrated).

Within the political economy of aging framework, policy and policy debates are examined as socially constructed "problems," narratives, and labels of old people and the demographics of aging and their contested policy remedies. Power inheres in the capacity of strategically located agents to define "the problem" and to press their views into public consciousness and law. Interactions and outcomes in critical political economy are understood within a "conflict paradigm" in which policy outcomes are the product of coercive forces of power that compete for dominance (and do or do not win). The outcomes may (1) give older adults the looking glass self-image of devalued, sense of worthlessness, and disempowerment (Rodin & Langer, 1980); (2) render their needs and lives neglected and invisible, as well as subject to social control; and/or (3) increase the dependency, hardship, and even shorten the life expectancy of older persons. Beyond the older persons themselves, social policy is consequential for social structure and social change.

See also: Intersubjectivity, Micro-levels, Postmodernism

Further Reading

Blumer, H. (1969). *Symbolic interaction.* Englewood Cliffs, NJ: Prentice-Hall.

Cooley, C. H. (1956). *Human nature and the social order.* Glencoe, IL: The Free Press.

Estes, C. L. (1979). *The aging enterprise: A critical examination of social policies and services for the aged.* San Francisco, CA: Jossey-Bass.

Estes, C. L. (1980). Constructions of reality. *Journal of Social Issues, 2*(36), 117–132.

Gubrium, J. F. & Holstein, J. A. (2000). The self in a world of going concerns. *Symbolic Interaction, 23*(2), 95–115.

Marshall, V. W., Martin-Matthews, A., & McMullin, J. A. (2016). The interpretive perspective on aging. In V. L. Bengtson & R. Settersten Jr. (Eds.), *Handbook of theories of aging* (3rd edition) (pp. 381–400). New York: Springer.

Mead, G. H. (1938). *The philosophy of the act.* Chicago, IL: University of Chicago Press.

Rodin, J. & Langer, E. (1980). Aging labels: The decline of control and the fall of self-esteem. *Journal of Social Issues, 36*(2), 12–29.

Rose, A. M. (1964). A current theoretical issue in social gerontology. *The Gerontologist, 4*(1), 46–50.

Strauss, A. L. (1993). *Continual permutations of action.* New York: Aldine DeGruyter.

Interaction Ritual Chains (IRCs)

The interactional processes through which rituals generated in individual and group interactions produce charged emotional energy. Interaction rituals are an essential analytic category in a critical perspective on old age and aging policy. Rituals produce symbols of group membership, connecting and mediating group structure and beliefs. Emile Durkheim's term, "collective effervescence," is the emotion produced by and through ritual, including the sacred (e.g., religion) and the secular, through which anger and solidarity may be conjoined.

Ritual ingredients may include a common action or event in which two or more persons are physically assembled in the same place so that they affect each other by bodily co-presence and their attention, and the shared mood of emotional experience is focused. Intensification occurs. Ritual outcomes include group solidarity and symbols of sacred relationships, righteous anger for violations. "The key process is participants' mutual entrainment of emotion and attention, producing a shared emotional/cognitive experience. . . . [It is] a micro-situational production of moments of intersubjectivity" (Collins, 2004, p. 48).

Interaction rituals are foundational to understanding the organization and trajectories of social movements, and the ideological campaigns within them. Crediting Durkheim, Goffman, and Mead, Collins (2004) illuminates the social phenomena of the circulation of symbols (e.g., wild police dogs biting black protesters) through "self-reinforcing" interaction rituals in which "the presence of memory is charged up" (p. 95) and mutual focus is concentrated. The central formulation is:

> Human beings are emotional energy seekers, thereby linked to those interactions and their derivative symbols that give the greatest EE in the opportunities presented by each person's social networks. . . . Human beings are active, excitement seeking, magnetically attracted to where things are happening. . . . We are deeply socially constituted beings. . . . Symbols make up the very structure of our consciousness.
>
> (Collins, 2004, pp. 373–374)

There are power rituals and status rituals with order-givers and order-takers during which individuals may win or lose emotional energy (EE). Outcomes of IRCs are influenced by power, material, and other resources that may constrain or unleash EE, through processes of "emotional entrainment" (Collins, 2004, p. 171). "EE is an empirical variable . . . EE is the continuum from enthusiasm, confidence and initiative at the high end, down to passivity and depression at the low end. EE . . . empirically [is] in the flow of consciousness and in one's bodily sensations" (pp. 133–134).

For two IRC analytic examples (Estes, 2017) directly related to the politics and policy of aging, *see* Social Movements; see also Collins (2004, Figures 2.1 and 4.1, pp. 48 and 147).

See also: Affect, Consciousness Raising, Co-presence, Culture, Emotional Energy, Politics, Social Movements

Further Reading

Collins, R. (2004). *Interaction ritual chains*. Princeton, NJ: Princeton University Press.

Estes, C. L. (2017). Older US women's economic security, health & empowerment. In S. Dworkin, M. Gandhi, & P. Passano (Eds.), *Women's empowerment and global health* (pp. 232–250). Oakland, CA: University of California Press.

Intergenerational Contract

An agreement of mutual assistance between generations as exemplified in the concept of social insurance and as a necessary component of broad-based society and State, public, and private programs in general (Arber & Attias-Donfut, 2000). Different people will experience different levels of need at different times in their lives. Differential contributions by circumstance and a common agreement of mutual assistance have been guiding principles integral to democratic Western welfare states.

In *Ties that bind*, Kingson, Hirshorn, and Cornman (1986) provide an overview of the relationship between generations, contending that protecting the ongoing welfare of all age groups is required to overcome the challenges of aging demographics and the uncertainties of life. Economics, politics, and cultural norms and values are pivotal in setting the balance between how much risk we ask to be borne by individuals and families and how much risk should be mutually shouldered through societal institutions and policy such as social insurance and social provisioning.

Major debate over welfare states highlights two divergent views regarding the intergenerational contract. One view accords validity to a State and society building upon a foundation of "the social," the commons (*generational interdependence*). Another view accords validity to State and society that builds upon the foundation of individual responsibility and "the atomistic individual" (*generational accounting*) (Williamson, Watts-Roy, & Kingson, 1999).

The two perspectives differ profoundly regarding (1) what kind of society and civilization we want to live in and to leave as our legacy to future generations; (2) how much we value the protection of minority rights and the survival of diverse communities (Kingson, Cornman & Torre-Norton, 2009; Rogne et al., 2009); and (3) who should bear the risk and responsibility for the problems that members of society confront. These involve questions about whether the individual is to blame for the unfolding life events and situations and/or whether there are risks for which no individual can prepare and no one should be denied assistance. Examples of major risks and harms that are larger than single individuals and families are the more "structural" events and conditions such as hurricanes Harvey and Katrina, global warming, the outsourcing and disappearance of jobs, the deindustrialization of communities, the Great Recession with bank and hedge fund Wall Street crashing that eradicated trillions in housing equity and life savings, and the laws that incentivize corporate inversions to avoid US taxes.

Generational Interdependence versus Generational Accounting: Reframing the Debate

"Generational interdependence" understands society from the perspective that "we are all in this together." It recognizes the social, economic, physical, and human developmental necessity of solidarity within and across generations and the utmost benefits of universal coverage by pooling risk across our broad population.

In direct contrast, the "generational accounting" frame prioritizes individual responsibility in which each individual and each generation is responsible for him- or herself alone – ignoring the certainty that no individual or generation has ever succeeded entirely on their own – independent of material and societal arrangements, benefits, institutions, and conditions across time. Generational accounting supports the false idea that what we achieve is solely due to our own effort, with nothing owed to our cumulative advantages and disadvantages throughout our lifespan. Anyone who has borne or cared for another human being, a child, grandchild, or other person, knows this is an untenable assumption – although perhaps compatible with three notions: (1) the "universal" white male privileged citizen; (2) ignoring and accepting the "impossible choice" (Lewis, 1995) and "forced choice" (Glenn, 2010) for women between mothers/caregivers and workers and poverty and gross inequities for women of color (Arber & Attias-Donfut, 2000, p. 10; Ginn & Arber, 2000, pp. 134–136) and unmarried, single women; and (3) the denial of the persistent and deeply damaging institutionalized racism that is still within our societies, from the womb, education, neighborhood, health, and economic pathways and social networks.

From a *critical political economy perspective*, "the social" is central to recognizing the material, symbolic, and normative realities of the contributions within and across generations in every person's life course. Commitment to the social also offers the possibility of personal growth and self-esteem, contributing to the whole beyond sustainable measure. There is value for mutual and collective problem-solving and commitment to our place in the world. Intergenerational interdependence offers the possibility of deepening the humane experience of old age and aging, disability and illness through relationally respectful interconnection. All people across the life course and the globe have a vested stake in aging policy as we are all aging, and we are inextricably linked to others who will enter or have entered old age. Younger people must proactively advocate for the preservation and protection of their human needs (and civil rights) in young and old age. These younger voices, with those in mid-life and older age, constitute a potentially powerful intergenerational resistance needed to successfully contest attacks against social insurance programs. The present period is one of heightened precarity of large swathes of the population, with particular population groups morbidly and mortally threatened. The immorality of denial and inaction is untenable.

See also: Ageism, Age Rating, Care Penalty, Choice, Cumulative Advantage/Disadvantage, Equity, Generational and Intergenerational Consciousness, Power, Precarity, Privilege, The Social

Further Reading

Arber, S. & Attias-Donfut, C. (2000). *The myth of generational conflict: The family and state in ageing societies* (1st edition). London: Routledge.

Estes, C. L. & Associates. (2001). *Social policy & aging: A critical perspective*. Thousand Oaks, CA: Sage.

Ginn, J. & Arber, S. (2000), Gender, the generational contract and pension privatization. In S. Arber & C. Attias-Donfut (Eds.), *The myth of generational conflict* (pp. 133–136). London: Routledge/ESA Studies in European Societies.

Glenn, E.N. (2010). *Forced to care: Coercion and caregiving in America*. Cambridge, MA: Harvard University Press.

Kingson, E. R., Cornman, J. M., & Torre-Norton, A. L. (2009). The future of social insurance: Values and generational interdependence. In L. Rogne, C. L. Estes, B. Grossman, B. Hollister, & E. Solway (Eds.), *Social insurance and social justice: Social security, Medicare and the campaign against entitlements* (pp. 95–108). New York: Springer.

Kingson, E. R., Hirshorn, B. A., & Cornman, J. M. (1986). Ties that bind: The interdependence of generations. Newport Beach, CA: Seven Locks Press.

Lewis, J. (1995). Égalité, différence et rapports sociaux de sexes dans les États providence du XXe siècle. In *La place des femmes* (pp. 407–422). Paris: La Découverte.

Rogne et al., (2009) (See Carroll L. Estes' Selected Works, Appendix 4 p. 395.)

Walker, A. (Ed.) (1996). *The new generational contract: Intergenerational relations, old age and welfare*. Hove, Sussex: Psychology Press.

Williamson, J., Watts-Roy, D. M., & Kingson, E. R. (1999). *The generational equity debate*. New York: Columbia University Press.

Intergenerational Intersubjectivity

Expands on the concept of generational consciousness (the idea of a shared epistemological standpoint in chronological cohorts), proposing that something radical and psychologically expansive happens when two generations come together relationally in dialogue and solidarity. Through contact with alterity and exposure to the Other, there is a synthesis of epistemes.

> Only the being whose otherness, accepted by my being, lives and faces me in the whole compression of existence, brings the radiance of eternity to me. Only when two say to one another with all that they are, "It is Thou," is the indwelling of the Present Being between them.
>
> (Buber, 2003, p. 35)

This dictionary is created through an intergenerational intersubjectivity, as Carroll and Nicholas have 48 years spanning their births (with Maggie Kuhn as our guide). Reflecting on epistemic advantage, witnessing and experiencing cultural revolutions and personal traumas ties us as a pair to think dynamically and expand the scope of our perceptions.

Critical implications for aging scholars, activists, and policy-makers include questions of who comes together (and how) to define and meet the needs of aging peoples.

See also: Co-presence, Generational and Intergenerational Consciousness, Interaction Ritual Chains/IRCs, Public Sociology, Solidarity

Further Reading

Buber, M. (2003). *Between man and man*. New York: Routledge.

Internalization/ Internalized Oppression

Describes a process of believing external messages or realities as inner-personal truths. Psychoanalytic theories of internalization have located this process as fundamental in one's concept and development of a self. Feelings of worthiness, goodness, and belonging are interactional and extend through nurturing and care.

Internalized oppression is a theory of how the stigma, discrimination, and violence (via classism, racism, heterosexism, patriarchy, anti-Semitism, etc.) can manifest as beliefs and behaviors. Lorde (1984, p. 142) talks about how this leads to self-isolation, proposing:

> In order to be whole, we must recognize the despair oppression plants within each of us . . . [a]nd we must fight that inserted piece of self destruction that lives and flourishes like a poison inside of us, unexamined until it makes us turn on ourselves in each other. . . . [W]e can lessen its potency by the knowledge of our real connectedness, arcing across our differences.

Liebow (2016) posits that internalized oppression encompasses more than a loss of agency and manifests as a loss of "moral identity," solidifying self-beliefs of deviance and criminality.

See also: Ageism, Oppression, Pedagogy, Racism

Further Reading

Liebow, N. (2016). Internalized oppression and its varied moral harms: Self-perceptions of reduced agency and criminality. *Hypatia, 31*(4), 713–729.

Lorde, A. (1984). Age, race, class, and sex: Women redefining difference. In *Sister outsider: Essays and speeches* (pp. 114–123). Freedom, CA: Crossing Press.

Intersectionality/ Intersectional Knowledge

A theoretical framework which posits that multiple and heterogeneous social categories of identities (e.g. race, ethnicity, sexual orientation, socioeconomic status) intersect

at the micro level of individual experience to reflect multiple interlocking systems of privilege and oppression at the macro-, social-structural level (e.g., racism, sexism, heterosexism, ageism).

Intersectionality was coined by legal scholar Kimberle Crenshaw (1989), and is rooted in black feminist scholarship. Collins (2015) proposes that intersectionality exists as a field of study of power relations, an analytical strategy for finding new solutions through new perspectives, and as critical praxis – a way of implementing plans and manifesting social change. Previous and related theories include a broad landscape of critical race theory (Delgado & Stefancic, 2013), racial formation theory (Omi & Winant, 2015), and systemic racism theory (Elias & Feagin, 2016), and feminist standpoint theories.

"Individuals & groups differentially placed within intersecting systems of power have different points of view on their own and others' experiences with complex social inequalities, typically advancing knowledge projects that reflect their social locations within power relations" (Collins, 2015, p. 14). This acknowledges that the breadth of experiences within structures of power is expansive and that input from many sources and an understanding of many issues must be present for solutions to be found.

See also: Standpoint Theories

Further Reading

Cho, S., Crenshaw, K. W., & McCall, L. (2013). Toward a field of intersectionality studies: Theory, application, and praxis. *Signs, 38*(4), 785–810.

Collins, P. H. (2015). Intersectionality's definitional dilemmas. *Annual Review of Sociology, 41*(1), 1–20.

Collins, P. H. & Bilge, S. (2016). *Intersectionality*. Cambridge: Polity Press.

Crenshaw, K. W. (1989). Demarginalizing the intersection of race and sex: A black feminist critique of antidiscrimination doctrine, feminist theory and antiracist politics. *University of Chicago Legal Forum, 140*, 139–167.

Delgado, R. & Stefancic, J. (2013). *Discerning critical moments*. In M. Lynn & A. D. Dixson (Eds.), *Handbook of critical race theory in education* (pp. 23–33). New York: Routledge.

Elias, S. & Feagin, J. R. (2016). *Racial theories in social science*. London: Routledge.

Omi, M. & Winant, H. (2015). *Racial formation in the United States*. New York: Routledge.

Yeh, J. C. (2018). Contemporary cultural norms from the vantage point of a younger woman of color. *Generations, 41*(4), 97–103.

J

Jeopardy

Entails risk, danger, and threat. Frances M. Beal (1970) coined the term "double jeopardy" to describe the experience of a black woman, exploited by both racism and sexism. Dr. Jacquelyne Johnson Jackson (1971) built on the theory in her article, "The blacklands of gerontology," where she developed the concept of "quadruple jeopardy" – being black, female, old, and living in poverty. This describes the exponential risks of holding these identities and being failed by society and the welfare state.

The US Constitution knows that multiple jeopardy is unfair, hence the "double jeopardy" clause in the Fifth Amendment, which prohibits the government from prosecuting individuals more than one time for a single offense or imposing more than one punishment for a single offense. Yet, for the lived experiences of those with multiple intersections of disadvantage and oppression, there are few protections to limit exposure to jeopardy and precarity.

Critical perspective: The most vulnerable are those jeopardized through experiencing multiple/intersecting oppressions. People of color, people in poverty, people with disabilities, women, trans/gender queer people, and others' negotiating marginalized identities have the most to lose from aging and old age policies that reproduce and accentuate social and economic divisions and disparities in life expectancy, chronic illness, and quality adjusted life years (QALYs). These modern injustices extend from the United States' deep roots in white supremacy.

See also: Blacklands, Intersectionality, Quality-adjusted Life Years (QALYs), Precarity, Racism, Risk, White Supremacy

Further Reading

Beale, F. (1970). Double jeopardy: To be black and female. In T. C. Bambara (Ed.), *The black woman, an anthology* (pp. 109–122). New York: Pocket Books.

Jackson, J. J. (1971). The blacklands of gerontology. *The International Journal of Aging and Human Development, 2*(3), 156–171.

Jackson, J. J. (1980). *Minorities and aging.* Belmont, CA: Wadsworth.

Justice

An ideal of equality and the steps required to promote it.

Competing perspectives on justice abound. For example, philosopher John Rawls (1971) in his influential classic discusses justice as fairness, using the model of the social contract as an alternative to traditional nineteenth-century utilitarianism. He and his followers argue for equality to reign unless inequality fulfills the greater civic interests. In a recent compendium of his lectures, Rawls discusses the tension between liberty and equality as well as the inherent injustice in the United States' public institutions (see Rawls, 2001).).

Amartya Sen (2011), in *The idea of justice*, reasons that a perfect society is impossible and argues for a focus on active reduction of injustice. He contends that a functional theory of justice can be developed in the process of debates over what is just or unjust.

A major way of defining justice is first to recognize through feeling and listening to experiences of injustice. We propose that central to our concept of justice is equality and respect for diversity. These are sometimes difficult to verbalize and publicize, as they are tender and susceptible to dominant backlash. Central to emancipatory gerontology is a question of definition: Whose conception of justice is valued through implementation, and how do notions of right and wrong justify punitive action?

Amid the competing perspectives, state welfare schemes administer programs, dispense important goods and services, and establish laws relevant to attaining social justice. All welfare states have the potential redistribution as a core tenet to promote social justice.

Moral imperatives of justice may be announced, legitimizing, and masquerading contests for social control and power. Wallerstein raises concerns about jurisdiction and who defines problems and who proposes solutions. When we think of punishment as part of justice, who do we deem fit to engage in punishment and where do we find it merited? According to Howard Zinn, there is a power that governments cannot suppress (2007, p. 168):

Let us not be disconsolate over the increasing control of the court system by the right wing. The courts have never been on the side of justice, only moving a few degrees one way or the other,

unless pushed by the people. Those words engraved in the marble of the Supreme Court, "Equal Justice Before the Law" have always been a sham.

No Supreme Court, liberal or conservative, will stop the war in Iraq or redistribute the wealth of this country, or establish free medical care for every human being. Such fundamental change, the experience of the past suggests, will depend on the actions of an aroused citizenry, demanding that the promise of the Declaration of Independence – an equal right to life, liberty, and the pursuit of happiness – be fulfilled.

Issues of justice for the older population remain vital, since economic and social inequality continues to grow in the USA, affecting large numbers of racial and ethnic minorities, women, and those living on low incomes. Needs, rights, and justice are three separate concepts to consider. For critical gerontologists, it is vital to promote social justice and to combat inequalities that derive from the organization of society.

The Elder Justice Act was enacted in 2010 as part of the ACA with bipartisan support for a coordinating council to make recommendations to the US Department of Health and Human Services (DHHS) secretary related to elder abuse, neglect, and exploitation. The book features more details regarding the dimensions of support provided by this Act in our Legislative Appendix.

See also: Blacklands, Cognitive Liberation, Collective Impact, The Commons, Ecologies, Empowerment, Oppression, Resistance, Right to Have Rights, Socialism, Voice(lessness)

Further Reading

Fraser, N. (2014). *Justice interruptus: Critical reflections on the "postsocialist" condition.* New York: Taylor and Francis.

Isbister, J. (2001). *Capitalism and justice.* Bloomfield, CT: Kumarian Press.

McCormick, P. T. (2003). Whose justice? An examination of nine models of justice. *Journal of Religion & Spirituality in Social Work: Social Thought, 22*(2–3), 7–25.

National Archives. Retrieved from www.archives.gov.

Oyez. Retrieved from www.oyez.org (website for Supreme Court media).

Rawls, J. (2001). *Justice as fairness: A restatement,* ed. Erin Kelly. Cambridge, MA: Harvard University Press.

Rogne, L., Estes, C., Grossman, B., Hollister, B., & Solway, E. (2009). *Social insurance and social justice: Social Security, Medicare, and the campaign against entitlements.* New York: Springer.

Schraad-Tischler, D. (2011). *Social justice in the OECD – How do the member states compare? Sustainable governance indicators 2011.* Bertelsmann Stiftung. Retrieved from https://news.sgi-network.org/uploads/tx_amsgistudies/SGI11_Social_Justice_OECD.pdf.

Sen, A. (2011). *The idea of justice.* Cambridge, MA: Harvard University Press.

Supreme Court of the U.S. Retrieved from www.supremecourtus.gov.

Walker, C., Walker, A., & Sinfield, A. (2011). The legacy of Peter Townsend. In A. Walker, A. Sinfield, & C. Walker (Eds.), *Fighting poverty, inequality and injustice* (pp. 1–27). Bristol: Policy Press.

Zinn, H. (2007). A power governments cannot suppress. In *The Supreme Court* (pp. 163–168). San Francisco, CA: City Lights Books.

K

Kinship

Builds from an experience of closeness and connectedness in social relationships between family and friends. This includes the bonds that tie people through belonging and affinity.

Kinship can be born into or developed over time through processes of mutual recognition, trust, and reliance. These bonds are deeply affected by cultural trauma and marginalization. The State plays a role in defining family through means-testing social support (Temporary Aid to Needy Families, Supplemental Nutrition Assistance Program) as well as economic policies such as tax incentives (relief for married couples, caregiver tax credits, housing regulations and rental codes, and estate taxation).

Experiences of caregiving and receiving are fundamental to the development and maintenance of kinship ties. Paid caregivers become part of the social fabric of those they care for and vice versa. Besides the financial economy of care, these dyads form meaningful relationships, sharing stories and experiences that are mutual transmissions of effective care and concern. Family members of older adults receiving care often develop relationships with caregivers as well, as paid caregivers relieve family members (especially women) who may have previously shouldered the majority of the care work.

Forced to care (Nakano-Glenn, 2010) describes the imperative (and lack of choice) for kin in caregiving positions in a society directed by policies (articulated and/or naturalized) which promote or require that families and kinship networks will do at least 80 to 90 percent of that unpaid care work with no substantial relief or alternative from the State. Paid care workers are from marginalized care groups, exploited, vastly underpaid without benefits, career ladders, or security (as those they care for may die and the job concluded unexpectedly). We argue that this marginalization and the desire and need to develop mutual recognition and trust in this intimate relationship of care reflect and project a psychic violence into the dyad. This relational trauma impoverishes and endangers both people. The hardship of being forced, coerced, and arguably underpaid to care correlates with shorter life expectancy, illness, and impoverishment. Negative feelings in the dyad and the phenomena of abuse and neglect exist within this framework of coercion.

Reciprocity stands in contrast to the inequality engendered in unpaid care work. Elders prefer to have paid caregivers that relieve dependence on families which may not be able to care. The societal pressures toward self-reliance and independence are extremely strong and can have an outsized impact on the behavior of individuals as they strive to not be a "burden." *Reciprocity* protects kinship ties from being run down and worn out. This requires a strong welfare state.

See also: Caregiving, Ethnogerontology, Family, Interaction Ritual Chains, Networks, Psychoanalytic Social Theory, Zero Years

Further Reading

Cicourel, A. (2015). Collective memory, a fusion of cognitive mechanisms and cultural processes. *Revue De Synthèse, 136*(3), 309–328.

Dannefer, D. & Phillipson, C. (2010). *The SAGE handbook of social gerontology* (1st edition). Los Angeles, CA: Sage.

Fry, C. L. (2003). Kinship and supportive environments of aging. *Annual Review of Gerontology and Geriatrics, 23,* 313–333.

Jagose, A. & Hall, D. E. (2013). *The Routledge queer studies reader*. New York: Routledge.

Meyer, M. H. & Parker, W. M. (2011). The changing worlds of family and work. In R. A. Settersten Jr. & J. L. Angel (Eds.), *Handbook of sociology of aging* (pp. 263–277). New York: Springer.

Nakano-Glenn, E. N. (2010). *Forced to care*. Cambridge, MA: Harvard University Press.

Knowledges

Socially generated and collectively gathered. Often in our culture people accept knowledge as factually legitimate based only upon the empirical demonstrations of proof or upon judgments of proclaimed experts and/or those who possess high status and power. The less the knowledge base is verifiably, empirically proven, the greater the influence of social, economic, and political factors in the acceptance of "data" as knowledge (i.e., as "social facts" in the sense of Emile Durkheim). In critical thinking, knowledge grows through dialectical processes situated within and across historical time, space, and place.

Berger and Luckmann (1966) argue, "[a]s definitions of reality become widely shared, they are institutionalized as part of the '*collective stock of knowledge*'" (p. 67). Such knowledge and expert opinion take on the character of objective reality, regardless of inherent validity or perhaps alternative reality.

Knowledge is weighted with power. The "sociology of knowledge" and "science and technology studies" accord legitimacy to multiple ways of knowing, methods of understanding, and standpoints. We use the plural, *knowledges*, to announce the multiple ways in which awareness, understanding, and knowing occur and may inform (dispute or contradict) one another. This is a strength of multidisciplinary and interdisciplinary approaches and the value of collaboration across knowers who draw from divergent epistemological lenses, approaches (e.g., inductive, deductive, positivist, interpretive), and disciplines (Max Weber's concept of *verstehen*).

Maggie Kuhn charged that aging policy was misguided because knowledge of the aged was garnered from young gerontologists who "objectified" older persons as "subjects" but did not understand the individual and collective experience of aging, ageism, infantilization, and commodification. She railed against methods, theories, and policies based on objectified "subjects."

The challenge to the "one universal truth" of objective knowledge is illuminated in the very concepts of intersectionality, identity politics, cultural wars and epistemic oppressions of race, ethnicity, class, gender, ability, and age. In *Black feminist consciousness*, Patricia Hill Collins (2002) serves notice to white feminists that they do not possess the universal truth about being a woman while black. Even earlier than this, freed slave Sojourner Truth interrogated the intersections of race and gender in her famous "Ain't I a woman?" speech at the 1851 Women's Convention in Akron,

Ohio – one of the earlier recorded accounts of the intersectionality perspective.

The present "alternative fact" and "fake news" period threatens the political, economic, and cultural foundations of knowledge(s).

See also: Discourse, Epistemology, Framing, Intersectionality, Levels of Analysis, Postmodernism, Relations of Ruling, Standpoint Theories, Think Tanks

Further Reading

Berger, P. L. & Luckmann, T. (1966). *The social construction of reality*. Garden City, NY: Doubleday.

Collins, P. H. (2000). *Black feminist thought: Knowledge, consciousness, and the politics of empowerment* (revised 10th Anniversary 2nd edition). New York: Routledge.

Collins, P. H. (2002). Some group matters: Intersectionality, situated standpoints, and black feminist thought. In T. Lott & J. Pittman (Eds.), *A companion to African-American philosophy* (pp. 205–229). Hoboken, NJ: Blackwell.

Collins, P. H. (2015). No guarantees: Symposium on Black Feminist Thought. *Ethnic and Racial Studies*, *38*(13), 2349–2354.

Frank, T. (2002). *New consensus for old*. Chicago, IL: Prickly Paradigm Press.

Katz, S. (1996). *Disciplining old age: The formation of gerontological knowledge*. Charlottesville, VA: University Press of Virginia.

Kuhn, T. S. (2008). *The structure of scientific revolutions*. Chicago, IL: University of Chicago Press.

Sanbonmatsu, J. (2004). *The postmodern prince: Critical theory, left strategy, and the making of a new political subject*. New York: Monthly Review Press.

L

Labeling

Key in pathologization and stigmatization, and fits alongside discourse, framing, and rhetoric.

Becker (1974) demonstrates through labeling theory that what is considered deviant is socially and structurally constructed. Critical gerontologists question the specific labels employed that confer values upon older adults as a demographic. These include the following.

Greedy Geezer

Greedy geezer was a term coined in 1988 by British journalist Henry Fairlie to informally dismiss the excessive wants of older adults.

Silver Tsunami

Silver tsunami was a phrase used by *The Economist*, *Forbes*, and many other publications to describe aging populations throughout regions and across the globe to frame them as an impending, catastrophic threat. Barusch (2013) uses Google's Ngram-Viewer to track the use of "Silver tsunami" in its 8000 iterations and poses the question, "How do you stop a metaphor?"

Baby Boomer

Baby boomer is a widely used term to describe individuals born just after World War II when the USA saw an increased birth rate. In media and political rhetoric, the baby boomers are often alluded to as the cause of an impending crisis, as their aging increases the aged population at a more rapid rate than previous generations.

Critical lenses may employ discourse analysis to unpack power relations and issues of subject/speaker within these words. Labels are associative, imply worth, and become legacies in and of themselves.

See also: Abjection, Baby Boomers, Crone, Discourse, Framing, Rhetoric, War on Women

Further Reading

Barusch, A. S. (2013). The aging tsunami: Time for a new metaphor? *Journal of Gerontological Social Work, 56*(3), 181–184.

Becker, H. S. (1974). Labelling theory reconsidered. *Deviance and social control*. London: Tavistock, pp. 41–66.

Labor

Productive activity carried out with a specific purpose either compensated or uncompensated. Traditionally formal labor (wage labor) is emphasized over uncompensated labor (caregiving), especially in economics.

Compensation and provision of wage labor is negotiated through the labor market.

Like any market, the labor market contains inherent imbalances in favor of buyers or sellers, depending on the interaction. As it stands currently in the USA, the labor market favors buyers of labor (employers) over the sellers of labor (employees). This market state is described as one in which buyers exert monopsony power. The US labor market's growing tendency toward monopsony derives from three primary sources: business and corporate consolidation, anti-competitive regulation, and low worker mobility (Council of Economic Advisors, 2016). These combine to force wages down and hinder the ability of workers to earn an equitable share of income. It is one of the main factors contributing to economic inequality in the USA.

Labor is highly gendered. Women are expected to do far more uncompensated labor in the form of caregiving and childrearing. The Pew Research Center (2015) conducted a survey on family makeup and care dynamics. They found that women shouldered a disproportionate share of family responsibilities compared to men and were significantly more likely to be the sole parent responsible for those responsibilities. This is one of the factors contributing to the wage gap between male and female workers. The labor market and labor itself in the USA has largely failed to keep pace with changing norms and socials trends, especially with regard to evolving family choices and care.

For all workers, wages have largely failed to rise in the past several decades. In inflation adjusted terms, the average salary for US workers has risen only extremely modestly since the 1970s. Meanwhile, executive pay has ballooned rapidly, currently sitting at an average of $13 million per year, 204 times larger than the yearly pay of the average worker (Chamberlain, 2015). Despite stagnant wage growth over the past two decades, the US economy has grown enormously. The gains from this growth have overwhelmingly accrued to the top 10 percent of earners, especially the top 1 percent (Piketty & Saez, 2003).

With the election of Donald Trump and undivided Republican control of the House of Representatives and Senate, progressives expected a new assault on workers and their relative well-being. From massive tax cuts for the rich to national right-to-work legislation, the potential for damage to the average worker is HUGE (to borrow a phrase). Attacks on labor, working people and the middle class may be seen in the uprooting by President Trump of many of the protections and advancements that President Obama made via administrative directives to the Department of Labor and other federal agencies. The Trump Administration's initiative to merge the Department of Labor and the Department of Education into the "Department of Education and Workforce" entails an erasure of the very word "labor." We argue that this demonstrates the disconnect and devaluing of labor rights and practices (as well as the decimation of the public education system) as the neoliberal agenda advances privatization and exploitation. The administrative crumbling of the nation-state demonstrates the eroding commitment to providing opportunity and support to the American people.

Abraham Lincoln's Challenge to Capitalism

> Labor is prior to, and independent of, capital. Capital is only the fruit of labor, and could never have existed if labor had not first existed. Labor is the superior of capital, and deserves much the higher consideration.
>
> (Lincoln's First Annual Message to Congress, December 3, 1861)

The Labor Movement

The Labor Movement has a long and global history. Through protests, strikes, and electoral movements, laborers have created the protections that workers rely on today. The work week, workers' compensation, minimum wage, overtime pay, and unions are just a few of the safeguards and protections won by the Labor Movement. Over the past 50 years, work has shifted significantly away from industrial labor, which lends itself particularly well to unionization, and toward the service and other sectors.

In the United States, Labor politics have become nearly exclusively associated with the Left and elements within the Democratic Party. Meanwhile, the Republican Party has embarked on a widespread campaign of corporate welfare from the Reagan Administration onwards, including a variety of actions designed to intentionally hamper the power of unions and workers. The most damaging and common of these methods is Right to Work legislation which forbids unions from compelling membership in contracts with private or public employers. This effectively cripples a union's ability to collect dues and allows for free riding.

A whiff of a potential weakening of the unadulterated hegemony of neoliberal free market dominance is seen in Britain's Labour Party's surprising revival by winning 32 new seats in the House of Commons in the June 2017 General Elections and the losses in Prime Minister May's Conservative Party. Labour's banner was "For the Many Not the Few" in which Labour vowed to nationalize the railroads, make universities free again, and inject billions into the National Health Service by raising taxes on companies and the top 5 percent of income earners. While the Labour Party failed to achieve a majority in the UK, their activation of young voters suggests a strong position moving forward.

See also: Class, Education, Exploitation, Precarity

Further Reading

Chamberlain, A. (2015). *CEO to worker pay ratios: Average CEO earns 204 times median worker pay*. Retrieved from www.glassdoor.com/research/ceo-pay-ratio/.

Cohen, P. (2016). A bigger economic pie, but a smaller slice for half of the U.S. *The New York Times*, December 6. Retrieved from www.nytimes.com/2016/12/06/business/economy/a-bigger-economic-pie-but-a-smaller-slice-for-half-of-the-us.html?_r=0.

Council of Economic Advisors. (2016). *Issue brief: Labor market monopsony: Trends, consequences, and policy responses*. Washington, DC: Council of Economic Advisors.

Pew Research Center. (2015). *Raising kids and running a household: How working parents share the load.*. Retrieved from www.pewsocialtrends.org/2015/11/04/raising-kids-and-running-a-household-how-working-parents-share-the-load/.

Piketty, T. & Saez, E. (2003). Income inequality in the United States, 1913–1998. *The Quarterly Journal of Economics, 118*(1), 1–39.

The Left

A political orientation favoring liberal ideals of democratization and equality. There is not one Left; rather various groups which situate themselves in opposition to the forces of the Right. These groups tend to believe that the equitable distribution of resources promotes the public good, and that markets (and corporations) require regulations to protect workers and the commons.

As a set of political movements, the Left has delivered a variety of victories. Most of the worker protections that we now take for granted were won by organizers and unions who put their livelihoods and safety on the line. The Vietnam War protests of the 1960s were driven by the Left and helped to fundamentally change the way Americans viewed both the war at hand but also American foreign policy more generally. From environmental regulation to racial equity, the Left has been the driving force behind political progress in the United States.

The Alt-Right latches onto this image, exaggerates and hystericizes the Left's promotion of safe spaces and intentionality as oppressive censorship and meaningless identity politics.

Richard Flacks (1988) identifies the Left as the primary source of progress in the United States over the past century. In his view, the Left is defined by a progressive worldview that seeks to continually advance the project of democratization and social progress. Bill Domhoff (2017), in his blog from the Trump front lines, suggests a Liberal–Left Alliance to counter-punch the egregious and injurious roll back of democracy and the US welfare state that is underway.

See also: Alt-Right, The Commons, Feminism, Political Parties and Platforms, Social Insurance

Further Reading

Domhoff, W. G. (2017). Can corporate power be controlled? Steps toward a constructive liberal–left alliance. Retrieved from www2.ucsc.edu/whorulesamerica/change/liberal_left_alliance.html.

Flacks, R. (1988). *Making history: The American left and the American mind.* New York: Columbia University Press.

Legitimacy

The right to exist and concerns respect and authority to have a voice (key to agency).

Sources of legitimacy may derive from tradition, charisma, or bureaucratic rationality; these dimensions explicate the relationship between authority and legitimacy (Weber, 1946). "Legitimacy attaches not merely to individual actions and relationships but to institutionalized systems of power and domination. . . . Embedded in legitimacy claims . . . is a truth claim, which, once challenged, undermines the deference legitimacy otherwise secures" (Silbey, 2006).

Politics is a dynamic struggle for legitimacy. The legitimacy problems of the State, capitalism, and democracy have been transported into all aspects of social policy for the aging, and particularly targeted against the bedrock programs of Social Security and Medicare (Estes, 1991, 2011). The social production and construction of legitimacy (and alternatively, the deconstruction of legitimacy) is profoundly significant. Once announced via Reagan's presidential Congressional message that the "government is the problem," there have been continuous and deepening high-stakes battles concerning the role of government. The State's legitimacy issues and its responses occur in socio-historical-materialist time, and reflect the power struggles ongoing. Across time and presidential administrations and dominant Congressional parties, the legitimacy problems are numerous. State and party responses include: the imposition of deficit reduction ideology and law; tax cuts for the wealthy and the call for more of them; funding cuts in politically weak programs; policies to stimulate the market; erosion of government entitlements; devolution of federal fiscal responsibility; deficit reduction to constrain social spending; and a health policy and health reform agenda of market stimulation, privatization, for-profit managed care, and individual responsibility (Estes, 1991).

Delegitimizing the governing State has direct consequences for aging policy, as exemplified by the vigorous attacks, and budget proposals and Congressional votes that threaten Medicare, Social Security, Medicaid, and the ACA Repeal (Estes, 2011). A capstone illustration of attacks on the legitimacy of the governing State came from the ranking minority member of the Senate Finance Committee, Senator Charles Grassley, as he declared during the Health Care Reform debate that "government is not a competitor for health insurance. With a public option, government is a predator" (Grassley, 2009).

Reflection on the Past Ten Years of the United States' Presidency and Congress

A legitimacy crisis unfolded over the eight years of Obama's Presidency as the Republicans in the House and Senate became the "Party of No," opposing almost anything that the President proposed, including stonewalling and denying his constitutional right to appoint a justice to the US Supreme Court when a seat was vacated as a result of the death of Justice Scalia. It was a period during which GOP behavior was variously characterized as an "insurrectionist party" (Lofgren, 2013), Nancy Pelosi called them "legislative arsonists" and worse. The period reveals the extent to which legitimacy is grounded in norms rather than in actual law or policy.

The central GOP cause has been the defunding and privatization of Social Security, Medicare, and Medicaid. These are the most popular and meaningful welfare state programs, yet states debate their funding while simultaneously shoveling out trillions to the private corporate winners of military, medicine, and prison contracts. The engorgement and accumulation of the nation's richest are on pace with parallel and skyrocketing inequality in almost every dimension of human life in America. Unabashed corporate and individual greed is obvious. It is tantamount to big capital's going out on strike against the USA, and performing disloyalty (e.g., by avoiding taxes) to the nation that made their fortunes possible. It is a *virtual strike against US labor, the middle class, young and old, all of us*. What is the strike? It is the taxpayer revolt of, by, and for the richest and wealthiest individual and corporate members among us. Shocking tax avoidance schemes accelerate in full view. With a wink and a nod, there is a "ho-hum" response to the well-documented outsourcing, corporate inversions, offshore shell companies withholding trillions of dollars,

whose intellectual capital and sweat was born in the USA. It is the disowning and disavowal of "the social," i.e., the responsibility to the larger society from which the labor and intellect was produced and from which their now privately "owned" riches have been realized and materialized.

What about the US government shutdown over Congress's own Congressionally self-constructed and imposed crisis of debt limits? And "fiscal cliffs"? And its tax cuts for the wealthy? Congressional legitimacy is on trial because of its failure to carry out three jobs: (1) passing the federal budget; (2) making sure the USA pays its bills (especially for things already legislated and bought via federal policy); and (3) keeping the lights on rather than ruling by government shutdown (real or threatened).

Instead, we are told that we must find "pay fors" for any money that is appropriated that does not meet certain conditions. "Pay fors" mean that whatever is in the budget must be paid for somehow by cutting something else we value dearly (*Note*: this is a Congressionally mandated rule). Examples are proposals in the 114th Congress to have highway funds paid for by deducting benefits from Social Security, from the women's violence shelters, from food stamps, or other perilous proposals. Is this a form of extortion?

State legitimacy is challenged through the construction of crisis framings. The deficit crisis framing has proven particularly effective, especially in conservative circles. In the aftermath of the conservative resurgence in the Reagan era, Republicans adopted deficits and debt crisis framings to attempt to undermine the legitimacy of social programs in the United States. The ideological underpinnings of the conservative movement dictate that government should have a limited role, with cuts to social insurance and public assistance.

Regarding the national debt and its effect on the economy, legitimacy carries serious material consequences. The value and stability of US debt is important to the global economy and is based on the assumption that the USA will honor its obligations and pay its debt. In 2011, the United States credit rating was downgraded to just below AAA (outstanding) by Standard and Poor's due to political brinkmanship in the budget negotiations. Since then, threats of government shutdowns and actual shutdowns have become a real possibility. Although the USA has avoided default, damage has still been done to the reputation of the US fiscal situation.

A legitimacy crisis of the governing State engulfed the USA following the 2016 elections, and the GOP trifecta of the 2017 presidency, the White House, Congress, and the Supreme Court. Looming is an "epic" legitimacy crisis not only of the State, but also of Democracy and The American Dream.

See also: Agency, Biomedicalization, Capitalism, Crisis, Critical Theory, Delirium, Democracy, Domination, Devolution, Empire, Governance, Hegemony, Ideology, Medical Industrial Complex, Power, The State, Subaltern

Further Reading

Clayman, S. E. (2017). The micropolitics of legitimacy. *Social Psychology Quarterly*, *80*(1), 41–64.

Estes, (1991) (See Carroll L. Estes' Selected Works, Appendix 4 p. 394.)

Estes, C. L. (2011). Crises in old age policy. In R. A. Settersten Jr. & J. L. Angel (Eds.), *Handbook of sociology of aging* (pp. 297–320). New York: Springer.

Grassley, C. (2009). Government is not a competitor, it's a predator. . *Kaiser Health News*, August 25. Retrieved from http://khn.org/morning-breakout/grassley-2/.

Habermas, J. (1975). *Legitimation crisis* (trans. T. McCarthy). Boston, MA: Beacon Press.

Lofgren, M. (2013). *The party is over: How Republicans went crazy, Democrats became useless, and the middle class got shafted*. New York: Penguin Group.

Silbey, S. (2006). Legitimacy. In B. S. Turner (Ed.), *The Cambridge dictionary of sociology* (p. 332). Cambridge: Cambridge University Press.

Weber, M. (1946). *From Max Weber: Essays in sociology*, translated and edited by H. H. Gerth and C. W. Mills. New York: Oxford University Press.

Weber, M. & Whimster, S. (2004). *The essential Weber: A reader*. New York: Routledge.

Leninist Strategy

A political theory of acquiring power and legitimacy through control of messaging and framing.

Lenin was one of the primary leaders of the Russian Revolution, the leader of the country post-revolution, and the first leader of the Soviet Union. He is one of the most influential Communist activists of history and one of Communism's most revered figures. Lenin was particularly politically innovative and developed a revolutionary structure that relied on a vanguard of party activists and officials to lead the proletariat toward socialism and revolution.

Privatizing Social Security

In the *Cato Journal*, Butler and Germanis (1983) proposed a Leninist strategy to move to "a private Social Security system in such a way as to . . . neutralize . . . the coalition that supports the existing system" (p. 555), observing that "Lenin recognized that fundamental change is contingent both upon a movement's ability to create a focused political coalition and upon its success in isolating and weakening its opponents" (p. 547). Privatizing Social Security will require "mobilizing the various coalitions that stand to benefit from the change . . . [t]he business community, and the financial institutions in particular" (p. 553).

Privatizing Medicare

The Leninist strategy is equally applicable to Medicare privatization adherents as well, as Speaker Gingrich argued in support of replacing the single payer government health insurance with individual vouchers to purchase private insurance care, and that would install the mechanism for a budget cap on Medicare financing, subjecting this open-ended Medicare entitlement to intense partisan political wrangling as a replacement for the base benefit coverage assured since its founding.

While the strategies proposed may be utilized by proponents and opponents of privatization, re-forming, and outright repeal of bedrock provisions in either program, a critical perspective points to the asymmetrical (unequal) access to power resources of money, ownership of the means of communication, and the cultural production of ideas through concentrated media, technology, and other resources.

A resistance movement against privatization in both programs has been evolving since the 1980s and had achieved rhetorical and political traction with rising expectations during the Obama second term and the Hillary Clinton election campaign (Estes, 2017). The Trump presidency is a major blow to the social insurance proponents seeking to preserve and improve both Social Security and Medicare, as well as Medicaid and the Affordable Care Act.

For all sides, the key principles of the Leninist strategy pertain to: (1) create focused political coalitions; (2) isolate and weaken opponents; (3) mobilize business and financial groups, and advocates; (4) propose the policy change; (5) neutralize the opposition; and (6) plan and work for the long haul to be a successful revolutionary. The difference is that the table is set with vastly unequal resources, occupied by wildly divergent power sources. Alford's (1975) analytic fits: there are three broad categories of interests in play: (1) dominant structural

interests, built into the way the system works; (2) competing structural interests; and (3) repressed interests (in health care these are "equal health care" advocates).

See also: Discourse, Framing, Legitimacy, Media Watch, Power, Propaganda, Socialism

Further Reading

Alford, R. (1975). *Health care politics*. Chicago, IL: University of Chicago Press.

Butler, S. & Germanis, P. (1983). Achieving a "Leninist" strategy. *Cato Journal*, *3*(2), 547–556.

Estes, C. L. (2017). Older US women's economic security, health and empowerment. In S. Dworkin, M. Gandhi, & P. Passano (Eds.), *Women's empowerment and global health* (pp. 232–250). Oakland, CA: University of California Press.

Levels of Analysis

Heuristic categories used in social science research that typically include micro, meso, and macro levels, to point to the location, size, and scale of inquiry focus to provide nuance and perspective to the study of social phenomena.

Social scientists have delineated different heuristic scales of social and environmental contexts that encompass individuals, groups, and communities, which help to think analytically and critically about society at micro to macro levels (nations, global economic systems). Conceptually, the levels of analysis may be thought of as individuals nested within "layers" of the community, which constitutes society. Of course, these levels need not be mutually exclusive areas of analysis. The boundaries between them are permeable, porous, and plastic from molecular to global scales. Social scientists seek to understand the pathways and mechanisms that form relationships between micro, meso, and macro levels, such as institutionalization, legitimation of ideas, classification and categorization, embodied and structured power relations, racism, sexism, classism, xenophobia, and more. The meanings of micro, meso, and macro are shaped by the intent of the analysis (Huber, 1991). An example of a cross-level analysis might examine how macro-global sectors dominate World Bank loan requirements, influencing nation-states and local systems, and an individual's access to health care.

See also: Agency, Consciousness Raising, Co-presence, Doxa, Empowerment Ideology, Imperative, Microfication, Praxis, Political Economy, Resilience, Zeitgeist

Further Reading

Clegg, S., Boreham, P., & Dow, G. (2013). *Class, politics and the economy*. London: Routledge.

Collins, R. (2000). Situational stratification: A micro-macro theory of inequality. *Sociological Theory*, *18*(1), 17.

Huber, J. (1991). *Macro–micro linkages in sociology*. Newbury Park, CA: Sage.

Siddiqi, A., Kawachi, I., Keating, D. P., & Hertzman, C. (2013). A comparative study of population health in the United States and Canada during the neoliberal era, 1980–2008. *International Journal of Health Services*, *43*(2), 193–216.

Life Course Perspective

Refers to a set of approaches to studying age and human development across the lifespan that focus on a range of ways in which age, generation, cohort, and context, including social norms and roles, organize the experience of aging. There are two main approaches, one focused on the life course as *individual life trajectories* (Elder, 2018; Dannefer, 2003); and another focused on the life course as a *social institution* (Kohli, 2007) including age-graded roles and life changes.

Life course analysis opens up understandings of the aging process, particularly in view of the notions of contingency and inequality, constrained by the particular sociohistorical context and by ongoing social dynamics such as cumulative advantages and disadvantages over a lifetime (Dannefer, 1987, 2003). With attention to cohort and intra- and inter-cohort variations and the availability of nationally representative longitudinal datasets, it is possible to examine life course trajectories with specificity both for the individual level and for collective and institutional properties such as inequality and relationships to race/racism and gender/sexism (Dannefer, Huang, & Estes, 2017).

Life course analysis intersects with the political economy of aging and critical gerontology. In the political economy of aging, the broad sociocultural, economic, and political arrangements and conflicts are "macro-historic conditions" (Pearlin, 2010) that are central in understanding one's "life chances" in old age and aging (Estes, 2001). Just as race and gender are social constructs that are systemic and coercive features of society, so are the intersections of social class, inequality, and age. Concepts of cohort location and cohort effect are central, given that cohorts are socially and economically diverse (Dannefer, 1987).

Gene–environment work and epigenetics are influencing the frameworks of human development and the life course, as interdisciplinary and multidisciplinary research brings this theory and research squarely into clinical trials, precision medicine, and the translational sciences. Axes of life course analysis are robust in this gene–environment world, but there is a noteworthy cautionary critique against *reductionist logic* in some of it that ignores or discounts the social constitution of what are assumed to be immutable genetic effects.

See also: Big Data, Cumulative Advantage/Disadvantage, Gene–Environment, Intersectionality, Stress

Further Reading

Baars, J., Dannefer, D., Phillipson, C., & Walker, A. (2016). *Aging, globalization and inequality.* Amityville, NY: Routledge.

Crimmins, E. M. (2015). Physiological differences across ageing populations reflecting early life and later life nutritional status and later life risk for chronic disease. *Journal of Population Aging, 8,* 51–69.

Dannefer, D. (1987). Aging as intracohort differentiation: Accentuation, the Matthew effect, and the life course. *Sociological Forum, 2*(2), 211–236.

Dannefer, D. (2003). Cumulative advantage/disadvantage and the life course: Cross-fertilizing age and social science theory. *The Journals of Gerontology Series B: Psychological Sciences and Social Sciences, 58*(6), 327.

Dannefer, D. (2011). Age, the life course, and the sociological imagination: Prospects for theory." In L. George (Ed.), *Handbook of aging and social sciences* (7th edition (pp. 3–16). San Diego, CA: Academic Press.

Dannefer, D. (2017). Precarity, inequality, and the problem of agency in the study of the life course. *Innovations in Aging, 1*(3), 1–10.

Dannefer, D., Huang, W., & Estes, C. L. (2017). Life course. In B. S. Turner (Ed.), *The Wiley Blackwell encyclopedia of social theory.* Hoboken, NJ: Wiley-Blackwell.

Elder, G. H. (2018). *Children of the great depression; Social change in life experience.* New York: Routledge.

Estes, C. L. (2001). Political economy of aging: A theoretical framework. In C. L. Estes and Associates (Eds.), *Social policy & aging: A critical perspective* (pp. 1–22). Thousand Oaks, CA: Sage.

Ferrer, I., Grenier, A., Brotman, S., & Koehn, S. (2017). Understanding the experiences of racialized older people through an intersectional life course perspective. *Journal of Aging Studies, 41,* 10–17.

Kohli, M. (2007). The institutionalization of the life course: Looking back to look ahead. *Research in Human Development, 4*(3–4), 253–271.

Maddox, G. L. & Campbell, R. T. (1985). Scope, concepts, and methods in the study of aging. In R. H. Binstock & E. Shanas (Eds.), *Handbook of aging and the social sciences* (2nd edition) (pp. 3–31). New York: Van Nostrand Reinhold.

Pearlin, L. (2010). The life course and the stress process: Some conceptual comparisons. *Journal of Gerontology Series B: Psychology and Social Sciences, 65B*(2), 207–215.

Life Expectancy

The estimated number of years until death. It is part of calculating the length of the lifespan, central in conceptualizing *longevity*.

There are several metrics for the estimation, which can shift and account for multivariable factors such as disease and illness, stress, race, gender, and economic security. The difference in life expectancy between demographics is known as the longevity gap.

In spite of major advances in medicine, the longevity gap between the richest and poorest people over age 50 has doubled in the past few decades (Bosworth, Burtless, & Zhang, 2016; University of Michigan Health and Retirement Study).

Laura Carstenson and Linda Fried (2012) urge us to think about longevity instead of aging, and that, as a society, we need to work toward making older persons financially secure, mentally sharp, and physically fit at 85+.

Rising economic disparity in life expectancy is empirically undisputed for both men and women (Brookings Institution; Tavernise, 2016). There is a measured gradient aligned with the richest 10 percent with the longest life expectancy, contrasted with the poorest 10 percent having the shortest life expectancy; and this holds for both men and women (life expectancy calculated at years remaining at age 50).

Raising the retirement age past 67 and the age of eligibility for Medicare past 65 will significantly impact low-income individuals' life expectancy and will widen the longevity gap.

Recent data affirm health disparities by income and race/ethnicity, and – for the first time in almost two decades – a decline in overall life expectancy. The expected age at death in the top and bottom income percentiles differs by 10.1 years for women and 14.6 years for men (Dzasu, 2017). Also significant are the disparities in life expectancy by US county, which shows that a 20-year gap exists between counties with the highest (87 years) and lowest (67 years) life expectancies (Dwyer-Lindgren et al., 2017). Counties in central Colorado had the highest life expectancies, while counties with Native American reservations had the lowest life expectancies. Compared to other countries, life expectancy at birth in the USA was nearly 79 years, compared to 81 in the European Union (World Bank). More than 30 nations have life expectancies exceeding ours, including Hong Kong and Japan (the highest at 84 each), as well as France, Iceland, Italy, Singapore, Spain, Sweden, and Switzerland (at 83 each). Even Cuba, with many fewer resources for health care than in the USA, beats us (at 80). The poorest men in America have life expectancies similar to men in Honduras and Paraguay.

Recent work by Case and Deaton (2017) examining life expectancy and morbidity by race, income, age, region, and educational attainment has found that middle-aged (45–54) whites without college degrees, especially those in rural areas, experienced a marked decline in life expectancy from 1999 to 2013. In the follow-up to their landmark 2015 study, Case and Deaton (2017) attributed this decline to increasing deaths from common health conditions like heart disease and diabetes as well as a significant uptick in the number of "deaths of despair" (suicide, alcoholism, and drug overdose). Bor, Cohen, and Galea (2017) note that the "steeper gradient" between low income and poor health is correlated with "distal factors" of "unequal access to technological innovations, increased geographical segregation by income, reduced economic mobility, mass incarceration, and increased exposure to the costs of medical care" (p. 1475).

The role of social policy in life expectancy has been acknowledged. Arno and colleagues (2011) find that the implementation of Social Security in 1940 and subsequent improvements in the program are associated with improvements in individual and population health.

With regard to race, ethnicity, and migration, many questions of life expectancy pertain to the concepts and theories of the "race crossover" (Jackson et al., 2011), hardiness (Kelley-Moore & Ferraro, 2004), and the Salmon Bias and Hispanic Paradox (Markides & Eschbach, 2005).

See also: Demography, Health Disparities, Inequality

Further Reading

Arno, P. S., House, J. S., Viola, D., Sohler, N., & Schechter, C. (2011). Social Security and mortality: The role of income support policies and population health. *Journal of Public Health Policy, 32*(2), 234–250.

Bor, J., Cohen, G. H., & Galea, S. (2017). Population health in an era of rising income inequality: USA 1980–2015. *The Lancet. 389*(10077), 1475–1490.

Bosworth, B., Burtless, G., & Zhang, K. (2016). *Later retirement, inequality in old age, and the growing gap in longevity between rich and poor.* Washington, DC: Brookings Institution.

Bound, J., Geronimus, A. T., Rodriguez, J. M., & Waidmann, T. A. (2015). Measuring recent apparent declines in longevity: The role of increasing educational attainment. *Health Affairs (Project Hope)*, *34*(12), 2167–2173.

Carstensen, L. L. & Fried, L. P. (2012). The meaning of old age. In J. Beard, S. Biggs, D. Bloom, L. Fried, P. Hogan, A. Kalache, & J. Olshansky (Eds.), *Global population ageing: Peril or promise?* (pp. 15–17). World Economic Forum: Global Agenda Council on Ageing Society.

Case, A. & Deaton, A. (2017). *Mortality and morbidity in the 21st century*. Washington, DC: Brookings Papers on Economic Activity.

Crimmins, E. M. (2015). Lifespan and healthspan: Past, present, and promise. *The Gerontologist*, *55*(6), 901–911.

Dwyer-Lindgren, L., Bertozzi-Villa, A., Stubbs, R. W., Morozoff, C., Mackenbach, J. P., van Lenthe, F. J., & Murray, C. J. L. (2017). Inequalities in life expectancy among US counties, 1980 to 2014: Temporal trends and key drivers. *JAMA Internal Medicine*, *177*(7), 1003.

Dzasu, V. J. (2017). National Academy of Medicine (NAM), Email to NAM members on Vital Directions for Health and Health Care discussion papers.

Isaacs, K. P. & Choudhury, S. (2017). *The growing gap in life expectancy by income: Recent evidence and implications for the Social Security retirement age*. Washington, DC: Congressional Research Service.

Jackson, J. S., Hudson, D., Kershaw, K., Mezuk, B., Rafferty, J., & Tuttle, K. K. (2011). Discrimination, chronic stress, and mortality among Black Americans: A life course framework. In *International handbook of adult mortality* (pp. 311–328). Dordrecht: Springer.

Kelley-Moore, J. A. & Ferraro, K. F. (2004). The black/white disability gap: Persistent inequality in later life? *The Journals of Gerontology Series B: Psychological Sciences and Social Sciences*, *59*(1), S34–S43.

Markides, K. S., & Eschbach, K. (2005). Aging, migration, and mortality: Current status of research on the Hispanic paradox. *The Journals of Gerontology Series B: Psychological Sciences and Social Sciences*, *60*(Special_Issue_2), S68–S75.

McClellan, M., McGinnis, J. M., & Dzau, V. J. (2016). Vital directions for health and health care. *JAMA, the Journal of the American Medical Association*, *316*(7), 711.

National Academies of Sciences, Engineering, Medicine. (2017). *Communities in action: Pathways to health equity*. January 11. Retrieved from http://nationalacademies.org/hmd/Reports/2017/communities-in-action-pathways-to-health-equity.aspx.

Tavernise, S. (2016). Disparity in life spans of the rich and the poor is growing. *The New York Times*, February 12.

World Bank data: Life expectancy at birth. Retrieved from https://data.worldbank.org/indicator/SP.DYN.LE00.IN.

Liminality

Describes the state or quality of being in between, being marked by ambiguity. This can speak to physical territories, temporal locations, or material conditions. Examples include being in between the workforce and retirement (planned or forced), the time spent between being insured or partial insurance, and this can also speak to dialectical tension produced through occupying contradictory locations (being highly educated and out of the workforce).

See also: Blacklands, Colonialisms, Epistemology, Intersectionality, Queer, Spheres, Transgressive

Further Reading

Thomassen, B. (2009). The uses and meanings of liminality. *International Political Anthropology*, *2*(1), 5–27.

Long-term Care, Long-term Services and Supports (LTSS)

Describes a network of services and supports needed as a result of severe impairment/disability or long-term illness. This may include assistance with "activities of daily living" (ADLs) such as eating, dressing, bathing; and extend to what are called "instrumental activities of daily living" (IADLs) such as preparing food, managing money, and cleaning.

The short history of long-term care in the USA is that it is, always has been, and continues to be women's work at no or low pay, without benefits, and with caregiver sacrifices on every front: economic, physical, psychological, and the increased morbidity and mortality of burdened informal caregivers. About 80 percent of all long-term care is provided by informal (unpaid) caregivers, mostly women. Formal providers of care are also mostly female, often racial, ethnic, and immigrant minorities, who work for low wages, most often with no formal benefits. The situation prompted Estes (2014) to say, "The US is 'free-riding' on the backs of women and people of color under every [LTC] plan enacted in the last five decades" (p. 97).

Regrettably this situation remains essentially unchanged, although local and state innovations and programs continue to proliferate, many with demonstrably positive outcomes with long-term care and Medicare policy debated (Blumenthal et al., 2003). In 2010 the Community Living Assistance Supports and Services Act (CLASS) was enacted as part of the ACA. As Ted Kennedy's legacy, CLASS was designed on the social insurance principle, but was fiscally flawed by not being mandatory. CLASS was passed as a voluntary LTC benefit program, a compromise deemed essential to the passage of the ACA at the time. Soon thereafter, the Obama Administration and opponents determined that the Act was not politically or fiscally feasible due to its structural problems of adverse risk selection, making it unsustainable within the private insurance underwriting principles and paradigm. CLASS was repealed by Congress, dashing the hopes of advocates pushing for a federally administered program available to all citizens that would provide cash benefits to help pay for long-term care services and supports. It was modeled after the German LTC system, but, as already noted, in the US case was doomed as a voluntary program, without mandatory universal financing through payroll taxes.

See also: Administration on Community Living (ACL), Caregivers/Caregiving, Care Penalty, Medicaid, Medicare, No Care Zone

Further Reading

Blumenthal, D., Moon, M., Warshawsky, M., & Boccuti, C. (Eds.). (2003). *Long-term care and Medicare policy: Can we improve the continuity of care?* Washington, DC: National Academy of Social Insurance.

Estes, C. L. (2014). The future of aging services in a neoliberal political economy. *Generations, 38*(2), 94–100.

Harrington, C., Jacobsen, F. F., Panos, J., Pollock, A., Sutaria, S., & Szebehely, M. (2017). Marketization in long-term care: A cross-country comparison of large for-profit nursing home chains. *Health Services Insights, 10*, 1–23.

Hudson, R. B. (2014). The aging network and long-term services and supports: Synergy or subordination? *Generations, 38*(2), 22–29.

Poo, A-J. (2015). *The age of dignity: Preparing for the elder boom in a changing America.* New York: The New Press.

Poo, A-J. (2017). Caregiving in America: Supporting families, strengthening the workforce. *Generations, 40*(4), 87–93.

Shura, R., Siders, R. A., & Dannifer, D. (2011). Culture change in long-term care: Participatory action research and the role of the resident. *The Gerontologist*, *51*(2), 212–225.

Thomas, K. S. & Applebaum, R. (2015). Long-term services and supports (LTSS): A growing challenge for an aging America. *Public Policy & Aging Report*, *24*, 56–62. www.thescanfoundation.org.

Losses

Include irretrievable opportunities, relationships, death, and deprivations of meaning.

There are many ways to consider loss as part of aging. Medical gerontological and geriatric research focuses on loss as biological deterioration and cell decay (senescence). Cognitive scientists and psychologists examine impairments to memory, mood, and loss of selfhood in Alzheimer's, dementia, and delirium. Functionalist sociological investigations look at loss of identity (through retirement and withdrawal from social spheres) and loss of friendship and kinship networks (as the longer people live, the more likely they are to experience others' deaths). Critical gerontology considers marginalization, loss of rights, dignity, and visibility.

A radical reframing of loss from the medical location of geriatric syndrome is to understand that all of these aforementioned losses (and threat of loss) are part of a journey, which is integral to personal growth, psychic, and spiritual development. It is foundational to what we regard as wisdom, living through multiple joys and surviving many traumas – a deepening of epistemic perspective.

History projects, especially oral collections such as StoryCorps, provide opportunities to gather rich narratives from aging peoples. In this way, social policy that promotes funding the arts may be understood to support the aging experience (as well as the intergenerational experience).

See also: Cumulative Advantage/Disadvantage, Epistemology

Maggie Kuhn

The self-proclaimed "wrinkled radical" who founded the aging activist group the Gray Panthers.

Margaret Eliza Kuhn (1905–1995), better known as Maggie, was active as an early theorist in the Sociology of Knowledge of Aging, producing provocative critiques of the scientific pursuits of gerontologists. In scholarly and professional convocations, she challenged the dominant gerontological and medical practices. Kuhn worked on stages and platforms with Dr. Robert Butler, the first director of the National Institute on Aging, and author of the 1975 Pulitzer Prize book *Why survive? Being old in America*. Both Kuhn and Butler are credited with the concept of "agism." Kuhn denounced "society [as] agist. . . . It is also racist and sexist. Agism is the arbitrary discrimination against people on the basis of their chronological age" (Kuhn, in Hessel, 1977, p. 15).

Anti-Vietnam War rallies drew Kuhn, who encouraged the "elders of the tribe" to take the risks of arrests that young students could not. She blazed a parallel path of critical left theorizing and trenchant structural analysis while she simultaneously attracted overflowing public audiences. In every media possible of her day, Kuhn promoted creative opposition to what she described as the objectification, individualization, and trivialization of the condition of old age in America and the culpability of gerontologists in such portrayals (Estes & Portacolone, 2009).

In 1972, she co-founded the activist group the Gray Panthers, committed to "a strong ethical-moral base in our social analysis and social strategy" (Kuhn, in Hessel, 1977, p. 123). Kuhn was a television hit on the *Tonight Show* starring Johnny Carson, talking frankly about the sexual and intellectual vitality she enjoyed as an old woman. Maggie was committed to the common welfare by undoing the institutionalized racist, sexist, classist, and ageist forces governing social policy and public perception. It required a process to radicalize and increase political awareness.

Kuhn and the Gray Panthers implemented a "media watch," as she railed against the dominant discourse that portrayed old age as inherently weak and diminished. As senior centers were touted by some as positive spaces for older adults, Kuhn attacked policy that supported (in her words) "playpens" and other pacification techniques. She rejected the infantilization and dehumanization of older adults: "We are not wrinkled babies, succumbing to trivial, purposeless waste of our years and our time" (Kuhn, in Hessel, 1977, p. 14).

Kuhn truly embodies the profile of Burawoy's "organic public sociologist" (Burawoy, 2005, p. 11), immersed in her causes and vigorously interacting with counter-publics. As an organic intellectual, working on the ground with and from the people, she was all about praxis and social justice. She delivered not only critiques of the paradigms and theories employed by gerontologists (including disengagement and activity theories), but also critiques of the disempowering and distancing research methods focused on the individual level and in ways that objectify human beings who are old. Instead, she suggested studies of the social consequences of victim blaming and investigation to reveal the injurious acts of the power elites, profiteers, and "knowledge definers" (Kuhn, 1977). In the 24 years following her forced retirement from the Presbyterian Church, Maggie Kuhn not only contributed to social gerontology, but also forwarded the work of younger scholars, including Carroll Estes. Kuhn's theoretical insights are deeply inscribed in the contemporary academic discourse in six areas: (1) identity politics, (2) intersectionality, (3) cultural and media studies in the cognitive sciences, (4) the political economy of aging, (5) the sociology of knowledge of gerontology, and (6) critiques of globalization and imperialism (Estes & Portacolone, 2009).

Tangible successes of the Gray Panthers social movement include the 1978 amendment to the Age Discrimination in Employment Act, raising the mandatory retirement age from 65 to 70 years. Nevertheless, as Horowitz (1970) notes, revolutionaries sustain themselves through their therapeutic stance of struggle, not the tangibility of results, as outcomes are never certain or sustained. Kuhn exemplified this stance, since she rejected the traps of the centralization of power and bureaucratic elitism in her movement, and shared both the joys and sorrows of the struggle with a diverse network committed to the cause.

See also: Age Discrimination in Employment Act, Gray Panthers, Organic Intellectual, Outrageous Act of the Day, Watch Dogs/Watch Bitches

Further Reading

Burawoy, M. (2005). For public sociology. *American Sociological Review*, 70(1), 4–28.

Estes, C. & Portacolone, E. (2009). Maggie Kuhn: Social theorist of radical gerontology. *International Journal of Sociology and Social Policy*, 29(1/2), 15–26.

Hessel, D. T. (1977). *Maggie Kuhn on aging: A dialogue*. Philadelphia, PA: Westminster Press.

Horowitz, D. (1970). *Empire and revolution*. New York: Random House.

The Market

A sphere of competition, touting its potential for innovation and growth. The market stands in direct contrast to the commons. In this sphere goods and services (and even social and environmental initiatives) are commodified and traded.

Market fundamentalism is a critical term that describes a strong adherence to free market and laissez-faire ideology. The term has been used most prominently by George Soros, Joseph Stiglitz, John Quiggin, and Fred Block.

George Soros, a billionaire investor and political philanthropist, used the term "market fundamentalism" in his 1998 book *The crisis of global capitalism*, in which he posits that over-confidence in market forces is the cause of various economic crises throughout the latter portion of the twentieth century. Joseph Stiglitz, similarly, criticized the market fundamentalism of the International Monetary Fund, and the neoliberal Washington Consensus more generally, in his acceptance essay for the Nobel Prize for Economics in 2001. Quiggin emphasizes very similar themes to Stiglitz, holding that market fundamentalists seek to imbibe their ideology with rational elements to lend their arguments legitimacy and delegitimize those of their opponents. Fred Block offers a deeper analysis of the calculus that has driven the adoption of market fundamentalism on the Right. He explains that the ideology became popular among Republicans in the 1970s and 1980s as a convenient way to appeal to both business interests and social and religious conservatives simultaneously.

Protectionism is an economic stance or system that favors the security of domestic industries over profit from foreign goods/labor through duties or quotas imposed upon importations. "Fiscally conservative" economists routinely cite this as a hindrance to the rapid growth, while those on the Left state that while it restricts opportunities for exploiting precarity in "developing nations," *protectionism* supports local economies. A similar debate exists between conservatives and progressives regarding the relationship of the welfare state to the market. A critical reframing of social insurance programs is to consider the amount of money that becomes infused into local economies as a *social stimulus*. Social Security Spotlight, a project by the National Committee to Preserve Social Security and Medicare, illustrates the economic impact of the $1.6 trillion of benefits that are spent and recirculated in each state (Arno & Maroko, 2016).

See also: Capitalism, Commodification, The Commons, Domination, Economics, Exploitation, Financialization, Ideology, The Left, Neoliberalism, Privatization, Welfare State

Further Reading

Arno, P. & Maroko, A. (2016). *Social Security Spotlight*. The National Committee to Preserve Social Security and Medicare. Retrieved from http://socialsecurityspotlight.org.

Block, F. (2004). *Reframing the political battle: Market fundamentalism vs. moral economy*. Berkeley, CA: Longview Institute.

Quiggin, J. (1997). Rationalism and rationality in economics. *Queensland Economic Review, 3*, 4–5.

Soros, G. (1998). *The crisis of global capitalism: Open society endangered*. New York: Public Affairs.

Stiglitz, J. E. (2001). Joseph E. Stiglitz – biographical. Retrieved from www.nobelprize.org/nobel_prizes/economic-sciences/laureates/2001/stiglitz-bio.html.

Media Theory

A multidisciplinary approach which employs sociocultural and political theoretical lenses to investigate various media.

The focus may include analyses of communication, networks, representation, and participation. Media theory also "keeps the pulse" of society and technological advances, identifying the discursive potential of connectivity. In other words, it offers some new opportunities for speech. Mechanical and digital reproduction, social media, and the widespread availability of media technologies have challenged traditional notions of authenticity and ownership over content (and content creation).

Critical gerontology has many opportunities to consider how continually developing technologies, entertainment, and social networking mediates the lives of older adults. *What does Twitter mean to an 80-year-old grandmother of two? What does it mean to her grandchildren?* Key questions can examine both intergenerational participation and inequalities on social media platforms, how aging cohorts adapt to new technologies, and the role of the marketplace and advertising in shaping these seemingly "open" networks.

See also: Co-presence, Digital Sphere, Media Watch, Networks, Textuality, Tweetstorm

Further Reading

Benjamin, W., Arendt, H., Zohn, H., & Wieseltier, L. (2007). *Illuminations* (reprinted edition). New York: Schocken Books.

Bulajić, V. V. (2007). *Database aesthetics: Art in the age of information overflow*. Minneapolis, MN: University of Minnesota Press.

Debord, G. (1977). *Society of the spectacle*. Detroit, MI: Black & Red.

McLuhan, M. & Fiore, Q. (1967). *The medium is the message*. New York: Random House.

Media Watch

The practice of identifying and calling attention to problematic and harmful representations in media.

Groups in the United States and around the world dedicate themselves to documenting and exposing sexist, racist, and dangerous published content.

Of particular note to critical gerontology is the monitoring and identification of ageism in the media. Ageism can take many forms. Dr. Frank Nuessel identifies four – two linguistic and two symbolic – actionable forms of ageism in the media (Nuessel, 1982).

1. Distortion: the attribution of negative characteristics to the elderly.
2. Degradation: the depiction of the elderly as inferior.
3. Exclusion: the elimination of the elderly from depictions.
4. Subordination: the depiction of the elderly as subservient.

There are a variety of groups that take a critical approach to media. Mediawatch.com represents one such organization. Over its 30 years of existence it has sought to challenge media stereotypes and to promote media literacy, with a special focus on media literacy in K-12 education. Other watchdogs are more political. Media Matters, for instance, is an explicitly political organization devoted to researching and correcting conservative misinformation. Media criticism and correction also come from within the media itself. An example of this is *On the Media*, a weekly radio show produced by WNYC and syndicated on public radio. The show is devoted to examining the media and its effect on society, and has been on the air in some form since 1995.

The idea of monitoring the media for harmful misinformation and stereotypes has been elevated in the wake of the continued spread of "fake news," propaganda, and ideological media. The *Oxford English Dictionary* even named "post-truth," denoting an emphasis on feeling over fact, as its word of the year in 2016. In response to the spread of "fake news" on its platform and mounting public pressure, Facebook announced in late 2016 that it would partner with third-party fact checkers like Snopes.com to flag untrue content on the site. Though the interest and emphasis on getting rid of "fake news" is well intentioned, it does not address the underlying problems plaguing media. As the US population has become increasingly politically polarized, media corporations and the tailored consumption of ideologically, politically entrenched media has followed suit, compounding the chasm of cultural separation.

See also: Ageism, Maggie Kuhn, Propaganda, Watch Dogs/Watch Bitches

Further Reading

Katz, J. (2016). "Duck dynasty" vs. "modern family": Mapping the U.S. cultural divide. *The New York Times*, December 27.

Mitchell, A., Gottfried, J., Kiley, J., & Matsa, K. E. (2014). *Political polarization & media habits*. Pew Research Center.

Nuessel, F. (1982). The language of ageism. *Gerontologist, 22*(3), 273–276.

Wahl, O. F. & Roth, R. (1982). Television images of mental illness: Results of a metropolitan Washington media watch. *Journal of Broadcasting, 26*(2), 599–605.

Medicaid

The health insurance program serving low-income Americans. The program is a partnership between states and the federal government. It is hard to overstate the importance of this program which provides health care to the most vulnerable Americans.

Medicaid was created in 1965 to provide health coverage to low-income people and families. The program is administered by states and funded through a combination of state funds and federal funds. The funding level received by a state varies primarily according to per capita income. Wealthier states receive less funding while poorer states receive more funding as a proportion of their costs.

In 2009 as part of the Affordable Care Act, the Obama Administration began an effort to expand Medicaid. The Obama expansion increased federal subsidies to states and expanded access to the program, attempting to reach more people who could not previously qualify for Medicaid but still could not afford private insurance. The expansion faced significant opposition from Republican governors who refused to accept the more broad eligibility requirements and extra funding. Most states accepted the expansion, but some states did not do this right away, and as of October 2017 there were 19 states that still rejected the expansion. The Kaiser Family Foundation (2018) estimates that this leaves 2,200,000 people in this so-called "coverage gap."

Medicaid's benefits are huge. The program has been especially beneficial for children. In 2016 a study by NBER (National Bureau of Economic Research) researchers found that not only does Medicaid-provided early childhood health care have a significant positive effect on lifetime health outcomes, it also provides significant financial benefit to the government, as it eliminates much of the need for disability benefits later in life (Goodman-Bacon, 2016). Another study, conducted by the *New England Journal of Medicine* in 2012, found that the expansion of Medicaid under the ACA was associated with a marked decrease in mortality rates in the states that instituted it. Predictably, the decrease in mortality rates was especially strong in counties with higher rates of poverty (Sommers, Baicker, & Epstein, 2012). For individuals with chronic conditions and disabilities, Medicaid is incredibly important, as it allows a degree of financial stability and personal independence that is rare for chronically ill or disabled people in the health care system.

The provision of long-term care is one of the most important aspects of Medicaid. The expansion of Medicaid under the ACA was key in solidifying and increasing the breadth of these services across the country. Many states have used the authorities and resources granted under the ACA to expand their long-term care systems and launch Managed Long-Term Services and Supports. These MLTSS programs provide services to vulnerable populations and allow for a high degree of coordinated care. This has been associated with more desirable outcomes for patients and a better quality of life (Dobson et al., 2017).

The future of Medicaid is unclear, to say the least. The benefits of the expansion under the ACA are extensive and well documented, and yet many Republicans, including a number of governors, continue to oppose it. With undivided Republican control of government, attention has turned back to conservative proposals to convert the program into block grants. This would likely lead to significant budget cuts and would hurt the stability and efficacy of the program in the long run as funding becomes dislocated from services.

Presently (2018), Medicaid covers anyone who meets its federal state eligibility requirements, around 75 million adults and children, and the associated costs borne mainly by federal dollars with a state (variable) match. Virtually every proposal put forward by the Republican Congress in

2017 involved some sort of a cut in Medicaid funding and/or reductions of eligibility.

> Part of the austerity vultures' plan to eviscerate Medicaid is by block-granting it. Instead of guaranteeing each state the money it needs to operate its Medicaid program, it would give each state a fixed (smaller) amount of money, no matter how many new people qualified because of a recession, or how much medical care was needed because of an epidemic. In return, states would be allowed to cut eligibility and medical benefits as needed to accommodate the smaller federal payments. Now that the $1.5 trillion tax cut to corporations and the rich has passed, the plan was to chop up Medicaid and Medicare in the Spring. But as this article shows, the austerity vultures are already preparing the states for block granting.
> (Lyon, 2018)

See also: Block Grants, Social Insurance, Welfare State

Further Reading

Center for Consumer Engagement in Health Innovation. Retrieved from www.healthinnovation.org/.

Dobson, C., Gibbs, S., Mosey, A., & Smith, L. (2017). *Demonstrating the value of Medicaid MLTSS programs.* National Association of States United for Aging and Disabilities.

Garfield, R., Damico, A., & Orgera, K. (2018). *The coverage gap: uninsured poor adults in states that do not expand Medicaid.* June 12. The Kaiser Family Foundation. Retrieved from www.kff.org/medicaid/issue-brief/the-coverage-gap-uninsured-poor-adults-in-states-that-do-not-expand-medicaid/.

Goodman-Bacon, A. (2016). *The long-run effects of childhood insurance coverage: Medicaid implementation, adult health, and labor market outcomes* (No. w22899). National Bureau of Economic Research.

Hwang, A. (2018). What's next for Medicare-Medicaid enrollees? Center for Consumer Engagement in Health Innovation, December 6. Retrieved from www.healthinnovation.org/news/newsletter/health-innovation-highlights-december-6-2018/full-edition#dc.

Liserv of Don McCanne of Physicians for a National Health Program (PNHP): www.pnhp.org/news/quote-of-the-day.

Lyon, M. (2018). Re. using Medicaid Section 115 waivers to take away health care 1 [Electronic mailing list message, January 12]. Retrieved from https://pairlist2.pair.net/mailman/listinfo/quote-of-the-day.

McDonnell, D. D. & Graham, C. L. (2015). Medicaid beneficiaries in California reported less positive experiences when assigned to a managed care plan. *Health Affairs (Project Hope), 34*(3), 447–454.

Rosenbaum, S., Riley, T., Bradley, A. L., Veghte, B. W., & Rosenthal, J. (2017). *Strengthening Medicaid as a critical lever in building a culture of health.* Washington, DC: National Academy of Social Insurance.

Sommers, B. D., Baicker, K., & Epstein, A. M. (2012). Mortality and access to care among adults after state Medicaid expansions. *The New England Journal of Medicine, 367*(11), 1025.

Medicare

A single-payer federal health insurance program for persons aged 65 years and older. Medicare also covers individuals with end-stage renal disease and those who are classified as disabled under Social Security (after a two-year waiting period).

In 1965, President Lyndon B. Johnson signed Medicare into law (H.R. 6675), issuing former President Truman, who had envisioned a universal health care program, the very first Medicare card during a ceremony to commemorate the event. In 1965, the budget for Medicare was around $10 billion and 19 million individuals signed up for Medicare during its first year. Today, Medicare covers approximately 59 million beneficiaries (Kaiser Family Foundation, 2017).

A Critical Look

Medicare offers fairly basic coverage, yet many (young people especially) often assume that older adults receive a much greater level of care and coverage than the program offers. The coverage is difficult to understand, as Medicare features many parts.

Part A

- Hospital "inpatient" coverage which ends after 60 days per "benefit period," includes skilled nursing, home health care post hospitalization, hospice care, and first three pints of blood.
- Eligible if individual or spouse contributes 40 quarters (10 years) of Medicare deductions from payroll.

Part B

- Eighty percent approved rate for "medically necessary" doctor visits, ambulance services, outpatient mental health care, medical equipment, diagnostic tests, and preventative tests.
- One hundred percent approved rate for Clinical Lab Services, Home Health Services.
- A monthly premium of between $104.90 and $121.80, an annual deductible of $166.
- Premium increases for individuals with an income of $85,000 and over $170,000.

Part C

- Medicare Advantage Plans are HMO- or PPO-type plans offered by private organizations and approved by Medicare. They "provide all of your Part A

Part B coverage. They generally offer additional benefits, such as vision, dental, and hearing, and many include prescription drug coverage. These plans often have networks, which mean you may have to see certain doctors and go to certain hospitals in the plan's network to get care . . . Medicare Advantage Plans, with or without prescription drug coverage, vary depending on where you live."

Medigap

- Private policies for individual purchase that are allowed under Medicare (for those who can afford them) that may cover (all or part of) deductibles, co-insurance, and co-pays related to Parts A and B. If you have a Medicare Advantage Plan then you cannot purchase Medigap.

Part D

- Covers prescription drugs, voluntary coverage but there are "late enrollment penalties." Deductibles, premiums, and co-pays vary widely by state and type of policy, insurance plans offered/negotiated, and the ability to pay (individual affordability). These prices and coverage are subject to change, as are formularies on an annual basis.

Tim Diamond (2018) writes about the disembodiment of Medicare policy. He posits that there is no plan for one body or the whole individual. One finds her or his body on different pages, in different parts of various plans with certain time frames and restrictions on services in place. We wonder who can understand what parts they need and what parts are covered in deciphering (and advocating) for care. Trying to parse what coverage exists induces one's eyes to cross! Many berate themselves for not understanding a system on which they rely.

Fortunately, there are now health counselors through SHIP who assist in identifying and guiding "consumers" through this plan.

Raising the Age of Eligibility

One of the most consistent solutions presented to reduce the cost of Medicare is an increase in the age of eligibility. In its most recent incarnation this proposal has made its way into Speaker Paul Ryan's "Better Way" plan, which includes a proposal to raise the eligibility age to 67. The impact of this would be devastating on its own and could be extremely damaging if combined with the repeal of the ACA. The American Research Corporation has looked into the impact of this proposal and found that it would result in significant decreases in insurance rates for persons aged 65 to 66. Currently the uninsured rate among this group is less than 2 percent with a majority insured through Medicare. If eligibility was changed to 67, the uninsured rate for this group would rise to 18.7 percent if the ACA is maintained or 37 percent if the ACA is repealed. Those with very low incomes and few assets can qualify for Medicaid while those with significant resources can purchase private insurance; however, those individuals caught in between are left with no real options.

Medicare for all is a rallying cry by many Americans. Although widely debated, it is a realistic option for the USA according to an economic analysis by PERI researchers (Pollin et al., 2018), as stated below (Pollin et al., 2018, Abstract)

> The most fundamental goals of Medicare for All are to significantly improve health care outcomes for everyone living in the United States while also establishing effective cost controls throughout the health care system.

See also: Medicaid, State Health Insurance Assistance Programs (SHIP), Social Insurance, Social Security

Further Reading

Arno, P. S. (2017). *Impact of raising eligibility age of Medicare.* Washington, DC: National Committee to Preserve Social Security and Medicare Foundation.

Center for Consumer Engagement in Health Innovation. Retrieved from www.healthinnovation.org/.

Diamond, T. (2018). Who are you in Medicare and you? Examining this second person. In C. Wellin (Ed.), *Critical gerontology comes of age: Advances in research and theory for a new century* (pp. 62–78). New York: Routledge.

Hwang, A. (2018). What's next for Medicare-Medicaid enrollees? Center for Consumer Engagement in Health Innovation, December 6. Retrieved from www.healthinnovation.org/news/newsletter/health-innovation-highlights-december-6-2018/full-edition#dc.

Kaiser Family Foundation. (2017). The facts on Medicare spending and financing. Retrieved from www.kff.org/medicare/issue-brief/the-facts-on-medicare-spending-and-financing/.

Marmor, T. R. (2000). *The politics of Medicare.* 2nd Ed. Hawthorne, NY: Aldine De Gruyter.

Oberlander, J. (2003). *The political life of Medicare.* Chicago, IL: University of Chicago Press.

Pollin, R., Heintz, J., Arno, P., Wicks-Lim, A., & Ash, M. (2018). *Economic analysis of Medicare for all.* Amherst, MA: University of Massachusetts Press. Retrieved from www.peri.umass.edu/.

Medical Industrial Complex (MIC)

The network of industries and interests that comprise medical care, coverage, and research. In 1969 Ehrenreich and Ehrenreich introduced the Medical Industrial

Complex in an article and following book *The American health empire*, a report from the consumer activist organization Health-PAC, to describe the multi-billion-dollar industry of medicine and medical care.

The term harks back to Dwight D. Eisenhower's concept of the Military Industrial Complex, which Marc Pilisuk (1965) identified as a structurally embedded barrier to peace which permeates all American institutions. A point of connection between both MICs is veterans' services, where medical care and military service (and often trauma or injury) form a billion-dollar project, employing people, and using federal money to purchase prescription drugs and medical supplies.

A key element today is the Medicare industrial complex (MIC) (Vladeck, 1999). However, the pharmaceutical industry is the largest, unregulated, and costly part of the MIC which extends to other elements of the complex. It affects the actuarial models and prices determined by insurance programs (public and private). This impacts which drugs doctors can prescribe and patients can afford to take. The politics of formularies is a study in itself. Formularies determine which drugs are included (i.e., paid for by insurance) and which drugs are not covered (paid for out of pocket). The "market value" cost of drugs to the public and to government and insurance payers (which may be completely independent of R&D and the government's investment in the basic research) is politicized and contentious, especially for life-saving, life-altering products.

The Aging Enterprise, which includes the large segment of the now trillion-dollar medical industrial complex, assures that the needs of the aged will be processed and treated as a commodity. Many of the resulting commodities, especially medical services, are sold for profit.

The costs of health care and services continue to rise in the United States. In 2016 Americans spent a combined $3.35 trillion on health care, or $10,345 per person. In 2013 health care spending accounted for 17 percent of GDP, an insane figure, especially considering that the next closest comparable country was France, with 11.6 percent. Despite exceptionally high health care spending per person in the United States, health outcomes consistently underperform compared to other high-income countries. In short, Americans spend more and get less.

See also: Cross-national Comparisons, The Market, Political Economy

Further Reading

Alonso-Zaldivar, R. (2016). $10,345 per person: U.S. health care spending reaches new peak. *PBS Newshour*, July 13. Retrieved from www.pbs.org/news-hour/rundown/new-peak-us-health-care-spending-10345-per-person/.

Jacoby, S. (2011). *Never say die*. New York: Pantheon Books.

Pilisuk, M. & Hayden, T. (1965). Is there a military industrial complex which prevents peace? Consensus and countervailing power in pluralistic systems. *Journal of Social Issues, 21*(3), 67–117.

Squires, D. A. & Anderson, C. (2015). *U.S. health care from a global perspective: Spending, use of services, prices, and health in 13 countries* (No. 15). New York: Commonwealth Fund.

Vladeck, B. C. (1999). The political economy of Medicare. *Health Affairs, 18*(1), 22–36. doi:10.1377/hlthaff.18.1.22.

Memory

The process by which we store and recall information and experiences. Memory is important for the formation of the self as well as a location within a cultural identity. Culture manifests and holds the memory of the people.

Most old age studies in the orthodox gerontological canon concerned with memory focus on the biological degradation of the brain. However, senescence and decline are just aspects of memory and aging. Memory exists in an interpersonal sphere: dynamic practices of telling and listening, cultural traditions, and the preservation of artifacts.

Remembering the past and being able to construct a narrative are crucial aspects to consciousness raising. This is key to organizing and synthesizing resistance. Trauma (on any level) threatens to extinguish memory, and central to healing is the struggle of remembering. Colonization and genocide do their best to dislocate and disembody generations of memories and to destroy epistemologies.

See also: Cognitive Liberation, Consciousness Raising, Culture, Epistemology, Knowledges, Resistance, Trauma

Further Reading

Cicourel, A. (2015). Collective memory, a fusion of cognitive mechanisms and cultural processes. *Revue De Synthèse, 136*(3), 309–328.

Davies, B. (1992). Women's subjectivity and feminist stories. In C. Ellis & M. Flaherty (Eds.), *Investigating subjectivity: Research on lived experience* (pp. 53–76). Newbury Park, CA: Sage.

Furtado, H. T. (2015). Against state terror: Lessons on memory, counterterrorism and resistance from the global south. *Critical Studies on Terrorism, 8*(1), 72–89.

Maruna, S. & Ramsden, D. (2004). Living to tell the tale: Redemption narratives, shame management, and offender rehabilitation. *Healing plots: The narrative basis of psychotherapy* (pp. 129–149). Washington, DC: American Psychological Association.

Men

A gendered demographic subset of a larger population who, as a group, hold a disproportionately larger share of power and capital. A major point of discussion in

aging research centers around life expectancy and the fact that men live shorter lives than women. Life expectancy varies by race, ethnicity, and class, with longevity positively correlating to privilege and economic security.

Critical scholars look to cultures of masculinity which repress emotional sharing and processing as possible factors in health disparities, morbidity, and mortality. A study by Coates and Herbert (2008) links male traders' testosterone levels with market performance, implicating how biological feedback in risk and reward is part of the sexed/gendered power structures in commerce. Calasanti (2004) writes that feminist gerontology can critically explore masculinity across the lifespan, locating how "arrangements that maintain privilege in young adulthood and middle age can lead to poor health in old age" (Calasanti, 2004, p. 305).

"Masculinism" is a concept Arthur Brittan uses to denote "the ideology that justifies and naturalizes domination" (Brittan, 1989, pp. 147–148). As white males with no college education gained ascendancy with their 72 percent support of Trump's presidential election, many wondered if and how class solidarity could resist the rise of super-wealthy rulers. Connell (2005) recognizes that multiple masculinities work together to legitimize and maintain privilege; however, despite being deeply embedded in power structures, masculinities can be strategically challenged to disrupt privilege and promote gender democracy.

The watershed of the #MeToo campaign, featuring women voicing their experiences of victimization and naming their perpetrators, led to the firings, divestment, and retiring of prominent (and powerful) men in entertainment and politics. Democratic senators Al Franken (Minnesota) and John Conyers (Michigan) resigned following allegations of sexual misconduct. The 2017 Alabama Senate race between Doug Jones (D) and Roy Moore (R) showcased the dynamics of the #MeToo disruption, especially as Trump and the RNC (Republican National Committee) threw in their endorsements in spite of the mountain of testimonials about Moore's inappropriate and predatory contact with underage women. Election results showed that Senator Doug Jones secured the vote through the strong turnout of black women and men. Most white women and men voters supported Moore in spite of the controversy, claiming that there was a liberal conspiracy. This further demonstrates the strong linkage between whiteness and masculinism proposed by Brittan (1989).

See also: Gender, Life Expectancy, The Market, Patriarchy, Privilege, War on Women

Further Reading

Brittan, A. (1989). *Masculinity and power.* Oxford: Blackwell.

Calasanti, T. (2004). Feminist gerontology and old men. *The Journals of Gerontology Series B: Psychological Sciences and Social Sciences, 59*(6), 305.

Coates, J. M. & Herbert, J. (2008). Endogenous steroids and financial risk taking on a London trading floor. *Proceedings of the National Academy of Sciences of the United States of America, 105*(16), 6167–6172.

Connell, R. W. (2005). *Masculinities* (2nd edition). Berkeley, CA: University of California Press.

Jackson, D. (2016). *Exploring aging masculinities: The body, sexuality and social lives.* London: Palgrave Macmillan.

Mental Health

Describes psychological well-being and care.

Emotional well-being is facilitated by strong relationships, freedom of expression, and security. Mental health implicates physical and cognitive functioning, as symptoms of depression, anxiety, and trauma manifest themselves throughout the body and brain.

Mental illness can include prolongation of those symptoms as well as addiction, and sociopathy (unfettered narcissism).

The ACA promotes "mental health parity" which stipulates that insurers must cover mental illness just as they cover physical illness. Critical practitioners can consider how bias perpetuated through ageist stereotypes of older clients as stubborn and less likely to change (as well as fat discrimination, classism, racism) is a threat to parity/equality in treatment, as well as part of the symptomatology and suffering.

Critical perspectives question the powerful role of associations and diagnostic criteria as tools of social control. When healing is in the service of getting people back to work and not back into their bodies and fostering community, we as a people must interrogate these simplistic notions of wellness.

See also: Cognitive Liberation, Epistemology, Stereotype Threat, Trauma

Further Reading

Kessler, E. M. & Schneider, T. (2017). Do treatment attitudes and decisions of psychotherapists-in-training depend on a patient's age? *The Journals of Gerontology Series B:* gbx078, https://doi.org/10.1093/geronb/gbx078.

Methodologies

Ways of studying reality; the procedures of research; the ways scientists investigate reality using systematic data collection techniques, predicated on paradigmatic assumptions.

There is almost always a methodology that is well suited to study a problem. Methodologies incorporate theoretical and analytic strategies and assumptions that legitimate the procedures and techniques for data collection and accord preferences for different analytic processes and levels of analysis, as well as the research questions addressed. The selection of a methodology is deliberate and reflects the research purpose. The choice of methodologies locates a research project, indicating what is possible for the research to achieve, what the research can ask, what the research can hope to have answered, and how the research is to be done.

Politics situate methodology within and outside the academy. For instance, quantitative and qualitative inquiry are both important for thinking about and studying social reality. Some scholars argue that the philosophical assumptions underpinning quantitative and qualitative inquiry differ, and as such, the methods of inquiry differ. Luker (2008) characterizes the methods of quantitative inquiry as "canonical social science" because it is the dominant culture of most social scientists. She characterizes the methods of qualitative inquiry as "salsa-dancing social science." There are many varieties of qualitative (as there are quantitative) research. Luker proposes that the methods of salsa-dancing social scientists can be innovative, critical, and challenge some of the most cherished assumptions of the dominant professional culture in which social scientists work, as well as the dominant culture of the larger society in which we all live.

The global community of scholars is between these two extremes, searching for a new middle ground while moving in several directions at the same time. On the one hand, there has been a call for more scientifically based research with an evidence-based research movement. On the other hand, there are renewed calls for social justice inquiry from critical social science traditions. Validity and reliability, the gold standard of science, have become the targets (and substance) of sustained and contested dialogues both within and across disciplines. These may be characterized as "paradigm wars" in which evidence-based knowledge is severely challenged (and impugned). Teddlie and Tashakkori (2003) identify three paradigm wars, or periods of conflict: the

postpositivist-constructivist war against positivism (1970–1990); the conflict between competing postpositivist, constructivist, and critical theory paradigms (1990–2005); and the current conflict between evidence-based methodologists and the mixed-methods, interpretive, and critical theory schools (2005 to the present).

Critical perspectives on methodologies emerged during the 1960s, attributed in measure to the failure of mainstream disciplines and theories to anticipate or explain the explosive ruptures of the civil rights, peace, women's movements, and social unrest and upheavals. Studies in social problems (Becker, 1963) and the sociology of knowledge (Gouldner, 1973) called out the failures of the dominant social science theories and methods. Harsh attacks were leveled at the shibboleths of positivism and value-free claims of objectivity dominating the social sciences. As the ideological objectivity and epistemological validity of classical methods and theories were challenged, students and faculty *questioned the authority* of the "received" traditional theoretical and methodological perspectives that reflected the voices and values of the predominantly white male academic establishment. According to Dubbin, McLemore, and Shim (2017, p. 498),

> critical research is explicitly and empirically grounded in prior evidence that the structure and content of social life disproportionately burdens some groups over others as a result of their social position, which provides the "jumping-off" point for further research (Thomas, 1993). Using a critical lens, the researcher examines the power relations that structure how everyday life is experienced within a particular lived environment and investigates the structures that regulate and legitimate specific ways of being, communicating, knowing and acting
>
> (Madison, 2005; Simon & Dippo, 1986).

Postcolonial critiques, postmodernism, standpoint epistemology, critical pedagogy, the Frankfurt School, and critical and radical race, ethnicity, feminist, black feminist, LGBTQ, political economy of aging, and intersectional scholarship cutting across disciplines have surged. Methods were unmasked as theory, while the hegemony of quantitative and deductive social sciences was redefined as problematic. The distance between theory, method, and practice narrowed with growing commitment inside and outside the academy to interrogating the diversity and interconnectedness of different spheres, spaces, sectors, and communities of society (Brown & Strega, 2005). One result has been the tidal wave of qualitative, interpretive, constructivist lines of inquiry. With this has come the legitimation of methods and theoretical approaches that lift and deepen our understanding of the meaning and experience of race, ethnicity, class, gender, age, and (dis)ability in US society.

Simultaneously, quantitative methods, statistical advances, and big data are growing, and mixed methods are blooming. Denzin and Lincoln (2017, p. 2) write:

Enter Teddlie and Tashakkori's third moment: Mixed methods and evidence-based inquiry meet one another in a soft center. C. Wright Mills (1959) would say this is a space for abstracted empiricism. Inquiry is cut off from politics. Biography and history recede into the background. Technological rationality prevails.

Sociologists of knowledge, science and technology studies, and philosophy are moving their respective fields forward, backward, or sideways as the "humanities" examines and re-examines itself through these new lenses. The potential emancipatory and empowering role of knowledge (Habermas, 1971) has gained ascendancy, as has the appreciation of the generative relation of the subject to the world, formal linguistic self-consciousness, epistemic phenomenology, symbolic forms, communication, and meaning.

Critical approaches to gerontology have helped shape methodological approaches adopted in empirical studies. Gerontologists with a commitment to social change have increasingly engaged with participatory methods of doing research, and it is receiving rapidly growing interest in aging as elsewhere (Minkler, 2000). It is a paradigmatically different approach to the researcher and the respondent, and reflects a broader shift to engage older people in the production of gerontological knowledge, such as by using methods like photovoice and photo elicitation (Yeh, 2012), and to engage older people in the dissemination of gerontological knowledge and in the development of policy and practice (Shura, Siders, & Dannefer, 2011; Buffel, 2018). Supporters of a participatory approach argue that older people's involvement in research processes can lead to their empowerment. There are, however, still limitations and challenges pertaining to the use of this research method. Ziegler and Scharf (2014, p. 158) identify three common concerns for both critical gerontology and participatory action research:

First, both approach favor critical thinking in relation to issues around social justice, social inequality and marginalization. Second, both share the goal of bringing about social change: participatory action research in terms of transformation primarily through community action (Kesby et al, 2007), critical gerontology mainly through policy-level change (see, for example, Phillipson and Scharf, 2004; Scharf et al, 2005; Walker, 2009). Third, critical gerontologists engage in reflection on their own roles in the production of knowledge relating to their research themes (Baars, 1991; Minkler and Holstein, 2008). The reflexive approach represents a vital part of the participatory action research tradition, with its challenges and limitations having been subject to wide debate among practitioners in development studies, geography and other disciplines

> (Pain, 2004; Nicholls, 2009; Smith et al, 2010).

In life course and aging studies there is a gene–environment science that bridges the biological (genetic and cellular) to the social, behavioral, and policy sciences. Empirical work has distributional and human rights consequences. The definition, treatment, and processing of old age and the experience of aging can be informed by earnest attention to the ways in which inequality and disparities manifest across race, ethnicity, class, gender, and ability. Novel, innovative and radical technical advances and translational frameworks, including big data, open up vast possibilities for the science, practice, and policy of gerontology. Yet, the baseline knowledge, assumptions, and new ways of science are not neutral in themselves; approaches often fail to consider their own relationship to processes of marginalization and domination (especially as much of the biological research overlaps with big money backing anti-aging innovation). The work ahead is monumental given the vast inequalities and the entrenchment of cumulative disadvantage.

See also: Anti-aging, Big Data, Cross-national Comparisons, Cumulative Advantage/Disadvantage, Gene–environment, Positivism, Quality-adjusted Life Years (QALYs)

Further Reading

Becker, H. S. (1963). *Outsiders: Studies in the sociology of deviance.* New York: The Free Press.

Brown, L. & Strega, S. (2005). *Research as resistance.* Toronto, ON: Canadian Scholars' Press.

Buffel, T. (2018). Older coresearchers exploring age-friendly communities: An "insider" perspective on the benefits and challenges of peer-research. *The Gerontologist.* doi:doi:10.1093/geront/gnx216.

Cicourel, A. V. (1964). *Method and measurement in sociology.* Oxford: Free Press of Glencoe.

Denzin, N. K. & Lincoln, Y. S. (2017). *Handbook of qualitative research* (5th edition). Thousand Oaks, CA: Sage.

Dubbin, L., McLemore, M., & Shim, J. K. (2017). Illness narratives of African Americans living with coronary heart disease: A critical interactionist analysis. *Qualitative Health Research, 27*(4), 497–508.

Gouldner, A. (1973). For sociology. *American Journal of Sociology, 78*(5), 1063–1093.

Habermas, J. (1971) *Knowledge and human interests,* trans. Jeremy J. Shapiro. London: Heinemann.

Kahana, E., Slone, M. R., Kahana, B., Langendoerfer, K. B., & Reynolds, C. (2017). Beyond ageist attitudes: Researchers call for NIH action to limit funding for older academics. *The Gerontologist,* gnw190.

Luker, K. (2008). *Salsa dancing into the social sciences: Research in an age of info-glut.* Cambridge, MA: Harvard University Press.

Minkler, M. (2000). Using participatory action research to build healthy communities. *Public Health Reports, 115*(2–3), 191–197.

Rowles, G. D. & Shoenburg, N. E. (2002). *Qualitative gerontology: A contemporary perspective.* New York: Springer.

Shura, R., Siders, R. A., & Dannefer, D. (2011). Culture change in long-term care: Participatory action research and the role of the resident. *The Gerontologist, 51*(2), 212–225.

Sprague, J. (2016). *Feminist methodologies for critical researchers* (2nd edition). Lanham, MD: Rowman & Littlefield.

Teddlie, C. & Tashakkori, A. (2003). *Handbook of mixed-methods in social and behavioral research.* Thousand Oaks, CA: Sage.

Yeh, J. (2012). Through their eyes: Using photovoice and photo elicitation in research with LGBQ older adults. *The International Journal of Aging and Society, 1*(3), 85–106.

Ziegler, F. & Scharf, T. (2014). Community-based participatory action research: Opportunities and challenges for critical gerontology. In J. Baars, J. Dohmen, A. Grenier, & C. Phillipson (Eds.), *Ageing, meaning, and social structure: Connecting critical and humanistic gerontology* (pp. 157–180). Bristol: Policy Press.

Microaggressions

Subtle and often unintentional remarks or responses which articulate stereotypes, distinguish otherness, and invalidate the experience of the Other. These, as with stereotype threat, may lead to negative health outcomes for people receiving them (Hall & Fields, 2015).

Sue et al. (2007) locate three forms: microassaults, microinsults, and microinvalidations. Donovan et al. (2013) develop "macroaggression" as a term to describe "blatant" and "egregious" acts of racism (e.g., slurs, overt discrimination, unfounded accusations of criminal acts). Dover (2016) identifies oppression, dehumanization, and exploitation as three sources of injustice that "provide the social structural foundation for individual acts of microaggression" (p. 575). These actions embed and entrench white supremacy and heteropatriarchy.

Caregivers and health care providers can deliver microaggressions on those they care for, so this is an important component of clinical training: drawing awareness and consciousness to microaggressions, listening to how they've been perceived and received, and addressing guilt and culpability in a way that does not further burden those having experienced said microaggression. Critical gerontological theory can further explore the relationship between alienation and intersectionality, namely the conflagrating exposure to ageism for marginalized aging peoples, especially in the context of emerging dependency needs as it relates to cumulative disadvantage and widening health inequalities.

See also: Ageism, Alienation, Oppression, Racism, Stereotype Threat, Violence, White Supremacy

Further Reading

Donovan, R. A., Galban, D. J., Grace, R. K., Bennett, J. K., & Felicié, S. Z. (2013). Impact of racial macro- and micro-aggressions in Black women's lives: A preliminary analysis. *Journal of Black Psychology, 39*(2), 185–196.

Dover, M. A. (2016). The moment of microaggression: The experience of acts of oppression, dehumanization, and exploitation. *Journal of Human Behavior in the Social Environment, 26*(7–8), 575–586.

Grace, R. K., Felicié, S. Z., Bennett, J. K., Donovan, R. A., & Galban, D. J. (2013). Impact of racial macro- and micro-aggressions in black women's lives: A preliminary analysis. *Journal of Black Psychology, 39*(2), 185–196.

Hall, J. M. & Fields, B. (2015). "It's killing us!" Narratives of black adults about microaggression experiences and related health stress. *Global Qualitative Nursing Research, 2*, 1–14.

Pierce, C. (1970). Offensive mechanisms. In F. B. Barbour (Ed.), *The black seventies* (pp. 265–282). Boston, MA: Porter Sargent.

Sethi, B. (2016). Microaggressions of caregiver employees: What has social work got to do with it? *Diversity & Equality in Health and Care, 13*(5), 365–371.

Sue, D. W., Capodilupo, C. M., Torino, G. C., Bucceri, J. M., Holder, A. M. B., Nadal, K. L., & Esquilin, M. (2007). Racial microaggressions in everyday life. *American Psychologist, 62*(4), 271–286.

Microfication

The overestimating of agency and tendency to focus on immediate aspects of everyday life while larger issues of political and social location, that define and set parameters of daily experience, remain invisible.

This focus on the micro stems from psychologistic and quantitatively oriented social science, and has two sources. According to Baars and colleagues (2006, p. 4):

> First, work in constructivist and humanistic traditions typically *substitutes* microsocial or narrative analysis for microanalysis, rather than seeking to conjoin the micro and macro. This practice ignores the degree to which microprocesses are shaped by macro level forces that are beyond the control and often beyond the sphere of knowledge of the experienced realities of everyday life. Second, related to the first, is the neglect of the centrally important reality of power. Key to understanding both individual aging and the development of age, as a property of social systems is a recognition of the centrality of power. Power is at work in determining, for examples, which ideologies of age become accepted within popular or scientific discourse and which individuals have the best odds to "age successfully."

Microfication is a process that struggles to understand the individual as part of the collective. It sees individual attributes and strengths as being possibly deterministic, rather than shaped by macro-level social forces. Reflected in austerity politics which proposes piecemeal solutions that restrict choice, microfication places responsibility on the individual and ignores the importance of the collective. The microfication of aging services exists because microfication is an ideological mechanism that distills the worth of an idea, rationalizes the existing paradigms of aging, and misrepresents deeper sources of structural failures and State violence as exposed by Estes (1979) in *The aging enterprise*.

Critical Reflections

Any term defined in isolation lends itself to collapsing understanding into microfication; "going big" as C. Wright Mills urges us involves identifying complexity and making linkages between ideas. A question for readers to consider is how might the balkanization of disciplines, expertise, and professionalization favor approaches entrenched in microfication?

Further Reading

Baars, J., Dannefer, D., Phillipson, C., & Walker, A. (Eds.). (2006). *Aging, globalization and inequality: The new critical gerontology*. New York: Routledge.

Estes, C. L. (1979). *The aging enterprise: A critical examination of social policies and services for the aged*. San Francisco, CA: Jossey-Bass.

Hagestad, G. & Dannefer, D. (2001). Concepts and theories of aging. In R. Binstock (Ed.), *Handbook of aging and the social sciences* (pp. 3–21). New York: Academic Press.

Military Industrial Complex

Comprises the alliance of military and industrial interests. The term originates from C. Wright Mills, who argued in his 1956 book *The power elite* that dominating corporate interests undergirding military and industry established a "permanent war economy" that threatened democracy. President Eisenhower echoed this call in his 1961 farewell address.

Eisenhower warned the nation that the arms industry was a necessity of modern security; however, it posed a significant threat if left unchecked. "In the councils of government, we must guard against the acquisition of unwarranted influence, whether sought or unsought, by the military-industrial complex. The potential for the disastrous rise of misplaced power exists and will persist" (Eisenhower, 1961). It is telling that Eisenhower may originally have intended to describe the phenomena as the "Military Industrial Congressional Complex," pinpointing the operative mechanism of the relationship. Congress, with its vulnerability to lobbying and moneyed influence, combines with porous public/private lines in the defense sector to create the juggernaut that is US defense spending.

In the United States, defense spending is considered sacrosanct. The unrelenting participation of the USA in the "War on Terror" renews itself with cycles of outrage, fear, and aggression fueled by drone warfare and immigration battles. It conveniently offers opportunities to private contractors making the concept of the Military Industrial Complex undeniably salient today.

The mere act of proposing cuts to military spending is derided as unpatriotic and dangerous. US military spending is by far the highest of any country in the world. In fact, yearly military spending in the USA is roughly the same size as the military spending of the next seven highest countries combined (National Priorities, 2016). And still, Trump wanted to raise the military budget 10 percent while slashing the EPA, the NEA, and most other social programs.

See also: Commodification, Financialization

Further Reading

Eisenhower, E. (1961). The farewell address. Retrieved from www.eisenhower.archives. gov/research/online_documents/farewell_ address.html.

Mills, C. W. (1956). *The power elite*. New York: Oxford University Press.

National Priorities. (2016). U.S. military spending vs. the world. Retrieved from www.nationalpriorities.org/campaigns/ us-military-spending-vs-world/.

Misogyny

Concerns the hatred of women. It encompasses prejudice which announces itself through defamation, discrimination, and abuse.

The first female Democratic nominee for President, Hillary Clinton, faced unprecedented hate from her opposition, as conservatives rallied with cries (and billboards) to "lock-her-up." Her opponent accused her of playing "the woman card," insinuating she was trying to attain preferential treatment or special attention because of her gender.

The crone represents the ultimate manifestation of misogyny across the lifespan. The wise and wizened woman is seen as an untrustworthy witch, devoid of beauty. She doesn't need a man or have anything for him to use, so she poses a threat to patriarchy and is held in contempt. The sources go back to Greek myths and philosophers in which even women's voices were considered unsanitary and dangerous (Beard, 2017).

See also: Abjection, Crone, Feminism, Gender, Men, Patriarchy, War on Women

Further Reading

Beard, M. (2017). *Women & power: A manifesto*. New York: Liveright.

Moral Hazard

Implies fraud or immoral behavior when there is a benefit from insurance. This refers specifically to the intentional (or reckless) exposure to risk when insurance covers the cost of the risk.

Economists in the 1960s used the term "moral hazard" to describe inefficiencies in insurance programs that encourage risk-taking, rather than providing coverage for existing or inherent risk. This has become the center of the debate regarding medical care: Do individuals seek unnecessary or exorbitantly costly care when the cost is covered by insurance? Many economists argue that co-insurance, co-payments, and deductibles increase the out-of-pocket spending of consumers and disincentivize exposure to risk (in other words, increasing individual responsibility and limiting opportunities for the moral hazard). In fact, this has been a convenient rationale to raise co-pays and deductibles for consumers. However, social scientists note that these disincentives become barriers for the most vulnerable populations – the poor, the elderly, and the chronically ill – and furthermore create a stigmatic divide between welfare programs and marketplace coverage. The "disincentives" go beyond correcting for what is understood as overuse or indulgence; these barriers affect use which may include routine health services essential for early detection and preventive care of severe (and costly) disease.

In 2003, John Nyman published *The theory of demand for health insurance.* His principal contribution has been to recognize that insurance-induced health care utilization, on balance, results in an increase in *social welfare.* This directly contradicts the argument of mainstream neoclassical health economics for the past 40 years.

A critical reframing of moral hazard considers how money lenders and investors capitalize on risk through speculation and financialization, as was seen in the subprime mortgage crisis. Here, we might understand that the *immorality* lies in predatory practices which exploit insecurity and capitalize on precarity. We recognize the contradiction that this immorality is not challenged and is built into legal and economic structures and practices. The shrewdness of the "titans of Wall Street" and business "sharks" often garners admiration within the corporate world instead of raising concern. Working-class movements like Occupy function as the concerned conscience that demands accountability, as the working class bears the weight of these gambles.

See also: Occupy, Pensions/Retirement Plans, Precarity

Further Reading

Arrow, K. (1963). Uncertainty and the welfare economics of medical care. *The American Economic Review, 53*(5), 941–973.

Kelman, S. & Woodward, A. (2013). John Nyman and the economics of health care moral hazard. *ISRN Economics.*

Swartz, K. (2010). *Cost-sharing: Effects on spending and outcomes.* Robert Wood Johnson Foundation: The Synthesis Project. Retrieved from www.rwjf.org/en/library/research/2011/12/cost-sharing-effects-on-spending-and-outcomes.html.

Morality

The discernment and distinction between right and wrong, reflective of societal values and constructed largely through dominant paradigms. Morality is not a static position, rather a dynamic and constant struggle for definition. Often moral outrage reaffirms existing power structures, such as the disdain in the ageist narratives toward "greedy geezers," in which older adults are seen as threats to the resources of working people. On the other hand, moral outrage can mobilize resistance.

There are philosophical and ethical questions regarding the construction of morality. Do non-working, older, poor, black, queer, and/or disabled people have moral rights? Are these equal rights? These questions and answers are often framed as human rights and split from conversations of morality.

Moral outrage can quickly mobilize the delegitimation of a candidate for public office, as seen in the 2016 presidential election. Less than 24 hours after the release of footage showing Donald Trump proclaim his star power and privilege to grab a woman by her vagina, pundits declared he could no longer win the election. Quickly many in the Republican Party called for him to step down, yet months later many of these politicians welcomed him into office at his inauguration. Politics showcases that morality and hypocrisy are not mutually exclusive.

George Lakoff directly links morality and politics in the language we use to the conceptual frames they instill in us (another framework of heuristics). He identifies the "Moral Hierarchy" instilled in family life which produces one of two logics: the nurturant family vision (embraced on the Left political spectrum) and the strict father vision (embraced on the Right political spectrum and inherent in authoritarianism). Dominant paradigms, often articulated through popular culture, value certain bodies and lives more than others. The moral hierarchy, according to Lakoff (2016), follows:

God above Man, Man above Nature, The Disciplined (Strong) above the Undisciplined (Weak), The Rich above the Poor, Employers above Employees, Adults above Children, Western culture above other cultures, America above other countries. The hierarchy extends to: Men above women, Whites above Nonwhites, Christians above non Christians, Straights above Gays.

This is how Trump's xenophobic rants about Mexicans being rapists, banning Muslims, or his vendetta against five young black men who were acquitted of rape did not incite widespread moral outrage. It was the view on women, arguably white and married women, which destabilized his base. We offer these points not to draw equivalencies between discrimination and systems of oppression, rather to illustrate that morality extends through hierarchical valuations of decency.

See also: Affect, Ageism, Authoritarianism, Black Lives Matter, Framing, Human Rights, Heuristic, Xenophobia

Further Reading

Lakoff, G. (2016). A minority president: Why the polls failed, and what the majority can do. Retrieved from https://georgelakoff.com/2016/11/22/a-minority-president-why-the-polls-failed-and-what-the-majority-can-do/.

Myth

Defined as a functional narrative or widely held belief accepted regardless of contradictory evidence.

Traditionally recognized as establishments of antiquity and belonging to the realm of classical study, there are theories of how myths exist and operate in contemporary discourse, culture, and the realm of the symbolic. Roland Barthes (1972) examined how social values symbolically manifest in modern myths and how these become speech acts which frame and structure ideologically cohesive beliefs (adhering to a schema that serves the dominant power's interests). This includes "hiding the hand" of power, rewriting histories, and naturalizing authority.

"Debunking" myths means challenging the validity of an unquestioned belief or value and examining the means and motives which perpetuate their acceptance. This provides opportunities for subverting and rejecting stereotypes. Critical gerontology interrogates functionalist and ageist myths. Maggie Kuhn (in an interview in 1989) exemplified this, calling out:

The first myth is that old age is a disease, a terrible disease that you never admit you've got, so you lie about your age. Well, it's not a disease – it's a triumph. Because you've survived. Failure, disappointment, sickness, loss – you're still here.

Another particularly powerful myth is that older people selfishly hoard their resources and withdraw from participating in society. This myth attacks elders and undermines intergenerational relations' need for cooperation, exchange, and interdependence. Similarly, in the push for Social Security privatization, the deficit hawks propose mythologies of austerity as essential solutions to fixing debt – as if debt were not a component of the capitalist gods they serve.

See also: Ageism, Contradiction, Social Construction, Spirits of Capitalism, Statistical Panic, Symbols

Further Reading

Barthes, R. (1972). *Mythologies* (trans. A. Lavers). New York: Hill and Wang.

Hindman, M. (2008). *The myth of digital democracy* (1st edition). Princeton, NJ: Princeton University Press.

Nativism

A political position favoring the interests of native-born citizens over those of immigrants and those without established citizenship. The "native" in this sense does not refer to indigenous peoples; rather it speaks to the territoriality of the colonists as manifested through nationalism and exceptionalism.

Nativism has a long history in the United States and has played a prominent role in US policy at various points. From the Know Nothings to the John Birch Society, Nativist movements in the United States tread a delicate line between covert and overt prejudice.

Critical gerontology recognizes the aging experience as one informed by power, oppression, and marginalization. A human rights perspective posits that the right to grow old should not be predicated on citizenship. For advocates of freedom and equity, these critical perspectives ground analyses which combat the nativist frames of political policy and discussion.

See also: Alienation, Citizenship, Colonialisms, Human Rights, Immigration, Marginalization, Oppressions, Power, Xenophobia

Necropolitics

Encompasses the politics of death and dying, which can include natural causes,

intentional causes, and geopolitical events resulting in genocide, war, and famine.

Mbembe (2008, p. 12) notes that necropolitics asks:

> [U]nder what practical conditions is the right to kill, to allow to live, or to expose to death exercised? Who is the subject of this right? What does the implementation of such a right tell us about the person who is thus put to death and about the relation of enmity that sets that person against his or her murderer? . . . What place is given to life, death, and the human body? How are they inscribed in the order of power?

For critical gerontology, this realm of politics and health care includes patient directives, the Right-To-Die Movement/debate, as well as holding critical implications for the economic incentives which motivate insurance panels and hospitals to limit expenses or extend life.

See also: Colonialisms, Death

Further Reading

Mbembé, J. A., & Meintjes, L. (2003). Necropolitics. *Public Culture*, *15*(1), 11–40.

Wilson, M-M. G. (2004). Commentary: Clash of the Titans: Death, old age, and the devil's advocate. *The Journals of Gerontology Series A: Biological Sciences and Medical Sciences, 59*(6), M612–M615.

Neoliberalism

A political philosophy and practice of shifting control and responsibility from the public sector to the private. Key terms and features of neoliberalism include the market, privatization, destruction of social welfare programs (the welfare state), free trade, deregulation, and inequality.

Bourdieu writes of "the work of inculcation," how praise of the free market and framing of its benevolence becomes a "symbolic drip feed." Through this lens, neoliberalism's steady advances convince people of privatization's rightful place in policy. However, public opinion continues to shift and resistance has mounted (*see* Occupy, Black Lives Matter, Gray Panthers).

Neoliberalism became the dominant ideology in international development in the Reagan era and extends into the present day. Groups like the World Bank, International Monetary Fund, and World Trade Organization encourage countries to adopt free market reforms in exchange for access to financial resources and trade agreements. Neoliberalism within these "developing" economies has had varying levels of success; while raising the gross domestic product (GDP), wealth is not evenly distributed and arguably produces a great deal of hardship for workers.

Neoliberalism has significantly shaped the nature of health care in the United States and especially on inequality in health outcomes. When compared with the Canadian health system, health care in the United States is far less equitable due to the overwhelming pressure of market forces (Siddiqi et al., 2013). Neoliberal health reform, including Obamacare, is consistent with the framework of a worldwide agenda developed by the World Bank, International Monetary Fund, and other international financial institutions (Waitzkin, 2011). The neoliberal approach promotes market-driven health care in order to open private access by multinational corporations to vast public sector health and social security trust funds. Neoliberal ideology claims quality and efficiency of corporate management of medical services in the private marketplace.

Neoliberalism has changed the meaning of citizenship within states. "Rather than being seen as the ultimate defenders of the rights of their citizens, states came to be perceived as clients in a global bourse [stock market]" (Centeno & Cohen, 2012, p. 325). Of grave concern is that the cult of individualism has "expunged from our collective consciousness" the guiding cultural ideas undergirding "fairness in bargaining and compensation, the possibility that workers have inalienable protections from their employers and the potential benefit of collective action" (Centeno & Cohen, 2012, p. 331). This is nowhere more starkly apparent than on the Trump agenda in which social insurance (Social Security, Medicare, Medicaid), health care (ACA, women's rights, patient rights), and civil rights (for sexual minorities, racial equality, labor rights) and responsibilities are on the line as deregulatory measures, tax cuts, and private contracting advance.

See also: Black Lives Matter, Capitalism, Colonialisms, Globalization, Gray Panthers, Inequality, The Market, Medical Industrial Complex, Occupy, Prison Industrial Complex, Privatization, Spirits of Capitalism, Workfare

Further Reading

Bourdieu, P. (1998). *Acts of resistance against the tyranny of the market.* New York: The New Press.

Centeno, M. A. & Cohen, J. N. (2012). The arc of neoliberalism. *Annual Review of Sociology, 38*(1), 317–340.

Estes, C. L. (2014). The future of aging services in a neoliberal political economy. *Generations, 38*(2), 94–100.

Polivka, L. (2011). Neoliberalism and postmodern cultures of aging. *Journal of Applied Gerontology, 30*(2), 173–184.

Siddiqi, A., Kawachi, I., Keating, D. P., & Hertzman, C. (2013). A comparative study of population health in the United States and Canada during the neoliberal era, 1980–2008. *International Journal of Health Services, 43*(2), 193–216.

Waitzkin, H. (2011). *Medicine and public health at the end of empire.* Boulder, CO: Paradigm.

Networks

Social structures consisting of a set of actors, organizations, or other entities that have ties to one another.

Social networks manifest formally and informally. They can exist in and out of real space, often occupying virtual/cyberspace, which creates and promotes social interactions (communication and support) between actors. Networks can function as platforms for the persuasion and consciousness raising of key stakeholders in policy and practice. The formation, structuring, and deployments of networks are a critical dimension of power.

The "Network Society" is "transforming *the fundamental dimensions of human life: time and space* . . . extending the productive capacity of working hours while superseding spatial distance in all realms of social activity . . . [opening] up unlimited horizons of creativity and communication" (Castells, 1994, p. 1). There is connectivity and access which disrupts the elite's ownership of knowledge/data/communication (and the restrictions engendered by elite establishments). However, digital technologies exist within infrastructure (capital, goods, and nation-states), embedded in established systems of power,

and there are limits imposed by advertisements, censorship, algorithms designed to direct and promote consumption of digital content.

Networks are integral to understanding power and counter-power. Emirbayer (1997) posits that social networks are "interstitial," existing between communities and systems. He writes, "Transactions unfolding within social networks are not always symmetrical in nature: flows are often 'directional' in content and intensity, with significant implications for actors' differential access to resources" (p. 299). This variation and heterogeneity of what constitutes a network (ideas about actors, identity, and location) gives rise to several theories, including observations about the stipulations for participation, networks' abilities to tolerate or accept difference, and shared values.

Two types of networks analyzed by Karatzogianni and Robinson (2010) are *reactive* and *affinity*. Reactive networks join in opposition to outside forces, forming connections between "insiders." Social cohesion is maintained through alienation of outsiders, which accords to the values and formations of fascism.

In contrast, affinity networks open to others and expand through bringing together different players/groups. The affinity network composition is informal and "is by definition voluntary, and it functions by resonances and attractions, not forced participation . . . affinity rather than hegemony" (Karatzogianni & Robinson, 2010, p. 145). Affinity networks sometimes arise when reactive networks push out actors, who reform and relate, grounded in their otherness, not shutting them out and not forcing participation.

In aging policy the concept of an aging network describes the agencies and provider systems created, facilitated, and sparsely funded through the Older Americans Act for community-based services available to older and disabled persons (Montgomery &

Blair, 2016). Critical gerontologists can employ the theoretical frameworks of the *network society, reactive networks*, and *affinity networks* to study the values that these services, organizations, and policy pieces promote or claim to provide.

See also: Aging Enterprise, Alienation, Fascism, Older Americans Act, Organization, Power

Further Reading

Castells, M. (1994). *The informational city: Information technology, economic structuring, and the urban-regional process*. Hoboken, NJ: Wiley-Blackwell.

Castells, M. (2015). *Networks of outrage and hope: Social movements in the internet age* (2nd edition). Malden, MA: Polity Press.

Emirbayer, M. (1997). Manifesto for a relational sociology. *The American Journal of Sociology, 103*(2), 281–317.

Estes, C. L. & Swan, J. H. (1993). *The long-term care crisis*. Thousand Oaks, CA: Sage.

Karatzogianni, A. & Robinson, A. (2010). *Power, resistance, and conflict in the contemporary world: Social movements, networks, and hierarchies*. London: Routledge.

Lievrouw, L. (2011). *Alternative and activist new media*. Malden, MA: Polity Press.

Montgomery, A. & Blair, E. (2016). *The aging network in transition: Hanging in the balance*. Washington, DC: National Academy of Social Insurance.

No-care Zone

A subjective, economic, cultural, and/or political space in which those needing care are denied it by virtue of exclusion or insufficient resources stipulated by public policy (or lack thereof).

The inability to pay for services or to fit into existing policy expectations (i.e., eligibility) is an intentional exclusion through public policy. Limited resources and social values work in tandem to create a reality that denies care. Class, race, gender, and sexuality along with age become constellated in the implicit and explicit constructions of exclusion that appear in medical standards and legal practices.

As the entry on the market illustrates (and the concept of precarity supports), gaps in coverage are part of the hegemonic order. They keep a working underclass desperate and more readily available to exploit. A critical lens locates no-care zones across the lifespan, theorizing the impact and significance on lived experience.

See also: Affordable Care Act (ACA), Hegemony, The Market, Oppression, Precarity, Zones

Further Reading

Estes, C. L., James Swan & Associates. (1993). *The long term care crisis: Elders trapped in the no-care zone*. Newbury Park, CA: Sage.

O

Occupy

A social movement organized in New York to protest the domination and control of Wall Street and power brokers representing the 1 percent over the 99 percent (Byrne, 2012; Van Gelder, 2011). This spread to a national movement which mobilized millions, many of whom had been dispossessed of their homes through foreclosure via the subprime mortgage crisis.

The messages varied throughout the vast, decentralized movement; yet at its core Occupy values the rights of people and nature over corporate rights. Methods of the movement included: speak out on issues that means most to you; study and teach non-violent techniques; claim and reclaim space, *occupy* it; "Be the media" and record the struggle by video. Occupied spaces create community and togetherness, lessening fear. Castells (2015, pp. 10–11) writes that these spaces:

> are usually charged with the symbolic power of invading sites of state power or financial institutions. . . . By taking and holding urban space, citizens reclaim their own city, a city from where they were evicted by real estate speculation & municipal bureaucracy. . . . The control of space symbolizes the control over people's lives. . . . By constructing a free community in a symbolic space, social movements create a public space, a space for deliberation, which ultimately becomes a political space, a space for sovereign assemblies to meet and to recover their rights of representation.

Maggie Kuhn seized her opportunity with Johnny Carson, electrifying TV's famous host by vociferously shaming his performance of Aunt Blabby, an ageist caricature of an old biddy. She shocked the public and the Federal Communications Commission by departing from expectations that she would be polite and compliant. She was opinionated and not afraid of vulgarity. With Gray Panthers media watch and her charismatic voice and action, Maggie radicalized consciousness of ageism in US politics and policy. Occupying the airwaves resists efforts from the Right to advance privatization.

See also: Ageism, Leninist Strategy, Maggie Kuhn, Resistance, Social Movements

Further Reading

Brown, L. & Strega, S. (2005). *Research as resistance*. Toronto, ON: Canadian Scholars' Press.

Byrne, J. (2012). *The occupy handbook*. New York: Back Bay Books.

Castells, M. (2015). *Networks of outrage and hope: Social movements in the internet age* (2nd edition). Malden, MA: Polity Press.

Van Gelder, S. (2011). *This changes everything*. San Francisco, CA: Berrett-Koehler.

Older Americans Act (OAA)

The Older Americans Act was signed into law in July of 1965. The Act aimed to provide services and support for older people and has since been reauthorized several times, most recently in 2016, under President Obama.

The law created the Aging Network, a group of agencies including the Administration on Aging and a number of state and local aging and assistance agencies. Currently, the Administration on Aging falls under the purview of the Administration for Community Living which is overseen by the Department of Health and Human Services.

The Administration for Community Living (ACL) provides and funds a variety of services for older Americans. Meal programs, case management, in-home short-term and long-term care, and disease prevention programs represent just some of the efforts undertaken by the various agencies within the Aging Network.

The Administration for Community Living oversees the following programs:

- Administration on Aging
- Administration on Disabilities
- National Institute on Disability, Independent Living, and Rehabilitation Research
- Administration for Community Living
- Center for Integrated Programs
- Center for Management and Budget
- Center for Policy and Evaluation

See also: Administration for Community Living (ACL), Policy

Further Reading

https://acl.gov/About_ACL/Organization/Index.aspx.

www.aoa.gov/SOS_[rpgra,s/OAA/.

Older Women's League

Founded in 1980 in Des Moines, Iowa after the WHCOA pre-conference by Tish Sommers and Laurie Shields. The League, known as OWL, aims to advocate for mid-life and older women and to combat the lack of women's voices and attention to women's roles in aging policy.

Tish Sommers noted that little attention was being paid to the ways in which aging was different and difficult for women. The Older Women's League has a national office, and a California state organization, as well as other local entities. A particularly active one is located in San Francisco, CA.

See also: Ageism, Networks, Resistance

Further Reading

Huckle, P. (1991). *Tish Sommers, activist, and the founding of the older women's league*. Knoxville, TN: University of Tennessee Press.

Hutchinson, S. L. & Wexler, B. (2007). Is "raging" good for health? Older women's participation in the raging grannies. *Health Care for Women International, 28*(1), 88–118.

Ontology

Studies reality, searching to locate objective and material truths. Distinct from epistemology, ontology concerns itself less with how things come into being and focuses on what exists. This approach describes much of the biomedical science's focus on cell life and death (e.g., gene expression, senescence, and telomeres).

Critical realist ontology is one of the more prominent approaches to ontology within the social sciences. It may be seen as a response to more positivist and empiricist schools of scientific thought, and emphasizes a deeper and more nuanced approach to social scientific inquiry. In particular, critical realism advocates for the examination of the origins and structure of the social world and of social systems and phenomena. This generally takes the form of an effort to consider phenomena in a broader context and to generalize beyond simple causal relationships. Socioeconomic stratifications, discrimination of all kinds, and other social factors must be examined simultaneously and with attention to one another.

See also: Critical Realism, Epistemology, Intersectionality, Postmodernism

Further Reading

Bhaskar, R. (2008). *A realist theory of science.* London: Routledge.

Oppression

Describes the violence toward and domination of groups of people who suffer disadvantage, coercion, or exploitation by people with more power. Those perpetrating and perpetuating this domination are referred to as the *oppressors*, and those abused by those with power are known as the *oppressed*.

Oppression may only be contested when it is named, as the dominant discourse routinely depoliticizes and naturalizes experiences of oppression, rendering them ordinary and expected parts of daily life. Oppression may be contested when it is named in safe or safer spaces away from the surveillance of oppressive policing structures and people.

The social work dictionary, edited by Robert L. Barker, suggests that oppression operates in a way which renders the oppressed "less able to compete with other social groups" (Barker, 2003). Patricia Hill Collins (2000) locates oppression as occurring within a "matrix of domination," which extends through four domains of power: the structural, disciplinary, hegemonic, and interpersonal.

Critical gerontologists can consider how stigma and degrading stereotypes coexist within policy that leaves older adults precarious on multiple levels. These analyses extend further questions for students, activists, and scholars about how oppression manifests through precarity and abjection, and impacts the organizing of social movements and solidarity.

See also: Abjection, Domination, Inequality, Power, Precarity, Social Movements, Solidarity

Further Reading

Barker, R. L. (2003). *The social work dictionary.* Washington, DC: NASW Press.

Collins, P. H. (2000). *Black feminist thought* (2nd edition, revised 10th anniversary edition). New York: Routledge.

Organic Intellectual

One who springs forth from elite exclusion and into the public sphere to share knowledges and affect change. This stands in contrast to the traditional ivory tower scholar. The quest of organic intellectuals is to create "a grounded, radical hegemonic re-thinking and politics" for advancing social change (Sassoon, 2000).

Organic intellectuals openly identify and act with oppressed classes, races, genders, and other oppressed (subaltern) groups and identities. Their work is extraordinarily difficult because it requires transforming the "pessimism of the intellect" into the "optimism of the will" (Sassoon, 2000). This framework illustrates the academic ground gained by feminists which for gerontological thought has promoted the critical importance of standpoint theory (Burawoy, 2016).

Intellectuals, including notables in America's literary culture (Whitman, Twain,

Thoreau, Melville) and resistance artists, have historically played key roles in the politicization of intellectuals and the successes of the American Left (Flacks, 1988, pp. 116–119). The 1960s civil rights revolt, and Trump's resistance works (ongoing), illuminate the interfaces of cultural radicalism, political engagement, and collective intellectual leftism. New arenas and possibilities for the success of organic intellectuals are evolving on the ground, in cyberspace, and in public consciousness. Focal points of energy are the erosion of legitimacy of established authority and the ideology of white superiority and the transparency of historical blockage of rights of peoples of color and other vulnerable groups in the USA.

See also: Hegemony, Ideology, Public Sociology, Standpoint Theory, The State, Think Tanks

Further Reading

Burawoy, M. (2016). Sociology as a vocation. *Contemporary Sociology: A Journal of Reviews, 45*(4), 379–393.

Flacks, R. (1988). *Making history*. New York: Columbia University Press.

Sassoon, A. S. (2000). *Gramsci and contemporary politics*. London: Routledge.

Organizations (Selected)

Groups comprising people who unite with a common mission, sharing resources, knowledges, and labor. Organizations can play pivotal roles in social movements as vanguards of justice. The entry for institutions expounds upon this idea of group which function as mainstays of cultural values and stewards of societal direction.

The following mentioned here are advocacy organizations which direct efforts and/or service across several levels. Critical gerontologists' knowledge of this landscape offers opportunities for participation and advancement of research and advocacy. Many of the following groups utilize existing research on aging populations and services, conduct their own research, or partner together to advance their advocacy through big data analyses on aging experiences.

AARP

The 37 million-plus organization of older adults (age 50+). It is part of the corporate Medical Industrial Complex (MIC) and was the architect of Medicare Part D (which favored and institutionalized big pharmaceuticals through out-of-pocket spending), 2016 controversy funding ALEC (the rightwing lobby group that advocates for privatization and defunding of social insurance programs). AARP may be described as "joined at the hip" in the MIC, with its selling of Medigap, Medicare Part C, and Medicare Part D insurance coverages, generating billions of revenue annually. As a co-branding partner of numerous other enterprises (cell phones, travel businesses), AARP is a profitable business. It is also the umbrella for an active policy think tank and a foundation, each contributing to aging policy.

Leadership Council of Aging Organizations (LCAO)

A coalition with 72 member organizations, the LCAO is dedicated to providing a voice for seniors on important issues. The organizations themselves, and LCAO, engage in a variety of advocacy efforts on many different issues (for more details *see* Coalitions).

National Committee to Preserve Social Security and Medicare (NCPSSM)

Founded in 1982, NCPSSM comprises: (1) a policy, lobbying, and advocacy entity (C-4 tax status); (2) a political action committee (PAC tax status); and (3) a foundation for education and research (C-3 philanthropic tax status). NCPSSM is completely member funded and has helped to prevent successive privatization and benefit cut proposals from being enacted. NCPSSM provides continuous policy and legislative analyses. NCPSSM is a founding member of Social Security Works and the Leadership Council of Aging Organizations.

National Council on Aging

Seeks to serve seniors in a variety of different realms. The Council conducts advocacy on issues related to aging in addition to partnering with a wide array of other organizations to provide services and community resources.

Older Women's League

Delivers a Mother's Day policy brief to Congress every year on Capitol Hill. The report focuses on inadequacies of Medicare and Social Security (e.g., not covering caregiving years and the consequences of being out of the workforce).

See also: Big Data, Coalitions, Institutions, Resistance, Social Movements

Outrageous Act of the Day

A framework and strategy for resistance suggested by Maggie Kuhn, who encouraged members of the Gray Panthers to do something outrageous every day. She advised:

> The older you get the more outrageous you can be because you have nothing to lose.
>
> – Maggie Kuhn

An instructive example from Maggie's own life was the protest staged during the Annual American Medical Association convention in Chicago in 1974. In response to the AMA's failure to provide useful health education for older persons and the Association's reticence to advocate for just policies, Maggie and a variety of allies staged a protest on the steps of the hotel where the AMA delegates were staying. They picketed the entrance and performed a guerrilla theater routine in which they dressed an actor up as the "sick AMA" and then attempted to treat and resuscitate them. The faux patient was only cured once wads of money were removed from their body (Kuhn, Long, & Quinn, 1991, p. 157).

Maggie Kuhn also obtained a press pass at the AMA convention in 1974 which she used to publicly interrupt the President of the AMA in front of the Association's delegates and to present a letter containing demands from the Gray Panthers. Maggie said of the incident:

> Go to the people at the top – that is my advice to anyone who wants to change the system, any system. . . . Leave safety behind. Put your body on the line. Stand before the people you fear and speak your mind – even if your voice shakes. . . . Well-aimed slingshots can topple giants.
>
> (Kuhn, Long, & Quinn, 1991, p. 159)

Author's Reflection

Maggie once told me that one might resist a grave obstacle with inappropriate levity. While there is arguably great variation in what is considered *outrageous*, here's my outrageous act today: donning my Pink Pussy Hat. I wear it because at the core of this "Social Security crisis" and deficit mania is masculinist thinking embedded in the dominant "rational man" economics. What are you outraged about today and how will you show it?

See also: Gray Panthers, Resistance

Further Reading

Hutchinson, S. L. & Wexler, B. (2007). Is "raging" good for health? Older women's participation in the raging grannies. *Health Care for Women International, 28*(1), 88–118.

Kuhn, M., Long, C., & Quinn, L. (1991). *No stone unturned.* New York: Ballantine.

P

Patriarchy

The term for a society or system in which men hold power exclusively or hegemonically. Patriarchy pervades political, religious, cultural, and economic institutions, limiting the authority of women and those identified as non-men. The materialist relations of patriarchy are male exploitation of women's labor.

The family and women's reproductive functions (biological and social) represent a primary locus of women's oppression. Feminists of different theoretical "waves" may emphasize different relational and causal paths to understanding patriarchy as ideology and dominance. Weedon (1987, pp. 2–3) argues,

> The term "patriarchal" refers to power relations in which women's interest are subordinated to the interests of men. These power relations take on many forms, from the sexual division of labour and the social organization of procreation to the internalised norms of femininity by which we live. Patriarchal power rests on the social meaning given to biological sexual difference.

For aging, the power structure and violence of the patriarchy illustrates the gendered dynamics of oppression across the life course. The violence of social control manifests and extends through multiple traumas of cumulative disadvantage, inequality, and the toll of gendered expectations. For practitioners this extends to looking at who holds power in decision-making and who is expected to obey. A further critical analysis locates who benefits *or does not* from the aging enterprise.

See also: Domination, Feminism, Men, Power, Privilege

Further Reading

Gamble, S. (2000). *The Routledge critical dictionary of feminism and postfeminism*. New York: Routledge.

Weedon, C. (1987). *Feminist practice and poststructuralist theory*. Oxford: Blackwell.

Pedagogy

The theory, and also a praxis of education. As the older population cohort in the United States becomes more diverse it is critical that gerontology adopt pedagogy that effectively addresses issues of racial and socioeconomic equity.

Emancipatory knowledges develop from what bell hooks (1994) identifies as "engaged pedagogy." She writes, "Conditions of radical openness exist in any learning situation where students and teachers celebrate their abilities to think critically, to engage in pedagogical praxis" (hooks, 1994, p. 202). This occurs when the teacher carries an awareness of their body's power and a duty to transform their academies so that "the way we live, teach, and work can reflect our joy in cultural diversity, our passion for justice, and our love of freedom" (p. 34). The concept of lifelong learning, modeled and championed by Maggie Kuhn, exemplifies that access and participation in education is more than a developmental stage. Learning functions collectively and through the generations.

Pedagogy is the critical point of praxis in the Freirean sense, especially as studying education can emancipate it from certain bounds of the market which threaten its reflexivity. Educational institutions can and should regard how processes of hiring, tenure, and retirement affect representation among faculty. These institutions also have an imperative to extend representational robustness to the classroom, holding a complicated responsibility in making education accessible to all. A commitment to equity and inclusion requires radical rethinking about (dis)ability, financial barriers, social jeopardies, and safety – both physical and emotional.

Advocates for the right to public education challenge the privatization initiatives through vouchers which threaten public funding on a state and national level. Primary education is critical and capable of radical/emancipatory practice. Similarly, threats to access exist via state discretion protecting private (charter) schools' discriminatory practices. The Trump era's Secretary of Education, Betsy DeVos, publicly affirmed the availability of federal funding via vouchers to private and religious schools, extending state discretion to discriminate as to codes of conduct, which can include sexuality and gender presentation. Advocacy for undocumented students

and international scholars was especially relevant in the Trump era of mass deportation and the "Muslim-Ban."

See also: Consciousness Raising, Education, Emancipatory, Epistemology, Praxis

Further Reading

Berila, B. (2015). *Integrating mindfulness into anti-oppression pedagogy*. New York: Routledge.

hooks, b. (1994). *Teaching to transgress*. New York: Routledge.

Karasik, R. J. & Kishimoto, K. (2016). Is gerontology ready for anti-racist pedagogy? A survey of educators' practices and perspectives. *Gerontology & Geriatrics Education*, 1–18.

Pensions/Retirement Plans

Retirement pension plans in the USA may be classified as defined benefit or defined contribution plans, and within each type there are multiple variations. The Bureau of Labor Statistics in the Glossary of Employee Benefit Terms (2017) states:

> *Defined benefit* plans determine payments according to a fixed formula based on salary, years of service, and age. *Defined contribution* plans determine the value of individual accounts on the basis of the amount of money contributed and the rate of return on the money invested.

Defined benefit pension plans provide guaranteed benefits for employees meeting eligibility criteria. Pension contributions are from the employer/sponsor (sometimes also requiring worker contributions) and a specified pension payment, lump sum (or combination thereof) promised on retirement rather than depending directly on individual investment returns.

In the private sector, until the 1980s, defined benefit plans were often funded exclusively by employer contributions. For very small companies with one owner and a handful of younger employees, the business owner generally received a high percentage of the benefits. In the public sector (e.g., University of California), defined benefit plans usually require employee contributions.

Government jobs and/or jobs protected with a strong union still offer pension plans to many, but since the 1980s private sector corporations retreated from offering defined benefit pensions, citing the high long-term costs, and instead have replaced them with defined contribution plans 401(k)s (*see below*). This means a dramatic rise in the proportion of defined contribution pension plans. Significantly this has occurred simultaneously in tandem with the decline in jobs with benefits, the rise in the flexibilization of work, part-time work, unemployment in major industrial sectors, and the outsourcing of US jobs overseas.

A defined contribution plan is a retirement savings program sponsored by an employer, which lets workers save and invest a piece of their paycheck before taxes are taken out. With the 401(k), the individual determines how and where the money is invested. 401(k) plans are named for a tax code which stipulates that these assets are untaxed until the money is withdrawn from the account. If that occurs before a certain age, heavy penalties must be paid. (*Note*: there are other types such as the Roth IRA that have different rules.)

The 401(k) has been heralded as a boon or a bane, depending on one's economic analyses and policy proposals. Ghilarducci, Saad-Lessler, & Reznik, (2018) expose the instability and "reactive behavior" that 401ks exhibit in response to recessions and economic shocks.

Individual Retirement Accounts (IRAs) offer several plans with varying incentives for individuals to contribute assets and savings to their own retirement outside of employer sponsorship. These can be invested in stocks and bonds. The ability to invest and to do so well is related to financial, educational, and other networks and resources.

Critical Perspective:

Many of these retirement plans follow in the tradition of individualism and free market ideology, often with little or no assistance to a person trying to prepare for retirement security. To varying degrees these pension plans and their brokers play on speculation and competition. Absolutely required (but not guaranteed by law) is one's access to resources beyond money (money management expert help with financial literacy) and security that your assets and income have stability. These are enormous barriers for those who do not occupy positions of privilege and connection (such as lower income people, women, and people of color, and even a large portion of middle-income people). Both 401ks and IRAs contribute to Wall Street profits and markets.

Only half of private workers have any kind of employer-sponsored retirement plan. Between 1989 and 2013, the percentage of workers with a defined benefit plan decreased from 22 to 7 percent; the percentage with defined contribution plans increased from 15 to 32 percent, and the percentage with both types of plans fell from 10 to 6 percent (Munnell, 2014).

In cases of corporate bankruptcies, some or all of the invested pension benefits may be lost to workers, depending on The Pension Benefit Guarantee Corporation (PBGC) and legal actions. In the case of 401k plans, worker contributions are voluntary and the risk of managing these funds is borne by individuals in volatile markets. Many workers who have access to 401ks do not participate and even fewer contribute the maximum amount allowed in them.

In addition, 401K and assets may be withdrawn by the worker (with penalties) and may be depleted significantly when other financial needs arise such as job loss or illness. Even the "Fiduciary Rule" that requires brokers to take their clients' best interests into account when guiding investment decisions concerning their retirement monies is threatened in Congress by policy-makers beholden to financial interests that seek to abolish the regulations of Wall Street. Private pension securitization schemes increase the reliance of workers on equity markets and serious risks of exotic instruments and portfolios that few understand. Soederberg (2010) critiques this increasing marketization of labor and disempowering exploitative relationships between financial capital and workers' pension funds.

Congress has shown its willingness to trade off private pension security for tax cuts and deficit politics. The overt politicization of retirement plan policies and regulations is a danger seen in tax reform proposals that could drastically cut tax subsidies, limiting worker contributions to 401ks. Other deleterious tax reform measures may exempt employers from contributing to these plans or their being involved in the costs of managing them.

Retirement plans are of little concern for the super-wealthy, whose incomes and assets of hundreds of millions of dollars exempt them from worrying about the need for reliable, fixed retirement income guarantees. This situation underscores the urgency of protecting and improving universal social insurance programs such as Social Security and Medicare as well as Medicaid. The prospects for these programs have been dimmed by the passage of the 2018 Tax Cuts and Jobs Act that most benefits corporations and the top 2 percent of Americans, and ramps up pressure from deficit hawks to eviscerate programs for the most vulnerable, like SSI, SNAP, as well as the disabled. For the aging, there are many who are "becoming poor for the first time in old age" (Kevin Prindeville, quoted in Samuels, 2018).

See also: Financialization, Moral Hazard, Poverty, Retirement, Social Security

Further Reading

Bureau of Labor Statistics. (BLS). (n.d.). Employee Benefits Survey. National Compensation Survey: Glossary of Employee Benefit Terms. Retrieved from www.bls. gov/ncs/ebs/glossary20162017.htm.

Ghilarducci, T. (2006). The end of retirement. *Class: The Anthology*, 503–511.

Ghilarducci, T. (2008). *When I'm sixty-four: The plot against pensions and the plan to save them.* Princeton, NJ: Princeton University Press.

Ghilarducci, T. (2010). The solution to the pension crisis is more pensions. *Perspectives on Work*, *14*(1–2), 34. Published by the Labor and Employment Relations Association (LERA). Retrieved from www. economicpolicyresearch.org/images/ docs/Teresa_Ghilarducci/The_Solution_ to_the_Pension_Crisis.pdf.

Ghilarducci, T. (2014). Private pensions, December 1. In *Oxford handbook of U.S. social policy*. Oxford: Oxford University Press. Retrieved from www.oxfordhand-books.com/view/10.1093/oxfordhb/ 9780199838509.001.0001/oxfordhb-9780199838509-e-031.

Ghilarducci, T. (2015). The welfare state: A terrible name for an essential system. *The Atlantic*, December 3. Retrieved from www.theatlantic.com/business/archive/ 2015/12/the-welfare-state-a-terrible-name-for-an-essential-system/418500/ ?0t3noghn72co.

Ghilarducci, T., Saad-Lessler, J., & Reznik, G. (2018). Earnings volatility and 401(k) contributions. *Journal of Pension Economics and Finance*, *17*(4), 554–575.

Gorman, M. (2018). Gen X women: The time is now to embrace health savings accounts. *Forbes*, November 30. Retrieved from www.forbes.com/sites/megangorman/2018/11/30/gen-x-women-the-time-is-now-to-embrace-health-saving-accounts/#5227360f2f74.

Hardy, M. & Hazelrigg, L. (2007). *Pension puzzles: Social security and the great debate.* New York, NY: Russell Sage.

Munnell, A. H. (2014). 401 (k)/IRA holdings in 2013: An update from the SCF. Retrieved from http://crr.bc.edu/wp-content/uploads/2014/09/IB_14-15.pdf.

O'Brian, E. (2018). Retirees are caught off-guard by these two major expenses. Don't let them bring down your retirement. *Money*, December 3. Retrieved from http://time.com/money/5469429/retirees-are-caught-off-guard-by-these-two-major-expenses-dont-let-them-bring-down-your-retirement/.

Phillipson, C. (2009). Pensions in crisis: Aging and inequality in a global age. In L. Rogne, C. L. Estes, B. R. Grossman, B. A. Hollister, & E. Solway (Eds.), *Social insurance and social justice: Social Security, Medicare, and the campaign against entitlements* (pp. 319–339). New York: Springer.

Rappaport, A. M. (2018a). Realities of retirement: Family is very important. *Investments and Wealth Monitor.* Retrieved from https://investmentsandwealth.org/getattachment/e7f180d5-a6ed-41d5-be57-9ddd23cc0dde/IWM18NovDec-RealitiesOfRetirement.pdf.

Rappaport, A. M. (2018b). What retirees do and say: Insights about decumulation strategies. *Benefits Quarterly of the International Society of Certified Employee Benefits Specialists.* Retrieved from www.iscebs.org/Resources/BQ/Pages/BQ-executive-summaries-2018.aspx.

Russell, J. W. (2014). *Social insecurity: 401(k)s and the retirement crisis.* Boston, MA: Beacon Press.

Samuels, A. (2018). This is what life without retirement savings looks like. *The Atlantic*, February 22.

Soederberg, S. (2010). Cannibalistic capitalism: The paradoxes of neoliberal pension securitization. In L. Panitch, G. Albo, & V. Chibber (Eds.), *The crisis this time: Socialist register 2011* (pp. 224–241). New York: Monthly Review Press.

The Society of Actuaries. (n.d.). Financial perspectives on aging and retirement across the generations. Retrieved from www.soa.org/research-reports/2018/financial-perspectives-aging-retirement/.

People of Color (POC)

An umbrella term for persons of non-white racial identity. This collective identification serves to organize against white supremacy, signaling a solidarity in resisting whiteness.

The label of POC encompasses many different identities. It signals the diverse negative effects of systemic racism and the strength called upon to reclaim one's humanity. Though different brown and black oppressed groups face unique challenges in society, the forces that are fundamentally responsible for those challenges can be identified (i.e., white supremacy and the systemic structure of racism). The POC label may also be useful in describing the aggregate effects of policy, such as the proposed lowering of the retirement age, which would disproportionately affect POC because of inequities in labor and generational inheritance, as well as the inseparable realities of health inequality and the racial wealth gap.

See also: Black Lives Matter, Colonialisms, Health Disparities, Intersectionality, Oppression, Racial Wealth Gap, White Supremacy

Further Reading

Cho, S., Williams, K., Crenshaw, K., & McCall, L. (2013). Toward a field of intersectionality studies: Theory, application, and praxis. *Signs, 38*(4), 785–810.

Omi, M. & Winant, H. (2008). Once more with feeling: Reflections on racial formation. *PMLA Theories and Methodologies, PMLA, 123*(5), 1565–1572.

Performativity

A theory proposed by Judith Butler (1993) about how our gendered identities are constituted in part by who we are expected to be and what we are allowed to say/do.

The way we walk and talk is embodied through a performance, which constitutes one way of understanding our identities. This is largely informed by who we are allowed to be, and for women the desired (or expected) roles have historically been restricted to those of ingénue, mother, and crone. Butler (2010) theorizes that sexuality is also performed. Language that speaks to this includes gay/queer/masc/butch/femme/high-femme aesthetics, and action.

Age is also an identity that becomes represented and constructed through performativity. Because age is enacted in all interactions, age is often rendered invisible and seemingly biologically and chronologically natural. As people age, society and biology inscribe visible and invisible codes on the body. The body becomes a negotiating receptor, accepting and resisting the social meanings produced internally and externally about growing older (Goffman, 1963; Laz, 2003).

The notion of "doing age" is such that age is "a performance in the sense of something requiring activity and labor" (Laz, 1998, p. 86). Conceptualizing age as performed clarifies how norms and roles work in social situations because they "are resources that individuals draw on in interaction. They are among the tools we use to act our age; they do not themselves constitute age" (Laz, 1998, p. 101). "Doing age" does not ignore the "fact" of chronological time. Rather, it enables the possibility to examine the process whereby chronological

time is made "factual" and to see the consequences of our aging *as if* chronology were natural. To "act one's age" or to live in a world where one acts a subjective age that others desire or ridicule is to understand that our performance of age, whether we do it well or poorly, is always collective and social. This is the realm of intergenerational intersubjectivity, and ideological values of worth and abjection have vast implications for how we connect with others through the course of our lives.

In the case of older adults, identity management is vital for surviving a culture that generally forces them to become disengaged or obedient subjects over time (Powell & Wahidin, 2007). However, performativity is not totally just about facing coercive threats to play a certain role. The performativity of young, old, and aging bodies is a way in which "practices of the self" are used to negotiate the simultaneous changes associated with chronological time and continuity of the self. This means there can also be joy in celebrating one's embodiment, and shifting sense of gender and sexuality, throughout the journey of age. This joy is about entering space and unrestricted movement and ability to build, play, and dream with others.

Concluding Critical Reflections

What does it mean to recognize performativity in a world where the prevailing ideology is that women should be seen and not heard? Restriction of autonomy bears relation to feelings of success or failure, and furthermore a general sense of self in the world. Rape is a form of social control that violently performs and silences patriarchal dominance; it is meant as a repatriation into silence. Elder abuse, which may include rape, is also a mechanism and function of social control that refuses to value or honor the subjectivities of older adults.

See also: Ageism, Gender, Grievability, Intergenerational Intersubjectivity, Intersectionality, Sexuality

Further Reading

Butler, J. (1993). *Bodies that matter*. New York: Routledge.

Butler, J. P. (1997). *Excitable speech: A politics of the performative*. New York: Routledge.

Butler, J. (2010). Performative agency. *Journal of Cultural Economy*, 3(2), 147–161.

Goffman, E. (1959). *The presentation of self in everyday life*. New York: Anchor Day Books.

Goffman, E. (1963). *Stigma: Notes on the management of spoiled identity*. Englewood Cliffs, NJ: Prentice-Hall.

Goodman, E. (2015). Caitlyn Jenner's Vanity Fair cover is not just a display of sexism. *Boston Globe*, June 10. Retrieved from www.bostonglobe.com/opinion/2015/06/10/caitlyn-jenner-vanity-fair-cover-display-ageism-not-just-sexism/nzfrBvHSnxAGZDf3gwe9lK/story.html.

Laz, C. (1998). Act your age. *Sociological Forum*, 13(1), 85–113.

Laz, C. (2003). Age embodied. *Journal of Aging Studies*, 17(4), 379–526.

Powell, J. & Wahidin, A. (2007). Understanding aging bodies: A postmodern dialogue on bio-medicine, body, and cultural representations of identity. In J. Powell and T. Owen (Eds.), *Reconstructing postmodernism: Critical debates* (pp. 141–151). New York: Nova Science Publishers.

Siverskog, A. (2015). Ageing bodies that matter: Age, gender and embodiment in older transgender people's life stories. *NORA – Nordic Journal of Feminist and Gender Research*, 23(1), 4–19.

Swinnen, A. M. C. & Port, C. (2013). Ageing, narrative and performance: Essays from the humanities. *International Journal of Ageing and Later Life*, 7(2), 9–15.

Plasticity

A term that refers to the distinctly "wide-open" and malleable nature of human development and aging, which includes biomarkers as well as psychological and social characteristics.

Sickness, aging, and health in general are inextricably linked to social situation and environment. Integrating cumulative advantage/disadvantage (CAD) theory into analysis of biological data reveals the human body not as a static subject but rather as an evolving entity shaped by experiences, environment, and society. In this frame the body is the cumulative sum of the experiences of the individual.

Breaking down the barrier between the study of social factors of health and the study of physical biological factors of health is critical to understanding the ways in which social and political structures tangibly affect the everyday well-being of people. This burgeoning field of study allows for the tangible measurement in individual bodies of the effects of adverse policy and social structures. The question moving forward is how to use this quantification of CAD to influence political power and produce better lives for individuals. The concept of plasticity is embedded within structures of power, and much of the literature on the biological frontier of plasticity ignores how opportunity and oppression go well beyond the "gene–environment" and play defining roles in what are identified as the "social determinants of health."

See also: Cumulative Advantage/Disadvantage, Gene–Environment, Social Determinants of Health, Telomeres

Further Reading

Dannefer, D. (2008). The waters we swim: Everyday social processes, macrostructural realities, and human aging. *Social Structures and Aging Individuals: Continuing Challenges*, 3–22.

Douthit, K. & Marquis, A. (2010). Biosocial interactions in the construction of late-life health status. In D. Dannefer (Ed.), *The SAGE handbook of social gerontology* (p. 329). Thousand Oaks, CA: Sage.

Policy

A plan or system of legislation, executive orders, rules, and regulations that are proposed, accepted, and adopted by governing powers.

Social policy incorporates its implementation. The import of attending to social policy is that it has pervasive and invasive effects on life and living every day and every night. Within the framework of critical theory, policy is neither neutral, nor is it consensual or static. Social policies are just that; they are social. As such, policies result from the winning amalgams of economic, political, and sociocultural conflicting processes and forces interacting during any given sociohistorical period (Estes & Associates, 2001). As the outcome of struggles, conflicts, and dominant power relations of the period, it reflects and instantiates the structures and culture of advantage and disadvantage that are enacted through class, race/ethnicity, gender, ability, age, and intersectionalities. Social policy itself is a key determinant of the life chances and conditions of individuals and population groups, neighborhoods and communities, and states, including the elderly (Estes & Associates, 2001) and across generations and around the world. Social justice, equality, democracy, and the public interest are each irreversibly and dialectically related to and intertwined with policy. Who makes the decisions is essential. We are reminded that C. Wright Mill's famous treatise on *The power elite* tells us that it comprises political, economic, and military

men. In 2017 USA the power of the military and its ascendancy in our government is noteworthy.

A–Z entries on capitalism, the State, ideology, power, and agency are core to social policy and the critical political economy of aging. Policies originate from and implicate ongoing ideological wars, visible and invisible power operating through social forces seeking to preserve the status quo or to transform it, radically or incrementally. Networks of policy advocates, policy wonks, and think tanks draft and message legislation and talking points. Social media activists are 24/7 active in efforts to sway policy and public opinion, exposing and proposing policy. On the Right, a coordinated and powerful entity is the American Legislative Exchange Council (ALEC) that provides state legislators with pre-written bills ready for state policy-makers to introduce. ALEC's conservative agenda promotes deregulation, corporate interests, and social issues like anti-abortion. In a similar echo chamber are deficit hawks, Wall Street, the Fix the Debt, Taxpayer Revolt folks and foundations. For social policy, Progressives look to Public Citizen, The Center for American Progress, Demos, the NAACP, National Organization for Women, and multiple civil rights, labor, and social justice organizations and foundations. "Citizens United," the Supreme Court decision that money is free speech, is foundational in how social policy gets done via the structure and processes of government functioning and political elections. Congressional members are understaffed given the import and breadth of their responsibilities and public expectations in a democracy. Money in politics intensifies the reliance of both parties, on lobbyists and private sector actors in shaping policy, particularly on highly specialized issues.

See also: Affordable Care Act, Americans with Disabilities Act, Medicaid, Medicare, Social Security

Further Reading

Domhoff, G. W. (2006). *Who rules America?* (5th edition). Boston, MA: McGraw-Hill.

Estes, C. L. & Associates. (2001). *Social policy & aging: A critical perspective.* Thousand Oaks, CA: Sage.

Mills, C. W. (2000). *The power elite.* Oxford: Oxford University Press.

Public Citizen News. (2017). Shining a light on Trump's corruption and corporate take-over, annual report. *Public Citizen News,* 38(1), 5–14.

Stone, D. A. (2002). *Policy paradox.* New York: Norton.

Zweigenhaft, R. L. & Domhoff, G. W. (1998). *Diversity in the power elite.* New Haven, CT: Yale University Press.

Political Economy

A theoretical perspective that examines the relations between political, economic, social, and cultural processes and institutions and how the State relates to and reflects power and ideology emanating from within these broad domains – and with what distributional consequences and for whom. Political economists study the mobilization and operation of power resources and the politics of contention surrounding laws, policies, norms, legitimacy, and practices of the State, the Market, and the peoples who are the public. Fundamental to critical political economy is a moral philosophy that embraces the normative values of social justice, fairness, equality, rights, democracy, and "the social" defined by an imperative of preserving the commons and the interdependence reflected in the phrase, "We're all in this together." Ideology, dominance, resistance, and inequality are keynotes in this work.

For the field of aging, critical political economy is integral to understanding the aging process, experience, and "life chances" over the life course, both individual and aggregated. Just as race, ethnicity, gender, and citizenship are social constructs that are systemic and potentially coercive features of society, instantiated in visible and invisible ways (e.g., institutional racism, patriarchy, nativism), so are the intersections of social class and age (including heterogeneous subpopulations). These intersections represent a crucial nexus for cumulative dis/advantage. The political economy of aging emphasizes power struggles and conflicts in systems of governance (the State, parties, democracy, and social movements), economic production and distribution (e.g., capitalism, global financialization), and the production of ideas (e.g., ideology, media, religion, education). The construction of old age, and societal processing and treatment of older persons, has been coined "the aging enterprise" (Estes, 1979). A major link to life course analysis investigates how the old are commodified and their needs exploited via profit-oriented markets, such as the medical-industrial complex (Estes, 1979, 1991; Estes & Associates, 2001).

Race, ethnicity, class, gender, and ability are recognized as crucial dimensions of old age and aging. In the political economy perspective, these are understood to be individual characteristics or attributes, and also as systemic features of the organization of society. Key elements involve the roles and effects (on old age and aging individuals and their families) of governance systems and the power struggles therein (e.g., the State), economic production (e.g., capitalism and globalization), and the production of ideas (e.g., ideology, systems of communication, and cultural production) (Estes, 2018). In broad outline the political economy of aging emphasizes:

- The socially and structurally produced nature of aging and the lived experience of old age as these are influenced by the individual and interlocking systems of oppression composed of gender, social class, race, ethnicity, ability, nativism, and generation.

- Ideology as a central element in the social, cultural, economic, and political processing and treatment of the old and aging in society and its distributional outcomes.
- The social production, social control, and management of gender-based, race and ethnicity-based old age dependency by the larger organizations and institutional forces of patriarchy and racism, and the State.
- The role, functions, actions, and consequences of the gendered and racial state as constructed, reproduced, and magnified under global and financial capitalism.
- The aging enterprise and the medical industrial complex and their responsibility in the disparate access to treatment, and outcomes of preventive, health and chronic illness, and mental health care, particularly for disadvantaged and marginalized aging and disabled persons, indeed all persons of all ages in US society.
- Critical reflexivity and feminist and antiracist methodologies and epistemologies in the production of gerontological knowledges.

Marxist Political Economy

Arguably the most significant alternative school of political economic thought, Marxist political economy describes a wide variety of frameworks and schools. In general, Marxist political economists agree on the flaws of capitalism and the necessity of a transition to socialism or communism of one kind or another. It should be noted that a transition to socialism may mean anything from a more robust social safety net to a belief in utopian Communism. Beyond these basic tenants there is significant diversity of thought within the larger field (O'Hara, 1999, p. 712).

Weberian Political Economy

Max Weber's overarching conceptual framework is one of conflict theory in which his tripartite theory of power rests on the accumulation of resources within each of three theoretically independent large domains of class, status, and party/politics. In real life, each of these domains comprises multiple arenas in which power may be constructed, accumulated, won, or lost in conflicts and power struggles over social problems and other issues. Weber emphasized the import of social forces and culture and religion on the formation of capitalist economies, the role of the State as the ultimate legitimate arbitrator of force, coercion and violence within the governing framework, the quickening and pervasive effects of rationalization through bureaucracy, accounting, and depersonalization under rational capitalism, and the crucial significance of legitimacy in the formation, operation, evolution, and survival of organizations and institutions of class, status, and party/politics. Weber was also committed to sociologists elucidating the effects of such forces and their power resources on personal meanings and social interaction in everyday life. Thus, Weber is noted for his affinity with subsequent US pragmatism, interactionism, and interpretive methodological innovations that followed.

See also: Class, Conflict Theory and Consensus Theory, Critical Realism, Emancipatory, Intersectionality, Medical Industrial Complex, Oppression, Power, The Social, The State

Further Reading

Estes, C. L. (1979). *The aging enterprise: A critical examination of social policies and services for the aged*. San Francisco, CA: Jossey-Bass.

Estes, C. L. (1991). The new political economy of aging. In M. Minkler & C. L. Estes (Eds.), *Critical perspectives on aging: The political and moral economy of growing old* (pp. 19–36). Amityville, NY: Baywood Publishing.

Estes, C. L. (2018). The critic comes of age: Part II. In C. Wellin (Ed.), *Critical gerontology comes of age: Theory and research for a new century* (pp. 19–34). New York: Routledge.

Estes, C. L. & Associates. (2001). Political economy of aging: A theoretical framework. In *Social policy & aging: A critical perspective* (pp. 1–23). Thousand Oaks, CA: Sage.

Estes, C. L. & Phillipson, C. (2007). Critical gerontology. In *Encyclopedia of gerontology* (pp. 330–336). New York: Elsevier.

O'Hara, P. A. (Ed.). (1999). *Encyclopedia of political economy*. London: Routledge.

Walker, A. & Foster, L. (Eds.). (2014). *The political economy of ageing and later life: Critical perspectives*. Northampton, MA: Edward Elgar, pp. 3–26.

Political Parties and Platforms

Coalitions of people and groups who at surface level agree along ideological lines. They cooperate politically to change governing regulations and laws, blocking attempts from opposing parties, as they maintain, dismantle, or expand the power of the State.

There have been several parties throughout the history of the United States; however, today there are two behemoths which dominate elections: Republicans and Democrats. Money spent campaigning (i.e., "war chests") enables candidates affiliated and vetted by the party to attract votes. This spending (collected through contributions of individuals and the endorsements of private companies) includes advertisements and research on manipulating public opinion. The political

and economic power of a party means that those belonging must also conform in order to receive resources. This involves contestations and maneuvering within the party, and these are often less visible to the public.

Platforms are the declared principles and initiatives of the party released each presidential election cycle detailing what the party desires to accomplish and how it plans to do so.

A cross comparison of the platforms announced for 2016 Conventions is shown in the following table.

In many ways, the two American political parties have become defined by what they oppose rather than by any affirmative propositions. The first-past-the-post voting system with single non-transferable voting in the United States, in which the winner of 214 electoral votes is guaranteed the presidency and each person is allowed to vote for only one candidate, mathematically guarantees the dominance of the two main parties. The two-party split frames stances and political maneuvers in terms of partisanship, with both parties impotently insisting that their platforms represent "human rights" not "partisanship issues." Both Democrats and Republicans invoke this moralism and the framing of a rights perspective when it is politically expedient, and it is a strategy in itself that is not removed from partisanship.

Third parties have come and gone and have never been particularly successful. The two most notable third-party campaigns were run in 1912 by Theodore Roosevelt and the Bull Moose Party and in 1992 by Ross Perot as an independent. In both cases these runs effectively delivered the presidency to the Democratic candidate, Woodrow Wilson with only 42 percent of the vote in 1912 and Bill Clinton with a similarly paltry 43 percent of the vote in 1992. Third parties have played important roles in disrupting the distribution of votes and

Table P1

The Republican Platform	The Democratic Platform
• Exclaims American exceptionalism an "exemplar of liberty for the world to see." • Frames economic liberty (the free market) as indivisible from personal freedom: "We believe political freedom and economic freedom are indivisible." • The Constitution is not flexible; it is an "enduring covenant" and the sovereignty is "endowed by creator." • State restriction of the market and reduction to military entail crisis. • Privatize and cut public funding for social insurance programs (i.e., Social Security and Medicare).	• Values unity, especially in the context of economic recovery from the "Great Recession." • Points to many being left behind economically, a "racial wealth gap," and income inequality. • Suggests market regulation is necessary: "We firmly believe that the greed, recklessness, and illegal behavior on Wall Street must be brought to an end." • Expand social insurance programs like Social Security. • Campaign finance reform is necessary. • Diplomacy makes the world safer. • Identifies climate change as a threat.

complicating "easy wins" for either party. In 2000, the Green Party received much focus for its role in drawing away Democrat voters from Gore, and many believed that this "cost the election." Similar debate surrounded the 2016 election with regard to schisms within the Democratic Party and third parties. The Tea Party has also played a significant role in radicalizing the Right, making more moderate Republicans shift their platform in order to keep their seats, as their constituents became more concerned with legislation that was anti-abortion, religious freedom and discrimination, and pro-gun focused.

See also: Alt-Right, Discourse, Framing, Ideology, The Left

Further Reading

Cohen, M. (2008). *The party decides*. Chicago, IL: University of Chicago Press.

Positivism

A philosophy of science which holds that objective accounts of the real world can be observed and revealed. August Comte (1798–1857) is the acknowledged founder of positivism and he also invented the term "sociology" to describe his proposed "positive" science of society.

Positivism is within the empiricist tradition of research inquiry, and holds that the methods of science, based on systematic observations and experiments, can give us knowledge of the laws about society and social phenomena. This approach tends to be deductive and linear in its process, working from concepts already specified in theory to test in people's everyday lives. Building on nineteenth-century discoveries in probability theory with observations drawn from a sample that has been selected from some larger population, positivist research characteristics include: a presumed neutral stance of the researcher, being statistically logical, hypothesis testing, cause-and-effect-oriented (e.g., measures independent and dependent variables), and findings to be revealed via controlled or pre-structured measurements (e.g., experimental designs like randomized control trials and random probability sampling, or quasi-experimental designs like cohort and case control studies). The goals of positivist research are to predict, measure, replicate, verify, and generalize findings, which can be reductive and deterministic. Metaphysical speculation is rejected, and the methods can never penetrate to the inner "essences" or "natures" of things.

Postpositivism

Postpositivism holds that only partially objective accounts of the world can be produced, since all methods are flawed. Postpositivist researchers will likely view inquiry as a series of logically related steps, believe in multiple perspectives from participants rather than a single reality, and espouse rigorous methods of data collection and analysis. They will engage in qualitative research methods, may use multiple levels of data analysis for rigor, employ computer programs to assist, and write their studies in the form of scientific reports, with a structure resembling quantitative approaches (e.g., problem, questions, data collection, results, conclusion). Quantitative researchers and funding agents largely prize the approach of positivism, demonstrated among scholars with prior quantitative research training, and in fields such as the health sciences in which qualitative inquiry is a newer approach to research and must be couched in acceptable terms.

This is not to conflate positivism and quantitative work, as if empirical measures are essentially positivistic. There is much critical work that is quantitative in illustrating inequality (e.g., Picketty's historical analyses of trends within capitalism) and multifaceted health metrics across domains that look at disparities (e.g., Dannefer's work on cumulative (dis)advantage). Conversely, qualitative work may be done with an uncritical positivistic mindset – numerous ethnographies such as Anselm Strauss' work exhibit these tendencies.

See also: Essentialism, Functionalism, Methodologies, Reductionism, Statistical Panic, Theories of Aging

Further Reading

Lemert, C. (Ed.). (2016). *Social theory: The multicultural, global, and classic readings* (6th edition). Philadelphia, PA: Westview Press.

Postmodernism

A broad movement in thought, following enlightenment and modernism, which expressed skepticism concerning authority assumed in knowledge. This movement focused on the production of knowledge through social and political forces embedded in power and history. Responding to legacies of domination and narrow definitions of legitimacy, *postmodern* traditions extend through the critical movements of *postcolonialism, postmaterialism*, and *post-structuralism*.

See also: Colonialisms, Feminism, Social Construction of Reality

Further Reading

Lemert, C. (Ed.). (2016). *Social theory: The multicultural, global, and classic readings* (6th edition). Philadelphia, PA: Westview Press.

Leonard, P. (1997). *Postmodern welfare*. London: Sage.

Lyotard, J. (1984). *The postmodern condition: A report on knowledge* (trans. G. Bennington & B. Masumi). Minneapolis, MN: University of Minnesota Press.

Sanbonmatsu, J. (2004). *The postmodern prince: Critical theory, left strategy, and the making of a new political subject*. New York: Monthly Review Press.

Turner, B. S. (1990). *Theories of modernity and postmodernity*. Newbury Park, CA: Sage.

Poverty

A state of deprivation, lacking the resources necessary to sustain. Definitions shift depending on standards of living, which differ greatly across culture and national identity.

Poverty Threshold

Ever since the "War on Poverty" was declared in 1965, the United States has used a measure of poverty that was acknowledged to be inadequate and simplistically designed. It has never been a measure of income adequacy, but instead has served as a proxy measure of destitution. Nevertheless, many public programs link benefits and financing to this poverty measure, despite the fact that the federal poverty line is about half the cost of a basic standard of living for many older adults (Wallace & Molina, 2008).

Every year, the US Department of Health and Human Services releases the Federal Poverty Level (FPL). The FPL sets a threshold, providing a uniform measure of income that factors in family size and adjusts for inflation. The poverty threshold serves different purposes, which include tracking poverty over time across demographic groups and determining eligibility for federal assistance programs and tax relief. The U.S. Census Bureau also calculates the Supplemental Poverty Measure (SPM) (www.census/gov/topics/income-poverty/supplemental-poverty-measure.html). The SPM poverty thresholds vary by accounting for geographic area, homeownership, financial resources, liabilities, taxes and value of in-kind benefits (e.g., food stamps), and out-of-pocket medical spending.

Conflict and power struggles characterize the measurement (and measures) of poverty, since they determine eligibility for many federal and state programs. In 2007, the Elder Economic Security Initiative (EESI) was launched in Massachusetts with the goal of redefining the discussion away from poverty and toward economic security. The EESI developed an alternative to the federal poverty line, the Elder Economic Security Standard index (Elder Index), which corrects many of the problems of the federal measure. The FPL is uniform across all parts of the country, based on 1955 consumption patterns of families, that assumes a fixed ratio of food costs to other costs. The Elder Index, in contrast, is county specific to reflect local variations in costs; is based on current consumption patterns of older adults; and is calculated on the actual costs of housing, medical care, food, and transportation with the relative balance of costs varying according to their true costs. Experts have debated ways to fix the FPL for years, and yet Congress has done nothing. The EESI initiative is working with community-based organizations, local and state governments, and service providers to incorporate the Elder Index into programs, planning, and policies from the ground up. Shortly after being introduced, it was used to successfully advocate for increasing the asset limit for Medicaid home- and community-based services in Massachusetts and was adopted as a planning tool by the United Way of the (San Francisco) Bay Area, some Area Agencies on Aging, and the State of California. The goal is to build momentum from the ground up so that the federal government is eventually pressured into also moving policy based on a goal of income adequacy for all older adults.

In aging policy, controversy surrounds the components of the Federal Poverty Level (FPL), which advocates claim vastly underrepresent the true expenses of older persons. Most alarmingly, medical expenses are excluded from the poverty measure. For elders, medical costs far surpass those of younger persons (three to five times) because the "out-of-pocket costs" for older persons under Medicare are rising rapidly. Medical care inflation is higher than other sectors, exposing elders (on fixed incomes) to unaffordable out-of-pocket spending on health care.

Medicaid is a federal state program, meaning that it allows for a substantial role for state discretionary policy, although there are also uniform federal Medicaid requirements. Medicaid, as a means-tested (welfare assistance) program, is subject to multi-state variation that allows for the politics to determine the relative "welfare generosity" that characterizes different geopolitical environments. Thus, the criteria and implementation of Medicaid programs differ by state, producing different eligibility criteria for the same income elder or other potentially eligible family member in different states.

"Extreme poverty" has surfaced in the current lexicon (Edin & Shaefer, 2015) with "evidence of the dramatic growth in extreme poverty since welfare reform." "It is time for policymakers to accept this fact and finally start the process of reforming a reform that left so many behind" (Shaefer & Edin, 2018, p. 26). The impact on single women, aging, and their children going forward through the life cycle will be deeper cumulative disadvantage, mortality, and morbidity (Deaton, 2018). Based on new World Bank data, "5.3 million Americans . . . are absolutely poor by global standards," while life expectancy in the USA in "the Mississippi Delta and much of Appalachia . . . is lower than in Bangladesh and Vietnam" (Deaton, 2018).

In the 114th and 115th Congress, Democratic efforts to expand and improve Social Security have variously incorporated measures to replace the FPL (poverty level) currently in use. Stalled conservative reform efforts on Social Security incorporated the Chained-CPI, to replace the FPL, that social insurance advocates insist would decrease benefits to those who need them most. In 2017 Congressman Garamendi and others introduced bills requiring the use of the CPI-E for poverty income measurement to update the index to better reflect elder expenses, including medical costs. Other proposed legislation (House and Senate) to expand and improve Social Security also incorporated the CPI-E (*see* Legislative Appendix). The 2017 Tax Reform and Jobs Act smuggled in the Chained-CPI as the federal policy measure for calculating Cost of Living adjustments (COLAs) going forward. This will reduce the cash income benefits for the majority of Social Security recipients, as well as limit the contributions younger generations can make toward their retirement security. This will widen inequality – big data illustrate the realities of cumulative advantage/disadvantage, as jeopardies increase for already vulnerable populations.

See also: Class, Cost of Living Adjustment (COLA), Cumulative Advantage/Disadvantage, Debt, Food Security, Health Disparities, Inequality, Jeopardy, Medicaid, Welfare State

Further Reading

Cubanski, J., Koma, W., Damico, A., & Neuman, T. (2018). How many seniors live in poverty? (November 19). Retrieved from www.kff.org/medicare/issue-brief/how-many-seniors-live-in-poverty/.

Deaton, A. (2018). The US can no longer hide from its deep poverty problem. Retrieved from www.nytimes.com/2018/01/24/opinion/poverty-united-states.html?em_pos=small&emc=ed.

Edin, K. J. & Shaefer, H. L. (2015). *$2.00 a day: Living on almost nothing in America.* New York: Houghton Mifflin Harcourt.

Elder index. Retrieved from www.ncoa.org/economic-security/money-management/elder-index/.

Herd, P., Favreault, M., Harrington Meyer, M., & Smeeding, T. M. (2018). A targeted minimum benefit plan: A new proposal to reduce poverty among older Social Security recipients. *RSF: The Russell Safe Foundation Journal of the Social Sciences, 4*(2), 74–90.

Herd, P., Favreault, M., Smeeding, T., & Harrington Meyer, M. (2018). A targeted minimum benefit plan (MBP): A new proposal to reduce poverty among older Americans. AARP. Retrieved from www.aarp.org/content/dam/aarp/ppi/2018/a-targeted-minimum-benefit-plan.pdf.

Romig, K. (2018). Social Security lifts more Americans above poverty than any other program (updated November 5). Washington, DC: Center on Budget and Policy Priorities (CBPP).

Shaefer, H. L. & Edin, K. J. (2018). Welfare reform and the families it left behind. The next round of welfare reform. *Pathways: A Magazine on Poverty, Inequality and Social Policy*, 22–27. Stanford, CA: The Stanford Center on Poverty and Inequality.

Torres, S. (2014). Aging women, living poorer. *Contexts*, *13*, 72–74.

U.S. Census. (n.d.). Retrieved from www.census.gov/data/tables/time-series/demo/income-poverty/historical-poverty-thresholds.html.

U.S. Census. (n.d.). Retrieved from www.census/gov/topics/income-poverty/supplemental-poverty-measure.html.

Wallace, S. P. & Molina, L. C. (2008). *Federal poverty guideline underestimates costs of living for older persons in California*. Berkeley, CA: UCLA Center for Health Policy Research.

Wallace, S. P., Padilla-Frausto, D. I., & Smith, S. (2013). Economic need among older Latinos: Applying the Elder Economic Security Standard™ Index. *Journal of Cross-Cultural Gerontology*, *28*(3), 239–250.

Power

The potential to act, acquire, and control. There are different dimensions and articulations of power: social, political, economic, and cultural. Weber (1978) locates power as the ability to "control others, events, or resources; to make happen what one wants to happen in spite of obstacles, resistance, or opposition." Feminist theorists have called this "power over" and have extended analyses of power relations through patriarchy. Critical race theorists understand power through the systemic racism of the State and society through slavery, segregation, subjugation, incarceration, and police violence as social control. Cultural white superiority permits the impunity of individual whites against persons of color.

Domination and privilege are two terms which characterize where power resides in the hierarchical strata of those who have access and control.

Power is foundational to aging policy, problem framing, agenda setting, implementation, outcomes, and the political struggles surrounding it.

Weber's classic definition of power (see *Economy and society*, ch. 1) is that it is the ability to force one's own will in the face of opposition, the likelihood that, despite resistance, one actor has the ability to impose his own will over another. Weber observes that power is "sociologically amorphous" "in the sense that it covers a multitude of situations and qualities. The concept of domination is more precise" (Agevall & Swedberg, 2016, p. 261).

Castells (2016) examines power relationships through "the formation of a new social structure . . . the network society." Consistent with Weber, power is "the relational capacity that enables certain social actors to asymmetrically influence," shape and institutionalize social structures.

"Power structure" and "Power elite" are related terms. Power structure analysis attends to identifying who is making decisions, controlling and aggregating resources, mobilizing influence and control. C. Wright Mills cites three major institutional sectors in the *The power elite* (1956/2000): The Military, the Executive Branch (Presidential Administration), and the Captains of Industry. (Note: C. W. Mills was excoriated for arguing that Congress was a second level of power.) The Trump Cabinet mirrored

Mills' delineation of the composition and dangers of the higher circles among the power elite. Feagin and Ducey (2017) analyze the white power elites of US and global power, understood as part of larger systemic racism around the world. Domhoff et al.'s (2018) recent power elite book reaffirms and updates data indicating the continuing and deepening force of power elites in new formations in the USA. According to Garsten and Sörborm (2018), the World Economic Forum (WEF) is situated within a system of "discretionary governance" in which organizations construct ideas and influence formal authorities. WEF is a brokering organization, with no formal mandate to implement positions. Networking relationally, across business, politics, and civil society, such organizations are powerful (discreet) agenda-setting agents in global relations.

See also: Capitalism, Class, Conflict, Domination, Ethnicity, Feminist, Inequality, Intersectionality, Medical Industrial Complex, Microaggressions, Military Industrial Complex, Prison Industrial Complex, Privilege, Race, The State, White Supremacy

Further Reading

Agevall, O. & Swedberg, R. (2016). *The Max Weber dictionary: Key words and central concepts*. Redwood City, CA: Stanford University Press.

Alford, R. R. & Friedland, R. (1985). *Powers of theory: Capitalism, the state, and democracy*. New York: Cambridge University Press.

Beard, M. (2017). *Women and power: A manifesto*. New York: Liveright.

Berger, B. K. (2005). Power over, power with, and power to relations: Critical reflections on public relations, the dominant coalition, and activism. *Journal of Public Relations Research, 17*(1), 5–28.

Castells, M. (2016). A sociology of power: My intellectual journey. *Annual Review of Sociology, 42*(1), 1–19.

Domhoff, G. W. (2014). *Who rules America? The triumph of the corporate rich* (7th edition). San Francisco, CA: McGraw Hill.

Domhoff, G. W., Campbell, J. L., & Cox, R. W. (2018). *Studying the power elite: Fifty years of who rules America?* New York: Routledge.

Feagin, J. R. & Ducey, K. (2017). *Elite white men ruling: Who, what, when, where, and how*. New York: Routledge.

Garsten, C. & Sörborm, A. (2018). *Discreet power: How the world economic forum shapes market agendas*. Stanford, CA: Stanford University Press.

Johnson, A. G. (2000). *The Blackwell dictionary of sociology*. Malden, MA: Wiley-Blackwell.

Mills, C. W. (2000). *The power elite*. Oxford: Oxford University Press. (Originally published 1956.)

Weber, M. (1978). *Economy and society*. Berkeley, CA: University of California Press.

Praxis

Primarily known as Paulo Freire's idea of how consciousness raising happens through a dynamic process of reflection and action where ground is gained through the wisdom of experience. Praxis operates as a dynamic interplay between reflexive knowledge and social action.

How does what I know impact what I do? Does it change things? What are my limitations, and how can I learn more to move forward?

The Frankfurt School had been interested in the relationship between theory and praxis but they paid more attention to critical theory than to praxis. According to Habermas, Marx had a tendency to reduce social praxis to work. Marxist praxis has a goal of challenging alienation and promoting growing into more humanness, which we can extrapolate to mean freer articulations of the many parts of self in the potential multiplicity of interaction and social identities.

Collins (2015) posits intersectionality as a critical praxis. In this frame intersectionality helps to ground and link grassroots actions and advocacy with scholarship to produce a recursive cycle of consciousness raising.

See also: Consciousness Raising, Empowerment, Intersectionality, Resistance Movements

Further Reading

Bottomore, T. B. (1983). *A dictionary of Marxist thought*. Cambridge, MA: Harvard University Press.

Collins, P. H. (2015). Intersectionality's definitional dilemmas. *Annual Review of Sociology, 41*(1), 1–20.

Freire, P. (1970). *Pedagogy of the oppressed*. New York: Herder & Herder.

Precarity

Entails insecurity, where safety and stability are uncertain. This is a reality of those without housing security or financial resources, including those without a social safety net.

The portmanteau, Precariat (a contraction of "precarious" and "proletariat"), speaks to a subset of the population who have no security or stable use value. What are they good for? Marx says they are exploited for the cheapness of labor they supply in capitalist societies. Capitalism thrives on having a surplus army of those who have no work: they contribute to (1) suppressing wages through increasing demand for work, and (2) willingness through desperation to supply labor at low wages. As globalization incentivizes companies to find cheaper labor (via outsourcing), displaced workers join this surplus army, experiencing precarity.

The concept of worker precariousness may be observed through the lens of the great financial crisis and recession of 2008, which caused a lack of ready access to paid employment, protection from arbitrary firing, long-term job stability, and adequate living wages. It renewed recognition of the plight of precarious elders, who are stranded without resources and must acquiesce to devaluation in the context of mass exploitation (of all workers).

Social insurance being restricted, contingent upon work history, citizenship status, and regulated through means-tested gradations of care contributes to the desperation (and potential to exploit) workers. In this way the welfare state is a threat to precarity and capitalism.

While some, like Guy Standing (2016), associate the precariat with the rise of authoritarianism, Richard Seymour (2012) contends that precariousness is shared:

> The precariat is not a dangerous, exotic, alien thing, not an incipient class to be patronised into existence. It is all of us. Every one of us who is not . . . a financial capitalist, not a government minister or senior civil servant, not a top cop or guest at a Murdoch dinner party, not a judge or news broadcaster – not a member, in other words, of the "power bloc", the capitalist class in its fractions, and the penumbra of bourgeois academics and professionals that surrounds it. We are all the precariat.

Similarly, the focus on older adults voting for Brexit in the UK and for Trump in the USA pathologized the precarity, while few (if any) provisions were made for solutions or extended support to older people (Grenier, Phillipson & Settersten Jr., 2018). Indeed, UK's Prime Minister May simultaneously proposed an "Alzheimer's Tax" on elders who received nursing home care.

See also: Capitalism, Globalization, Health Care, Housing, Inclusion/Exclusion, Labor, Welfare State

Further Reading

Becker, G. (1997). *Disrupted lives: How people create meaning in a chaotic world*. Berkeley, CA: University of California Press.

Bourdieu, P. (1998). *Acts of resistance against the tyranny of the market*. New York: The New Press.

Estes, C. L. & DiCarlo, N. B. (2019) *Exploitation and the State in precarity, USA: Social and psychic trauma across generations*. Working paper. San Francisco, CA: UCSF Institute for Health & Aging.

Grenier, A., Lloyd, L., & Phillipson, C. (2017). Precarity in late life: Rethinking dementia as a "frailed" old age. *Sociology of Health & Illness, 39*(2), 318–330.

Grenier, A., Phillipson, C., & Settersten Jr. R. (Eds.). (2019). *Precarity and ageing: Understanding changing forms of risk and vulnerability in later life*. Bristol: Policy Press.

Portacolone, E. (2013). The notion of precariousness among older adults living alone in the U.S. *Journal of Aging Studies, 27*(2), 166–174. doi:10.1016/j.jaging.2013.01.001.

Seymour, R. (2012). We are all precarious – on the concept of the "precariat" and its misuses. *New Left Project*, February 10. Retrieved from www.newleftproject.org/index.php/site/article_comments/we_are_all_precarious_on_the_concept_of_the_precariat_and_its_misuses.

Standing, G. (2016). *The precariat: The new dangerous class*. London: Bloomsbury Academic.

Prison Industrial Complex

The network of business and government forces which construct prisons that incarcerate and employ millions of people within the USA.

The privatization of prisons coincides with an increase in the number of people living in imprisonment. This entails aging in imprisonment or aging with a history of imprisonment. The psychosocial stressors and political (and economic) disenfranchisement of imprisoned people are manifold, such as not being able to vote, or contribute significantly to earning years for Social Security and disability (because typically they earn only $1.30/hour).

Actors in resistance movements often risk jail time. After 30 days of incarceration your Social Security benefits cease, so if you age into Social Security years while in prison your dependents cannot collect any benefits during that time – only if you were already collecting. While prisons can prevent violent offenders from hurting others in society, prison and jail time are historic mechanisms of fascist states' measures of social control.

The Prison Industrial Complex has taken on an entirely new facet in the past several decades with the proliferation of private prisons and private contracts for prison services. This has accompanied the War on Drugs and a slew of tough-on-crime legislative initiatives at the state and federal level. Michelle Alexander (2012) identifies mass incarceration as a key mechanism of racial oppression, illustrating the federal government's complicity in private enterprises profiting off black and brown pain. These points are carried forward in the private detention centers holding undocumented immigrants in the name of "due process," where individuals and families languish in limbo.

See also: Commodification, Financialization, Privatization

Further Reading

Alexander, M. (2012). *The new Jim Crow: Mass incarceration in the age of colorblindness*. New York: The New Press.

Fellner, J., Vinck, P., & Human Rights Watch (Organization). (2012). *Old behind bars: The aging prison population in the United States*. New York: Human Rights Watch.

Miller, R. J., Miller, J. W., Djoric, J. Z., & Patton, D. (2015). Baldwin's mill: Race, punshiment, and the pedagogy of repression, 1965–2015. *Humanity and Society*, *89*(4), 456–475.

Nkansah-Amankra, S., Agbanu, S. K., & Miller, R. J. (2013). Disparities in health, poverty, incarceration, and social justice among racial groups in the United States: A critical review of evidence of close links with neoliberalism. *International Journal of Health Services*, *43*(2), 217–240.

Stuart, F. & Miller, R. J. (2017). The prisonized old head: Intergenerational socialization and the fusion of ghetto and prison culture. *Journal of Contemporary Ethnography*, *46*(6), 673–698.

Privatization

The process of transferring responsibility and resources from the public sector to the private sector. It may be a shift from some level of government to one or more of several private arenas: (1) the non-profit sector, (2) the for-profit sector, and (3) individuals and their families, friends, or unpaid caregivers. Privatization generally imposes the power of the logic of capital and its ideology of efficiency and quality. An oft-repeated declaration is that "government is the problem, not the solution." The biggest battles in aging politics over many decades stem from the campaign to take Social Security and Medicare private. Newt Gingrich famously said about Medicare, we must make it a voucher and thereby "drown it in the bathtub" (Estes, 1991; Estes & Associates, 2001).

From a critical perspective the problem with privatization is that it transfers and solidifies ownership from public to private sector entities that use their authority to exploit and profit from the public's dependence on a needed good or service (Dutta, 2015). Privatization is a key process of US capitalism that has been rapidly accelerated with globalization, permitting cross-border movements of finance, trade, deregulation, and competition, labor flexibilization, tax

inversions and avoidance, and direct and indirect investments.

The imposition of privatization as an ideology and its implementation through policy has produced "an altered form of the welfare state" in which the role of the State is being shifted from one of serving the public interest to one of bankrolling and mediating between vast US corporate stakeholders. Privatization breaks the constraints on the use of public resources for the common good. Indeed, the common good is a blurred and controversial, contested, even "foreign" notion. The "collective," "the social," and "the communal" have receded from public consciousness and even the right to our respective subjective identities.

Privatization disproportionately hurts poor individuals and families, often by creating or increasing new user fees; decreasing wages and benefits by contract labor; and increased socioeconomic and racial segregation, stigma, and inequality.

Old Age Policy and Privatization

Social Security and Medicare, Medicaid, and the Affordable Care Act have each been battlegrounds for and against the welfare state, in which the public sector has a legitimate and cherished role in the protection and provision of rights, opportunities, and assurance of stability and continuity of a humane society as a collective and individual project of social development. A series of presidential and Congressional commissions, public and private, have considered but failed to agree on recommendations to privatize Social Security and Medicare.

A dominant and ideological view imposed by corporate elites in the USA is that the market is more efficient and "better" for society than the State. Bitter conflicts ensue among global actors and capital, the weakened nation-state, and members of society and citizens who are reduced to commodifiers as consumers and customers.

The privatization movement has become entrenched through political struggles over the morality and affordability of social insurance and the value of collectively pooled risk versus individual responsibility. The privatization movement is so well entrenched that it may be defined as institutionalized. The institutionalization of a social movement encompasses both its process of formation and evolution as well as its outcomes, including the inculcation and adherence over time to value systems that become relatively stable and that both prescribe and constrain certain activities or behavior, such as the conceptualization and implementation of certain policy approaches (Jary & Jary, 2000, pp. 306–307).

See also: Capitalism, Commodification, Globalization, The Market, Medical Industrial Complex, Neoliberalism, Political Economy, Social Insurance

Further Reading

Dutta, M. J. (2015). *Neoliberal health organizing: Communication, meaning, and politics.* Walnut Creek, CA: Left Coast Press.

Estes, C. L. (1991). The Reagan legacy: Privatization, the welfare state and aging. In J. Myles & J. Quadagno (Eds.), *States, labor markets, and the future of old-age policy* (pp. 59–83). Philadelphia, PA: Temple University Press.

Estes, C. L. & Associates. (2001). *Social policy & aging: A critical perspective.* Thousand Oaks, CA: Sage.

In the Public Interest. (2016). *Report: how privatization increases inequality.* September. Oakland, CA.

Jary, D. & Jary, J. (2000). *Collins web-linked dictionary of sociology.* New York: Harper-Collins. (Originally published 1991.)

Leonard, P. (1997). *Postmodern welfare.* Thousand Oaks, CA: Sage.

Privilege

A right or benefit extended to someone or a community based on special qualifiers.

Privilege manifests through intersections of opportunity and access to power. Just as marginalization and jeopardy may be understood through intersectionality, privilege may be conceived of as constructed through various identities. Positions of privilege include white, male, cisgendered, heterosexual, able-bodied, and having access or control over material resources (class privilege).

Privilege often operates unconsciously. Individuals and communities with privilege often hold these positions without much thought or concern about how they are maintained through systems of oppression and exploitation. Sociological studies of inequality look in particular at how inequality and marginalization occur through exclusion and exploitation based on age, disability, ethnic or racial category, gender, sexual orientation, religion, and/or social class. Goffman (1983) and Collins (2004) identify deference and demeanor as codes of conduct that maintain privilege, and as Hallet (2007) notes in his study on definitional power.

Zoe Leonard's (1992) poem, "I want a president," calls for a leader who knows marginalization and the denial of privilege – someone with AIDS, on the margins, someone "with no air-conditioning, a president who has stood in line at the clinic, at the DMV, at the welfare office, and has been unemployed and laid off and sexually harassed and gay-bashed and deported."

See also: Class, Domination, Oppression, Power, White Supremacy

Further Reading

Collins, R. (2004). *Interaction ritual chains.* Princeton, NJ: Princeton University Press.

Goffman, E. (1983). The interaction order: American Sociological Association, 1982 presidential address. *American Sociological Review, 48*(1), 1–17.

Hallett, T. (2007). Between deference and distinction: Interaction ritual through symbolic power in an educational institution. *Social Psychology Quarterly, 70*(2), 148–171.

Leonard, Z. (1992). "I want a president."

Twine, F. W. (2013). *Geographies of privilege.* New York: Routledge, pp. 8–10.

Productive Aging

The greater capacity to integrate the self, and to be in community with aging, leading toward wellness and self-care of the individual.

From a critical perspective, healthy and productive aging have been conflated, and the mantras of "healthy" and "productive" may be seen imposing a "compulsory normative" moral agenda that suits the needs of a capitalist system which values productivity from the standpoint of profit-making, subsidies for the Medicare industrial complex, and the commodification of everything aging.

Productive aging and healthy aging, as advanced by most gerontologists and geriatricians, act directly and indirectly as code words for social control and social labeling of what is good or bad, what costs society. It reflects "the Western embrace of the individual as self-sustaining, autonomous, and the unfettered agents of limitless power" (Hagestad & Dannefer, 2001).

The scientific discourse of healthy aging is laden with ageism, discriminatory labels, and fear of death. Nevertheless, it has been adopted by the WHO, UNESCO, the UN, and other international entities concerned with the "pandemic" of "greedy geezers" and aging and old age as a mortal threat to the global economy, and to families, societies, and communities everywhere. It is the trending mantra of many if not most gerontological and geriatric researchers and practitioners. Its associated terms are: successful

aging, optimal aging, productive aging, and the dialectics of normal aging. Rowe and Kahn (1987) broke the stranglehold of "normal aging" in gerontology, challenging the assumptions of normative disengagement as a natural and inevitable part of aging.

While it is important to work on one's and others' health, the term wellness by itself offers a limited uncritical perspective about what being well means. It may lend support to policies that blatantly ignore the social and structural barriers to individual and family wellness – hence facilitating exploitation of the self (blaming the victim), while serving capitalism and profit. It is compatible with surveillance monitoring (self and other). If you're not doing what you should be doing, then "off with your head." It is a double-edged sword.

A more critical perspective on wellness would insist that if you aren't still producing you still have value to society, and human rights. And who owns production and the difference between what is defined and imposed as use value and exchange value? A related issue is who is defined as a wellness failure or risk (perhaps uninsurable), and by whom?

See also: Functionalism, Healthy Aging, Positivism, Reductionism

Further Reading

Estes, C. L., Biggs, S., & Phillipson, C. (2003). Productive ageing, self-surveillance, and social policy. In *Social theory, social policy and ageing* (pp. 63–78). Maidenhead, Berks: Open University Press.

Estes, C. L., Mahakian, J. L., & Weitz, T. A. (2001). A political economy critique of "productive aging". In C. L. Estes & Associates. *Social policy & aging: A critical perspective* (pp. 187–199). Thousand Oaks, CA: Sage.

Hagestad, G. & Dannefer, D. (2001). Concepts and theories of aging. In R. Binstock (Ed.), *Handbook of aging and the social sciences* (pp. 3–21). New York: Academic Press.

Rowe, J. W. & Kahn, R. L. (1987). Human aging: Usual and successful. *Science*, *237*(4811), 143–149.

Propaganda

Misleading or selective information employed to foster bias or sway opinion. It may idealize a public figure, or sensationalize an event (turning it into a crisis). A recent development is "fake news" in the "post-truth" era. Incorrect or politicized reporting (i.e., Breitbart) and the stating of fiction as fact confuse the public.

This also correlates to "gaslighting" which describes a psychological manipulation and dismantling through cycles of enticement, rejection, and blame – a sort of seducing the scapegoat and then asking the goat to slaughter itself. This involves destabilizing and delegitimizing a target.

See also: Alt-right, Ideological State Apparatus, Watch Dogs/Watch Bitches

Psychoanalytic Social Theory

Involves a combined approach from psychoanalytic and social theory to interrogate the relationship between psychic and structural elements. Examples include critically examining how policy and welfare provisions may function as repressive tools with regard to internalizing shame, devaluing/dismantling developmental supports to maintain the precarity, and manipulating desire for consumption.

Major contributors include:

- The Frankfurt School, which used Freudian theory to understand how "political power imprints itself upon the internal world of human subjects" (Elliott, 2013, p 140). Theodor Adorno proposed the "Authoritarian Personality."
- Erich Fromm, who sought to identify "the links between individual repression, cultural reproduction and ideological domination" (Elliott, 2013, p. 141).

- Herbert Marcuse, who argued that escalations in production resulted in higher levels of repression, and that patriarchy rested on a surplus of repression maintained through a "performance principle."
- Jacque Lacan, who theorized lack, a feeling of not having enough and incompleteness, which Jean-François Lyotard extrapolated as a motivator for consumption and a legitimator of capitalism. Louis Althusser used Lacan in conjunction with Marx to reimagine ideology as a process of identification inherent in subjectivity. Slavoj Žižek furthers this, theorizing *ideology* as fantasy filling in the void of the self.
- Feminists have employed Lacan and Freud to examine gender and critique patriarchal projections of what constitutes a self and desire. Julia Kristeva theorizes how the Other becomes *abject*.

Questions regarding motivation, power, and how vulnerable populations remain "out of sight, out of mind" and out of fields of study are relevant for critical gerontology. For old age policy we can consider how social exclusion is a manifestation of a narcissistic need to deny or kill off "weak" parts; furthermore, how this marginalization feeds into market forces of greed, where consumption and capital determine worth value.

Collaborator's Reflection

A lens for reflexivity, psychoanalysis, and praxis.

Increasingly, psychotherapists seek to incorporate social theories of identity (on oppression, imperialism, culture, generational trauma) into treatment for individuals and groups. Feminist psychoanalyst-scholar Jessica Benjamin (2004), looking at Otherness, allows her understanding of structural inequality and violence to inform her analyses of the psyche – locating the realm of this interplay of mirroring and mutual recognition on a level she deems "deep structure."

As the theorists mentioned above have employed psychoanalytic concepts into social analyses, critical gerontologists can incorporate these ways of questioning as they seek to examine the constant interplay of how the social order extends into the depths of unconscious process and yearning. This is a very interactionist framework that requires challenging oneself and others; transgressing against power and privilege – taking risks that threaten the status quo. The social justice concept of internalized oppression finds harmony with psychoanalytic concepts of how the self forms. Synthesizing understandings of *resistance* is another opportunity, i.e., thinking of *resistance* as (1) a struggle against submitting to the burdens laid by oppressive forces, and (2) an evasive response which is too much to consciously bear. How might shame be understood as a tool of social control, integral in a landscape of inequality?

See also: Abjection, Affect, Politics of, Authoritarianism, Delirium, Internalization, Intersubjectivity, Precarity

Further Reading

Benjamin, J. (2004). Beyond doer and done to: An intersubjective view of thirdness. *The Psychoanalytic Quarterly*, *73*(1), 5–46.

Elliott, A. (2013). Psychoanalytic social theory. In A. Elliott (Ed.), *Routledge handbook of social and cultural theory*. New York: Routledge.

Oliver, K. (2004). *The colonization of psychic space: A psychoanalytic social theory of oppression*. Minneapolis, MN: University of Minnesota Press.

Public Opinion, Polling

Surveys conducted with representative samples which attempt to ascertain public sentiment on particular issues. Polls come in many varieties and have proliferated over the course of the past century. Politicians, advocacy groups, and media organizations fund polling to run election campaigns, organize lobbying efforts, and illustrate demographic trends. In general, the public sees those paid for by media organizations while the others remain private. Public polling on specific policy proposals is often cited by politicians and advocacy groups to demonstrate public support for their agendas. A high degree of skepticism and contextualization is advisable in consuming opinion polling, as poll quality and biases vary significantly.

Public Opinion on Social Security

Social Security has consistently been the target of right-wing reform attempts since the Reagan era. Conservative lawmakers relentlessly propose cutting benefits and privatizing Social Security as solutions to the long-term costs of the program, in spite of a preponderance of polling data which suggest that Americans oppose benefit cuts and privatization, preferring plans to raise taxes to cover budget shortfalls. According to the Pew Research Center, 67 percent of Americans oppose benefit cuts to Social Security. The same survey found that opposition to benefit cuts remains significant across the ideological spectrum with even consistent conservatives opposing cuts by a significant margin (Pew Research Center, 2014, pp. 69–70).

In a 2016 poll of likely voters conducted by Lake Research Partners, 79 percent of respondents indicated that they support increasing Social Security benefits, 77 percent indicated opposition to raising the Social Security retirement age to 69, and 93 percent favored allowing Medicare to negotiate drug prices (National Committee to Preserve Social Security and Medicare, 2017).

When President Bush proposed changes to Social Security in 2005, the centerpiece being privatization, his reforms were initially greeted with mixed reactions. In February, 2005, the public was nearly split on his reforms, with 44 percent supporting them and 50 percent opposing them. By July, 2005 the prospects for Bush's proposal had gotten significantly worse as, despite a countrywide tour and press campaign, Americans' opinions of the reforms remained at 29 percent in favor and 62 percent opposed (Gallup, 2016). Bush's attempt at privatization had failed.

Columbia University political scientist Dorian Warren finds a low predictive impact of public opinion on policy decision-making (See Oligarchy Rule by the Wealthy Few: the one percent), as he observes that buying influence is now a constitutional right under the Supreme Court's McCutcheon decision.

See also: Social Insurance, Social Security

Further Reading

Cook, F. L. & Czaplewski, M. B. (2009). Public opinion and social insurance: The American experience. In L. Rogne, C. L. Estes, B. R. Grossman, B. A. Hollister, & E. Solway (Eds.), *Social insurance and social justice: Social Security, Medicare and the campaign against entitlements* (pp. 251–278). New York: Springer.

Gallup. (2016). In depth: Topics A to Z: Social Security. Retrieved from www.gallup.com/poll/1693/social-security.aspx.

National Committee to Preserve Social Security and Medicare. (2017). *Support for Medicare and Social Security*. National Committee to Preserve Social Security and Medicare.

Pew Research Center. (2014). *Political polarization in the American public*. Pew Research Center.

Walker, E. A., Reno, V. P., & Bethell, T. N. (2014). *Americans make hard choices on Social Security: A survey with trade-off*

analysis. National Academy of Social Insurance.

Public Sociology

A type of sociology that seeks to make the field more accessible and more applicable to a broader set of people and experiences. This often involves engaging the general public and organic intellectuals in dialogue with traditional intellectuals.

Michael Burawoy warns that "sociology has become detached from its early mission in social reform and social justice. . . . [and that what is required is] an engagement with the profound and disturbing trends of our time" (Burawoy, 2005, pp. 4, 20). He calls for a strong critical sociology and public sociology that is presently subaltern. The sociological field of power is "a more or less stable hierarchy of antagonistic knowledges" in which there is:

[A] ruling coalition of professional and policy sociology and a subaltern mutuality of critical and public sociology. This pattern of domination derives from the embeddedness of the discipline in a wider constellation of power and interests. In our society, power and money speak louder than values. . . . In the US capitalism is especially raw with a public sphere that is not only weak but overrun by armies of experts and a plethora of media.

(Burawoy, 2005, p. 18)

Burawoy (2005, p. 18) argues that sociology needs to create:

[T]he space to manufacture a bolder and more vital vision. . . . Instead of driving the discipline into separate spheres we might develop a variety of synergies and fruitful engagements. . . . The subaltern knowledges (critical and public) should be allowed breathing space to develop their own capacities and to inject dynamism back into the dominant knowledges.

The efforts of public sociology naturally run against many of the larger trends within society over the past several decades. The pursuit of a public discipline is complicated by general tendencies toward privatization and proprietization. In this societal lens public pursuits are devalued, in part because they are often associated with more diverse and egalitarian points of view (Guinier & Torres, 2009). This does not mean that public sociology is doomed; rather that it faces serious challenges that can be overcome in an effort to expand sociological dialogue to a wider spectrum of voices.

See also: Organic Intellectual, Sociology

Further Reading

Agger, B. (2000). *Public sociology*. Lanham, MD: Rowman & Littlefield.

Burawoy, M. (2005). For public sociology. *American Sociological Review, 70*(1), 4–28.

Clawson, D. (2007). *Public sociology: Fifteen eminent sociologists debate politics and the profession in the twenty-first century*. Berkeley, CA: University of California Press.

Guinier, L. & Torres, G. (2009). *The miner's canary: Enlisting race, resisting power, transforming democracy*. Cambridge, MA: Harvard University Press.

Land, K. C. (2008). Whither public sociology? *Contemporary Sociology, 37*(6), 507–511.

Schwartz, P. (2008). The contested territory of public sociology. *Contemporary Sociology, 37*(6), 512–515.

Q

Quality-adjusted Life Years (QALYs)

A measure of time and quality of life an individual enjoys as a result of medical or social intervention. Health-adjusted life years (HALYs) serves as an umbrella concept to determine the burden of disease, which also includes a focus on disability-adjusted life years (DALYs). The data are used to determine the cost-effectiveness of interventions. The basic premise is that:

1 year of life lived in perfect health $\times$ 1 utility value $= 1$ QALY

The imprecision of the idea of "perfect health" makes this measure problematic and limits its applicability to heterogeneous populations and the varying values associated with dimensions of health. Furthermore, QALYs and DALYs fail to account for those with chronic illness or stress factors such as poverty. Gold, Stevenson, and Fryback (2002) note that these measures "discriminate against people with limited treatment potential (e.g., those with preexisting disability or illness); and they fail to account for qualitative differences in outcomes (e.g., lifesaving versus health improving) because of the way in which morbid and mortal outcomes are aggregated" (p. 128). Because of the economics which undergird the functionalist orientation of mainstream medicine, critical scholars and advocates for/from marginalized communities need to question the applicability and utility of measurements of "quality."

Other critical questions include extending an analysis of QALYs to include unpaid caregivers who spend years caring for a dependent person. The stress and/or economic toll that comes with being confined in a caregiving position has direct and indirect implications for health costs.

See also: Health Disparities, Medical Industrial Complex, Methodologies, Zero Years

Further Reading

Gold, M. R., Stevenson, D., & Fryback, D. G. (2002). HALYs and QALYs and DALYs, oh my: Similarities and differences in summary measures of population health. *Annual Review of Public Health*, *23*(1), 115–134.

Harris, J. (1987). QALYfying the value of life. *Journal of Medical Ethics*, *13*(3), 117.

Koch, T. (2000). Life quality vs the "quality of life": Assumptions underlying prospective quality of life instruments in health care planning. *Social Science & Medicine*, *51*(3), 419–427. Retrieved from www.ncbi.nlm.nih.gov/pubmed/10855928.

Queer

Reclaimed by many of those people who celebrate and own their existence as resistance to heteropatriarchy. It has been conventionally defined as unusual or strange, used derisively as a pejorative insult to castigate gender and sexually nonconforming people. *Queering* is a term which originally suggested spoiling or ruining, but has gained popular ground as a term to describe subverting and transgressing the social order. The definitional power has been wrested from the oppressor.

Queer theory is a burgeoning field of gender studies, questioning the essentialism of gender and the norms regarding monogamy, binary sexualities, and health.

One key idea of queer theory is that sex, gender and sexual orientation do not often line up in the consistent ways that are often presumed: man, masculine, hertosexual; man, feminine, homosexual; woman, masculine, homosexual; women, feminine, heterosexual. There is no necessary, or even a probable, connection between these terms.

(Branaman, 2013, p. 92)

See also: Subversive, Transgressive

Further Reading

Branaman, A. (2013). Feminist and post-feminist theories. In A. Elliott (Ed.), *Routledge handbook of social and cultural theory* (p. 92). New York: Routledge.

Jagose, A. & Hall, D. E. (2013). *The Routledge queer studies reader*. New York: Routledge.

R

Race/Racism

Race

A socially constructed categorical definition of identity based on ancestry and physical appearance.

Throughout the world and in the USA, white people have used race to understand their colonial endeavors. The social sciences have helped shift dominant paradigms which understood race as a biological reality that proved essential differences between groups.

Postmodern theories in particular have complicated and called out science's role in legitimating racial disparities. Emerging psychological study and gene theories have reinvigorated perspectives on how trauma, including the trauma of racial oppression, is passed on down generations – challenging ideals of equal opportunity and potentially informing new practices of equity.

Racial Formation Theory

A framework for examining race and society first outlined by Omi and Winant in 1986 establishes race as socially constructed and based in political, economic, and social institutions and factors (Omi & Winant, 2015).

Omi and Winant describe race as a construction that is constantly changing and being reinvented. Race has no meaningful biological foundation; rather it is enforced, like other forms of identity, as a means of social categorization. The purpose of this categorization if clear, like most cases in which one group seeks to define an "other" racism and race, serves to benefit dominant groups at the expense of less dominant groups. This process creates and solidifies political, social, and economic institutions in favor of the dominant groups creating a system of institutional racism. In this way racism and racist institutions are a fundamental aspect of American society, inextricable from the founding and history of the nation.

The theory also emphasizes that class alone cannot explain the inequity produced by racism. Economic factors combine with political and social factors to produce and perpetuate racism. Racism is not limited to one or another sphere of life and society; it universally applies to every aspect of society.

Key concepts relevant to critical aging policy and politics are "racial projects" and "anti-racist projects." Projects "are defined as racist if it *creates or reproduces structures of domination based on racial signification and identities*" (Omi & Winant, 2015, p. 128, italics in original). Anti-racist projects "are those that *undo or resist structures of domination based on racial significations and identities*" (Omi & Winant, 2015, p. 129, italics in original).

Racism

The prejudice or discrimination based on racial difference. It operates at multiple levels of the individual, social institutions, ideology, the State, even the globe.

Systemic Racism

A theory developed by Joe Feagin (in Feagin, Vera, & Ducey, 2015, p. 221) offers:

> [A] framework of oppression that encompasses . . . the unjustly gained economic and political power of whites . . . the continuing resource inequalities across the color line, and the prevailing white racial frame with its racist ideologies, attitudes, images, emotions, and inclinations to discriminate.

Anti-racist Social Theory

Major US forbearers of anti-racist theory include W. E. B. DuBois who analyzed racial oppression and wrote of white supremacy and the institutionalized racist order until his death in 1963. DuBois argued that all major US institutions were constructed as part of a racist order, including globally. Anna Julia Cooper described "jungles of barbarism" created by white Americans. Oliver C. Cox linked racism and capitalism, and how racialized classes emerged from the labor exploitation of African Americans, writing until his death in 1974. Patricia Hill Collins and bell hooks are credited with anti-racist feminist theory.

See also: Abjection, Black Lives Matter, Blacklands, Colonialism, Honky Gerontology, Inequality, Intersectionality, Jeopardy, Neoliberalism, Oppression, Power, Racial Wealth Gap, The Social, The State (*see* Racial State), Structure, White Supremacy

Further Reading

Benjamin, R. (2016). Innovating inequity: If race is a technology, postracialism is the genius bar. *Ethnic and Racial Studies*, *38*(13), 2227–2234.

Benjamin, R. (2017). Cultura obscura. Race, power, and "culture talk" in the health sciences. *American Journal of Law and Medicine*, *43*, 225–238.

Elias, S. & Feagin, J. R. (2016). *Racial theories in social science*. London: Routledge.

Emirbayer, M. & Desmond, M. (2015). *The racial order*. Chicago IL: University of Chicago Press.

Feagin, J. R. (2006). *Systemic racism*. New York: Routledge.

Feagin, J. R. & Elias, S. (2013). Rethinking racial formation theory: A systemic racism critique. *Ethnic and Racial Studies*, *36*(6), 931–960.

Feagin, J. R., Vera, H., & Ducey, K. (2015). *Liberation sociology* (3rd edition). Boulder, CO: Paradigm.

Omi, M. & Winant, H. (2015). *Racial formation in the United States*. New York: Routledge.

Racial Wealth Gap

Describes the disparity in income and wealth between racial and ethnic groups. In the United States racial wealth gaps are large and consistent. In 2013, the wealth of a typical white household was 13 times that of a typical black household. This disparity extends to retirement income and savings but is much less severe, though still present, in Social Security benefits (Veghte, Schreur, & Waid, 2016).

The factors that create the racial wealth gap vary but mostly have to do with access to various institutions and the compounding effect that lack of access has on an individual's ability build and sustain wealth, especially over the course of multiple generations. Lower rates of educational attainment, especially lower rates of college graduation, combine with less sizable intergenerational wealth transfer, and higher levels of unemployment to compromise the ability of African Americans to earn as much as their white peers. Lower earnings and institutional disadvantages in turn produce lower rates of homeownership which effectively locks many African American families out of an important wealth-building tool. These factors are compounded over the course of generations, constantly reinforcing the racial wealth gap which has grown significantly over the past several decades (Shapiro, Meschede, & Osoro, 2013). Health disparities also shape divisions in wealth, as illness pulls resources from people and their families (e.g., through caregiving, time off work).

See also: Health Disparities, Inequality, Racism

Further Reading

Rockeymoore, M. (2014). Beyond broke: Why the racial wealth gap matters. *HuffPost*, February 29. Retrieved from www.huffingtonpost.com/dr-maya-rockeymoore/beyond-broke-why-the-income-inequality_b_5229888.html.

Shapiro, T. M. (2017). *Toxic inequality: How America's wealth gap destroys mobility, deepens the racial divide, and threatens our future.* New York: Basic Books.

Shapiro, T., Meschede, T., & Osoro, S. (2013). *The roots of the widening racial wealth gap: Explaining the black–white economic divide.* Institute on Assets and Social Policy.

Veghte, B. W., Shreur, E., & Waid, M. (2016). *Social Security and the racial wealth gap.* National Academy of Social Insurance.

Radical (and Radical History)

Connotes an extreme departure from the norm, a challenge to the status quo. It describes a political, cultural, economic, theoretical, and/or methodological stance distinct from liberal, conservative, and neoliberal platforms. It may propose dismantling and reforming a system, which may occur on the Left or the Right, or other extreme poles of the normal, the usual, the taken-for-granted.

Radical gerontology problematizes mainstream theories and assumptions, interrogating the roots of dominant ideologies and power structures. It queries how the medical industrial complex dictates curriculum, establishes legitimacy through channels of elite professionalization, and channels funding for scholarships. Being interpretative with social sciences (grounded theory and ethnomethodologies) in the 1960s was radical to the positivism that reigned over academia.

While there are multiple radical traditions across disciplines of academic study, we want to advance the concept of *radical history* as part of emancipatory gerontology – key in examining power and privilege, reckoning with legacies of colonial violence and domination.

Radical History

An approach to the study of history that emphasizes the political aspects of the discipline as well as advocacy and the study of the histories of marginalized peoples.

Howard Zinn, late author of *The politics of history*, describes his "determination to emphasize the lives of those still wanting the necessities of existence (food, shelter, dignity, freedom)." Radical history, as proposed by Howard Zinn (1970), reaches the kind of "awareness that moves people in humanistic directions" through "a value-laden historiography." Radical history aims to "untie our minds, our bodies, our disposition to move."

Arguing against the search for "a nonexistent objectivity," Zinn urges a historiographical "retrogressive subjectivity." This means departing from the "privileged observer" position, mindful of the discipline's tendency to see and write history from the top or the middle. Zinn writes history that touches us, and may pull us out of lethargy. Zinn (1970[2012], pp. 87–100) identifies five benefits of radical historical analysis.

1. We can intensify, expand, and sharpen our perception of how bad things are for victims of the world (awareness of what is wrong).
2. We can expose the pretensions of governments to either neutrality or beneficence (disabuse ourselves of the confidence that we can depend on governments to rectify what is wrong).
3. We can expose the ideology that pervades our culture, the rationale for the going order. (e.g., the sanctity of economic inequality, war, racism).
4. We can recapture those few moments in the past which show the possibility of a better way of life than that which has dominated the Earth so far.
5. We can show how good social movements can go wrong, how leaders can betray followers, how rebels can become bureaucrats, and how ideals can become frozen and reified.

Radical historical theory and analysis is a commendable and consistent guide for much-needed work in critical aging policy, the political economy of aging, and critical gerontology more broadly.

See also: Consciousness Raising, Critical Theory, Emancipatory, Epistemology, Pedagogy, Political Economy

Further Reading

Estes, C. L. (2018). A first generation critic comes of age: Part II. In C. Wellin (Ed.), *Critical gerontology comes of age*. New York: Routledge.

Feagin, J. R. & Vera, H. (2015). *Liberation sociology*. Boulder, CO: Paradigm.

Takaki, R. T. (1993). *A different mirror*. Boston, MA: Little, Brown.

Walker, A., McCarthy, T. P., & Chomsky, N. (2012). *The indispensable Zinn: The essential writings of the people's historian*. New York: The New Press.

Zinn, H. (1970). *The politics of history*. Boston, MA: Beacon Press.

Rationalization

A deeply ingrained characteristic of Western states and their economic organization and politics. Max Weber wrote of the Protestant Ethic and the Spirit of Capitalism in terms of the legitimacy of bureaucratization and the attachment to formal rules and the rational through quantitative calculation (e.g., calculability in capital accounting). Rationalization is experienced in the rationalization of daily life and in the maddening acceleration of efficiency measures, depersonalization of speaking to computerized customer services. Rationalization is a mode of domination in industrialization, computerization, and all things digital. Authority of the law and regulation and decision (or lack of it) hides behind "impersonal" rules, decisions of superiors over subordinates, affecting the accumulation of power through social control, scientific management, by experts, professionals, managers, and supervisors.

Weber and Clegg describe a set of factors that demand the "calculability of results," including "a 'formally free' labour force, the appropriation and concentration of the physical means of production as disposable private property; the representation of share rights in organizations and property ownership; and the 'rationalization' . . . the market, technology, and the law" (Clegg, 1975, p. 114; see also Weber, 1948, p. 182). Autonomous, coercive, technocratic administrative actions are accorded the equivalent of legal authority. Rationalization produces technical and resource constraints upon the State, society, and the people – these constraints have been identified as an "iron cage," a metaphor for being imprisoned by a depersonalized bureaucratic process. The use of the rationalization of global financial systems and techniques (e.g., hedge funds) that are so complicated they may not be understood by those who buy or sell them.

A case in aging policy is the survival-induced movement of non-profit human services agencies to mimic the behavior of for-profits, including use management and the rationing of care, to be more efficient (and rational) in order to compete on price by adopting market segmentation and "creaming" of low-risk, lower cost patients. It was the Reagan Administration's 1980s change of rule-making to permit for-profits to compete with non-profits for Older Americans Act funding that changed the character and face of the aging network, opening the way for the Medicare managed care policies and then Medicaid that subsidize the medical industrial complex and the aging enterprise to the tune of trillions of dollars. To the extent that systemic irrationalities and inefficiencies result, a range of crisis tendencies emerge (e.g., the exploding costs of US medical care, difficulties in ensuring access to needed care for all). Technology continues to be a driving force in both the rationalization and commodification of health care, also being reproduced in global markets to snuff out and compete with other nations' universal health care systems.

See also: Digital Sphere, The Market, Positivism, Statistical Panic

Further Reading

Clegg, S. (1975). *Power, rule and domination.* London: Routledge & Kegan Paul.

Estes, C. L. & Alford, R. L. (1990). Systemic crisis and the nonprofit sector: Toward a political economy of the nonprofit health and social services sector. *Theory and Society, 19*(2), 173–198.

Estes, C. L., Wallace, S. P., Linkins, K. W., & Binney, E. A. (2001). The medicalization and commodification of aging and the privatization and rationalization of old age policy. In C. L. Estes (Ed.), *Social policy and aging: A critical perspective* (pp. 45–60). Thousand Oaks, CA: Sage.

Polivka, L. & Estes, C. L. (2009). The economic meltdown and old age politics. *Generations, 33*(3), 56.

Weber, M. (1927). *General economic history* (trans. F. H. Knight). New York: Adelphi.

Weber, M. (1948). In Mills, C. W., Gerth, H. (Eds.), *From Max Weber: Essays in sociology.* London: Routledge.

Reductionism

Focuses analyses (both theoretical and methodological) at a simple level, often privileging the individual while ignoring the social or collective dimensions.

Hagestad and Dannefer's (2001) critique of gerontology as resplendent with "microfication" is a core element of critical thinking and research. Disengagement theory and other organismic-developmental theories reinterpret socially produced patterns of "normal" development and aging as anchored in the organism's internal growth and aging processes. The focus on the cellular reflects the "misconception that the biological sphere of human functioning is somehow disconnected from ecology of proximal and dystal systems of human activity" (Douthit & Marquis, 2010, p. 340).

See also: Devolution, Essentialism, Framing, Functionalism, Gene–Environment, Healthy Aging, Heuristics, Methodologies, Microfication, Positivism

Further Reading

Douthit, K. & Marquis, A. (2010). Biosocial interactions in the construction of late-life health status. In D. Dannefer & C.

Phillipson (Eds.), *The SAGE handbook of social gerontology* (pp. 329–342). Los Angeles, CA: Sage.

Hagestad, G. & Dannefer, D. (2001). Concepts and theories of aging. In R. Binstock (Ed.), *Handbook of aging and the social sciences*. New York: Academic Press.

Refugees

Persons who "owing to well-founded fear of being persecuted for reasons of race, religion, nationality, membership of a particular social group or political opinion, is outside the country of his nationality and is unable or, owing to such fear, is unwilling to avail himself of the protection of that country" (Defined by Article 1 of the 1951 UN Convention).

Older displaced people are especially vulnerable, particularly in times of conflict or in the aftermath of natural disasters. Physical limitations may impose serious restrictions upon their ability to make the long and frequently very dangerous journeys typical of many refugees. The United Nations High Council on Refugees (UNHCR) estimates that older refugees make up 8.5 percent of the overall refugee population. These individuals are highly dependent on their families and social connections, and often struggle to adapt to unfamiliar people and surroundings, especially when they are separated from their friends and family.

Since 2011, five million Syrians have fled their country as refugees. Right-wing groups insist on rejecting their resettlement, convinced that Islam will overwhelm native populations. There are also critical implications for the relationship between the United States and the Global South in light of the Trump Administration and Campaign's attack on undocumented immigrants. Thousands of people crossing the border without documentation do so because the endemic corruption, poverty, and violence in their homelands threaten their existence.

Much of this precarity is a result of US manipulation or participation, arming coups and supporting regime changes. Indigenous populations face particular challenges, struggling to exist in nations which have forced them out, exploited their precarity, or committed genocide (e.g., the 170,000 people who died in Guatemala from 1960 to 1996). How can these vulnerable survivors not be seen as anything but refugees?

See also: Citizenship, Globalization, Statelessness, War, Xenophobia

Further Reading

Aiyar, S., Barkbu, B., Batini, N., Berger, H., Detragiache, E., Dizioli, A., & Topalova, P. (2016). *The refugee surge in Europe: Economic challenges*. International Monetary Fund.

Hollifield, M., Fullilove, M. T., & Hobfoll, S. E. (2011). Climate change refugees. In I. Weissbecker (Eds.), *Climate change and human well-being. International and cultural psychology*. New York: Springer.

United Nations High Commissioner for Refugees. *Safeguarding individuals: Older people*. Retrieved from www.unhcr.org/en-us/older-people.html.

Relationships

The interpersonal connections and alliances formed throughout life, crucial to emotional development, sharing resources, and navigating oppressive social barriers.

Two social psychology models illustrate the dimensions of mainstream gerontological investigation.

(1) The Convoy Model (Kahn & Antonucci, 1980) emphasizes the importance of emotional closeness across the lifespan and life course, offering empirical measures to six qualitative dimensions, particularly in relation to age, race, gender, and

socioeconomic status (SES). They relate to who is there for older adults for confiding, reassurance, respect, sick care, talk with when upset, and talk about health. These questions are key in determining systems of support upon discharge from hospital or in the wake of a serious medical diagnosis.

(2) Socioemotional Selectivity Theory (Carstensen, 1995) contends that older people develop smaller and closer networks with age, focusing on bonds which matter and eschewing superficial relating. This confronts previous models that theorized disengagement as decline in old age; however, this could be considered as an adaptation that extends from the disengagement model.

Earlier entries on caregiving and family demonstrate the complexities of monetized interdependence. Critical reflection is important for relationships of all kinds, including relations between and among races, ages, classes, and genders. Emirbayer and Desmond (2012) argue that our understanding of social order will remain unsatisfactory so long as we fail to turn our analytic gaze back on ourselves and inquire critically into the hidden presuppositions that shape our thought. Emirbayer and Desmond (2012, p. 577) state:

> For reflexive thinking to survive and, what is more, to be employed widely in the interest of scientific truth, analysts must produce works that *challenge, deepen, and further* its current standards, for what constitutes reflexive thinking, we argue, entails much more than observing how one's social position affects scientific analyses or the political imagination.

To advance emancipatory gerontology, moving toward theoretical clarity and reflexivity in our concept of the social world, human agency needs to be radically reconceptualized. Emirbayer and Mische (1998) call for a relational pragmatics – more adequate theorization of the temporal nature of human experience. Because "[a]ctors are always living simultaneously in the past, future, and present, and adjusting the various temporalities of their empirical existence to one another (and to their empirical circumstances) in more or less imaginative or reflective ways" (p. 1012), this lays the basis for a more dynamic understanding of the capacity that actors have to mediate the structuring contexts within which action unfolds.

This perspective also "opens up the possibility to conceive of moral and practical issues regarding human freedom, creativity, and democracy in a more satisfactory and powerful way" (Emirbayer & Mische, 1998, p. 1012). Emirbayer and Mische (1998) argue that norms and values are by-products of actors' engagement with one another in ambiguous and challenging circumstances. Problematic situations can become resolved "only when actors reconstruct the temporal-relational contexts within which they are embedded and, in the process transform their own values and themselves" (Emirbayer and Mische, 1998, p. 1013).

To conceive of the social world in processes, as dynamic, unfolding relations, Emirbayer (1997) calls for a "transactional" and "relational" perspective because "human beings do not create unitary societies but a diversity of intersecting networks of social interaction" (p. 295). In his manifesto for a relational sociology, Emirbayer (1997) identifies three transpersonal, relational contexts within which all social action unfolds: social structure, culture, and social psychology.

Extending Emirbayer's (1997) arguments further, for critical thinkers seeking to develop a relational mode of gerontological inquiry requires (1) exploring more aggressively the analytical levels of culture and collective emotions, (2) striving to maintain theoretical consistency across levels of analysis in efforts at theory-building, and (3) beginning to systematize some of the alternative ways in which central issues and problems have been thematized from within gerontology.

See also: Agency, Critical Realism, Generational and Intergenerational Consciousness, Gerontological Imagination, Intergenerational Intersubjectivity, Knowledges, Structure, Sociology

Further Reading

Antonucci, T. C., Ajrouch, K. J., & Birditt, K. S. (2014). The convoy model: Explaining social relations from a multidisciplinary perspective. *The Gerontologist*, *54*(1), 82–92.

Carstensen, L. L. (1995). Evidence for a lifespan theory of socioemotional selectivity. *Current Directions in Psychological Science*, *4*(5), 151–156.

Emirbayer, M. (1997). Manifesto for a relational sociology. *American Journal of Sociology*, *103*(2), 281–317.

Emirbayer, M. & Desmond, M. (2012). Race and reflexivity. *Ethnic and Racial Studies*, *35*(4), 574–599.

Emirbayer, M. & Mische, A. (1998). What is agency? *American Journal of Sociology*, *103*(4), 962–1023.

Kahn, R. L. & Antonucci, T. C. (1980). Convoys over the life course: Attachment, roles, and social support. In P. B. Baltes & O. Brim (Eds.), *Life span development and behavior, volume 3* (pp. 253–267). New York: Academic Press.

Relations of Ruling

A feminist structural and interactional analysis of power relations offered by Canadian Sociologist Dorothy Smith. It problematizes the "experiencing of life that is not already defined within the ruling relations," and promotes an analysis which is grounded "in the actualities of women's lived experience." Smith writes (1999, p. 76):

> In these relations, the particularity of individuals, their actual situation and site of work, the ephemerality of the lived moment, and so on, disappear. Their disappearance is itself an accomplishment of what particular people do. . . . From this standpoint, the ruling relations themselves, including the social organization of knowledge, are problematized for investigation.

Smith (1999) warns of the danger of a social science that is captured by and envisioned through the relations of ruling and the limitations of gendered and raced knowledges and epistemologies. This can be challenged by "A sociology . . . method of inquiry that extends and expands what we can discover from the local settings of our everyday/*everynight* living" (p. 74). She questions:

> [H]ow is it that language and discourse appear as if they were autonomous systems, forgetting the irremediably local historicity of speakers, readers and writers? How can we take up post structuralism's discovery of how discourse speaks to us?
>
> (Smith, 1999, p. 76)

Smith calls for a scientific procedure that preserves the subject as actor and experiencer. Smith looks at the *three effects of distinctively women's work*. First, it relieves men of the need to take care of their bodies or their homes, freeing them to the world of the abstract; frees men to be *abstract*. Second, women's work is perceived not as self-chosen and willed, but "natural" and emotional labors of love. Women's work is *natural*. Women are alienated from their own experiences as they only have the conceptual schemes of the ruling masculine to define themselves. Work on feminist standpoint theory and the epistemic advantage (Harding, 1996), queer theory, heteronormativity, (dis)ability, signal important developments for inclusion in the study of aging, politics, and policy.

See also: Feminism, Knowledges

Further Reading

Harding, S. (1996). Standpoint epistemology (a feminist version): How social disadvantage creates epistemic advantage. *Social Theory and Sociology: The Classics and Beyond*, 146–160.

Smith, D. E. (1996). The relations of ruling: A feminist inquiry. *Studies in Culture, Organizations, and Society*, 2, 171–190.

Smith, D. E. (1999). *Writing the social: Critique, theory, and investigations*. Toronto, Ontario: University of Toronto Press.

Reproduction, Social

A concept that embraces the *work* of (1) biologically reproducing and nurturing members of society, including maternity, pregnancy, and childrearing, to create educated, healthy, knowledgeable, and able human beings, and (2) structuring and providing societal conditions, resources, policies, benefits, and services to support and facilitate (or not) the reproduction of individuals, communities, and society across time, space, and place.

The requisite of social reproduction is understood as work that engages and affects our society, economy, and way of life involving care, education, and nurturance across the life course. There is strong empirical evidence that these caregiving and social reproduction responsibilities exact a high price on women. There is evidence that care work and needs across generations is increasing, as social supports from the State

are diminishing and uncertain. Many families confront the challenges of multiple generations of older family members (Gelfand, Olsen, & Block, 1978).

Nancy Folbre (2001), a feminist economist, notes that "[t]he invisible hand of markets depends upon the invisible heart of care. Markets cannot function effectively outside the framework of families and communities built on values of love, obligation, and reciprocity" (p. 4). Classical market economists' and Marxist treatment of reproduction are criticized for their conceptualizations of productivity in ways that ignore or marginalize the central contribution of women's reproduction work as foundational to the economy and capitalism.

From a critical feminist political economy perspective, we know that women's contribution to social reproduction and its *non-recognition* illustrates how men of power, acting through the State and society, have appropriated reproduction via physical and legal control of women and children. The divisive history of conflict over women's reproductive freedom is unremitting in US policy, including the right of individual women to decide whether and when to have children. These struggles and the policy contests that accompany them are inscribed in the vulnerable situation and inequalities of mid-life and older women and the families that depend on them, and the need to care for them. Race, class, ethnicity, ability, gender, and age are pivotal.

An area of "social reproduction feminism" builds on Benston's political economy of women's liberation in which she argues that "household labor, including child care, constitutes a huge amount of socially necessary labor" for commodity production under capitalism (Benston, 1969). This is foundational to understanding women's oppression in capitalist society. Fraser (2016) highlights racialized capitalism as central to expropriation and exploitation of the work and care provided by women of color.

What does this have to do with aging? As described in multiple A–Z concepts, we know that women's disadvantage and inequality reproduce disadvantage and inequality in mid-life and old age, but in magnified and accumulated form. The structural order and the power of one's social location is the best predictor of outcomes in aging and old age. Key characteristics of race, ethnicity, gender, class, ability, and age and their intersectionalities persist as the strongest determinants of health and retirement security. Policies for the old and aging are crucial in alleviating the worst of some of these effects, but the big structural status quo remains in place.

See also: Care Penalty, Cumulative Advantage/Disadvantage, Dependency Ratios, Family Gender, Ideology, Patriarchy, Social Determinants of Health, War on Women, Welfare State

Further Reading

Arber, J. (2000). Rewriting class, race, and gender: Problems in feminist rethinking. In M. M. Ferree, J. Lorber, & B. B. Hess (Eds.), *Revisioning gender* (pp. 44–49). Walnut Creek, CA: Rowman & Littlefield.

Benston, M. (1969). The political economy of women's liberation. *Monthly Review, 21*(4).

Dickinson, J. & Russell, B (Eds.). (1986). *Family, economy & state: The social reproduction process under capitalism*. Toronto, Ontario: Garamond Press.

Folbre, N. (2001). *The invisible heart: Economics and family values*. New York: New York University Press.

Foster, J. B. & Clark, B. (2018). Women, nature & capital in the industrial revolution. *Monthly Review, 69*(8), 1–24.

Fraser, N. (2016). Expropriation and exploitation in racialized capitalism: A reply to Michael Dawson. *Critical Historical Studies, 3*(1), 168–178.

Fraser, N. (2017). Crisis of care? On the social-reproductive contradictions of contemporary capitalism. In T. Bhattacharya (Ed.), *Social reproduction theory: Remapping class, recentering oppression* (pp. 21–46). London: Pluto Press.

Gelfand, D., Olsen, J., & Block, M. (1978). Two generations of elderly in the changing American family: Implications for family services. *The Family Coordinator, 27*(4), 395–403.

Ginn, J., Street, D., & Arber, S. (Eds.). (2001). *Women, work, and pensions: International issues and prospects*. Buckingham: Open University Press.

Vogel, L. (1983/2016). *Marxism and the oppression of women*. Chicago, IL: Haymarket Books.

Resilience

The capacity to bounce back or overcome trauma.

"Resilience" in gerontological literature has been defined as "flourishing despite adversity" (Hildon et al., 2009). Another perspective is that it is "a motivating force and intuitive process that facilitates a sense of personal control and freedom" (Richardson, 2002).

Adversity is measured by "circumstances that produce a significant average decrease in quality of life" (e.g., functional limitations, life getting worse in health and stress domains, negative life events, and a decline in general living circumstances) (Hildon et al., 2009). While resilience may be a recognition of recovery and strength, it may also frame an oppressive expectation such as the "pick yourself up by the bootstraps" puritan ideology and victim blaming. The discourse of resilience exhibits similar tendencies of microfication, and the reductionist emphasis on individualism. Resilience as part of healing must be located not just at an individual level but also on the collective. Communities, culture, and institutions are players in resilience, especially in responses to communities recovering from natural disasters.

Resilience may also be an attribute, condition, or situation produced at the macro level of nation-state policy as exemplified by how nations use tax and transfer policies to redistribute market-based income, which, in the USA, has produced a rise in Gini coefficient (rise in inequality) after taxes and transfers, lower equality in provision of social goods (e.g., health care and education), and less cohesiveness across race/ethnic and class-based groups. These comparative differences show up in life expectancy and other health outcomes (e.g., Canada and the USA). Similarly, neighborhood characteristics and institutional racism and sexism are shown to be related to health and economic outcomes.

Emancipatory gerontology beckons research and discourse to shift from romanticizing resilience toward examining the role of social insurance programs and the welfare state in preventing exposure to trauma and facilitating resilience factors through material support.

See also: Gene–Environment, Levels of Analysis, Stress, Trauma

Further Reading

Hildon, Z., Montgomery, S. M., Blane, D., Wiggins, R. D., & Netuveli, G. (2009). Examining resilience of quality of life in the face of health-related and psychosocial adversity at older ages: What is "right" about the way we age? *The Gerontologist, 50*(1), 36–47.

Richardson, G. E. (2002). The metatheory of resilience and resiliency. *Journal of Clinical Psychology, 58*(3), 307–321.

Resistance

Pushes back against dominant forces, struggling for power and privilege where it is denied.

A cornerstone of critical perspectives on aging policy is the conflict between forces and structures of power and those of resistance through agency; that is, resistance by and through one's human and collective subjectivity and ability to act. Resistance involves questioning authority and the legitimacy of regimes that shut down and close off ways of thinking, knowing, and doing that embrace and foster human development across the intersectionalities of the life course.

Resistance on the Left is in the fight against Social Security privatization campaigns, particularly during and since the George W. Bush era. Carroll Estes (2017) documents a number of progressive social movement developments. These are threads upon which the social insurance defenders are building:

1. The strengthening of grassroots advocates in tandem with the stance of House Speaker/Leader Pelosi's "just say no" campaign against Social Security privatization and the "no cuts" campaigns of social insurance proponents from 2005 to 2016.

2. The success in preventing Social Security beneficiary cuts during the Reagan through Obama presidencies in the face of deficit hawks and conservative and media crowds framing "the Washington consensus." (This pushback occurred in spite of the lukewarm and wavering support from two Democratic presidents, Bill Clinton and Barack Obama).

3. The rise of new modes of resistance in social media, the blogosphere, and on the ground (e.g., Occupy, Black Lives Matter).

4. The development of critical intellectual frameworks networking through Google groups, progressive think tanks, and the increasing accessibility to and effective analytics and public dissemination of big data on the distributional effects of policy "Choices" and nonexistent choices.

5. The strengthening of emancipatory politics through mobilized bases of community and their consolidation through coalitional actions in response to the onslaught of monied conservative foundations, think tanks, and the Tea Party.

The Trump election and presidency re-energized old and stimulated new resistance efforts, reaching into and across the fourth estate media, scientists, women, and racial, ethnic, and immigrant communities – and the historic EU and NATO alliances. Disruption, fear, and the uncertainty of displacement open up the possibility of mass rebellion. Disorientation and decentering but the unimaginable unreality may also re-energize "the social, the community, the collective, human rights." This is where critical aging policy stands.

Non-violent Resistance

The Albert Einstein Institution's website features a list of 198 methods of non-violent (meaning not physically violent) resistance. These methods include non-violent protest and persuasion, non-cooperation (social, economic, and political), and non-violent intervention. Listed below are categories within these realms. More comprehensive descriptions and historical examples of each may be found in volume two of *The politics of nonviolent action* by Gene Sharp.

The Methods of Non-Violent Protest and Persuasion

- Formal Statements
- Communications with a Wider Audience
- Symbolic Public Acts
- Pressures on Individuals
- Drama and Music
- Processions
- Honoring the Dead
- Public Assemblies
- Withdrawal and Renunciation

The Methods of Social Non-Cooperation

- Ostracism of Persons
- Non-cooperation with Social Events, Customs, and Institutions
- Withdrawal from the Social System

The Methods of Economic Non-Cooperation: Economic Boycotts

- Actions by Consumers
- Action by Workers and Producers
- Action by Middlemen
- Action by Owners and Management
- Action by Holders of Financial Resources
- Action by Governments

The Methods of Economic Non-Cooperation: The Strike

- Symbolic Strikes
- Agricultural Strikes
- Strikes by Special Groups
- Ordinary Industrial Strikes
- Restricted Strikes
- Multi-industry Strikes
- Combination of Strikes and Economic Closures

The Methods of Political Non-Cooperation

- Rejection of Authority
- Citizens' Non-cooperation with Government
- Citizens' Alternatives to Obedience
- Action by Government Personnel
- Domestic Governmental Action
- International Governmental Action

The Methods of Non-Violent Intervention

- Psychological Intervention
- Physical Intervention
- Social Intervention
- Economic Intervention
- Political Intervention

Figure R1 Resistance

Political art and social satire can be a powerful way of keeping track of current events and critiquing "non-change." Brian McFadden, cartoonist for *The New York Times*, captures the Zeitgeist of 2013 with a critique of the status quo.

What is startling is the applicability of McFadden's 2013 comic representation of the current Zeitgeist. The headlines hold up remarkably well as a mirror of today's US precarious times.

See also: Emancipatory, Human Rights, Precarity, Solidarity, The Social, Zeitgeist

Further Reading

Arno, P., Knapp, K., Russo, S., & Viola, D. (2015). Rising food insecurity and conservative policy in the US: Impact on the elderly. *World Journal of Social Science Research*, ISSN 2375–9747 (Print) ISSN 2332–5534 (Online) Vol. 2, No. 1, 2015. www.scholink.org/ojs/index.php/wjssr.

Bourdieu, P. (1998). *Acts of resistance: Against the tyranny of the market*. New York: The New Press, p. 91.

Estes, C. L. (2017). Older US women's economic security, health and empowerment: The fight against opponents of Social Security, Medicare and Medicaid. In S.L. Dworkin, M. Gandhi, & P. Passano (Eds.), *Women's empowerment and global health* (pp. 232–250). Berkeley, CA: University of California Press.

Montgomery, N. & Bergman, C. (2017). *Joyful militancy: Building resistance in toxic times*. Baltimore, MD: AK Press.

Sharp, G. (1973). *The politics of nonviolent action: Part one: Power and struggle*. Boston, MA: Porter Sargent Publishers.

www.aeinstein.org/nonviolentaction/198-methods-of-nonviolent-action/.

Retirement

The point at which an individual leaves the labor force.

Two framings of retirement outside of the US:

> *Jubilación* is the Spanish term for retirement. Though the term has a more positive feel than retirement, older people in the Spanish-speaking world face the same problems of insufficient resources once they leave the workforce.
>
> *Redundancy* is the British term for forced retirement as a State policy, retirement as a State institution. The State encouraged older adults to sacrifice their place in the workforce so that younger workers would have opportunities.

Retirement in the United States evolves within and alongside major changes in the labor force and social policy. These include workers' demands for eight-hour workdays, unionization, workplace safety protections, and Social Security, as well as major economic events and trends such as depressions, recessions, booms, and globalization. The institution of retirement provided a path out of the labor market, opening up jobs for younger workers, and created a position for older adults which has been termed by Townsend (1981) as structured dependency. The subject of the history of retirement demonstrates how policy structures the life course for many.

Mandatory retirement changed in the USA in 1986 through an amendment to the Age Discrimination in Employment Act of 1967; however, previously, State penalties (which still exist for air traffic controllers at age 56 and pilots at age 61) existed to prevent work past certain ages which "opened up" labor markets for unemployed young people (generational conflict). Redundancy hints at obsolescence and excess, and the term may be understood as violent in that it carries political and economic ideological (pro)opposition in the landscape of austerity (i.e., balancing/cutting).

Traditional retirement has been replaced by older adults facing limited "retirement" options, or having insubstantial retirement security and returning to the workforce for the "gig economy." Retirement as a point of departure from the labor force is a complexly constructed "choice." This may or may not be the end of labor, as many, especially women, face informal labor and responsibilities long after retirement, and many facing or experiencing precarity in retirement "choose" to return to the workforce (O'Rand, 2018).

Reagan initiated reforms that attempted to eliminate what he called "double dipping," the simultaneous drawing of Social Security benefits and public pensions. The Windfall Elimination Provision and Government Pension Offset mandate that retired public workers or their dependents and spouses have their Social Security benefits adjusted downward depending on the size of the benefits they draw from their pension and on how many years of Social Security eligible work they completed. This has been a key factor in dismantling the three-legged stool into a two-legged stool, which is discussed in the entry for Social Security.

See also: Age Discrimination in Employment Act, Choice, Labor, Pensions, Precarity, Social Security

Further Reading

Ghilarducci, T. & Moore, K. (2015). Racially disparate effects of raising the retirement age. *Working Paper Series 2015-3*. Schwartz Center for Economic Policy Analysis and Department of Economics, the New School for Social Research.

Graebner, W. (1980). *A history of retirement*. New Haven, CT: Yale University Press.

O'Rand, A. (2018). *Age and inequality: Diverse pathways through later life*. Abingdon, Oxon: Routledge.

Samuels, A. (2018). This is what life without retirement savings looks like. *The Atlantic*, February 22.

Society of Actuaries (2013). *Impact of retirement risk on women*. Women's Institute for Secure Retirement.

Townsend, P. (1981). The structured dependency of the elderly: A creation of social policy in the twentieth century. *Ageing and Society*, *1*(1), 5–28.

Rhetoric

The way things are said, the synthesis of ideas and turns of phrase to build an argument, convey an idea, persuade, or inspire.

An example is the turn of phrase "The Divided States of America," which confronts the formal and familiar understanding of "United" with the contradicting reality of deep political division. This appeared in the *Huffington Post*, *The New York Times*, and *Time* magazine.

See also: Affect, Discourse, Framing, Heuristic

Right to Have Rights

Describes the guaranteed legitimacy of entitlements. This focuses on how the State extends protection and safeguards the rights of people. It is foundational to *human rights perspectives*.

Sommers (2008, p. 118) posits, in *Genealogies of citizenship: Markets, statelessness, and the right to have rights*, that:

> [C]itizens [are] being expelled from the rights-bearing terrain of the rule of law, from protection by the social state (usually called the welfare state) and from access to the public sphere. These are the socially excluded . . . people [who] have

lost meaningful membership in civil society and political community – that which confers recognition and rights.

It is a result of decades in the USA of "systematically degrading the public sphere and subjecting the institutions of the state to conquest by market fundamentalist regimes [which] are transforming the foundations of citizenship from social and non-contractual to contractual and market driven ones" (p. 118). Critical questions concern the cost of survival and the recognition of dignity outside of labor/consumer model.

See also: Citizenship, The Commons, Human Rights, Legitimacy, Statelessness

Further Reading

Sommers, M. R. (2008). *Genealogies of citizenship: Markets, statelessness, and the right to have rights*. New York: Cambridge University Press.

Risk

A state in which something of value or importance may be won or lost. In the field of gerontology this is generally applied to health care and physical well-being, though it can also apply to financial well-being.

In American discourse, risk is framed within capitalist ideology of individualism and the sanctity of the market. Risk is something to avoid, and is an impediment to profits, business, and income and wealth accumulation. The rejection of universal risk pools like original intentions of Medicare and Social Security indicates the dominant market ideology's defense and dependence upon the avoidance of risk (or if it cannot be avoided, the provision of special economic subsidies and market incentives to "pay" business to treat people who are sick, disabled, homeless, disadvantaged by race, color, ethnicity, class, age, deformity).

Risk is the basis of insurance underwriting through actuarial models designed to detect and project "risk." This allows companies to "hedge" corporate risk and to protect corporations, providers, and institutions from "adverse selection" of customers who may actually use the services or need the benefits. There are special "risk corridors" in health insurance, special segmenting of patients, customers, and "covered lives" so that both markets and profit-making may be assured for medical/health insurance ventures. Before the ACA, insurers could refuse to cover particular diseases and conditions (preconditions or projected possible conditions). The common design of private medical care is to go to great lengths to avoid the sick, the likely to be sick, the chronically ill, those more likely to actually use your health care services.

Actuarially determined risk produces the perverse incentive to avoid paying for health promotion and disease prevention, because in the current dynamic health insurance markets, even though you may have someone likely to be sick later, because of plan changes and drug formulary changes these patients may be encouraged to drop out of your health insurance plan by the next open enrollment period. Indeed, practices can "discourage" the sick from continuing with a particular plan (although it was against the law in ACA). Health services research shows that older adults who are sicker in Medicare Managed Care move off of these plans and on to traditional Medicare. As there is age grading in health insurance, with elders more likely to incur higher costs, provisions exist which state that health insurers and plans may charge up to three times what those under the age of 65 pay. Long-term care insurers presently have no requirement prohibiting increased premiums for the increased age of persons.

The "universal risk pool" is the cornerstone of universal health coverage by single payers. Universal risk pool coverage is most economically efficient and affordable for societies. The core commitment and principle is that "We are all in this together." It is structurally designed as mandatory for all to participate in order to enable all to be covered, sick and well, poor and rich, all by race, ethnicity, sexuality, gender, immigrant status, age, and ability. All IN: the universal risk pool means no "opting out" – no third-party payers raking off marketing and profit "margins" that elevate the costs of medical and health care, and deter long-term preventive health practices and treatment. Where such systems exist, the State does not tend to be seen as "bad," evil, or "the problem" (e.g., Norway).

In the USA the migration of risk has been from the family to the State; and from the State to the individual. "Going bare," meaning going without insurance coverage, is increasingly a problem in the face of this risk shifting. The individualization of risk transfers responsibility or accountability away from the corporation, leaving the individual facing precarity. This loss of buffering of the individual and community and society is called the Risk Shift (Hacker, 2008).

Classic policy examples of risk shifting are "devolution," Block granting Medicaid and welfare services, increased state discretion on eligibility criteria and benefits provided. This creates the potential of 58,000 jurisdictions, each with variable policies, services, and lack of accountability because (1) there is little or no transparency, and (2) the most powerful interests with the most at stake are able to impose their lobbying to their advantage, while (3) the most vulnerable, the weakest, are likely to have the least ability to organize to defend their interests and needs.

The National Academy of Social Insurance (NASI) has identified three major risks with regard to inequality and aging (2017): (1) long-term care services and supports, (2) caregiving and the gender gap in retirement security, and (3) non-standard work (which characterizes the largest segment of new jobs). Non-standard work means there is no identifiable employer and the risk is borne by the non-standard worker.

See also: Age Rating, Ageism, Austerity, Capitalism, Choice, Class, Commodification, Crisis, Framing, Individualism, Precarity, Privatization

Further Reading

Beck, U. (1992). *Risk society: Toward a new modernity.* Thousand Oaks, CA: Sage.

Edelman, M. J. (1977). *Political language.* New York: Academic Press.

Estes, C. L. & Newcomer, R. J. (1983). *Fiscal austerity and aging: Shifting government responsibility for the elderly.* Beverly Hills, CA: Sage.

Faux, J. (2010). *Global class war: How America's bipartisan elite lost our future – and what it will take to win it back.* Hoboken, NJ: Wiley.

Hacker, J. S. (2008). *The great risk shift.* Oxford: Oxford University Press.

Herd, P. (2009). The two-legged stool: The reconfiguration of risk in retirement income security. *Generations, 33*(3), 12–18.

Lupton, D. (Ed.). (1999). *Risk and sociocultural theory: New directions and perspectives.* Cambridge: Cambridge University Press.

Russell, J. W. (2014). *Social insecurity: 401 (k) s and the retirement crisis.* Boston, MA: Beacon Press.

Veghte, B. W., Shreur, E., & Bradley, A. (2017). *Report to the new leadership and the American people on social insurance and inequality.* Washington, DC: National Academy of Social Insurance.

S

Scarcity

Speaks to not having enough resources to adequately meet individual and collective needs.

Scarcity is constructed and framed through crisis which necessitates responses of sacrifice and cultures of austerity. In response to limited access to resources, competition is naturalized as practical for survival. Haste and competition become key to survival. Alternative paths toward integration which value the calm, reflective, and non-reactive are ignored. The mentality of scarcity obscures and suppresses opportunities for cooperation and investment.

Scarcity is key in market turbulence. The abstraction of financial capital promotes volatility and economic insecurity. The uncertainty of scarcity itself provides additional opportunities for capital flight, generating markets promising security but failing to deliver. Scarcity fuels its delirious replication. The world, for instance, may be producing enough food to feed its population, but unequal access or distribution of that resource can obscure realities of bounty or sufficiency.

The ideology of scarcity is a core economic principle in the philosophy of financial capitalism and with it the assumption that the allocation of rewards of the capitalist market by differential race, class, and gender is not aberrational but an expected and positive product of the basic inherent value of persons of different race, class, and gender to society. It is a meretricious notion that those who are most valuable to society deserve most are that inequalities in wealth and income and health are an unfortunate but requisite by-product by a system that promotes the best for all (via the "invisible hand" of the market). At the *micro* level individuals are held responsible for their attributes and social condition. At the *meso* level institutions of law, education, medicine, and economic organization are seen as inherently steeped in systems of inequality in order to advance the goals of these various institutions. At the *macro* level the ideology, which in the US case is hegemonic and dominant, supports the continuance of institutions which produce inequality in the advance of profit and the maldistribution of precarity.

See also: Austerity, Citizenship, Crisis, Delirium, Neoliberalism, Precarity, TINA

Sexism

Prejudice and discrimination based on gender in the society. Pateman (2018) critiques traditional Western thought about the State as if it were derived from an original contract. Relevant to considerations of the marriage contract, the employment contract, the welfare and global contract – as well as the intergenerational social contract debates surrounding Social Security, Medicare, and "we are all in this together."

See also: Feminism, Gender, Wage Inequality, War on Women

Further Reading

Pateman, C. (2018). *The sexual contract* (30th Anniversary edition). Stanford, CA: Stanford University Press.

Sexuality

The expression of libidinal and erotic desire. It is constructed not just through its expression (or repression), but largely by how it is received and accepted (or rejected). The core of sexuality centers on concepts of embodiment and gendering, where performativity is celebrated. One might argue that the physical pleasure of sexuality is contingent upon the dignity of desire, while conservative perspectives narrowly disparage physical pleasure as compulsive and animalistic, without regard for the sensuality of consent.

In his *History of sexuality* (1976, 1984; see 2012), Michel Foucault advances sexuality as a concept within Western society. He identifies fluidity and repression as key factors in sexuality, and traces the ways in which society and cultural forces, more than biological ones, determine the acceptable spectrum of sexualities.

Connell and Dowsett (1992) take a similar approach to gender and sexuality. In particular they examine the ways in which sexuality influences social structure and power dynamics. Sexuality and gender identity have become political battlefields in the United States; the claiming of sexual identity has become an inherently political act.

Gerontological study about sexuality and aging has overturned the myth of the sexless older adult. Much of health policy focuses on the sexual and reproductive health of young people, ignoring the reality that many older adults have the desire and capability to have sex. Research provides a basis of legitimacy for advocates to challenge the inadequacy of practice standards entrenched in ageist tropes of sexlessness (Taylor & Gosney, 2011). Critical gerontologists, and organizations like SAGE, who promote the valuing of marginalized sexualities, have also played an important role in identifying how nursing homes and care workers often fail to recognize or serve gay, lesbian, bisexual, queer, and trans older adults (Adams & Tax, 2017).

See also: Epistemology, Feminism, Gender, Men, Patriarchy, Women

Further Reading

Adams, M. & Tax, A. D. (2017). Assessing and meeting the needs of LGBT older adults via the Older Americans Act. *LGBT Health*, *4*(6), 389–393.

Connell, R. W. & Dowsett, G. W. (Eds.). (1992). *Rethinking sex: Social theory and sexuality research*. Philadelphia, PA: Temple University Press.

Connell, R. W. & Messerschmidt, J. W. (2005). Hegemonic masculinity: Rethinking the concept. *Gender and Society*, *19*(6), 829–859.

Dowsett, G. W. (2003). Some considerations on sexuality and gender in the context of AIDS. *Reproductive Health Matters*, *11*(22), 21–29.

Foucault, M. (2012). *The history of sexuality (Vols 1–3)*. London: Vintage.

Taylor, A. & Gosney, M. A. (2011). Sexuality in older age: Essential considerations for healthcare professionals. *Age and Ageing*, *40*(5), 538–543.

Originally known as Senior Action in a Gay Environment, and later Services & Advocacy for GLBT Elders, SAGE was founded to create a network of support for these older community members, first in New York City and then nationwide. Learn more at www.sageusa.org/.

The Social

A concept which speaks broadly to philosophical, ideological, and normative principles that declare certain mutual rights, privileges, and responsibilities of members and citizens of nation-states. "The Social" embraces what is considered essential grounding for a civilized nation and democratic society and what is expected and contributed by the members of that society, as well as the reciprocal commitments between the society and State with its people.

Inextricably, *the Social* embeds the concept of and right to self-development of individual human beings. As Richard Flacks (1988, p. 126) observes, self-development is the:

> growth in the capacity of the individual to find and express meaning in his or her life, to believe that one's life counts both for specific others and for some larger, historically relevant purpose, that one is a person of worth and accomplishment. . . . [It] is constituted by the establishment of *identity* – the sense that one's life has to do with a meaning defined by heritage that one is true to and carrying forward, or by a vision of the social future that one is trying to contribute to. Second, self-development has to do with the growth in the *actualization* of one's potentials in the sense that one has talents, abilities, and qualities that are valuable to others and that one is using with increasingly good effect. . . . [Further] Economic and social marginality blocks self-development. The economically excluded and socially uprooted cannot follow the prescriptions of official culture to find meaning and self-worth.

Stated another way, to acknowledge *the Social* is to acknowledge that the "self-realization of individuals as social beings" occurs in the context of social interactions through which we are a part of a larger collective community and society. We are not "atomized individual agents" (Walker, 2006, p. 74; See also Honneth, 1994). We are profoundly influenced by our birth cohort, historical moment, and generation, as these are conditioned by the institutions of governance, the economy, education, job markets, global processes and forces of racism, ageism, sexism, ability, social class, and geopolitical location.

A critical approach to social policy and aging takes as given that "the material and human reproduction of society involves relations and processes of interdependence" (Twine, 1994, p. 29) throughout the life course. Over time, *the Social* is expressed and lived socially and culturally through race, ethnicity, class, gender, ability, and nation.

The argument against *the Social* is the ideology of extreme individualism. It reflects and comports with market ideology, as if the individual is solely and independently responsible for his or her success or failure. It ignores the vastly different opportunities available to the individual from circumstances of birth, parents, families, and communities of origin to the social, political, economic, cultural attributes and cumulative advantages and disadvantages across the life course (Estes, 2013).

See also: The Commons, Democracy, Digital Sphere, Generations, Networks, Power, Oppression, Resistance

Further Reading

Dannefer, D. (2011). Long time coming, not here yet: The possibilities of the social in age and life course studies. In R. A. Settersten Jr. & J. L. Angel (Eds.), *Handbook of sociology of aging* (pp. 633–643). New York: Springer.

Estes, C. L. (2013). The disappearance of the social in the USA. Paper presented at the *International Association of Gerontology & Geriatrics (IAGG)*. Seoul, Korea.

Ferge, Z. (1997). The changed welfare paradigm: The individualization of the social. *Social Policy & Administration, 31*(1), 20–44.

Flacks, R. (1988). *Making history*. New York: Columbia University Press.

Honneth, A. (1994). The social dynamics of disrespect: On the location of critical theory today. *Constellations, 1*(1), 255–269.

Twine, F. (1994). *Citizenship and social rights: The interdependence of self and society*. London: Sage.

Walker, A. (2006). Reexamining the political economy of aging. In J. Baars, D. Dannefer, C. Phillipson & A. Walker (Eds.) *Aging, globalization and inequality: The new critical gerontology* (p. 74). Amityville, N Y: Baywood Pub. Co.

Social Construction of Reality

A theory in the sociology of knowledge credited to Berger and Luckmann (1966). Indebted to Alfred Schutz, George Herbert Mead, phenomenology, social psychology, and symbolic interactionism, we know that the "definition of the situation" is of enormous consequence across contentious areas of individual, peer, community, and policy spheres, often invoking race, sexuality, ethnicity, age, ability, class, and gender.

Knowledge is socially generated; it comes from the questions asked, the collection, ordering, and interpretation of data, and the organization, work, and opinions of the scientific community who, themselves, are competing, experts of power, stature, and potential wealth. Although socially generated, this interpretation and ordering of knowledge takes on the character of objective reality.

As W. I. Thomas said, "if something is believed to be real, it is real in its consequences." "Although socially generated, knowledge and expert opinions take on the character of objective reality, regardless of whether or not they are valid". This applies to gerontological knowledge and, as these definitions are widely shared, they become part of the "Collective stock of knowledge" (Berger & Luckmann, 1966, p. 60). Labeling theory (Becker, 1963, p 11) informs us that social problems and by definition the intervention policies and programs are "created by society . . . by making the rules whose infraction constitutes deviance" or normality. Hence, the development of interventions is intertwined with the "societal reaction" (i.e., by the *reactions* of others). Social constructionism is now an influential perspective in gerontology and geriatrics.

As Estes has long argued, the central dimension of power is key to crisis definition and management by the State and capital. Estes argues that definitions of reality that hold political or economic dominance in old age policy are part of discursive intellectual and power struggles. As important social constructions of reality are, as in their potential for stereotyping, blaming, and institutionalizing "cause and effect," we are discovering that these constructions of reality profoundly affect the *life course experience of each of us*. A large literature attests that there are significant consequences for people of "how others think of us:" concepts such as "the looking glass self," "learned helplessness," "sense of personal control," and "self-esteem" reflect the import of definitions and labels at a very deep personal and interpersonal level.

Estes' work on political economy of aging contends that *Whoever controls the dominant constructions of reality controls an important part of destiny: the ability to define problems and the ability to limit what is considered as the realistic, appropriate, feasible policy solution*. To wit: the crises of Social Security, demographic aging, and federal deficit are endemic and emblematic of "The Social Construction of Crisis" (Estes, 1979, 1983, 2011).

Conservatives speak to their base. When progressives move to the Right, they activate and reinforce conservative values and positions. Simply negating the other side's frames only reinforces them. In short, constructions of reality and frames are all about power relations and the way into the American psyche without physical bloodshed.

Further Reading

Becker, H. S. (1963). *Outsiders: Studies in the sociology of deviance.* New York: The Free Press.

Berger, P. L. & Luckmann, T. (1966). *The social construction of reality.* Garden City, NY: Doubleday.

Estes, C. L. (1979). *The aging enterprise: A critical examination of social policies and services for the aged.* San Francisco, CA: Jossey-Bass.

Estes, C. L. (1983). Social Security: The social construction of a crisis. *Milbank Memorial Fund Quarterly/Health and Society, 61*(3), 445–461.

Estes, C. L. (2011). Crises and old age policy. In R. A. Settersten Jr. & J. L. Angel (Eds.), *Handbook of sociology of aging* (pp. 297–320). New York: Springer.

Lakoff, G. & Johnson, M. (2008). *Metaphors we live by.* Chicago, IL: University of Chicago Press.

Mannheim, K. (1936). *Ideology and Utopia.* New York: Routledge & Kegan Paul.

Mannheim, K., Erös, J. S., & Stewart, W. A. C. (1957). *Systematic sociology.* London: Routledge & Kegan Paul.

Thomas, W. I. (1970). *The unadjusted girl.* Santa Fe, NM: Gannor.

Wolfson, M. H. (2006). Neoliberalism and social security. *Review of Radical Political Economics, 38*(3), 319–326.

Social Contract

The concept that government and citizens have a range of responsibilities toward one another and that the fulfillment of these responsibilities represents the foundation of an equitable and stable society.

The concept dates back to the classical world with salient discussions on the subject by Roman and Greek scholars. Key thinkers about social contracts are Hobbes, Locke, and Rousseau. Hobbes posited the idea of "natural law" to explain the formation of society. In his view humans live in a natural and constant state of war. Society is simply a contract between free men to abrogate this state of war and live by a commonly accepted set of rules. Locke and Rousseau built upon this framework, arguing that humans give up a certain amount of their rights in return for civil rights predicated on the defense of the community's collective rights. Locke advocated the notion of fundamental inalienable rights granted by God while Rousseau emphasized self-rule according to the "general will." Locke's inalienable rights concept eventually made its way into the United States Declaration of Independence, and both he and Rousseau were cited as major influences by America's founding fathers.

Today the social contract is under threat from myriad globalized corporate and quasi-governmental financial entities and nation-states challenged by their powers. Who does the contract exist between? And where does its legitimacy reside? Social Security and Medicare, two programs often referred to as parts of the American social contract, are in danger of being undone. Social contract adherents argue that both programs need to be improved and enlarged, not diminished.

Pateman's classic, *The sexual contract* (1988), highlights the gendered nature of the social contract and women's historical exclusion from declarations of the rights of the individual and the citizen. She cites social contracts of exclusion in the employment contract (e.g., equal wages), the marriage contract, the property contract, and the sexual contract (to women's bodies). Patriarchal rights are "continuously renewed and reaffirmed through actual contracts in everyday life" (Pateman, 1988, p. 114; Pilcher & Whelehan, 2004, pp. 150–154). White feminist analyses of the social contract are incomplete as to their exclusions and discrimination by race and ethnicity (Madison, 1991). Even critical analyses of the social and sexual contract provide the dominant white Eurocentric and ethnocentric perspectives, with little examination of the exclusionary contractual rights in slavery, the diaspora of Native Americans, and the treatment of immigrants as aliens, illegals, and the Other.

A prime example in old age policy is the 1935 origins of Social Security, which for decades initially precluded the coverage of domestic and agricultural workers, effectively denying retirement security to the majorities of African American and Mexican migrant workers working in the USA (Poole, 2006). At its founding, there were other exclusions of different elements of the working population, many of which were later gradually added over time (DeWitt, 2010).

See also: Generations, Intergenerational Contract, Justice, Medicare, Social Security

Further Reading

DeWitt, L. (2010). The decision to exclude agricultural and domestic workers from the 1935 Social Security Act. *Social Security Bulletin, 70*(4). Washington, DC: Office of Retirement and Disability Policy, Social Security Administration.

Geyman, J. (2006). *Shredding the social contract.* Monroe, ME: Common Courage Press.

Madison, A. (1991). The social contract and the African American elderly. *Urban League Review, 15*(2), 21.

Pateman, C. (1988). *The sexual contract.* Cambridge: Polity Press.

Pilcher, J. & Whelehan, I. (2004). *50 Key concepts in gender studies.* Thousand Oaks, CA: Sage.

Piven, F. F. & Cloward, R. A. (1997). *The breaking of the American social compact.* New York: The New Press.

Poole, M. (2006). *The segregated origins of Social Security: African Americans and the welfare state.* Charleston, NC: University of North Carolina Press.

Social Determinants of Health

Include an array of social conditions and experiences which impact (or determine) health (Wallace & Estes, 2019).

Practitioners in community clinics are particularly aware of how housing, access to food, transportation, and educational and employment opportunities affect the health and wellness of the communities they serve. On very practical levels it becomes clear how "medical compliance" (that is, taking medications or continuing treatments) relates to stable living conditions. This text explores the relationships between psychic wellness, trauma, and precarity (Estes & DiCarlo, 2019).

Social insurance programs are essential in addressing (and on a material level providing funding for) these social determinants. For example, the Medi-Medi program refers to people who are dual-eligible beneficiaries of Medicare and Medicaid. There are approximately 9.2 million people who are dually eligible for Medicare and Medicaid, either because they are younger than 65 years of age, disabled, and poor or because they are 65 or older and are poor or have exhausted their non-housing assets paying for health care. This population tends to be in poorer health and require more care compared to non-dual-eligible beneficiaries because of their complex needs. Medi-Medi program participants make up approximately 16 percent of Medicare enrollees and about 15 percent of Medicaid enrollees, accounting for 27 and 39 percent of

Medicare and Medicaid spending, respectively (Meyer, 2012).

See also: Climate Change, Food Security, Housing, Precarity, Resilience

Further Reading

Braveman, P. & Gottlieb, L. (2014). The social determinants of health: It's time to consider the causes of the causes. *Public Health Report, 129*(Suppl. 2), 19–31.

Estes, C. L. & DiCarlo, N. (2019). Precarity, USA: The State, Trauma and Ageing. In A. Grenier, C. Phillipson, & R. Settersten Jr. (Eds.), *Precarity and ageing: Understanding changing forms of risk and vulnerability in later life.* Bristol: Policy Press.

Institute of Medicine. (2016). A framework for educating health professionals to address the social determinants of health. Washington, DC: National Academies Press. Retrieved from www.nap.edu/catalog/21923/a-framework-for-educating-health-professionals-to-address-the-social-determinants-of-health.

Magnan, S. (2017). Social determinants of health 101 for health care: Five plus five. NAM Perspectives. Discussion Paper. Washington, DC: National Academy of Medicine.

Meyer, H. (2012). The coming experiments in integrating and coordinating care for "Dual Eligibles." *Health Affairs, 31*(6), 1151–1155.

Wallace, S. P. & Estes, C. L. (2019). Older people. In B. S. Levy (Ed.), *Social injustice and public health* (3rd edition). New York: Oxford University Press

World Health Organization. (2017). Social determinants of health. Retrieved from www.who.int/social_determinants/en/.

Social Insurance

A system created by nation-states to insure and insulate families and individuals against the loss of income or savings that may result from retirement, poor health, unemployment, disability, or the death of a breadwinner.

In contrast to means-tested public welfare, which generally offers only temporary assistance, social insurance is intended to provide long-term sustained benefits over a lifetime. It provides individuals and their families with a protective floor that insulates

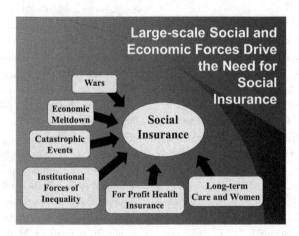

Figure S1 Social Insurance
Source: Estes (2005).

them from financial risk (Altman, 2005). Under US Social Security, social insurance benefits are based on employee-employer contributions, reducing dependency and constituting an "earned right" (Bethell, 2000) based on a beneficiary's and eligible worker's family members work history.

Social insurance participation is compulsory for all workers, ensuring the universal nature of these programs in the United States. Social Security and Medicare ensures that everyone is protected and that the programs remain financially stable. There is no distinction made or risk penalty paid between high-risk individuals and low-risk individuals, unlike in a private insurance market. Through universal participation, risk is sufficiently spread throughout the entire system to provide it with financial stability (Bethell, 2000). This is the strength of a universal risk pool, which covers the vast majority of working Americans and their families.

Underlying the concept of social insurance is the notion of the intergenerational compact. For a system like Social Security to function, every generation from young to middle age to elderly must participate and contribute. The young and healthy are expected to contribute, knowing that they will receive benefits once they are eligible to receive and need them. Princeton Dean and Provost J. Douglas Brown, a major architect of Social Security, describes the intergenerational compact as "The fundamental obligation of the government and citizens of one time and the government and citizens of another time to maintain a contributory social insurance system" (Brown, 1977, pp. 31–32).

In current policy debates social insurance is matched against the ownership society. While social insurance generalizes risk, in an ownership society risk is a responsibility delegated to the individual or family. In a fully privatized system, the few who are advantaged prosper, the many

disadvantaged suffer, and society loses the intergenerational and intra-group cohesion and solidarity provided by social insurance (Cornman, Kingson, & Butts, 2005). More than a practical solution to a complex problem of resources, social insurance also represents an attempt at actualizing justice and equity on a national scale. It also acknowledges that economic risk is not due solely to individual work history but also to large, even catastrophic, conditions and events for which the individual has little or no responsibility (see the above figure). Even weather events such as fires, floods, tornadoes, the 9/11 events, and human ravages of wars may trigger the need for social insurance.

The Great Depression and the intervening decades, including the Great Recession of 2007, illuminate the import of social insurance for a society, as late Social Security Commissioner Robert M. Ball stated (2000):

- It is universal: Everyone in paid employment is covered.
- It is an earned right: Eligibility for benefits at the benefit rate is based on an individual's past earnings and contributions.
- It is wage related: Benefits are calculated to maintain a relationship between an individual's standard of living in and out of work.
- It is contributory and self-financed: Contributions pay for benefits. This gives contributors a moral claim on future benefits.
- It is redistributive: To ensure minimum benefit adequacy, lower earners receive modestly higher benefits than would their wages alone.
- It is not means-tested, making it possible to add to private savings and assets.
- It is wage-indexed and portable, following worker from job to job.
- It is inflation-protected with automatic cost-of-living adjustments.
- It is compulsory, compelling all of us to contribute to our own future security.

There are distinctly disparate goals for social insurance compared to privatization.

Most significantly, social insurances, as a group, are public programs of the nation-state, for which all financial books are open, transparent, and accountable to all Americans. The principles of morality, fairness, and democracy may be invoked in the guardianship and trust for these vital programs (Rogne et al., 2009; Veghte, Shreur, & Bradley, 2017).

In light of the robotization of labor and potential jobless economies, there have been renewed proposals for universal income, supported by experts such as E. O. Wright (2010) and Robert Reich (2016). They advocate for a universal basic income (UBI), also known as a basic income guarantee (BIG) or a negative income tax. A program designed around this concept would provide a basic annual income to all citizens with which they could purchase food, housing, and other necessities. This would allow individuals to make choices in their best interests rather than out of desperation or precarity. UBI programs of varying types have been implemented throughout the world, although they tend to fit into four broad categories:

1. Growth Dividends: Temporary programs that distribute money annually as a way of collectivizing the benefits of economic growth. Payments are generally relatively small, cannot replace welfare, and are not meant to last in perpetuity. Such programs have been successfully implemented in Macau and Singapore.
2. Poverty Reduction: Cash-based assistance meant to supplement or replace existing welfare programs and put families and individuals above a specific poverty threshold. The Chinese Dibao program is the largest example, although other countries have experimented with cash assistance of various kinds.
3. Resource Dividends: Distributes dividends from resource extraction activities, contracts, and taxes to residents. This model has been adopted by various oil states in the Middle East, although citizenship and eligibility restrictions there make it hard to argue that the programs are truly universal. It has also been functioning in Alaska since 1982.
4. Unconditional Benefits: Long-term benefits provided to every citizen on a monthly or annual basis regardless of employment, income, or any other identifier. This has never been instituted on a national level although small pilot programs exist, most notably in Finland.

See also: Cross-national Comparisons, Medicaid, Medicare, Public Opinion Polling, Risk, Social Security

Further Reading

Altman, N. J. (2005). *The battle for social security: From FDR's vision to Bush's gamble.* New York: Wiley.

Ball, R. M. with Bethel, T. (Ed.). (2000). *Insuring the essentials: Bob Ball on Social Security.* NY: The Century Fund Press.

Bethell, T. N. (Ed.). (2000). *Insuring the essentials: Bob Ball on Social Security.* New York: The Century Foundation Press.

Berkowitz, E. D. (2003). *Robert Ball and the politics of Social Security.* Madison, WI: University of Wisconsin Press.

Brown, J. D. (1957). *The idea of Social Security. Original speech. Bureau of Old Age & Survivors Insurance, Committee on Economic Security. History Archives.* Baltimore, MD: Social Security Administration/SSA.

Brown, J. D. (1977). *Essays on social security.* Princeton, NJ: Industrial Relations Section, Princeton University.

Cornman, J. M., Kingson, E. R., & Butts, D. (2005). Should we be our neighbors' keeper? *Church & Society, 95*(3), 34–41.

Estes, C. L. (2005). Debate on the privatization of Social Security. Paper presented at the Annual Meeting of the

Gerontological Society of America, Washington, DC.

Estes, C. L. (2011). Crises and old age policy. In R. A. Settersten Jr. & J. L. Angel (Eds.), *Handbook of sociology of aging* (pp. 297–320). New York: Springer.

Reich, R. (2016). Why we'll need a universal basic income. Retrieved from http://robertreich.org/post/151111696805.

Rockeymoore, M. & Lui, M. (2013). Social security as a civil right. *Nationaljournal. Com.*

Rogne, L., Estes, C. L., Grossman, B., Hollister, B. A., & Solway, E. (Eds.). (2009). *Social insurance and social justice: Social Security, Medicare and the campaign against entitlements* (pp. 115–147). New York: Springer.

www. SSRN. *Social Security Pensions & Retirement Income Journal.*

Veghte, B. W., Shreur, E., & Bradley, A. (2017). *Report to the new leadership and the American people on social insurance and inequality.* Washington, DC: National Academy of Social Insurance.

Wright, E. O. (2006). Two redistributive proposals – universal basic income and stakeholder grants. *Focus, 24*(2), 5–7.

Wright, E. O. (2010). *Envisioning real utopias.* London: Verso.

Social Isolation/ Loneliness

Living without or away from others and a result of limited opportunities for connections.

The number of older adults living alone continues to rise in the United States. Elderly individuals who live alone frequently experience a high degree of social isolation and loneliness. Despite this, the desire to be self-sufficient in old age and the inherently individualistic nature of American culture creates immense social pressure for the elderly to live alone.

One solution used to counteract the loneliness experienced by the elderly are senior-specific housing options. These provide opportunities for socialization but usually limit the elderly from more general community engagement and almost completely eliminate intergenerational interaction. Portacolone and Halpern (2016) argue that the value of senior-specific housing is predicated largely on the incredible difficulty that seniors face living alone in conventional housing and the societal pressures that promote age segregation and self-sufficiency.

Solo living presents a variety of challenges for older individuals. They confront issues of memory loss, declining physical strength, and waning financial resources. As a result, many seniors living alone sustain themselves at an extremely delicate equilibrium point, living a fundamentally precarious life (Portacolone, 2013; Portacolone et al., 2018).

See also: Housing, Precarity

Further Reading

Klinenberg, E., Torres, S., & Portacolone, E. (2012). *Aging alone in America.* New York: Council on Contemporary Families Briefing Paper.

Portacolone, E. (2011). The myth of independence for older Americans living alone in the Bay Area of San Francisco: A critical reflection. *Ageing and Society, 31*(5), 803–828.

Portacolone, E. (2013). The notion of precariousness among older adults living alone in the US. *Journal of Aging Studies, 27*(2), 166–174.

Portacolone, E. & Halpern, J. (2016). "Move or suffer": Is age-segregation the new norm for older Americans living alone? *Journal of Applied Gerontology, 35*(8), 836–856.

Portacolone, E., Perissinotto, C., Yeh, J. C., & Greyson, S. R. (2018). "I feel trapped": The tension between personal factors of social isolation and the desire for social integration among older residents of a high-crime neighborhood. *The Gerontologist, 58*(1), 79–88.

Social Movements

Arise in relation to conflicting values, economic interests, politics, and cultural communities. Social movements require developing a case for a cause. Making the case for the cause often involves challenging the status quo and confronting the normalized view (doxa) that there is no alternative (TINA) to how "the system" works. The idea of resistance must engage the imagination of those who seek the movement and requires confronting power and challenging power elites, whose perspectives and interests are built into the framing, operating, and defending of the status quo.

Acquiescence to "the normal" is fundamental in reproducing how our systems work, such as health insurance. The dominant definition of "how things work" often limits our thinking about alternatives, thereby constraining consciousness and motivations to rebel or challenge the status quo in policy and other institutions such as the State and how the market works. Agency may be expressed and mobilized to defend or counter dominant ideologies, centers of power, and the institutions built up over time. Agency may be activated and engaged via many paths, events, processes, and structures, including media, even virally. As attested to in a vast literature, broad alliances of people may become aware, connected, and drawn in by shared concerns of people they know and to whom they may relate. Social movement literature tends to focus on one or two related areas: (1) the how and why of Social Movement Organizations (SMOs) as a field, including the mobilization process, structure, strategy, competing SMOs, allies, and coalitions, and (2) the effects and impact of social movements.

In aging policy as in social movement actions generally, we have learned that it is easier to say "NO" on the front end of a proposal to privatize rather than to change a policy or regulation once enacted. An example is former House Speaker Nancy Pelosi's resolve to "just say no" to Social Security privatization every time it came up during the G. W. Bush presidency. It succeeded for its time. Yet the GOP effectively used the same strategy for the Obama presidency, even nullifying the filling of a Supreme Court vacancy. The difficulty of unraveling legislation once implemented is seen in the tortured Repeal Obamacare (the ACA) movement, even under GOP control of Congress and White House, which appears endless.

Agency is exercised when activists step up and out on the vanguard of events, both accidentally and intentionally, catalyze awareness of the possibility of stopping the unacceptable by being present and yelling. A strategy to mobilize agency is overt in President Trump's and GOP pronouncements and leaks that begin with extreme, if not outrageous, unthinkable, even deplorable discourse, appointees, and rule changes, legal or questionable. Persistence, talking point consistency, and repetition reproduce the possibility of normalizing the most confrontative language and tear down of the moment. From twitter rants to White House negotiations, the bigger the reaction, disarray, disrespect, the better. Public trust and the legitimacy of officeholders have declined as opinion polls validate. Trump's strategy shows not only the political uses of outrage, but also the sly "wearing down" of the public with vulgarity and hate speech. The important point is the relationship between agency and social movements.

The sparks of resistance exist in social events, political discourse, and the imposition of actions of major threatening social consequence. The relationship between socially generated panic and resistance movements is underscored; the seeds are in the daily digest of social and mainstream media, fanned by political intrigue, fears of treachery, economic theft by the powerful, and the threatened demise of the democratic idea and sanctity of the franchise. Movements stimulate counter-movements, waxing and waning across geopolitical space and historical time. Cyberspace and nuclear threats abound while money literally talks, gerrymanders political districts, and suppresses votes.

Manuel Castells is in the forefront of power analyses of the network society that is restructuring both capitalism and the State; it has profoundly altered societies around the globe through the "relentless interaction, constituting technologically and culturally, instant communities of transformative practice." With it, the social production and sharing of meaning occurs through "digital networks of horizontal, unfettered communication" that fits the cultural social movements of the 1960s expressing autonomy and freedom and extending it across multiple arenas of social life (Castells, 2016, p. 6). The internet age has generated new forms of power that can be galvanized through counter-power that "is enacted by reprogramming networks around alternatives and values, and/or disrupting the dominant switches while switching networks of resistance and social change" (Castells, 2014, p. 9).

Of relevance to critical aging are major theoretical advances in feminist social reproduction, critical race and postcolonial work, queer theory, and discourses of identity and embodiment across multiple arenas. Social movements on climate change and the limits and exhaustion of nature (pro- and anti-science) call out the intergenerational stakes and dangers for all living things and the planet as a whole.

An innovative analytic approach to resistance movements is found in Randall Collins' treatise on Interaction Ritual Chains/

Case #1 Campaigns of Deficit Crisis Construction – Deconstruction Networks

- Fix the Debt rituals: Partisan Congressional "hostage taking" via promised budget cuts and think tank crisis framing and proposals
- Social Security, Disability, Medicare, Medicaid, Health Insurance (ACA)
- Congressional rituals: Inter–intra party stand-offs
- Government shutdowns, fiscal cliff rituals, running the fiscal clock out
- Demands for Social Security and Medicare trade-offs and "pay fors" to cut already earned Social Security or Medicare benefits, by attacking some other high value target (e.g., infrastructure or a fix for dreamers facing deportation)
- President-Congressional – Intra- and inter-party threats and deal-making

---

Case #2 Campaigns For and Against Social Security Privatization

- Social relations: ways in which people interact with one another
- Rituals: testimonies, hill briefings, rallies, networks of outrage, hope, and despair
- Social media (Google groups, gray literature), blogs, YouTube, Twitter, Facebook
- Coalitions: intersectional constituencies and alliances (LGBTQ, Race, Ethnicity, Gender, Ability, Immigrants, Age) and issues (e.g., inequality, global warming)
- Rituals of anniversaries: Eightieth birthday of Social Security and fiftieth birthday of Medicare, Medicaid, and Older Americans Act

IRCs (2004). In battles over entitlements, Social Security, Medicare, and Medicaid, the openings to and evolution of social movement resistance are shaped by IRCs, including the messaging and policy campaigns that promote consciousness raising and co-presence or sharing with others (virtually or in person). Social interactions stimulate emotional energy (EE) like an electrical charge, as interaction rituals may form around and through conversations in particular places, websites, internet cafés, demonstrations, list serves, blogs, and spaces such as www.entitledtoknow. org or www.socialsecurityworks.org. These become "occupied spaces" that create communities, overcome fear, and stimulate vital forms of "symbolic power" in what are networks of outrage and hope (Castells, 2014, pp. 10–11). Two cases highlight applied dimensions of interaction ritual chain and networking perspectives in aging policy (Estes, 2017).

The reader is invited to develop Social Movement Cases for Black Lives Matter/ BLM, Gender, and other issues of concern.

See also: Agency, Capitalism, Civil Rights Movement, Domination, Ideology, Interaction Ritual Chains, Intersectionality, Networks, Power, The State, TINA (There is No Alternative)

Further Reading

Amenta, E. (2001). *When movements matter: The Townsend plan and the rise of Social Security.* Princeton, NJ: Princeton University Press.

Brown, J. D. (1957). Original speech at Princeton University, Bureau of Old Age & Survivor's Insurance. Committee on Economic Security. SSA History Archives.

Brown, P., Zavestoski, S., McCormick, S., Mayer, B., Morello-Frosch, R., & Altman, R. (2004). Embodied health movements: New approaches to social movements in health. *Sociology of Health and Illness, 26*(1), 50–80.

Castells, M. (2014). *Networks of outrage and hope: Social movements in the internet age.* Malden, MA: Polity Press.

Castells, M. (2016). A sociology of power: My intellectual journey. *The Annual Review of Sociology, 42,* 1–19. www.annualreviews.org.

Collins, R. (2004). *Interaction ritual chains.* Princeton, NJ: Princeton University Press.

Della Porta, D. (2016). *Oxford handbook of social movements.* Oxford: Oxford University Press.

Estes, C. L. (1979). *The aging enterprise: A critical examination of social policies and services for the aged.* San Francisco, CA: Jossey-Bass.

Estes, C. L. (2011). Crises and old age policy. In R. A. Settersten Jr. & J. L. Angel (Eds.), *Handbook of sociology of aging* (pp. 297–320). New York: Springer.

Estes, C. L. (2017). Older US women's economic security, health and empowerment: The fight against opponents of social security, Medicare and Medicaid. In S. L. Dworkin, M. Gandhi, & P. Passano (Eds.), *Women's empowerment and global health* (pp. 232–250). Berkeley, CA: University of California Press.

Estes, C. L., with DiCarlo, N. B. (2016). Social movements and social knowledges: Gerontological theory in research, policy and practice. In V. L. Bengston & R. Settersten Jr. (Eds.), *Handbook of theories of aging* (pp. 87–106). New York: Springer.

McAdam, D., Tarrow, S., & Tilly, C. (2001). *Dynamics of contention.* Cambridge: Cambridge Press Syndicate of the University of Cambridge.

Mobilizing Ideas/Activists & Scholars debate. Retrieved from www.mobilizingideas. wordpress.com.

Ross, J. & Lowery, W. (2017). Turning away from street protests: BLM Washingtonpost, May 4.com/national.

Svihula, J. & Estes, C. L. (2008). Social security privatization: An ideologically structured movement. *Journal of Sociology and Social Welfare, 35*(1), 43–103.

West, D. (2013). *Social movements in global politics*. Cambridge, MA: Polity Press.

Zald, M. (2000). Ideologically structured action: An enlarged agenda for social movement research. *Mobilization, 5*(1), 1–16.

Social Security

Officially known as the Old-Age, Survivors, and Disability Insurance Program (OASDI). In the United States, Social Security provides benefits to citizens over the age of 65, the dependents and spouses of deceased qualifying individuals, and the disabled. All must meet qualifications of formal work, defined by the number of quarters in the labor market for which employees and employers contribute FICA payroll taxes. FICA stands for Federal Insurance Contributions Act under the Social Security Act.

To understand the program, it is instructional to revisit *The idea of Social Security* by Princeton economist and Social Security architect Dean J. D. Brown (1957):

> The depression of 1932 proved once for all, even to the most conservative elements of America, that the forces of economic competition and change were too inherent in our system of political economy to rely upon prevention alone for the protection of our citizens against distress caused by loss of earnings. At long last, they began to realize that the emphasis had to shift, so far as the wage earner was concerned, to a system of benefits payable as a matter of right, regardless of the degree to which the employer or the Government succeeded in eliminating the disastrous effects of the physical hazards of life.

Social Security is extremely important to America's older retirees and their families. Most – 61 percent – of retirees rely on it for one-half or more of their monthly income. Social Security is accurately dubbed America's most successful anti-poverty program. It lifts millions of elders out of poverty. Without Social Security benefits 40 percent of American Seniors would live below the poverty line. For persons of color, the low income, and those most disadvantaged women and children, it is a vital lifeline of daily existence.

It is important to distinguish Social Security from other public assistance programs. Social Security, as a form of Social Insurance, is universal, an earned right, wage related, contributory, self-financed, redistributive, means-untested, wage indexed, inflation protected, and compulsory.

The Vital Role of Social Security as Economic Stimulus and Economic Stabilizer

Social Security provides a large economic stimulus in the US economy. This benefits communities, states, and the nation as a whole as it exerts a stabilizing effect on the economy due to the steady level of guaranteed benefits from Social Security (Arno & Maroko, 2016).

Since Social Security benefits are spent and cycle through the economy there is a cumulative impact, which increases aggregate economic activity as recipients spend their benefits on goods and services.

> The businesses that receive these dollars use them to pay their owners and employees, purchase additional items to sell, and pay rent, taxes, and the other normal costs of doing business. Their suppliers in turn use the revenue they receive to pay their employees, suppliers, and so forth.

This is known as an economic multiplier effect. In 2014 Social Security contributed $1.6 trillion nationally to the US economy as benefits were spent and generated additional economic activity in every community and state in the nation (www.SocialSecuritySpotlight.org) . In this pivotal way Social Security operates as a large and continuous economic stimulus to the US economy. It is appropriately called an essential economic stabilizer, particularly in times of financial crises such as the Great Recession of 2007 (Arno, Maroko, & Estes, 2017).

See also: Inequality, Poverty, Social Insurance, Welfare State

Further Reading

Altman, N. & Kingson, E. (2011, Nov 11). Reflections on the importance of security – social security – on the 10th anniversary of 9/11. *HuffPost*, November 11. Retrieved from www.huffingtonpost.com/nancy-altman/reflections-on-the-import_b_957225.html.

Arno, P. S. & Maroko, A. R. (2016). *Economic impact of social security*. Washington, DC: National Committee to Preserve Social Security and Medicare Foundation.

Arno, P. S., Maroko, A. R., & Estes, C. L. (2017). Social Security: The nation's biggest (hidden) economic stimulus. Paper presented at the American Society on Aging (March). Chicago, IL: ASA.

Bethell, T. N. (Ed.). (2000). *Insuring the essentials: Bob Ball on Social Security*. New York: Century Foundation Press.

Brown, J. D. (1957). *The idea of Social Security. Original speech. Bureau of Old Age & Survivors Insurance, Committee on Economic Security. History Archives*. Baltimore, MD: Social Security Administration/SSA.

Galbraith, J. K. (2010). In defense of deficits. *The Nation*, March 4.

Herd, P., Favreault, M., Harrington Meyer, M., & Smeeding, T. M. (2018). A

targeted minimum benefit plan (MBP): A new proposal to reduce poverty among older Social Security recipients. *RSF: The Russell Sage Foundation Journal of the Social Sciences, 4*(2), 74–90.

Isaacs, K. P. & Choudhury, S. (2017). *The growing gap in life expectancy by income: Recent evidence and implications for the social security retirement age*. Washington, DC: Congressional Research Service. www.SocialSecuritySpotlight.org.

Social Security Disability Insurance (SSDI)

Provides benefits to disabled individuals based on Social Security qualification of either them or their family. A related program is Supplemental Security Income (SSI): a means-tested federal-state program that provides qualified beneficiaries income to those who are blind, disabled, or aging. The operations of these two programs are shown in Table S1:

See also: Americans with Disabilities Act (ADA), Disability, Supplemental Security Income (SSI)

Further Reading

Arnone, W. & Veghte, B. (2017). Disability protection IS part of Social Security. May 24. Washington, DC: National Academy of Social Insurance (NASI).

Bauer, B. (2017). SSI and SSDI: What are these benefits and how do they differ. National Council on Aging Blog.

Chart book: Social security disability insurance. (2016). Retrieved from www.cbpp.org/research/social-security/chart-book-social-security-disability-insurance.

Mitra, S., Palmer, M., Kim, H., Mont, D., & Groce, N. (2017). Extra costs of living with a disability: A systematized review and agenda for research. *Disability and Health Journal*. doi:10.1016/j.dhjo.2017.04.007.

Table S1

Factor	SSI (Means-tested)	SSDI (Social Security)
Eligibility based on	Age (65+) *or* blindness (any age) *or* disability (any age) *and* limited/no income and resources	Disability *and* sufficient work credits through own/family employment
When benefits begin	First full month after the date the claim was filed or, if later, the date found eligible for SSI	Sixth full month of disability; six-month period begins with the first full month after the date SSA decides the disability began
Average benefit (monthly)	$542 (as of January 2017)	$1,171 (as of January 2017)
Maximum benefit (monthly)	$735/$1,103 (single/married couple) in 2017 (based on income)	$2,687 in 2017 (based on work history)
Health insurance	Automatically qualifies for Medicaid upon receipt of SSI (in most states)	Automatically qualifies for Medicare after a 24-month waiting period from time benefits begin (no waiting period for persons with ALS)

(National Council on Aging Blog, April 6, 2017)

Socialism

A theory and practice of governing which allows communities to share in the means of production and distribution of resources. Social democracies feature social and economic systems which generally aim to eliminate poverty and provide universal coverage for services like healthcare and education. Right-wing framings of socialism disparage these systems as dangerous to the free market and to economic expansion through unfettered capitalist competition.

The most popular programs were lambasted as "socialism" when introduced, and perhaps they warrant the title – but they are also wildly popular. The right wing's complete rejection of socialist principles ignores the advantages of social insurance and social justice features to most citizens and the inequalities created by free market systems. The word "Socialism" is deployed as an invective by some conservatives in order to advance the certain political death of an idea, policy, or practice that is proposed such as Medicare for All (Waitzkin & Working Group, 2018).

Cross-national comparisons of the Scandinavian Democratic Socialist countries – Sweden, Norway, and Denmark – tout decreases in measures of inequality and the strength of social insurance programs and stronger wage equality. In the United States, Democratic Socialists of America gained traction and members following the Trump election. One of their members, Alexandria Ocasio-Cortez (D.-NY), became the youngest woman to be elected to Congress, demonstrating an effective progressive campaign.

Bornat and colleagues (1985) have developed a socialist *Manifesto for Old Age* to address many facets of ageism, and the structurally induced impoverishment and lack of care provisions for elders and their caregivers and the serious inequities by race, ethnicity, class, gender, and sexualities. Emancipatory gerontology can continue in the tradition of this clarion call, for redressing inequalities, establishing access and opportunity regardless of means, and moving from austerity toward generosity.

See also: Capitalism, Collective, Democracy, Fascism, Social Insurance

Further Reading

Albo, G. & Panitch, L. (2018). *Rethinking democracy: Socialist register (2018)*. New York: Monthly Review Press.

Bornat, J., Phillipson, C., & Ward, S. (1985). *A manifesto for old age*. London: Pluto Press.

Eagleton, T. (2011). *Why Marx was right*. New Haven, CT, and London: Yale University Press.

Estes, C. L. (1982). Ageing & society. Retrospective on C. Phillipson, *Capitalism and the construction of old age*.

Phillipson, C. (1982). *Capitalism and the construction of old age*. London: Macmillan.

Waitzkin, H. & Working Group. (2018). *Heath care under the knife: Moving beyond capitalism for our health*. New York: Monthly Review Press.

Sociology

A discipline composed of many approaches and theoretical frameworks oriented to studies of human relationships, culture, identity, consciousness, institutions, and social structures in society. It recognized that the social world encompasses multiple levels of systemic processes, each with its own force and each involving the dynamics of power and knowledge construction.

Mills (1959) criticized the "grand theory" and "abstracted empiricism" of mainstream academic sociology. The sociological imagination embodies "the idea that the individual can understand his own experience and gauge his own fate only by locating himself within his period, that he can know his own chances in life only by becoming aware of those of all individuals in his circumstances" (p. 5). The task and promise is "to grasp history and biography and the relations between the two within society . . . as a form of self-consciousness" (p. 7). A central point is the linkage between personal troubles and social issues, the individual and the structural.

Burawoy (2005, p. 4) identifies four types of sociological work. He writes:

> [W]e discover antagonistic interdependence among four types of knowledge: professional, critical, policy, and public. In the best of all worlds the flourishing of each type of sociology is a condition for the flourishing of all, but they can just as easily assume pathological forms or become victims of exclusion and subordination. This field of power beckons us to explore the relations among the four types of sociology as they vary historically and nationally, and as they provide the template for divergent individual careers. Finally, comparing disciplines points to the umbilical cord that connects sociology to the world of publics, underlining sociology's particular investment in the defense of civil society, itself beleaguered by the encroachment of markets and states.

In critical aging policy, Estes' writing incorporates all four types of sociology (Estes, 2008). In the genre of professional sociology, she has studied (1) ideological constructs and frames such as "Social Security as the problem," the Social Security system as "bankrupt;" and elders as "greedy geezers," and (2) the agents of power and conflict (power elites, economic dominants, and institutional structures, including the State) behind winning and losing ideas, policies, and peoples. As a policy sociologist, she examines how Social Security, Medicare, and long-term care policy "work" and the outcomes of policy options for diverse and vulnerable individuals and groups. As a critical sociologist, she attempts to demystify the systems of domination that produce injustice and inequality in aging through policy. As a public sociologist, she brings critical perspectives into public dialogue and action, working to subvert the disempowerment of women and other disadvantaged and vulnerable elders through State policy. At this level of social practice in action (praxis), scholars think, write, and work as part of a larger virtual collective of organic intellectuals, those who investigate, speak out, and collaborate with (and on behalf of) oppressed communities (Gramsci, 1971).

See also: Gerontological Imagination, Public Sociology, The State

Further Reading

Burawoy, M. (2005). For public sociology. *American Sociological Review, 70*(1), 4–28.

Estes, C. (2008). A first generation critic comes of age: Reflections of a critical gerontologist. *Journal of Aging Studies, 22*(2), 120–131.

Gramsci, A. (1971). *Selections from the prison notebooks of Antonio Gramsci.* London: Lawrence & Wishart.

Mills, C. W. (1959). *The sociological imagination.* Oxford: Oxford University Press.

Solidarity

Grounded in unity or mutuality. It means standing with people, resisting dominant forces that seek to isolate and weaken. Unity and collaboration are crucial for social movements to sustain themselves. Shows of solidarity in boycotting, marching, and lending economic support are ways in which people have pushed for fair labor, housing, and aging rights. Solidarity reminds us of Emile Durkheim's insight concerning the collective conscience and the function of religion and ritual practices, in binding people to society and consensus being a mechanism of legitimacy. For social institutions, interaction ritual chains help integrate people and promote social integration, institutionalization, and interaction order (Goffman, 1983; Collins, 2004).

Solidarity can include the practice of allyship, where those with privilege align empathy and devote resources to marginalized people. An example is provided by Maggie Kuhn, who chained herself to the White House fence in 1980 demonstrating solidarity with black people who were grossly under-represented at the first White House Conference on Aging.

However sustainable, anti-oppressive solidarity among heterogeneous populations must recognize that unity does not mean sameness. Recognizing difference in power and privilege is key to allyship. Allies can support each other in their practice by demonstrating patience and kindness, especially as they explore and challenge discrepancies between the intent and impact of their activism.

See also: Coalitions, Collective Impact, Family, Kinship, Resistance

Further Reading

Angel, R. J. & Angel, J. L. (2017). *Family, intergenerational solidarity, and post-traditional society.* New York: Routledge.

Baars, J., Dannefer, D., Phillipson, C., & Walker, A. (Eds.). (2006). *Aging, globalization and inequality: The new critical gerontology.* New York: Routledge.

Collins, R. (2004). *Interaction ritual chains.* Princeton, NJ: Princeton University Press.

Durkheim, E. (2010). From mechanical to organic solidarity. In *Sociology: Introductory readings* (pp. 25–29). Originally published in Durkehim, E. (1893/1964). *The division of labor in society.* New York: The Free Press.

Goffman, E. (1983). The interaction order: American Sociological Association, 1982 presidential address. *American Sociological Review, 48*(1), 1–17.

Smith, J., Chatfield, C., & Pagnucco, R. (1997). *Transnational social movements and global politics: Solidarity beyond the state.* Syracuse, NY: Syracuse University Press.

Spheres (Public/Private, Subaltern, Security)

Public vs. Private

Public vs. private describes a dichotomy of representation, understanding, and duty. "Lives" are often discussed in these dialectics, suggesting a discrepancy between public and private life. People venture out into a world where their identities and personalities are analyzed through how they perform various roles (of parents, leaders, citizens, celebrities, and villains). This split becomes more unstable with more abject or restrictive definitions of identity. This was at the heart of the debate over whether a woman like Hillary Clinton could be just the right balance of strong and vulnerable if she could or would give access to a private self – and furthermore if her refusal to give said "access" made her cold and withholding or professional and disciplined. This calls out a related critical literature on the family, patriarchy, and the public versus private (D'Entreves & Vogel, 2000; Landes, 1998). Important concepts are male/female roles, responsibilities, privilege, ideologies, power, cumulative advantage and disadvantage across the life course, by race, ethnicity, gender, class, ability, and age.

Subaltern Sphere

Subaltern sphere describes a population, collective, or space outside of hegemonic discourse and control. Critical gerontology as fields of knowledge, critical practice, and radical activism are examples of work that are pushing the boundaries of our taken-for-granted normalizing and perpetuation of what is dysfunctional and runs counter to the Social in the public interest. Currently there is the danger of domination of our disciplines and advancement when money and power speak louder than values (Burawoy, 2005).

Spheres of Security

Chernof (2011) uses spheres of security as a framing device for considering Long-term Care and Supportive Services (LTSS) in the USA. The spheres of (1) income security, (2) health security, and (3) functional security are the primary foci of policy-makers on issues of age and aging. Chernof (2011) points to significant gains in the areas of income security and health security while acknowledging a general lack of progress on the issue of functional security. Social Security provides a base level of income security to older Americans while Medicare and Medicaid provide resources in the area of health security. Of notable concern, access to programs addressing functional security are significantly lacking, although the underfunded Older Americans Act and limited provisions in the ACA encourage the development of spotty initial steps toward the sphere of functional security.

See also: Critical Theory, Family, LTSS, Public Sociology, Resistance, The Social, Zones

Further Reading

Burawoy, M. (2005). For public sociology. *American Sociological Review, 70*(1), 4–28.

Chernof, B. (2011). The three spheres of aging in America: The Affordable Care Act takes on long-term-care reform for the 21st century. *Generations, 35*(1), 45–49.

D'Entreves, M. & Vogel, U. (Eds.). (2000). *Public and private: Legal, political, and philosophical perspectives.* London: Routledge.

Landes, J. (Ed.). (1998). *Feminism, the public and the private.* Oxford: Oxford University Press.

Spirits of Capitalism

The ideological currents and beliefs which undergird our capitalist systems. These change over time, responding to industrial, technological, and medical advances.

The *first spirit of capitalism*, as proposed by Weber, is that salvation is earned through hard work. What is known as the Protestant Work Ethic is grounded in the belief of a good afterlife that is ensured by sacrificing pleasure and avoiding sin (especially sloth and gluttony). Industrialization ushered in a *second spirit of capitalism*, characterized by an accumulation of material wealth as a manifestation of hard work.

Biomedical research and revolutions in genetic manipulation have already or may soon usher in a *third spirit of capitalism*, where increasingly capital goes to warding off death and disease. It becomes less about working hard to deserve a heaven, and more about working hard to maintain safety/security organized around preventing death or the loss of individual agency. This is the push in synthetic biology around engineering genetic material and around advancing anti-aging medicine, yet there is also the pull of disease as a market for profit.

See also: Agency, Anti-aging, Capitalism, Ideology, The Market, Zeitgeist

Further Reading

Akerlof, G. A. & Shiller, R. J. (2010). *Animal spirits: How human psychology drives the economy, and why it matters for global capitalism*. Princeton, NJ: Princeton University Press.

Boltanski, L. & Chiapello, E. (2005). The new spirit of capitalism. *International Journal of Politics, Culture, and Society, 18*(3), 161–188.

Du Gay, P. & Morgan, G. (Eds.). (2014). *New spirits of capitalism? Crises, justifications, and dynamics*. Oxford: Oxford University Press.

Weber, M. (1904/1905/1930). *The Protestant ethic and the spirit of capitalism*. New York: Scribner.

Standpoint Theories (ST)

Challenge the scientific knowledge production of those who experience, know, hear, speak, and construct theory, methodologies, analyses, and interpretations of the dominant white male standpoint in their respective disciplines. ST accords validity and scientific legitimacy to the epistemological advantage of using one's own standpoint as women, blacks, ethnics, Jews, or other previously subjugated unheard voices as writers and thinkers.

The founding principles of standpoint theory are that material life, not only structures, sets limits on our understandings of social relations. The knowledge available to ruling elites is partial, while the social relations of which we are a part and perhaps privileged to possess set limits on what we know: situated knowledge. ST calls for a more embodied and reflexive knowledge.

Standpoint theory is a major contribution of feminist critical theory linking the production of knowledge and the practices of power. Proponents of ST challenge the neutrality of expert knowledge about women that objectifies, pathologizes, and subjugates women because it is innocent of the epistemological understanding of women's lived experiences, meaning, and struggles, day and night. Theorists have variously advanced ST as a philosophy of science, and epistemology, a methodology, and a political strategy. ST is credited with producing oppositional knowledge and shared consciousness. A radical notion of ST is that oppressive conditions are a valued source of critical insight. Pioneering this work have been feminist scholars Nancy Hartsock, Donna Haraway, Dorothy Smith, and Patricia Hill Collins.

ST is also a central element in the frameworks of race and ethnicity studies. The richness of intersectionality theory and knowledge is indebted to advances of and within ST. W. E. B. Dubois' "double consciousness," Collins' black feminist consciousness (1986), and the "bifurcated consciousness" of women in sociology are all examples of this. Collins' classic work in particular speaks to African American women's knowing as "outsider within" power relations and the perspective of "stranger status" in understanding self, family, and society through low paid domestic help.

In gerontology, Gray Panthers (GP) co-founder Maggie Kuhn criticized the objectification and alienation by scholars studying the elderly methods and theories trivialized of what and who older persons are and what they experience. Maggie and Gray Panthers used critical theory to lambast gerontologists for their microscopic gaze, ageism, distancing methods, depersonalization, stereotyping, and ignorance of the condition of old age in America.

See also: Class, Ethnicity, Feminist/Feminism, Intersectionality, Jeopardy, Race

Further Reading

Collins, P. (1986). Learning from the outsider within: The sociological significance of black feminist thought. *Social Problems*, *33*(6), S32.

Estes, C. & Portacolone, E. (2009). Maggie Kuhn: Social theorist of radical gerontology. *International Journal of Sociology and Social Policy*, *29*(1/2), 15–26.

Harding, S. G. (2004). *The feminist standpoint theory reader: Intellectual and political controversies*. Hove, Sussex: Psychology Press.

The State

Comprised of multiple institutional sectors, structures, and sites (legislative, executive, judicial, military, educational) and individual organizational agencies. The State has power to: (1) allocate and distribute scarce resources to ensure the survival and growth of the economy; (2) mediate between the different needs and demands across different social groups; and (3) ameliorate social conditions that could threaten the existing order and/or disturb the power of entrenched vested interests. Offe and Ronge (1982) emphasize the State's interest in promoting private accumulation of wealth and capital reinvestment due to State dependency on capital's support for or resistance to taxation. In democracies, the will of the electorate is challenged by this reality and the need to mobilize resources to counter it.

A major challenge to nation-states is their accountability for two roles: the success of the economy and the defense of their homeland and people. O'Connor (1973) contends that the United States has contradictory functions that spend the State into fiscal crisis: advancing the subsidies to and profits of capital, while addressing the needs of a growing citizenry displaced by global capitalism. Debate and tensions center on the role of the State, as actors actively participate in these struggles, asserting their relative power and interests.

As Manuel Castells (2015, p. 8) says,

> [T]he network[s] of power constructed around the state and the political system . . . play a fundamental role in the overall networking of power. . . . The stable operation of the system and the reproduction of power relationships in every network, ultimately depend on the coordinating and regulatory functions of the state . . . it is via the state that different forms of exercising power in distinct social spheres relate to the monopoly of violence as the capacity to enforce power in the last resort. So, while communication networks process the construction of meaning on which power relies, the state constitutes the default network for the proper functioning of all other power networks.

In the political economy of aging (Estes & Associates, 2001), theories of the State reside within the conflict paradigm (see the works of Max Weber, Karl Marx, Antonio Gramsci, and Randall Collins), which posits that the social order is held together by the dominance of certain groups, interests, and forces over others. Jill Quadagno (1999) describes the United States' shift to a "capital investment state" in which public benefits are restructured to coincide to provide advantage to the private for-profit sector. State policy actions and outcomes reflect who wins and who loses among the forces of dominance and resistance.

Feminist theorists have shown that the State is an actor in the sexual politics of male dominance through law, policy, and practice (MacKinnon, 1989), via "state masculinism" (Brown, 1995) imposed through controls over reproduction, through the regulation of pornography, through women's greater dependence on the State for survival, and through relations of distribution (Acker, 1988, 1992). Connell (1987) argues that the State does more than regulate institutions and relations like marriage and motherhood; it manages them. The State actually constitutes "the social categories of the gender order" as "patriarchy is both constructed and contested through the state." This is occurring through relentless attacks on women's health rights via highly charged legislative abortion restrictions imposed in many American states, and constitutional and existential challenges to the ACA. President Trump's Cabinet, Supreme Court, and federal judiciary picks are the whitest and most socially conservative male dominated in decades, underscoring the power of the State and its multiple judiciary and administrative apparatuses to restore and reinforce patriarchal rule of law consistent with neoconservative and anti-woman ideologies.

State power over women intersects with old age policy. First, women are more dependent than men upon the nation-state all across the life course; thus, women of all ages are more vulnerable than men to swings in State policy driven by larger political, economic, and global forces. Second, women's dependency on the State increases with age, motherhood, divorce, widowhood, and living alone, while demands for women's unpaid labor in caregiving accelerate, requiring many to curtail or quit paid work. This leads to further impoverishment (Harrington-Meyer & Herd, 2007). Third, U.S. policy produces a "gendered distribution of old age income" (Harrington-Meyer, 1990, 551; Estes, Biggs, & Phillipson, 2003/2009; Estes, O'Neill, & Hartmann, 2012).

Black feminist analyses validate that the distinctly unequal gendered and raced distribution of old age income that is enforced through a two tiered State policy: (1) one that is means-tested, welfare based, and variable by state of residence that serves low-income women and families, and high percentages of racial minorities (e.g., SSI and TANF); and (2) another (e.g., Social Security) that is for women who are married and/or work in covered employment (but who generally earn less than men). As a consequence, older women, comprising three-quarters of the elderly poor, receive a smaller dollar amount from every retirement income source than older men, with women of color being the worst off (Estes, O'Neill, & Hartmann, 2012).

Sociologists of race and ethnicity have shown that institutions and the organization of the State and its laws and sanctions reflect central and historical racial formation and exclusion from the society. The dynamics of civil society and the social institutions are examined with a primary focus on the role of the State in constructing and extending racial formations and enforcing racial exclusion (Goldberg, 2002).

Omi and Winant (2015) portray the State as central in the allocation of power along racial lines and in shaping the racial dynamics of civil society. They emphasize the shift in racial politics from racial domination to racial hegemony culminating in the current "color blind racial hegemony," acting as if there is no racism in society so no need for affirmative actions. Omi and Winant illuminate the State's role in racial projects, consisting of political socialization, race consciousness, racial identity-making, and group boundary formation. Feagin's (2006, pp. 6–8) systemic racism perspective underscores white-on-black oppression, centuries old, as an "independent social reality" in the operating structures and counter-forces; the relationships between them; and that permit (or not) patterns of social change and lack thereof. The word "systemic" denotes an "organized societal whole with many interconnected elements." Critical race theory seeks to expose the links between capitalism and systemic racism (Elias & Feagin, 2016).

President Trump's first senior counselor and chief strategist, Steve Bannon, announced in 2017 the President's intention to "deconstruct the state administrative apparatus." Under the mantra of unfettered markets, Trump's billionaire Cabinet members were appointed with the designated purpose of deconstructing, defunding, and neutering the regulatory mission, capacity, and priorities of major State administrative agencies they lead such as the EPA, FCC, FAA. This is similar to the 1980s Reagan Administration playbook during which high-level officials bashed and trashed the governing State, civil service, public services, and even security intelligence services. Such attacks have been part of vigorous (and successful) efforts to cut taxes for corporations and the wealthy and to transfer massive State program subsidies to private hands, while individualizing personal responsibility. Trump's overt and brazen accusations from the top appear to be designed to delegitimize independent sources of State authority and suppress vital public data. Withering partisan attacks on the Congressional Budget Office, the FBI, and the media have sharpened vitriol and distrust.

Louis Althusser, French critical scholar, described the State's multiple means, or apparatuses through which to advance support of a nation-state and society's economic system and conditions of production. Althusser's (2014) list of institutions that comprise the Ideological State Apparatus (ISA) includes: the religious ISA (the system of the different churches); the educational ISA (the system of the different public and private 'schools'); the family ISA (the systems of marital, gender, and sexual regulation and policy); the legal ISA (laws and courts); the political ISA (the political system, including the different parties); the labor/trade-union ISA; the communications ISA (press, radio, television, internet, and FCC); and the cultural ISA (literature, the arts, sport, religious). In addition, there is the State apparatus which functions "by violence": the police, armies, prisons, and cyberwars.

Althusser's critical analyses appear to be applicable to considerations of old age and aging policy. Key elements of the ideological and administrative state apparatus have been intentionally decentered, unhinged, and rendered dysfunctional by its leaders – and with no certainty regarding the unintended consequences that may be devilish to life and living on the planet (to wit the anti-science denials of climate science warnings).

According to Howard Zinn (2007, p. 11),

America's future is linked to how we understand our past. . . . I hope to awaken a great consciousness of racial injustice, sexual bias, class inequality and national hubris. I also want to bring into the light the unreported resistance of people against the power of the Establishment: the refusal of the indigenous to simply disappear: the rebellion of black people in the antislavery movement and in the more recent movement against racial segregation; the strikes carried out by working people all through American history.

See also: Ideology, Patriarchy, Political Economy, Power, Propaganda, Race/Racism, Welfare State

Further Reading

Acker, J. (1988). Class, gender, and the relations of distribution. *Signs*, *13*(3), 473–493.

Acker, J. (1992). Gendered institutions – From sex roles to gendered institutions. *Contemporary Sociology*, *21*, 565–569.

Althusser, L. (2014). *On the reproduction of capitalism*. London: Verso.

Brown, W. (1995). *States of injury*. Princeton, NJ: Princeton University Press.

Bourdieu, P. (2001). *Masculine domination*. Stanford, CA: Stanford University Press.

Castells, M. (2015). *Networks of outrage and hope: Social movements in the internet age* (2nd edition). Malden, MA: Polity Press.

Connell, R. (1987). *Gender and power*. Cambridge, MA: Polity Press.

Elias, S. & Feagin, J. R. (2016). *Racial theories in social science*. New York: Taylor and Francis.

L. Estes & Associates, (2001) (See Estes' Selected Works, Appendix 4 p. 395.)

Estes, C. L. (2006). Critical feminist perspectives, aging and social policy. In J. Baars, D. Dannefer, C. Phillipson, & A. Walker (Eds.), *Aging, globalization, and inequality: The new critical gerontology* (pp. 81–102). Amityville, NY: Baywood Publishing.

Estes, C. L., Biggs, S., & Phillipson, C. (2003). *Social theory, social policy and ageing: A critical introduction*. Maidenhead, Berks: McGraw Hill Education.

Estes, C. L., O'Neill, T., & Hartmann, H. (2012). *Breaking the Social Security glass ceiling: A proposal to modernize women's benefits*. IWPR Report #D502. Washington, DC: Institute for Women's Policy Research, National Committee to Preserve Social Security and Medicare Foundation, and the NOW Foundation.

Feagin, J. R. (2006). *Systemic racism: a theory of oppression*. New York, NY: Routledge.

Goldberg, D. T. (2002). *The racial state*. Malden, MA: Blackwell.

Harrington Meyer, M. (1990). Family status and poverty among older women: The gendered distribution of retirement income in the United States. *Social Problems*, *37*(4), 551–563.

Harrington Meyer, M. & Herd, P. (2007). *Market friendly or family friendly? The state and gender inequality in old age*. New York: Russell Sage Foundation.

MacKinnon, C. A. (1989). *Toward a feminist theory of the state*. Cambridge, MA: Harvard University Press.

O'Connor, J. (1973). *The fiscal crisis of the state*. New York: St. Martin's Press.

Offe. C. & Ronge, V. (1982). Theses on the theory of the state. In A. Giddens & D. Held (Eds.) *Classes, power, and conflict*. (pp. 249–256). Berkeley: Univ. of California Press. Also published in *New German Critique*, (6), 137–147.

Omi, M. & Winant, H. (2015). *Racial formation in the United States*. New York: Routledge.

Quadagno, J. (1999). Creating a capital investment welfare state: the new American exceptionalism, *American Sociological Review*, 64 (1): 1–11.

Zinn, H. (2007). *A power governments cannot suppress*. San Francisco, CA: City Light Books.

State Health Insurance Assistance Programs (SHIPs)

Independent state programs that help seniors navigate Medicare, Medigap, Medicare Advantage, and Medicaid.

US federal health systems and plans can be complicated and many people have trouble assessing their eligibility and options. To help alleviate this problem every state has an assistance program that is free for all seniors to utilize and is funded by the federal government.

In California the program is called HICAP, the Medicare Health Insurance Counseling and Advocacy Program, which provides beneficiaries with unbiased individual assistance and advocacy related to their Medicare benefits as well as community education opportunities. Federally funded and administered through states and territories, SHIP programs run through the US Administration on Community Living (ACL).

Approximately 10,000 Americans become eligible for Medicare each day, increasing the need and demand for SHIP assistance. Over the past two years, more than 7 million people with Medicare received help from SHIPs. Understanding the A, B, C, and D of Medicare is an overwhelming, isolating experience for older adults and people with disabilities. SHIPs provide local, in-depth insurance counseling to Medicare beneficiaries and families, including coverage options, fraud and abuse issues, billing problems, appeal rights, and enrollment in low-income protection programs.

Because of the labor-intensive, in-person nature of SHIP work and high demand, volunteers assist paid staff. SHIP assistance goes to Medicare Advantage and Part D prescription drug plans, local and state agencies, the Centers for Medicare and Medicaid Services, the Social Security Administration, and members of Congress and their staffs.

Making informed decisions among an average of 20+ prescription drug plans and 19 Medicare Advantage plans, and Medigap supplemental insurance policies, saves money and improves access to quality care, particularly given the significant differences in premiums, cost sharing, provider networks, and coverage rules at stake.

See also: Administration for Community Living (ACL), Medicaid, Medicare

Further Reading

www.medicare.gov/Contacts/#resources/ships.

States' Rights

Concerns the authority and jurisdiction of each state and their power to set and determine elements of their own governance. The federal government and its three branches each have roles defined by the American Constitution, with roles and powers not defined by the Constitution left to state governments. The result of this somewhat vague delegation of powers to the states is a constant conflict of authority between state governments and federal authorities on matters of regulation, programmatic control, and general policy.

States' Rights are "the principle that the states should oppose the increasing authority of the national government . . . [It was] most popular . . . before the Civil War" (Ginsberg et al., 2017, pp. 87–88) and by southern states in defending slavery and contesting racial desegregation and voting rights.

States' Rights versus the US Constitution are vigorously tested in state and federal court systems, with the US Supreme Court ultimately ruling on the constitutionality of cases

The Reagan era brought with it a new conservative commitment, laced in rhetoric and ideology, to reducing the role of the federal government in the name of conservative ideals. This did not stem the growth of government size, which continued to increase under Reagan (Bivens, 2016). It did however succeed in crippling a number of federal programs and shifted a huge amount of power on social policy back to state governments. This devolution of power to the states is the core tenet of New Federalism that continues to stoke struggles over States' Rights to this day.

Medicaid is perhaps the most instructive program exhibiting the dynamics of the relationship between the federal government and the states. The program is funded in combination by the federal government and state governments, and participation, on the part of the states, is theoretically voluntary. Eligibility and other aspects of the program are determined by the states with the federal government covering 55 to 100 percent of the cost of the program for each state. Under the ACA Medicaid coverage and funding was expanded by the federal government with heavy opposition from Republican governors. After the multifaceted Supreme Court decision in *NFIB v. Sebelius* Republican governors were able to reject the Medicaid expansion for their individual states while continuing to receive pre-ACA Medicaid funding as the federal government was prevented from halting all Medicaid assistance as leverage to force a state to accept the expansion. This illustrates an important point. Though the federal government has broad authority to provide funding for a wide range of state-run programs, it can rarely mandate how states actually utilize that funding. In this way, the interaction between the federal government and states can act as a choke-point for social programs. Regardless of federal will to act on some particular issue, policy-makers at the state level can reject or dilute executive and Congressional efforts. This has proved to be an effective strategy for Republican-run states to sabotage environmental legislation, social programs in aging, and immigration reform.

New Federalism

New Federalism is an effort toward the devolution of responsibility and power from the federal government to state governments on matters of social policy. The changes entailed in this ideology have broad, harmful effects on social programs and the individuals who utilize them, and are intended to affect a particular political agenda. From a critical perspective, Estes (1983, pp. 255–260) points out how reductions in the federal role in domestic social policy serve important political and economic functions, six of which are outlined below. In the Nixon and Reagan presidential eras, there was strong policy commitment to shifting responsibility and monies from the federal, to state, local governments, and – wherever possible – to increasing individual responsibility for addressing the problems and issues that were being addressed. Over time, similar related policy initiatives have been advanced under a plethora of other names, such as block grants, revenue sharing, devolution, decentralization, privatization, cost containment, and deficit reduction.

First, decentralized and highly discretionary non-national programs tend to neutralize and weaken political mobilization of the powerless by shifting the focal point for social action from a more easily mobilized national effort to the hundreds and thousands of state and local jurisdictions.

Second, the decentralization in policies provides a mechanism for the devolution of responsibility for policy-making from government (the public sector) to the private sector through interest group influence (Lowi, 1971). Block grants to states, a feature of New Federalism, provide extremely broad powers to the states in language that may have many interpretations, thus opening up major opportunities for political actors, powerful interests, and state and local administrators to make policy in the implementation process.

Third, the decentralization of social programs under current new federalism policies places human service demands on the most fiscally vulnerable levels of government decision-making. Unlike the federal government, state and local governments have to balance their budgets annually. No deficit spending is permitted, which makes them subject to extreme budget restraints due to federal funding cuts and state tax policy. Decisions about services for the poor are located precisely where pressures to limit public spending on social programs are greatest and necessarily the most conservative.

Fourth, decentralization supplants national policy goals and commitments with the more variable state and local policy choices, particularly with regard to programs for the poor of all ages. There is little assurance of consistency, uniformity, or equity of policy for powerless groups across different states.

Fifth, as policy choices about human service cutbacks are increasingly made at the state and local levels, cutbacks and their impact on the poor and aged are extremely difficult to document. The reduction of trustworthy, available state-level data, in the name of eliminating red tape, serves only to obfuscate changes in services and programs.

Sixth, decentralization assures that the dominant economic and political interests will not be challenged when policies are variably created and inconsistently implemented across divergent state and local entities. Both the increasing number of policy decisions made by administering agencies and the heightened intensity of interest group and private interest politics tend to minimize even the influence of political leaders on public expenditures and priorities.

The entire system of state devolution through block grants is presupposed on the notion that lawmakers will respond to increasing needs with increased funding. This has never been the case. Of the 13 major housing, health, and social services block grant programs only two have received increased funding since 2000 to reflect rising need. In fact, the average funding change across the 13 programs has been a 27 percent reduction since 2000 (Shapiro et al., 2016). Federal lawmakers feel little pressure to maintain funding to programs once they

have been converted to block grants, and the ability to respond to fluctuations in needs is largely eliminated by this process.

Supreme Court Justice Louis Brandeis is known for popularizing the saying that states should serve as "laboratories of democracy." The divergent approaches of states with regard to a wide variety of issues can be instructive in examining the effects that different policy has on citizens (Ginsberg et al., 2017).

One noteworthy recent laboratory experiment comes from Kansas. In 2012 Kansas Governor Sam Brownback cut Kansas' income tax from 6 to 4.5 percent and instituted a tax exemption for operators of LLCs at the urging of Heritage Foundation economists and former Reagan Administration advisors Stephen Moore and Arthur Laffer. Brownback believed, as did Laffer and Moore, that the tax cuts would spur economic growth and pave the way for eventually eliminating the income tax entirely in Kansas (Mazerov, 2016).

Regardless of the lofty intentions behind Brownback's plan, the effect has been fiscal disaster. The significant economic growth envisioned by Moore and Laffer failed to materialize and the state suffered successive budget crises. Kansas' GDP has lagged significantly behind the national average through 2016 and employment gains were modest compared to the United States as a whole (Mazerov, 2016). Kansas had its bond rating downgraded twice since 2013 as it remained in a perpetual state of budget crisis. Virtually every social program has suffered in Kansas. Higher education, health and aging services, and Medicaid have all seen tens of millions of dollars' worth of cuts in the effort to compensate for reduced state revenues (Lowry, 2015). The State of Kansas' public schools got so bad that in 2016 Kansas' Supreme Court ruled that the underfunding of poorer schools was not only inequitable but unconstitutional (Bosman, 2016). The economic effects on the state were so dire that the conservative Kansas legislature voted tax increases in 2017, overriding the governor's veto in doing so.

Minnesota and Wisconsin offer one of the purest comparisons of the effects of disparate economic policies. In 2011 Republican Scott Walker was elected Governor of Wisconsin, replacing a Democratic predecessor, and Democrat Mark Dayton was elected Governor of Minnesota, replacing a Republican predecessor. Since then the two governors have pursued remarkably different policies. Walker has enacted $4.7 billion of tax cuts, eliminated collective bargaining for public employees, and pursued a general policy of deregulation. Dayton has raised the minimum wage and increased taxes on the top 2 percent of earners to finance education and infrastructure (Ratliff, 2016).

Though it is impossible to attribute the relative performance of the two states solely to the policies of their governors, Minnesota seems to have performed significantly better economically than Wisconsin since 2011 while providing more social services. Minnesota has added more jobs than Wisconsin despite a smaller population and has seen much lower increases in poverty and child poverty rates than Wisconsin (Ratliff, 2016). While Wisconsin has had to cut education funding and has struggled to reduce its uninsured rate, largely due to Scott Walker's extreme resistance to the ACA, Minnesota has increased funding for education and improved insurance rates significantly (Jacobs, 2014). The divergent performances of Wisconsin and Minnesota suggest that an aggressive pro-business tax-cutting agenda is not the ideal path toward growth or citizen well-being. It is perhaps telling that when Scott Walker spoke at the 2016 Republican National Convention he was not included in the night devoted to economic policy and growth. After Wisconsin and Michigan Republican Governors lost their 2018 races, their GOP state legislators passed legislation to deny the newly elected Democratic Governors multiple powers and authority before they took office. This States' Rights battle is sure to be contested in Court.

See also: ACA, Austerity, Block Grants, Devolution, Education, Medicaid, Privatization, The State

Further Reading

Bivens, J. (2016). Why is recovery taking so long – and who's to blame? August 11. Retrieved from Economic Policy Institute, www.epi.org/publication/why-is-recovery-taking-so-long-and-who-is-to-blame/.

Bosman, J. (2016). Kansas parents worry schools are slipping amid budget battles. *The New York Times*, June 1. Retrieved from www.nytimes.com/2016/06/01/us/kansas-parents-worry-schools-are-slipping-amid-budget-battles.html.

Estes, C. L. (1983). Perspectives of a political economist. In C. L. Estes, R. J. Newcomer, & Associates, *Fiscal austerity and aging: Shifting government responsibility for the elderly* (pp. 255–270). Beverly Hills, CA: Sage.

Ginsberg, B., Lowi, T. J., Weir, M., & Tolbert, C. J. (2017). *We the people: An introduction to American politics* (11th Core edition). New York: W. W. Norton.

Jacobs, L. R. (2014). Right vs. Left in the Midwest. *The New York Times*, Sunday Review, July 17. Retrieved from www.nytimes.com/2013/11/24/opinion/sunday/right-vs-left-in-the-midwest.html.

Lowi, T. J. (1971). *The politics of disorder* (Vol. 71). New York: Basic Books.

Lowry, B. (2015). Kansas Gov. Sam Brownback cuts Medicaid reimbursements, higher-ed spending. July 22. Retrieved from *The Wichita Eagle*, www.kansas.com/news/politics-government/article78450362.html.

Mazerov, M. (2016). Kansas' tax cut experience refutes economic growth predictions of Trump tax advisors. August 12. Retrieved from Center on Budget and Policy Priorities, www.cbpp.org/research/federal-tax/kansas-tax-cut-experience-refutes-economic-growth-predictions-of-trump-tax#_ftn19.

Ratliff, M. (2016). Wisconsin vs. Minnesota: What the data show. July 20. Retrieved from Center for Economic and Policy Research, http://cepr.net/blogs/cepr-blog/wisconsin-vs-minnesota-what-the-data-show.

Shapiro, I., DaSilva, B., Reich, D., & Kogan, R. (2016, March). *Funding for housing, health, and Social Services block grants has fallen markedly over time.* Center on Budget and Policy Priorities, March.

Statelessness

Means losing the protections of a nation-state as well as a claim to rights or entitlements.

Hannah Arendt (1951, p. 273) understood:

> the existence of a right to have rights . . . and a right to belong to some kind of organized community, only when millions of people emerged who had lost and could not regain these rights. Stateless people could see . . . that the abstract nakedness of being nothing but human was their greatest danger . . . the loss of home and political status became identical with expulsion from humanity altogether.

Complex and highly varied national laws regarding nationality across the world combine with international conflicts and displacements to produce vast numbers of stateless individuals. Migrant workers, refugees, and persecuted ethnic and religious minorities are especially vulnerable to losing or simply never receiving national status. The UN Refugee Agency estimates that there are 10 million stateless people around the world with approximately one-third of that number comprising children (UNHCR, 2016).

See also: Neoliberalism, Inequality, Inclusion/Exclusion.

Further Reading

Arendt, H. (1951). *The origins of totalitarianism.* New York: Schocken Books.

Somers, M. R. (2008). *Genealogies of citizenship: Knowledge, markets, and the right to have rights.* New York: Cambridge University Press.

UNHCR. (2016). Statelessness around the world. Retrieved from United Nations High Committee on Refugees, www.unhcr.org/en-us/statelessness-around-the-world.html.

Statistical Panic

Arises from neurotic obsession with calculating risk. Kathleen Woodward (2008) proposes the term "statistical panic" to describe the phenomenon of fear inspired by statistics, particularly those focused on *crisis*: numerical or empirical odds of disaster, illness, or collapse. This can help explain the fascination with election polls, and the frenzy of stock market and policy proposals to scale back or privatize social insurance.

We see this in the rhetoric of falling off of the fiscal cliff, and critically we can wonder at how fears of the "silver tsunami" drive empirical data to concretize the unknown of the inevitable. Societal fears of growing older, also located and labeled in individuals as *gerascophobia*, exist within the context of the numerical data generated by gerontological institutions – much of this research focuses on illness, suffering, and mortality.

Ziliak and McCloskey (2008) argue in *The cult of statistical significance* that many of the "tests" do not test, and many of the "estimates" fail to estimate – the blind reliance and devotion toward empiricism lacks validity.

See also: Big Data, Demography/Demographics, Framing, Functionalism, Rhetoric

Further Reading

Woodward, K. (2008). *Statistical panic: Cultural politics and poetics of the emotions.* Durham, NC: Duke University Press.

Ziliak, S. & McCloskey, D. N. (2008). *The cult of statistical significance: How the standard error costs us jobs, justice, and lives.* Ann Arbor, MI: University of Michigan Press.

Stereotype Threat (ST)

Describes the social psychological phenomenon in which stereotypes influence behavior of the stereotyped individual (Steele & Aronson, 1995). Stereotypical expectations manifest themselves *vis-à-vis* age, race, ethnicity, sexuality, and ability. In terms of aging, research:

> offer[s] evidence that ST consumes working memory resources in the elderly. More importantly, we rely on a process dissociation procedure (PDP) and show for the first time that ST undermines the controlled use of memory and simultaneously intensifies automatic response tendencies. These new findings indicate that seemingly concurrent models of ST are actually compatible, and offer further reasons to pay special attention to aging stereotypes during standardized neuropsychological testing.
> (Mazerolle et al., 2017)

A related concept is Ambiguous Discrimination Stress (ADS), in which people are unsure whether the unfair treatment they receive is due to racial discrimination or bias or not. This uncertainty is a stress that oppressed and marginalized groups carry

in many spaces, especially predominantly white ones.

See also: Abjection, Alienation, Dementia, Inequality, Jeopardy, Microaggression, Racism, Violence

Further Reading

Desrichard, O. & Köpetz, C. (2005). A threat in the elder: The impact of task-instructions, self-efficacy and performance expectations on memory performance in the elderly. *European Journal of Social Psychology, 35,* 537–552.

Hess, T. M., Auman, C., Colcombe, S. J., & Rahhal, T. A. (2003). The impact of stereotype threat on age differences in memory performance. *Journal of Gerontology: Psychological Sciences, 58B*(1), 3–11.

Kang, S. K. & Chasteen, A. L. (2009). The moderating role of age-group identification and perceived threat on stereotype threat among older adults. *International Journal of Aging and Human Development, 69*(3), 201–220.

Levy, B. (1996). Improving memory in old age through implicit self-stereotyping. *Journal of Personality and Social Psychology, 71*(6), 1092–1107.

Mazerolle, M., Régner, I., Barber, S. J., Paccalin, M., Miazola, A. C., Huguet, P., & Rigalleau, F. (2017). Negative aging stereotypes impair performance on brief cognitive tests used to screen for predementia, *The Journals of Gerontology Series B: 72*(6), 932–936. https://doi.org/10.1093/geronb/gbw083.

Rahhal, T. A., Hasher, L., & Colcombe, S. J. (2001). Instructional manipulations and age differences in memory: Now you see them, now you don't. *Psychology and Aging, 16*(4), 697–706.

Steele, C. M. & Aronson, J. (1995). Stereotype threat and the intellectual test performance of African Americans. *Journal of Personality and Social Psychology, 69*(5), 797–811.

Stein, R., Blanchard-Fields, F., & Hertzog, C. (2002). The effects of age-stereotype priming on the memory performance of older adults. *Experimental Aging Research,* *28*(2), 169–181.

Thomas, A. K., Smith, A., & Mazerolle, M. (2018). The unexpected relationship between retrieval demands and memory performance when older adults are faced with age-related stereotypes. *The Journals of Gerontology Series B: Psychological Sciences and Social Sciences,* March. https://doi.org./10.1093/geronb/gby031.

Stress

Arises when individuals are overwhelmed by an environment or interaction. It can result in physical illness like headaches, muscle tension, and stomach problems. Anxiety and depression also arise from repeated exposure to stress, and chronic stress may lead to diabetes, high blood pressure, and heart disease.

Len Pearlin's stress process paradigm (Pearlin et al., 1981) influenced studies on social structure and mental health, showing how enduring stressors in ordinary daily life may deplete the very social and psychological resources that might otherwise mitigate the damaging emotional impact of such stressors. Pearlin's longitudinal and life course studies substantiate that social stratification is related to differences in the mental health risks of psychological distress – as is also shown in the mental health effects on informal caregivers to persons with AIDS and to those with Alzheimer's Disease.

The Folkman Model (Lazarus & Folkman, 1984) identifies the transactional process of meaning-based coping with positive outcomes. It is part of a resilient process that reduces the effects of negative life events; it is associated with the creation of positive emotions, positive reappraisal, and life goals.

See also: Allostatic Load, Health Disparities, Resilience, Trauma, Violence

Further Reading

Lazarus, R. S. & Folkman, S. (1984). *Stress, appraisal, and coping.* New York: Springer.

Pearlin, L. I., Menaghan, E. G., Lieberman, M. A., & Mullan, J. T. (1981). The stress process. *Journal of Health and Social Behavior,* *22*(4), 337–356.

Pearlin, L. I., Mullan, J. T., Semple, S. J., & Skaff, M. M. (1990). Caregiving and the stress process: An overview of concepts and their measures. *The Gerontologist,* *30*(5), 583–594.

Structure

May be defined as recurring patterns of social practices. Enduring, orderly patterns of social relationships and behaviors form the basis of social structure. Social arrangements and social roles in which we are engaged in our daily lives constitute the social structures we know well. Social structure also comprises observable patterns in social practices. As such, structure refers to systems of stratification and difference. Many structures are formally authorized, creating power differences and "rights" that are culturally, politically, and/or economically recognized as legitimate ways of ordering and doing things. They may be informally or formally sanctioned institutions, customs, norms, and practices governing everyday life and functioning. The concepts power structure and class structure are possibly most familiar in our lexicon.

We see and experience hierarchies through structure and the practices they create. Structures by organization, practice, and policy of Social Security and Medicare are consequential. They signal who is on top, who has the authority and legitimacy; and who has the "discretion" to impose and interpret (or reject) rules and rights.

Structural gender and sex roles are built into the practice and history of the nuclear family. Race and color have been structured through slavery and exclusion/inclusion via immigration status, imposing difference by ethnicity, nation of origin, and the treaties, lands and rights of indigenous peoples. Microaggressions exemplify patterns of behavior that signal the structures of domination and subordination. Federal, state, and local policy create structures of management, implementation, and regulation.

Structures embed a form of reification, the concretizing of patterns of social relations in our minds; they become what we come to see and accept as permissible and impermissible. Once embedded, social structures are extremely difficult to change, to reverse, or to break open. Deep structure is a theoretical space where we can examine how the psyche and social structures reflect struggles for and against wholeness as a society and ourselves as a self.

Dominant structural interests are built into the way the system works. Dominant interests do not need to be exercised in order to be present, represented, or enforced; they already reside in the policy and operations pertinent thereto. For those interests that are not dominant, they may be competing interests vying for dominance or repressed interests. It is the repressed interests that have to exert much more energy, resource mobilization, and voices to be heard (Alford, 1975). Agency and structure are often posed as opposites, although they are dialectical processes within any power field that produces policy agendas, laws, and all types of sanctions.

Related to the structure of aging policies, a critical perspective examines the operation of powerful structural interests legitimized by law and regulation, and the existing practices and rules within and across state and non-state entities and actors. Illustrating a dominant structural interest, physicians hold dominant authority in medical care decisions and are the legal prescribers of prescription drugs. Doctors are charged with powers, authority, and privileges of certifying illness and disability by and for the State. Registered nurses, even nurse practitioners, have competing interests, roles, and competencies, but they are circumscribed by the exclusive rights of MDs except in legally adjudicated circumstances.

Throughout aging policy, there is structural complexity both within and between different elements of the federal, state, and local governments and different corporate and non-profit sectors. This is further complicated by the larger global economic and financial systems of capitalism that have been granted rights and powers through trade and other transnational agreements. An example is the World Bank's and International Monetary Fund's requirement that governments in developing countries dismantle and privatize their public health systems as a condition of loans.

Varying theoretical perspectives utilize the concept of structure differently. Marx's distinction between base and superstructure locates the base in relations of production (e.g., work conditions negotiated between employer and employee) and the superstructure as the cultural, social, and political relationships which arise from labor relations. Weber introduced the idea of structuralism, which proposes that these relations, values, and power structures reciprocally inform and "structure" each other. For Emile Durkheim (1985/1964, *The rules of sociological method*), social structures are a material "social fact," meaning that they are external to and coercive over individual actors. In functionalist thinking (Parsons, 1949) social structures are "positive" and "requisite" to social integration and maintenance of the social order. Constructionist theorists (Berger & Luckmann, 1966) argue that interactional processes of social actors (agency) are pivotal (if not primordial) in constructing (and deconstructing) social structures. Social structures are the creation of active human beings. Estes (1979; Estes & Associates, 2001) observes that coercive conflicts over the dominant and competing ideologies, power, and structures in society show how social policy is contested and implemented (or not) in and through social structures. Social structures are highly consequential for the lives of people and communities across the lifespan.

See also: Class, Ideology, Ideological State Apparatus, Microaggressions, Power, Relations of Ruling, States' Rights, The State

Further Reading

Alford, R. R. (1975). *Health care politics: Ideological and interest group barriers to reform.* Chicago, IL: University of Chicago Press.

Berger, P. L. & Luckmann, T. (1966). *The social construction of reality.* Garden City, NY: Doubleday.

Durkheim, E. (1985/1964). *The rules of sociological method.* New York: The Free Press.

Estes, C. L. (1979). *The aging enterprise.* San Francisco, CA: Jossey-Bass.

Estes, C. L. & Associates. (2001). *Social policy & aging: A critical perspective.* Thousand Oaks, CA: Sage.

Parsons, T. (1949). *Social theory and social structure.* New York: The Free Press.

Structured Dependency Theory

Stems from Peter Townsend's classic treatise on "The structured dependency of the elderly" which posits that the dependency of the elderly in the twentieth century is "being manufactured socially and its severity is unnecessary" (Townsend, 1981, p. 5). As defined before, dependency is a state of need that often places one in a position of subordination. Illness, disability, and impaired mobility often place one in a position of reliance. Critical perspectives question how this reliance is manufactured and exploited, questioning how design and accessibility support or limit participation.

Consistent with the critical perspectives of Estes (1979), Walker (1980), and Phillipson (1982), this means that dependency is manufactured and could therefore be revised or at least ameliorated to some extent. An aging policy example is the "imposition . . . of earlier retirement, the legitimation of low income, the denial of rights to self-determination in institutions, and the construction of community services for recipients assumed to be predominantly passive" (Townsend, 1981, 5–28 in FR). Central problems are "the management of modern economies and the distribution of power and status in such economies" (Townsend, 1981, p. 23). Sociological analyses of abjection and social exclusion provide frameworks for exploring the ideological mechanisms promoting the structuring of dependency for older adults.

See also: Dependency, Political Economy, Social Construction of Reality

Further Reading

Estes, C. L. (1979). *The aging enterprise: A critical examination of social policies and services for the aged.* San Francisco, CA: Jossey-Bass.

Phillipson, C. (1982). *Capitalism and the construction of old age.* London: Macmillan.

Townsend, P. (1981). The structured dependency of the elderly: A creation of social policy in the twentieth century. *Ageing and Society, 1*(1), 5–28.

Walker, A. (1980). The social creation of poverty and dependency in old age. *Journal of Social Policy. 9*(1), 49–76.

Walker, A. & Foster, L. (Eds.). (2014). *The political economy of ageing and later life: Critical perspectives.* Northampton, MA: Edward Elgar.

Subjective Aging

A term developed to describe a more personal and existential point of view on aging that incorporates an individual's psychological sense or personal aging within the immediate sociocultural context of aging (which is often entrenched and internalized through ageism). Subjective age is commonly termed perceived age, self-perceived age, or self-perception of age. According to Gendron, Inker, & Welleford (2018, p. 619):

Subjective age empirically measures self-perception of age by evaluating how old a person feels, thinks, or appears as a phenomenological variable to study outcomes such as psychological well-being, life satisfaction, or overall health. Subjective age measures can encompass person-oriented measures or context-oriented measures. Person-oriented measures include feel age (the age a person feels), look age (the age a person thinks they look), do age (the age a person perceives themselves to act), or interest age (the age a person perceives to reflect their interests) (Uotinen, 2005). Context-oriented measures involve a specific comparison with another individual or group. Subjective age can be operationalized in a variety of ways. Examples from recent literature include "How old do you feel", "How old do you feel when you look at yourself in the mirror?", and "How old do you, yourself, feel inside?" (Hughes, Geraci, & De Forrest, 2013; Kleinspehn-Ammerlahn, Kotter-Grühn, & Smith, 2008; Rubin & Berntsen, 2006).

Research on subjective age is not limited to one culture or geographic area. Subjective age can be informed by relation to others, constructed through interaction and intersubjectivity. For instance, people of the same chronological age may report feeling very different ages, regardless of their numerical age. The social constructions of young and old as subjectivities can also be informed by culture. Cross-cultural interpretations of what it is to be old, and therefore a sense of one's subjective age, can vary from one culture to another. While gerontologists widely accept the paradigm that growing older is a complex, interactive, and multidirectional process, Gendron, Inker, and Welleford (2018, p. 619) ask:

If we accept these multidirectional paradigms for growing older, then we need to consider what we are actually asking when we ask, the question "how old do you feel?" Are we inadvertently conflating a neutral description (age or old age) with a feeling? What does old feel like? Is feeling old intended to capture the accumulation of wisdom, life experience, and knowledge, or is feeling old intended to capture physical and/or mental decline? Given the alternative interpretations of aging as growth, maintenance, or decline, it seems that we cannot truly know what we are measuring when using the variable of subjective age in this manner unless we know how respondents are thinking about what it means to them to be or feel "old". This leads us to one challenge with the subjective age variable: it presupposes that being 80 or 60 or 40 has a normed meaning and experience, such that people can measure themselves against this in order to answer whether they feel they are older or younger than this. But what does it actually mean to be or feel or look 80? The heterogeneity of the experience of growing older, or the age paradox, means that this will be different for each of us, depending on a complex web of factors including genetics, epigenetics, cohort, personal life experiences, and choices. So how do respondents know what an 80 year old should look like, feel like, or be like?

See also: Intergenerational Intersubjectivity, Temporality

Further Reading

Chudacoff, H. P. (1992). *How old are you? Age consciousness in American culture.* Princeton, NJ: Princeton University Press.

Diehl, M., Wahl, H. W., Brothers, A., & Miche, M. (2015). Subjective aging and awareness of aging: Toward a new understanding of the aging self. *Annual Review of Gerontology and Geriatrics, 35*(1), 1–28.

Gendron, T. L., Inker, J., & Welleford, A. (2018). "How old do you feel?" The difficulties and ethics of operationalizing subjective age. *The Gerontologist, 58*(4): 618–624.

Kaufman, S. R. (1986). *The ageless self.* Madison, WI: University of Wisconsin Press.

Settersten Jr., R. A. & Hagestad, G. O. (2015). Subjective aging and new complexities of the life course. *Annual Review of Gerontology and Geriatrics, 35*(1), 29–53.

Subversive

A quality of resistance. It disrupts the order of things, challenges the status quo. It does not respect the establishment, but rather questions the revered legitimacy of established (and dominant) powers.

See also: Disruption, Legitimacy, Queer, Resistance

Supplemental Security Income (SSI)

A vital component of the safety net that provides cash assistance to the most vulnerable Americans who either are not eligible for Social Security or whose benefits are too low to provide a subsistence income. Meagre monthly SSI income averages $541. Administered by the Social Security Administration, SSI is aimed to reduce poverty and provide essential support. In 2017 it covered 8+ million older Americans and people with disabilities, including 1.2 million children with disabilities (CBPP, 2018). Long-term low-wage workers and individuals who spend many years in unpaid caregiving roles depend on SSI to help pay for housing, food, and out-of-pocket medical expenses, among other things. Over 2.7 million SSI recipients also receive Social Security OASDI benefits.

Today, one's income must be well below the Federal Poverty Level to qualify for SSI. The current countable savings/asset limit is just $2,000 ($3,000 for a couple) per calendar year and the income limit is approximately $750 ($1,100 for a couple) a month. Both of these limits were established in 1972 and the asset limit has been frozen for more than four decades. The SSI Restoration Act was introduced (but not passed) in 2017 to provide much-needed and long overdue updates for SSI eligibility. SSI legislation remains stymied in bipartisan political struggles.

See also: Disability, Social Insurance, Social Security

Further Reading

Center on Budget and Policy Priorities (CBPP). (2018). Supplemental Security Income (SSI). January 29. Retrieved from www.cbpp.org/sites/default/files/atoms/files/1-29-18ssi.pdf.

Consortium for Citizens with Disabilities (CCD). (2018). Preserve SSI: A vital part of our Social Security system. January. Washington, DC: CCD Social Security Task Force.

info@c-c-d.org.

www.c-c-d/org.

www.ssa.gov/disabilityssi/ssi.html.

Symbolic

A realm of representation and meaning.

On one level symbols are understood as non-textual pictographic elements, painted on walls of caves or sewn onto flags. Critical theory locates symbols as containing pathways to layers of representation and meaning; how we come to see the Statue of Liberty as a symbol of welcoming freedom, or the noose as racial oppression and violence, and the Swastika as Aryan arrogance. It is important to note that symbols carry different meanings for different peoples and populations – the aforementioned symbols carry alternative meanings depending on the subject positioning of the participant-receiver. The immigrant grandfather from Sicily who came through Ellis Island perceives the Statue of Liberty through a vastly different epistemic lens than an immigrant from Central America in an ICE detention center in Texas. The symbolic violence of the noose and Swastika is deployed and celebrated by neo-Nazi white supremacists.

Studies of the symbolic include the work of linguists and semiotists such as De Saussure, Lacan, Levi-Strauss, and Derrida who deconstructed text for its symbolic qualities. Carl Jung located interactions and events as reiterative and defining of dynamics and archetypes. Freud parses out symbolic meaning in dream images and through mythology as symbolic of neurotic complexes (e.g., Oedipus). Hegel examines the symbolic dialectics of master and slave. Debord identifies the creation and consumption of spectacle, and Barthes innovates an understanding of myth as unconscious manipulations of power. Psychoanalytic understandings of the symbolic include gestures of mothering, the breast, holding, and their counterparts splitting, collapse, and the bad mother. Avant-garde artists in the 1920s illustrated a surreal ability to speak to and critique contemporary realities, especially post-World War I fascistic atrocities. We see the tragedy of Picasso's Guernica and Dali's hopeless nihilistic rotting as a symbolic manifestation of aggression and despair.

In identifying the symbolic, critical theorists look at constructions of meaning and dynamics of power and definitional dominance as well as the resistance of oppressed and silenced groups and transgressive turns against the doxa. In aging, we might look to how ageism is symbolically constructed through tropes of abjection and trivialization such as how grannies are dotty, geezers are frail, and the elderly are out of touch. In aging policy we can question what need and dependence symbolize in the context of means-testing, time limits, or penalties.

Resistance movements may themselves produce symbolic disruptions where access, flow, and ownership are stripped from public space and governance – and where compliance, morality, and benevolence stood. Presidents may do the same. Rituals take on symbolic meaning of trust, inclusion, participation, and belonging. The breaking from and renunciation of rituals (sacred and secular) may engender epic human and social consequences.

See also: Art as Resistance, Framing, Interactionism, Myth, Textuality

Further Reading

The sociology of symbolic power. A special issue in memory of Pierre Bourdieu. *Theory and Society* (December 2003), *32*, 5–6.

T

Telomeres

The genetic material at the end of a chromosome which serves as a protective function for the cell. By repeating units of DNA at the ends of chromosomes, telomeres act as buffers against the loss of protein-coding DNA during cell division. While telomere shortening happens naturally with aging, mounting research indicates that the process is accelerated by psychological and biological stress (Wojcicki et al., 2016; Blackburn & Epel, 2017). Stress and stress hormones deplete and impair this protective function which hastens cellular mutations, illness, and death. By 2017 at least two companies were offering consumer mail-order test kits for measuring telomere length.

Critical theory notes that systems of oppression appear and operate even at cellular levels, and call for research to examine intergenerational transmissions of trauma and genetic stress.

See also: Gene–Environment

Further Reading

Blackburn, E. & Epel, E. (2017). *The telomere effect: A revolutionary approach to living younger, healthier, longer.* New York: Grand Central Publishing.

Wojcicki, J. M., Olveda, R., Heyman, M. B., Elwan, D., Lin, J., Blackburn, E., & Epel, E. (2016). Cord blood telomere length in Latino infants: Relation with maternal education and infant sex. *Journal of Perinatology, 36*(3), 235–241.

www.yourgenome.org/facts/what-is-a-telomere.

Temporality

A philosophical framework of time and event progression.

In gerontology it generally describes chronometric (linear and measured) shifts from past, present, to future; however, cultural conceptualizations of time vary. Instead of age, time can be measured in periods such as reproductive years and labor participation. Cultural frameworks may also include non-linear frameworks of spiritual development, such as coming into consciousness, cycles of rebirth, and discovery.

Temporality also deals with perception and subjective experiences of time. In challenging chronometric frames of time, Baars (2015, p. 400) asserts that memory has its own temporal dimensions: "vividness is not determined by chronometric time: something that happened fifty years ago can be more vividly remembered than something that happened last summer."

See also: Epistemology, Knowledges, Liminality, Memory, Subjective Aging

Further Reading

Baars, J. (2013). Critical turns of aging, narrative and time. *International Journal of Ageing and Later Life, 7*(2), 143–165.

Baars, J. (2015). Time in late modern aging. In J. Twigg & W. Martin (Eds.), *Routledge handbook of cultural gerontology* (pp. 397–403). New York: Routledge.

Temporary Assistance to Needy Families (TANF)

Provides cash assistance to poor families. TANF was one of the centerpieces of President Clinton's welfare reform package and replaced the Aid to Families with Dependent Children program.

TANF made many changes to how family welfare worked but the two most important were devolution and work requirements. Under TANF, recipients are subject to work requirements: 30 hours of work per week for single-parent households and 35 to 50 for two-parent households within two years of joining the program. The program devolved from federal control to a set of block grants to states, who have significant leeway in determining the structure and benefits of the program.

TANF provides much-needed assistance for families struggling financially; however, the program is fundamentally flawed. Work requirements can be burdensome and unrealistic, especially as expanded childcare and educational resources have failed to materialize. Some states have managed to make the system work but many others have abused the devolution of responsibilities and diverted TANF funds to cover other state programs. Barely half of TANF funds spent by states in 2015 were spent on the program's core goals of basic assistance (26%), support of work-related activities (8%), and childcare (16%).

See also: Welfare State

Further Reading

Schott, L., Pavetti, L., & Floyd, I. (2015). *How states use federal and state funds under the TANF block grant.* Washington, DC: Center on Budget and Policy Priorities.

Textuality

Central to media studies, an interdisciplinary field in which psychoanalytic sociological frameworks and feminist scholarship are engaged in ferreting out the unthought and the unexplored.

Critical frameworks include Judith Butler's grievability and performativity, Laura Mulvey's theory of the gaze as a site of ownership, Donna Haraway's cyborg blurring the binary or organic and inorganic humanity, Jean Baudrillard's simulacra, and Randall Collins' interaction ritual chains and co-presence. Each offer critical lenses across their disciplines that could be employed in investigating these phenomena.

Media theory is concerned with textuality, especially that of the image, digital space, and communicative and connective mediums (telephonic and electronic, but also what is declared through the use of public and private space). Declarations of direction for participation, instruction for consumption, and restriction are examined.

Literary theory impels thinking on how things are objectified and inscribed through tropes and fetishes to be de-toothed or naturalized. Objectification/abjectification and fetishization are important lenses for viewing constructions of subjecthood.

An example of this study could be intergenerational bonds between elders in Britain mentoring children in India via teleconferencing. How colonial and postcolonial negotiations of power and worth become constellated, recapitulated, or resisted in this connection. And furthermore, what it means for a people to not have to share political or economic realities but to exist for each other on screens.

See also: Co-presence, Digital Sphere, Framing, Grievability, Interaction Ritual Chains, Tweetstorm

Theories of Aging

Understandings of aging, or explanations that lead to, and are driven by, cumulative knowledge on aging. Theories of aging ensure scientific and humanitarian advancements in gerontology by undergirding our knowledge and nurturing the future development of theory and practice in gerontology. According to Bengtson and Settersten Jr. (2016, p. 2):

> In some fields of the social sciences, it can be said that there are two primary types of theories: (a) theories of *explanation* of *why* and *how* something occurs – for example, cumulative advantage/disadvantage theories that explain *why* variability among older people partly reflects social inequalities, and *how* social processes generate those inequalities over time; and (b) theories of *orientation* that provide a worldview and even a set of explicit assumptions or propositions, which lead us to see and interpret aging phenomena in particular ways – for example, postmodern theory, feminist theory, critical gerontology, or the life-course perspective. Although the latter are often called "theories," they are, from another perspective, more often broader "paradigms" than theories. However, the frame and propositions they provide are extremely useful in developing more specific theories. In any case, both types are represented in gerontology today.

In addition to explaining and understanding aging, theory is important for pragmatic reasons in gerontology. Theories can contribute to the integration of knowledge over time. For instance, "[a] good theory identifies the problem and its most important components (concepts) based on the separate findings and empirical generalizations from research. It also describes the linkages among the concepts in a causal sequence, based on previous knowledge" (Bengtson & Settersten Jr., 2016, p. 3). This enables future investigators to test, refine, or refute theory, thus advancing future knowledge development. Theories can facilitate prediction by pointing to new research directions based on findings. Theories can also guide interventions to improve human conditions because it allows practitioners to apply or advance existing knowledge to solve problems at macro- to micro-social levels, such as through implementing public policies or designing service delivery.

In aging, theories have "undergone several pendulum shifts during the relatively short history of gerontology" (Bengtson & Settersten Jr., 2016, p. 4). The development of theory in gerontology is conventionally mapped as an unbroken path that advanced from medieval theology and ancient philosophy, to the foundation of modern medicine during the Enlightenment, and finally to the emergence of gerontology and geriatrics in the twentieth century (Achenbaum, 1995; Cole, 1992; Katz, 1996). By the early twentieth century, science had become the source of knowledge to provide explanations of aging as religious dogma and spiritual views were cast off. Discovering laws about normality and pathology as applied to the process of growing older became a focus to establish increasing scientific management over aging and the life course. Meanwhile, scientific and technical advancements in the medical profession, as well as increases in the realms of improved housing, labor practices, sanitation, potable water, food systems, and pollution, have coincided substantially with the advancement of human health and longevity. This is reflected by the growing body of literature, research, practice, and education seeking to bring psychological, sociological, and environmental contributions to gerontology in addition to the biological theories of aging (Achenbaum, 1995; Katz, 1996; Kontos, 2005).

Despite these developments, gerontology has been characterized by an imbalance between the accumulation of data and the development of theory (Baars, Dannefer, Phillipson, & Walker, 2006). Researchers interested in aging have collected tremendous amounts of data, driven by narrowly defined questions with little attention to basic assumptions or larger theoretical issues. According to Baars and colleagues (2006):

An absence of theoretical development is surely not surprising for a fairly young enterprise that seeks to capture a complex empirical reality; especially one that draws from many disciplines, and that is preoccupied with urgent practical problems (Hagestad & Dannefer, 2001). Yet the lack of attention to theory has meant that research questions have often been informed by an uncritical reliance on images and assumptions about aging drawn from popular culture or from traditions and paradigms of theory that are considered outdated within the broader discourses of behavioral and social theory. When such assumptions are used to guide the formulation of research questions and research designs, the results can be what has been termed "dust-bowl empiricism" (Birren, 1988), unintended reductionisms or other fallacies that misspecify the level of analysis and, therefore, missed opportunities to pursue the most revealing aspects of the subject matter in question (Hendricks, 1999) (pp. 1–2).

For example, many discussions have charted the long-term tension between activity and disengagement theories of aging. From a critical perspective, these theories continue the invisibility of the overarching hegemony of culture and State, and therefore an implicit, if not explicit, assumption that the State is benign, as Chris Phillipson often and eloquently puts it. Dannefer (2011), has also dealt with broader implications of reductionism in theories of aging and has identified two different strands of life-course theory, a North American social-psychological strand that tends to veer toward reductionism and a European structural strand that tends to veer toward institutionalization of the life course.

Estes, Binney, and Culbertson (1992) contend that social forces outside of and within the field threaten the promise of the "gerontological imagination" and both the practice and promulgation of theory in gerontology. Beginning around the 1970s, critical theory challenged traditional theories and perspectives within the study of aging (Estes & DiCarlo, 2016; Baars et al., 2006). As noted by Estes, Biggs, and Phillipson (2003/2009, p. 2), this was a response to three major concerns arising from research into old age:

First, the need for a clearer understanding of what various researchers identified as the "social construction of dependency" in old age. This was seen to have resulted from the development of services associated with the welfare state, from the continued financial impoverishment of a large section of the elderly population, and from the systematic stereotyping of older people (or "ageism" as coined by Robert Butler (1975) in the late 1960s). Second was the critique of the biomedical model, a view that associated growing old with physical and mental deterioration and disease. Third was the individualistic focus of traditional gerontology, and the lack of attention to social structure and economic relationships.

Since the initial development of the political economy of aging (Estes, 1979; Walker

& Foster, 2014) to the present, a critical lens has opened to the humanities as well as to social science, public health, and policy-based disciplines. Feminist perspectives on gender, race, and ethnicity have exerted greater influence on studies of aging, and globalization and migration have been recognized as factors in transforming the lives of older people in developed and developing countries (Estes with DiCarlo, 2016; Baars et al., 2006). This has opened the analysis of aging in terms of power, ideology, and stratification, as well as the expanding global reach of such forces. Moving further into the twenty-first century, the discourse and praxis of gerontology continue to make it an authoritative mode of knowledge production on aging as well as an influence on policy-making (Estes, 1979).

A Teaching Appendix for *Ageing A–Z* contains charts that belong in a gerontologist's Toolkit on Theories of Aging in the US. The Teaching Appendix also contains a brief overview of the rise of gerontology to critical gerontology in the USA, 1900 to the present (Yeh, DiCarlo, & Estes, 2019).

See also: Critical Theory, Cumulative Advantage/Disadvantage, Disengagement, Ethnogerontology/Ethnogeriatrics, Feminism/Feminist, Functionalism, Gerontological Imagination, Healthy Aging/Active Aging, Life Course Perspective/Theory, Political Economy, Productive Aging, Reductionism, Structured Dependency Theory

Further Reading

Achenbaum, W. A. (1995). *Crossing frontiers: Gerontology emerges as a science.* New York: Cambridge University Press.

Baars, J. (2010). Time and ageing: Enduring and emerging issues. In D. Dannefer & C. Phillipson (Eds.), *The SAGE handbook of social gerontology* (pp. 367–376). Thousand Oaks, CA: Sage.

Baars, J., Dannefer, D., Phillipson, C., & Walker, A. (2006). Introduction: Critical

perspectives in social gerontology. In J. Baars, D. Dannefer, C. Phillipson, & A. Walker (Eds.), *Aging, globalization, and inequality: The new critical gerontology* (pp. 1–16). Amityville, NY: Baywood Publishing.

Bengtson, V. L. & Settersten Jr., R. A. (Eds.). (2016). *Handbook of theories of aging* (3rd edition). New York: Springer.

Bengtson, V. L., Rice, C. J., & Johnson, M. L. (1999). Are theories of aging important? Models and explanations in gerontology at the turn of the century. In V. L. Bengtson & K. W. Schaie (Eds.), *Handbook of theories of aging* (pp. 3–20). New York: Springer.

Cole, T. (1992). *The journey of life: A cultural history of aging in America.* New York: Cambridge University Press.

Dannefer, D. (2011). Long time coming, not here yet: The possibilities of the social in age and life course studies. In R. A. Settersten Jr. & J. L. Angel (Eds.), *Handbook of sociology of aging* (pp. 633–643). New York: Springer.

Dannefer, D. (2011). Age, the life course, and the sociological imagination: Prospects for theory. In R. H. Binstock & L. K. George (Eds.), *Handbook of aging and the social sciences: A volume in handbooks of aging* (seventh edition) (pp. 3–16). New York: Academic Press.

Dannefer, D. & Settersten Jr., R. A. (2010). The study of the life course: Implications for social gerontology. In D. Dannefer & C. Phillipson (Eds.), *The SAGE handbook of social gerontology* (pp. 3–15). Thousand Oaks, CA: Sage.

Estes, C. L. (1979). *The aging enterprise: A critical examination of social policies and services for the aged.* San Francisco, CA: Jossey-Bass.

Estes, C. L. with DiCarlo, N. B. (2016). Social movements and social knowledges: Gerontological theory in research, policy, and practice. In V. L. Bengtson & R. A. Settersten Jr. (Eds.), *Handbook of theories of aging* (third edition) (pp. 87–106). New York: Springer.

Estes, C. L., Biggs, S., & Phillipson, C. (2003/2009). Social theory and aging. In *Social theory, social policy and ageing* (pp. 1–23). London: Open University Press.

Estes, C. L., Binney, E. A., & Culbertson, R. A. (1992). The gerontological imagination: Social influences on the development of gerontology, 1945–present. *International Journal of Aging and Human Development, 35*(1), 49–65.

Estes, C. L., Swan, J. H., & Gerard, L. E. (1982). Dominant and competing paradigms in gerontology: Towards a political economy of ageing. *Ageing & Society, 2*(2), 151–164.

Katz, S. (1996). *Disciplining old age: The formation of gerontological knowledge*. Charlottesville, VA: University Press of Virginia.

Kontos, P. (2005). Multi-disciplinary configurations in gerontology. In G. J. Andrews & D. R. Phillips (Eds.), *Ageing and place: Perspectives, policy, and practice* (pp. 24–35). New York: Routledge.

Marshall, V. W. (1999). Analyzing social theories of aging. In V. L. Bengtson & K. W. Schaie (Eds.), *Handbook of theories of aging* (pp. 434–455). New York: Springer.

Quadagno, J. (2008). Theories of aging. In *Aging and the life course: An introduction to social gerontology* (pp. 24–48). New York: McGraw-Hill.

Walker, A. & Foster, L. (Eds.). (2014). *The political economy of ageing and later life: Critical perspectives*. Northampton, MA: Edward Elgar, pp. 3–26.

Yeh, J. C., DiCarlo, N. B., & Estes, C. L. (forthcoming). *The rise of gerontology to critical gerontology in the US, 1900 – present*. Institute for Health & Aging Working Paper, University of California, San Francisco.

Theories of Need

Encompasses theoretical frameworks that examine motivation and agency through human need. From a critical perspective, two compatible theories of need underscore that basic and universal human needs exist in culturally specific ways. First, there is a deep literature on the psychology of human needs, including Maslow's hierarchy. Second, Ryan and Deci (2017) bring forward Self-Determination Theory (SDT), in which basic psychological needs are articulated, drawing upon developmental, personality, social, and cognitive psychology. "SDT contends that needs for competence, relatedness and autonomy must be satisfied to achieve psychological growth, human integrity and human well-being" (Dover, 2017, p. 4).

Ian Gough's neo-Marxist criticism states that postmodernism is dislocated from real, working definitions of need. Departing from a focus on subjective, culturally specific definitions of needs and values, Doyal and Gough (1991; Gough, 1994) argue that humans have fundamental and objective, universal needs that follow a hierarchy of importance. They propose empirically attributable social indicators for evaluating countries and economies on how they meet those needs. Safety and physical health, along with autonomy, are the cornerstones of need (p. 53). These extend into mental health, cognitive skills, and opportunities for social participation. Basic physical needs that qualify the preconditions for autonomy include:

1. Adequate nutritional food and water
2. Adequate protective housing
3. Non-hazardous work environment
4. Non-hazardous physical environment
5. Appropriate health care
6. Security in childhood
7. Significant primary relationships with others
8. Physical security
9. Economic security
10. Safe birth control and childbearing
11. Appropriate basic and cross-cultural education

For critical gerontology, Dover (2017) raises a profound question: "Can human needs be met in a society which has one or more of the theorized social systems of oppression, dehumanization and exploitation?" This has serious implications for critical thought and praxis in aging. Does dividing or parceling the needs of older people as mere categories of "social problems" neglect or minimize attention to the foundational needs for health, safety, and autonomy? Theories of need provide a framework for developing holistic approaches to well-being that consider the material conditions and the social psychological needs of older people and their families and the society in which they reside.

See also: Human Rights, Justice, Oppression, Postmodernism, Right to Have Rights, The Social

Further Reading

Dover. M. A. (2016). Human needs: Overview. In C. Frankin (Ed.), *The encyclopedia of social work* (Electronic edition). New York: Oxford University Press & National Association of Social Workers (NASW).

Dover, M. A. (2017). A partial theory of human injustice: Oppression, dehumanization, exploitation, and systematic inequality in opportunities to address human needs (March). Unpublished mss.

Doyal, L. & Gough, I. (1991). *A theory of human needs.* New York: Guilford Press.

Gough, I. (1994). Economic institutions and the satisfaction of human needs. *Journal of Economic Issues, 28*(1), 25–66.

Ryan, R. M. & Deci, E. L. (2017). *Self-determination theory: Basic psychological needs in motivation, development & wellness.* New York: Guilford Press.

Theory of Change

Comprises a set of hypotheses, critical assumptions, and indicators that are posited as causal pathways of change toward achieving a goal. Networks of experts and foundations advanced these approaches as evaluation tools to legitimate the investment of philanthropic and non-profit organizations in policy advocacy and social action. Action research and community-based participatory projects worked in potentially controversial arenas. Theories of change specify the thinking that guides interventions and actions for testing and improvement under the logic of the evidence-based sciences (Organizational Research Services, 2004). An example of a theory of change model includes:

1. A statement of the current situation and major underlying causes affecting the impacted group. Ensures that every member of the endeavor is on the same page about the problem and its various interactions.

2. A desired long-term goal. Ideally a goal that is truly long term (10 to 15 years). Must be clearly defined and observable.

3. Domains of change. These are the main areas in which changes must be implemented to achieve the long-term goal(s).

4. Pathways of change which include breakthroughs and incremental changes. This is the map that tracks and predicts progress from the base state through to the long-term goal. It is important that it distinguishes between and includes both incremental changes and significant breakthroughs.

5. Stakeholders. These are the individuals and groups affected by the change or with an interest in change, community members, NGOs, government agencies, and others.

6. Indicators. The metrics by which progress is measured. They tell the story of how success will be recognized at each step in the pathway of change. Indicators should be defined for each prioritized breakthrough on the pathway of change, as well as the long-term impact

goal. Indicators should be operational (i.e., that they include enough detail to be measurable).

7. Assumptions. These are hypotheses of change, the mechanisms, phenomena, and relationships that the stakeholders believe will create change or contribute to the base state.

The approach. Groups and individuals may endeavor to change any number of aspects or outcomes of a particular community or region – and at systemic levels. Health, education, governance, social, and environmental factors can be targeted through theories of change with evaluation frameworks that specify measurable indicators for projects designed to produce cultural, social, behavioral, organizational, or policy change. Aging advocacy and civic engagement were targeted in the 2000s. Atlantic Philanthropies pushed evidence-based social change and advocacy initiatives around Social Security, health, communities of color, and the low income, as did the Ford Foundation, and others. In health care, Families USA, the Robert Wood Johnson Foundation, Commonwealth Fund, and H . J. Kaiser Jr. Family Foundation functioned as think tanks around which policy advocacy and evaluation science could mobilize.

Further Reading

CARE International. (2012). Defining theories of change. CARE International UK: Peacebuilding with Impact. Retrieved from www.care.org/sites/default/files/documents/PSJ-2012-CARE-Defining-Theories-of-Change-document.pdf.

Organizational Research Services. (2004). Theory of change: A practical tool for action, results and learning. Annie E. Casey Foundation. Aecf.org. Retrieved from www.aecf.org/m/resourcedoc/aecf-theoryofchange-2004.pdf.

Think Tanks

Groups comprising experts and researchers who engage in analysis and policy advocacy on a variety of very specific issues. Think tanks are a major and growing influence in ideological production with regard to public policy and aging, race, ethnicity, class, gender, and disability.

In particular, there has been an exponential growth in the number and influence of right-wing think tanks designed to push market fundamentalism and "drown the welfare state" in the bathtub.

Think tanks are an essential part of the "policy planning networks" identified by Domhoff (2006, p. 77) created by the corporate community via non-profit, theoretically non-partisan entities to articulate and promote their policy preferences to key political leaders (elected and non-elected), the media, allied interests, and the public. Think tanks and conservative foundations endowed by wealthy philanthropists are very influential in the USA (Stefancic & Delgado, 1996).

On Social Security and Medicare, and Medicaid, for example, the Heritage Foundation and Cato Institute have been determined, hostile, and effective. Each played pernicious roles in ideological framing, agenda setting, and messaging about the budget debt, bankruptcy, and demographic hysteria: "We cannot afford it." "The programs are unsustainable." "We are robbing our children's future," and the "Greedy Geezers are eating our greens." They have joined with the National Association of Manufacturers, the Chamber of Commerce, and others in their "There is no alternative" (TINA) march to Social Security privatization, and Medicare privatization (voucher/coupon care with House Speaker Paul Ryan as the cheerleader). Other heavy lifters are the $1 billion Peterson Foundation, the Koch brothers, and the "Fix the Debt" campaign orchestrated by the Committee for a Responsible Federal Budget.

At least four issues motivate right-wing think tanks in influencing aging policy: (1) tax cuts for the rich; (2) cutting corporate costs by eliminating employer matching contributions to employee contributions; (3) privatizing everything that is deemed as public, such as social insurance programs in order to transfer more risk to individuals, shrink the welfare state, and enrich private US and global financial markets; and (4) delaying and/or refusing to pay back monies borrowed from Social Security by cutting federal taxes for the wealthy. The election of Trump and a Republican-dominated Congress in 2016 presented these groups with a major opportunity to take down the bedrock social insurance and safety net programs.

Old and new non-partisan, progressive-leaning think tanks that have targeted the protection and strengthening of retirement and health security include the Center for American Progress, the Institute for Women's Policy Research, the Center for Global Policy Solutions, the Black Caucus Foundation, and the National Council of La Raza. These have been joined by many others and gained momentum during and after the Obama presidency, including Social Security Works.

The rightist turn of American politics in 2016 poses a major frontline test of the organization, tactics, and success of the Left resistance think tanks and broader progressive movements. Now mobilizing against the Right's efforts to dismantle and privatize social insurance through significant changes in Social Security and Medicare, think tanks on the Left are challenged as never before. The resistance and outrage pouring out in the media, and on the streets, have magnified the growth and intensity of social justice work in think tank form.

The formidable counter-attacks to public interest think tanks are manifested in the rising number and power of market fundamentalists engaging well-known scholars and programs through some of the most well-regarded "non-partisan" DC think tanks such as the Brookings Institution and the Urban Institute. Heritage and CATO are notable for decades of unabashedly promoting the privatization of Social Security and the demise of social insurance. The Heritage Foundation stocked the government early in the Trump era, ensuring a mainline defense against anything Obama and progressivism (Mahler, 2018). The deficit hawks are relentless in promoting crisis politics and the urgency of austerity, with a bullseye on "entitlements" of Social Security, Medicare and Medicaid, and other safety net programs. Renewed zeal followed the passage of the 2017 Tax Cut and Jobs Act and unceasing efforts to undo the Affordable Care Act by sabotage, regulatory changes, and legislation.

As Peter Overby describes, there are 400 think tanks in US Capitol city, and there is a "seismic shift [that] involves the funding for think tanks. Once they lived on broad grants, from foundations and reticent millionaires. But now, the funders are often wealthy business people – in modern jargon, philanthro-capitalists – notably many from the tech industry" (Overby, 2017). He chronicles the New America Foundation's scuttling of its Google-funded program on open markets, after criticisms of and fines for Google's monopoly practices were leveled by the European Union. On the progressive side, one result is the dedication of work under the Open Markets Institute, which continues the study and exposes market distortions via monopoly power and the pursuit of the restoration of traditional American monopoly law.

These developments are relevant to the aging, particularly insofar as they affect the framing, funding, and policy trajectory of bedrock programs of Social Security, Medicare, Medicaid, the Affordable Care Act, SSI and SSDI, and chronic and long-term care services and supports.

See also: Debt, Neoliberalism, Privatization, Resistance, Social Movements

Further Reading

Domhoff, G. W. (2006). *Who rules America?* (fifth edition). Boston, MA: McGraw-Hill.

Herman, E. (1997). No mercy: How conservative think tanks and foundations changed America's social agenda. *Journal of the History of the Behavioral Sciences, 33*(3), 309–310.

Mahler, J. (2018). All the right people: How one conservative think tank stocked the federal government for the Trump era. *The New York Times Magazine,* June 24, pp. 32–38, 51, 53.

Medvetz, T. (2012). *Think tanks in America.* Chicago, IL: University of Chicago Press.

Overby, P. (2017). Who controls think tanks? Shifts in funding highlights changes in the industry. Morning Edition, September 20. National Public Radio.

Stefancic, J. & Delgado, R. (1996). *No mercy: How conservative think tanks and foundations changed America's social agenda.* Philadelphia, PA: Temple University Press.

The Third Rail

A phrase to describe an untouchable topic or policy. Touch it and you get electrocuted as you would if you touched the electrified third rail on a commuter train track. The third rail has been used to describe Social Security as a program that is dangerous to attack or change, such as privatizing or means-testing the program. If beneficiaries, benefits, or the program structure are cut or modified in policy reform, these actions are perceived as producing severe negative political consequences for those who dare. Medicare has been seen as residing on the third rail as well, as hazardous to radically change. Widespread public support for both of these social insurance programs has

remained strong across all age, race, ethnicity, class, gender, and disability groups, and even largely across political party lines.

Medicaid and the Affordable Care Act have attained increasingly favorable status over time. Even with sustained attacks from the political Right, public opinion about these programs remains positive and stable (NASI, 2013). Before the 2016 elections these and other welfare state policy arenas were ultimately shielded by the proverbial third rail. Since the 2016 elections, the meaning and protection of the third rail is in full frontal assault from the highest levels of the US State, the President, his administration, and conservatives in both houses of Congress. The volatility of Trump Administration policy has whip-sawed many long-revered practices and institutions, often by mere presidential Tweets, contradictory and ambiguous. Precarity and destabilization has ascended to center stage of social policy for the aging and for virtually all social groups, perhaps except for those who are the wealthiest among us.

See also: Ideological Advocacy Coalitions, Networks, Social Insurance

Further Reading

NASI. (2013). *Strengthen Social Security: What do Americans want?* Washington, DC: National Academy of Social Insurance.

TINA (There Is No Alternative)

The slogan of conservatives, made famous by Great Britain's Prime Minister Margaret Thatcher in the 1980s and mimicked by President Ronald Reagan. Her framing of policy options was that the only alternative to any problem of the government was in the free market. TINA undermined the legitimacy of public services such as

National Health Insurance, public housing, and retirement pensions.

Social action is indivisible from social constructions of reality. The importance of social constructions of reality, of discourses, ideological messages in real world politics is immense. TINA is the construction of realty that government is the problem and capitalism is the solution, garnering the persistent and consistent backing of international finance capital.

Bauman and Donskis (2016) find TINA lurking in "liquid evil," depicted as the "black holes" of privatized and deregulated social spaces in which forceful individualization and mutual estrangement replace cooperation and solidarity.

In the USA, TINA has been the mantra of the conservative Right to support radical change to the foundations of Social Security. In 1983, the *CATO Journal* published an article by Stuart Butler and Peter Germanis, "Achieving a 'Leninist' strategy," which advocated for the privatization of Social Security. The Heritage and CATO authors claimed that there is no alternative to free market capitalism and neoclassical Chicago School economic theory. The definition of the problem characterized Social Security as in crisis, going bankrupt, and fiscally unsustainable. Cuts and privatization were and are posed as the only alternative. The proffer is legitimacy for the privatization of virtually all public services and benefits under the banner of TINA. The same kind of strategy has been mirrored in persistent attempts to "reform" and privatize Medicare through vouchers and cost-cutting. A successful example of TINA under Medicare is the GOP's privatization of the Part D prescription drug program, while also prohibiting government price negotiations with the proprietary Rx industry.

See also: Austerity, Capitalism, Framing, Social Construction of Reality, Social Security

Further Reading

Bauman, Z. & Donskis, L. (2016). *Liquid evil.* Cambridge, MA: Polity Press.

Butler, S. & Germanis, P. (1983). Achieving a "Leninist" strategy. *CATO Journal, 3*(2), 547–556.

latimes.com/2012/Jan/13//business/la/-fi-hiltzik-20120113 Attacks on Social Security, Medicare borrow a strategy from Lenin.

Transgressive

Describes qualities in which movement is against and beyond boundaries. "It is that movement which makes education the practice of freedom." hooks (1994, p. 113) frames disruptions as opportunities to learn:

Confronting one another across differences means that we must change ideas about how we learn; rather than fearing conflict we have to find ways to use it as a catalyst for new thinking, for growth.

See also: Disruption, Resistance

Further Reading

hooks, b. (1994). *Teaching to transgress.* London: Routledge.

Trauma

A deeply disturbing experience, such as injury or loss. These "leave traces on our minds and emotions, on our capacity for joy and intimacy, and even on our biology and immune systems" (Van der Kolk, 2014, p. 1).

Trauma is marked belatedly by repetition in which the symbolic struggles to make sense of the Real. It is "an event . . . defined by its intensity, by the subject's incapacity to respond adequately to it, and by the upheaval and long-lasting effects that it brings about in the psychical organization"

(Laplanche, 1974, p. 465). It disrupts relationships and the capacity to form bonds, making it difficult to communicate and trust.

Feminist scholars look also at the political implications of trauma. The term "rape culture" emerged in the 1970s to describe how pervasive and normalized sexual crimes against women are in American society. The National Intimate Partner and Sexual Violence survey (Black et al., 2010) reports that nearly 1 in 5 women are raped in their lifetimes, versus 1 in 59 men. Cahill (2001, p. 132) writes, "Rape, in its total denial of the victim's agency, will, and personhood, can be understood as a denial of intersubjectivity itself. . . . The self is at once denied and . . . stilled, silenced, overcome." For generations, this gendered violence has kept women leaders (including scholars and politicians) bound to taking care of themselves and their sisters, requiring vast amounts of energy, time, and focus from which their male colleagues have been relatively free.

Different types of trauma – collective, historical, synergistic – are especially relevant to a critical understanding of aging.

Collective Trauma

Emile Durkheim posits that the very grounding of the social order, and the basis for solidarity and social cohesion, are held together by a group's norms, values, and rituals.

Environmental catastrophes (floods, tornadoes, hurricanes, massive oil spills, pipeline leaks, fires) produce psychic and physical injury, grief and trauma, flashbacks, loss of social anchors, and the struggle to find meaning and purpose for the community. Human actions such as wars, genocide, and economic depressions produce collective trauma as well – as may wildly unexpected political or cultural turns of events and outcomes (Pinderhughes, 2015). Collective trauma may describe the mind-numbing experience of being unable to find a job due to global outsourcing of industries. This results in the loss of homes, towns, and a way of life for millions of white middle-class males, and the decline of opportunities even for college-educated youth, particularly those of color. Hillary Clinton's supporters describe the trauma and fear they harbor in the situation where the "norm" has been redefined to feature the breach of "fundamental ethical norms, like 'don't threaten your opponent' and 'don't celebrate sexual assault'." In such traumatic situations, memories reactivate "of historical traumas linked with anti-democratic politics [and] . . . fascism" produced and a feeling that the "world is suddenly upended" (Gross, 2016, p. 8). Collective trauma in immigrant communities resulted from the 2017 Trump mandated raids and rampages of ICE and other deportation forces who rounded up suspected illegal immigrants and terrorized entire communities on US soil. This "moral panic" (Bauman, 2016) is an extreme form of anxiety that refugees (strangers at our door) have stirred up in the present historical moment of Brexit, ISIS, and Trump.

Historical Trauma

Wounds from previous generations carry into subsequent ones in the form of historical trauma. The experience of colonization/colonialisms, exploitation, and war often accompanied by sexual violence and substance dependency bleed through generations. On one level these are genetically encoded, and on another level they are socially (re)produced through existing power structures and reactive defensive and coping strategies. This is illuminated in DeGruy's (2005) work on how slavery and survival strategies appear in many black Americans' modern-day realities.

Critical practitioners can consider how compliance or suspicion with regard to the authority of care workers may be culturally/historically endowed protective mechanisms in vulnerable communities. Food hoarding or lack of documentation make sense in light of famine and persecution. While some might dismiss these as maladaptive, there are ways that survivors and their progeny intuitively protect themselves and their resources. The State is not trusted to be a stable entity founded on goodwill. The wisdom of these generations of survivors must be honored with compassion.

Synergistic Trauma

Howard Pinderhughes and colleagues (2015), a sociologist who studies community violence and prevention, proposes the term "synergistic trauma" to describe the accumulation of traumatic experience and exposure. This builds on the theory of complex trauma (Herman, 2015), which results from simultaneous or sequential occurrences of child maltreatment – including emotional abuse and neglect, sexual abuse, physical abuse, and witnessing domestic violence – that are chronic and beginning in early childhood.

These experiences in early childhood are found to be especially imperiling. Adverse Childhood Experiences (ACEs) refer to exposure to traumas during childhood. A CDC-Kaiser longitudinal study found correlations between these events and health behaviors/outcomes (Felitti et al., 1998). ACEs include:

- Recurrent physical abuse
- Recurrent emotional abuse
- Contact sexual abuse
- Having an alcohol or drug abuser in the household
- Having an incarcerated household member
- Having a household member who is chronically depressed, mentally ill, institutionalized, or suicidal
- Having a mother who was treated violently, such as witnessing your mother being a victim of domestic violence

- Having one or no parents, such as a parent who is out of the home either through death or divorce, and emotional and physical neglect.

As the number of ACEs increases so does the risk for conditions that follow the individual into later life:

- Alcoholism and alcohol abuse
- Chronic obstructive pulmonary disease
- Depression
- Fetal death
- Health-related quality of life
- Illicit drug use
- Ischemic heart disease
- Liver disease
- Poor work performance
- Financial stress
- Risk for intimate partner violence
- Multiple sexual partners
- Sexually transmitted diseases
- Smoking
- Suicide attempts
- Unintended pregnancies
- Early initiation of smoking
- Early initiation of sexual activity
- Adolescent pregnancy
- Risk for sexual violence
- Poor academic achievement.

Critical perspectives of trauma (see Pinderhughes, forthcoming), bridge systems of oppression to lived experience. Frameworks of restorative justice and collective healing combat delusions of superiority and separateness, encouraging empathic connections for the perpetrators, victims, and bystanders of trauma.

See also: Colonialism, Gene–Environment, Memory, Resilience, Resistance, Stress, War, Violence

Further Reading

Bauman, Z. (2016). *Strangers at our door*. Bristol: Polity Press.

Black, M. C. et al. (2010). *The national intimate partner and sexual violence survey (NISVS): 2010 summary report*. National Center for Injury Prevention and Control: Division of Violence Prevention.

Cahill, A. J. (2001). *Rethinking rape*. Ithaca, NY: Cornell University Press.

DeGruy, J. (2005). *Post traumatic slave syndrome*. Portland, OR: Uptone Press.

Felitti, V. J., Anda, R. F., Nordenberg, D., Williamson, D. F., Spitz, A. M., Edwards, V., & Marks, J. S. (1998). Relationship of childhood abuse and household dysfunction to many of the leading causes of death in adults: The adverse childhood experiences (ACE) study. *American Journal of Preventive Medicine, 14*(4), 245–258.

Fink, B. (1997). *A clinical introduction to Lacanian psychoanalysis*. Cambridge, MA: Harvard University Press.

Gross, N. (2016). Are Americans experiencing collective trauma? *The New York Times: Sunday Review*, December 18, p. 8.

Herman, J. L. (2015). *Trauma and recovery* (second edition). New York: Basic Books.

Laplanche, J. (1974). *The language of psychoanalysis*. New York: Norton.

Pinderhughes, H. (forthcoming). *Dealing with danger: How inner-city youth cope with the violence that surrounds them*. Philadelphia, PA: Temple University Press.

Pinderhughes, H., Davis, R., & Williams, M. (2015). Adverse community experiences and resilience: A framework for addressing and preventing community trauma. Oakland, CA: Community Trauma Prevention Institute.

Van der Kolk, B. (2014). *The body keeps the score: Brain, mind, and body in the healing of trauma*. New York: Viking Press.

Trolling

Internet slang for those who inflame or provoke outrage by saying hyperbolic vile things on the web. Feminist activists who write blogs or participate in social media regularly get trolled on their platforms and in message boards. Their voices are derogatorily labeled "social justice warriors," denoting excess zealotry and therefore to be dismissed.

The conventional wisdom among activists is "Do not feed the trolls," as they eat up emotional energy, and engaging them only encourages them.

See also: Alt-Right, Digital Sphere

Tweetstorm

Describes a flurry of Twitter posts, or tweets, designed to support a "trending" idea that influences public opinion for or against an issue or candidate.

Social Security Works organized tweeting on policy topics, calling it a "Tweetnado." The power of the Twitter hashtag is its ability to hyperlink ideas and to show the varying landscape of a single word or concept. Tweetstorms may also be used to document injustice. Hashtags such as #cronesolidarity have been used to create a radical feminist aging alliance.

Hashtags are also used to launch social media campaigns instigating social movements such as #blacklivesmatter, #sayhername, #CarryThatWeight, #metoo, and #OccupyWallStreet. In aging policy, several hashtags have linked a support base for critical ideas. For example, Maya Rockeymoore promotes the #inclusionrevolution. Social Security Works and The National Committee to Preserve Social Security & Medicare have produced #ScrapTheCap seeking to boost revenues for and benefits under Social Security.

A disturbing development is the detection by the US intelligence community and others of Bots that produce and reproduce millions of messages through Tweetstorms and other social media; giving the erroneous distortion of trending public views the use of Bot campaigns is a fake disfiguring of US democratic values, processes, and communications. Russian interferences (plural is intended here) in US elections have been tracked to the successful deployment of Bots and other techniques across social media in propaganda campaigns to sway public opinion and disrupt democratic processes, including vote preferences.

See also: Digital Sphere, Framing, Textuality

U

Underground

Describes a space or spaces where transgressive or subversive ideas may circulate or events may occur. The Underground Railroad prior to the Civil War and the Weather Underground of counter-cultural resistance in the 1970s are two well-known examples of this.

In the context of geographies, it can be an alternative and hidden channel extending through liminal spaces. The Underground itself possesses a quality of liminality.

See also: Liminality, Subversive

United States Constitution

The formational document of the United States, replacing the unwieldy Articles of Confederation in 1789. It sets forth the function and structure of American government as a federal republic. The system put in place by the Constitution relies on a separation of powers, implementing checks and balances to prevent tyrannical forces, as deemed by the founders from driving government policy. In practice the convoluted structure of governance in the United States empowers smaller, more entrenched groups and requires incredibly high thresholds for significant changes in governance.

The meaning of constitutional provisions is ultimately interpreted by the Supreme Court. In 1937, the Court ruled that Social Security, and the expanded federal powers necessary to fund and implement it, was constitutionally sound. Justice Benjamin J. Cardoza stated on the subject, "Only a power that is national can serve the interests of all" (Koff & Park, 1999, p. 165). This decision solidified the federal government's role in providing social insurance for the elderly and others, a function that it serves to this day.

The first amendment of the Bill of Rights added to the Constitution guarantees freedom of speech and of the press. This permits a crucial capacity for speaking to power. Critiquing dominant forces, unveiling brutality, and documenting exploitation are part of a long tradition in journalism and scholarship and are enabled by the first amendment. This right is the only hope for capitalism to have something akin to a conscience.

Following his 2016 presidential election, Donald Trump mounted a sustained and vitriolic assault on the press and freedom of speech. Journalist Christiane Amanpour (2016) spoke of being chilled by Trump's attacks: "We must fight against the normalization of what is unacceptable." In late 2017, internal White House advice to the Centers for Disease Control (CDC) dissuaded staff from using words and phrases such as "evidence-based," "vulnerable," and "diversity" in CDC reports. This is understood as an attempt to discredit and silence scientific conclusions that are or may be unfavorable to Trump Administration policies. Censorship is a word that comes to mind, although an ongoing campaign to promote anti-science discourse is an apt description as well.

See also: Priviledge, Right to Have Rights, Social Security, States' Rights

Further Reading

Amanpour, C. (2016). Journalism faces an "existential crisis" in Trump era. *CNN*, November 23. Retrieved from www.cnn.com/2016/11/23/opinions/christiane-amanpour-journalism-in-trump-era/.

Koff, T. H. & Park, R. W. (1999). *Aging public policy: Bonding the generations* (second edition). Amityville, NY: Baywood Publishing.

V

Veterans (with contribution by Natalie Purcell)

Those who have served in the military, now retired from combat or service. The population of living US veterans is estimated at approximately 20 million (National Center for Veterans Analysis and Statistics (NCVAS), 2017; Veterans' Affairs Office of Policy and Planning, 2017). Although the twenty-first century has seen the longest war in US history (Astore, 2017), the number of living veterans in the United States has gradually declined as fewer Americans serve in the country's now all-volunteer military. The veteran population has dropped by approximately 50 percent since 1980 (Livingston, 2016), and the Department of Veterans Affairs projects that it will decrease by another 30 percent or more over the next 20 years (NCVAS, 2017). At the same time, the population of veterans is changing, with increasing numbers of women serving in the military (including in combat roles). Today, racial and ethnic minority groups comprise over 23 percent of veterans, a number that is projected to increase to over 32 percent in the next two decades (NCVAS, 2017).

Veterans tend to have higher rates of chronic disease and common health conditions like diabetes and cancer compared to the general population (Eibner et al., 2016), some of which is attributable to their military service and combat exposures. Veterans are also more likely to struggle with serious mental illnesses, especially post-traumatic stress disorder or PTSD (American Psychological Association, 2007; Tanielian & Jaycox, 2008). Notably, nearly a quarter of Iraq War veterans met the diagnostic criteria for PTSD eight years after deployment (Vasterling et al., 2016). However, Traumatic Brain Injury (TBI), resulting from blasts or other impacts to the head, is known as the signature wound of the Wars in Iraq and Afghanistan (Snell & Halter, 2010), affecting approximately 17% of post-9/11 US military veterans (Lindquist, Love, & Elbogen, 2017). Other problems commonly linked to military service include alcohol and substance abuse, relationship difficulties, and various reintegration challenges (American Psychological Association, 2007; Tanielian & Jaycox, 2008). Sometimes known as "moral injury," many veterans also grapple with spiritual wounds in the aftermath of war's violence (Purcell et al., 2016; Shay, 1994).

Veterans who are honorably discharged from the US military are entitled to certain benefits for their service. Benefits from the Veterans' Administration (VA) include college tuition (GI Bill), government-paid health care, and special disability pay for those wounded in combat. The VA health care system is the largest public health care system in the United States. Approximately 8.9 million veterans are enrolled in VA health care, and over 5 million veterans rely on VA for care each year (Veterans' Affairs Office of Policy and Planning, 2017). The VA provides care that is comparable and, by many common quality measures, superior to care delivered in the private sector (Blay et al., 2017; O'Hanlon et al., 2017). However, limited resources and high-profile scandals have driven ongoing efforts to privatize veterans' health care (Gordon, 2017). In general, long-standing veterans' advocacy organizations, such as the American Legion and the Veterans of Foreign Wars, have advocated for improving VA health care, rather than privatizing care or eliminating a public health care option for veterans.

VA has responded, in part, with a "Whole Health" initiative, which focuses on delivering personalized, integrated, biopsychosocial care to veterans, and improving access to peer support, health coaching, and complementary and integrative care modalities (Shulkin, 2016; United States Department of Veterans' Affairs, 2017). The Whole Health transformation is consistent with VA's efforts to meet the unique needs of the veteran population with tailored initiatives, such as its homelessness eradication efforts (U.S. Department of Housing and Urban Development-VA Supportive Housing Program; Veterans' Health Administration Office of Mental Health, 2017a) and its justice outreach program for incarcerated veterans (Veterans' Justice Outreach Program; Veterans' Health Administration Office of Mental Health, 2017b).

For the families of many veterans, Social Security represents an important source of income security. Nearly one in five recipients of Social Security is a veteran. When a service member dies their family is usually eligible to receive survivor benefits through Social Security until their children have completed high school. The widow of a service member, with or without children, is also entitled to benefits through the Department of Veterans' Affairs for life or until remarriage. The families of American contractors killed while working abroad may also receive Social Security benefits and are additionally protected by federally mandated workers' compensation (Reno, Cardwell, & Lavery, 2006). Veterans also rely on Social Security for disability insurance and income later in life. In addition, for just under half of all veterans receiving disability insurance, Social Security benefits represent over three-quarters or more of their total income.

See also: Military Industrial Complex, Social Insurance, Social Security, Trauma

Further Reading

American Psychological Association. (2007). *The psychological needs of U.S. Military service members and their families: A preliminary report.* American Psychological Association. Association Presidential Task Force on Military Deployment Services for Youth, Families and Service Members. Retrieved from www.apa.org/about/policy/military-deployment-services.pdf.

Astore, W. J. (2017). The longest war in American history has no end in sight. *The Nation*, February 28. Retrieved from www.thenation.com/article/the-longest-war-in-american-history-has-no-end-in-sight/.

Blay, E., DeLancey, J. O., Hewitt, D. B., Chung, J. W., & Bilimoria, K. Y. (2017). Initial public reporting of quality at Veterans Affairs vs. non-Veterans Affairs hospitals. *JAMA Internal Medicine, 177*(6), 882–885. https://doi.org/10.1001/jama internmed.2017.0605.

Eibner, C., Krull, H., Brown, K. M., Cefalu, M., Mulcahy, A. W., Pollard, M., & Farmer, C. M. (2016). Current and projected characteristics and unique health care needs of the patient population served by the Department of Veterans Affairs. *Rand Health Quarterly*, *5*(4). Retrieved from www.ncbi.nlm.nih.gov/pmc/articles/PMC5158228/.

Gordon, S. (2017). *The battle for veterans' healthcare: Dispatches from the frontlines of policy making and patient care*. Ithaca, NY: Cornell Publishing.

Lindquist, L. K., Love, H. C., & Elbogen, E. B. (2017). Traumatic brain injury in Iraq and Afghanistan veterans: New results from a national random sample study. *The Journal of Neuropsychiatry and Clinical Neurosciences*, *29*(3), 254–259. https://doi.org/10.1176/appi.neuropsych.16050100.

Livingston, G. (2016). Profile of U.S. veterans is changing dramatically as their ranks decline. November 11. Retrieved from www.pewresearch.org/fact-tank/2016/11/11/profile-of-u-s-veterans-is-changing-dramatically-as-their-ranks-decline/.

Military Health Policy Research. Retrieved from www.rand.org/pubs/monographs/MG720.html.

National Center for Veterans Analysis and Statistics. (2017). *Veteran population projections 2017–2037*. United States Department of Veterans Affairs. Retrieved from www.va.gov/vetdata/.

O'Hanlon, C., Huang, C., Sloss, E., Price, R. A., Hussey, P., Farmer, C., & Gidengil, C. (2017). Comparing VA and non-VA quality of care: A systematic review. *Journal of General Internal Medicine*, *32*(1), 105–121. https://doi.org/10.1007/s11606-016-3775-2.

Purcell, N., Koenig, C. J., Bosch, J., & Maguen, S. (2016). Veterans' perspectives on the psychosocial impact of killing in war. *Counseling Psychologist*, *44*(7), 1062–1099. https://doi.org/10.1177/0011000016666156.

Reno, V. P., Cardwell, A., & Lavery, J. (2006). *Survivor benefits for families of deceased servicemembers and overseas contract workers*. National Academy of Social Insurance.

Shay, J. (1994). *Achilles in Vietnam: Combat trauma and the undoing of character*. New York: Simon and Schuster.

Shulkin, D. J. (2016). Beyond the VA crisis: Becoming a high-performance network. *New England Journal of Medicine*, *374*(11), 1003–1005. https://doi.org/10.1056/NEJMp1600307.

Snell, F. I. & Halter, M. J. (2010). A signature wound of war: Mild traumatic brain injury. *Journal of Psychosocial Nursing and Mental Health Services*, *48*(2), 22–28. https://doi.org/10.3928/02793695-20100107-01.

Social Security works for veterans and active military members. (2016). Social Security Works. Retrieved from www.socialsecurityworks.org/2016/04/04/social-security-works-for-veterans-and-active-military-members/.

Tanielian, T. & Jaycox, L. H. (2008). *Invisible wounds of war: Psychological and cognitive injuries, their consequences, and services to assist recovery*. RAND Center for Military Health Policy Research. Washington, DC: RAND Corporation.

United States Department of Veterans' Affairs. (2017). About Whole Health – VA patient centered care [general information]. Retrieved from www.va.gov/PATIENTCENTEREDCARE/explore/about-whole-health.asp.

Vasterling, J. J., Aslan, M., Proctor, S. P., Ko, J., Marx, B. P., Jakupcak, M., & Concato, J. (2016). Longitudinal examination of posttraumatic stress disorder as a long-term outcome of Iraq War deployment. *American Journal of Epidemiology*, *184*(11), 796–805. https://doi.org/10.1093/aje/kww151.

Veterans' Affairs Office of Policy and Planning. (2017). National Center for Veterans' Analysis and Statistics [Homepage]. Retrieved from www.va.gov/vetdata/.

Veterans' Health Administration Office of Mental Health. (2017a). U.S. Department of Housing and Urban Development-VA

Supportive Housing (HUD-VASH) Program – Homeless Veterans [general information]. Retrieved from www.va.gov/homeless/hud-vash.asp.

Veterans' Health Administration Office of Mental Health. (2017b). Veterans Justice Outreach Program – Homeless Veterans [general information]. Retrieved from www.va.gov/homeless/vjo.asp.

Violence

Administered force intended to hurt, violate, or kill.

Violent attacks may not be consciously intentional, as seen in microaggressions, and the violence of racist ideologies is a major oppressive force with which American ethnic minorities need to contend. Pinderhughes (1997) examines the development of racial identities and racism in youth, focusing on the reverberations of racial violence at a community level. He proposes that community- and school-based education are essential for disrupting the indoctrination of intolerance. This extends to questions in later life, such as (1) how do older adults, especially those relying on people of color caregivers, confront the violence they perpetrate or perpetuate; and, of course, (2) how do caregivers and other care professionals, such as doctors, psychotherapists, and physical therapists, reflect on their positions of privilege and consider the stereotypes they hold that they threaten their clients?

Critical theorists locate violence at State and societal levels. Structural violence (Galtung, 1969) considers how violence and injustice are embedded in the landscape of policy. As described elsewhere, violence is normalized and part of the doxa – everyday and everynight assaults on the personhood and dignity of individuals exists through patriarchal and classist systems that perpetuate exclusion, exploitation, and sexual violence. Structural violence operates like a bear trap waiting to snap – like the donut hole in Medicare prescription drug coverage – or a neglected and inadequate safety net, like COLAs that do not keep pace with actual increases in the cost of living.

There are ideological dimensions of violence as well. Terror events inspire fear and panic more than other forms of violence, though the actual threat may be statistically significantly less. Heightened fears about terror attacks reinforce xenophobia, which can distract from concerns about more pernicious events, like legislation withdrawing the social safety net. Millions of uninsured individuals face premature death, though it makes less splashy headlines than gruesome, yet isolated, bombings or shootings.

Arguments over what constitutes violence also frame scholarship and theory of social movements. Shon Meckfessel (2016) examined the debates regarding destruction of property and rioting and how these are framed in social movements. He identifies how non-violence is proposed and privileged as morally righteous. A relevant consideration is that riots may represent little or no more danger than sanctioned State violence.

A new appreciation of violence recognition is in sexual violence against girls and women. Intimate partner violence (IPV) is a public health concern. The cumulative social costs of IPV are "Serious threats to economic security and opportunity and contribute to women's economic inequality" according to the Institute for Women's Policy Research (IWPR) in its Economic Security for Survivors Project (Bocinski, 2017). IPV contributes to eroding wages, rising medical bills, and the tightening financial grip of partners. Wendy Max and colleagues (2001) calculate US national expenditures and consequences. Gun violence through mass shootings is a tragic and rising problem, for which the power of the NRA has for decades successfully repressed Congressional action, and even publicly funded research, with limited exceptions (Max & Rice, 1993; Max, 1999).

The #metoo sexual harassment/abuse, hate crimes, and mass shootings signal the urgency of US and global action for the security and protection from predatory violence against targeted individuals and groups. The Trump Administration deployed ambivalent and minimalist steps by disbanding initiatives and funding cuts for the Violence Against Women Act (VAWA) administered under the Department of Justice. VAWA's mission embraces the prevention and protection of the targeting of groups such as women, children, immigrants, and LGBT persons. The 2013 VAWA Act reauthorization included increases in visas available to battered immigrant women fleeing their abusers, new non-discrimination protections for LGBT survivors of violence, and a provision granting tribal courts the authority to prosecute non-Native Americans who abused Native women on tribal land. However, Trump's Attorney General (AG) Jeff Sessions voted against the VAWA reauthorization when he was a US Senator. The AG who runs the Department of Justice (DoJ) is charged with guarding and overseeing VAWA violations. Due to an unusual historic paradox, the first Trump AG reflected the contradictory structural location of vetoing a bill that he was later charged with carrying out as AG.

The State's violence against undocumented immigrants, and those seeking asylum, manifested through detention centers, family separations, and coercive measures for "self-deportation." Simultaneously, Trump AG Jeff Sessions attacked former qualifications for special groups fleeing persecution for those escaping domestic violence and gang violence. AG Sessions was fired after 2018 mid-term elections, and replaced by Interim AG and legal battles.

See also: Crisis, Framing, Microaggressions, Oppression, Racism, Resistance, The State, Stereotype Threat, Trauma, War, War on Women

Further Reading

Bocinski, S. G. (2017). *The nation*, (9/20). Economic Security for Survivors Project. Washington, DC: IWPR.

Castañeda, E. & Schneider, C. L. (Eds.). (2017). *Collective violence, contentious politics, and social change: A Charles Tilly reader*. New York: Routledge.

Galtung, J. (1969). Violence, peace, and peace research. *Journal of Peace Research*, 6(3), 167–191.

Max, W. (1999). Economic analysis of firearm injuries in California. Fifth National Handgun Epidemic Lowering Plan (HELP) Network Conference, San Francisco, February 5–6.

Max, W. & Rice, D. (1993). Shooting in the dark: Estimating the cost of firearm injuries. *Health Affairs* (winter), 171–185.

Max, W., Rice, D. P., Finkelstein, E., Bardwell, R. A., & Leadbetter, M. S. (2001). The economic toll of intimate partner violence against women in the United States, 1995. *Violence and Victims*, 19(3), 259–272.

Meckfessel, S. (2016). *Nonviolence ain't what it used to be: Unarmed insurrection and the rhetoric of resistance*. Edinburgh: AK Press.

Pinderhughes, H. (1997). *Race in the hood*. Minneapolis, MN: University of Minnesota Press.

Voice(lessness)

Refers to the power of expression and communication or lack thereof.

Voice articulates agency, presence, and desire. It is affect made known and embodied. Voicelessness is deprivation of opportunity or capacity for speech or speech acts. It is rendered through trauma which shuts off expression. Culturally this appears through the preferential distribution of social support or public goods, and material income deprivation for others. Impoverished people spend energy and time struggling for survival. They get pushed out of desirable spaces and moved to the outskirts of communities, becoming less visible and valued. The net effect is to silence their voices.

In the field of aging, one of the prime examples of "voicelessness" is nursing home residents, many of whom are accomplished professionals and all of whom are rich in life experience, but are virtually never asked about anything except, e.g., whether they want pudding or cake. The topic of elder abuse and the voicelessness of nursing home residents have stimulated major efforts to improve quality of care and culture change, as illustrated by Shura et al. (2010).

See also: Agency, Cognitive Liberation, Desire, Discourse, Power, Resistance, Trauma

Further Reading

Shura, R., Siders, R. A., & Dannefer, D. (2010). Culture change in long-term care: Participatory action research and the role of the resident. *The Gerontologist, 51*(2), 212–225.

Wage Inequality

Describes the gap between earners, especially between those that do similar work or have similar experience or merits, defined by the slogan "Equal Pay for Equal Work." The inequality can be located through intersections of gender and race. Inequalities in pay show how employers use cost-cutting strategies, exploiting the status quo, and precarity, adopting what they can get away with, to increase wage inequality.

A decade of legislation sought to close the gap. The Lilly Ledbetter Fair Pay Act (2009) allows recourse for gendered wage inequality for 180 days following the last paycheck. Obama's 2014 Fair Pay and Safe Workplaces order prohibited wage discrimination among federal contractors. In 2017, Trump revoked the 2014 order and blocked other initiatives designed to minimize wage inequality.

Since wage income informs the dollar amount of Social Security benefits one receives upon retirement, discrimination resulting in lower wages in early life manifests itself in lower benefit amount received in later life. In addition, as older workers increase their years in the workforce, wage inequality is a lens with which to see race, ethnicity, gender, class and other discrepancies, fairness, and favoritism in pay over the lifespan. The wage gap between women of color and white men is very high, with African American women earning about 67 cents to a white man's dollar and Latina women earning 62 cents to a white man's dollar (Hegewisch & Williams-Baron, 2017). The large wage gap between black and brown men compared to white men is a similar case of persistent and institutionally sanctioned practices that advantage white males' earnings.

Occupations themselves are classed, gendered, and raced setting up the systemic framework for wage inequality. Caregiving, teaching, and predominantly female-led occupations earn considerably less than male-dominated engineering, science, and white-collar careers. The gender wage gap adds to the significant poverty of children, especially for people of color and single mothers experiencing multiple jeopardies (Hegewisch & Williams-Baron, 2017).

See also: Cumulative Advantage/Disadvantage, Inequality, Jeopardy, Oppression, Racial Wealth Gap, War on Women

Further Reading

Hegewisch, A. & Williams-Baron, E. (2017). *The gender wage gap by occupation 2016 and by race and ethnicity*. Washington, DC: Institute for Women's Policy Research/ IWPR.

War

An effort to attack or defend against the Other. The discourse of war is a declaration that legitimizes violence and is an act of framing (Butler, 2009). It is a crusade against a threat, be it another country or an ideological battle on drugs, poverty, women, or people of color. It is part of how reactive networks utilize scarcity, crisis, and terror to form cohesive identities which wards off outsiders and limits opportunities for insiders to articulate difference (Karatzogianni & Robinson, 2017).

Nor is warfare simply framed. Chomsky and Fraser provide a Human Rights framing on war-making in *The new military humanism: Lessons from Kosovo* (1999). Therein humanism is used as a smokescreen for powerful countries to pursue their own agendas through violent means. Piven (2004) illuminates the domestic costs of war at home and how war is a power strategy employed to advance the business agenda at home and rollback social spending. Klein (2007) details the uses of public disorientation following massive collective shocks – terrorist attacks, natural disasters, nuclear war threats – to advance undemocratic and unpopular economic shock therapy, globally and in the USA. War's impacts on modern society are multifaceted. On the heels of the Korean War, President Eisenhower warned against a growing military-industrial complex, an industry of war-profiteering where for-profit contractors structurally penetrate governmental agencies and agendas. Former vice-president Dick Cheney was previously the head of Halliburton, a contractor that received billions in income from prosecution of wars against Iraq and Afghanistan. Whether he directly earned anything from the wars engaged during his time in office is unclear, but the fact remains that war greatly benefited his company's growth and highlights the permeable barrier between public and private entities in the defense sector.

For veterans of war there are tiers of privilege in medical care and educational access. This is complicated by historical discrimination against women and LGBTQ populations who were barred from, or restricted in, military service, and further complicated by the class dynamics of military recruitment and the draft. The burden of war, especially in terms of sacrifice of life, lies most heavily on the working class. The differentiated provision of post-military services into later life for certain populations further increases this burden.

Many people displaced by war seek refuge in other countries that may not have social insurance coverage to assist them in old age. They also may be unable to draw upon social programs to help themselves and their families. Through this process war creates large populations of geographically, financially, and socially dislocated people, including the elderly.

See also: Neocolonialism, Statelessness, Trauma, Veterans

Further Reading

Binney, E. A. & Estes, C. L. (1988). The retreat of the state and its transfer of responsibility: The intergenerational war. *International Journal of Health Services, 18*(1), 83–96.

Butler, J. (2009). *Frames of war: When is life grievable?* New York: Verso.

Chomsky, N. & Fraser, N. (1999). *The new military humanism: Lessons from Kosovo.* Monroe, ME: Common Courage Press.

Karatzogianni, A. & Robinson, A. (2017). Schizorevolutions versus microfascisms: The fear of anarchy in state securitisation. *Journal of International Political Theory, 13*(3), 282–295.

Klein, N. (2007). *The shock doctrine: The rise of disaster capitalism.* New York: Metropolitan Books.

Piven, F. F. (2004). *The war at home: The domestic costs of Bush's militarism.* New York: The New Press.

War on Women

Centers on US efforts to deny and obliterate women's rights to (1) reproductive choice; (2) equal gender access to health care; (3) protections of women's and girls' equal gender benefits and coverage under social and health insurance and safety net programs; and (4) protections against sex and gender discrimination and violence in the workforce, home, community, and society. Each of these fronts of the war is particularly harmful to mid-life and older women, people of color, and low- or no-income wage earners and caregivers (Estes, 2017/2018).

Trump's election reawakened public consciousness and media coverage of the resurging War on Women. It is credited with inspiring multiple post-inaugural million women marches in the USA and abroad. Women everywhere donned the new women's symbol of resistance: pink pussy hats.

War on Women is the appropriate name for the waves of attacks on the economic security, health security, the empowerment of women, and relentless efforts to further undermine the most vulnerable women by State policy-makers and powerful stakeholders in the United States. House Leader Nancy Pelosi and Senator Barbara Boxer popularized the term during the 2010 Congressional elections. Pelosi launched the campaign, "When Women Succeed, America Succeeds." When Republican presidential candidate Donald Trump accused Democratic nominee Hillary Clinton of playing the woman card, she exclaimed, "Deal me in!"

Figure W1 War on Women
Source: Illustration by Tyler Feder @tylerfeder.

The political and legislative conflict is between those supporting the rights and needs of women and girls against many forms of sex and gender discrimination, including the right to privacy and individual choices with regard to their own bodies versus those seeking to: (1) reclaim the patriarchal rights of men to impose State control and religious restrictions over women and their bodies, and (2) advance market fundamentalism without regard to the health and economic consequences to vulnerable women of color, low-income and single mothers and grandmothers disadvantaged by the market and its power brokers. The governmental plan for defunding Planned Parenthood is taken as a material symbol of War on Women.

See also: Affordable Care Act (ACA), Medicaid, Medicare, Reproduction, The Social, Social Security

Further Reading

Brody, E. M. (2003). *Women in the middle: Their parent-care years*. New York: Springer.

Estes, C. L. (2017/2018). Women's rights, women's status, and women's resistance in the age of Trump. *Generations: Journal of the American Society on Aging, 41*(4), 36–44.

McCammon, H. J., Taylor, V., Reger, J., & Einwohner, R. L. (Eds.). (2017). *The Oxford handbook of U.S. women's social movements activism*. Oxford: Oxford University Press.

Traister, R. (2018). *Good and mad: The revolutionary power of women's anger*. New York: Simon & Schuster.

Watch Dogs/Watch Bitches

Progressive monitors observing and calling out unjust representation in media. Watch dogging and watch bitching in the public interest is a pivotal element of praxis in the critical gerontologists' and public intellectuals' tool-box. Muckraking and whistle-blowing are an honorable part of radical movement history that require teaching in the academy and through activist and practitioner mobilization.

As an example, Maggie Kuhn and the Gray Panthers (GPs) Media Watch viewed broadcast television for jokes, portrayals, and discourse that denigrated older persons. This opened the way for Kuhn's testimony before the Federal Communications Commission (FCC) on ageism in the media, and indirectly, to the successful passage of the Age Discrimination Act. Maggie Kuhn's famous TV rebuke of Johnny Carson's ageism in his portrayal of "Aunt Blabby" captured headlines for FCC regulatory action and policy change.

Watch dogging and watch bitching provides the content, the delineation of the treatment, the exposure of a situation in a different light (and sunlight). Witnessing and empathy are key processes in social movement mobilization. Even morality may be recaptured and guided into consciousness and action. The expansion of the Right's conservative vanguard would not be possible without making rights a centerpiece of watching and witnessing campaigns, firmly linking politics and morality as George Lakoff (2004/2014) posits. From the Left perspective, examples of watch dogging and watch bitching build off of Black Lives Matter, Occupy/the 99 percent, the bears on melting icebergs, Martin Luther King's addresses on Black/Negro/African American rights as human rights, Hillary Clinton's Beijing pronouncement that women's rights are human rights, and US Attorney General Loretta Lynch's stand on transgender rights as human rights.

Watch dogging in the public interest is a re-energized preoccupation. During the 2016 presidential elections, the airwaves, blogosphere, and all forms of media filled the public space (including smut newsstand magazines) with heretofore unimagined disinformation, lies, fake news, alternative facts, hacktivist products, and foreign and US intelligence interventions. Disruption of the existing, usual, "normal" "social order" and social expectations was a winning strategy of the right wing, imposing and capturing breaking news. Concepts of trolling, doxxing, fake news, and alternative facts fill the dialogue of the moral agents installed in the 115th and 116th Congress and the White House, giving new meaning to the cliché "There is a new Sheriff in town." A humorous media catchphrase quotes Congressional and White House GOP-ers as acting, not as the nation's watch dogs on national security (e.g., Russian meddling), but being the President's "lapdogs."

See also: Anonymous, Discourse, Framing, Praxis, Trolling

Further Reading

Lakoff, G. (2004/2014). *The all new don't think of an elephant! Know your values and frame the debate.* White River Junction, VT: Chelsea Green Publishing.

Welfare State

A system in which the State assumes responsibility for the protection and promotion of the social and economic well-being of its citizens through pensions, grants, programs, and other benefits. Welfare states may provide an array of housing, health care, and employment insurance for their citizens. Western welfare states have shielded workers from biographical or market exigencies and employed economic policies to regulate and stimulate growth (Piven & Cloward, 1997, p. 12). Social rights in welfare states were won largely through labor movements.

Esping-Andersen (1990) differentiates welfare states by organizational logic, their capacity to loosen labor market dependence, their effects on social stratification, and the relations between State and market. His contribution is linking State regimes with stratification outcomes in three models: (1) residual welfare states (USA, Canada, UK), (2) conservative welfare states (Germany, France, Italy), and (3) social democratic welfare states (Scandinavia). Feminist scholar Jane Lewis and others countered Esping-Andersen's models with gender-specific typologies based on states' treatment of women as wives, mothers, and workers (Lewis, 1992; O'Connor, Orloff, & Shaver, 1999). European welfare states may be classified as strong, moderate, or weak in terms of a "male breadwinner" model, depending on women's entitlement as citizen, mother, and/or worker.

Since Ronald Reagan's 1980 election, aging policy has steadily embraced the privatization of public and non-profit services and of vast State subsidies of the welfare state Medicare program through the medical industrial complex (Estes, 1991). Financial institutions of transnational capitalism such as the International Monetary Fund and the World Bank began undermining the welfare state entitlements as a condition of providing international development loans all over the world (Estes & Phillipson, 2002). The banks' claim was that being part of the global community required opening up a state's health and other services to private corporate markets in health and social services – in many cases actually dismantling universal state provision of health care (Mendoza, 2015).

Ferge (1997) aptly characterizes the changed welfare paradigm as "the individualization of the social" through which global changes in welfare state objectives and principles moved from modern to neo-liberal, privatization, and means-testing. It is notable that this transition has occurred despite public disapproval. It has produced deleterious changes in the erosion of generational solidarity and rising inequalities, with profound implications for social and health security. Consolidation and intervention of financial transnational capitalism has diminished the role of the welfare state in developed and developing nations. The State's role is increasingly centered on mediating conflicts over financing of care and support for vulnerable and other deserving groups such as older people versus free markets and their unfettered capital flight and offshore tax avoidance schemes. Elected politicians have avoided explicit steps to mitigate massive job outsourcing, contracting, and excessive corporate pay. Diminishing corporate responsibility is matched with ambiguous loyalty of corporations to the nation-state and its people.

The contemporary US welfare state is reviled by politicians on the Right, especially targeting Franklin D. Roosevelt's most successful and pervasively popular social insurance program, Social Security. Conservatives have bashed the term "welfare state" as if it were a dirty word and have done the same in trashing the once-revered word "entitlement." Progressives have adopted this messaging, promoting concepts like "earned benefit." For five decades, the stated mission of conservative think tanks and policy-makers has been to destroy the welfare state as instituted by Roosevelt in the 1930s and Lyndon B. Johnson in the 1960s. Social Security, Medicare, and Medicaid are continuously assailed by policy-makers on the Right as inimical to individual freedom and responsibility. Beginning in 2017, the Trump Administration took actions (and inactions) to dismantle the welfare state through crafted executive orders, Cabinet appointees, deregulatory changes, federal agency closures, and startling budget cuts to social programs.

Virtually neglected in welfare state attacks coming from the conservative Right is the fact that there are different experiences of the welfare state according to social class, race, ethnicity, ability, age, and gender. Bach (2017, p. 5) observes that the welfare state "privileges some and subordinates others." There is limited literature on the "hidden," "submerged" forms of "welfare for the wealthy." There are marked "administrative inequalities" across class characterizing benefits of US social welfare provision and administration. There is "hyper-regulation" (punitive and risky) for those at the bottom or on the lower middle rungs of the income and social status order. The Welfare State:

> distributes significant benefits regressively, to households with substantial wealth. . . . Those who are economically disadvantaged are . . . subject to a social welfare state that is meager, punitive, and tremendously risky for those who receive its benefits. . . . But for those with economic privilege, the story is quite different. Families and individuals with significant economic privilege benefit disproportionately from a whole host of cash and near-cash benefits that are neither meager nor punitive. . . . Benefits for the rich function as nearly invisible entitlements.
>
> (Bach, 2017, p. 3)

Trump's 2017 Tax Reform and Jobs Act is a classic illustration of the structured entitlement advantage to the wealthy and Wall Street.

A critical gerontological perspective on the welfare state starts from the fact that the American institutions supporting the welfare of American citizens are limited compared to more robust institutions in Western Europe. Nevertheless, under pressures from globalization and other forces, structural adjustment policies have challenged and curtailed welfare state policies in the European Union as well. Critical gerontologists note that, even in most generous nations, welfare state, regulations, and benefits impose social control as well as offer potential pathways for empowerment (Piven & Cloward, 1993). In the USA the State continues to impose male over female preferences in key policy domains, ensuring a masculinist state (Brown, 1992) and major inequities by race, ethnicity, class, gender, ability, and age (Estes, 2005, 2017/2018). This exemplifies and contradicts the notion of the welfare state as guardian of rights and basic needs of all citizens as well as visions of empowerment, liberty, and the reduction of market-based inequality (Walker, 2011).

See also: Globalization, Ideology, Privatization, The Social, The State

Further Reading

Aspalter, C. (2008). Understanding European social policy. March 1. Retrieved from SSRN: https://ssrn.com/abstract= 2665512 or http://dx.doi.org/10.2139/ ssrn.2665512.

Bach, W. A. (2017). Poor support/rich support: (Re)viewing the American social welfare state. *Florida Tax Review* (spring).

Brown, W. (1992). Finding the man in the state. *Feminist Studies, 18*(1), 7–34.

Esping-Andersen, G. (1990). *Three worlds of welfare capitalism.* Cambridge: Polity Press.

Estes, C. L. (1991). The Reagan legacy: Privatization, the welfare state, and aging in the 1990s. In J. Myles and J. S. Quadagno (Eds.), *States, labor markets, and the future of old age policy* (pp. 59–93). Philadelphia, PA: Temple University Press.

Estes, C. L. (2005). Women, ageing and inequality: A feminist perspective. In M. Johnson (Ed.), *Cambridge handbook of age and ageing* (pp. 525–529). Cambridge: Cambridge University Press.

Estes, C. L. (2017/2018). Women's rights, women's status, women's resistance in the age of Trump. *GENERATIONS: Journal of the American Society on Aging, 41*(4), 36–44.

Estes, C. L. & Phillipson, C. (2002). The globalization of capital, the welfare state, and old age policy. *International Journal of Health Services, 32,* 279–297.

Estes, C. L. & Philipson, C. (2007). Critical gerontology. In J. Birren (Ed.), *Encyclopedia of age, aging, and the aged* (pp. 330–336). San Diego, CA: Academic Press.

Ferge, Z. (1997). The changed welfare paradigm: The individualization of the social. *Social Policy & Administration, 31*(1), 20–44. doi:10.1111/1467–9515.00035.

Gamble, A. (2016). *Can the welfare state survive?* Cambridge: Polity Press.

Gough, I. (1980). *The political economy of the welfare state.* London: Macmillan.

Judt, T. (2015). *When the facts change: Essays, 1995–2010.* London: Cornerstone.

Lewis, J. (1992). The decline of the male breadwinner model. *Journal of European Social Policy. 2*(3), 159–173.

Mendoza, K-A. (2015). *Austerity: The demolition of the welfare state and the rise of the zombie economy.* Oxford: New Internationalist Publishers.

O'Connor, J. S., Orloff, A. S., & Shaver, S. (1999). *States, markets, families: Gender, liberalism and social policy in Australia, Canada, Great Britain, & the U.S.* New York: Cambridge University Press.

Pascall, G. (2008). Gender policy. In P. Abrahamson & C. Aspalte (Eds.), *Understanding European social policy* (ch. 10). Taiwan: China: Casa Verde Publishers.

Piven, F. F. & Cloward, R. A. (1985). *The new class war.* New York: Pantheon Books.

Piven, F. F. & Cloward, R. A. (1993). *Regulating the poor.* New York: Vintage.

Piven, F. F. & Cloward, R. A. (1997). *The breaking of the American social compact.* New York: The New Press.

Walker, A. (2011). Social quality and welfare system sustainability. *The International Journal of Social Quality, 1*(1), 5–18. doi:10.3167/IJSQ.2011010102.

Wilson, W. J. (2017). Why sociologists matter in the welfare reform debate. *Contemporary Sociology*, *46*(6), 627–634.

White House Conference on Aging (WHCOA)

White House Conferences on Aging, first held in 1961, and again in 1971, 1981, 1995, 2002, 2005, and 2015, have aimed to convene a variety of groups and individuals to reach a "call to action." The tenor, organization, and character of these events have varied, as has the sincerity (or lack therof) for a call to action on the part of the different presidential administrations that were prodded or pleased to hold a WHCOA.

Managing the demands from aging advocates for a strong public government commitment and new resources for the aged has defined nearly every conference. Over different presidential administrations, the once-a-decade WHCOA has opened up hopes and expectations and simultaneously shut them down. Some presidential administrations have worked assiduously to narrow the opportunities for the voices of elders and their advocates as well as the approved topics. The impetus to exercise as much social control as possible has been tempting. Ronald Reagan's 1981 WHCOA was a particularly raucous one in that regard. Efforts to suppress the agenda by Reagan's WHCOA team backfired, energizing participants into mass protests under the wise guidance of two influential Republicans, Dr. Arthur Fleming and former Social Security Commissioner Charles Schotland.

The 2005 WHCOA, chaired by G. W. Bush appointee Dorcas Hardy, set two overarching issues:

(1) "the fiscal realities of Federal, State, and local budgets demand that we rethink old ways of doing business . . . and are diligent in executing changes.

Just adding new entitlements and funding will only make real problems more difficult to solve;" and (2) "the responsibility for creating and implementing solutions is not solely a Federal responsibility" (2005 WHCOA Final Report). Conference delegates were greeted with the framing that the "tomorrow's older population . . . will be healthier and wealthier/[and] will be better educated and desire to make contributions beyond traditional retirement."

(WHCOA, 2015, Executive Summary, p. 7)

The 2015 WHCOA, with Nora Super at the helm as Executive Director, focused on technology and entrepreneurship, with a major lineup of corporate speakers. A letter from 74 Congressional signatories, including liberal leaders Bernie Sanders, Elizabeth Warren, John Conyers, and John Lewis, told President Obama that "more than half (53 percent) of today's working Americans are not expected to have sufficient resources upon retirement to maintain their standard of living." They urged the expansion of Social Security on its eightieth birthday in 2015. Obama's "neglect" in not supporting the expansion of Social Security benefits was frustrating. It was not until near the end of Hillary Clinton's 2016 presidential campaign that Obama generally supported Social Security expansion. The ongoing affordable housing crisis for seniors was also largely missing from the 2015 WHCOA, as the conference emphasized a neoliberal agenda of commercialization and market-based initiatives (Kleyman, 2015). A primary feature was public–private partnerships between the government and corporations. This set the tone for much of the conference, but did not inspire confidence or foster engagement from long-time advocates who in previous WHCOAs used the opportunity for energizing grassroots at all geopolitical levels (state, local levels, rural, American Indian nation). The tightly controlled corporate agenda from business and government elites prevailed.

The WHCOA appears to have become a social control vehicle utilized to manage and reduce expectations, replete with opportunities to instill conservative austerity and personal responsibility messages. Whether and how the WHCOA will exist in the future, if at all, is unknown.

Robert Blancato, an involved and influential leader in WHCOAs for decades, offers insights into such national conferences going forward. Blancato observes that those White House conferences that did leave positive impressions in 1971 and 1995 encouraged advocacy at the delegate level and focused on specific important policy issues. In 1971 it was President Nixon at the distinct urging of his Director, Dr. Arthur Flemming, who endorsed an initial funding level of $100 million for the new Older Americans Act nutrition program. In 1995 House Speaker Newt Gingrich and delegates, motivated by a deep and visceral disdain for the so-called Contract with America, passed resolutions repudiating the contract and reaffirming support for Social Security and Medicare. The delegates produced an historic resolution which five years later became the National Family Caregiver support program.

Blancato recommends that future conferences be forums that involve both Congress and the White House, returning to a delegate selection process that gives strong advocates a chance to be chosen. The political and policy environment of the time must be reflected and responded to by the delegates. It must be a forum that reaffirms the value of social insurance programs and reflects, in composition and content, the increasing diversity of the aging population.

See also: Citizenship, Maggie Kuhn, Power, Social Movements, Voicelessness

Further Reading:

Kleyman, P. (2015). Will commercialization be Obama's legacy on aging? *New America Media*, July 17. Retrieved from http://newamericamedia.org/2015/07/will-commercialization-be-obamas-legacy-on-aging.php.

The White House. (2015). *Fact sheet: The White House Conference on Aging*, July 13. Office of the Press Secretary. The White House. Retrieved from https://obamawhitehouse.archives.gov/the-press-office/2015/07/13/fact-sheet-white-house-cor.

White Supremacy

Describes the ideological position that white people are the best and deserve the most. It's entrenched in the political and economic landscape of American society, built on the backs of people of color who have past and presently been enslaved and exploited. Slavery, segregation, discrimination, violent policing, and incarceration are mechanisms of a white state.

White Privilege

Whiteness is a location of structural advantage, of race privilege. Second, it is a "standpoint," a place from which white people look at ourselves, at others, and at society. Third, "whiteness" refers to a set of cultural practices that are usually unmarked and unnamed (Frankenberg, 1993, p. 1). Feagin (2006, p. 25) writes:

> Central to the persistence of systemic racism has been the development of a commonplace white racial frame . . . an organized set of racialized ideas, stereotypes, emotions and inclinations to discriminate. . . .The frame and associated discriminatory actions are consciously or unconsciously expressed in the routine operations of racist institutions of this society.

Whiteness is inherited, automatic, and often unquestioned access to opportunities, rights, and security denied to those identified as not white. Key to this has been the development of a set of ideas and stereotypes about race that serve as conscious and unconscious foundations for bias. Definitions of whiteness can change throughout time and place (i.e., Jews, Latinos, people with transnational and international identities), but a key characteristic as McIntosh (1988) identifies is an ability to be unaware of one's race and privilege. It seems natural and with no dire need for reflection – the dominant group need not articulate its power explicitly or examine itself publicly. As visibility of people of color in positions of leadership and black power increases, there have been accompanying vocal backlashes of white supremacy in which pride, arrogance, and fear of the Other are made explicit. CNN commentator Van Jones locates the election of Donald Trump and his backing from white Americans as the "whitelash" for having a black president (Obama) in the White House (CNN live, November 9, 2017). White privilege also extends here in the laxness of response to those articulating white supremacy, as well as silence in the face of the continued murders of unarmed people of color by police (who are acquitted time and again). When people of color denigrate whiteness, they are often met with extreme force, and when white people voice their hatred they expect to be protected by "free speech."

In gerontology, white privilege appears in policy which neglects and perpetuates inequality for aging people of color. For example, raising the retirement age disproportionately affects people of color as they have been disproportionately restricted or only given access to physically demanding jobs which have worn out their bodies sooner than the majority of their white white-collar counterparts. We can also think about inequalities and disproportionate black populations in incarceration. As well

as policy for housing, where access to housing and generational transmission of wealth is constellated in poverty, trauma, statelessness, since the 400 years where black people were kept in slavery.

White privilege also appears in the tone-deaf appropriation of black culture and arts, such as Social Security Works rap performed by white elders in which they wear gold chains, Rocco Wear, and appear on streets covered in graffiti. Some might also see the naming of the Gray Panthers as a symbolic co-opting of the Black Panthers' defiance and strength. This is complicated by the fact that Maggie Kuhn worked with, and alongside, Black Panthers in aging and in multiple civil rights initiatives throughout the East and West USA.

White privilege comes with a luxury of denial and discomfort where an ownership of guilt doesn't necessarily lead to dialogue or responsiveness to the Other's needs. The burden of absolving this guilt is placed on people of color pardoning privilege and less of a white ownership of extending that privilege.

See also: Blacklands, Black Lives Matter (BLM), Microaggressions, Racism, Stereotype Threat, Violence

Further Reading

Blumer, H. (1958). Race prejudice as a sense of group position. *Sociological Perspectives, 1*(1), 3–7.

Feagin, J. R. (2006). *Systemic racism.* New York: Routledge.

Frankenberg, R. (1993). *White women, race matters.* London: Routledge.

McIntosh, P. (1988). *White privilege and male privilege: A personal account of coming to see correspondences through work in women's studies.* Wellesley, MA: Wellesley College Center for Research on Women.

Perry, P. (2007). White universal identity as a "sense of group position". *Symbolic Interaction, 30*(3), 375–393.

Worker's Compensation

A form of insurance that provides benefits to employees injured during the course of their work.

Worker's Compensation is the oldest form of Social Insurance in the United States. It is required in 49 states, with Texas being the only state that allows employers to "opt out" of the program. Plans in the states that do require Worker's Compensation cover a variety of costs, including medical care, disability benefits, and wage replacement.

The system by which benefits are delivered varies from state to state but most are fairly complex and inefficient when it comes to paying for and delivering medical care. Claims are generally routed through the legal system and the costs of processing them are immense.

See also: Disability, Labor, Social Insurance

Workfare

Describes when receipt of welfare benefits is contingent upon work status. This is true under the Temporary Assistance for Needy Families (TANF) program and to work history requirements to receive Social Security Insurance or Disability Insurance. Survivors' benefits also depend upon the qualifying work history of the deceased provider.

Much of the Medicaid policy and debate concerns how to incentivize work and discourage unemployment. The political Right contends that the social safety net endangers the will to work, encourages laziness and dependency, threatens the Puritan work ethic, and thereby increases program costs. This ideology supports racial stereotypes regarding the inherent difficulty in controlling unwilling Others. This promotes the role of the State as the strict father needed to correct and discipline for individual human

failure (Lakoff, 2014). Neoliberal ideology is invoked with renewed vigor in the Trump Administration's guidance to states allowing them to implement work requirements for Medicaid waiver programs. Howard Gleckman writes in *Forbes* about "What Medicaid's work requirement means for seniors, people with disabilities and their caregivers." Kentucky leads the way and at least ten other states are applying for the Medicaid work requirement. Medicaid 1115 waivers allow for state discretion in offering benefits to particular populations for dental and vision care and long-term care services and supports. NHeLP (2018) sued CMS, the Medicaid administering agency in DHHS. From a critical political economy perspective, instituting work requirements uniformly for Medicaid would be a gigantic negative shift, especially for low-income families and children and those near age 65 with health conditions that keep them from working, including those taking early retirement who wait for or don't qualify for SSDI, as well as their dependent children, grandchildren, and family caregivers. The disadvantages of race, ethnicity, gender, and class are compounded in such bold moves against access to health care.

See also: Cumulative Advantage/Disadvantage, Crisis, Long-term Care, Medicaid, No-care Zone, SSDI, The State, Stateless, States' Rights, TANF

Further Reading

Gleckman, H. (2018). "What Medicaid's work requirement means for seniors, people with disabilities and their caregivers. *Forbes*, January 19. Retrieved from www.forbes.com/sites/howardgleckman/2018/01/19/what-medicaids-work-requirement-means-for-seniors-people-with-disabilities-and-their-caregivers/#16b61c22206c.

Kaiser Family Foundation. (2017/2018). Medicaid Fact Sheets. www.kff.org/medicaid/work.

Lakoff, G. (2014). *The all new don't think of an elephant! Know your values and frame the debate*. White River Junction, VT: Chelsea Green Publishing.

National Health Law Program. (2018). Letter to CMS (J. Perkins, January 11). Washington, DC: NHeLP. Retrieved from www.healthlaw.org/issues/medicaid/medicaid-work-requirements.

Tweet @seemaCMS #transformingMedicaid January 11, 2018.

Xenophobia

The fear of outsiders.

The status category and role of loyal citizen "acts as a legitimizing concept for the ideology of xenophobia (exclusion of the stranger), [on] which the very (local) notion of national citizenship is based" (Grossman et al., 2009, p. 121). By its nature, it is "related in the expectation of an internalized sense of duty and responsibility to maintaining the social (and economic and cultural) order. . . . [N]ormative expectations, that if broken are means for varying degrees of degradation of citizenship status"(Grossman et al., 2009, p. 121). It comes with negative sanctions that may be called "alien" in both meaning and privilege.

In critical perspective, xenophobia invokes hostility, discrimination, even violence against the "Other." It may result in denial of education and other benefits of the State, and even imprisonment. The political, economic, and cultural struggles have placed immigration policy at the center of controversy for many within US borders. The Trump Presidency has given new meaning to the individual and collective fear, disruption, and trauma that xenophobic public policy imposes upon family, community, and all institutions of society. Brutal enforcement, roundups, detention, expulsion, and police raids trash human rights.

See also: Citizenship, Deportation, Fascism, Human Rights, Immigration, Military Industrial Complex, Nativism, Networks, Prison Industrial Complex, Racism, Refugees

Further Reading

Grossman, B. R., Solway, E., Estes, C. L., Rogne, L., & Hollister, B. A. (2009). One nation, interdependent: Exploring the boundaries of citizenship in the history of Social Security and Medicare. In L. Rogne, C. L. Estes, B. Grossman, B. Hollister, & E. Solway (Eds.), *Social insurance and social justice: Social Security, Medicare, and the campaign against entitlements* (pp. 115–147). New York: Springer.

Youth

A quality or state of being associated with the young, advanced through beliefs about beauty, potential, and desirability.

Youth is socially constructed and socially and culturally variable. Populations that experience early death from community violence or hazardous labor conditions have different concepts of what it means to be young and survive into old age.

Youth, as construed by anti-aging industries and research, is constructed as a worthier investment than already matured and older populations.

One of the fundamental problems of aging policy is demonstrating intergenerational connections and linking the well-being of older people to that of younger people. This challenge is especially important for social insurance programs like Social Security, which provides value to young people both in the form of survivor benefits and future benefits, including disability. Child and youth survivor benefits are an essential source of income for the dependents and families of the recently deceased. Paul Ryan, Speaker of the House, says he was able to go to college with the survivor benefits he received after his father's death. Survivor benefits of college or trade school were deleted as a Social Security benefit by Ronald Reagan, depriving and further disadvantaging youth whose parent had died or became disabled. Advocates for Social Security expansion support reinstating this vital educational benefit. Immigrant youth are plagued by their uncertain futures as DACA swings in hot political winds.

The political activism of youth offers the possibility of social change. The events of mass gun violence and student deaths in 2017/2018 and the protests of students, teachers, families, and communities could dislodge the seemingly unstoppable and intransigent success of the National Rifle Association (NRA) in Congress and State houses. The assumed political passivity of youth could be an erroneous stereotype. Repeated school and church shootings are occurring in confluence with an awakening youth consciousness seen in protest marches and discourse. Digital resources are engaging and linking youth with older generations via multiple platforms, including #MeToo, DACA, Black Lives Matter, college debt, and global warming.

See also: Anti-aging, Children, Framing, Generation, Generational and Intergenerational Consciousness

Further Reading

Price, T. (2012). Social Security does more than just protect the elderly. The Roosevelt Institute: Blog.

Rockeymoore, M. (2012). Selling out America's youth: An open letter to Alan Simpson. *HuffPost*, December 10. Retrieved from www.huffingtonpost.com/dr-maya-rockeymoore/an-open-letter-to-alan-si_b_2270726.html.

Ruddick, S. (2003). The politics of aging: Globalization and the restructuring of youth and childhood. *Antipode, 35*(2), 334–362.

A young person's guide to Social Security. (2016). Washington, DC: Economic Policy Institute, National Academy of Social Insurance.

Z

Zeitgeist

Translated from the German as "spirit of the time," it describes general cultural currents, trends, and events that mark a time distinct from others.

The concept was first suggested by philosopher Georg Hegel who proposed that the primacy of context informs agency, as individuals act in accordance with power and what is available to them at the time. Zeitgeist is thus both a structural force and a structuring one. Prevailing beliefs and values influence emerging ones; and recursively, new beliefs change the way we understand the existing order.

The term "Zeitgeist" can describe intellectual trends and how these relate to the dominant social order. An example would be how positivism and empiricism produce and qualify phenomena in a fashion that agrees with the commodification and market ideologies of capitalism.

Currently, the Zeitgeist of empowerment and visibility of marginalized and racialized Others such as Black Lives Matter exists alongside a Zeitgeist of capitalism and authoritarianism as played out through terrorism, global imperialism, militarization, and privatization. This multiplicity of time spirits of the current age complicates the telling of a single story of it (as identified by Chimimanda Ngozie Adiche), but provides opportunities to recognize intersectionality, and occasionally to question epistemological blind spots.

Whether one uses one term or a combination to describe ideology, discourse, event, or Zeitgeist, these terms are just vessels and frames to differentiate and develop thought, not stake down truth. As language goes in and out of vogue, as vernacular becomes official, as profane terms vacillate between being radical, popular, and tame, so too does theoretical language and jargon. The poetics of variation keep critical thought alive!

See also: Black Lives Matter, Intersectionality, Social Movements, Spirits of Capitalism

Zero Years

The material evidence of the low/no value accorded to caregiving under US Social Security policy. No caregiving years are credited as "work" under Social Security benefit calculations. As reported by the Institute for Women's Policy Research, these are called "Zero Years" (no credit) under Social Security in calculations toward the 35 years of work history and benefit level. Unlike the USA, 32 of 35 OECD nations accord some form of credit for caregiving under their retirement systems. Legislation has been proposed to deal with this issue in the 114th and 115th Congressional sessions but was bottled up by the GOP House Speaker Ryan, so these proposed legislative remedies were not assigned to any committee or the House Floor for consideration. With the 2018 mid-term election of Democratic House Speaker, it is expected that proposed legislation addressing zero years and other improvements will be advanced to committees and the House Floor for votes.

See also: Caregiving/Caregivers, Care Penalty, Precarity, Quality Adjusted Life Years (QALYs)

Further Reading

Estes, C. L., O'Neill, T., & Hartmann, H. (2012). *Breaking the Social Security glass ceiling: A proposal to modernize women's benefits*. Washington, DC: NCPSSM Foundation, NOW Foundation, & IWPR.
Institute for Women's Policy Research. Retrieved from https://iwpr.org.
Rockeymoore, M. & Lui, M. (2011). *Plan for a new future: The impact of social security reform on people of color*. Washington, DC: Commission to Modernize Social Security.

Zones

Define areas or scopes of commonality. These can reference geographical territories and localities, geopolitical and economic alliances such as the Eurozone, or theoretical and subjective spaces that share sociopolitical realities or cultural imaginaries.

Hagestad (1999) uses the term "gray zone" to describe the shared border between sociology and gerontology. Rowles (1981) proposes "surveillance zones," describing the area outside of the home where older people feel supported in the sightlines of neighbors who can observe their needs. *Blue Zones* is framing for areas in which people tend to live longer and in good health, identified as "longevity hotspots." The absence of care or support is recognized in our entry for the No-care Zone (Estes, Swan, & Associates, 1983). Political journalism research identifies zones of consensus, legitimate controversy, and deviance (Clayman, 2017) that are consequential for political discourse.

Wild Zone Feminists argue that because our society and language are androcentric, women are pushed to the margins, relegated and regulated, unable to speak in their own words. Elaine Showalter's (1981) "Feminist criticism in the wilderness" builds on the anthropologist Edward Ardner's "wild zone." Showalter uses it as a space in which women's experience does not lie within the dominant male cultural paradigm. Women can only reach this in fantasy; instead women write from two literary traditions at the same time: a mainstream male-dominated tradition, and the muted tradition of female endeavors.

Retirement communities and respite care are not considered a public good in the USA. This allows for the creation of exclusive zones, curated or gated for those elderly with ample resources. There are dozens of retirement colonies in Mexico, South and Central America, where older US adults with financial resources find the quality of life is higher and the cost of living lower than in the United States. Critical questions arise around the stratifications of citizenship and the privatization and commodification of aging expatriate communities, augmenting economic disparity and gentrification as well as promoting neocolonialism.

See also: Blacklands, Gentrification, Liminality, Neocolonialism, No-care Zone

Further Reading

Clayman, S. E. (2017). The micropolitics of legitimacy. *Social Psychology Quarterly, 80*(1), 41–64.
Estes, C. L., Swan, J. S., & Associates. (1983). *The long-term care crisis: The no-care zone*. Thousand Oaks, CA: Sage.

Hagestad, G. O. (1999). A gray zone? Meetings between sociology and gerontology. *Contemporary Sociology*, *28*(5), 514–517.

Kanthak, J. F. (2003). Feminisms in motion: Pushing the "wild zone" thesis into the fourth dimension. *Literature Interpretation Theory*, *14*(2), 149–163.

Rowles, G. D. (1981). The surveillance zone as meaningful space for the aged. *The Gerontologist*, *21*(3), 304–311.

Showalter, E. (1981). Feminist criticism in the wilderness. *Critical Inquiry*, *8*(2), 179–205.

IV

Closing

Aging A–Z began with what we considered salient policy topics that were changing with mind-warping speed. We found ourselves in the middle of a new politics of the absurd. We moved from thinking about austerity to specifying modes of cruelty coded through public and private policy. We found our focus on devolution and disparities through states-rights block grants to complement the gerrymandering and voter suppression tactics designed for xenophobia and racism to operate – direct attacks against universal rights. It is shocking but not unbelievable to see the tie-ins between nationalism, white supremacy, and authoritarianism. Our critical perspectives are rooted in our own experience of living through moments where it seems we were standing (sinking?) on quicksand. Could a woman's right to choose (*Roe*) vanish? Could the promise of health care insurance without pre-existing conditions disappear? Was the President of the USA driving traumatic experiences of family separation at the border? Did we almost have a woman president, only to elect a braggadocios perpetrator of sexual assault?

Such events have informed our evolving epistemology, bringing us into acute awareness of domination and oppression, as well as our own experiences of privilege and marginalization. More than our intersubjective experience, we have benefitted from our intergenerational collaboration. We have named and danced around difference and similarity in opportunity, class, sexuality, gender, and our inherited and lived traumas. These experiences have palpably informed the book given, emboldened by our witnessing of the harrowing stories of others surviving these times.

We reiterate that *Aging A–Z* is not the definitive account of the challenges facing this country and the world. If anything, through our work we hope to encourage readers to embrace the indefiniteness of a single story and to look to those in jeopardy for the solutions. The terms presented will always be in a process of definition and redefinition. We need readers to interpret and contest the possible applications: they are not for one method or practice. In this way, we imagine that possible uses for this text are for widening the scope of classroom instruction, helping to situate dissertations and theses within a context (and history) of scholarship, and to deepen gerontological and geriatric practice in medical and community settings. We hope for activists and policy-makers to divine new approaches to solving systemic issues, to see the need for representation of diverse and older voices as crucial to progress. For these reasons we have balanced and grounded *A–Z* in structural analysis and theories of social movements.

As we gain a firmer understanding of *where* we are and *who* we are, we can begin to fathom *what to do next*. For some this may include becoming more involved in democratic processes such as voting, attending town halls, or running for office. For others, this may mean sharing financial resources and extending privilege to elevate people of color poor, disabled, women, and trans voices. Action also includes going to the street, occupying space, and challenging authoritarianism – not easy things to do in an increasingly militarized police state. Regardless of what readers decide to *do next*, we hope that it certainly involves questioning power and the status quo that relegates aging issues to the medical realm and ignores their place in *the social*.

Toward Emancipatory Gerontology

Emancipatory gerontology aims to advance knowledge and the realization of dignity, access, equity, healing, and social justice through individual and collective agency and social institutions. An imperative is accessible public knowing of the individual and social consequences of major policy and institutional forces in relation to aging and generations across the life course.

Scholarship from the perspective of public goods alters the way we think, examine, and work. Our engagement is drawn to social facts on the ground as well as to big data and information on interstitial and other levels. It will shape how we see, analyze, and understand human interconnections and consequences at the individual, family, neighborhood, community, nation-state, and global levels. Implications redound to the framing of the questions investigated, the methods, the science and technology, risk, social movements, social action, and agency at the collective and individual levels.

The present historic moment is characterized by mounting individual and collective precarity that is manifested in debate over *The Right to Have Rights*. Critical perspectives are challenging assumptions and ways of framing and doing what we do. Scientific standpoints are sensitized to race, ethnicity, gender, class, sexualities, (dis)abilities, immigrant and indigenous peoples and their intersectional ties. Structure and agency are implicated in the material and symbolic experiences of advantage and disadvantage, which cumulate over our lifetimes, generations, communities, and world. Emancipatory gerontology will benefit from the work of critical theorists who join critique, conflict, and crisis debates with focus on social struggles as sources of emancipatory (and alt-regressive and non-emancipatory responses (Jaeggi, 2017; Fraser & Jaeggi, 2018).

Imperative also is consideration of the Anthropocene – the new human-dominated geological epoch of human impact on geology and ecosystems (Crutzen & Stoermer, 2000) and the ecological emergency expressed through cumulating environmental hazards. The Anthropocene signals the human age and humanity's role and effects on the "really existing" material conditions of climate change threatening the planet, non-human life and clean air, soil, and water.

Theory, research, and practice demand attention to inequality, power, and action. Real-world nano, micro, meso, and macro levels provide the lens for our science and society. Critical vigilance and analysis is required to understand the effects of the dizzying and relentless rhetoric and actions designed to undo, unravel, and obliterate US institutions of the State and democracy. Explicit administrative steps in the Trump era are intended to abrogate (or extinguish) the protection and extension of the human rights space embedded in the public and the social. There appears to be little regard for the consequences of the march to permanently malign trust and truth in the undoing of the administrative state apparatus, nor does there appear to be serious concern about the effects on the human and non-human species. Emancipatory gerontology and its coming of age is the unequivocal charge of this historical moment.

References

Bellamy, J. & Clark, B. (2018). The robbery of nature. *Monthly Review: An Independent Socialist Magazine, 70*(3), 1–20.

Crutzen, P. J. & Stoermer, E. F. (2000). The Anthropocene. *Global Change Newsletter, 41*, 17–18.

Fraser, N. & Jaeggi, R. (2018). *Capitalism: A Conversation in critical theory*. New York: John Wiley & Sons.

Jaeggi, R. (2017). Crisis, contradiction, and the task of a critical theory. In B. Barggu & D. Bottici (Eds.), *Feminism, capitalism and critique*. Basingstoke: Palgrave Macmillan.

Collaborator's Reflection

A–Z employs the critical framework of the political economy and announces novel cross-theoretical approaches for gerontology within domains of what we locate as psycho-analytic social theory, the politics of affect, and theories of abjection and delirium. This is one of the original contributions of *A–Z* that values pain and confusion as part of a process. Our shared commitment is to foster a critical imagination, decenter whiteness, and advance praxis that promotes generational healing and advances the reality of a just society.

We have wondered, during the process of writing this treatise, what an A–Z would have looked like ten years ago. It could not have been the same book, as the framework developed and applied to the 2016 election and the Trump Administration became a critical mission of resistance. Through the process of collaboration and navigating institution, I have developed more of an appreciation for intersectionality and a wariness of white liberalism. I found new ways to ask for help and to listen to the fear and concern of others. This has included becoming more aware of the microaggressions I perpetrate frequently with people of color in my circles, as well as developing responses to others' microaggressions. I imagine these were always present but they have erupted spectacularly in the Trump era as a widely shared response of white people trying to figure out their unconscious complicity in white supremacy. These are complicated in proximity to the emboldened white nationalists and racists who have been observed on social media harassing and threatening brown and black peoples.

In the course of writing this book, I hadn't anticipated how much my relationship with my home state of West Virginia could or would change. Since my exodus I have newfound sorrow and compassion for those in Appalachia who have been sold addictive opiates with impunity by big pharma. From my perspective on the Left Coast, these people have been largely abandoned by mainstream coastal progressives who view too many of the working-class and poor white population as uncouth racists beyond hope. This does little to challenge whiteness, since racial supremacy is steeped in class. As inequality deepens in regions of Appalachia, it is critical that progressives strengthen social welfare.

V

A–Z Acknowledgments

There are many individuals to whom we are indebted for this encyclopedic endeavor. Key scholars who profoundly shaped Estes' graduate and postgraduate work and baseline theoretical framework undergirding *Aging A–Z* are Randall Collins, and the late Herbert Blumer, Alvin Gouldner, James O'Connor, and Fred Koenig.

Detailed scholarly reviewers offered critique and discovery of new topics and literatures. With permission to cite them are the immense contributions of Dale Dannefer, Teresa Ghilarducci, Chris Phillipson, and Alan Walker. None of them bear responsibility for the perspectives taken here, but much credit for invigorating our imaginations. The author and collaborator alone bear the responsibility for *A–Z* content. Jarmin Yeh merits special acknowledgment for constructing, rewriting, and strengthening myriad Glossary entries.

Contributing to the writing, review, and improvement of specific *A–Z* Glossary entries are: Peter Arno, Robert Blancato, Ryon Cobb, Ellen Daniell, David Gelfand, Brooke Hollister, Julene Johnson, Jessica Kelly Moore, Barbara Koenig, Ben Libbey, Marty Lynch, Sara Palmer, Howard Pinderhughes, Elena Portacolone, Natalie Purcell, Kathy Sykes, and Meg Wallhagen.

Aging A–Z draws upon career-long research and publications with many students, post-docs, and colleagues over the past five decades, including Robert Alford, Simon Biggs, Ted Benjamin, Elizabeth Binney, Julia Bradsher, Liz Close, Chiquita Collins, Richard Culbertson, Catherine Dodd, Mary Foley, Pat Fox, Lenore Gerard, Sheryl Goldberg, Charlene Harrington, Mauro Hernandez, David Lindeman, Karen Linkins, Steve Lohrer, Milena Nelson, Robert Newcomer, Marj Plumb, Leah Rogne, Jon Showstack, Erica Solway, Jim Swan, Steve Wallace, Tracy Weitz, Chris Wellin, Juanita Wood, and Jane Sprague Zones.

Before the title "policy wonk" was invented, Estes was privileged to receive close mentoring from three originals, Robert Ball, Philip R. Lee, and Dorothy Rice, each of whom brought forth social insurance and the public interest via the Big Four: Social Security, Medicare, Medicaid, and national health insurance. Notable Congressional sheroes and heroes are US Senator Mazie Hirono and US House members Jared Huffman, Barbara Kennelly, Nancy Pelosi, Jackie Speier, and Mike Thompson.

Colleagues and scholars whose work influenced us include Nancy Adler, Jacqui Angel, Toni Antonucci, Jan Baars, Liz Blackburn, Toni Calasanti, Stephen Crystal, Timothy Diamond, Elise Epel, Madonna Harrington Meyer, Pamela Herd, Martha Holstein, James Jackson, Paul Kleyman, John Myles, Virginia Olesen, Jill Quadagno, Anne Showstack Sassoon, Donna Zullman, and the late Anselm Strauss and Josh Wiener. Social justice activists fomenting critical resistance in support of social insurance are Nancy Altman, Eric Kingson, Terry O'Neill, Max Richtman, Maya Rockeymoore, and Kate Villers. Sonoma County Supervisor Shirlee Zane models power in the local state.

Offering continuous encouragement for all things health and mind are Dr. Christina Dumbadse, Linda Illsley, and Dr. Ho Lam Tsang. Special advisors and mentors include Dr. Nancy Milliken, Dixie Horning, Dr. Ellen Weber, The Glide Foundation's Reverend Cecil Williams and Janice Mirikitani, Justice Judith McConnell, Kay Sprinkel Grace, and Shirley Chater. Current Dean Katherine Gillis, UCSF School of Nursing, and the late Margretta Styles were role models without peer.

Invaluable support was rendered by Wendy Max, Director, UCSF Institute for Health and Aging (IHA) and Howard Pinderhughes, Chair, UCSF Department of Social and Behavioral Sciences (SBS) and administrative staff: Regina Gudelunas, Cynthia Mercado-Scott, Yana Peterson, Brandee Woleslagle, and Patrice Bryant. IT wizard Doug McCracken guided us through computer glitches and repeatedly "saved Carroll and the book." Sean Dickerson organized the manuscript in Google Docs, employing librarian magical powers. Stephanie Wilkinson, Carroll's former UCSF administrative analyst, organized chaos. Endless unnamed and named support came from Kelly Roberts and Yolanda Duarte.

Aging A–Z is inflected throughout by the mentorship of two courageous women, each of whom knew who she was and what she was fighting for: Maggie Kuhn, co-founder of the Gray Panthers, and Tish Sommers, co-founder of the Older Women's League. Wrinkled Radical, Maggie Kuhn, imparted our mantra that "everything is connected," especially young and old. She implored us to "Do our homework; Go to the roots; Go to the top; and to Speak our mind even though our voice may shake." We hope to carry this forward intergenerationally through emancipatory gerontology.

My mother and mystery author, Carroll Cox Estes, spoke through the written word when it was too dangerous for women to speak verbally. There is no way such profound mentoring can be adequately recognized. My dad, US Federal Judge Joe Estes, sparked my policy obsession. My daughter, Duskie Lynn Estes, made the impossible *A–Z* Odyssey a reality. My granddaughters, Brydie and Mackenzie, inspire all of us. Special credit for the exquisite culinary arts behind *Aging A–Z* belongs to ZAZU Kitchen + Farm, the Piglet Food Truck, Black Pig Meat Co. and the dazzling feats of Celebrity Chefs Duskie Estes and my son-in law, John Stewart. My extended family is a great source of strength: the Philip R. Lee clan, Margi Lee, Amy Lee, and Dr. Catherine Lee, my niece, Lise Luttgens, and late Aunt Margaret Estes.

DiCarlo wishes to thank friends and family, including, but not limited to: Louella, Ruth Fiscella, Melinda DiCarlo, Rose Marie and Roy Pfeiffer, Rafael Velázquez, Talia Davidow, Audrey Webb, and Linda Shapiro. Michael Joyce and Nancy Giunta were instrumental in sharpening critical perspectives and sowing seeds of intellectual confidence. All were involved in supporting this endeavor.

Dean Birkenkamp, Senior Sociology Editor for Routledge: Taylor & Francis was and is invaluable in "bringing *A–Z* home," advising, reading, editing, and strengthening the book. Mitch Allen, who originally signed the book contract under Left Coast Press, redirected the book to Routledge and suggested the idea of an A–Z dictionary. Mitch advised and edited from his new venture, Editorial Roadside Service. We are amazed that *A–Z* has become a living text in what we experience as a seemingly endless encyclopedia.

VI

Appendix

1

Teaching and Learning from *Aging A–Z* Appendix

Critical pedagogy is a teaching method that aims to help challenge and actively struggle against any form of social oppression and its related norms, values, and beliefs. It is a theory method which serves to allow students to gain a critical awareness of the established social order and social relations to critique and to change it. A critical pedagogy views education as inherently political. A vision of justice and equality as a basis for education is important for the liberation from oppressive social relations.

It follows, therefore, that the approach to pedagogy on aging should be a critical one, focusing on participatory approaches to learning, emancipatory knowledge, and the application of that knowledge in the public arena to create social change. This teaching and learning appendix is designed to help foster the development of "transformative intellectuals" (Aronowitz & Giroux, 1985) who recognize the power relations and political struggles embodied in the debates on aging and who see their roles as actors in efforts to advance social progress and the common good. *A–Z* encourages a roving, hyperlinked eye for the interrelatedness of theory, resistance, practice, and policy. It may be used to guide teaching and learning for the classroom, community forums, and group trainings.

Advancing Standards of the Field

AGHE, the Academy for Gerontology in Higher Education, has developed and adopted a guiding set of Gerontology Competencies for Undergraduate and Graduate Education. These Competencies may be understood as working together to inspire and deepen one's gerontological imagination. The areas of study are spread as follows:

CATEGORY I Foundational Competencies to All Fields of Gerontology

I.1 FRAMEWORKS FOR UNDERSTANDING HUMAN AGING:

Utilize gerontological frameworks to examine human development and aging.

I.2 BIOLOGICAL ASPECTS OF AGING:

Relate biological theory and science to understanding senescence, longevity, and variation in aging.

I.3 PSYCHOLOGICAL ASPECTS OF AGING:

Relate psychological theories and science to understanding adaptation, stability, and change in aging.

I.4 SOCIAL ASPECTS OF AGING:

Relate social theories and science of aging to understanding heterogeneity, inequality, and context of aging.

I.5 THE HUMANITIES AND AGING:

Develop comprehensive and meaningful concepts, definitions, and measures for the well-being of older adults and their families, grounded in the Humanities and Arts.

I.6 RESEARCH AND CRITICAL THINKING:

Distinguish factors related to aging outcomes, both intrinsic and contextual, through critical thinking and empirical research.

CATEGORY II Interactional Competencies across Fields of Gerontology

II.1 ATTITUDES AND PERSPECTIVES:

Develop a gerontological perspective through knowledge and self-reflection.

II.2 ETHICS AND PROFESSIONAL STANDARDS:

Adhere to ethical principles to guide work with and on behalf of older persons.

II.3 COMMUNICATION WITH AND ON BEHALF OF OLDER PERSONS:

Engage, through effective communication, older persons, their families, and the community in personal and public issues on aging.

II.4 INTERDISCIPLINARY AND COMMUNITY COLLABORATION:

Engage collaboratively with others to promote integrated approaches to aging.

CATEGORY III Contextual Competencies across Fields of Gerontology

III.1 WELL-BEING, HEALTH, AND MENTAL HEALTH:

Promote older persons' strengths and adaptations to maximize well-being, health and mental health.

III.2 SOCIAL HEALTH:

Promote quality of life and a positive social environment for older persons.

III.3 PROGRAM/SERVICE DEVELOPMENT:

Employ and design programmatic and community development with and on behalf of the aging population.

III.4 EDUCATION:

Encourage older persons to engage in lifelong learning opportunities.

III.5 ARTS AND HUMANITIES:

Promote engagement of older people in the arts and humanities.

III.6 BUSINESS AND FINANCE:

Address the roles of older persons as workers and consumers in business and finance.

III.7 POLICY:

Employ and generate policy to equitably address the needs of older persons.

III.8 RESEARCH, APPLICATION, AND EVALUATION:

Engage in research to advance knowledge and improve interventions for older persons.

This list along with more specific subsets may be found on AGHE's website: www.

aghe.org/images/aghe/competencies/
gerontology_competencies.pdf.

Coursework Examples Utilizing A–Z Concepts

Aggregating the critical concepts can assist teaching faculty and students in building coursework which expands levels of analysis. Examples of how concepts may be employed and aggregated on specific courses and subject areas are as follows:

- History of Social Welfare (example concepts):
    - Affordable Care Act (ACA/Obamacare)
    - Austerity
    - Disability
    - Devolution
    - Exploitation
    - Fascism
    - Social insurance
    - Social Security
    - Welfare state
- Women's Studies
    - Intersectionality/intersectional knowledge
    - Feminism/feminist
    - Oppression
    - Praxis
    - Privilege
    - Social construction of reality
    - Zero years
- Race, Gender, and Inequality
    - Caregiving
    - Exploitation
    - Fascism
    - Feminism/feminist
    - Men
    - Misogyny
    - Performativity
    - Power
    - Race/racism
    - Racial wealth gap
    - Social insurance
    - Social Security
    - Trauma
    - War on women
- Race, Sexuality, and Society
    - Ethnicity
    - Exploitation
    - Intersectionality
    - Microaggressions
    - Queer
    - Race/racism
    - Sexuality
    - Stereotype threat
    - Trauma
    - War on women
- The Psychology of Aging
    - Abjection
    - Ageism
    - Exploitation
    - Gene–environment
    - Life course perspective
    - Resilience
    - Stress
    - Subjective aging
    - Trauma
- Political Economy of Person and Environment
    - Capitalism
    - Class
    - Discourse
    - Ideology
    - Power
    - Race
    - Relations of ruling
    - The State
    - Structure
- Inequality and the Life Course Perspective
    - Class
    - Commons, the
    - Cumulative advantage/disadvantage
    - Gender
    - Health disparities
    - Housing
    - Human rights

- HIV/AIDS
- Race/racism
- Racial wealth gap
- White supremacy
- Conceptual Foundations of Social Policy
  - Austerity
  - Capitalism
  - Colonialisms
  - Cost of Living Adjustment (COLA)
  - Crisis
  - Debt
  - Discourse
  - Framing
  - Ideology
  - Insurance/reinsurance
  - Political economy
  - Social reproduction
  - The State
  - TINA (There is No Alternative)

  A–Z concepts may also be used to *analyze and respond to* current events and public issues.

- Natural Disasters, such as Hurricanes Harvey and Maria (2017)
  - Climate change
  - Crisis
  - Event
  - Housing
  - Grievability
  - Precarity
  - Resilience
  - Trauma
- Elections
  - Demagogue
  - Democracy
  - Discourse
  - Framing
  - Media watch
  - Morality
  - Networks
  - Political parties and platforms
  - Propaganda
  - Rhetoric

- Immigration Legislation, such as The Dreamers Act (DACA)
  - Colonialisms
  - Globalization
  - Immigration
  - Race/racism
  - Violence
  - White supremacy
  - Xenophobia

Social Work Coursework

Promoting social work values through the study of social welfare:

- Abjection
- Ageism
- Agency
- Aging in community/aging in place
- Austerity
- Block grants
- Caregiving/caregivers
- Choice
- Collective impact
- Crisis
- Culture
- Democracy
- Discrimination
- Ecologies
- Empathy
- Empowerment
- Entitlement
- Equality
- Equity
- Exploitation
- Family
- Food (in)security
- Gender
- Generational and intergenerational consciousness
- Gentrification
- Health disparities
- Healthy aging/active aging
- HIV/AIDS
- Home care
- Honky gerontology

- Housing
- Human rights
- Ideology
- Immigration
- Individualism
- Inequality
- Intergenerational contract
- Intersectionality/intersectional knowledge
- Jeopardy
- Justice
- Kinship
- Levels of analysis
- Life course perspective
- Mental health
- Micro-aggressions
- Morality
- Oppression
- Policy
- Poverty
- Power
- Privilege
- Race/racism
- Relationships
- Resilience
- Stress
- Structure
- Subjective aging
- Theories of aging
- The State
- Trauma
- Wage inequality
- Welfare state
- Violence

Nursing Coursework

Focusing on care grounded in an analysis that promotes respect and personhood:

- Ableism/TABS
- Affordable Care Act (ACA/Obamacare)
- Ageism
- Allostatic load
- Alzheimer's disease
- Anti-aging
- Bioethics
- Biomedicalization

- Caregiving/caregiver
- Choice
- Culture
- Death
- Delirium
- Dementia
- Disability
- Disengagement
- Ecologies
- Embodiment
- Empathy
- Empowerment
- Epigenetics
- Equality
- Equity
- Family
- Food (in)security
- Gender
- Gene–environment
- Grievability
- Health disparities
- Healthy aging/active aging
- HIV/AIDS
- Homecare
- Housing
- Human rights
- Inequality
- Intersectionality/intersectional knowledge
- Jeopardy
- Levels of analysis
- Life course perspective
- Life expectancy
- Long-term care, Long-term Services and Supports (LTSS)
- Medical industrial complex
- Mental health
- Morality
- Policy
- Poverty
- Power
- Productive aging
- Quality-adjusted life years (QALYs)
- Resilience
- Social determinants of health
- Social isolation/loneliness
- Stress
- Subjective aging

- Telomeres
- Theories of aging
- Trauma
- Veterans

The breadth and specificity of topics and subjects in *A–Z* make possible an ongoing re-imagining of the field of gerontology and social policy. See examples and *Create your own courses*!

- Psychoanalytic social theory: psychic and structural foundations of sociocultural difference
- Developments in anti-racist pedagogy and practice
- Political discourse and generational framings
- Resistance Movements: Age, Solidarity, and Allyship.

Theories of Aging: A Sample Syllabus

(as developed by Jarmin Yeh)

For educators seeking to construct a syllabus on theories of aging, this template is a teaching tool with examples of how to organize theories of aging and utilize A–Z concepts and their related readings. To approach this course with a critical pedagogy entails co-learning with others, self-reflection, and asking (for example) the

following set of questions with each theory examined.

- How is aging framed and understood by this theory?
- What types of assumptions about individuals and society underpin this theory of aging? What is overlooked?
- What types of social problems or social processes does this theory seek to explain, illuminate, or resolve?
- How has this theory been taken up in professional practice or policy realms, with what implications, and for whom?
- Where does the locus of power lie within this theory? How does change occur according to this theory?
- How does this theory relate to your own experiences of aging? How does this theory challenge your understanding of aging?
- What are the benefits of this theory? What are its limitations?

To develop your critical lens and reflexivity, writing memos (or "notes to self") about anything you think may be good to track is recommended. Memos should include basic facts *plus* all kinds of theoretical ideas and thoughts you have, including possible new directions to take next. Your memos become an analytic archive of your thinking process. These are seeds that can lead to the beginnings of new ideas, concepts, methods, papers, and proposals.

Week	Learning objectives and critical thinking	Relevant A–Z concepts
1	**Getting started: Unleashing your gerontological imagination** • Link biography and history, personal with public. • Find your standpoint and voice in gerontology. • Discuss how aging is constructed by the social.	• Age/aging • Critical realism • Culture • Empowerment • Gerontological imagination • Intersectionality/intersectional knowledge • Organic intellectual

Week	Learning objectives and critical thinking	Relevant A–Z concepts
	Activity • Watch *Conversation portrait: The perverse pleasures of obituaries*. Available online at http://vimeo.com/13346929. New York Public Library (2010). • After watching the video, students will write their own obituaries and discuss them. *Critical thinking* • Reflecting on the process of writing your obituary, what was an insight you gained from this activity? • How do your insights contribute to your gerontological imagination? • What were the major historical events of your life course? How did they affect your future aging self?	• Pedagogy • Public sociology • The social • Standpoint theories
2	**Developing a critical lens: A foundation for analysis** • Understand the history of social theory development in gerontology. • Develop a critical lens to analyze social theory and its relationship to adult aging. *Critical thinking* • Do gerontologists need theories? • How does social theory influence gerontology? • What do social theories in aging hope to achieve? What are their limitations? • How are aging people represented in contemporary media? Who offers the representations?	• Agency • Digital sphere • Discourse • Doxa • Epistemology • Hegemony • Honky gerontology • Levels of analysis • Methodologies • Microfication • Ontology • Praxis • Rhetoric • Sociology • Structure • Temporality • Theories of aging • Zeitgeist
3	**The modern world and aging** • Understand how the rise of modernization influenced theory development in the sciences and in aging. • Identify social theories that underpin modernist theories of aging.	• Big data • Demography/demographics • Essentialism • Functionalism • Geographies • Positivism

(Continued)

Week	Learning objectives and critical thinking	Relevant A–Z concepts
	Critical thinking	• Reductionism
	• What historical, social, economic, cultural, and political influences contributed to the rise of gerontology and the development of theories of aging?	• Social construction of reality
		• Spheres (public/private, subaltern, security)
	• What do modernist theories of aging seek to explain? What are their limitations?	
4	**Biological influences on theories of aging**	• Ableism/TABS
	• Relate biological theory and science to understanding senescence, longevity, and variation in aging.	• Allostatic load
		• Anti-aging
		• Biomedicalization
	• Identify the influences of biological theories on understanding aging.	• Disengagement
		• Embodiment
		• Epigenetics
	Critical thinking	• Gene–environment
	• Some scientists believe that the human lifespan can be extended far beyond its current limits. What do you think of this idea? Do the theories of aging seem to support it?	• Healthy aging/active aging
		• Life expectancy
		• Losses
		• Plasticity
		• Quality-adjusted life years
	• Many people who undergo cosmetic surgery are motivated by a wish to maintain or regain their once youthful appearance. Do you think a concern with the outward signs of aging is a positive or negative social trend?	• Telomeres
		• Temporality
	• If government officials want to promote social equality, at what stage of the life course should they intervene?	
	• How might social policy in early childhood affect later life outcomes?	
4	**Psychological influences on theories of aging**	• Abjection
	• Relate psychology theories and science to understanding adaptation, stability, and change in aging.	• Ageism
		• Exploitation
		• Interactionism
	• Identify the influences of psychological theories on understanding aging.	• Intergenerational intersubjectivity
		• Life course perspective
		• Mental health
	Critical thinking	• Micro-aggressions
	• How do our self-perceptions influence our experiences of growing older?	• Psychoanalytic social theory
		• Resilience

Week	Learning objectives and critical thinking	Relevant A–Z concepts
	• How does society's perceptions of older people influence our experiences of growing older? • What stereotypes of older adults might be founded in symptoms of age-related disorders? What do these stereotypes say about our society? • What is the relationship between abjection and exploitation?	• Stress • Subjective aging • Trauma
5	**Demographic influences on theories of aging** • Relate demography theories and science to understanding the heterogeneity, inequality, and context of aging. • Identify the influences of demographic theories on understanding aging. *Critical thinking* • The proportion of working-age Americans to retired Americans has been dropping for several decades as the result of declining fertility and mortality rates. Should the government encourage couples to have more children? • What is the utility of categorizing people into cohorts or generations? What are its limitations? • What kinds of political activity should we expect from baby boomers or older generations? From younger generations?	• Age rating • Dependency and dependency ratio • Generation • Labeling • Productive aging • Social contract • Stereotype threat • Structured dependency theory
6	**Pushing and pulling around a critical turn** • Understand how contemporary events influenced critical theory development in the social sciences and in aging. • Identify social theories that underpin critical theories in aging. *Critical thinking* • What historical, social, economic, cultural, and political influences contributed to the rise of critical theory development in the social sciences? How did these influences contribute to theory development in aging?	• Ageism • Civil Rights Movement/Civil Rights Act • Critical theory • Culture • Democracy • Emancipatory • Embodiment • Ethics • Ethnogerontology/ethnogeriatrics • Interactionism • Intersectionality/Intersectional knowledge

(Continued)

(Continued)

Week	Learning objectives and critical thinking	Relevant A–Z concepts
	• What do critical theories of aging seek to explain? What are their limitations? • What social movements have older Americans participated in? How have these movements affected theory formation on aging? • How might postmodern concepts and fields of study inform big data research?	• Knowledges • Maggie Kuhn • Misogyny • Oppression • Patriarchy • People of color • Performativity • Postmodernism • Privilege • Queer • Race/racism • Radical (and radical history) • Resistance • Sexuality • Social movements • Subversive • Symbolic • Theory of change • War • War on women
7	**Political economy of aging** • Understand how this theory considers the reproduction of social inequalities. • Identify how public policies are an outcome of social struggles and dominant power relations. *Critical thinking* • What is the relationship between age and social status? • How does this theory consider the ways in which race, class, and gender affect the social status of older adults? • What concepts have been used in debates about government spending on older adults? • What types of markets, policies, and products have emerged to serve problems of aging and older adults? • What do industrial complexes (e.g. Military, Medical, Prison) have to do with the political economy of aging?	• Aging enterprise • Austerity • Capitalism • Class • Conflict theory and consensus theory • Cost of living adjustment • Crisis • Debt • Discourse • Economics • Financialization • Framing • Ideological advocacy coalitions • Institutions • Labor • Medical industrial complex • Military industrial complex • Necropolitics • Neoliberalism • Pension/retirement plans • Political economy

Week	Learning objectives and critical thinking	Relevant A–Z concepts
	• How do social policies inform or support each other? Discuss how Housing, Medicare, and Social Security work in tandem or in opposition for supporting older adults. Are there other social policies or programs which seem interconnected?	• Power • Precarity • Prison industrial complex • Privatization • Race • Social insurance • Spirits of capitalism • The State • Structure • TINA (There is No Alternative) • Welfare state
8	**Feminist theories of aging** • Relate feminist theory and science to understanding the role of the gendered state and the reproduction of patriarchal systems. *Critical thinking* • How does the State, capital, and the sex/gender system conjointly produce and reproduce the dominant institutions that render older women vulnerable and dependent throughout their life course? • What is the relationship between the labor market and retirement and women's aging? • How are theories of masculinity related to theories of feminism in aging?	• Feminism/feminist • Intersectionality/intersectional knowledge • Men • Misogyny • Patriarchy • Relations of ruling • Reproduction, social • Resistance • Sexism • Social movements • Standpoint theories • Wage inequality • War on women • Zero years
9	**Inequalities and aging** • Understand how interlocking systems of oppression are related to aging. • Understand how the theory of cumulative advantage/disadvantage explains gender, racial, and ethnic differences in well-being among older adults. *Critical thinking* • What health disparities can you identify in the people within your community? How are they defining your community? Does this include your workplace? • What can the government do to increase the economic security of minority group members in their old age?	• Aging in community/aging in place • Blacklands • Class • Commons, the • Cumulative advantage/ disadvantage • Dependency and dependency ratio • Equality • Equity • Gender • Gentrification • Health disparities • HIV/AIDS • Housing • Human Rights

(Continued)

(Continued)

Week	Learning objectives and critical thinking	Relevant A–Z concepts
	• What can be done to improve the well-being of minority groups that does not involve the government? • How do the ideas of the political economy and the social status accorded to people fit together to affect them as they grow older? • What are civil rights and how do they relate to the social safety net?	• Inequality • Intersectionality/intersectional knowledge • Jeopardy • People of color • Poverty • Precarity • Queer • Racial wealth gap • Race/racism • Sexuality • Structured dependency theory • Trauma • Violence • Wage inequality • Welfare state • White supremacy • Xenophobia
10	**Globalization and aging** • Identify global challenges to the nation-state and implications for policy on aging. • Describe the mechanisms that help or hinder caring across borders, global care chains, and institutional responses to old age. *Critical thinking* • How does transnational aging, migration, and aging in developing countries affect nation states and aging policies at global to local levels? • Demographers recognize the contributions immigrants make to a developed nation's population structure, yet many Americans feel threatened by immigrants. What is the relationship between immigration and aging? What can be done to improve the immigrant's public image? • What are the intergovernmental organizations and interest groups that represent older adults around the world, and what have they accomplished? • How do global phenomena affect people's individual experiences of growing older? The experiences of families? The experiences of communities?	• Citizenship • Colonialisms • Ecologies • Ethics • Family • Freedom • Gentrification • Geographies • Globalization • Governance • Human rights • Immigration • Inclusion/exclusion • Inequality • Labor • Nativism • Neoliberalism • Poverty • Race/racism • Refugees • Violence • War • White supremacy • Xenophobia

Partial Chart of Theories of Aging

This partial chart may be useful as a teaching tool to accompany a course on theories of aging.

Chart A1 Rise of Gerontology to Critical Gerontology in the USA, 1900 to the Present
(selected elements from Yeh, DiCarlo, & Estes, forthcoming)

Themes	Rise of gerontology Circa 1900 to 1965	Legitimating gerontology Circa 1945 to present	Critical gerontology Circa 1970 to present
Notable gerontological moments	1904 – "Gerontology" coined by biologist, Eli Metchnikoff. 1909 – "Geriatrics" coined by physician, Leo Nascher.	1945 – The Gerontological Society [of America] was established. 1954 – The Gerontological Society [of America] became an affiliate of the American Association for the Advancement of Science.	1970 – Gray Panthers, founded by Maggie Kuhn, to confront ageism and social justice through multigenerational advocacy. 1971 – National Caucus on the Black Aged (NCBA), formed by Hobart Jackson, Robert Kastenbaum, and Jacquelyne Johnson Jackson, to confront racial inequities through minority aging advocacy.
Dominant gerontological theories	Disengagement, activity, continuity theories; life cycle, life course, lifespan theories; human/adult development theories	Successful, productive, normal, healthy, active aging theories; age stratification theories (e.g., cohort, birth order, generational focus); biosocial and bioecological models; environmental gerontology.	Political economy of aging, cumulative advantage/ disadvantage and inequality theories, feminist/race/ethno gerontologies, cultural gerontology.
Main mode of gerontological action	Discover laws about normality and pathology as applied to growing older.	Scientific management and control over aging and the life course; shape possibilities for aging well and for social participation; promote societal integration and social harmony.	Bridge dichotomy between agency and structure; identify cultural and symbolic beliefs/meaning in old age; problematize intergenerational conflict; fight power struggles over social

(Continued)

(Continued)

Themes	Rise of gerontology Circa 1900 to 1965	Legitimating gerontology Circa 1945 to present	Critical gerontology Circa 1970 to present
			systems and social structures; ideological transformations; resist exploitation and oppression; seek social justice; solidarity with marginalized, disenfranchised, and disadvantaged people and groups.
Criticisms	Individualistic; ignores large-scale collective social explanations in aging process; reinforces alienation and dependency in old age; promotes ageism, age segregations, separation of older adults from society; homogeneity of aging assumed.	Homogeneity of older adults assumed (i.e., white middle-class American). In its process of legitimation, it maintains the status quo of society (e.g., women less valuable than men; older women less valuable than younger women; people of color less valuable than white people; LGBTQ people less valuable than straight people). An excess of structure confines the possibilities of adult aging to age stages and stereotypes.	Self-critical; accused by other traditions as idealistic. An excess of fluidity disconnects aging from the material basis of experience and can lead to insecurity and risk. Holds the potential to undermine the economic and cultural foundations that substantially improved quality of life for older people during the modern era.

Further Resources and Reading

Aronowitz, S. & Giroux, H. (1985). *Education under siege. The conservative, liberal and radical debate over schooling.* South Hadley, MA: Bergin & Garvey.

Brown, P., Cohen, A. L., Bradley, D. B., Bennett, C. R., Dawson, A., & Estes, C. L. (2016). Women In Gerontology Legacy Project (June). Women's Task Force. Washington, DC: Gerontological Society of America and AGHE.

Cianciolo, P. K. (2009). Teaching collaborative learning and continuing education strategies about Social Security and Medicare. (pp. 399–416) in Rogne, L., Estes, C. L. et al. (Eds.), *Social insurance and social justice.* New York: Springer.

Damron-Rodriguez, Interviewed by Erica Hegland. (2015). Part of the Women In Gerontology Legacy Project (WIGL) [Video File]. Retrieved from https://youtu.be/nQQZfT8KwFk.

Estes, C., interviewed by C. R. Bennet. (2014). Part of the Women in Gerontology Legacy Project (WIGL) [video file]. Retrieved from https://youtu.be/wEJs_J8SJQs.

Estes, C. L., Grossman, B. R., Rogne, L., Hollister, B., & Solway, E. (2008). Teaching Social Insurance in Higher Education. Occasional Papers. Number 6. AARP. Washington, DC: AARP.

Grabinski, C. J. (2009). Beyond lectures and tests: Facilitating applied and interactive social insurance learning experiences in gerontology courses. (pp. 417–433) in Rogne, L., Estes, C. L. et al. (Eds.), *Social insurance and social justice*. New York: Springer.

Mayo, P. (1999). *Gramsci, Freire and adult education. Possibilities for transformative action*. London and New York: Zed Books.

Yeh, J. C., DiCarlo, N. B., & Estes, C. L. (forthcoming). The rise of gerontology to critical gerontology in the US, 1900 – present. Institute for Health & Aging Working Paper, University of California, San Francisco.

2
Practice Toolkit
(as developed by Nicholas DiCarlo)

Acknowledging Age, Disability, and Working with Strengths
- Debunking popular myths and learning about stereotypes.
- Thinking about the voices behind stories.

Critical thinking
- What are the cultural fears of aging? How does an older client understand their strengths and limitations? What are fears regarding timelines of frailty and decline?
- How do patients understand their right to determine the care they receive?
- What is the relationship between a client's agency and functional myths of self-reliance?
- How can dependency be understood and normalized as part of the human experience?
- Which stories are celebrated and which are silenced?

Trauma, Inequality, and Vulnerable Populations
- Understand how interlocking systems of oppression are related to aging.
- Understand the practitioner's privilege and its relationship to oppressed populations.
- Build critical analyses of how trauma manifests through systems of oppression and carries through generations.

Critical thinking
- What are structural barriers to people receiving care?
- How does "evidence-based practice" legitimize Western practices and discourage the use of "unproven" cultural traditions of healing?
- How does functionalism determine or frame the goals of care?
- What are trauma-informed practices in your workplace?

- Abjection
- Ageism
- Alzheimer's disease
- Americans with Disabilities Act
- Disability
- Functionalism
- Micro-aggressions
- Myth
- Oppression
- Psychoanalytic social theory
- Precarity
- Productive/successful aging
- Resilience
- Statistical panic
- Stereotype threat

- Citizenship
- Deportation
- Equality
- Equity
- Gender
- Health disparities
- Housing
- Human rights
- HIV/AIDS
- Immigration
- Inequality
- People of color
- Poverty
- Power
- Precarity

- What makes care "culturally competent"?
- Are the people being cared for reflected in those caring for them?
- How do practitioners both challenge and support each other to become aware of their blind spots?

- Privilege
- Racial wealth gap
- Race/racism
- Rape
- Refugees
- Resilience
- Sexuality
- Stress
- Trauma
- Violence
- Wage inequality
- War
- White supremacy
- Xenophobia

Critical Care, Medical Environments, and Social Welfare

- Builds on trauma-sensitive practice, deepening awareness of sociocultural difference, and privilege at an institutional level.
- Finding context for and re-conceptualizing "health behavior."
- Thinking about how care may be employed as a method of social control.
- Understanding the role and impact of "pathology" for clinical work.
- Learning about emerging theories of illness.

Critical thinking

- What are the financial incentives behind providing a certain type of care?
- Who involved in caregiving is compensated and how? How secure are the networks of informal care, and how do these relate to class privilege?
- At which levels of analysis does the patient or practitioner lose a sense of purpose and understanding?

- Aging Eenterprise
- Caregiving
- Class
- Culture
- Dementia
- Domination
- Gene–environment
- Institutions
- Levels of analysis
- Long-term care
- Medical industrial complex
- Medicare
- Social Security
- The State
- Telomeres
- Welfare state

3
Legislative Appendix
(as co-developed with Ben Veghte)

The following sections detail some of the legislative landscape around social policy and social insurance programs serving older Americans. The first section charts the history of the Elder Justice Act (2010), the second names the bills introduced in the 114th Congress, and the third lists the bills introduced in the 115th Congress with additional detail as to what the Acts specifically address. This illustrates the process of introducing and reintroducing legislation, which is a crucial component of resistance movements from progressives. Whether or not the legislation is passed, it stands as a record of what can be, anchoring the progressive legislation as part of a written history.

The Elder Justice Act

- It was enacted in 2010, as an amendment to the Affordable Care Act.
- The bill's authorization expired at the end of fiscal year 2014.
- In 2015, Rep. Peter King (R-NY) and eight co-sponsors introduced H.R. 988, the Elder Justice Reauthorization Act, which died in the 114th Congress.
- In 2017, Rep. King and four co-sponsors introduced H.R. 2639, an updated version of the Elder Justice Reauthorization Act.
- In 2017, Reps King and Suzanne Bonamici (D-OR) created an Elder Justice Caucus in the House of Representatives.

According to the Congressional Research Service, the Elder Justice Act's "organic" authority continues, because it has received appropriated funds. The Elder Justice Initiative has developed an improved data system to track incidences of elder abuse. The Act created an Elder Justice Coordinating Council comprising various relevant federal agencies. Funding is the big challenge, particularly for Adult Protective Services (APS). The Department of Justice is conducting sweeps to break up scams. EJA funding through Social Service Block Grants (SSBGs) is imperiled to the extent that SSBG survives the political axe (Blancato, 2018).

Further Reading

Blancato, R. (2018). Personal communication, March 1.

Elder Justice Act Summary. (2017). Factsheet retrieved from www.elderjustice coalition.com.

The Supplemental Security Income Restoration Act (2017)

The Supplemental Security Income Restoration Act was introduced in the 113th, 114th, and 115th Congresses by Congressman Raúl M. Grijalva.

This Act aims to help low-income seniors and people with disabilities by updating the program's eligibility rules (which have largely remained unchanged since Nixon signed the eligibility rules into law (1972)). The Act would allow the following:

- Individuals will be able to save up to $10,000 (couples: $20,000) for emergencies such as car repairs, new roofs, and other unexpected expenses without losing benefits.
- Individuals will be able to receive up to $114 monthly from other sources such as Social Security benefits or pension payments without a corresponding loss in benefits.
- Individuals who are able to work will be able to earn up to $377 monthly without being penalized.
- Individuals who live in households with others, including family members, will no longer be penalized with lower benefits through the in-kind support and maintenance provision.
- Individuals who transfer assets (even small amounts of money to a family member) will no longer suffer harsh penalties.
- Couples will receive their full SSI benefit, totaling twice the individual rate, rather than a reduced marriage penalty rate of $1103.
- State and local earned income tax credits and child tax credits will be excluded from income calculations in the same manner as general tax payments.

Further Reading

Policy Issue Brief on Supplemental Security Income Restoration Act of 2017. Provided by Justice in Aging. Retrieved from www.justiceinaging.org.

Health Care Provisions in the Bipartisan Budget Act of 2018

On February 9, Congress passed the *Bipartisan Budget Act of 2018* which includes changes to several Medicare programs, and provides funding for other health programs that support low-income older adults, people with disabilities, and their families. Below is a summary of these health-related provisions.

Funding for Outreach to Low-income Medicare Beneficiaries

The law provides an additional two years' funding to State Health Insurance Assistance Programs (SHIPs), Area Agencies on Aging, Aging and Disability Resource Centers, and the National Center for Benefits and Outreach Enrollment to conduct outreach and enroll low-income Medicare beneficiaries. This funding for targeted outreach is separate from annual appropriations for SHIPs.

Funding for Community Health Centers and CHIP

The law guarantees funding for community health centers (CHCs) and the National Health Service Corps for 2018 and 2019, and authorizes the Secretary of HHS to award supplemental grants to CHCs to implement models to improve access to primary care. Congress also approved additional funding for the Children's Health Insurance Program (CHIP), guaranteeing the program's funding through 2027.

Medicare Therapy Cap Repeal

The law permanently repeals the payment cap on outpatient physical, occupational, and speech therapies effective January 1, 2018, and makes changes to the medical necessity review process for these services.

Part D Donut Hole Closure

The law closes the Medicare Part D "donut hole" or coverage gap faster. Instead of 2020, the donut hole will now close in 2019, at which time beneficiaries will be required to contribute 25% percent to the cost of prescription drugs. This provision does not affect coverage for beneficiaries who receive the Part D low-income subsidy known as "Extra Help," since they already don't experience the donut hole. Justice in Aging • www.justiceinaging.org • FACT SHEET • 2.

Changes to Medicare Advantage for People with Chronic Conditions and Dual Eligibles

1. Special Needs Plans – The law permanently reauthorizes Medicare Special Needs Plans (SNPs). SNPs serve target populations with special needs, including individuals who are dually eligible for Medicare and Medicaid and individuals with chronic conditions.
2. VBID Models and Supplemental Benefits: The law expands testing of the Medicare Value-Based Insurance Design (VBID) model to all states by 2020. There are currently 11 plans in three states participating in the VBID model, which allows plans to offer supplemental benefits or reduced cost sharing to enrollees with specific chronic conditions. The law also expands the type of supplemental benefits which Medicare Advantage Plans may offer to chronically ill individuals beginning in 2020. These can include benefits that are not primarily health related as long as the benefit has a reasonable expectation of improving or maintaining the health or overall function of the individual.

Medicare Coverage of Speech-generating Devices

Congress enacted the Gleason Enduring Voices Act, guaranteeing Medicare coverage of speech-generating devices as routinely purchased durable medical equipment.

Medicare Home Health Benefit Changes

The law changes how Medicare will pay for home health services beginning in 2020. The home health payment episode will be reduced from 60 to 30 days and therapy thresholds will be eliminated. Beginning in 2019, Medicare will be allowed to base eligibility determinations for home health services on a review of the patient's medical record, including a home health agency's record, beginning in 2019.

Independence and Home Demonstration Program

Congress extended the Medicare Independence at Home demonstration by two years and increased the cap on the total number of participating beneficiaries.

Other Changes

To offset the costs of some of the above provisions, Congress chose certain changes that will be detrimental to the Medicare program and the health and financial security of older Americans and their families. These include the following:

1. Increase Medicare premiums for higher-income beneficiaries: Beginning in 2019, Part B and Part D premium contributions for beneficiaries with modified adjusted gross incomes (MAGIs) over $500,000 for individuals or over $750,000 for couples will increase from 80 to 85 percent.
2. Reduce the ACA Prevention and Public Health Fund by $1.35 billion over ten years.

Bills and Resolutions: 114th Congress (Selected)

- Social Security Expansion Act S. 731 – Bernie Sanders
- The Social Security 2100 Act H.R. 1391 and S. 1904 – Blumenthal & Larson
- Social Security Enhancement and Protection Act H.R. 1756 – Gwen Moore
- Protecting and Preserving S.S. Act. 6. 960 and H.R. 1811 – Hirono & Deutch
- Fair Adjustment and Income Revenue for S.S. Act H.R. 1984 – Peter DeFazio
- Keeping Social Security Solvent Act H.R. 2078 – Paul Tonko
- Social Security Fairness Act S. 1651 – Brown & Collins
- One Social Security Act H.R. 3150 – Xavier Becerra
- CPI-E Act of 2015 H.R. 3351 – Mike Honda
- Caregiver Credit Act H.R. 3377 – Nita Lowey
- SAFE Social Security Act S. 1940 – Brian Schatz
- SAVE -1 Time Social Security Increase – Elizabeth Warren
- House Resolution to Protect and Expand Social Security – Jan Schakowsky

Bills and Resolutions: 115th Congress (Selected and Annotated)

Social Security Expansion Act (S. 427, H.R. 1114) – Sen. Bernie Sanders (I-VT), Rep. Peter DeFazio (D-OR-4)

- Subjects earnings above $250,000 to the payroll tax and expands payroll tax to all earnings between the current cap and $250,000. Taxes investment income, switches to CPI-E, and boosts benefits by adjusting the benefit formula.

CPI-E Act of 2017 (H.R. 1251) – Rep. John Garamendi (D-CA-3)

- Switches to CPI-E from CPI-W.

Protect our Widow and Widower Retirement Act (H.R. 1583) – Rep. Linda Sanchez (D-CA-38)

- Creates an alternative benefit for widows equivalent to 75 percent of the combined income while both spouses were alive.

Social Security 2100 Act (H.R. 1902) – Rep. John Larson (D-CT-1)

- Raises the payroll tax cap to $400,000. Introduces CPI-E, raises minimum benefit 125 percent, expands benefits, and raises threshold on taxation of benefits.

Protection of Social Security Benefits Restoration Act (S. 959) – Sen. Ron Wyden (D-OR)

- Repeals the 1996 Social Security garnishment rules. Prevents Social Security from being garnished for federal student debt, home loans owed to the VA, and food stamp overpayments.

Social Security Safety Dividend Act of 2017 (H.R. 67) – Rep. Sheila Jackson Lee (D-TX-18)

- Directs the Department of the Treasury to disburse a $250 cash payment to recipients of the government's various pension and social insurance programs in cases where there is no cost of living adjustment for a particular year.

Improving Access to Affordable Prescription Drugs (S. 771, H.R. 1776) – Sen. Al Franken (D-MN), Rep. Jan Schakowsky (D-IL-9)

- Lowers prescription drug prices through Medicare price negotiation, anti-price gouging measures, capping out-of-pocket costs, and increasing competition and innovation.

Medicare for All Act of 2017 (S. 1804) – Sen. Bernie Sanders (I-VT)

- Establishes a federally administered Medicare-for-all national health insurance program that will be implemented over a four-year period.

Expanded and Improved Medicare for All Act (H.R. 676) – Rep. Keith Ellison (D-MN-5)

- Establishes a Medicare for All program to provide health insurance for all U.S. residents.

Social Security Caregiver Credit Act of 2017 (S. 1255) – Sen. Christopher Murphy (D-CT)

- Extends credits to full-time caregivers of dependents and expands caregiver training programs.

Social Security for Future Generations Act (H.R. 2855) – Rep. Al Lawson (D-FL-5)

- Subjects earnings above $250,000 to payroll tax. Switches to the CPI-E from the CPI-W. Extends student benefit to age 22. Updates widow/widower benefit. Includes special minimum benefit.

Fair COLA for Seniors Act (H.R. 2896) – Rep. Richard Nolan (D-MN-8)

- Switches to the CPI-E.

Protecting and Preserving Social Security Act (S. 1600 and H.R. 3302) – Sen. Mazie Hirono (D-HI) and Rep. Ted Deutch (D-FL-22)

- Eliminates Social Security tax cap gradually over seven years, ultimately subjecting all earnings to payroll taxes. For higher earners, expands payroll tax to all earnings. Switches to the CPI-E from the CPI-W.

Social Security Administration Accountability Act (H.R. 5431) – Rep. Brian Higgins (D-NY-26)

- Requires Social Security Commissioner to include the number of pending cases at the hearing offices in each budget submission and to provide justification for any office closing. Requires GAO to study disability hearings process.

BASIC Act (H.R. 5302) – Rep. Peter DeFazio (D-OR-4)

- Pro-rates beneficiary's last month of benefits and increases the lump sum death payment by about $255; these new benefits will not violate the family maximum provisions.

Elder Poverty Relief Act (S. 2653) – Sen. Ron Wyden (D-OR)

- Beneficiaries aged 82 or older, SSI recipients at the full retirement age, and other Social Security and SSI recipients who have received benefits for 20 years or more will receive an additional $85 per month (increasing annually by 4 percent). Social Security beneficiaries with low monthly benefits at the full retirement age will receive additional benefits of approximately $944 per month, adjusted annually.

SWIFT Act (S. 3457) – Sen. Bob Casey (D-PA)

- Allows widow(er)s and surviving divorced spouses with disabilities to receive 100 percent of the survivor benefit regardless of their age, and lifts caps on these benefits. Enables widow(er)s and surviving divorced spouses caring for children to receive child-in-care benefits until the children are aged 18 or 19 if still in school, and requires the federal government to proactively provide information to widow(er)s and surviving divorced spouses about benefits for which they are eligible, claiming options, and important deadlines.

Strengthening Social Security Act (H.R. 6929) – Rep. Linda Sanchez (D-CA-38) and Rep. Mark Pocan (D-WI-02)

- Increases monthly benefits for current and future retirees. Switches to CPI-E from CPI-W. Phases out the Social Security tax cap. Increases widow(er)s' benefits to the greater of 75% of combined benefits, or the Primary Insurance Amount.

Maintain Access to Vital Social Security Services Act of 2018 (H.R. 7146) – Rep. Gwen Moore (D-WI-04)

- Requires SSA to operate a sufficient number of field offices and to employ an adequate number of personnel at each field office to provide convenient and accessible services to the public while minimizing wait times, and requires new reporting to Congress on these matters.

Affordable Medications Act and Improving Access to Affordable Prescription Drugs (S. 3411 and H.R. 1776) – Sen. Tina Smith (D-MN) and Rep. Jan Schakowsky (D-IL-9)

- Lowers the price of prescription drugs by ending the restriction that prevents Medicare from using its buying power to negotiate lower drug prices for beneficiaries, curbing drug company monopoly practices that keep prices high and prevent less expensive generics from coming to the market such as "pay-for-delay" agreements and price gouging. Increases transparency at drug companies. Caps out-of-pocket costs for drugs in health insurance plans. Funds innovation.

Further Reading

Policy Issue Brief on Social Security Legislation in the U.S. Congress provided by Social Security Works. Retrieved from https://socialsecurityworks.org/.

Outlook for the 116th Congress

In the 116th Congress, there will be a continuing evolution of Congressional debates, votes, negotiations, court decisions, and challenges at the federal and state levels regarding the ACA, Medicare for All, and Medicaid provisions.

With Democrats winning a strong majority in the House of Representatives, policies seeking to mitigate economic and health insecurity, for seniors and other segments of the population, will receive serious consideration on a variety of fronts. The Social Security 2100 Act, introduced by Congressman John Larson (D-CT-01) with more than 200 co-sponsors, expands benefits for millions, protects low income workers, and strengthens the trust fund by raising the payroll tax to wages above $400,000. With Rep. John Larson, a long-time proponent of Social Security expansion, as Chair of the Social Security Subcommittee of House Ways and Means, is holding hearings on expanding Social Security – Many Social Security expansion bills previously introduced in the 114th and the 115th congressess are likely to be reintroduced in the 116th Congress as well.

With the Affordable Care Act (ACA) being tentatively struck down by a federal judge in Texas on the grounds that its mandate requiring people to buy health insurance is unconstitutional, pressure is mounting on Congress to address the problem of health uninsurance and underinsurance. With regard to the ACA, a coalition of 17 Democratic attorneys general have asked Judge Reed O'Connor to clarify his ruling. The fate of the ACA will likely remain unresolved until it reaches the Supreme Court. In the meantime, the Department of Health and Human Services has said that it will continue to administer and enforce all aspects of the ACA until the issue is definitively resolved. Democrats in the House and the Senate introduced resolutions to allow the House and Senate Counsels to intervene in that lawsuit, expressing the sentiments of those bodies that the ACA's consumer protections and Medicaid be maintained and strengthened.

With Democrats taking control of the House, Medicare expansion is likely to receive far more intense consideration than in the 115th Congress. Of the 40 new Democratic Members of the House, virtually all ran on expanding Medicare (and Social Security). Rep. Pramila Jayapal (D-WA) and Rep. Deborah Dingell (D-MI) will continue to co-chair the Medicare for All Caucus, created in July 2018, to which 71 House members now belong. The Medicare for All Act and the Expanded and Improved Medicare for All Act are sure to be reintroduced into the Senate and House, respectively, and the latter is likely to include coverage of long-term services and supports as well as health care. Continued efforts to control drug prices are ongoing, including a new measure to be introduced by Sen. Bernie Sanders (I-VT) and Rep. Ro Khanna (D-CA): the Prescription Drug Price Relief Act.

Further Reading

Altman, N. (2018). Personal communication, December 18.

Medicare for All Congressional Caucus. (2018). Retrieved from https://jayapal.house.gov/medicare-for-all.

The New York Times. (2018). Texas judge strikes down Obama's Affordable Care Act as unconstitutional. Retrieved from www.nytimes.com/2018/12/14/health/obamacare-unconstitutional-texas-judge.html.

Pollin, R. et al. (2018). Economic analysis of Medicare for All. Retrieved from www.peri.umass.edu/publication/item/1127-economic-analysis-of-medicare-for-all.

4

Carroll L. Estes' Selected Works

Carroll Estes' work embraces four types of sociology that Burawoy has identified as: (1) traditional (professional) sociology, (2) policy sociology, (3) critical sociology, and (4) public sociology. Public sociology and critical sociology are *subaltern*, meaning subordinate, marginalized, in lower status of the discipline. Critical sociology is the *"conscience of professional sociology."* Public sociology is the *"conscience of policy sociology."* Burawoy warns of the "growing gap between the sociological ethos and the world we study," asking, "For whom and for what do we pursue our discipline?" (Burawoy, M. (2005). *American Sociological Review*, *70*(1), 4–28).

Selected Works: Estes Reference List

1. Estes-Thometz, C. L. (1963). *The decision-makers: The power structure of Dallas.* Dallas, TX: Southern Methodist University Press.
2. Estes, C. L. (1979). *The aging enterprise: A critical examination of social policies and services for the aged.* San Francisco, CA: Jossey-Bass.
3. Estes, C. L. (1979). Toward a sociology of political gerontology. *Sociological Symposium*, *26*, 1–25.
4. Estes, C. L. (1980). Constructions of reality. Special Issue: Old age: Environmental complexity and policy interventions. *Journal of Social Issues, 36*(2), 117–132.
5. Estes, C. L., Swan, J. H., & Gerard, L. E. (1982). Dominant and competing paradigms in gerontology: Towards a political economy of aging. *Ageing and Society, 2* (Part 2), 151–164 (July).
6. Estes, C. L. (1983). Social Security: The social construction of a crisis. *Milbank Memorial Fund Quarterly/Health & Society, 61*(3), 445–461.
7. Estes, C. L., Newcomer, R. J., & Associates. (1983). *Fiscal austerity and aging: Shifting governmental responsibility for the elderly.* Beverly Hills, CA: Sage.
8. Estes, C. L., Gerard, L., Zones, J., & Swan, J. H. (1984). *Political economy, health, and aging.* Boston, MA: Little Brown.
9. Estes, C. L. & Alford, R. (1990). Systemic crisis and the nonprofit sector: Toward a political economy. *Theory and Society, 19*(2), 173–198.
10. Estes, C. L. (1991). The Reagan legacy: Privatization, the welfare state, and aging in the 1990s. In J. Myles and J. S. Quadagno (Eds.), *States, labor markets, and the future of old age policy* (pp. 59–93). Philadelphia, PA: Temple University Press.
11. Estes, C. L. (1991). The new political economy of aging: Introduction and critique. In M. Minkler & C. L. Estes (Eds.), *Critical perspectives on aging: The political and moral economy of growing old* (pp. 19–36) Amityville, NY: Baywood.

Table A2 Estes' Selected Publications by Type of Knowledge (Mixed Categories May Apply)

Professional Sociology/Gerontology	Policy Sociology/Gerontology

Professional Sociology/Gerontology
- *The Decision Makers* (Book, 1963)
- *The Aging Enterprise* (Book, 1979)
- "Toward a Sociology of Political Gerontology" (1979)
- "Constructions of Reality" (1980)
- "Dominant and Competing Paradigms in Gerontology" (1982)

Policy Sociology/Gerontology
- *Fiscal Austerity and Aging* (Book, 1983)
- "Social Security/Social Construction of a Crisis" (1983)
- *The Long Term Care (LTC) Crisis* (Book, 1993)
- "Politics of LTC Reform/Clinton Plan" (2003)
- "Chronic Care/What Learned?" (2003)
- "Older People/ Social Injustice" (2019)

Critical Sociology/Gerontology
- *Political Economy, Health and Aging* (Book, 1984)
- "Systemic Crisis and the Non-profit Sector" (1990)
- "The Reagan Legacy" (1991)
- "New Political Economy of Aging" (1991)
- "The Gerontological Imagination" (1992)
- "Critical Gerontology & the New Political Economy of Aging" (1999)
- *Social Policy and Aging* (Book, 2001)
- "The Globalization of Capital, the Welfare State and Old Age Policy" (2002)
- "Social Security Privatization and Older Women" (2004)
- *Social Theory, Social Policy and Ageing* (Book, 2003/2009)
- "Crises and Old Age Policy" (2011)
- "Exploitation and the State in Precarity USA" (2019)

Public Sociology/Gerontology
- *Social Justice and Social Insurance* (Book, 2009)
- "The Economic Meltdown and Old Age Politics" (2009)
- *Breaking the Social Security Glass Ceiling* (2012)
- "Future of Aging Services in a Neoliberal Political Economy" (2014)
- "Older U.S. Women's Economic Security, Health, and Empowerment" (2017)
- "Women's Rights, Women's Status, and Resistance in the Age of Trump" (2017–18)
- *Aging A–Z: Concepts toward Emancipatory Gerontology* (Book, 2019)

Note: Table A2 Publications include Estes' sole authored, co-authored, and co-edited works (citations of authorship, co-authorship, and editorship of selected works are given below).

12. Estes, C. L., Binney, E. A., & Culbertson, R. A. (1992). The gerontological imagination: Social influences on the development of gerontology, 1945 – present. *International Journal of Aging & Human Development, 35*(1), 49–65.

13. Estes, C. L., Swan, J. H., & Associates. (1993). *The long-term care crisis: Elders trapped in the no-care zone.* Newbury Park, CA: Sage.

14. Estes, C. L. (1999). Critical gerontology and the new political economy of aging. In M. Minkler & C. L. Estes (Eds.), *Critical gerontology: Perspectives from political and moral economy* (pp. 17–35). Amityville, NY: Baywood.

15. Estes, C. L. & Associates. (2001). *Social policy & aging: A critical perspective.* Thousand Oaks, CA: Sage.

16. Estes, C. L. & Phillipson, C. (2002). The globalization of capital, the welfare state, and old age policy. *International Journal of Health Services, 32*(2), 279–297.

17. Estes, C. L., Biggs, S., & Phillipson, C. (2003/2009). *Social theory, social policy, and ageing: A critical introduction.* Maidenhead, Berkshire: Open University Press.

18. Lynch, M., Estes, C., & Hernandez, M. (2003). Chronic care initiatives: What we have learned and implications for the Medicare program. In D. Blumenthal, M. Moon, M. Warshawsky, & C. Boccuti (Eds.), *Long-term care and Medicare policy* (pp. 151–174). Washington, DC: National Academy of Social Insurance/Brookings Institution Press.

19. Estes, C. L., Wiener, J. M., Goldberg, S. C., & Goldenson, S. (2003). The politics of long term care reform under the Clinton health plan. In P. R. Lee & C. L. Estes (Eds.), *The nation's health* (7th edition) (pp. 213–220). Sudbury, MA: Jones & Bartlett.

20. Estes, C. L. (2004). Social Security privatization and older women: A feminist political economy perspective. *Journal of Aging Studies, 18*(1), 9–26.

21. Grossman, B., Solway, E., Hollister, B., Estes, C. L., & Rogne, L. (2009). One nation, interdependent. In L. Rogne, C. L. Estes, B. R. Grossman, B. Hollister, and E. Solway (Eds.), *Social insurance and social justice: Social Security, Medicare and the campaign against entitlements* (pp. 115–147). New York: Springer.

22. Polivka, L. & Estes, C. L. (2009). The economic meltdown and old age politics. *Generations: Journal of the American Society on Aging, 33*(3), 56–62.

23. Estes, C. L. (2011). Crises and old age policy. In R. A. Settersten Jr. & J. L. Angel (Eds.), *Handbook of sociology of aging* (pp. 297–320). New York: Springer.

24. Estes, C. L., O'Neill, T., and Hartmann, H. (2012). *Breaking the Social Security glass ceiling: A proposal to modernize women's benefits.* Washington, DC: NCPSSM Foundation, NOW Foundation, and Institute for Women's Policy Research.

25. Estes, C. L. (2014). Future of aging services in a neoliberal political economy. *Generations: Journal of the American Society on Aging, 38*(2), 94–100.

26. Estes, C. L. (2017). Older US women's economic security, health and empowerment. In S. L. Dworkin, M. Gandhi, & P. Passano (Eds.), *Women's empowerment and global health* (pp. 232–250). Berkeley, CA: University of California Press.

27. Estes. C. L. (2017/2018). Women's rights, women's status, women's resistance in the age of Trump. *Generations: Journal of the American Society on Aging, 41*(4), 36–44.

28. Estes, C. L. (2018). A first-generation critic comes of age revisited. In C. Wellin (Ed.), *Critical gerontology comes of age* (pp. 19–34). New York: Routledge.

29. Wallace, S. P. & Estes, C. L. (2019). Older people. In B. Levy (Ed.), *Social injustice and public health* (3rd edition). New York: Oxford University Press.

30. Estes, C. L. & DiCarlo, N. B. (2019). *Exploitation and the State in precarity, USA: Social and psychic trauma across generations.* Working paper. San Francisco, CA: UCSF Institute for Health & Aging.

31. Estes, C. L. with DiCarlo, N. B. (2019). *Aging A–Z: Concepts toward emancipatory gerontology.* New York: Routledge.